969-7790 BURRELL

6159

JOHN PRICE

D.E. LARSEN

142/ 16, 17

APPLE

FILES

esc

up ↑

space bar once

move arrow

correct

doesn't work over 40 characters

LOOPS

INITIALIZE

BODY

INCREMENT

TEST

I BIT

SPACE BAR ERASES.

6-E — ◻

6 Z - ZOOM

249

PAGE 34

49

55

56

61

121

161

183

227

236-237

240

RND NUMBERS FROM 1–6

LET X = RND(0) * 6 + 1

LET Y = INT(X)

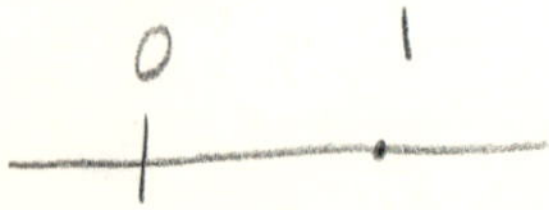

HOUGHTON MIFFLIN COMPUTER EDUCATION PROGRAM

Computer Programming in BASIC

David L. Myers, Senior Author
Valarie A. Elswick
Patrick W. Hopfensperger
Joseph P. Pavlovich

HOUGHTON MIFFLIN COMPANY • BOSTON
Atlanta Dallas Geneva, Ill. Lawrenceville, N.J. Palo Alto Toronto

Authors

David L. Myers, Computer Coordinator and Mathematics Teacher, Winsor School, Boston, Massachusetts.

Valarie A. Elswick, Mathematics and Computer Programming Teacher, Roy C. Ketcham High School, Wappingers Falls, New York.

Patrick W. Hopfensperger, Mathematics and Computer Programming Teacher, Homestead High School, Mequon, Wisconsin.

Joseph P. Pavlovich, Mathematics Department Chairperson and holder of the Richard King Mellon Chair, Shady Side Academy, Pittsburgh, Pennsylvania.

Editorial Adviser

Thomas J. Plati, Computer Coordinator K-12, Shrewsbury Public Schools, Shrewsbury, Massachusetts.

Teacher Consultants

John J. Joyce, Mathematics and Computer Programming Teacher, Winchester High School, Winchester, Massachusetts.

Leslie A. Leibovitch, Computer Coordinator and Mathematics Department Chairperson, Olive Vista Junior High School, Sylmar, California.

Carolyn P. Ott, Division Chairperson for Trade and Industrial and Computer Programming Teacher, Walton High School, Marietta, Georgia.

Dorothy Peterson, Mathematics Department Chairperson and Computer Programming Teacher, Jefferson High School, Cedar Rapids, Iowa.

Hector Rios, Computer Coordinator, North East Independent School District, San Antonio, Texas.

Printed in U.S.A.
ISBN: 0-395-36082-x
ABCDEFGHIJ-KR-93210/898765

Using This Book

This book is intended to be used in a BASIC computer programming course for high school students. The material in the book is flexible enough to be used in either a one-semester or a two-semester course and in a variety of settings.

Each section of the book contains pencil-and-paper exercises that rely directly on the syntax rules and techniques presented in that section. In addition, there are more difficult exercises that require students to modify programs and to write their own programs. Students can solve these problems without using a computer, or they may be required to enter, debug, and print copies of their solutions to hand in. The book also provides suggestions for projects, which are more involved or difficult problems requiring several hours of student programming effort.

The lab activities at the ends of most sections all involve active use of a computer. They have several purposes — to reinforce and extend the material presented in the book, to provide some model programs, and to show students how they can discover on their own the capabilities of the computer they are using. The lab activities are important, but not all of them need to be done by every student. The choice of which lab activities to assign must be based on the interests of the teacher, the background of the students, and the availability of time and computers. Notes in the teacher's manual provide guidance in the selection of exercises and lab activities, as well as pacing of the course.

Different computers, of course, use different versions of BASIC. The commands used for graphics are particularly variable. This book describes the versions of BASIC used on *Apple* computers, *TRS-80* computers, and *IBM* personal computers. The differences among these machines are spelled out in detail. The book can be used with computers other than the three mentioned, but the teacher will need to point out to students the changes applicable to their machines.

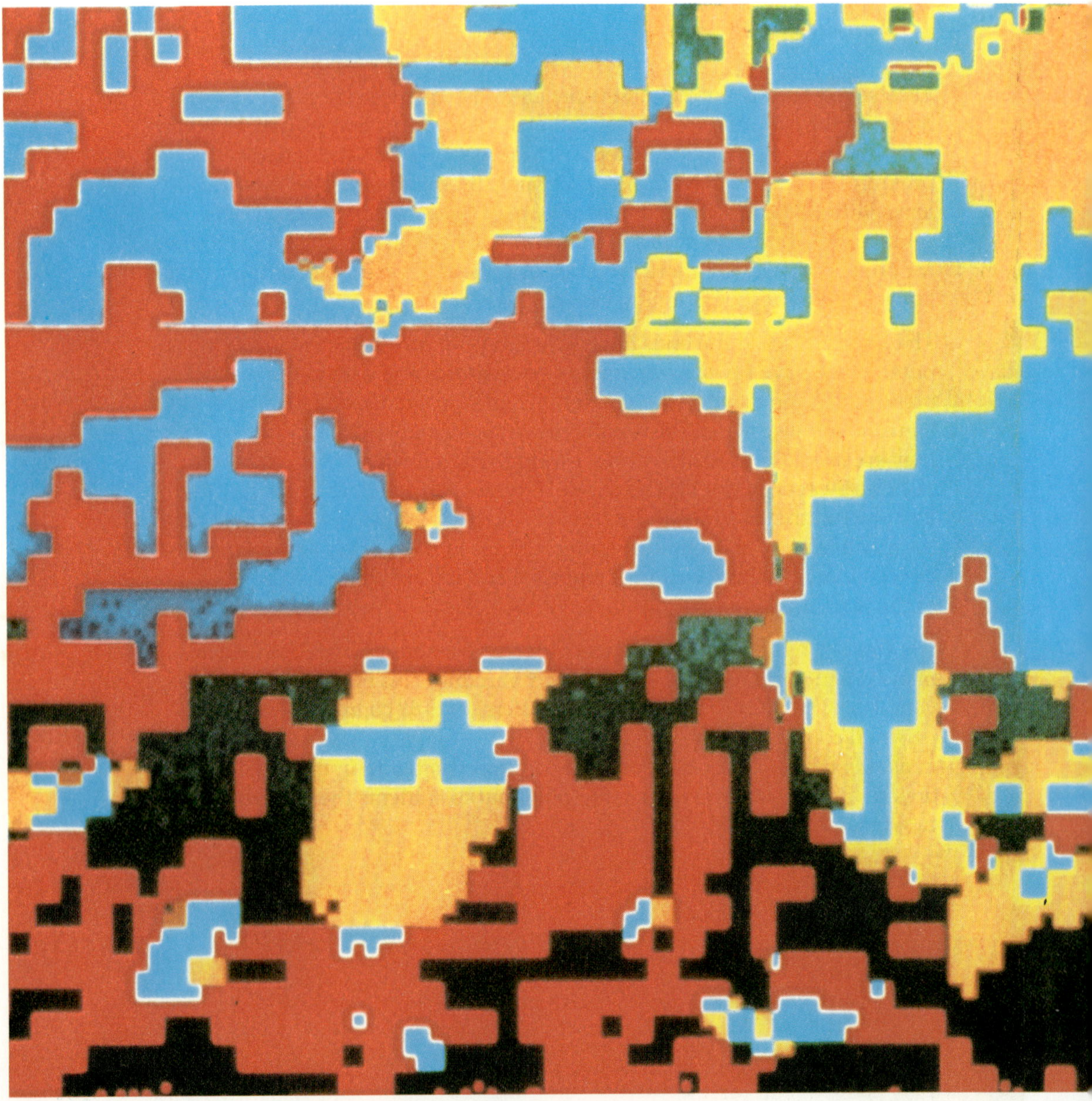

Table of Contents

Chapter 1 About Computers

Chapter 2 Computer Output

Chapter 3 Computer Input

Chapter 6 Formatting; Graphics

Chapter 7 Numeric Functions

Chapter 8 String Functions

Chapter 9 Arrays

Chapter 10 Sorting; Searching

Chapter 11 Files

CHAPTER

1 About Computers

This intricate computer graphic, entitled Escher, *was created by the computer artist David Em. The pattern suggests the work of the Dutch artist M. C. Escher (1898–1972), who often explored geometric principles in his designs.*

Introduction

This textbook is about *programming;* that is, giving detailed instructions to a computer to make it perform various tasks. You will be using the computer language BASIC, which is similar to English, but has a relatively small vocabulary and very rigid grammatical rules.

To be an effective *programmer,* you need to have a general understanding of computers; how they were developed, how they work, how you can communicate with them, and how they are affecting society today.

1-1 From Pebbles to Chips . . .

A computer is an electrical and mechanical device that processes or manipulates information. The information that it uses can be any combination of letters and numbers; it could be a play of Shakespeare, the latest stock market report, or numbers describing the orbit of a satellite. The computer handles the information and carries out mathematical operations following a set of internally-stored instructions. This set of instructions is called a *program.* You will be learning how to write BASIC programs in this book.

The history of the computer fittingly begins with humankind's learning to count and do simple calculations. Over the past 6000 years of recorded history, the methods of doing calculations have changed greatly. In the early days, human beings counted with the aid of their fingers, pebbles, sticks, and even used charcoal to mark on cave walls.

The earliest *mechanical* calculating devices probably resembled the *abacus.* Invented by the Chinese and adapted by many cultures, the abacus dates back to about 3000 B.C. It is still in use today in several areas of the world.

An important development in mechanical calculation was the gear-driven adding machine. Blaise Pascal, a French mathematician, invented one in 1642. A few of the working models he produced still exist today.

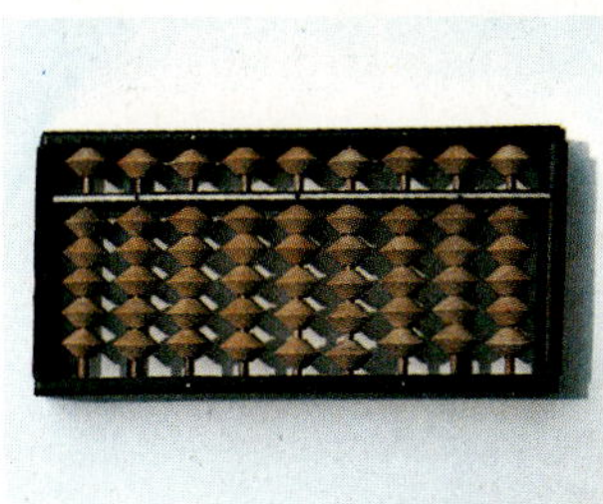

Abacus

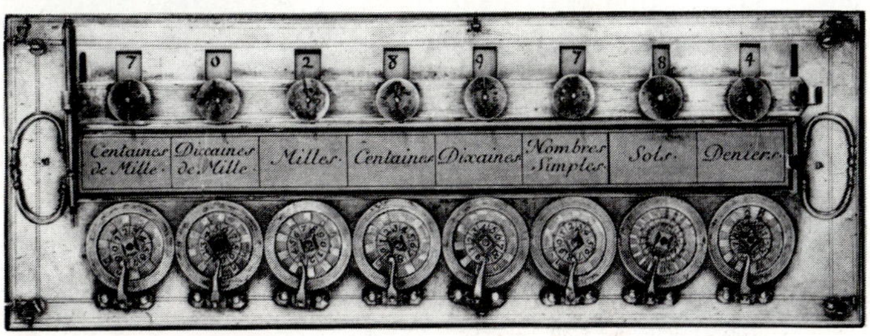

Pascal's adding machine

An essential step in the development of computers was finding a way to represent information and instructions in a form that a machine could use. During the Paris World's Fair in 1801, Joseph Jacquard exhibited a weaving loom he had designed that used a system of punched cards to control the patterns to be woven into the fabric. The punched cards functioned like a modern computer program; they allowed the weaver to communicate with the machine to produce a desired design or pattern, just as a computer program communicates the programmer's wishes to the computer. Of course, the computer is a *generalized* calculating device, rather than a specialized machine.

Jacquard's loom

The next significant event in the development of the computer resulted from joining together the physical representation of information with a general calculating machine. The English inventor Charles Babbage designed a "difference engine" to help compute various mathematical tables and an "analytic engine" that was to run on a punched card system similar to Jacquard's. His "analytic engine" of the 1830's was to perform arithmetic operations, store information, and print the results. Unfortunately, the machinists of his time could not produce accurate enough parts for his machines to work.

Babbage's difference engine

A less ambitious but more practical device using punched cards was invented by Herman Hollerith in 1889. He devised a coding procedure for the United States Census Office and a machine that could interpret the code. The machine processed numbers when they were punched into cards. His invention was used to tabulate the U.S. Census of 1890 and formed the basis of the techniques used to handle large collections of numbers.

Hollerith's tabulating machine

In the late 1930's a powerful computing device was designed by Howard Aiken of Harvard University. Called the Mark I, this computer used relays, which are electrical switches like those in old telephone switchboards. The Mark I computer was designed to solve equations of advanced calculus and began operation in 1944.

About the same time, the world's first *electronic* digital computer was developed at the University of Pennsylvania by John Mauchly and J. Presper Eckert. This machine, the ENIAC (Electronic Numerical Integrator and Calculator), contained 18,000 vacuum tubes like those used in radios and television sets of the late 1940's and early 1950's. The switches of the ENIAC (the vacuum tubes) were much faster than those of the Mark I because they had no moving parts; they relied entirely on the motion of electrons.

Vacuum tubes

Mark I computer

The Mark I and the ENIAC were programmed by physically connecting electrical wires in the proper order. The final conceptual step in developing modern computers was accomplished in 1949 under the leadership of John von Neumann of Princeton University. He urged that programs be stored inside the computer, by setting the electronic switches, rather than externally by means of electrical connections. This allowed more flexibility and greater speed. Virtually all modern computers use the "stored program concept."

ENIAC computer

The vacuum tubes used in the computer systems of the 1940's generated a considerable amount of heat and burned out frequently. The technological developments of the next several decades helped to eliminate the problems of heat and unreliability while at the same time providing tremendous increases in speed and capacity.

Transistors were first developed by Bell Laboratories in 1947. Transistors perform the same electronic function as vacuum tubes but are smaller, use less power, and are much more reliable. Near the end of the 1950's, transistors started to replace vacuum tubes in computers. As a result, reliability improved and cost decreased.

One remarkable characteristic of transistors is that they can be made very small. This has allowed engineers and scientists to develop photographic

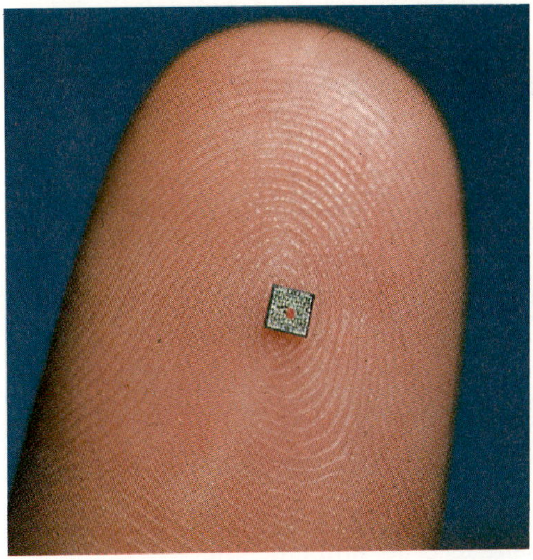

A microchip

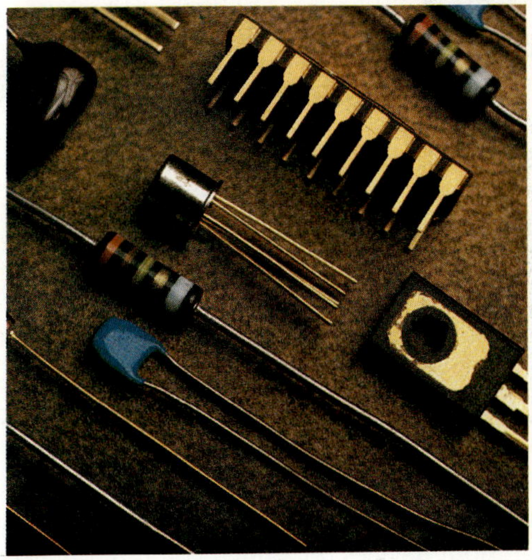

Transistors

techniques to produce hundreds and even thousands of transistors and other electronic components on a single small piece, or *chip*, of silicon crystal. All of the components are tied together into a single *integrated circuit*. These chips can be manufactured very inexpensively and can contain a circuit equivalent in power to entire computers of the 1950's (which often filled large rooms). The latest and smallest of these chips, called *microchips*, were first developed in the 1970's. Microchips form the heart of the microcomputers that are so popular today in homes, schools, offices, factories, and even in individual toys and games.

1-2 How the Computer Works

To understand how a computer works, you need to know something about its *hardware* and *software*. *Hardware* is the term used to describe the actual physical equipment of the computer system. The term *software* is used to describe programs or sets of instructions that the computer is to follow.

Although there are many types of computer systems available today, they each contain the same four basic parts: input, storage (or memory), processing, and output.

An input device is used to enter data (information) and instructions into the computer. The computer stores this information in its memory as it is entered. Then the processing unit, following instructions also stored in memory, operates on the information. The output device is needed to communicate the results or solutions to the user of the computer.

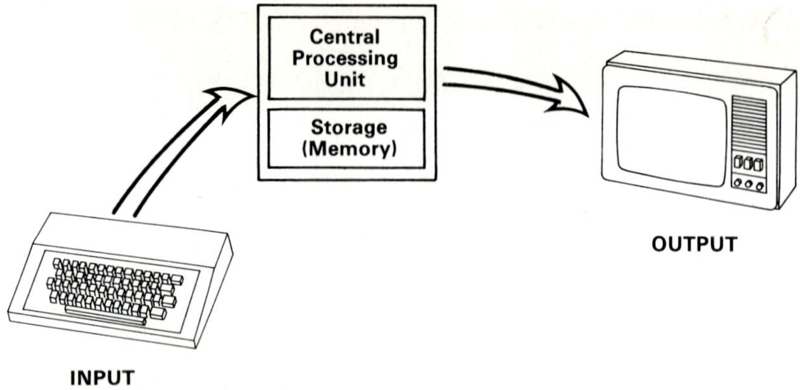

Parts of a computer system

Input devices vary depending on the type of computer being used. Examples of input devices for a microcomputer are the cassette recorder and tape, the disk drive and floppy (flexible) disk, a typewriter-like keyboard, and a telephone modem. A program or data may come from a tape or floppy disk, it may be typed at a keyboard, or it may be sent to the computer from another computer via phone lines and a telephone modem.

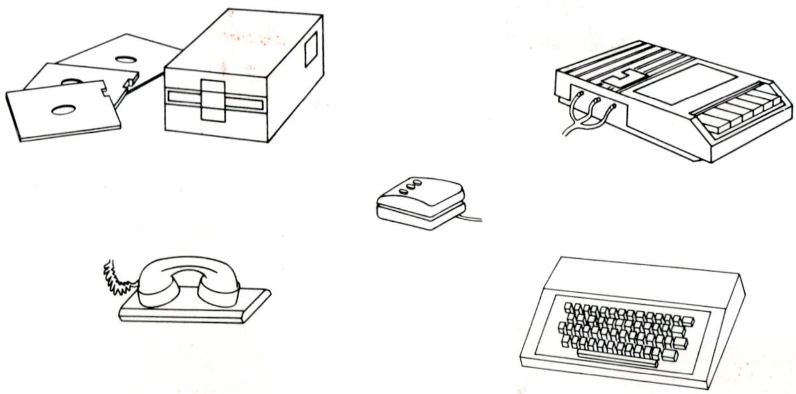

Input devices

In a microcomputer, the processing unit, usually referred to as the CPU *(central processing unit),* is the "heart" or "brain" of the computer. It is usually contained on a single chip (the "microprocessor" chip) within the computer casing. The CPU controls the input and output devices, performs needed arithmetic operations, and routes the information being processed from input to memory to output.

The storage unit of a microcomputer consists of two types of memory, RAM and ROM. RAM *(random-access memory)* can be changed while the computer is operating; it is used to store information and programs that come from the

A circuit board

user by way of the input devices. Information stored in RAM will be lost if the power to the system is interrupted or turned off. ROM *(read-only memory)* cannot be changed by the user or by the computer. It contains the *control program* for the computer, which interprets information and carries out commands. The control program in ROM cannot be lost if the computer is turned off.

A computer must have an output device if the user is to learn the results of the calculations and data processing carried out by the CPU. Usually, the most important output device of a microcomputer is the display screen (also known as the "cathode ray tube," or CRT). Results can also be sent to magnetic tape or to disk. Printers are another important output device. Printers produce a written copy of the results. Less essential but often used input/output (I/O) devices include remote terminals, plotters, time clocks, and voice synthesizers.

A plotter

It is important to realize that hardware is useless without software. The programs of a microcomputer, whether stored on a floppy disk or a cassette tape or in the computer's memory, contain the instructions for everything the computer is capable of doing.

1-3 Communicating with the Computer

The methods used to communicate with a computer are very important. The computer must receive instructions in a form that it has been programmed to accept and to which it can respond.

The computer itself cannot understand a human language such as English. It is built (that is, its electronic circuits are arranged) to respond to instructions in *machine language.* Machine language is based on coding in the binary number system. (See the Computer Language Feature on page 64.) The binary number system uses only 0's and 1's to represent numbers. These digits — 0 and 1 — can easily be related to the electronic components of the computer, where the current (or switch) is either on (represented by 1) or off (represented by 0). Although the computer understands machine language, human beings sometimes have difficulty with it; an instruction telling an Apple computer to add one number to another looks like this: 10101101 00001010 00000011 01101101 00000111 00000011 10001101 00001000 00000011.

Clearly, it would be easier for a human being to communicate in a familiar language like English. Of course, the computer does not understand English (a very complicated language, if you think about it), so a compromise was reached. Languages less complicated than English but easier for a programmer to work with than machine language were invented. In this book, you will learn to use the BASIC language to communicate with computers.

BASIC (Beginner's All-purpose Symbolic Instruction Code) was first developed in the early 1960's as a general purpose computer language. It was, and is today, a language that you can learn without having a strong technical or scientific background. BASIC is the most popular language used for microcomputers. Any computer language that a human can understand easily,

English → BASIC → Machine Language

such as BASIC, is called a *high-level language.* Many other high-level computer languages have been developed. You can learn a little about Logo, Pascal, and others in the Computer Language features at the end of each chapter of this book.

BASIC is sufficiently close to English that you will not have much trouble learning it. (For example, you can make the computer add two numbers together by typing LET X = A + B.) The computer is not in such a fortunate position; BASIC is very far from machine language. To bridge the gap between the two languages, a control program, called the *BASIC interpreter*, has been written for your machine. In most microcomputers, it resides in ROM and rapidly translates your directions, expressed in BASIC, into machine language instructions that your computer can use.

There are two major aspects to the process of learning programming: You will learn the vocabulary and rules of BASIC, and you will learn how to think of problems in terms that can be expressed in BASIC and solved by the computer. These two aspects of programming will be covered side-by-side in this text. If your interest in programming continues, you will probably learn other high-level languages such as Pascal or COBOL later in your education. Your study of BASIC will make that task much easier.

1-4 The Computer's Role in Society

Advances in technology over the last five to ten years have removed many of the fears that people formerly had about computers. Many people once considered computers to be a threatening, powerful force understood by few. Today, both at home and in the arcades, people have found computers to be exciting and fun to use. In today's society it is important to develop your understanding of computers beyond the recreational stage.

The continuing advances in computer technology have begun to have profound effects on our educational system, job and career opportunities, the way we spend our money, and many other aspects of our daily lives. The computer's ability to process information and to help solve problems quickly and accurately is here to stay. The computer is a powerful tool; you should learn how to use this tool as effectively as possible.

In education, the availability of microcomputers has had a tremendous effect at both the elementary and secondary levels. Students at various grade levels are using special software packages to help them learn a variety of subjects. Computer literacy is becoming an essential part of education. Programming in high-level languages is being taught at all grade levels.

Career opportunities in computer-related fields are many and varied, including: programmers to tell computers what to do, operators to run them, engineers to design them, factory workers to make them, technicians to repair them, and sales people to sell and install them.

Because our society deals with so much information, computers can be found and are being used in almost every career you might imagine: salesclerking in a store, checking car engines, diagnosing disease, and predicting the weather. Continuing advances in computer technology will provide new applications of computers in many fields.

Computers are profoundly influencing our daily lives. Computers help to run telephone systems, schedule doctor's appointments, and keep track of how quickly people pay their bills. There are small computers in home appliances, cars, and games. It is difficult to find an area of our lives that is not touched by computers. The more you know about computers — how they work and how to communicate with them — the better prepared you will be for the future.

Installation of a flight-control computer

Computers in the classroom

Computer-assisted textile design

Chapter Summary

The history of the computer begins with mankind's learning to count and do simple calculations. The earliest mechanical calculating device probably was the *abacus,* invented by the Chinese about 3000 B.C. Here are some of the significant events leading to the development of the computers of today:

Blaise Pascal, a French mathematician and physicist, invented a gear-driven adding machine in 1642.

Joseph Jacquard designed a weaving loom that used punched cards (similar to a modern computer program) to control patterns woven into fabric. His loom was exhibited during the Paris World's Fair in 1801.

During the 1820's and 1830's, the English mathematician and inventor Charles Babbage designed a "difference engine" to compute mathematical tables, and an "analytic engine" to do calculations, store information, and print the results of the calculations.

Herman Hollerith invented a machine to process numbers contained on punched cards. The machine was used to tabulate the 1890 U.S. Census.

MARK I, a computer using *electrical relays,* was developed in the 1930's by Howard Aiken of Harvard University.

ENIAC, a computer using *vacuum tubes,* was developed in the 1940's by John Mauchly and J. Presper Eckert at the University of Pennsylvania.

Bell Laboratories in 1947 developed the *transistor,* which replaced vacuum tubes in computers during the 1950's.

Microchips, developed in the 1970's and forming the heart of computers today, are small pieces of silicon crystal containing miniaturized components that have been fused into a single unit known as an *integrated circuit.*

A *computer* is an electrical and mechanical device that processes and manipulates information. A *computer program* is a set of instructions that a computer can follow.

Hardware refers to the actual physical equipment of a computer system and *software* refers to a program that can be followed by a computer.

The CPU *(central processing unit)* controls the flow of data through the four parts of a computer system: input, storage (memory), processing, and output.

The storage unit of a microcomputer consists of two types of memory, RAM and ROM. RAM *(random-access memory)* can be changed while the computer is operating; ROM *(read-only memory)* cannot be changed by the user or the computer.

BASIC, a high-level language, is the most popular language used today for communicating with microcomputers.

Computer Applications

The Home of the Future

The Computerized Home

Computerized devices like this sewing machine may be commonplace in future homes.

You arrive home from school and approach the door to your house. You punch a secret code into a keypad on the door frame and the door automatically opens. A familiar voice says, "Hi, Sue, your mother went to the grocery store and will be home about five." You look around. No one is in sight but you don't seem worried; it is just your home computer "talking." This scene describes one function the home computer will perform for people living in a computerized home. The computerized home will more than likely contain a central computer that can speak and respond to human speech, control utilities and appliances, communicate directly with other computers, and provide information from world-wide sources. The computer will be an important tool for the family at work and at play.

Computerized monitoring system for home-security alarms

Much of the technology necessary to run a computerized home has already been developed. In the early 1970's, the microchip was introduced. The microchip is a small piece of silicon crystal containing electronic circuitry that can execute programs. Because of its small size, the microchip has revolutionized many consumer products. Most auto manufacturers have installed microchips that can monitor engine controls, fuel consumption, and even tune the radio. In the home, microchips are used to run microwave ovens and control cooking times. With a microchip at the core, a computer system has been developed that can control and monitor a home's heating and cooling, its security and fire alarms, its lights, appliances, and electronic devices such as t.v.'s and stereos. The computer system has built-in telephone circuits that allow a person to call the computer by phone and tell it what time to turn on the oven to start dinner or what radio station should be playing at a particular time. The phone capabilities also allow the computer to signal the police or fire department automatically when the security or fire alarm is set off. If all of these applications can be performed now, can you imagine what new functions the computer will perform in the home of the future?

Communications Revolution

Perhaps the biggest change in the home of the future will result from the communications revolution that could make it increasingly easier to perform many kinds of work at home. Through ordinary telephone lines and satellite broadcast receivers, a worker may be able to access vast data banks of large computers anyplace in the world. Some think the future home will be an "electronic cottage." Instead of commuting to the factory or the office to work, many of us could stay home and perform our job there. Some sociologists predict that many people might prefer to work at home, given the proper communication technology, which includes the home computer.

People who enter data, type, work with numbers, or prepare invoices could easily shift to the home. A secretary could take dictation at home over the phone, type the text on a home computer terminal, and then send the completed text to the office over the telephone lines. An accountant might use the home computer to balance ledger sheets, and a stock broker might use it to buy and sell stocks. In the future, engineers, draftsmen, lawyers, writers, insurance agents, investment counselors, academic researchers, and others might do some or all of their work at home through the use of a computer and telecommunications.

Computer Tasks

The computer system in the home of the future may do much more than help people conduct business. It probably will monitor nearly all household devices, control air systems, access larger computer data bases, and perform routine chores (most likely by means of a household robot). People will be able to use the computer to store all home records, keep track of appointments, phone numbers, household repairs, and lists of things-to-do. With the computer performing all of these tasks, people can spend more time on other activities.

Many future homes will use solar panels to provide heat and hot water.

Pilot

The computer language Pilot was first developed in San Francisco in the late 1960's. It was designed as a computer-aided-instruction language for teachers to use in writing programs for testing and teaching. The intent was to create a language that would make it easy to write *interactive* programs, that is, programs that would carry on a "conversation" with the user in a friendly question-and-answer format. With this feature, the programmer can write educational programs without dealing with all the details required in manipulating character strings. All that the teacher need do is tell the computer that she or he will be working with strings (words), and Pilot's built-in instructions for dealing with words will take care of the rest. Thus, the teacher is free to concentrate on the text being written, without having to pay as much attention to syntax as would be necessary with a language such as BASIC or Pascal. Pilot's ability to "converse" enables it to be used creatively to write poems and short stories.

Here are some Pilot language commands:

- T: Print *text* on the screen.
- A: *Accept* an answer typed by the user.
- M: *Match* keyword with typed answer.
- J: *Jump* to another program line.

The example below is a Pilot program that uses these commands:

```
T:  How many ways can you arrange the letters in CAT?
*TRY : A
M:  6, Six
TY: That's correct!
TN: Sorry, try again.
JN: *TRY
T:  Question #2 is . . .
```

The first line of the Pilot program asks the user a question, which is displayed on the screen. The purpose of the second line is twofold: the *TRY instruction indicates that this line can be jumped to later and the letter A accepts an answer to the question. Line (3) tests whether the digit "6" or the word "Six" matches any of the words in the answer. If there is a match, the TY command (Y stands for *yes*) prints the message "That's correct!". If there is no match, the TN command (N stands for *no*) prints the message "Sorry, try again."; the JN command in the next line jumps the program back to the *TRY instruction.

There are other Pilot instructions that can be used to keep track of the number of right and wrong answers typed by the user.

The major advantage of Pilot lies in its ability to manipulate text and character strings. If all you want to do is print text information on the screen, BASIC's handling of words as simple strings of characters works fine as well. If you want, however, to compare, move around, or in other ways process text, then Pilot is a better choice for a programming language.

Performing math calculations with Pilot can be difficult, since it was not designed to do more than simple arithmetic computations. Also, Pilot provides no way of storing or processing large quantities of data (like with arrays in BASIC), so solving problems that require organization of large amounts of information is extremely difficult. The language is very *modular* (that is, each task can be done separately in the program), but difficulties can arise when individual modules are linked together.

Even though Pilot was developed for teachers, many students enjoy using it to write tests for each other. Writing a test with Pilot can help the programmer learn logical and structured programming design as well as the subject matter of the test.

Student taking test developed by teacher using Pilot

CHAPTER

2 Computer Output

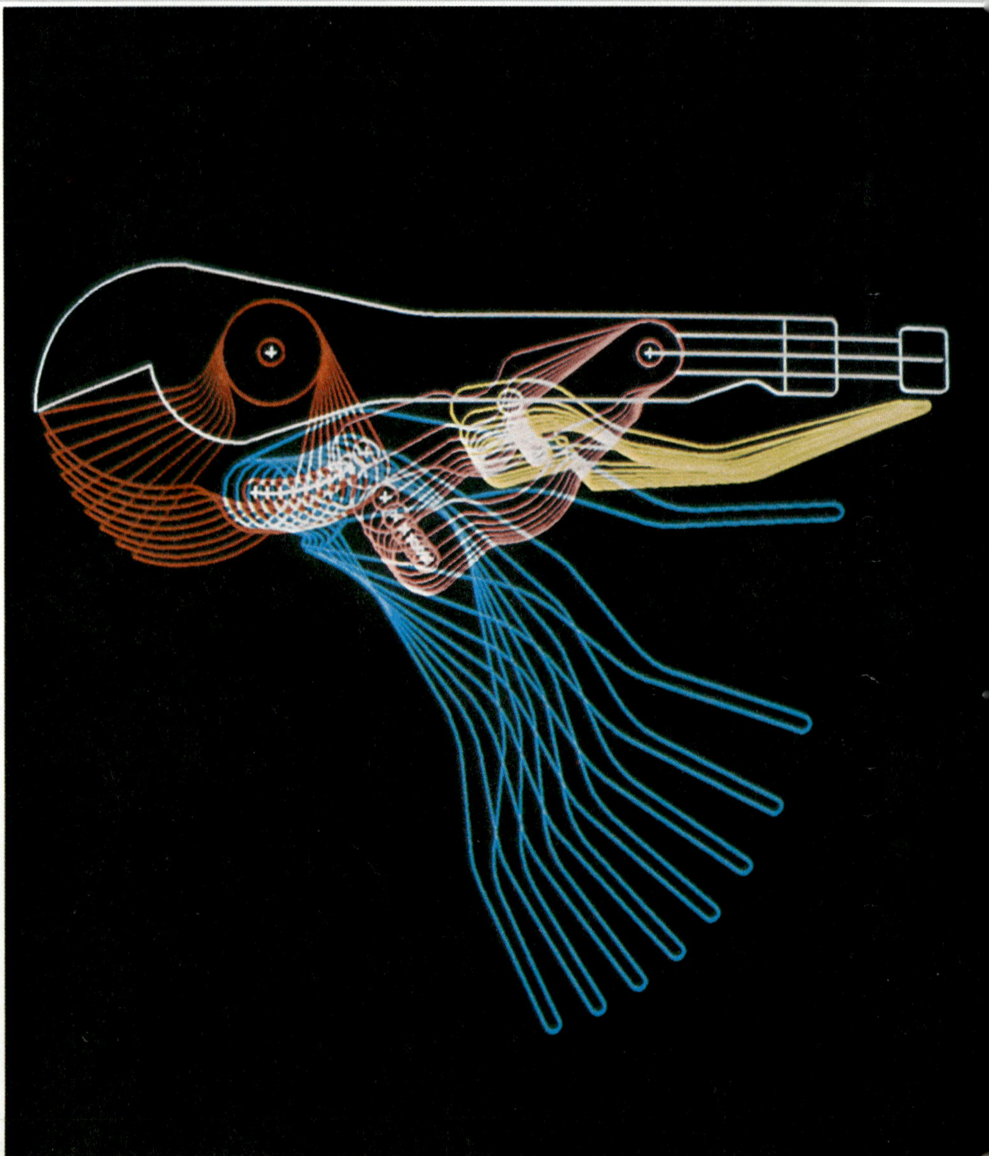

Engineers use computer graphics in designing tools. Here, animation is used to analyze the movements of the parts of pliers.

Introduction

As mentioned in Chapter 1, we will use the computer language BASIC in this book. It is one of the most commonly used programming languages today. Different computers have different versions of BASIC; whenever possible, we will use a general form that will work on most computers. Where there are significant differences, we will give the necessary changes for the *Apple, IBM,* and *TRS-80* microcomputers. For other machines, differences can be explored in the Lab Activities that appear throughout the book.

In the first two sections of this chapter, you will learn how to use the computer as a calculator. Certain words in the BASIC language can be used to give the computer instructions, or *commands,* that it will perform as soon as you press the <RETURN> or <ENTER> key after typing the command. When a computer is used in this fashion, it is said to be in *immediate mode.* Later in the chapter, you will see how to store instructions in the computer's memory as a *program,* a technique that makes the computer a much more useful and powerful tool than a simple calculator. In the final section of this chapter, a short introduction to *graphics* is presented for the *Apple, IBM,* and *TRS-80* microcomputers.

2-1 The PRINT Command

One of the most useful words in the BASIC language is PRINT. The PRINT command allows the computer to communicate with you. It can be used to display on the screen any combination of letters, numbers, and symbols (such a combination is called a *string*), or to evaluate numerical expressions and show the results on the screen. When strings are used with the PRINT command, they must be enclosed in quotation marks, as in the following example:

Example 1

a.
```
PRINT "HELLO THERE"          ← command
HELLO THERE                  ← output
```

b.
```
PRINT "NOW WE CAN COMMUNICATE"      ← command
NOW WE CAN COMMUNICATE              ← output
```

The result, or *output,* of a PRINT command appears on the screen beneath the command on the next line. PRINT causes the computer to display on the screen exactly what is typed inside the quotation marks, including spaces, as you can see in Example 2 on the next page. (The small shaded rectangles in that example are used to represent spaces in this book.)

Example 2

a. PRINT "YOU ARE SMA■A■A■RT" ← command
YOU ARE SMA■A■A■RT ← output

b. PRINT "6■■■+4" ← command
6■■■+4 ← output

Operations in BASIC

You can form numerical expressions using the operations of addition, subtraction, multiplication, division, and exponentiation (taking powers). The following special symbols are used in BASIC:

Operation	Symbol in BASIC	Example in Arithmetic	Example in BASIC
Addition	+	4 + 9	4 + 9
Subtraction	—	13 — 2	13 — 2
Multiplication	*	3 × 5	3 * 5
Division	/	16 ÷ 2	16 / 2
Exponentiation	↑ or ∧	3^2	3 ↑ 2 or 3 ∧ 2

(*Note:* In this book we will use the symbol ↑ for exponentiation.)

The next example shows how to use the PRINT command and the operation symbols above to calculate values of numerical expressions.

Example 3

a. PRINT 4 + 9 — 2
11

b. PRINT 3 * 5
15

Notice that the numerical expressions in Example 3 are not enclosed in quotation marks. If quotes were used, then the computer would PRINT the strings 4 + 9 — 2 and 3 * 5 rather than the values 11 and 15.

Making Corrections

If you make a typing mistake and have not yet pressed the < RETURN > or < ENTER > key, you can correct that mistake by using the backspace key. Each time the backspace < ← > key is pressed, it causes the computer to move back one character to the left of the cursor. (The *cursor* is the solid or blinking rectangle, underline, or other symbol that indicates where the next character will appear on the screen.) Note that the backspace key, unlike most of the keys on the keyboard, does not cause any new characters to appear on the screen; it merely moves the cursor to the left. When the cursor is properly positioned on your mistake, type the correct character, then finish typing the rest of the line. (*Note:* Many computers have other special keys, called *cursor keys,* for correcting mistakes. Some, for example, have a forward-arrow <→> key that can be used to recopy the characters passed over by the use of the backspace <←> key.) The process of making changes and corrections is called *editing.*

Avoiding Pitfalls

1. When PRINTing strings, be sure to enclose them in quotation marks.
2. Do *not* enclose in quotation marks any numerical expression you want the computer to evaluate.
3. If PRINT (or any other command in BASIC) is misspelled, the computer will print a SYNTAX ERROR message. (The exact form of the error message depends on the computer you are using. See page 658.) Syntax is the set of rules for putting together statements in a language. A SYNTAX ERROR in BASIC is caused by a sequence of characters that is not "meaningful" to the computer — that the computer has not been programmed to accept.

Summary

An *immediate mode command* is any instruction that the computer executes as soon as the <RETURN> or <ENTER> key is pressed.

The PRINT command can be used to display on the screen any *string* of letters, numbers, and symbols (enclosed in quotation marks), or to evaluate a numerical expression and display the result on the screen.

Exercises 2-1

In Exercises 1–8, predict the output of each command. In the case of a SYNTAX ERROR, correct the mistake.

A **1.** **a.** PRINT "2 + 3"
b. PRINT 2 + 3
c. TWO + 3

2. **a.** PRINT "FOUR TIMES SIX"
b. PRINT "4 × 6"
c. PRINT 4 * 6

3. a. PRINT "5 + EIGHT"
   b. PRINT 5 + 8
   c. DISPLAY "FIVE AND 8"

4. a. TYPE "SEVEN SQUARED"
   b. PRINT 7 ↑ 2
   c. PRINT 7 * 7

5. a. PRINT "SIX MINUS FOUR"
   b. PRINT 6 — 4
   c. PRINT "6 — 4"

6. a. PRENT "ONE-HALF"
   b. PRINT "1 / 2"
   c. PRINT 1 / 2

7. a. PRINT "WEA■■R■■Y"
   b. PRINT "WEA■R■Y"
   c. PRINT "■■■WEARY"

8. a. PRINT "STRO■O■NG"
   b. PRINT "STRO■■O■■O■■NGER"
   c. PRIMT "STRO■O■O■O■NGEST"

In Exercises 9–20, write a command that gives the indicated output.

B 9. HERE WE GO

10. THREE TIMES FIVE

11. 3 * 5

12. 15

13. (3)(5)

14. 3 × 5

15. 3 / 5

16. 3■■■ * ■■■5

17. I SAID, 'I'M FINE'

18. 8 / 4 = 2

19. $35.02 + $16.09

20. D■■■O■■■N■■■E

In Exercises 21–26, write a command using BASIC operation symbols that will find the value of each numerical expression.

21. $13 \times 50 \times 12$

22. $8 \div 4$

23. $16 - 8 + 7$

24. 500^2

25. $8 \times 5 \div 10$

26. $20^2 \div 100$

Lab Activity

Experimenting with Strings

Problems

1. Type each of the following commands into your computer (use the apostrophe key for the single quotation marks):

```
PRINT 'HOW ARE YOU TODAY? '
PRINT "I SAID, "HOW ARE YOU TODAY? " "
PRINT "I SAID, 'HOW ARE YOU TODAY? ' "
PRINT "I'M FINE ! ! "
```

Notice the output in each case. May single quotation marks be used to PRINT a string? What happens when the usual quotation marks are used *within* a string? How about single quotes within a string? Are the results surprising? Which of the commands above shows the correct method of PRINTing a direct quote within a string?

2. **a.** Starting at the left side of the screen (just press the < RETURN > or < ENTER > key to place the cursor there), type the letter A repeatedly to determine how many characters your screen can display on a single line.

b. What happens when you type too many letters to fit on one line on the screen? You should find that the extra characters are printed on the next line. This is called *wrap-around*. Experiment to see if wrap-around occurs if you try to PRINT a string (in quotation marks) that has too many characters.

c. Use the PRINT command to determine the number of lines that can be shown on your screen at one time. (Be sure to count lines the computer leaves blank!) What happens when you try to PRINT one more line? The top line should go off the screen and the rest of the lines move up. This is called *scrolling*.

3. Determine experimentally the maximum length of a string inside quotation marks in a PRINT statement.

2-2 Numbers in BASIC; Order of Operations

Numbers in BASIC

In BASIC, numbers may be written in three ways:

1. Integer form (5, −32, 1000, or 0, for example)
2. Decimal form (.372, 3.1416, −32.37, or .00089, for example)
3. Exponential form (E-form)

Exponential form, or *E-form*, is really scientific notation written in a slightly different way. In scientific notation the number 230000 can be expressed as 2.3×10^5, since multiplying by 10^5 moves the decimal point 5 places to the *right*. In BASIC, this number is written 2.3E + 05. (This is the way most computers *print* exponential form. When you type a number in exponential form, however, the plus sign in front of the exponent is not usually required, and the zero in front of the 5 is also optional.) Thus, a positive number in exponential form starts with a decimal between 1 and 10, followed by the letter E and a positive or negative integer (the exponent).

Example 1

$4.027E + 07 = 4.027 \times 10^7 = 40270000$ (moving the decimal point 7 places to the *right*).

A negative exponent causes the decimal point to be moved to the *left*, as shown in Example 2.

Example 2

$6.3E - 04 = 6.3 \times 10^{-4} = .00063$ (moving the decimal point 4 places to the *left*).

When there is a minus sign in front of the decimal, then the entire number is negative, as you can see in Example 3.

Example 3

$-5.68E - 10 = -5.68 \times 10^{-10} = -.000000000568$ (moving the decimal point 10 places to the left).

(*Note:* Some computers sometimes use a D in place of the E. The D stands for *double precision.* Numbers in D-form are evaluated in the same way as numbers in E-form.)

Computers differ in the number of decimal places they use. Most print at least 6 digits and calculate with at least 7-digit accuracy (see the Lab Activity). In this case, even if you type in more digits, the computer will retain only 7 of them. Some computers have double precision numbers with twice as many decimal places as usual; the number of digits retained by these computers is still limited, however.

You can type a number into the computer in any one of the three forms described earlier, and the computer will accept it. However, commas must *not* be included. For example, you should type 276321 rather than 276,321. (In Section 2–4, you will see that commas and other punctuation marks have a special use in BASIC.)

Order of Operations

In the previous section, you saw how to use the PRINT command to evaluate simple numerical expressions. More complicated expressions can also be evaluated in this way. How does the computer evaluate an expression such as 3 + 4 * 2, for example? It follows the usual rules of arithmetic. Since all multiplications are done before additions (if there are no parentheses), the computer will get

$$3 + 4 * 2 = 3 + 8 = 11.$$

Here are the rules governing the order in which operations are performed:

Order of Operations

First:	Perform all operations inside parentheses.
Second:	Evaluate all powers.
Third:	Perform all multiplications and divisions, in order from left to right.
Fourth:	Perform all additions and subtractions, in order from left to right.

In Example 4, these rules are used to evaluate two BASIC numerical expressions.

Example 4

a. $14 / 2 - 3 * 1 = 7 - 3$	Divide and multiply (left to right).
$= 4$	Subtract.
b. $3 + 5 \uparrow 2 * 4 = 3 + 25 * 4$	Evaluate all powers.
$= 3 + 100$	Multiply.
$= 103$	Add.

When a BASIC numerical expression contains parentheses, all operations in parentheses are done first, from the innermost parentheses outward. (Again, this is the same as in arithmetic.) Within each set of parentheses, operations are performed beginning with the second step listed in the rules for order of operations in the table above.

Example 5

a. $8 * 2 / (5 - 1) = 8 * 2 / 4$	Do parentheses first.
$= 16 / 4$	Multiply.
$= 4$	Divide.
b. $4 + (3 * 2 - 1) \uparrow 2 / 5 = 4 + (5) \uparrow 2 / 5$	Do parentheses first.
$= 4 + 25 / 5$	Evaluate all powers.
$= 4 + 5$	Divide.
$= 9$	Add.

Parentheses may always be added to make clear the meaning of an expression. If in doubt, use parentheses — they may make the difference between a correct answer and an incorrect one.

Avoiding Pitfalls

1. When evaluating numerical expressions on the computer, be sure to include necessary parentheses. For example, to evaluate the arithmetic expression $\frac{3 \times 10}{9 - 6}$, you need to type:

```
PRINT 3 * 10 / (9 — 6)
```

2. Be sure that every left parenthesis in a numerical expression has a matching right parenthesis, or a SYNTAX ERROR will result.

3. Remember that commas must not be included when typing numbers into the computer.

Summary

Numbers may be written in BASIC in any one of three forms: integer form, decimal form, or exponential form *(E-form)*. When evaluating BASIC numerical expressions, apply the same rules for order of operations as in arithmetic. Perform operations in parentheses first, from the innermost parentheses outward.

Exercises 2-2

A **1.** Express each of the following numbers in its integer or decimal form.

a. 5.0E + 07 **b.** 1.23E + 03 **c.** −1.23E + 03
d. −1.23E − 03 **e.** 3.0467E + 06 **f.** 3.001E − 06
g. 1.234E − 04 **h.** −1.234E − 04 **i.** 4.26305E + 08
j. 1E + 08 **k.** 1E − 08 **l.** 3E − 04

2. Evaluate each of the following BASIC numerical expressions.

a. 3 − 4 * 2 **b.** 3 − (4 * 2) **c.** 3 − 4 ↑ 2
d. (3 − 4) ↑ 2 **e.** 12 − 4 / 2 **f.** (12 − 4) / 2
g. 8 − 4 / 2 * 3 **h.** (8 − 4) / 2 * 3 **i.** 3 * 2 ↑ 3 * 2 − 2
j. (3 * 2) ↑ 3 * (2 − 2) **k.** 5 * (4 − 1) ↑ 2 **l.** (5 * (4 − 1)) ↑ 2
m. 16 − 4 / 4 + 2 **n.** (16 − 4) / (4 + 2) **o.** 16 − (4 / 4 + 2)
p. 6 * 3 − 3 ↑ 2 / 3 **q.** 6 * (3 − 3 ↑ 2 / 3) **r.** 6 * ((3 − 3) ↑ 2 / 3)

B **3.** Write each of the following using BASIC operation symbols. Then evaluate the expression.

a. $2 + 3 - 5$ **b.** $2 \times 3 - 5$ **c.** $2^2 - 5$
d. $9 - 3 \div 3$ **e.** $12 - 2 \times 3 \times 4$ **f.** $12 \div 3 - 4 \div 2$

g. $5^2 \times 2 + 5$
h. $6^{(1+2)}$
i. $2(3 + 4)$
j. $2 \times 3 + 2 \times 4$
k. $2(3 + 2 \times 4)$
l. $12(1 + .1)^2$
m. $2^3 - 24 \div 2 \times 6 + 3$
n. $-6 \times 12 \div 3^2 + 4 \times 3$
o. $2^4 - (24 \div 3 \times (1 + 2))$
p. $(8 - (2 \times 2)) \div 8 \times 2$
q. $10^2 \times 5 \div (-20 + 10)$
r. $-6 \times ((12 \div 3)^2 + 4) \div 3$

4. In each of the following, place parentheses to make the equality true.

a. 4 − 5 * 6 = −6
b. 6 * 2 − 3 * 5 = −30
c. 3 − 2 ↑ 2 + 6 = 7
d. 7 − 2 ↑ 3 − 1 = 25
e. 5 + 3 ↑ 2 / 2 = 32
f. 8 / 6 + 2 * 3 − 1 = 2

Lab Activity

Experimenting with Numbers

Problems

1. Determine the number of decimal places your computer uses by typing each of the following commands and recording the output:

```
PRINT 1.23456     (no quotation marks)
PRINT 1.234567
PRINT 1.2345678
PRINT 1.23456789
PRINT 1.234567891
PRINT 1.2345678912 , and so forth.
```

Continue to expand the decimal until your computer first PRINTS a number that is not identical to the one you typed. How many decimal places does your computer PRINT?

2. Type the following commands and record your computer's output:

```
PRINT 123456     (no quotation marks)
PRINT 1234567
PRINT 12345678
PRINT 123456789
PRINT 1234567891
PRINT 12345678912 , and so forth.
```

Continue to expand the number until your computer converts the number you type into exponential form. What is the maximum number of digits that your computer accepts before it automatically converts your positive number to exponential form? What is the *largest* positive number that your computer accepts without converting it to exponential form?

3. Determine the smallest positive number (a decimal) that your computer does not automatically convert to exponential form. Try the following:

    PRINT .01
    PRINT .001
    PRINT .0001 , and so forth.

4. If you type a number in exponential form, determine whether your computer *always* PRINTs it in exponential form. For example, if you type PRINT 8.2E + 03, is the output 8.2E + 03 or 8200?

5. The expression 342.02E + 08 is not in E-form, since it does not start with a decimal between 1 and 10. Type the following commands to determine what your computer does with these expressions:

    PRINT 342.02E + 08
    PRINT .034E + 06
    PRINT —628.5E — 03
    PRINT 6480E + 12

6. Use the PRINT command to discover the largest number your computer can handle. Try PRINT 1E + 15, then PRINT 1E + 20, and so forth, until your computer prints a message such as OVERFLOW ERROR.

7. In Problem 6, you found that there are limits on how large a positive number your computer can work with. Discover any limits it has for a smallest positive number: try PRINT 1E — 20, PRINT 1E — 25, and so forth, until your computer outputs the wrong number. What is the smallest positive number that the computer handles correctly? What number (an integer) is this extremely close to?

2-3 A First Program: RUN, LIST, NEW, HOME, CLS

In the first two sections of this chapter we used the computer in immediate mode to perform simple tasks one at a time (such as PRINTing strings or evaluating numerical expressions). You can make the computer perform much more complex tasks by storing an entire sequence of instructions — a *program* — in the computer's memory. Then, the computer will carry out the instructions in the program whenever and as many times as you tell it to do so.

A BASIC computer program consists of a set of instructions, or *statements*, each of which is preceded by a number, called a *line number*. Line numbers specify the exact order in which the statements of a program are to be performed, or *executed*; the statement with the smallest line number is executed first, followed by the statement with the second smallest line number, and so forth. The following program uses only PRINT statements (except in line 120) to display a funny face on the screen.

Program 1

Statement

```
10  PRINT  "FUNNY FACE"
20  PRINT  "          *********"
30  PRINT  "        **           **"
40  PRINT  "      **  --      --  **"
50  PRINT  "   ((**    @       @     **))"
60  PRINT  "     **                    **"
70  PRINT  "     **  SS      V     SS  **"
80  PRINT  "       **  SS        SS  **"
90  PRINT  "         **  SSSSS  **"
100  PRINT  "          **      **"
110  PRINT  "---MMM-----*****-----MMM---"
120  END
```

The line numbers tell the computer that the instruction following it is a *program statement* rather than an immediate mode command. For example, if you type PRINT "   *********", then the computer will immediately PRINT the spaces and stars on the screen. If instead you type the statement 20 PRINT "   *********", the computer will insert the instruction into the program that is currently in its memory.

The RUN Command

To instruct the computer to execute the statements in a program, you type the immediate mode command RUN. (RUN comes *after* a program has been entered, but it is not part of the program.) After typing in Program 1, if you type RUN, the output will be as follows:

```
RUN
FUNNY FACE
          *********
        **           **
      **  --      --  **
   ((**    @       @     **))
     **                    **
     **  SS      V     SS  **
       **  SS        SS  **
         **  SSSSS  **
          **      **
---MMM-----*****-----MMM---
```

In producing the output on the previous page, the computer executed the program statements in numerical order, from the smallest line number (10) to the largest (120). The END statement in line 120 tells the computer to stop executing the program. (*Note:* Most microcomputers do not require an END statement in a program; the computer simply stops when it finishes executing the last line. Since an END statement gives a program structure and helps to avoid confusion, however, we will always include one in our programs in this book.)

Do you see why it was necessary to write a program to make the computer display the funny face? What would happen if you typed the lines of Program 1 as immediate mode commands?

The LIST Command

You may be wondering why the line numbers in Program 1 are in multiples of 10. This is done so that you can insert extra lines into the program without having to renumber lines. For example, suppose you want to include more detail in the top portion of the face produced by the program. One way to do this is to type a statement, say with line number 15, as follows:

```
15 PRINT "            *****"
```

The computer will automatically insert line 15 in its proper numerical location in the program (between lines 10 and 20). The change will not be immediately visible on the screen, however. To see that the new line has been correctly inserted, you can type the immediate mode command LIST. LIST causes the computer to display the entire program currently in its memory, in numerical order. Here's a LISTing of the new version of the program:

```
LIST
10 PRINT "FUNNY FACE"
15 PRINT "            *****"
20 PRINT "          *********"
30 PRINT "        **         **"
40 PRINT "      **  --     --  **"
50 PRINT "   ((**    @     @    **))"
60 PRINT "    **                **"
70 PRINT "    **  SS   V   SS  **"
80 PRINT "      **  SS     SS  **"
90 PRINT "        **  SSSSS  **"
100 PRINT "          **     **"
110 PRINT "---MMM-----*****-----MMM---"
120 END
```

Now if you type RUN again, you can see the output of the revised program.

```
RUN
FUNNY FACE
              *****
            *********
          **         **
        **  --     --  **
     ((**    @       @    **))
       **                 **
       **  SS     V    SS  **
         **  SS      SS  **
           **  SSSSS  **
              **    **
---MMM-----*****-----MMM---
```

If you want to see just one line of a program, type LIST followed by the single line number. For example, if you type LIST 40 (for Program 1), then the computer displays:

```
40 PRINT "        **  --     --  **"
```

If you want to see several lines of a program, type LIST followed by the first and last line numbers of the desired part, with a hyphen between the two line numbers. For example, if you type LIST 50–80, then the computer displays:

```
50 PRINT "  ((**    @       @    **))"
60 PRINT "    **                 **"
70 PRINT "    **  SS     V    SS  **"
80 PRINT "      **  SS      SS  **"
```

There is not much point in LISTing only part of Program 1, since it is so short; but you will soon write programs whose LISTings do not fit on the screen all at one time. Partial listings will become very convenient.

Making Corrections

You can correct errors in a program line in several different ways:

1. Use the backspace key (or the special cursor keys — see Section 2–1, page 19) if you notice the error *before* you have entered the program line into the computer's memory (that is, before you have pressed the <RETURN> or <ENTER> key).

2. If you have already pressed < RETURN > or < ENTER >, retype the line using the same line number, making the necessary corrections as you type. The new version of the line will replace the previously typed one in the computer's memory. For example, if you type:

```
10  PRINT "WEIRD FACE"
```

and then `LIST 10 - 20`

the computer will display:

```
10  PRINT "WEIRD FACE"
15  PRINT "              *****"
20  PRINT "            *********"
```

3. If you want to delete a line from a program, simply type the line number and press the < RETURN > or < ENTER > key. For example, if you type:

```
100
110
```

and then `LIST 90 - 120`

the computer will display:

```
90  PRINT "          **  SSSSS  **"
120  END
```

The NEW Command

Suppose you want to type a second program. You must first erase the old program from the memory of the computer; otherwise the old program lines can become part of the new program. The easiest way to erase an old program is to type the immediate mode command NEW. NEW clears the computer's memory, ensuring that lines from a previous program will not affect the new program. On most computers, NEW does not clear the screen, just the memory of the computer. Thus, if you type in a program and then type NEW, the program may still be on the screen, but it will not be in the memory.

HOME and CLS

BASIC has a command for clearing the screen of all characters. On *Apple* computers, the command is HOME; on *IBM* and *TRS-80* computers it is CLS (which is an abbreviation for "CLear Screen"). Each of these instructions may be used as an immediate mode command or as a program statement.

Once the HOME or CLS instruction is executed, the cursor will appear in the top left-hand corner of the cleared screen. Note that clearing the screen does not clear the memory of the computer; any program that was in the computer before clearing the screen will still be there afterwards. If you want to clear the memory, then you must (also) type NEW.

Avoiding Pitfalls

1. Be sure you type BASIC words such as PRINT, RUN, LIST, and NEW correctly, or a SYNTAX ERROR will result.
2. Remember to type NEW before typing in a new program, or overlaps with lines in a previous program may occur.
3. Remember that clearing the screen does not clear the computer's memory. If you want to erase what is in memory, you must also type NEW.

Summary

A BASIC computer program consists of a set of instructions *(statements)*, preceded by numbers *(line numbers)*.

The RUN command tells the computer to execute all the statements in the program currently in memory.

The END statement tells the computer to stop executing the statements in a program.

The LIST command tells the computer to display, in order, the statements in the program currently in memory.

The NEW command tells the computer to delete the program currently in memory.

The CLS or HOME command tells the computer to clear the screen (but not the memory).

Statements may be inserted anywhere in a program by choosing line numbers between existing line numbers. Statements may also be added at the beginning or end of a program.

Statements in a program may be changed by retyping the line using the same line number, or deleted by typing the line number followed by <RETURN> or <ENTER>.

Exercises 2-3

A

1. How does the computer know whether an instruction you type is a program statement or an immediate mode command?
2. What command tells the computer to execute the statements in a program?
3. What statement in a program is used to stop execution of the program?
4. What command tells the computer to display the statements currently in memory?
5. What command clears the computer's memory?

In Exercises 6–13, correct any errors in the given statements.

6. `25 PRIMT "HOW ARE YOU, FRIEND"`
7. `10 PRINT "I'M FINE, THANKS`
8. `50 "PRINT" 6 ↑ 2`
9. `12 PRINT 56 / 2(3 + 2)`
10. `45 TYPE "SILLY MISTAKE"`
11. `15 PRINT 4 × 5 / 10`
12. `15 PRINT 12 * 3 / (5 + 7`
13. `24 PRINT "IS THIS CORRECT"?`

In Exercises 14–19, predict the output of each program.

14.
```
10 PRINT "2 + 6 = "
20 PRINT 2 + 6
30 END
```

15.
```
10 PRINT 3 * 33
20 PRINT "IS A SECRET AGENT"
30 END
```

16.
```
10 PRINT "ALPHABET"
25 PRINT "A"
35 PRINT "Z"
38 END
```

17.
```
5 PRINT 2
10 PRINT "2"
12 PRINT 2 * 2
16 PRINT "2 * 2"
20 END
```

18.
```
5 PRINT "PARENTHESES"
10 PRINT 1 + 2 ↑ 3
20 PRINT (1 + 2) ↑ 3
30 PRINT (1 + (1 + 2)) ↑ 3
35 PRINT "TRICKY"
45 END
```

19.
```
40 PRINT "TIME"
20 PRINT "STITCH"
27 PRINT "IN"
10 PRINT "A"
100 PRINT "NINE"
50 PRINT "SAVES"
200 END
```

In Exercises 20–27, write a program that has the output shown.

B **20.**

```
1
   2
      3
   2
1
```

21.

```
      Z
   Y
X
   Y
      Z
```

22.

```
    *     *
    *     *
* * * * * * * *
    *     *
    *     *
* * * * * * * *
    *     *
    *     *
```

23.

```
* BOX *
B     B

O     O

X     X
* BOX *
```

24.

```
NUMBER     SQUARE     CUBE
1          1          1
2          4          8
3          9          27
4          16         64
5          25         125
```

25.

```
       C
      CO
     COM
    COMP
   COMPU
  COMPUT
 COMPUTE
COMPUTER
```

26.

```
$ $ $ $ $ $ $ $

            $
        $
    $

$ $ $ $ $ $ $ $
```

27.

```
* * * * * * * *
* * * * * * * *
          * *
        * *
      * *
    * *
  * *
* * * * * * * *
* * * * * * * *
```

28. Write a program that PRINTs your name, address, and telephone number on four separate lines.

29. Write a program that PRINTs your initials in large block letters (like the letter Z in Exercise 27 — only bigger).

30. Write a program that PRINTs your first name in large block letters, then erases the screen and PRINTs the message HOW DID I DO?. (See Exercise 27 for an example of a block letter.)

Lab Activity

A Program to RUN

In this Lab Activity, you will type and RUN a program that will allow you to draw interesting designs that have the symmetry of snowflakes. The program contains many programming techniques and BASIC words that you have not learned yet. Don't worry about it — simply use the program and enjoy the designs. The program will be entered into the computer in several stages. First, type the following lines. (Several program lines differ for different computers; choose the version that applies to your machine.) LIST portions of the program after you have entered it to check for typing mistakes.

Apple

```
10  PRINT "DRAWING DESIGNS"
100  HGR2
200  HCOLOR= 3
210  LET X = 5
220  LET Y = 5
300  GOSUB 1000: REM * PLOT POINTS
310  GET A$
400  IF A$ = "I" THEN LET Y = Y + 1: GOTO 300: REM * MOVE UP
410  IF A$ = "J" THEN LET X = X - 1: GOTO 300: REM * MOVE LEFT
420  IF A$ = "K" THEN LET X = X + 1: GOTO 300: REM * MOVE RIGHT
430  IF A$ = "M" THEN LET Y = Y - 1: GOTO 300: REM * MOVE DOWN
440  IF A$ < > "Q" THEN GOTO 300
450  TEXT
460  END
1000  IF SQR(X * X + Y * Y) > 95 THEN LET X = .8 * X: LET Y = .8 * Y
1060  GOSUB 1500: REM * PLOT POINTS
1300  RETURN
1500  HPLOT 140 + X, 96 - Y
1600  RETURN
```

TRS-80

Here are the changes for *TRS-80* computers:

```
100  CLS
200  <—— delete
310  LET A$ = INKEY$: IF A$ = "" THEN GOTO 310
```

```
450  CLS
1000  IF SQR(X * X + Y * Y) > 23 THEN LET X = .7 * X: LET Y = .7 * Y
1500  SET(64 + X, 24 - Y)
```

IBM

Here are the changes for *IBM* microcomputers:

```
100  CLS
200  SCREEN 1, 1
310  LET A$ = INKEY$: IF A$ = "" THEN GOTO 310
450  SCREEN 0
1000  IF SQR(X * X + Y * Y) > 90 THEN LET X = .8 * X: LET Y = .8 * Y
1500  PSET(160 + X, 100 - Y)
```

Problems

1. RUN the program. Type the I, J, K, and M keys repeatedly and watch the points being plotted on the screen.
2. Type Q to end the program. Type RUN again. Draw a square. Draw a more complicated figure such as:

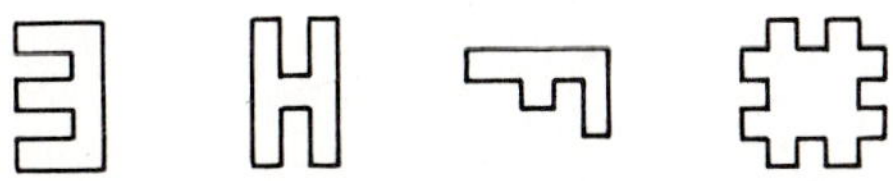

3. Type Q and then RUN the program again. Determine what the program does when you move the leading point toward the edge of the screen. (For a more interesting effect, don't approach the edge in a straight line; make several turns.) Move the leading point toward the edge in several different directions around the screen. What is the approximate shape of the border? (Line 1000 contains the instructions that cause this behavior.) Type Q again to end the program.
4. Your designs so far have probably not looked much like snowflakes. Snowflakes are very *symmetric* (that is, they repeat themselves in several different directions). To start putting some symmetry into your design add this line:

   Apple: `1510 HPLOT 140 + X, 96 + Y`

   TRS-80: `1510 SET(64 + X, 24 + Y)`

   IBM: `1510 PSET(160 + X, 100 + Y)`

   RUN the program and describe the effect this line has on the program.

5. To put more symmetry into your designs, add these lines:

Apple:
```
1520 HPLOT 140 — X, 96 + Y
1530 HPLOT 140 — X, 96 — Y
```

TRS-80:
```
1520 SET(64 — X, 24 + Y)
1530 SET(64 — X, 24 — Y)
```

IBM:
```
1520 PSET(160 — X, 100 + Y)
1530 PSET(160 — X, 100 — Y)
```

LIST the appropriate part of the program to see that the lines have been properly inserted. RUN this new version of the program and try drawing some designs. You might want to move the leading points to the edge of the screen and take advantage of the effect discovered in Problem 3.

6. The symmetry (repeated points) you saw in Problem 6 is called *reflection symmetry* because it results from *reflecting* points in certain lines, just as a mirror reflects images. Snowflakes also have *rotational symmetry,* which you can see by adding the following lines:

```
1010 LET XS = X
1020 LET YS = Y
1030 GOSUB 1500
1040 LET X = — .5 * XS — SQR (.75) * YS
1050 LET Y = SQR(.75) * XS — .5 * YS
1070 LET X = —.5 * XS + SQR (.75) * YS
1080 LET Y = — SQR(.75) * XS — .5 * YS
1090 GOSUB 1500
1200 LET X = XS
1210 LET Y = YS
1505 GOTO 1600
```

Note: On *TRS-80* computers also add these lines:

```
1024 LET X = SQR(.75) * XS + .5 * YS
1028 LET Y = .5 * XS + SQR(.75) * YS
```

RUN the new version of the program after checking your typing very carefully. Move the leading points and draw a three-way rotationally-symmetric design.

7. To restore the four-way reflection symmetry and finish the program, delete line 1505 from the program (just type 1505 with nothing after it). RUN the program and draw some snowflakes. (*Note:* On *TRS-80* computers also delete lines 1024 and 1028.)

8. See if you can find in the LISTing of the program which lines determine the starting position of the points being plotted. Change these values to see if you can get a snowflake to start near the edge of the screen rather than in the middle.

2-4 More about PRINT: Commas and Semicolons

Commas and semicolons have a special purpose in BASIC. When used in PRINT statements, they control where the output of a program will appear on the screen.

The Comma

When a comma is used to separate strings and numerical expressions in PRINT statements, it causes the output to be printed across the screen in *zones*. Some computers have three print zones, as shown below; others have four or more. The number of spaces within each zone also varies from computer to computer, but usually ranges from 14 to 16. (See the Lab Activity.)

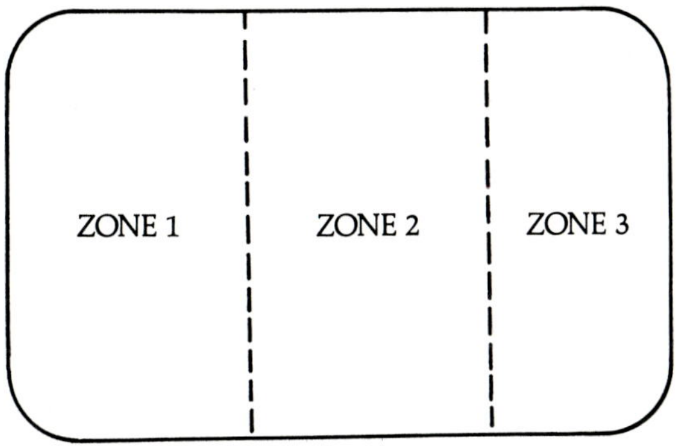

Program 1

Statement

```
10 PRINT "COMMAS", "ADD", "SPACE"
20 END
```

Output

```
COMMAS                    ADD                       SPACE
```

The commas in line 10 cause each string to be printed successively across the screen at the beginning of each zone. If there were more strings than zones in line 10, then the computer would automatically PRINT those extra strings beginning in the first zone of the next line.

Values of numerical expressions are also PRINTed in a zoned format when commas are used, as you can see in the output of Program 2.

Program 2

Statement

```
10  PRINT "ADD", "DIVIDE", "SUBTRACT"
20  PRINT 2 + 4, 2 / 4, 2 - 4
30  PRINT 4 + 2, 4 / 2, 4 - 2
40  END
```

Output

```
ADD            DIVIDE         SUBTRACT
6              .5             -2
6              2              2
```

(*Note: IBM* and *TRS-80* computers — but not *Apple* — leave a space in front of a number for a possible minus sign.)

Strings and values of numerical expressions can be PRINTed on the same line in a zoned format, as in the output of the following program.

Program 3

Statement

```
10  PRINT "2 + 3 =", 2 + 3
15  PRINT
20  PRINT "5 SQUARED:", 5 ↑ 2
25  PRINT
30  PRINT "5 * 5 = ", 5 * 5
40  END
```

Output

```
2 + 3 =        5

5 SQUARED:     25

5 * 5 =        25
```

Notice the PRINT statements in lines 15 and 25. Since these PRINTs are not followed by a string or a numerical expression, the computer puts a blank line between the output of lines 10 and 20 and lines 20 and 30. Note also how the use of strings in lines 10, 20, and 30 makes it clear what the output is about.

The Semicolon

Semicolons in PRINT statements also affect the form of the output, but in a different way. Semicolons are used to PRINT output close together.

STRINGS AND SEMICOLONS

When semicolons are used to separate strings in a PRINT statement, the computer prints the strings without adding space, as you can see in the output of Program 4.

Program 4

Statement

```
10  PRINT "SEMICOLONS"; "MERGE"; "STRINGS"
20  END
```

Output

```
SEMICOLONSMERGESTRINGS
```

There are two ways you can get proper spacing in output with strings. First, and simplest, is to include a space inside the quotation marks at the beginning or end of a string. For example, to separate the strings in Program 4, you could type:

```
10  PRINT "SEMICOLONS  "; "MERGE  "; "STRINGS"
```

or

```
10  PRINT "SEMICOLONS"; "  MERGE"; "  STRINGS"
```

The other method of spacing strings is to type spaces inside quotation marks and place them between the strings, set off by semicolons. Using this method in Program 4, you could type:

```
10  PRINT "SEMICOLONS"; "  "; "MERGE"; "  "; "STRINGS"
```

Each of these methods of separating strings would change the output of Program 4 to this:

```
SEMICOLONS MERGE STRINGS
```

NUMERICAL EXPRESSIONS AND SEMICOLONS

The effect of semicolons on numerical expressions in a PRINT statement varies somewhat from computer to computer (as shown on the next page). For example, suppose a program contains this line:

```
30  PRINT "ARITHMETIC:", 2 + 3; 2 - 3; 2 * 3
```

IBM and TRS-80 (The PET is the same as the IBM and TRS-80)

On *IBM* and *TRS-80* computers the output of line 30 would appear as follows:

```
ARITHMETIC:              5  -1  6
```

When PRINTing numbers both of these computers place a single space in front of and behind the number. If the number is negative, a minus sign is placed in the front space.

Apple

On *Apple* computers the output of line 30 would be this:

```
ARITHMETIC:              5-16
```

Since *Apple* computers do not add space before or after a number, you need to use strings consisting of spaces inside quotation marks to make the output clear. For example, in line 30 you would type:

```
30  PRINT "ARITHMETIC:", 2 + 3; "  "; 2 - 3; "  "; 2 * 3
```

Then the output would look like this:

```
ARITHMETIC:              5  -1  6
```

Punctuation at the End of a Line

When a comma or semicolon is typed at the end of a PRINT statement, it causes the computer to place the output of the next PRINT statement on the *same* line (unless the line is filled already). Here is an example:

Program 5

Statement

```
10  PRINT "5  4  3  2  1  0  ";
20  PRINT "BLAST OFF!"
30  END
```

Output

```
5  4  3  2  1  0  BLAST OFF!
```

Because of the semicolon at the end of line 10, the string BLAST OFF in line 20 is PRINTed in the output on the same line as the string in line 10. (Why is a space included after 0 in the string in line 10?)

The final program in this section uses PRINT statements to calculate the average number of points scored by each of five basketball players in their last three games. It also PRINTs the average of all five players as a team for the three games. Commas and semicolons are used throughout the program to make the output appear in a format that is easy to read.

Program 6

Statement

```
10  PRINT "PLAYER'S", "POINTS", "AVG.PTS."
20  PRINT "NICKNAME", "3 GAMES", "3 GAMES"
30  PRINT
40  PRINT "SUPERSHOT", "28 9   26", (28 + 9 + 26) / 3
50  PRINT "DUNKER", "21 16 8", (21 + 16 + 8) / 3
60  PRINT "LEAPER", "20 9   10", (20 + 9 + 10) / 3
70  PRINT "CHARGER", "15 11 7", (15 + 11 + 7) / 3
80  PRINT "FOULER", "10 9   14", (10 + 9 + 14) / 3
90  PRINT, , "--------"
100  PRINT, , "AVG. FOR"
110  PRINT, , "3   GAMES"
120  PRINT, , (28 + 9 + 26 + 21 + 16 + 8 + 20 + 9 + 10 + 15 + 11 + 7 + 10 +
9 + 14) / 15
130  END
```

Output

```
PLAYER'S            POINTS              AVG.PTS.
NICKNAME            3 GAMES             3 GAMES

SUPERSHOT           28 9   26           21
DUNKER              21 16 8             15
LEAPER              20 9   10           13
CHARGER             15 11 7             11
FOULER              10 9   14           11
                                        --------
                                        AVG. FOR
                                        3 GAMES
                                        14.2
```

Notice how the use of commas enables us to arrange the output in columns. In particular, notice in lines 90–120 how the use of two successive commas places the output in the third zone (since nothing is PRINTed in the first or second zone).

When the typed characters in a program statement do not all fit on one line (as in line 120), the extra characters are said to *wrap-around* to the next line on the screen.

Avoiding Pitfalls

1. When using commas in PRINT statements, remember that the number of strings and numerical expressions in each statement should not exceed the number of print zones on your computer (see the Lab Activity).
2. When using semicolons in PRINT statements, remember to include spaces at the beginning or end of strings, or use extra strings consisting of spaces inside quotation marks to get proper spacing in the output.

Summary

If you want the output of your program to be spread out in zones, use commas; if you want the output to be placed close together on a single line, use semicolons.

A comma or semicolon typed at the end of a PRINT statement causes the output of the next PRINT statement to be PRINTed on the *same* line (unless the line is filled already).

A statement such as 30 PRINT causes the computer to leave a blank line in the output of the program.

Exercises 2-4

In Exercises 1–14, predict the output of each program for your computer. (Be sure you know the number of print zones for your computer, as well as the size of each zone. Do the Lab Activity first.)

A

1.
```
10 PRINT 5, 3
20 PRINT "END"
30 END
```

2.
```
10 PRINT 5, 3,
20 PRINT "END"
30 END
```

3.
```
10 PRINT 5, 3, 1;
20 PRINT "END"
30 END
```

4.
```
10 PRINT 5; 3; 1;
20 PRINT "END"
30 END
```

5.
```
10 PRINT "EYE";
20 PRINT "  TO";
30 PRINT "  EYE"
40 END
```

6.
```
10 PRINT "EYE"; "  ";
20 PRINT "TO"; "  ";
30 PRINT "EYE"
40 END
```

7.
```
10 PRINT "SUM IS:  ";
20 PRINT 2 + 3
30 END
```

8.
```
10 PRINT "PRODUCT IS:"; "  ";
20 PRINT 2 * 3
30 END
```

9.
```
10 PRINT "ISN'T THIS A REALLY GREAT", "STRING?"
20 END
```

10.
```
10 PRINT 12; "  IS THE PRODUCT OF  "; "4 AND 3"
20 PRINT "BUT  "; 7; "  IS THE SUM OF"; "  ";
30 PRINT "4 AND 3"
40 END
```

11.
```
10 PRINT "HA", "HA", "HA"
20 PRINT "BOO"; "HOO", "BOO"; "HOO"
25 PRINT
30 PRINT "HA", "HA"; "HA","HA"
40 PRINT "BOO"; "HOO" , , "BOO"; "HOO"
50 END
```

12.
```
10 PRINT , 1, -2, 3
20 PRINT 1, -2, 3, 4
30 PRINT 1; "  "; -2, 3; 4
40 PRINT 1, -2; "  "; 3; 4
50 END
```

13.
```
10 PRINT "THE AVERAGE OF 75, 86, AND 91 IS :  "; (75 + 86 + 91) / 3
15 PRINT
20 PRINT (75 + 86 + 91) / 3; "  IS THE AVERAGE OF 75, 86, AND 91."
30 END
```

14.
```
10 PRINT "AREA OF A TRIANGLE"
20 PRINT
30 PRINT "BASE", "HEIGHT", "AREA"
40 PRINT 3, 4, 3 * 4 / 2
50 PRINT 10, 20, 10 * 20 / 2
60 END
```

B **15.** Write PRINT statements that give output similar to that shown in (a)–(e) below. You may use only the string MUR and the string consisting of one space.

a. `MUR            MUR            MUR`

b. `MURMURMUR`

c. `MURMUR         MURMUR         MURMUR`

d. `MUR MUR MUR MUR`

e. `MURMUR MURMUR MURMUR MURMUR`

16. Write a program that PRINTs your name on the first line of the screen, your street address on the third line, and your city and state on the fifth line.

17. Write a program that lists the names of five students, their mid-year and final exam grades, their average grade for the year, and the average grade for all five students. Have the output appear in a zoned format, similar to the following:

```
STUDENT'S          EXAM            AVERAGE
NAME               GRADES          FOR YEAR

WILLIAMS           88  82          85
DEANE              91  84          87.5
JACKSON            78  90          84
FIELDS             91  91          91
YOUNG              76  82          79
                                   --------
                                   TOT.AVG.
                                   GRADE
                                   85.3
```

Lab Activity

Exploring PRINT Zones

Problems

1. RUN the following program to discover the number of print zones on your computer.

```
10 PRINT "A", "A", "A", "A", "A", "A", "A", "A"
100 END
```

How many zones does your computer use? (Change line 10 so that the number of letter A's matches the number of print zones on your computer.)

2. Add the following line to the program to discover the length of each PRINT zone.

```
5 PRINT "12345678901234567890123. . ."
```

(Type the number of digits needed to fill one line on your screen when the program is RUN.)

RUN the program. Now compare the output from lines 5 and 10 to determine the number of characters that can fit into each zone (the *length* of each zone). Is each zone the same length on your computer?

3. Add the following line to the program to find out what happens when the first PRINT zone is more than completely filled up.

```
30 PRINT "ABCDEFGHIJKLMNOPQRST", "A"
```

RUN the program. What are the results?

4. Reduce the length of the first string in line 30 until the second zone is no longer affected. What is the longest string that can be PRINTed in the first zone that does not change the second zone?

5. Using a technique similar to that of Problems 3 and 4 above, determine the longest string that can be PRINTed in the second zone that will not affect the third zone. (If you have an *Apple* computer, the result of this experiment is most unexpected.)

2-5 An Introduction to Graphics

On most microcomputers, it is possible to produce *graphics* output; in addition to PRINTing letters, numbers, and the other usual characters, the computer can draw dots (that is, plot points) on the screen at any locations you specify. By writing a program that plots many points, you can make the computer draw a design or picture.

Each make of computer has its own unique graphics commands. The size of the dots and the colors available also vary from computer to computer. We will present here a short introduction to graphics on the *Apple, TRS-80,* and *IBM* microcomputers. More advanced graphics techniques for each machine will be presented later in the book, as you learn more of the BASIC language.

Apple Graphics

On *Apple* computers, there are two types (modes) of graphics; this section will introduce you to the simpler of the two — *low resolution graphics.* To draw pictures using low resolution graphics, you must first give the computer the instruction GR (an abbreviation of GRaphics), which can be either an immediate mode command or a statement in a program. The effect of the GR instruction is to clear the screen to black (any text on the screen disappears). All but the bottom four lines on the screen are then available for drawing. (PRINT statements may be used to output text to these bottom four lines.)

Next, you must tell the computer what color you want the dots (points) to be. This is done with the COLOR statement. COLOR is followed by an equals sign and the number of the color you want. There are fifteen colors available (if you count black and white); their numbers are given in the table below:

Color Table

0 = black	4 = dark green	8 = brown	12 = green
1 = magenta	5 = gray	9 = orange	13 = yellow
2 = dark blue	6 = medium blue	10 = gray	14 = aqua
3 = purple	7 = light blue	11 = pink	15 = white

As an example, the statement COLOR = 3 will set the color of subsequent dots to purple. The color of new dots may be changed at any time using the COLOR statement. Note that the color of any dots already on the screen will not change — only ones that are yet to be drawn. Also, if you have a black and white (or black and green or black and amber) screen, the colors will be varying shades of gray (or green or amber). In any case, the computer starts out with the color equal to 0 (black), so you *must* change the color initially to a number between 1 and 15 in order to produce anything other than invisible black dots on a black background.

To actually draw the dots on the screen, you type PLOT followed by two numbers separated by a comma. The two numbers specify where on the screen the dot will appear. Think of covering the screen with a 40 by 40 grid, similar to graph paper. The little rectangles of the grid (where the dots will go) are numbered from 0 to 39 in both the horizontal and vertical directions, as indicated in the diagram below. Any small rectangle on the screen can be specified by giving its horizontal coordinate *(column number),* followed by its vertical coordinate *(row number).* For example, PLOT 2, 6 will fill in the little rectangle shown in the grid with the color you have chosen.

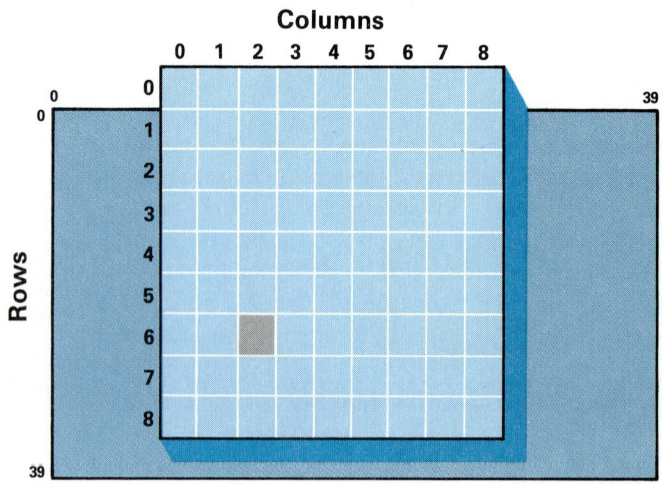

To leave graphics mode and return to typing, LISTing, and RUNning other programs, type the immediate mode command TEXT. (TEXT may also be used as a statement in a program.) The screen then will fill with some unusual symbols and characters. The HOME command can be used to clear the screen.

Here is an example of a simple program that uses COLOR and PLOT statements to draw a small orange and green box on the graphics screen (if you have a color monitor).

Program 1

Statement	Remark
10 GR	*Clear screen, enter graphics mode.*
20 COLOR = 9	*Orange points.*
30 PLOT 4, 4	*Plot points on edge of box.*
40 PLOT 5, 4	
50 PLOT 6, 4	
60 PLOT 6, 5	
70 COLOR = 12	*Green points.*
80 PLOT 6, 6	
90 PLOT 5, 6	
100 PLOT 4, 6	
110 PLOT 4, 5	
120 END	

Output

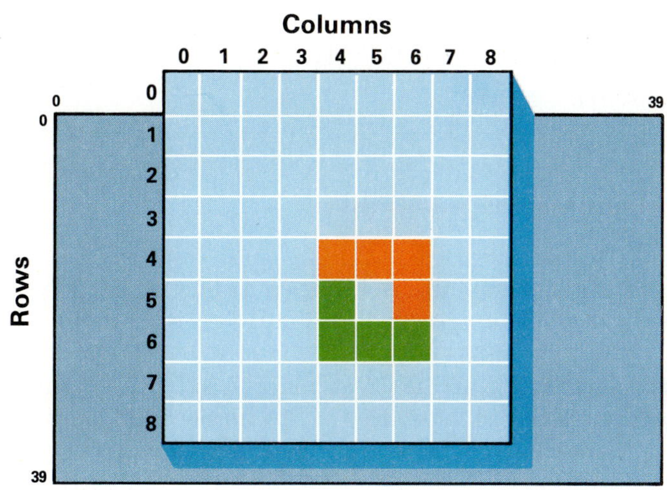

If you add the lines

```
115 TEXT
118 HOME
```

what will you see on the screen when you RUN Program 1?

Avoiding Pitfalls

1. Be sure to set the COLOR to a number between 1 and 15 before PLOTting points, or the points will be invisible.
2. If you specify a horizontal coordinate (column) less than 0 or greater than 39, or a vertical coordinate (row) less than zero or greater than 47, you will get an ILLEGAL QUANTITY error message and your program will stop.
3. If you use parentheses in a PLOT statement — PLOT (4, 12) for example — you will get a SYNTAX ERROR message and your program will stop.

Summary for the Apple

GR clears the screen to black and prepares the computer to do low resolution graphics.

COLOR = 7 tells the computer to plot subsequent points in light blue.

PLOT 15, 28 tells the computer to fill in the little rectangle in column 15 and row 28 with the current color.

TEXT causes the computer to leave graphics mode. HOME will clear the screen of the unusual symbols and characters.

(Exercises 2–5 are on page 55.)

TRS-80 Graphics

On *TRS-80* computers, text and graphics can be mixed on the screen. Only white dots (points) can be drawn unless you have the *TRS-80* color computer.

To start, you will usually want to clear the screen using CLS. To draw a small rectangular white dot on the screen, type SET (,), with two numbers inside the parentheses. The two numbers specify where on the screen the dot will appear. Think of covering the screen with a 128 by 48 grid, similar to graph paper. The little rectangles of the grid (where the dots will go) are numbered from 0 to 127 in the horizontal direction, and from 0 to 47 in the vertical direction, as indicated in the diagram below. Any small rectangle on the screen can be specified by giving its horizontal coordinate *(column number)*, followed by its vertical coordinate *(row number)*. For example, the instruction SET(2, 6) will fill in the little rectangle shown in the grid with a white dot.

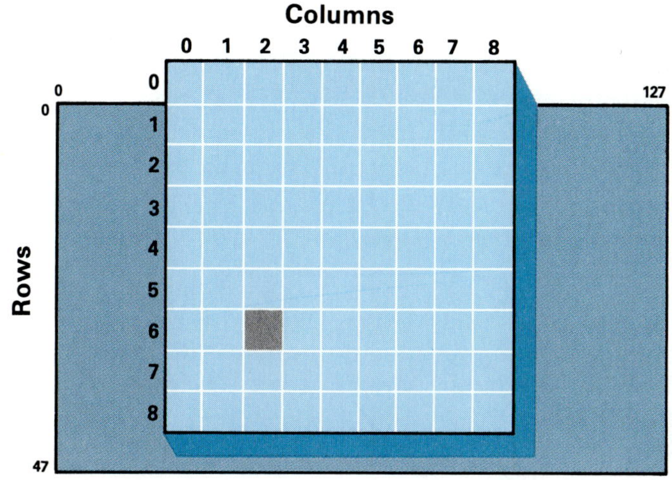

Here is an example of a simple program that uses SET instructions to draw a small box on the screen.

Program 2

Statement	Remark
10 CLS	*Clear screen.*
20 SET(4, 10)	*Plot points on edge of box.*
30 SET(5, 10)	
40 SET(6, 10)	
50 SET(6, 11)	
60 SET(6, 12)	
70 SET(5, 12)	
80 SET(4, 12)	
90 SET(4, 11)	
100 END	

Output

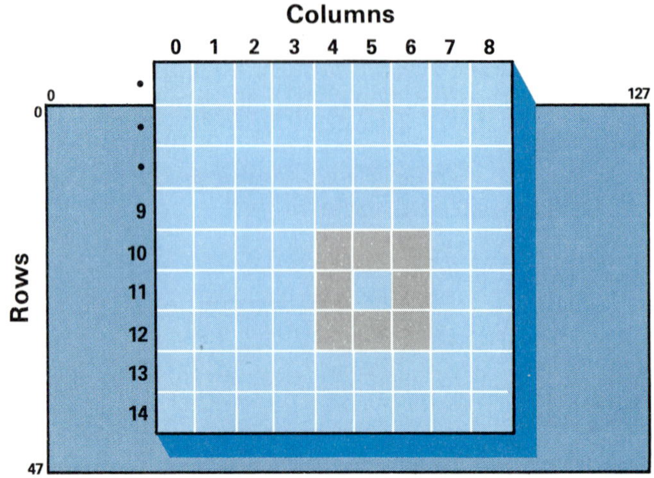

(*Note:* The READY prompt will always appear after the program is RUN. In Chapter 6 you will learn how to keep it off the screen and away from your finished picture.)

Avoiding Pitfalls

1. Be sure you enclose the numbers in the SET instruction in parentheses; otherwise, you will get a SYNTAX ERROR message and your program will stop.
2. If the first of the two numbers in a SET command is less than 0 or greater than 127, or if the second number is less than 0 or greater than 47, you will get an ILLEGAL FUNCTION CALL error and your program will stop.

Summary for the TRS-80

Use CLS to clear the screen before doing graphics.

The command SET(38, 29) causes the computer to plot a small white rectangle at the position with horizontal coordinate 38 (column number) and vertical coordinate 29 (row number).

(Exercises 2–5 are on page 55.)

IBM Graphics

There are two types of graphics capability on the IBM Personal Computer. In this section, you will learn how to use *medium resolution graphics* (a Color/Graphics Monitor is needed.)

To draw color pictures using medium resolution graphics, you must first give the computer the instruction SCREEN 1, 0, which can be either an immediate mode command or a statement in a program. SCREEN 1, 0 does not clear the screen (except the first time you use it), so you will usually want to use CLS.

Next, you must tell the computer what color you want the screen to be (this is called the *background* color) and select one of two *palettes* (a palette is the range of colors used by an artist in a painting) that contain the possible colors for the points that will be drawn. This is done with the COLOR statement. The form of the COLOR statement is:

COLOR *background, palette*

There are 16 background colors available (if you count black and white); their numbers are given in the table below:

Background Color Table

0	Black	8	Gray
1	Blue	9	Light Blue
2	Green	10	Light Green
3	Cyan	11	Light Cyan
4	Red	12	Light Red
5	Magenta	13	Light Magenta
6	Brown	14	Yellow
7	White	15	Bright White

Each palette contains 3 possible colors for the points that will be drawn on top of the background. The palettes are numbered 0 and 1 as you can see below:

Palette 0	Palette 1
Green (1)	Cyan (1)
Red (2)	Magenta (2)
Brown (3)	White (3)

For example, the statement

COLOR 1, 0

will set the background color to blue and allow you to draw points in any of the 3 colors listed under Palette 0. (*Note:* It is also possible to draw points in the background color — which will make the points invisible. You will see why this is a useful technique in Chapter 6, Section 6–5.) The background color, or the palette, or both, may be changed at any time using the COLOR statement with new color numbers.

To actually draw a point on the screen, you use the PSET statement. The PSET statement has this form:

PSET(X, Y), *color*

The *color* value you assign (either 1, 2, or 3) specifies the color of the point to be drawn based on the palette you selected in the COLOR statement. The values you give for the coordinates (X, Y) specify where on the screen the point will appear. Think of covering the screen with a 320 by 200 grid, similar to graph paper. The little rectangles of the grid (where the points will go) are numbered from 0 to 319 in the horizontal direction, and from 0 to 199 in the vertical direction, as indicated in the diagram below. Any small rectangle on the screen can be specified by giving its horizontal coordinate *(column number)*, followed by its vertical coordinate *(row number)*. For example, the lines

```
110 COLOR 1, 0          ← blue background, palette 0
120 PSET(2, 6), 2       ← on palette 0, color number 2 is red
```

will cause a red point to be drawn at coordinates (2, 6). The background color is blue, as you can see in the diagram.

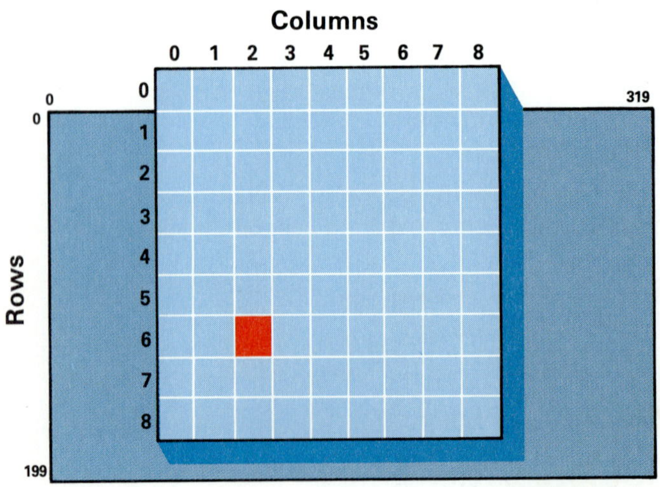

You may return to the text screen for typing, LISTing, and RUNning the same or other programs by typing SCREEN 0, 0. (*Note:* After you return to the text screen, the computer automatically allows only 40 characters on a line. If you want to type up to 80 characters on a line, type the immediate mode command WIDTH 80.)

If you prefer to draw points without color (that is, white points on a black background), type SCREEN 1, 1 rather than SCREEN 1, 0. No COLOR statement is needed, and no color value need be specified in the PSET statement. For example, the lines

```
100 SCREEN 1, 1
110 PSET(2, 6)
```

will cause a white dot to be drawn on a black screen in the 2nd column and 6th row.

Here is an example of a simple program that uses the COLOR and PSET instructions to draw a red and white letter L on a graphics screen with a blue background.

Program 3

Statement	Remark
10 CLS	*Clear screen.*
20 SCREEN 1, 0	*Medium resolution graphics, with color.*
30 COLOR 1, 0	*Set blue background; choose color from Palette 0.*
40 PSET(40, 10), 2	*Plot red points.*
50 PSET(40, 11), 2	
60 PSET(40, 12), 2	
70 PSET(40, 13), 2	
80 PSET(40, 14), 2	
90 COLOR 1, 1	*Set blue background; choose color from Palette 1.*
100 PSET(41, 14), 3	*Plot white points.*
110 PSET(42, 14), 3	
115 PSET(43, 14), 3	
120 PSET(44, 14), 3	
130 END	

Output

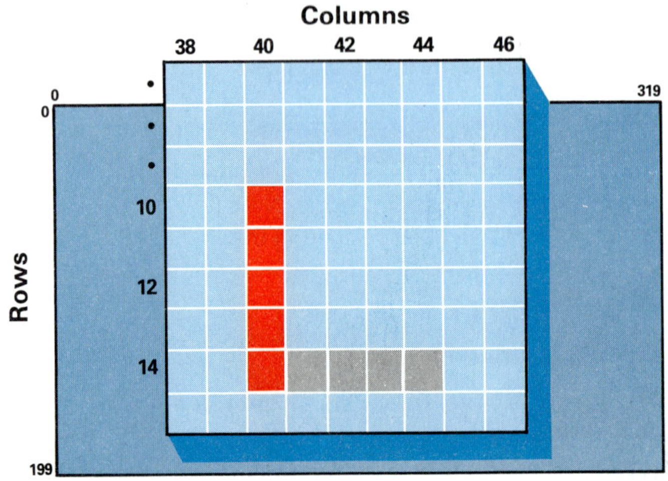

Avoiding Pitfalls

1. Be sure you enclose the numbers in the PSET instruction in parentheses; otherwise, you will get a SYNTAX ERROR message and your program will stop.
2. If you draw points in the same color as the background color, the points will be invisible.

Summary for IBM

SCREEN 1, 0 will allow you to do medium resolution graphics with color.

SCREEN 1, 1 will allow you to do medium resolution graphics, but without color.

The lines

```
100  COLOR 9, 0          ←—— light blue background, palette 0
110  PSET(190, 48), 1    ←—— on palette 0, color number 1 is green
```

will cause a green point to be drawn on a light blue background at coordinates (190, 48).

SCREEN 0, 0 will end graphics mode and return the computer to a 40 character per line text screen.

Exercises 2-5

A **1.** On a piece of graph paper, color in the points (rectangles) that would be plotted by each of the programs listed beneath your computer's name. (The graph paper only needs to cover the upper left-hand corner of the screen — about 10 by 10.)

Apple

a.
```
10 GR
20 COLOR = 15
30 PLOT 0, 0
40 PLOT 1, 0
50 PLOT 2, 0
60 PLOT 0, 2
70 PLOT 1, 2
80 PLOT 2, 2
90 END
```

b.
```
10 GR
20 COLOR = 15
30 PLOT 1, 4
40 PLOT 3, 4
50 PLOT 1, 6
60 PLOT 3, 6
70 PLOT 4, 5
80 END
```

TRS-80

a.
```
10 CLS
20 SET(0, 0)
30 SET(1, 0)
40 SET(2, 0)
50 SET(0, 2)
60 SET(1, 2)
70 SET(2, 2)
80 END
```

b.
```
10 CLS
20 SET(1, 4)
30 SET(3, 4)
40 SET(1, 6)
50 SET(3, 6)
60 SET(4, 5)
70 END
```

IBM

a.
```
10 SCREEN 1, 1
20 PSET(0, 0)
30 PSET(1, 0)
40 PSET(2, 0)
50 PSET(0, 2)
60 PSET(1, 2)
70 PSET(2, 2)
80 END
```

b.
```
10 SCREEN 1, 1
20 PSET(1, 4)
30 PSET(3, 4)
40 PSET(1, 6)
50 PSET(3, 6)
60 PSET(4, 5)
70 END
```

2. Correct the errors, if any, in each of the following statements. Use only the statements that apply to your computer.

Apple

a. `100 GR`
b. `100 PLOT (6, 12)`
c. `80 PLOT 6, 50`
d. `130 TEXT`
e. `70 COLOR = "GREEN"`
f. `35 COLOR (6)`

TRS-80

a. `100 SET(5, —7)`
b. `40 SET 3, 12`
c. `28 SET(140, 90)`
d. `100 CLR`

IBM

a. `100 SCREEN (1, 1)`
b. `20 SCREEN`
c. `50 COLOR 9, 2`
d. `85 PSET 3, 12`
e. `60 PSET(500, 65)`
f. `70 PSET(180, 56), 4`

B **3.** (*Apple* and *IBM*) Write the statements for your machine that will clear the screen, set up graphics mode, and plot a red point at coordinates (20, 30).

4. Write a program to draw each of the following figures in graphics mode on your computer.

a.

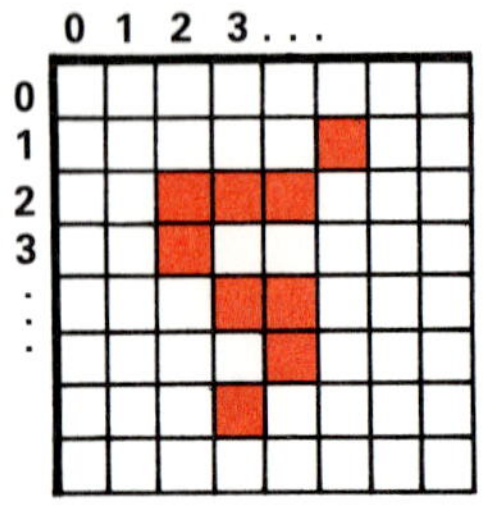

b.

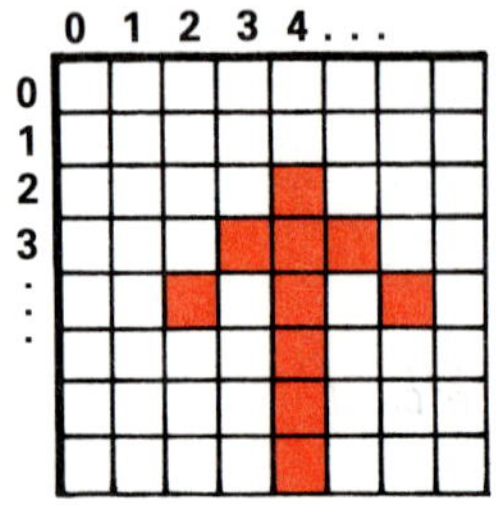

c.

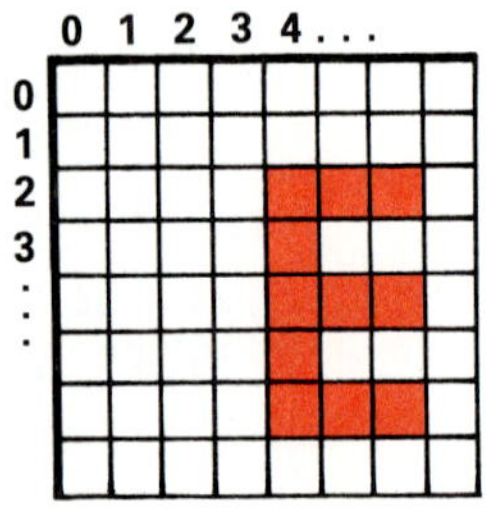

d.

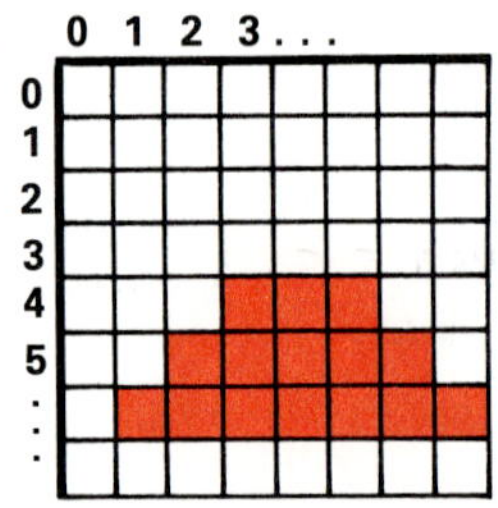

5. Write a program to draw your initials in large block letters in graphics mode. (See Problem 4(c) for an example of a block letter.)

6. Write a program to draw as accurate a circle as you can in graphics mode. (Draw the points on graph paper first.)

7. Write a program that will draw an *isosceles right triangle,* like the one at the right, in graphics mode. (An *isosceles right triangle* is a triangle with a right angle and two equal sides.)

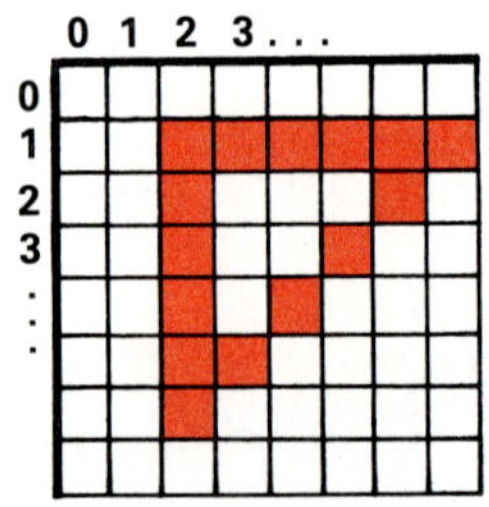

Lab Activity

A Coordinate Guessing Game

Type the following program into the computer. (Choose the version that applies to your machine.)

Apple

```
10 PRINT "HIT THE TARGET GAME"
20 PRINT
30 LET X = RND( - PEEK(78) - 256 * PEEK(79)): REM * RANDOMIZE
```

```
40  INPUT "READY TO PLAY?"; A$
50  IF LEFT$(A$, 1) = "N" THEN GOTO 210
60  GOSUB 500: REM * DRAW TARGET
70  LET NSH = 1: REM * NO. OF SHOTS
80  PRINT "TYPE SHOT IN THE FORM: COLUMN, ROW"
90  INPUT XS, YS
100  IF XS >= 0 AND XS <= 39 AND YS >= 0
       AND YS <= 39 THEN PLOT XS, YS
110  IF XL > XS OR XS > XL + 4 THEN GOTO 190
120  IF YT > YS OR YS > YT + 4 THEN GOTO 190
130  GR
140  TEXT
150  HOME
160  PRINT "YOU HIT THE TARGET IN  "; NSH; "  SHOT(S)"
180  GOTO 20
190  LET NSH = NSH + 1
200  GOTO 80
210  END
500  LET XL = INT(35 * RND(1)): REM * LEFT HORIZONTAL COORDINATE
510  LET YT = INT(35 * RND(1)): REM * TOP VERTICAL COORDINATE
520  GR
530  COLOR = 15: REM * WHITE
540  FOR X = XL TO XL + 4
550  PLOT X, YT
560  PLOT X, YT + 4
570  NEXT X
580  FOR Y = YT + 1 TO YT + 3
590  PLOT XL, Y
600  PLOT XL + 4, Y
610  NEXT Y
620  RETURN
```

TRS-80

```
10  PRINT "HIT THE TARGET GAME"
20  PRINT
30  RANDOM
40  INPUT "READY TO PLAY"; A$
50  IF LEFT$(A$, 1) = "N" THEN GOTO 210
```

Program continued on following page.

```
55  CLS
60  GOSUB 500: REM * DRAW TARGET
70  LET NSH = 1: REM * NO. OF SHOTS
80  PRINT @835, "TYPE YOUR SHOT IN THIS FORM: COLUMN, ROW";
87  PRINT @899, "             ";
90  PRINT @899, " "; : INPUT XS, YS
100  IF XS >= 0 AND XS <= 100 AND YS >= 0
       AND YS <= 38 THEN SET(XS, YS)
110  IF XL > XS OR XS > XL + 4 THEN GOTO 190
120  IF YT > YS OR YS > YT + 4 THEN GOTO 190
150  CLS
160  PRINT "YOU HIT THE TARGET IN  "; NSH; "  SHOT(S)"
180  GOTO 20
190  LET NSH = NSH + 1
200  GOTO 87
210  END
500  LET XL = RND(96): REM * LEFT HORIZONTAL COORDINATE
510  LET YT = RND(34): REM * TOP VERTICAL COORDINATE
540  FOR X = XL TO XL + 4
550  SET(X, YT)
560  SET(X, YT + 4)
570  NEXT X
580  FOR Y = YT + 1 TO YT + 3
590  SET(XL, Y)
600  SET(XL + 4, Y)
610  NEXT Y
620  RETURN
```

IBM

```
10  PRINT "HIT THE TARGET GAME"
20  PRINT
30  INPUT "READY TO PLAY"; A$
40  IF LEFT$(A$, 1) = "N" THEN GOTO 210
45  PRINT "TYPE A NUMBER BETWEEN THE GIVEN LIMITS"
50  RANDOMIZE
55  CLS
60  GOSUB 500: REM * DRAW TARGET
70  LET NSH = 1
80  LOCATE 22, 1: PRINT "TYPE SHOT IN THE FORM: COLUMN, ROW";
```

```
87  LOCATE 23, 1: PRINT"                    ";
90  LOCATE 23, 1: INPUT XS, YS
100  IF XS >= 0 AND XS <= 300 AND YS >= 0 AND YS <= 160 THEN PSET(XS, YS)
110  IF XL > XS OR XS > XL + 8 THEN GOTO 190
120  IF YT > YS OR YS > YT + 8 THEN GOTO 190
130  SCREEN 0, 0
150  CLS
160  PRINT "YOU HIT THE TARGET IN  "; NSH; "  SHOT(S)"
180  GOTO 20
190  LET NSH = NSH + 1
200  GOTO 87
210  END
500  LET XL = INT(292 * RND(1)): REM * LEFT HORIZONTAL COORDINATE
510  LET YT = INT(152 * RND(1)): REM * TOP VERTICAL COORDINATE
520  SCREEN 1, 1
540  FOR X = XL TO XL + 8
550  PSET(X, YT)
560  PSET(X, YT+ 8)
570  NEXT X
580  FOR Y = YT + 1 TO YT + 7
590  PSET(XL, Y)
600  PSET(XL + 8, Y)
610  NEXT Y
620  RETURN
```

Problems

1. RUN the program. Type in your guesses for the coordinates of the center of the target as two numbers separated by a comma, then press either the < RETURN > or < ENTER > key. (Do not type parentheses around the numbers.) Try to lower your score to a consistent level of 2 or 3.

2. To use a smaller target, RUN the program with these changes:

Apple

```
540  FOR X = XL TO XL + 2
560  PLOT X, YT + 2
580  PLOT X, YT + 1
590  PLOT XL + 2, YT + 1
600 }
610 } <---- delete
```

TRS-80

```
540  FOR X = XL TO XL + 2
560  SET(X, YT + 2)
580  SET(XL, YT + 1)
590  SET(XL + 2, YT + 1)
600 }
610 } <---- delete
```

IBM

```
540  FOR X = XL TO XL + 5
560  PSET(X, YT + 5)
580  FOR Y = YT + 1 TO YT + 4
600  PSET(XL + 5, Y)
```

Chapter Summary

An *immediate mode command* is an instruction that the computer executes as soon as the < RETURN > or < ENTER > key is pressed.

The PRINT command can be used to display on the screen any *string* enclosed in quotation marks or to evaluate a numerical expression and display the result.

A BASIC computer program consists of a set of instructions called *statements,* preceded by *line numbers.* Statements in a program may be changed by retyping the line using the same line number or deleted by typing the line number followed by < RETURN > or < ENTER >.

The RUN command tells the computer to execute the statements in the program currently in memory.

The LIST command tells the computer to display, in order, the statements in the program currently in memory.

The END statement tells the computer to stop executing the program.

The NEW command tells the computer to delete the program in memory.

The HOME (or CLS) command tells the computer to clear the screen.

In PRINT statements, use commas if you want the output of your program to be spread out in zones. If you want the output placed close together, use semicolons. A statement such as 20 PRINT causes a blank line to appear in the output of a program.

Numbers may be written in BASIC in integer, decimal, or exponential form *(E–form).* When evaluating BASIC numerical expressions, apply the same rules for the order of operations as in arithmetic. Perform operations in parentheses first, from the innermost parentheses outward.

Apple Graphics
See the summary on page 48.

TRS-80 Graphics
See the summary on page 50.

IBM Graphics
See the summary on page 54.

Chapter Test

1. Write a command using BASIC operation symbols that will find the value of each numerical expression.
   a. $8 \times 6 + 4$ b. $18 \div 2$ c. 6^2 d. $5 - 4^2$

2. Predict the output of each of the following commands.
   a. PRINT "10 + 3"
   b. PRINT 3 + 6
   c. PRINT "COUR■AGE"
   d. PRINT "3 ↑ 3"

3. Express each of the following in integer or decimal form.
   a. 7.1326E + 03
   b. 3.7105E − 04
   c. 2E + 05
   d. 3E − 04
   e. −3E − 03
   f. −6.3E + 03

4. Evaluate each of the following BASIC numerical expressions.
   a. 12 − 12 / 3 + 3 * 2
   b. 5 ↑ (2 * 2)
   c. (12 − 12 / 3 + 3) * 2
   d. 6 − (18 / 2 + 1) * 3
   e. (12 − 12) / 3 + 3 * 2
   f. 6 − 18 / (2 + 1)

5. Predict the output of the following program:

```
30 PRINT "THAN"
20 PRINT "NOW"
40 PRINT "NEVER"
50 END
10 PRINT "BETTER"
```

6. Predict the output of each of the following programs:

a.
```
10 PRINT "COMPUTERS..."
20 PRINT "5 * 3", "3 ↑ 4", "16 / 2"
30 PRINT 5 * 3, 3 ↑ 4, 16 / 2
40 PRINT
50 PRINT "DAZZLING!"
60 PRINT "FINISHED"
70 END
```

b.
```
10 PRINT "3 + 12 / 4 = ";
20 PRINT 3 + 12 / 4
30 PRINT
40 PRINT "THIS"; "  "; "IS"; "  ";
50 PRINT "AN EXAMPLE"
60 PRINT "EASY", "AS", "PIE"
70 END
```

7. Write a program in graphics mode to produce the output shown on the grid at the right.

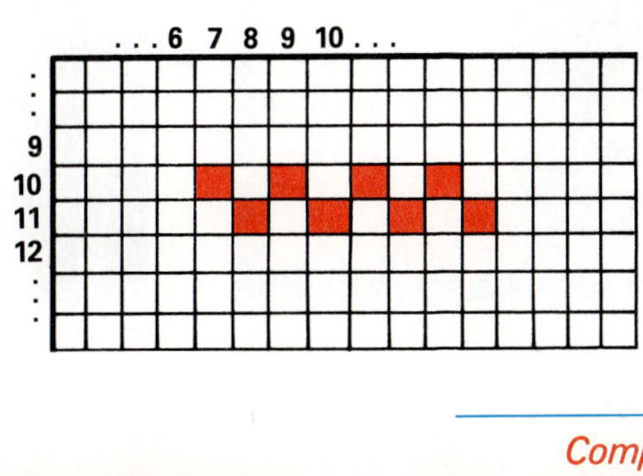

From Rossum's Robot to ???

When you hear the word robot, what comes to your mind? R2D2 of *Star Wars* fame, or perhaps some diabolical machine attempting to take over the world in a science fiction movie? Both of these examples portray a robot as an intelligent and rather sophisticated machine that is nearly human. But the robots that are being used today do not match our imagination. If you were to enter a car manufacturing plant, you probably would see rows of giant mechanical arms that are used to weld, sand, and paint car bodies. These arms have wrist, elbow, and shoulder mechanisms that allow them to move and swivel claw-like hands, so that they can perform the tasks mentioned above. These robot arms may be a far cry from your idea of a robot, but they do have something in common with R2D2; they have been programmed to do certain tasks.

The term robot comes from the Czechoslovakian word "robota", which means work. Its probable first use was in 1920 to refer to a mechanical worker in the play *Rossum's Universal Robots*. Since then many people have envisioned what a robot should be and what it should be able to do. Nowadays, most people agree that a robot is a mechanical device that has been programmed to perform specific tasks.

The fact that robots have computers as "brains" sets them apart from other machines. Robots can be programmed to do a variety of repetitious tasks automatically, making them more versatile than conventional machinery. If the robot arms in a car factory were not programmable, they might become obsolete with every newly-designed model. By giving the robot arms a new set of instructions, they can be made ready to weld and

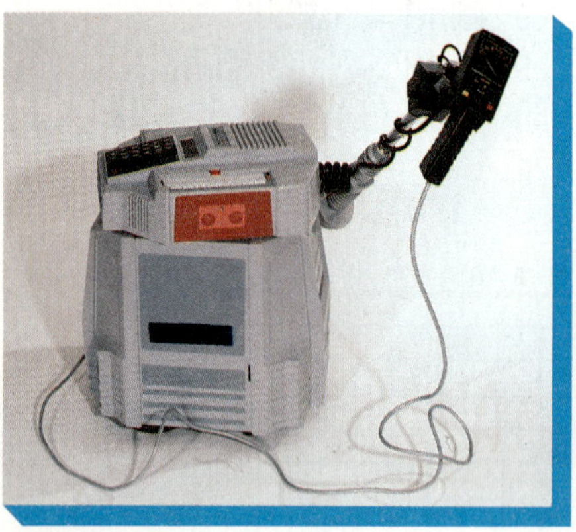

Household robot

Automobile assembly-line robots

Robot arm for welding

paint a different model of car. This reprogramming of robots can greatly reduce the cost of "retooling" an assembly line for every new model, and thus allow the car manufacturer to build more economical cars.

Robot Capabilities

The instructions for tasks that robots will perform must be very specific. Although it is a simple matter for you to reach down and tie your shoelace, imagine how many steps would be needed to instruct a robot to do this!

Besides their use in the auto industry, robots are commonly used today in tool and die casting, metal forging, welding, and in industries that assemble small parts into bigger ones. Many of the jobs that robots do are repetitious, but robots never get bored. They continue the same task in the same way until they are instructed to stop. Robots can perform tasks such as handling dangerous radioactive materials. In addition, they can perform tasks that require a high degree of accuracy. Neurosurgeons have used lasers in small robot arms to pinpoint the location of brain tumors.

A look into the near future shows robots that can collect garbage, pick fruit, prepare fast food, butcher meat, and shear sheep. Robots directed by spoken command will be able to perform tasks for people with physical handicaps. It is possible that before long you may have your own household robot to serve foods and do chores. Many of these activities require the robot to "see" and "feel." Improving the vision and refining the sense of touch of a robot are not simple problems to overcome, but engineers say they can be solved by electrical and mechanical technologies. Researchers have already developed a robot "skin" that will heighten a robot's sense of touch.

The robot is beginning to change the way the world works. In the future, robots will do the jobs that are better suited for robots — hazardous jobs and ones that are monotonous. This will free people to do safer and more interesting work.

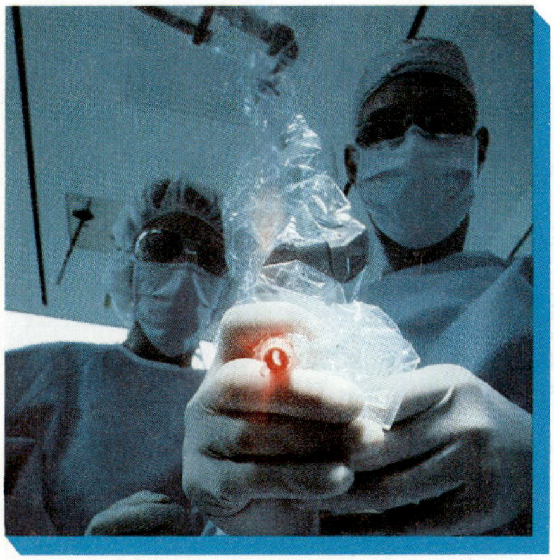

Robot arm with surgical laser

Computer Languages — Machine (binary)

Machine language is the most fundamental of all computer languages. It is the means of all communication with a computer system. The processing of all data and instructions by the computer is done in machine language code. If a program is written in any other language, the computer must translate it into machine language code first, before processing the instructions.

Machine language code is written using a combination of 0's (zeros) and 1's (ones). Each combination, usually eight digits long, is called a *byte.* The 0's and 1's that make up the byte are called *bits* (short for *b*inary dig*its*). *Binary* code dates back to the time when electronic digital computers were first developed. The processing and storing of data resulted from combining the principles involved in electrical switching and the properties of the binary number system. An electrical switch can either be turned on or turned off. In relation to the binary number system, a 0 is used to represent a switch that is turned off, which implies that current is kept from passing through the switch. A 1 is used to represent a switch that is turned on, indicating that current is allowed to pass through the switch. Therefore, a machine language instruction is really telling the computer how to set its internal switches to accomplish a particular task.

Off: 0

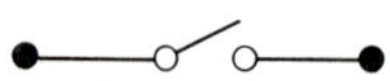

Switch open:
no current flow

On: 1

Switch closed:
current flows

You may be wondering how the computer translates the base-10 numbers that you are familiar with into combinations of 0's and 1's (bytes). First, recall that a base-10 number, say 865, can be represented in the following way:

$$865 = 8 \times 100 + 6 \times 10 + 5$$

or

$$865 = 8 \times 10^2 + 6 \times 10^1 + 5 \times 10^0$$

As you can see, each digit of a base-10 number represents the product of that digit and a power of 10. If the digits are numbered as shown below, then the exponent in the power of 10 associated with a digit is equal to the number of that digit minus 1.

8	6	5	
3rd digit	2nd digit	1st digit	

$$8 \times 10^2 = 8 \times 10^{3-1}$$
$$6 \times 10^1 = 6 \times 10^{2-1}$$
$$5 \times 10^0 = 5 \times 10^{1-1}$$

The base-2 system works in a similar way: Each digit represents the product of that digit and a power of 2. For example, the base-2 number 10101 has a base-10 value of 21 because

$$\begin{aligned} 10101 &= 1 \times 2^4 + 0 \times 2^3 + 1 \times 2^2 + 0 \times 2^1 + 1 \times 2^0 \\ &= 1 \times 16 + 0 \times 8 + 1 \times 4 + 0 \times 2 + 1 \\ &= 21. \end{aligned}$$

(Actually, the base-2 number 10101 is represented by 00010101, the initial three 0's complete the byte.) Do you now understand how binary numbers are constructed? Try writing the number 60 in binary form. (You should get 00111100.)

Letters and other keyboard characters are converted first to base-10 numbers (see the table of ASCII codes on page 428) and then into binary form. Writing machine language code for strings is tedious and time-consuming. For instance, the following code would be necessary to represent just the single string SPECIAL: 01010011 01010000 01000101 01000011 01001001 01000001 01001100. The first group of eight digits represent the letter S, the second the letter P, and so on.

Interior view of a computer chip

Early computers such as Univac had thousands of electrical switches.

CHAPTER

3 Computer Input

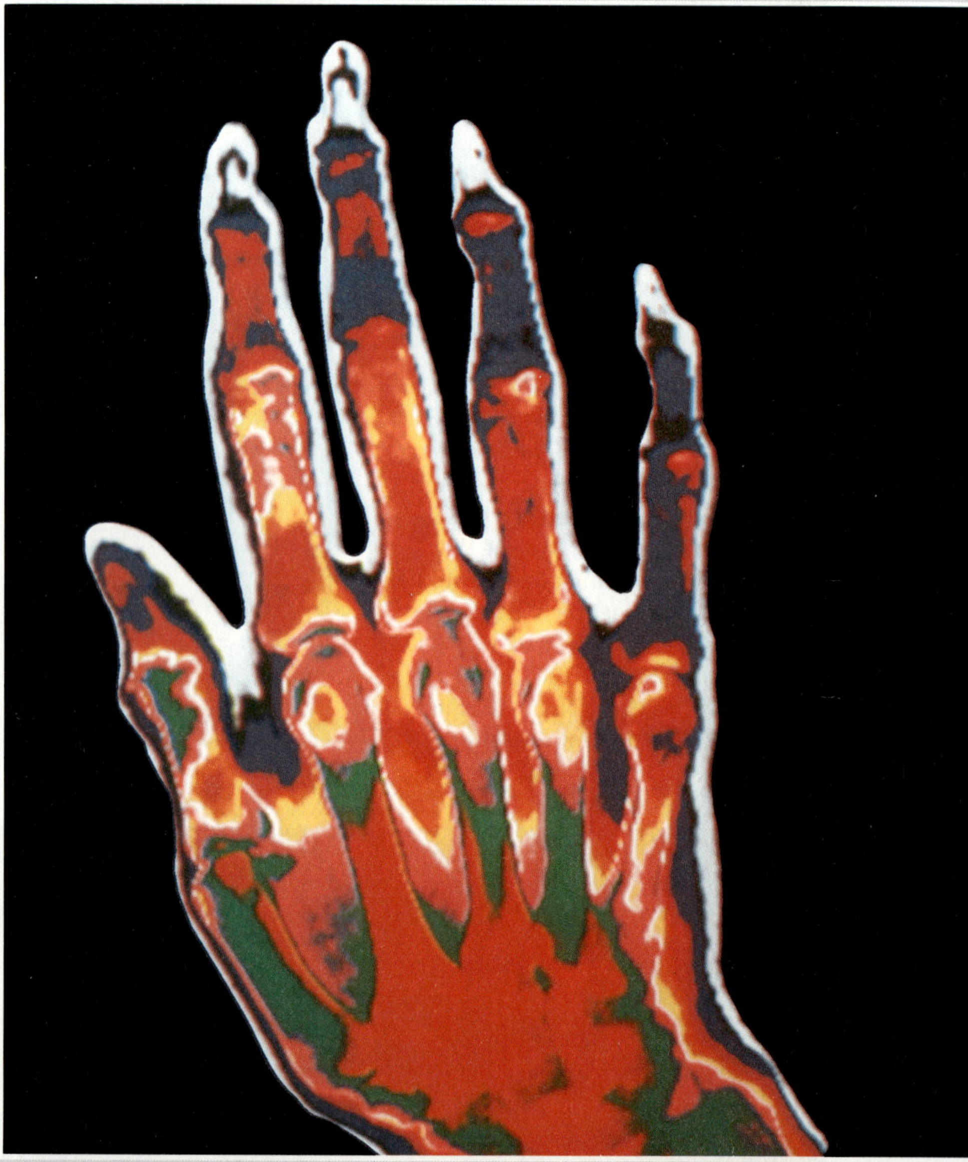

Computer-enhanced thermograms are used in the medical diagnosis of circulatory problems. The red areas in the hand above indicate hotter temperatures, and the green, blue, and black areas show colder temperatures.

Introduction

In Chapter 2, you learned how to store commands in the computer as programs for later execution. It is also possible — and useful — to store numbers and strings in the computer. This is done using *variables.* Variables are discussed in the first section below, and their uses are illustrated throughout this chapter.

3-1 Variables

The memory of your computer can be thought of as being divided into compartments, like mailboxes. You can store numbers or strings in the compartments, but you must first give each compartment (mailbox) you use a name, called a *variable.* The contents of the mailbox (the number or string) is the *value* of the variable. A variable that refers to a number must be a single letter of the alphabet, or a letter followed by other letters or the digits 0 to 9. Variables for strings are the same as for numbers, except that they must end with a dollar sign: $.

In the illustration below, the mailbox labeled with the variable A contains the number 5. We say that A has the value 5. The *string variable* A$ has as its value the string BLUE, the *numeric variable* Z9 has the value 17.3, and the string variable FOOD$ has the value APPLE.

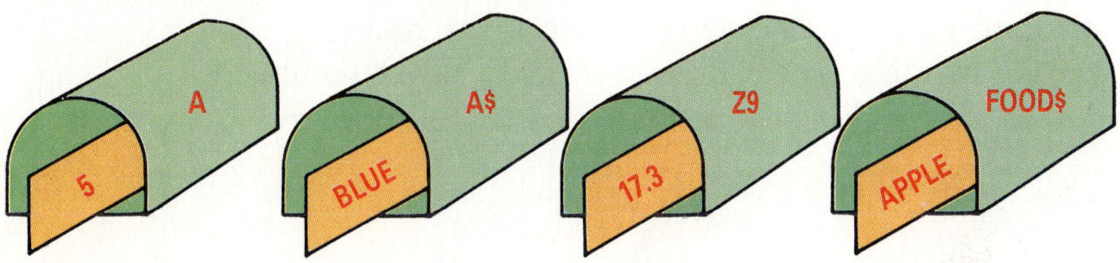

Here are some more examples of BASIC variables:

Y, X$, BD, B2, CX$, CD19, E2F1, LOB$, LOOK$

Many computers recognize only the first two characters of a variable. (See the Lab Activity for Section 3–2 to determine how your machine works.) On these computers, the variables LOB$ and LOOK$ will be considered the same, since the first two characters of each are identical. Note that even though the $ is not among the first two characters of these variables, the computer will recognize it and consider both LOB$ and LOOK$ to be the same string variable: LO$. Note further that a string variable and a numeric variable that are identical *except* for the $ will be considered as completely different; for example, LP and LP$ will have different values, one a number and the other a string. Although it is important to keep in mind the two-character limitation mentioned above, careful use of more than two characters in variables can help make your programs easier for others to understand.

Reserved Words

Commands in BASIC cannot be used as variables. Nor can these *reserved words* be used *within* variables on most computers. (See Problem 6 in the Lab Activity for Section 3–2.) For example, RUN, NEW$, and PRINT are not valid BASIC variables; nor are L*END* and RE*LIST* on most computers. Use of these variables will result in SYNTAX ERROR messages (even on computers that recognize only the first two characters of a variable). Refer to your computer's manual for a complete list of all the reserved words for your version of BASIC.

Avoiding Pitfalls

1. Remember that variables in BASIC must begin with a letter of the alphabet; 1A, for example, is not a valid variable.
2. Be sure that the last character of a string variable is the dollar sign: $.

Summary

A *variable* in BASIC is the name of a compartment in the memory of the computer. A variable consists of either a single letter, or a letter followed by other letters or the digits 0 to 9. A *string variable* must end with a $ and have a string as its value; a *numeric variable* must have a number as its value.

Exercises 3-1

A **1.** Tell whether each of the following variable names is legal. If not legal, give a reason why.

a. Y
b. Y4
c. 4Y
d. 1$
e. X1$
f. CD
g. D$C
h. XYZW
i. ADD+
j. LM21
k. PRINT
l. RUNNER
m. BB$
n. NUMBER
o. SEND
p. AB02$
q. COUNT
r. NEWS$
s. FEB?
t. MNY$

2. Tell whether each of the following represents a string variable or a numeric variable, and give its value.

a.
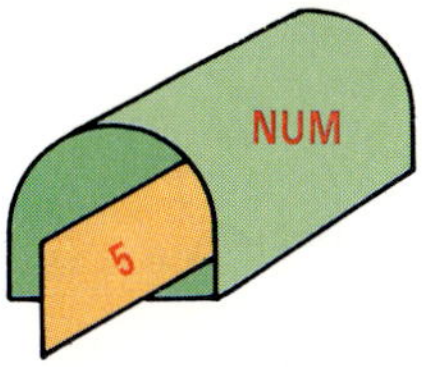

b.
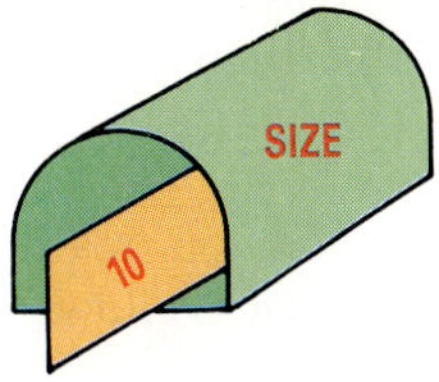

c.
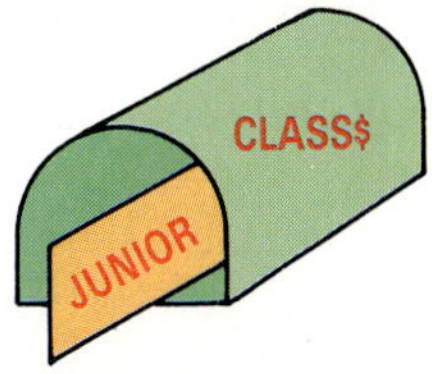

d.
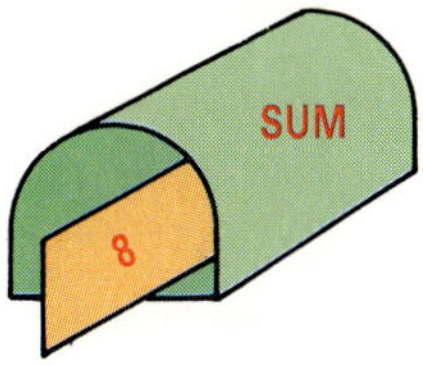

e.
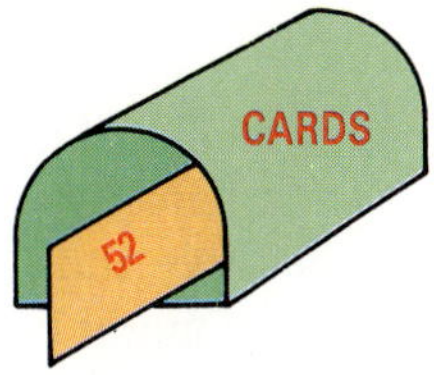

f.
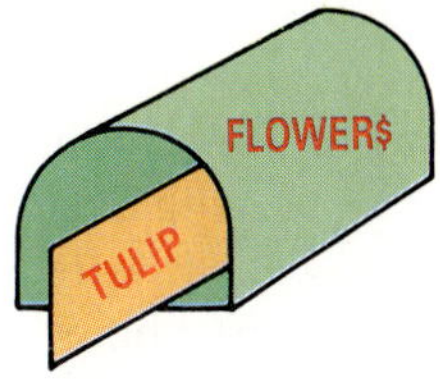

3. Find the error, if any, in each of the following. Give a possible correction.

a.
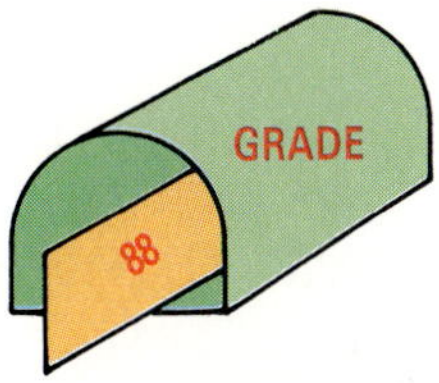

b.
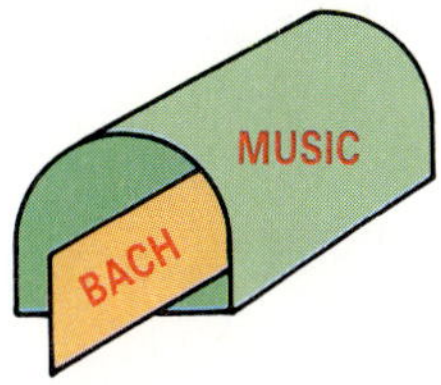

c.
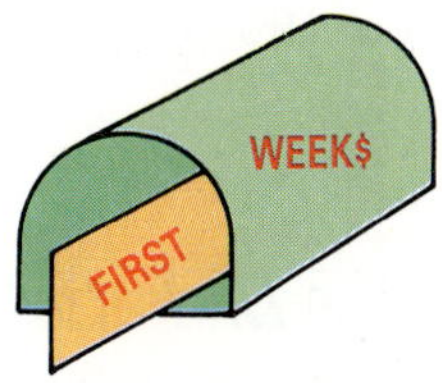

d.

e.
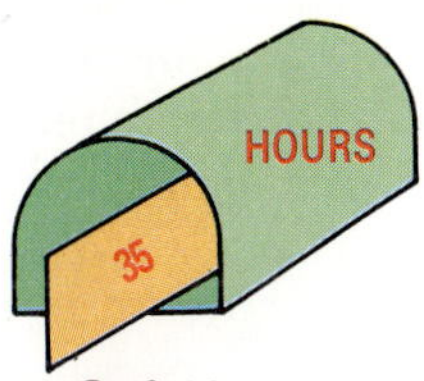

f.
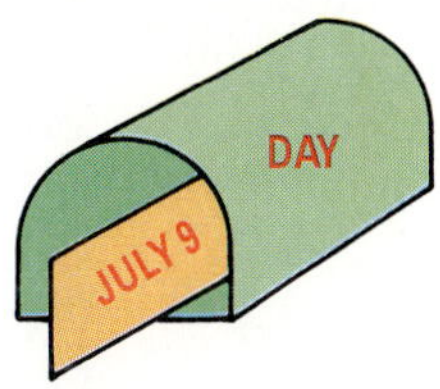

Lab Activity

Diskettes and Printers

Using Diskettes

Diskettes are made of thin plastic covered with magnetic material. Information is recorded as extremely small magnetized regions on the surface of the plastic disk. As the diskette rotates inside the drive, the magnetic specks come periodically within reach of a "head" that detects the magnetization and reads the information on the diskette.

When you turn on your computer with a diskette in the appropriate drive (this is called *booting* the diskette), a long control program called DOS (short for *Disk Operating System*) is read into your computer's memory. DOS interprets your diskette commands and relays information between the computer's memory and the diskette.

The commands available with DOS depend on your machine and the particular version of DOS you are using, but every DOS allows you to format diskettes, save programs, load programs, delete programs, and list the contents of a diskette.

Note that none of these commands will work unless DOS is *first* read into the computer by booting a diskette. If you experience any errors, check that your diskette has been inserted correctly in the drive and try again. If nothing works (including expert help), then your diskette might be ruined; bending, dust, extreme heat or cold, even fingerprints can ruin diskettes. Also, strong magnetic fields can affect diskette operation, so it is a good idea not to store diskettes near electronic devices such as television sets and stereos.

Formatting a Diskette

Unless you buy a diskette with programs already on it, you must format or *initialize* a blank diskette before it can be used. (Some indexing information must be recorded on it.) To format a new diskette or to reformat an old one (formatting completely erases any old information recorded on the diskette), do the following:

Apple

Make sure DOS is booted, then type NEW. Next, type into the computer a short program that will be RUN automatically whenever this newly formatted diskette is booted. The program need not do anything of interest, but commonly it gives a greeting or identifies the owner of the diskette. For example, you could type the following program replacing JOHN DOE with your own name.

```
10 PRINT "HI THERE!"
20 PRINT "DISKETTE INITIALIZED BY"
30 PRINT "JOHN DOE, 9 / 5 / 85"
40 END
```

Now, remove the diskette used to boot DOS and place the diskette to be formatted in the drive, then type: INIT HELLO. The program you typed will be called HELLO. After the whirring and clacking stops and the red light on the drive goes off, your diskette is ready for use.

IBM

Make sure DOS is booted in drive A (the one on the left), then type:

FORMAT B: / S

You will be instructed by the computer to insert the diskette to be formatted in drive B (the one on the right) and to press any key when ready to format. When formatting of the diskette is complete, the computer will offer the option of formatting other diskettes.

TRS-80

Make sure DOS is booted, then type: FORMAT. The computer will then ask these questions:

FORMAT WHAT DRIVE?

You should type the number of the drive that contains the diskette to be formatted; drive 0 is on the bottom and drive 1 is on the top.

DISKETTE NAME?

You should decide on and type a name that may be up to eight characters long, the first of which *must* be a letter. The other characters may be letters or numbers. (Actually, certain other keyboard characters are legal, but it is usually best to avoid them.)

MASTER PASSWORD?

You should type a password made up of from one to eight letters or numbers, starting with a letter. Be sure you remember this password; it is needed if you want to copy the contents of this diskette onto another diskette. If you just press the < ENTER > key in response to this question, then PASSWORD will automatically be assigned as the diskette's password.

Saving a Program

To save the program that is currently in memory on your diskette (you may want to type a short program to practice with), do the following:

Apple

Decide on a *name* up to 30 characters long, the first of which must be a letter, and the rest any character except a comma. Then type:

SAVE *name*

IBM

(At this point you should load BASIC into memory. Simply type the word BASIC after the A (or B) prompt.) Decide on a *name* up to 8 characters long, the first of which *must* be a letter, and the rest letters or numbers. There are some other keyboard characters that may follow the first letter, but many punctuation marks and operation symbols are not legal, so it is best to stick with letters or numbers. Now type:

SAVE "*name*"

(Be sure to include the quotation marks. If your diskette is in drive B, then type: SAVE "B: *name*")

TRS-80

(At this point you should load BASIC into memory. Simply type the word BASIC after the TRSDOS READY prompt.) Decide on a *name* up to 8 characters long, the first of which *must* be a letter, and the rest letters or numbers. There are some other keyboard characters that may follow the first letter, but many punctuation marks and operation symbols are not legal, so it is best to stick with letters or numbers. Now type:

SAVE "*name*"

(Be sure to include the quotation marks. If your diskette is in drive 1 (the one on the top), then type: SAVE "*name*:1")

Loading a Program

To load a program from your diskette into memory (thereby erasing any old program that was in memory), do the following:

Apple

Type: LOAD *name*, where *name* is the same one given to the program when it was SAVEd.

IBM

Type: LOAD "*name*", where *name* is the same one given to the program when it was SAVEd.

(If your diskette is in drive B, then type: LOAD "B:*name*")

TRS-80

Type: LOAD "*name*", where *name* is the same one given to the program when it was SAVEd.

(If your diskette is in drive 1, then type: LOAD "*name*:1")

Deleting a Program

To delete a program from your diskette, do the following:

Apple

Type: DELETE *name*, where *name* is the same one given to the program when it was SAVEd.

IBM

Type: KILL "*name*.BAS", where *name* is the same one given to the program when it was SAVEd.

(If your diskette is in drive B, then type KILL "B:*name*.BAS")

TRS-80

Type: KILL "*name*", where *name* is the same one given to the program when it was SAVEd.

(If your diskette is in drive 1, then type: KILL "*name*:1")

Listing the Contents of a Diskette

To see a listing of the programs stored on a diskette, do the following:

Apple

Type: CATALOG

IBM

Type: FILES

TRS-80

Type: CMD "D: *d*", where *d* is the drive number.

Using a Printer

If your computer has a printer attached, you can make a permanent paper copy of any program and of any PRINTed output.

To make a paper copy of a program LISTing, turn on the printer's power switch, then follow the instructions for your computer on the next page.

Apple

Type PR#1 to direct output to the printer (assuming that the printer card is plugged into slot 1 — check with your teacher), then type LIST. After the program has been LISTed on paper, type PR#0 to send output back to the screen.

IBM and TRS-80

Type LLIST instead of LIST.

To make a paper copy of the PRINTed output of a program, turn on the printer's power switch, then do the following:

Apple

Type PR#1 to direct output to the printer, then RUN the program. Type PR#0 to direct output back to the screen.

IBM and TRS-80

Use LPRINT in your program statements in place of PRINT, then RUN the program as usual.

3-2 The LET Statement

In the last section, you learned that variables are names for numbers or strings stored in the computer's memory. In BASIC, the LET statement is used to assign values to variables, as in the following program.

Program 1

Statement	Remark
10 LET A$ = "ADDITION"	*Stores the string ADDITION in the memory compartment called A$.*
20 LET B = 2 + 3	*Stores the number 5 in the memory compartment called B.*
30 PRINT A$	*PRINTs the value of A$.*
40 PRINT B	*PRINTs the value of B.*
50 END	

Output

```
ADDITION
5
```

In Program 1, the LET statement in line 10 assigns the string ADDITION to the variable A$. Notice that a string in a LET statement *must* be enclosed in quotation marks. In line 20, the computer first calculates 2 + 3 and then assigns the result to the variable B; that is, it stores the number 5 in a mailbox or memory compartment called B.

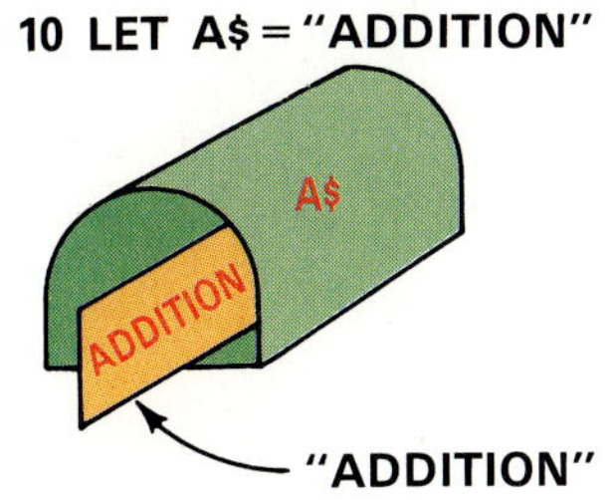

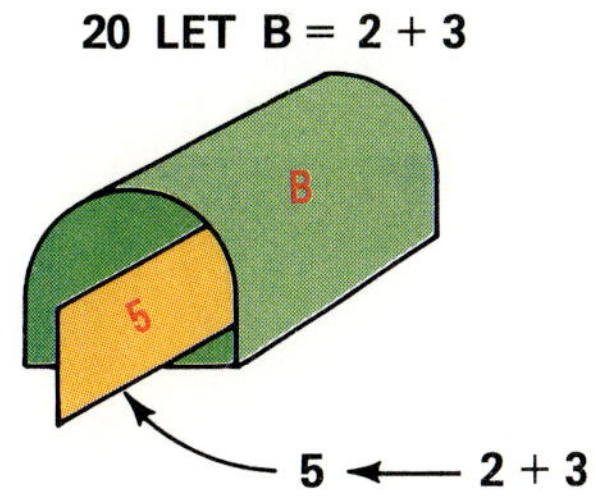

Lines 30 and 40 in the program PRINT the values of A$ and B. Note that the values of the variables remain the same after they are PRINTed.

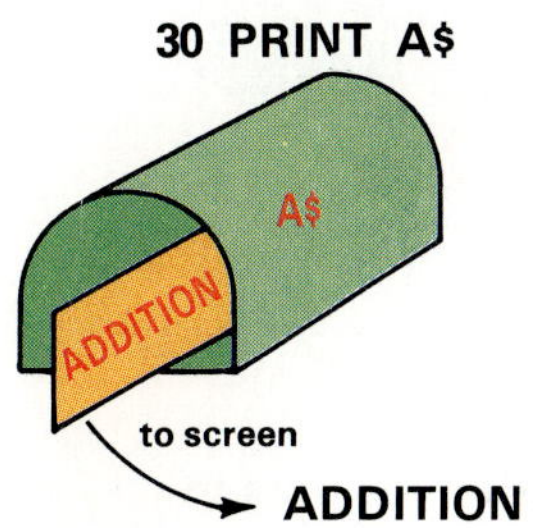

A LET statement has the following form:

LET *single variable = a string, variable,* or *BASIC numerical expression.*

A BASIC numerical expression may contain numbers, numeric variables, parentheses, and the operation symbols +, −, *, /, and ↑. Examples include the following:

2 + 3
D − 12.5
2 * (A / 3)
A − 4 ↑ 2 * 5

When the right side of a LET statement is a numerical expression, the computer calculates the value of the expression and stores the result in the memory compartment named by the variable on the left side of the equals sign. This is illustrated by line 30 of the program on the next page.

Program 2

Statement	Remark
10 LET A = 5	*Assigns the number 5 to A.*
20 LET B = 13	*Assigns the number 13 to B.*
30 LET C = (A + B) / 2	*Calculates (5 + 13) / 2 and assigns the result to C.*
*40 PRINT "AVERAGE OF "; A; " AND "; B;	
50 PRINT " IS "; C	
60 END	

Output

AVERAGE OF 5 AND 13 IS 9

The following diagram shows how line 30 works:

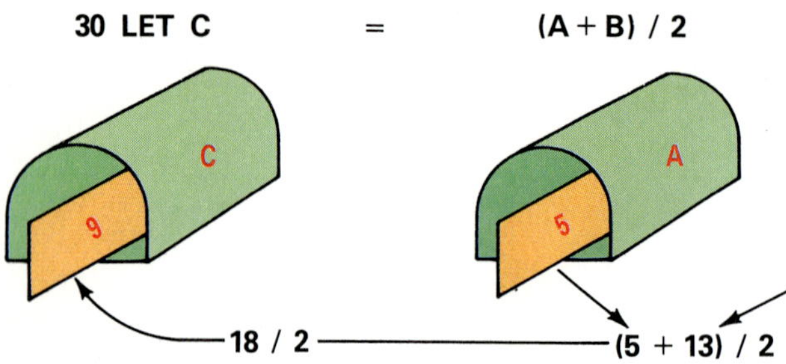

The final values stored in memory compartments A, B, and C are shown in the diagram below:

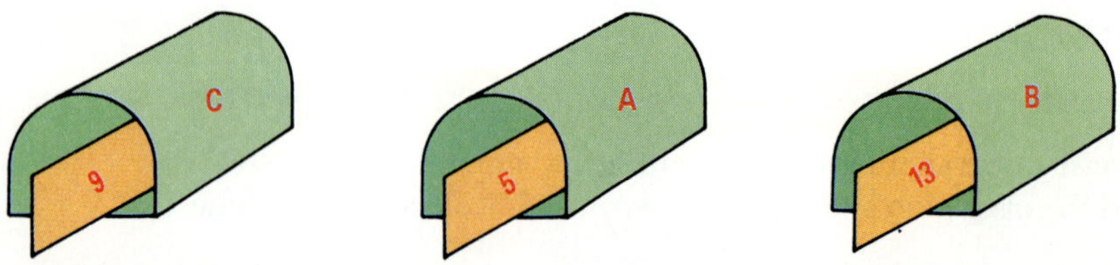

Notice the combination of strings and variables separated by semicolons in lines 40 and 50. PRINTing the output in this manner is clearer and more meaningful than merely PRINTing the number 9. Notice also that the variables A, B, and C are not enclosed in quotation marks. If lines 40 and 50 were combined and written 40 PRINT "AVERAGE OF A AND B IS C", then the

* In lines 40 and 50 we include spaces in the strings, even though some computers do not require them. In the programs in this book we will always include these spaces when strings and numbers will be PRINTed on the same line in the output.

output would be as follows:

AVERAGE OF A AND B IS C

In other words, variables within quotes are considered strings in BASIC.

In Program 2, suppose that line 30 were missing. Then when the computer executed line 50 it would not know the value of C. In this case the output would look like this:

AVERAGE OF 5 AND 13 IS 0

The value of C is 0 because in BASIC all numeric variables that have not been assigned a value are automatically given the value 0. All string variables that have not been assigned a value represent the *null string* — the empty string with no characters: "". If a null string is PRINTed, a blank line appears on the screen.

String variables may be placed within sentences, separated from other strings by semicolons, as in the following program.

Program 3

Statement	Remark
10 LET FRST$ = "JANE"	*Assign values to the string variables.*
20 LET SEC$ = "TOM"	
30 LET THRD$ = "DICK"	
40 LET FOUR$ = "MARY"	
50 PRINT "DEAR "; SEC$; ","	
60 PRINT	*Blank line.*
70 PRINT THRD$; " ASKED ME TO INVITE YOU"	
80 PRINT "TO "; FOUR$; " 'S HOUSE FOR A"	
85 PRINT "COMPUTER SESSION. SEE YOU AT 7!"	
90 PRINT	*Blank line.*
100 PRINT , , FRST$	*PRINTs the value of FRST$ in the third zone.*
110 END	

Output

```
DEAR TOM,

DICK ASKED ME TO INVITE YOU
TO MARY'S HOUSE FOR A
COMPUTER SESSION. SEE YOU AT 7!

                              JANE
```

It is possible to have a single variable on the right side of the equals sign in a LET statement. The following program illustrates this technique.

Program 4

Statement	Remark
10 LET A$ = "KEYS"	
20 LET B$ = "LOCKS"	
30 LET C$ = A$	*Assigns KEYS to C$.*
40 PRINT B$; " AND "; C$	
50 END	

Output

```
LOCKS AND KEYS
```

Line 30 needs some explanation. When the computer executes this line, it assigns the value of the variable A$ on the right side of the equals sign (KEYS) to the variable C$ on the left side of the equals sign:

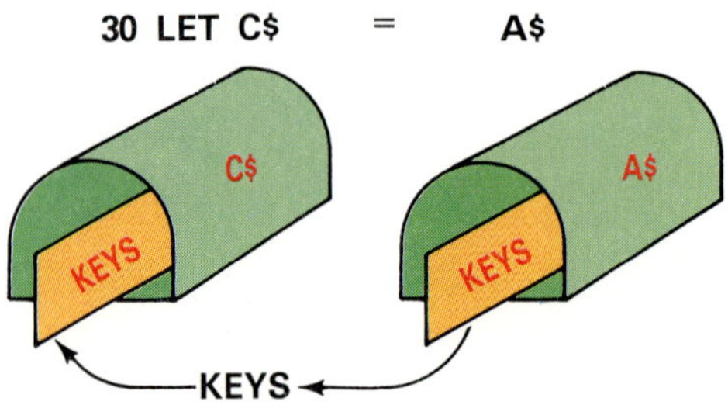

The result is:

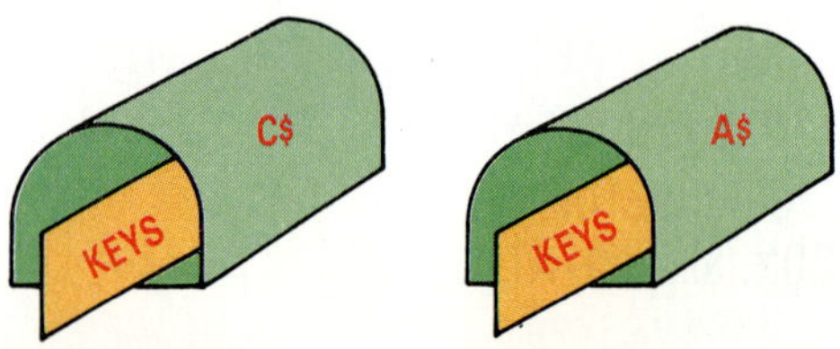

A LET statement changes the value only of the variable on the left side of the equals sign. Thus, the value of the variable A$ in the program above remains KEYS. Moreover, LET erases any value assigned earlier in the program to the left-hand variable. For example, if you add the line

```
25 LET A$ = "ROCKS"
```

to Program 4, then the old value of A$ will be replaced, and the output of the program will be LOCKS AND ROCKS.

The final program in this section shows how you can use the LET statement to make the computer count.

Program 5

Statement

```
10 LET D = 1
20 PRINT D
30 LET D = D + 1
40 PRINT D
50 LET D = D + 1
60 PRINT D
70 LET D = D + 1
80 PRINT D
90 END
```

Output

```
1
2
3
4
```

The statement LET D = D + 1 that occurs repeatedly in Program 5 does not make sense in mathematics (since D = D + 1 is impossible). The statement does have meaning in BASIC, however, since the left side is a single variable (D) and the right side (D + 1) is a valid BASIC numerical expression. In this program the initial value of D is 1 (from line 10). Then the statement LET D = D + 1 in line 30 adds 1 to the initial value of D and stores the new value, 2, at the same location. The old value of D, namely 1, is replaced.

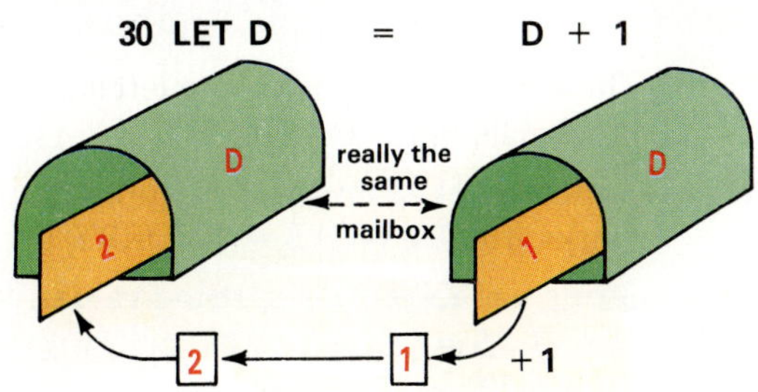

The result is:

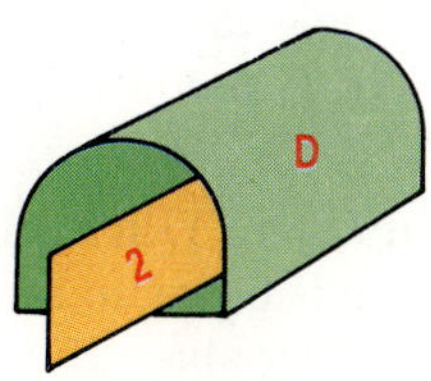

The LET statement in line 50 of Program 5 changes the value of D in a like manner from 2 to 3.

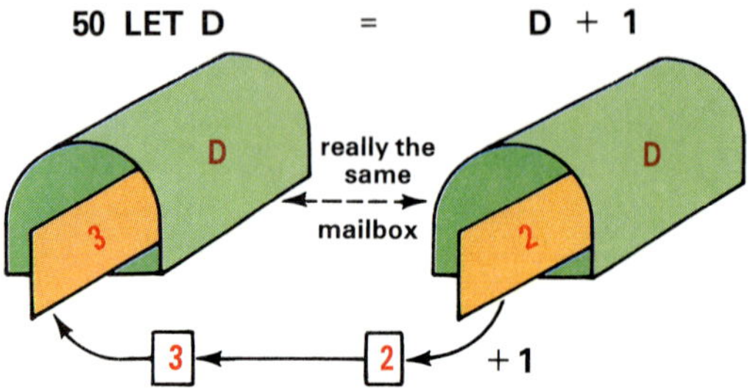

Result:

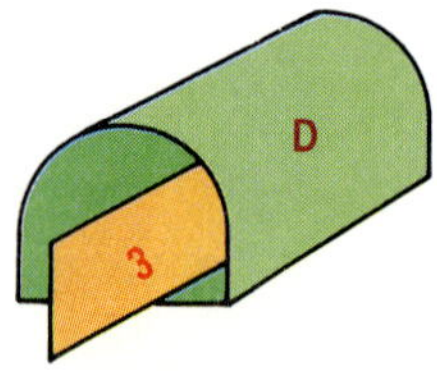

Finally, the LET statement in line 70 changes the value of D from 3 to 4. The counting method used in Program 5 is rather tedious. In Section 3–6, you will learn a much more efficient method of counting on the computer.

Avoiding Pitfalls

Here are some common *errors* in LET statements. A possible correction is given for each statement.

1. 10 LET 7 = A — The variable must be on the left side of the equals sign; 10 LET A = 7.

2. 10 LET WOE$ = WORRY — Strings must be enclosed in quotation marks; 10 LET WOE$ = "WORRY".

3. 10 LET B$ = 18 — String variables require string values; 10 LET B$ = "EIGHTEEN" or 10 LET B$ = "18".

4. 10 LET B = "EIGHTEEN" — The variable B is a numeric variable and requires a number value; 10 LET B = 18.

5. 10 LET E + 1 = E — Only a single variable may be on the left side of the equals sign; 10 LET E = E + 1.

The errors in (2), (3), and (4) usually result in a TYPE MISMATCH error. TYPE MISMATCH means that a statement is trying to assign a string to a numeric variable, or a number to a string variable.

Summary

The LET statement is used to assign values to variables. String values must be enclosed in quotation marks.

A LET statement has the form:

LET *single variable = a string, variable, or BASIC numerical expression*

A BASIC numerical expression may contain numbers, variables, parentheses, and operation symbols.

In BASIC, all numeric variables that have not been assigned a value are automatically given the value 0; all string variables that have not been assigned a value represent the null string (the string containing no characters at all).

The statement LET X = Y assigns the value of Y to the variable X. The value of Y does not change.

The statement LET D = D + 1 adds 1 to the present value of D and stores the new value in the same variable (compartment), D. The old value of D is replaced.

Exercises 3-2

A

1. Identify the *errors* in each of the following LET statements. Give a possible correction.

a. `10 LET 2B = 5`

b. `5 LET H$ = ORANGES`

c. `20 LET C5 = "MAYBE"`

d. `15 LET A$ = 3 + 6`

e. `15 LET M ↑ 2 = M`

f. `25 LET "TRUE" = TR$`

g. `40 LET 18 = AB`

h. `45 LTE A = B * C`

2. Predict the output of each of the following programs.

a.
```
10 LET A = 5
20 LET B = A ↑ 2
30 PRINT A; "  SQUARED IS  "; B
40 END
```

b.
```
10 LET Y = 4
20 LET Y = Y + 10
30 PRINT Y
40 END
```

c.
```
10 LET L = 4
20 LET F = 7
30 LET G = L + F - 2
40 PRINT G
50 END
```

d.
```
10 LET X1 = 5
20 LET X2 = 20
30 LET X3 = X1 * X2
40 PRINT X1; " * "; X2; " = "; X3
50 END
```

2. e.
```
10 LET Y=5
20 LET X=3 * Y
30 LET Z=2 * X
40 PRINT X, Y, Z
50 END
```

f.
```
10 LET A$=" TIMES "
20 LET B=12
30 LET C=B * B
40 PRINT B; A$; B; " IS "; C
50 END
```

g.
```
10 LET X=5
20 PRINT X
30 LET Y=7
40 LET X=Y
50 PRINT X
60 END
```

h.
```
10 LET A=2 * 3
20 LET B=3 ↑ 2
30 LET B=A * B
40 PRINT A, B
50 END
```

i.
```
10 LET A$="HIGH"
20 LET B$="LOW"
30 LET HI=84
40 LET LO=63
50 PRINT A$; " TEMP: "; HI
60 PRINT B$; " TEMP: "; LO
70 END
```

j.
```
10 LET X$="IN"
20 LET Y$="OUT"
30 LET P$=X$
40 LET X$=Y$
50 PRINT P$; " AND "; X$
60 END
```

3. What will the computer PRINT for each of the following programs?

a.
```
10 PRINT MO$
20 LET MO$="MONTH"
30 END
```

b.
```
10 PRINT AB
20 LET AB=1000
30 END
```

The chart below, called a RUN chart, can be used to predict the output of a program. Each variable is given a column in the chart, and the effect of each LET statement is recorded. Another column is reserved for the output from any PRINT statements.

Program

Statements

```
10 LET A=5
20 LET B=3
30 LET A=A+1
40 LET B=B−1
50 LET C=A * B
60 PRINT A, B, C
70 END
```

RUN chart

LINE	A	B	C	OUTPUT
10	5			
20		3		
30	5 + 1 = 6			
40		3 − 1 = 2		
50			6 * 2 = 12	
60				6 2 12

4. Predict the output of each of the programs on the following page by completing the RUN chart. (See the explanation above.)

a. Statements

```
10 LET X = 1
20 LET X = X + 1
30 PRINT X
40 LET X = X + 1
50 PRINT X
60 LET X = X + 2
70 PRINT X
80 END
```

LINE	X	OUTPUT
10		
20		
30		
40		
50		
60		
70		

b. Statements

```
10 LET K = 5
20 LET K = K - 1
30 PRINT K
40 LET K = K - 3
50 PRINT K
60 PRINT K - 1
70 END
```

LINE	K	OUTPUT
10		
20		
30		
40		
50		
60		

c. Statements

```
10 LET X = 1
20 LET Y = 2
30 LET X = X + Y
40 PRINT X
45 LET Y = 4
50 LET Y = Y + X
60 PRINT Y
70 LET X = X + Y
80 PRINT X
90 END
```

LINE	X	Y	OUTPUT
10			
20			
30			
40			
45			
50			
60			
70			
80			

d. Statements

```
10 LET E = 1
20 LET F = 3
30 LET G = E * F - 1
40 PRINT G
50 LET F = E + G
60 PRINT F
70 LET G = G + F
80 PRINT G
90 END
```

LINE	E	F	G	OUTPUT
10				
20				
30				
40				
50				
60				
70				
80				

In Exercises 5 through 9, use LET statements to assign the given values to variables.

B 5. Write a program to calculate the area A of a rectangle of length 16.2 cm and width 12.4 cm. (Area = length * width)

6. Write a program to calculate the area A of a circle with radius 4.8 cm. (Area = $\pi * r^2$; use $\pi \approx 3.14159$)

7. Write a program to calculate the average AVG of 6 test scores. The scores are 77, 88, 82, 91, 84, and 70.

8. Write a program to calculate the weekly salary S of a person who works 36 hours at a wage of $4.20 per hour.

9. Write a program to convert 100 yards to meters M. (1 in. = 2.54 cm)

10. Rewrite Program 5 (Section 2–4, page 41) using LET statements to assign a nickname to each of the players and to calculate the averages for the three games.

Lab Activity

Exploring Variables

Type, LIST, and then RUN the following program:

```
10 LET A1234 = 1.3
20 PRINT A1234
30 END
```

The output should be 1.3, as you would expect from your knowledge of variables.

Problems

1. Change lines 10 and 20 of the program by increasing the length of the variable as follows:

```
10 LET A12345678901234 = 1.3
20 PRINT A12345678901234
30 END
```

Does the program still work properly?

2. Continue to increase the length of the variable in lines 10 and 20 until an error message appears on the screen. How long can variables be on your computer? In general, the number of characters allowed is quite large.

Consider this program:

```
10 LET A=1
20 LET A1=2
30 PRINT A, A1
40 END
```

Most computers will consider A and A1 to be *different* variables, so that line 30 should give this output:

```
1                    2
```

Type the program and RUN it to verify this output.

3. Change lines 10 and 30 of the program above to:

```
10 LET A12=1
30 PRINT A12, A1
```

LIST the new version. On many microcomputers, the variables A1 and A12 are considered to be the same variable because their first two characters are identical. (Your computer should at least LIST the two variables as they appear in lines 10 and 20.) RUN the program. Are the values of A12 and A1 the same? Does your computer consider A1 and A12 to be different variables?

4. If the output in Problem 3 is: 1 2, then your computer looks at more than two characters in a variable. If that is true for your computer, increase the lengths of the two variables (keeping them identical except that one of them has one more character than the other) until your computer considers the two variables to be the same or until you are not allowed to add any more characters. Summarize the results.

5. Write a short program that tries to use the reserved word LIST as a variable. What does your computer do when you enter the program line containing LIST? What does your computer do when you LIST the program? When you RUN the program?

6. Write an experimental program that will help you determine whether your computer will allow you to place a reserved word *within* a variable (try P*LIST* or X*RUN*T, for example). If your computer rejects these variables, at what point do you find out — when you enter the program line with PLIST or XRUNT, when you LIST the program (look carefully), or when you RUN the program?

3-3 The INPUT Statement

In the previous section you learned one method of assigning values to variables — the LET statement. Recall the program, shown below, that used LET statements to calculate the average of two numbers:

Program 1

Statement

```
10  LET A = 5
20  LET B = 13
30  LET C = (A + B) / 2
40  PRINT "AVERAGE OF  "; A; "  AND  "; B;
50  PRINT " IS "; C
60  END
```

Output

```
AVERAGE OF 5 AND 13 IS 9
```

Suppose you now want to find the average of two other numbers, say 12 and 23. You could change lines 10 and 20 in Program 1 to

```
10  LET A = 12
20  LET B = 23
```

and then RUN the program a second time. If you wanted to find the average of many pairs of numbers, however, then changing the two lines would become rather tedious.

BASIC provides another way of assigning values to variables — the INPUT statement. This statement allows you to type values while a program is RUNning. Let's rewrite Program 1 above using INPUT statements:

Program 2

Statement	Remark
10 PRINT "AVERAGING PROGRAM"	
15 PRINT	*Blank line.*
20 PRINT "TYPE FIRST NUMBER:"	
30 INPUT A	*Assigns number you type to A.*
35 PRINT	
40 PRINT "TYPE SECOND NUMBER:"	
50 INPUT B	*Assigns number you type to B.*

```
60 LET C = (A + B) / 2                    Calculates the average.
70 PRINT                                  Blank line
80 PRINT "AVERAGE OF  "; A; "  AND  "; B;
90 PRINT "  IS  "; C
100 END
```

Output

```
AVERAGING PROGRAM

TYPE FIRST NUMBER:
? 5

TYPE SECOND NUMBER:
? 13

AVERAGE OF 5 AND 13 IS 9
```

The statement INPUT A in line 30 causes the computer to print a question mark (?) on the screen. The ? prompt indicates that the computer is waiting for you to type a single value for the variable immediately following the word INPUT — in this case A. Since A is a numeric variable, you should type a single number (numerical expressions like 5 + 6 are not allowed). Assume that you type the number 5, as shown above. Then when you press the < RETURN > or < ENTER > key, the computer assigns the number 5 to A and then goes on to the next line.

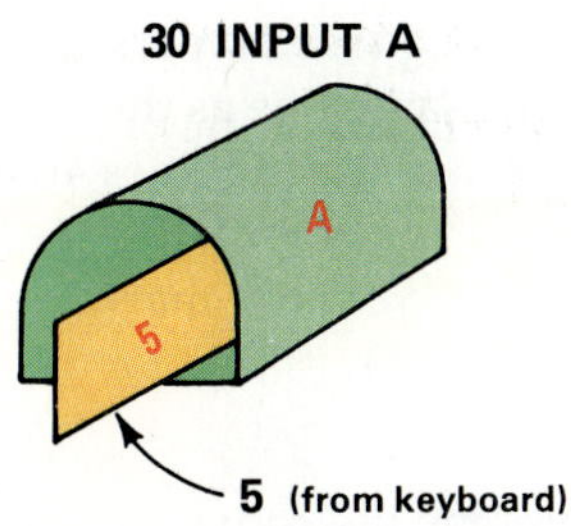

A similar sequence occurs when the computer arrives at the statement INPUT B in line 50; if you type 13 followed by a < RETURN > or < ENTER > key press, the value of B becomes 13. After the average is PRINTed in lines 80 and 90, the program ENDs. If you want to find the average of other pairs of numbers, you would simply RUN the program again for each pair. (In Section 3–6, you will learn how to make the computer repeat the same task over and over again. Then you will not have to RUN the program several times.)

The INPUT statement may also be used to assign values to string variables, as illustrated in Program 3 on the next page.

Program 3

Statement	Remark
10 PRINT "NAME PROGRAM"	
15 PRINT	
20 PRINT "WHAT IS YOUR FIRST NAME: ";	PRINTs message and waits for a value for FRST$.
30 INPUT FRST$	
40 PRINT "WHAT IS YOUR LAST NAME: ";	PRINTs message and waits for a value for LAST$.
50 INPUT LAST$	
60 PRINT	
70 PRINT "HELLO "; FRST$; " "; LAST$; "."	PRINTs message containing the value of FRST$ and LAST$.
80 PRINT "HOW ARE YOU TODAY?"	
90 END	

Output

```
NAME PROGRAM

WHAT IS YOUR FIRST NAME:   ? CHERYL
WHAT IS YOUR LAST NAME:   ? CLARK

HELLO CHERYL CLARK.
HOW ARE YOU TODAY?
```

The semicolon at the end of line 20 causes the question mark from the INPUT statement in line 30 to appear on the same line as the message PRINTed in line 20. (The same technique is also used in lines 40 and 50.) Notice that when you type in a string while the computer is executing an INPUT instruction, it is *not* necessary to type quotation marks around the string. (See the Lab Activity for some exceptions.)

As a final program in this section, let's combine the conversational friendliness of Program 3 with the computing of averages in Program 2. Before writing the program, let's outline our strategy. We divide the program into separate tasks, as follows:

1. Identify the user of the program.
2. Tell the user the purpose of the program.
3. Have the user type the two numbers to be averaged (test scores in this example).
4. Compute the average.
5. PRINT the result.

After writing the separate parts of the program as outlined, we combine the parts to get this program:

Program 4

Statement

```
5  PRINT "FRIENDLY AVERAGING PROGRAM"
10  REM * IDENTIFY USER
15  PRINT "WHAT IS YOUR FIRST NAME:  ";
20  INPUT FRST$
25  PRINT
30  REM * PURPOSE OF PROGRAM
40  PRINT "HELLO  "; FRST$; ".  THIS PROGRAM WILL CALCULATE THE"
50  PRINT "AVERAGE OF YOUR LAST 2 COMPUTER TEST SCORES."
55  PRINT
60  REM * ASK FOR LAST 2 TEST SCORES
65  PRINT "WHAT IS YOUR FIRST TEST SCORE:  ";
70  INPUT T1
75  PRINT "WHAT IS YOUR SECOND TEST SCORE:  ";
80  INPUT T2
85  PRINT
90  REM * COMPUTE THE AVERAGE
100  LET AVG = (T1 + T2) / 2
110  REM * PRINT THE RESULT
115  PRINT "CONGRATULATIONS  "; FRST$; "!  YOUR AVERAGE IS  "; AVG
120  END
```

Output

```
FRIENDLY AVERAGING PROGRAM
WHAT IS YOUR FIRST NAME:  ? BRET

HELLO BRET. THIS PROGRAM WILL CALCULATE THE
AVERAGE OF YOUR LAST 2 COMPUTER TEST SCORES.

WHAT IS YOUR FIRST TEST SCORE:  ? 85
WHAT IS YOUR SECOND TEST SCORE:  ? 77

CONGRATULATIONS BRET! YOUR AVERAGE IS 81
```

A new statement — REM — is used several times in Program 4. REM statements are explanatory REMarks placed in a program to help a user understand the program. (REMs also serve as reminders to the writer of a program, who may forget over a period of time what was intended in the program.)

When the computer encounters a REM, it ignores the rest of the line. REM statements may be placed anywhere in a program and will not affect how a program RUNs. REM statements are printed, however, anytime a program containing them is LISTed.

REM statements are one method of *documenting* a program. *Documentation* provides a description of the purpose of the program, the role of important lines, instructions on how to use the program, and other useful information related to the program. Messages in PRINT statements are another method of documenting a program. Any well-written program should include documentation.

Avoiding Pitfalls

1. If the computer is executing a statement such as 20 INPUT X and you type a string rather than a number, then an ERROR message (such as REENTER or REDO) results. The computer then prints another question mark (?) and waits for you to type a value for X. If you type a number, then the computer will assign the number to X and then go on to the next line in the program. If you type a string again, then the ERROR message is repeated and another ? is printed. (*Note:* Unlike most errors, this one does not stop the program.)
2. If the computer is executing a statement such as 20 INPUT N$ and you type a string containing a comma, then the computer interprets what you typed as two separate strings. For example, suppose you type the string: DOE, JOHN. Some computers will assign DOE to N$, print an ERROR message such as EXTRA IGNORED, and then continue execution of the program. Other computers will not accept the string at all and print an ERROR message such as REENTER or REDO, and wait for the new INPUT.
3. Beginning programmers sometimes use an INPUT statement such as 50 INPUT 46, intending to use the number 46 later in the program. This is incorrect and will cause a SYNTAX ERROR, since INPUT must be followed by a variable.
4. If you repeat the same variable in an INPUT statement that you used in an earlier INPUT (or LET) statement, the second value typed will replace the first.
5. If an INPUT statement contains a numeric variable, you may type only a single number. Numerical expressions such as

   6 / 3, or 2 * A − 1

   are not allowed.

Summary

The INPUT statement may be used to assign values to numeric or string variables.

The statement INPUT A causes the computer to print a ? and assign the number you type to the variable A.

The statement INPUT N$ causes the computer to print a ? and assign the string you type to the variable N$.

REM statements are explanatory remarks placed in a program to help a user understand the program. REM statements do not affect the RUN of a program.

Documentation should include the purpose of the program, the role of important lines in the program, instructions on how to use the program, and other useful information.

Exercises 3-3

A

1. Tell whether the following are valid INPUT statements.

a. `10 INPUT Y1$`
b. `20 INPUT Y + 2`
c. `15 INPUT ABC$`
d. `30 INPUT 23`
e. `50 INPUT "BUFFALO"`
f. `60 INPUT BUFF$`

2. Explain why the value shown for each INPUT will cause an ERROR message.

a.
```
10 INPUT CLR
? ORANGE
```
b.
```
20 INPUT NM$
? LOGAN, MARIA
```
c.
```
30 INPUT Y1
? 5 * 2
```

3. Predict the output of each of the following programs. Assume that you give correct responses to the questions asked.

a.
```
10 PRINT "WHAT IS YOUR FIRST NAME:  ";
20 INPUT F$
30 PRINT "YOUR MIDDLE INITIAL:  ";
40 INPUT I$
50 PRINT "YOUR LAST NAME:  ";
60 INPUT L$
70 PRINT
80 PRINT "HELLO  "; F$; "  "; I$; ".  "; L$
90 PRINT "WHAT'S FOR LUNCH TODAY?"
95 END
```

b.
```
10 PRINT "HELLO, WHAT IS YOUR NAME?"
20 INPUT N$
30 PRINT "NICE TO MEET YOU,  "; N$; "!"
40 PRINT "HOW OLD ARE YOU?"
50 INPUT A
60 PRINT "YOU KNOW,  "; N$; ",  I HAD A PET MOUSE"
65 PRINT "THAT WAS  "; A; "  YEARS OLD."
70 PRINT "BYE!!"
80 END
```

4. **a.** Predict the output of the following program. Assume that you type DOG for the first INPUT and FLEAS for the second.

```
10 PRINT "TYPE A NOUN:  ";
20 INPUT N1$
30 PRINT "TYPE ANOTHER NOUN:  ";
40 INPUT N2$
50 PRINT "MY  "; N1$; "  HAS  ";
60 PRINT N2$
70 END
```

b. Predict the output if you type GOLDFISH for the first INPUT, and TONSILS for the second.

5. Predict the output of the following program. Assume that you type REGULAR for the first INPUT and 10 for the second.

```
10 PRINT "PREMIUM OR REGULAR?"
20 INPUT TYPE$
30 PRINT "SORRY, I HAVEN'T GOT ANY  "; TYPE$
40 PRINT "I'VE GOT LEAD-FREE"
45 LET CST = 1.18
50 PRINT "HOW MANY GALLONS?"
60 INPUT NGAL
70 PRINT "THAT WILL BE  "; NGAL * CST
80 END
```

6. Give the output of the following program for the words you decide to type in response to the INPUT statements.

```
10 REM * THIS PROGRAM WILL WRITE A SHORT PARAGRAPH
20 REM * USING THE WORDS YOU TYPE FOR THE INPUT STATEMENTS.
25 REM * (SEE LINES 110–125.)
30 PRINT "NUMBER:  ";
40 INPUT NUM
```

```
45  PRINT "YEAR:  ";
50  INPUT YR
55  PRINT "FIRST NOUN:  ";
60  INPUT N1$
70  PRINT "ADJECTIVE:  ";
80  INPUT ADJ$
85  PRINT "SECOND NOUN:  ";
90  INPUT N2$
95  PRINT "VERB:  ";
100  INPUT VERB$
105  PRINT
110  PRINT "      YESTERDAY, WHICH WAS OCTOBER  "; NUM; ","; YR; ", I"
115  PRINT "DECIDED TO GO FOR A  "; N1$; ". THEREFORE, I PUT ON"
120  PRINT "MY  "; ADJ$; "  COAT, SADDLED MY  "; N2$; ", AND  "
125  PRINT VERB$; "  OFF."
130  END
```

7. Predict the output of the following program. Assume that you type 4 for the first INPUT, 6 for the second INPUT, and 7 for the third.

```
10  INPUT X
20  INPUT Y
30  INPUT X
40  PRINT X + Y
50  END
```

8. Predict the output of the following program. Assume that you type BARLEY for the first INPUT and OATS for the second.

```
10  LET PP$ = "WHEAT"
30  INPUT PP$
50  PRINT PP$
60  INPUT QQ$
70  LET QQ$ = PP$
80  PRINT QQ$
90  END
```

In Exercises 9–12, write a program to solve the given problem. Include several PRINT and REM statements so that a user will understand how the program works and how to use the program. Use strings with commas or semicolons to make the output clear.

B **9.** Write a program that INPUTs 3 numbers, then calculates and PRINTs their average.

10. Write a program that INPUTs the length S of a side of a square, then calculates and PRINTs the area of the square.

11. Write a program that INPUTs the length L and width W of a rectangle, then calculates and PRINTs both the perimeter P and the area A of the rectangle.

12. Write a program that INPUTs the temperature in degrees Fahrenheit F and converts the temperature to degrees Celsius C.

$$C = \frac{5}{9}(F - 32)$$

13. Write a program that calculates the amount A of money that you would have after investing P dollars (P is called the *principal*) at an annual interest rate of R percent for Y years. If interest is compounded T times a year, then the formula is

$$A = P\left(1 + \frac{R}{T}\right)^{TY}.$$

Use INPUT statements for the variables P, R, T, and Y.

Lab Activity

INPUT with Quotes, Commas, and Spaces

The following short program will help you discover how quotation marks and commas may be used on your computer when typing a string in response to an INPUT statement.

```
10 INPUT A$
20 PRINT A$
30 END
```

RUN the program, typing the string ME as the INPUT, to ensure that the program works correctly.

Problems

1. RUN the program and type the string "ME" (with the quotation marks). RUN the program again and type the string "OW". What does your computer do with the quotation marks?

2. RUN the program and type the string ME"OW. RUN the program again and type the string ME"OW"ME. Is it possible to have quotation marks in the middle of an INPUT string on your computer? Experiment further with the strings "ME"OW and ME"OW".

3. RUN the program and type the string ME,OW. RUN the program again and type ME,"OW". Finally, try the string "ME,OW". How should quotation marks be used if you want to INPUT a string containing a comma?

Type the following program:

```
10 INPUT A$
20 INPUT B$
30 PRINT A$; B$
40 END
```

4. RUN the program and type the string HELLO for the first INPUT and THERE for the second INPUT. What is the output?

5. RUN the program again, typing HELLO for the first INPUT and ■■■THERE for the second. Does your computer PRINT the leading spaces? RUN the program and type HELLO■■■ for the first INPUT and THERE for the second. Does your computer PRINT the trailing spaces? See if you can determine a way to type in strings so that the computer will *always* PRINT leading and trailing spaces.

3-4 More About INPUT

In the previous section you learned that INPUT statements are usually accompanied by PRINTed messages that tell the user what information is needed, as illustrated in this program:

Program 1

Statement

```
10 PRINT "TYPE YOUR FIRST NAME:  ";
20 INPUT FRST$
25 PRINT
30 PRINT "TYPE YOUR FAVORITE COLOR:  ";
40 INPUT CLR$
50 PRINT
60 PRINT "SURPRISINGLY,  "; FRST$; ",  "; CLR$;
70 PRINT "  IS MY FAVORITE, TOO!"
80 END
```

Output

```
TYPE YOUR FIRST NAME:  ? HELENA
TYPE YOUR FAVORITE COLOR:  ? RED
SURPRISINGLY, HELENA, RED IS MY FAVORITE, TOO!
```

As a programming convenience, most computers allow messages to be placed in INPUT statements. For example, in Program 1 on the preceding page we can combine the statements in lines 10 and 20, and also the statements in lines 30 and 40, to get this simpler program:

Program 2

Statement	Remark
10 INPUT "TYPE YOUR FIRST NAME: "; FRST$	*Prints message and assigns string typed to FRST$.*
15 PRINT	
20 INPUT "TYPE YOUR FAVORITE COLOR: "; CLR$	*Prints message and assigns string typed to CLR$.*
30 PRINT	
40 PRINT "SURPRISINGLY, "; FRST$; ", "; CLR$;	*PRINTs message containing the values of FRST$ and CLR$.*
50 PRINT " IS MY FAVORITE, TOO!"	
60 END	

Output

```
TYPE YOUR FIRST NAME:  ? BOBBY
TYPE YOUR FAVORITE COLOR:  ? BLUE
SURPRISINGLY, BOBBY, BLUE IS MY FAVORITE, TOO!
```

Notice in lines 10 and 20 that a message in an INPUT statement must be enclosed in quotation marks, then followed by a semicolon and a variable. On some computers, a message included in an INPUT statement will not cause a ? prompt to appear on the screen. On these machines, you can include any desired ? as part of the message. (In the programs in this book we will always show a ? prompt.)

If a message is too long to fit on a single line on the screen, it can be typed on two or more lines by using a PRINT statement along with an INPUT statement, as shown in lines 10 and 20 of Program 3 on the next page.

Program 3

Statement	Remark
10 PRINT "TYPE YOUR FIRST NAME, OR"	*PRINTs message.*
20 INPUT "A NICKNAME IF YOU PREFER: "; NN$	*Prints message and assigns string typed to NN$.*
30 INPUT "TYPE YOUR AGE: "; A	*Prints message and assigns number typed to A.*
40 PRINT	
50 PRINT NN$; " IS "; A; " YEARS OLD."	*PRINTs message containing the values of NN$ and A.*
60 END	

Output

```
TYPE YOUR FIRST NAME, OR
A NICKNAME IF YOU PREFER:   ? BECKY
TYPE YOUR AGE:   ? 15

BECKY IS 15 YEARS OLD.
```

INPUT with Several Variables

In all the INPUT statements you have seen up to now, only one variable has been assigned a value in each statement. Actually, it is possible to assign values to several variables in the same INPUT statement, as you can see in the following program:

Program 4

Statement

```
10 PRINT "TYPE YOUR FULL NAME (FIRST, MIDDLE, LAST)"
20 INPUT "AND AGE, SEPARATED BY COMMAS:   "; F$, M$, L$, A
30 PRINT
40 PRINT "LET IT BE KNOWN THAT:"
50 PRINT
60 PRINT F$; "   "; M$; "   "; L$
65 PRINT
70 PRINT "AGE   "; A
75 PRINT
80 PRINT "HAS PASSED THE DRIVER'S TEST."
90 END
```

Output

```
TYPE YOUR FULL NAME (FIRST, MIDDLE, LAST)
AND AGE, SEPARATED BY COMMAS:   ? DENNIS, R., STEVENS, 16

LET IT BE KNOWN THAT:

DENNIS R. STEVENS

AGE 16

HAS PASSED THE DRIVER'S TEST.
```

Variables in an INPUT statement must be separated by commas. Numeric and string variables may be combined in the same INPUT statement, as you can see in line 20 above. When this is done, you must type the strings and numbers to be assigned to the variables in exactly the same order in which the variables are listed, with commas between the values. For example, since the order of the variables in line 20 is F$, M$, L$, and A, you must type three strings followed by a number when the message appears on the screen. The four values must be separated by commas.

Avoiding Pitfalls

1. Remember that a message in an INPUT statement must be enclosed in quotes, then followed by a semicolon and one or more variables.
2. In an INPUT statement with more than one variable (such as INPUT X, A$, Y), the variables must be separated by commas. When you type values for the variables when the program is RUN, the values must also be separated by commas.
3. Suppose that you press the < RETURN > or < ENTER > key before typing enough numbers or strings to match the number of variables in an INPUT statement. Some computers assign the numbers or strings that have been typed to the corresponding variables, then print two question marks (??) and wait for you to type values for the remaining variables. Other computers instead print an ERROR message such as REENTER or REDO FROM START and wait for you to type the list of values over again.
4. Suppose that you type *more* numbers or strings than there are variables in an INPUT statement. Some computers assign the typed values (in order) to the variables in the statement and print an ERROR message such as EXTRA IGNORED, and then continue execution of the program. Other computers print an ERROR message such as REENTER or REDO FROM START and wait for you to type the list of values over again.

Summary

Messages may be placed within INPUT statements in the following form:

INPUT "message" ; *variable*

The message must be enclosed in quotation marks.

A message too long for one line of output may be typed on two or more lines using PRINT statements, and then an INPUT statement for the last line of the message.

Several variables may be assigned values in a single INPUT statement (for example, INPUT A$, B, FRST$, D). The variables must be separated by commas. The strings and numbers to be assigned to the variables must be typed in exactly the same order in which the variables are listed, with commas between the values.

Exercises 3-4

A

1. Tell whether the following are valid BASIC statements. If not valid, give a possible correction.

a. `10 INPUT "TYPE A NUMBER:  ; N`
b. `10 INPUT "X = "; X`
c. `10 INPUT BB, B$`
d. `10 INPUT "NUMBERS = "; X, Y, Z`
e. `10 INPUT A$; A1$; B`
f. `10 INPUT A$, 35`
g. `10 INPUT "A$"; B$`
h. `10 INPUT X; "  IS A BIG NUMBER."`
i. `10 INPUT "Y"; Y`
j. `10 INPUT "ANSWER:  "; A`

2. Rewrite each of the following programs to include the messages in the INPUT statements.

a.
```
10 PRINT "TYPE NO. OF WINTER COATS:  ";
20 INPUT NWC
30 PRINT "YOU HAVE  "; NWC; "  WINTER COATS?"
40 END
```

b.
```
10 PRINT "HOW MANY ITEMS?"
20 INPUT I
30 PRINT "WHAT IS THE COST PER ITEM?"
40 INPUT CST
50 PRINT "TOTAL COST IS:  "; I * CST
55 PRINT "WHAT A DEAL"
60 END
```

3. a. Rewrite the statements in lines 10–35 below using only one INPUT statement.

```
10  PRINT "TYPE NAMES OF THREE FRIENDS:  "
20  INPUT F1$
30  INPUT F2$
35  INPUT F3$
40  PRINT "YOU LIKE. . .
45  END
```

b. Complete line 40 so that the three INPUT names are PRINTed on the same line with commas and spaces between them, and a period at the end of the sentence.

4. If you were to RUN the following program and type YELLOW after the ? prompt, what would be the output of the program?

```
10  LET A$ = "RED"
15  LET A$ = "BLUE"
20  INPUT A$
30  PRINT "THE COLOR IS:  "; A$
40   END
```

B

5. Write a program that INPUTs a person's first name and last name, and then PRINTs them on the same line, last name first, with a comma and space between them.

6. a. Write a program that INPUTs three names, then PRINTs the names on *separate* lines in the reverse order from the order in which they were entered.

b. Change the program to PRINT the three names on the *same* line (in reverse order), with a comma and space between each name.

7. Write a program that INPUTs the number of nickels, dimes, and quarters a user has, then calculates and PRINTs the total amount of money in dollars and cents. Here is a sample output:

```
HOW MANY NICKELS, DIMES, AND QUARTERS DO YOU HAVE?
? 3, 2, 4
YOU HAVE 9 COINS THAT TOTAL $1.35.
```

8. Write a program that INPUTs the height of a user in feet F and inches I, and then converts the height to centimeters C (1 inch = 2.54 cm). Here is a sample output:

```
TYPE IN YOUR HEIGHT (FEET, INCHES):  ? 5, 6
WOW, YOU ARE 167.64 CENTIMETERS TALL!
```

9. Write a program that INPUTs the number of hours H a user works in a week and the amount of money M earned per hour. Have the program calculate and PRINT the user's salary for one week. Here is a sample output:

```
HOW MANY HOURS DO YOU WORK IN A WEEK:   ? 40
HOW MUCH MONEY DO YOU EARN PER HOUR:   ? 4.50
YOUR SALARY FOR ONE WEEK IS 180 DOLLARS.
```

10. Rewrite Program 5 (Section 2–4, page 41) using INPUT statements to enter the players' nicknames and the number of points scored in the last three games.

11. (Graphics) Write a program that INPUTs the X- and Y-coordinates of a point, then plots the point in graphics mode on the screen. If your computer has color, then have the program plot the point in any INPUT color.

Lab Activity

Being Creative

Write a short story of 50 to 100 words. When you are finished, delete three to five key nouns, replacing them with the variables N1$, N2$, and so on. Then delete three to five key adjectives, replacing them with the variables A1$, A2$, and so on. Do the same with several verbs, calling them V1$, V2$, and so on. Write a program that will allow a user to type strings for the missing nouns, adjectives, and verbs. (Use INPUT statements with appropriate prompting messages.) Have the program PRINT the story with these words in the appropriate positions in the text. (See Exercise 6, page 92 for an example of how this can be done.) RUN the program to see if it works correctly.

3-5 READ . . . DATA Statements

Thus far, you have learned two ways to assign values to variables: LET and INPUT. The LET statement assigns values from *within* a program, and the INPUT statement allows the user to supply the values while the program is RUNning. There is a third method that is particularly appropriate for assigning a large number of values; this method uses the statements READ and DATA. A DATA statement is essentially a list of values; the READ statement assigns these values to variables. The READ . . . DATA technique is illustrated in Program 1 on the next page.

Program 1

Statement	Remark
10 PRINT "PLANETS, PART 1"	
15 PRINT	
20 READ M$, V$, E$	*Assigns strings from DATA line to M$, V$, and E$.*
30 PRINT M$; " AND "; V$	
35 PRINT "ARE CLOSER TO"	
40 PRINT "THE SUN THAN "; E$; " IS."	
50 DATA MERCURY, VENUS, EARTH	*Three DATA values.*
60 END	

Output

```
PLANETS, PART 1

MERCURY AND VENUS
ARE CLOSER TO
THE SUN THAN EARTH IS.
```

The READ statement (line 20) causes the computer to search through the program, from the smallest line number to the largest, to find a DATA line (line 50). The computer assigns the first DATA value (MERCURY) to the first variable (M$). Then the computer assigns the second DATA value (VENUS) to the second variable (V$). Finally, the third variable (E$) is given the last DATA value (EARTH). The diagram below illustrates how the READ statement in line 20 assigns the DATA values to the variables.

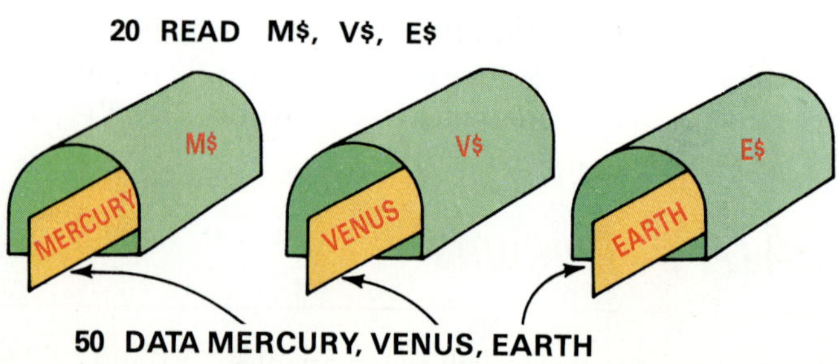

Notice that strings in a DATA statement ordinarily need not be enclosed in quotation marks, although most computers will accept them. (See the Lab Activity to discover when quotation marks *must* be used with strings in DATA statements.)

Both numeric and string variables may be used in a READ statement, as shown in Program 2 on the next page.

Program 2

Statement	Remark
10 PRINT "PLANETS, PART 2"	
20 READ N, E$, S$	*Assigns values from DATA line to N, E$, and S$.*
30 PRINT "OF THE "; N; " KNOWN PLANETS"	
40 PRINT E$; " RANKS THIRD IN DISTANCE";	
45 PRINT " FROM THE "; S$; "."	
50 DATA 9, EARTH, SUN	*Three DATA values.*
60 END	

Output

```
PLANETS, PART 2
OF THE 9 KNOWN PLANETS
EARTH RANKS THIRD IN DISTANCE FROM THE SUN.
```

As you can see in Programs 1 and 2, the strings or numbers in a DATA statement and the variables in a READ statement must be separated by commas.

Numbers in a DATA statement may be in integer, decimal, or exponential form, but expressions using operation symbols (such as 2 / 3, 5 + 2, and 4 * 3 − 1) are not allowed unless they are assigned to string variables. The DATA statements may be placed anywhere in a program, but are more commonly found at or near the end. This location makes the statements easier to find in case you want to change the information contained in them.

READ and DATA statements may appear on more than one line in a program, as in this revised version of Program 2.

Program 3

Statement	Remark
10 PRINT "MORE ABOUT PLANETS!"	
20 READ E$, S$	*Assigns strings from lines 50 and 52 to E$ and S$.*
25 READ N	*Assigns number from line 55 to N.*
30 PRINT E$; " IS ABOUT "; N; " MILLION"	
40 PRINT "MILES FROM THE "; S$; "."	
50 DATA EARTH	
52 DATA SUN	

Program continued on next page.

```
55  DATA 93
60  END
```

Output

```
MORE ABOUT PLANETS!
EARTH IS ABOUT 93 MILLION
MILES FROM THE SUN.
```

After the first DATA value (EARTH) is assigned to the first variable (E$), the computer looks for the next DATA statement (line 52). It then assigns the string SUN to the second variable (S$). Finally, in executing the statement READ N in line 25, the computer finds the next DATA value in line 55, and assigns the number 93 to the variable N.

The RESTORE Statement

At times you may want to use the same DATA values more than once in a program. Ordinarily, if your program has already used (that is, READ) all the values in all the DATA statements, any further READ statement will cause an OUT OF DATA error message and the program will stop. The RESTORE statement makes it possible to use DATA over again beginning with the first value listed.

Program 4

Statement	Remark
10 PRINT "RESTORING DATA"	
20 READ X, Y	
30 PRINT "TOTAL COST IS: "; X + Y	
40 RESTORE	*RESTOREs DATA values so that they can be used again.*
50 READ A, B	
60 PRINT "FIRST ITEM'S COST IS: "; A	
70 PRINT "SECOND ITEM'S COST IS: "; B	
80 DATA 1.65, 4.53	
90 END	

Output

```
RESTORING DATA
TOTAL COST IS:  6.18
FIRST ITEM'S COST IS:  1.65
SECOND ITEM'S COST IS:  4.53
```

The READ statement in line 20 assigns the value 1.65 to X and 4.53 to Y. The RESTORE statement in line 40 tells the computer to start READing the DATA again, beginning with the first value listed. Thus, the READ in line 50 assigns the first DATA value (1.65) to A, and the second (4.53) to B.

Avoiding Pitfalls

1. Numeric and string variables in a READ statement must match properly with numbers and strings in a corresponding DATA statement.
2. If there are *more* strings or numbers in all the DATA statements than there are variables in all the READ statements, then the computer will simply ignore the extra values.
3. If there are *fewer* strings or numbers in all the DATA statements than there are variables in all the READ statements (and RESTORE is not used), then the computer needs more values than you provided. Your program will stop and you will get an OUT OF DATA error message. You should change the program so that the number of DATA values matches the number of variables to be READ.
4. Beginning programmers might type a statement such as 20 READ 25, intending to use the number 25 later in the program. Remember that READ must be followed by one or more variables.

Summary

READ . . . DATA statements may be used to assign values to variables. For example, in the program

```
30 READ A$, B$, C$
40 DATA EARTH, WIND, FIRE
50 END
```

the READ statement assigns the string EARTH to A$, WIND to B$, and FIRE to C$.

Strings and numbers in a DATA statement and variables in a READ statement must be separated by commas. The order of the strings and numbers must match the order of the string and numeric variables.

DATA statements are usually placed at or near the end of a program.

The RESTORE statement allows you to use the same DATA more than once in a program.

Exercises 3-5

A **1.** Find the error(s) in each of the following programs. Give a possible correction.

a.
```
10 READ X; Y
30 PRINT X * Y
40 DATA 12, 20
50 END
```

b.
```
10 READ X, Y$
20 PRINT X, Y$
30 DATA CHARM, 12
40 END
```

c.
```
10 READ M, N
20 PRINT M / N
30 DATA 15, 2 / 3
40 END
```

d.
```
10 READ A1, X$, B2
15 PRINT A1, X$, B2
20 DATA —5, GAMMA
30 END
```

e.
```
10 READ X$, Y$, Z$,
20 PRINT "MONTHS"
30 DATA JAN, MAR, APRIL
35 END
```

f.
```
10 READ P, Q, R, S
20 PRINT P + Q + R + S
25 DATA 15, 22  10, 50
30 END
```

2. Rewrite the following programs using READ . . . DATA statements.

a.
```
10 LET A = 12
20 LET B$ = "   RED"
30 LET C$ = "   ROSES"
40 PRINT A; B$; C$
50 PRINT "EVEN DOZEN"
60 END
```

b.
```
10 LET A1 = 4
20 LET B1 = 10
30 LET C1 = 3
40 LET AVG = (A1 + B1 + C1) / 3
50 PRINT "AVERAGE:   "; AVG
60 END
```

3. Predict the output of each of the following programs.

a.
```
10 READ A1, A2, A3
20 LET SUM = A1 + A2 + A3
30 PRINT "SUM:   "; SUM
40 DATA 15, 8, 2
50 END
```

b.
```
10 READ A$, B$, C$
20 PRINT A$; "   IS A   "; B$
30 PRINT "AND A   "; C$
40 DATA PLUTO, DOG, PLANET
50 END
```

c.
```
10 READ J$, M$
20 READ N
30 PRINT J$; "   HAS AT   ";
35 PRINT "LEAST   "; N
40 PRINT M$
50 DATA JUPITER, MOONS, 16
60 END
```

d.
```
10 READ AB$
20 PRINT AB$; "   ";
30 READ CD$
40 PRINT CD$
50 DATA MARS, SATURN
60 END
```

e.
```
10 READ NM$, G1, G2, G3
20 PRINT NM$; " 'S ";
30 PRINT "GRADES ARE:  "
40 PRINT G1, G2, G3
50 DATA JEREMY
60 DATA 80, 93, 82
70 END
```

f.
```
10 READ A$, B$
20 READ C$
30 PRINT A$; "  AND  "; B$;
40 PRINT "  AND  "; C$
50 DATA ASTEROIDS
60 DATA COMETS, BLACK HOLES?
70 END
```

g.
```
10 READ A$
20 PRINT A$
25 RESTORE
30 READ B$
40 PRINT B$
50 RESTORE
60 READ C$
70 PRINT C$
80 DATA ALPHA, KAPPA, OMEGA
90 END
```

h.
```
10 READ X, Y, Z
20 LET PROD = X * Y * Z
30 PRINT "PRODUCT:  "; PROD
40 RESTORE
50 READ P, Q, R
60 LET SUM = P + Q + R
70 PRINT "SUM:  "; SUM
80 DATA 2, 1, 5, 3, 10, 6
90 END
```

4. Predict the output of Program 2 if the statements in lines 20 and 30 are interchanged (switched).

5. Predict the output of Program 3 if the variable N in lines 25 and 30 is changed to N$.

B

6. Write a program using READ . . . DATA statements that has the following output:

```
JACK'S GRADES ARE:  72, 84, 91, 85
JACK'S AVERAGE IS:  83
```

Use this DATA line: 100 DATA JACK, 72, 84, 91, 85

7. Write a program using READ . . . DATA statements that has the following output:

```
1 POUND IS APPROXIMATELY 454 GRAMS
10 POUNDS IS APPROXIMATELY 4540 GRAMS
```

Use this DATA line: 100 DATA 1, 454

8. Write a program using READ . . . DATA statements that has the following output:

```
DON'T FORGET ABOUT
NEPTUNE AND URANUS
```

Use this DATA line: 100 DATA NEPTUNE, URANUS, FORGET

9. Write a program using READ . . . DATA statements that has the following output:

```
IF A CAR TRAVELS 216 MILES
USING 6 GALLONS OF GAS,
THE CAR IS GETTING GAS MILEAGE
OF 36 MILES PER GALLON.
```

Use this DATA line: 100 DATA 216, 6

10. Write a program using READ . . . DATA statements that has the following output:

```
TODAY'S HIGH:  10 DEGREES CELSIUS
TOMORROW'S EXPECTED HIGH:  12 DEGREES CELSIUS
AVERAGE TEMPERATURE IS:  11 DEGREES CELSIUS
```

Use this DATA line: 100 DATA CELSIUS, 10, 12

11. Write a program using READ . . . DATA statements that has the following output:

```
NAME                    NUMBER
JENSEN                  612-4838
JONES                   214-6837
```

Use this DATA line: 100 DATA JENSEN, 612–4838, JONES, 214–6837

12. Rewrite Program 5 (Section 2–4, page 41) using READ . . . DATA statements. The DATA statements should contain the players' nicknames and the number of points scored in the last three games.

Lab Activity

DATA and Quotation Marks

Type, LIST, and then RUN the following program:

```
5  PRINT "ABOUT QUOTES"
10 READ A$
20 PRINT A$
30 DATA CANNOT
40 END
```

Is the output as you expect?

Problems

1. Change line 30 to

```
30 DATA CAN, NOT
```

and RUN the program. Since BASIC uses commas to separate values in a DATA statement, the computer assigns CAN to A$ and ignores the string NOT.

2. You can make the computer READ commas by enclosing an entire string in a DATA statement within quotation marks. For example, change line 30 above to:

```
30 DATA "CAN, NOT"
```

RUN this new version of the program. What is the output now? What does the computer do with the quotation marks?

3. Change line 30 again so that the output of the program will be this:

```
WE THINK, THEREFORE, WE EAT
```

4. Try this line in the program:

```
30 DATA I: GUESS
```

What does the computer do with this string when you try to RUN the program? Change the line so that the computer's output will be I:GUESS.

5. As you probably discovered earlier (see the Lab Activity for Section 3–3, page 95, Problems 4 and 5), BASIC ignores certain spaces in strings. Notice what the computer does with the spaces if you change line 30 to:

```
30 DATA ■■■■■ME
```

You can have the computer include leading spaces in a DATA string value by enclosing the string in quotation marks. Try 30 DATA "■■■■■ME" and verify that the spaces are now included.

6. Determine if the computer ignores spaces *within* a string in a DATA statement. Try this line:

```
30 DATA ME■■■■■YOU
```

Are the spaces PRINTed in this case?

7. Change the following lines to see what the computer does with spaces at the *end* of a string in a DATA statement:

```
10 READ A$, B$
20 PRINT A$; B$
30 DATA I■■■■■, YOU
```

What does your computer do with trailing spaces in a DATA string value?

3-6 The GOTO Statement

In all of the programs that you have seen so far, the computer executed the lines in numerical order, from the smallest line number to the largest, until it reached the END statement. The real power of the computer is unlocked if we control the order in which the lines in a program are executed. This is done with the instruction GOTO, as illustrated in the following program.

Program 1

Statement	Remark
10 PRINT "A FIRST LOOP"	
20 INPUT "TYPE YOUR FIRST NAME: "; F$	*Assigns name typed to F$.*
30 PRINT F$; ", THIS MESSAGE WON'T STOP!"	*PRINTs message.*
40 GOTO 30	*Executes line 30 next.*
50 END	

Output

```
A FIRST LOOP
TYPE YOUR FIRST NAME:  ? SHARON
SHARON, THIS MESSAGE WON'T STOP!
SHARON, THIS MESSAGE WON'T STOP!
SHARON, THIS MESSAGE WON'T STOP!
.
.
.
```

After requesting the user's name in line 20, the computer PRINTs the message in line 30 and arrives at line 40. There the statement GOTO 30 causes the computer to go back to line 30 and PRINT the message a second time. Then the computer arrives at line 40 again and the GOTO instruction causes it to go back to line 30, PRINT the message, and so on.

Lines 30 and 40, which the computer executes repeatedly, make up what is called a *loop*. Drawing arrows from one line to the next line that the computer will execute shows why this word is used:

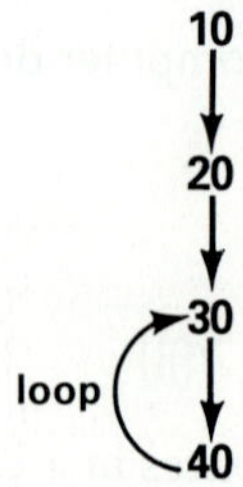

As you can see in the output of Program 1, the computer continues to PRINT the message

SHARON, THIS MESSAGE WON'T STOP!

over and over again. You can stop the RUN of the program by pressing the < BREAK > key or the < RESET > key. (*Note:* On some computers you must hold down the CONTROL < CTRL > key while pressing the < BREAK > or < RESET > key.)

Here is a slightly different version of Program 1.

Program 2

Statement	Remark
10 PRINT "A BIGGER LOOP"	
20 INPUT "TYPE YOUR FIRST NAME: "; F$	*Assigns name typed to F$.*
30 PRINT F$; ", PLEASE STOP THE PROGRAM!"	*PRINTs message.*
35 PRINT	
40 GOTO 20	*Executes line 20 next.*
50 END	

Output

```
A BIGGER LOOP
TYPE YOUR FIRST NAME:  ? ALAN
ALAN, PLEASE STOP THE PROGRAM!

TYPE YOUR FIRST NAME:  ? MELISSA
MELISSA, PLEASE STOP THE PROGRAM!

TYPE YOUR FIRST NAME:  ? JUAN
JUAN, PLEASE STOP THE PROGRAM!

TYPE YOUR FIRST NAME:  ? VANESSA
VANESSA, PLEASE STOP THE PROGRAM!
.
.
.
```

Notice the difference in the GOTO statements of Programs 1 and 2. In line 40 of Program 2 the computer is sent back to line 20 (rather than line 30, as in Program 1), where it is instructed to INPUT another name. The new name is then PRINTed in the message in line 30. Line 35 causes the computer to PRINT a blank line in the output. Then the GOTO 20 statement in line 40 sends the computer back to line 20 and the loop is repeated. This looping process will continue until the user stops the RUN of the program. Program 2 then has a bigger loop than the first; it looks like this:

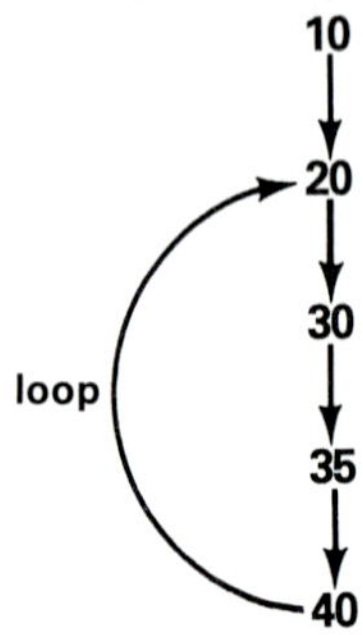

GOTO with READ . . . DATA

Loops are particularly useful in programs containing READ . . . DATA statements, as illustrated in Program 3 below.

Program 3

Statement	Remark
10 PRINT "TELEPHONE DIRECTORY"	
20 PRINT "NAME", "NUMBER"	*PRINTs column headings.*
30 READ N$, NUM$	*Assigns strings from DATA line to N$ and NUM$.*
40 PRINT N$, NUM$	
50 GOTO 30	*Executes line 30 next.*
60 DATA JACOBS, 876-3020, JENSEN, 413-6972	
65 DATA JONES, 612-0084	
70 END	

Output

```
TELEPHONE DIRECTORY
NAME           NUMBER
JACOBS         876-3020
JENSEN         413-6972
JONES          612-0084
OUT OF DATA IN 30
```

The loop in lines 30, 40, and 50 allows us to assign three different pairs of strings to N$ and NUM$ with only one READ statement, which is executed several times. The first time line 30 is executed, the READ statement assigns JACOBS to N$ and 876–3020 to NUM$. The next time line 30 is executed (the second time through the loop), the computer READs the DATA values from the place where it left off previously. This means that JENSEN is assigned to N$ and 413–6972 to NUM$. The third time through the loop, the READ statement assigns JONES to N$ and 612–0084 to NUM$. After these last two strings are PRINTed (line 40), the GOTO statement in line 50 sends the computer back to the READ statement in line 30. Since there are no more strings to be READ in the DATA list, the computer prints the message OUT OF DATA IN 30 and the program stops. (You will learn how to avoid this error in the next chapter.)

Counting Loops

By using the GOTO statement and a loop, we can have the computer perform repetitious tasks (such as counting) quickly and efficiently.

Program 4

Statement	Remark
10 PRINT "COUNTING PROGRAM"	
20 LET D = 1	*Initial value of D is 1.*
30 PRINT D	*PRINTs the value of D.*
40 LET D = D + 1	*Increases the value of D by 1.*
50 GOTO 30	*Executes line 30 next.*
60 END	

Output

```
COUNTING PROGRAM
1
2
3
4
.
.
.
```

As you may recall from an earlier version of this program (Program 5, page 79), the statement LET D = D + 1 in line 40 adds 1 to the present value of D (1) and stores the new value (2) in the same variable (D). The old value is replaced. In line 50 the GOTO instruction sends the computer back to line 30 and the new value of D (2) is PRINTed. The computer then continues through the loop, increases the value of D to 3, goes back to line 30, PRINTs 3, and so on. When a variable such as D is used in this manner, it is called a counting variable, or a *counter.*

Program 4 will continue to loop and PRINT numbers until you stop the RUN of the program. BASIC provides a method of leaving a loop automatically at any number you want, as you will see in the next chapter.

Avoiding Pitfalls

1. If your program has a line such as 50 GOTO 20 but there is no line 20, then the computer prints an ERROR message such as UNDEFINED STATEMENT ERROR IN 50. (Error messages vary. See page 658 for the message given on your computer.)
2. If a loop contains one or more READ statements, then each time through the loop the computer assigns as many DATA values as there are variables in the READ statements. Thus, if there are two variables, the total number of DATA values should be a multiple of two; if there are three variables, the total number of DATA values should be a multiple of three, and so on. Otherwise, an OUT OF DATA error message may result.
3. Beginning programmers sometimes use a GOTO instruction to send the computer to a DATA line rather than to a line with a READ statement. Remember that it is the READ statement that assigns values to variables.

Summary

A GOTO statement changes the order in which the lines in a program are executed. For example, the statement 40 GOTO 30 causes the computer to execute line 30 immediately after executing line 40.

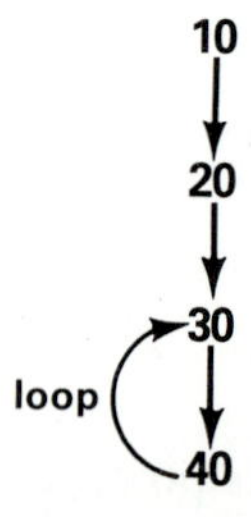

The statement LET D = D + 1 adds 1 to the present value of D and stores the new value in the same variable (D). A variable used in this way is called a *counter.*

To stop the RUN of a program, press the < BREAK > key or < RESET > key (the < CTRL > key must also be pressed on some computers).

Exercises 3-6

A **1.** In each of the following programs:

i. Tell the order in which the program lines are executed (for example, 10, 20, 30, 40, 30, 40, 30, 40, . . .).

ii. Predict the output.

a.
```
10 PRINT "ABC"
20 LET A$ = "CDE"
30 PRINT A$
40 GOTO 20
50 END
```

b.
```
10 LET X = 3
20 LET Y = 2
30 LET X = X + Y
40 PRINT X
50 GOTO 30
60 END
```

c.
```
10 PRINT "USELESS?"
20 PRINT "NOT REALLY"
30 GOTO 30
40 END
```

d.
```
10 PRINT "FORWARD"
20 GOTO 50
30 PRINT "XYZ"
40 LET X = 72
50 END
```

e.
```
10 PRINT "MORE COMPLICATED"
20 GOTO 50
30 PRINT "ABC"
40 PRINT "P"
50 GOTO 20
60 END
```

f.
```
10 PRINT "EVEN HARDER"
20 GOTO 50
30 PRINT "XX"
40 PRINT "ZZ"
50 GOTO 30
60 END
```

2. Predict the output, or give the ERROR message, for each of the following programs.

a.
```
10 PRINT "ERROR?"
30 PRINT "NO"
40 GOTO 20
50 END
```

b.
```
10 PRINT "MISTAKE?"
20 GOTO 40
30 GOTO 25
40 GOTO 25
50 END
```

c.
```
10 READ A, B
20 PRINT A + B
25 RESTORE
30 GOTO 10
40 DATA 3, 8, 6, 4
50 END
```

d.
```
10 READ A, B
20 PRINT A * B
30 GOTO 10
40 DATA 3, 10, 5, 8, 6
50 END
```

3. Predict the output of Program 3 if line 50 is changed to 50 GOTO 20.

4. Predict the output of Program 4 if line 50 is changed to 50 GOTO 20.

5. a. Predict the output of the following program. Assume that you type HOUND for the first INPUT and ORLEANS for the second.

```
10 PRINT "LIMERICK"
20 INPUT "NOUN:  "; NOUN$
30 INPUT "PLACE:  "; PL$
40 PRINT "THERE ONCE WAS A  "; NOUN$
50 PRINT "FROM  "; PL$
60 GOTO 40
70 END
```

b. Add the line 35 GOTO 60 to the program in (a). Change line 60 to 60 GOTO 20. Predict the output for any two strings you want the program to INPUT.

6. a. Predict the output of the following program. Construct a RUN chart. (Show at least 20 lines in the RUN chart.)

```
10 PRINT "RAPID"
15 PRINT "GROWTH"
20 LET X=0
30 PRINT X
40 LET X=X+5
50 GOTO 30
60 END
```

b. Change line 20 in the program in (a) to 20 LET X = 8. Construct a RUN chart and predict the output.

c. Change line 50 in the program in (b) to 50 GOTO 20. Construct a RUN chart and predict the output.

7. Predict the output of each program by constructing a RUN chart.

a.
```
10 PRINT "PLANETS AGAIN!"
15 LET C=0
20 READ PLNT$
30 LET C=C+1
40 PRINT "PLANET NUMBER  "; C; "  IS  "; PLNT$
50 GOTO 20
55 DATA MERCURY, VENUS, EARTH, MARS
60 DATA JUPITER, SATURN, NEPTUNE
65 DATA URANUS, PLUTO
70 END
```

b.
```
10 PRINT "GRADES"
20 PRINT "NAME", "AVERAGE"
30 READ NM$, G1, G2, G3
40 LET X = G1 + G2 + G3
50 LET Y = X / 3
60 PRINT NM$, Y
65 GOTO 30
70 DATA SEAVERS, 78, 91, 83, JEFFERSON, 90, 83, 91
80 DATA MARTINEZ, 85, 88, 79, MARKSON, 77, 92, 80
90 END
```

c.
```
10 PRINT "REAL GROWTH"
20 LET X = 2
30 LET Y = 7
40 PRINT X + Y
50 LET X = X + 2 * Y
60 LET Y = Y - 1
70 GOTO 40
80 END
```

d.
```
10 PRINT "TONGUE TWISTER"
20 READ A$, B$, C$, D$
30 PRINT A$; "  "; B$; "  "; C$; "  "; D$
40 LET A$ = "SANDY"
50 LET B$ = "SHORE"
60 RESTORE
70 GOTO 20
80 DATA SHE, SELLS, SEA, SHELLS
90 END
```

(Show at least 20 lines in the RUN chart in (c).)

B **8. a.** Write a program using a loop that has the following output:

```
BEST SONG
I WANNA HOLD YOUR HAND
I WANNA HOLD YOUR HAND
I WANNA HOLD YOUR HAND
.
.
.
```

b. Change your program in part (a) so that the output looks like this:

```
BEST SONG
I WANNA HOLD YOUR HAND
EVER HEAR IT?
I WANNA HOLD YOUR HAND
EVER HEAR IT?
.
.
.
```

9. Write a program using a loop that asks a user his or her favorite song, then PRINTs the title of the song repeatedly.

10. Write a program using a loop that has the following output.

```
I 1 A SKUNK.
I 2 A SKUNK.
I 3 A SKUNK.
I 4 A SKUNK.
.
.
.
```

11. Write a program using a loop to produce each output shown below.

a.
```
1  4
2  8
3  12
4  16
.
.
.
```

b.
```
1  2
2  4
3  8
4  16
.
.
.
```

Lab Activity

Line Editing

This activity explains how to edit program lines on the *Apple, IBM,* and *TRS-80* microcomputers. Choose the explanation below that applies to your computer.

Problems

Apple

1. Type the following program into the computer:

```
10  PRINT "A CRAZY PROGRAM"
20  PRINT "THE PORPOISE OF WHICH"
30  PRINT "IS TO SHOW YOU HOW TO DO EDIT
ING OF BASIC PROGRAM LINES WITHOUT RETY
PING EVERYTHING"
40  END
```

In line 30, just keep typing everything inside the quotation marks, with single spaces between the words; do not press < RETURN > until after the last quotation mark is typed.

2. As you know, you can change a line in a program simply by retyping it using the same line number, making the necessary corrections as you type. Another method is to use these keys:

   < ESC >, I, J, K, M, < → > (the forward arrow), and < RETURN >

   First, you need to learn how to move the cursor about the screen. To do this, first press the < ESC > key once. Then the keys

   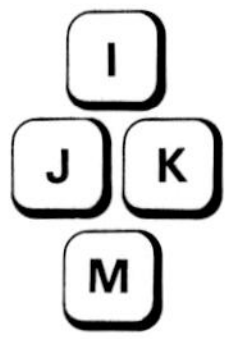

   will cause the cursor to move left, up, right, and down. Experiment with these keys to learn how to control the cursor's movement.

   Next, move the cursor to a clear space near the bottom of the screen. Press the < SPACE > bar to cancel the < ESC >, then try typing I, J, K, or M. What happens? Press < RETURN >. What is the computer's response?

3. Suppose you want to add a comma to the end of the string inside the quotation marks in line 10, so that it reads this way:

```
10  PRINT "A CRAZY PROGRAM,"
```

   First, type LIST to get a clear copy of the program on the screen. (If the program were longer, you could just LIST one or a few lines, as you learned to do in Chapter 2.)

   Now, press < ESC > and use the I, J, K, and M keys to position the cursor on the first character of line 10 (the number 1). Press the < SPACE > bar to cancel the < ESC >. You are now ready to re-enter the line, which you *could* do by retyping each old character and adding a comma before the last quotation mark. Instead, you can avoid retyping by having the computer *copy* the characters that are already there; this is done by using the forward-arrow key < → >. If the cursor is on the 1 and you press the < → >, the cursor moves to the 0 and the computer interprets this action exactly as if you typed the 1. Press the < → > repeatedly (or hold it down and press the repeat < REPT > key at the same time) to copy all the characters and spaces in the line until the cursor is on the last quotation mark. If the cursor goes too far, you can back it up using the back arrow < ← >. When the cursor is positioned on the quotation mark, type the comma and then another quotation mark. Now press < RETURN >. Move the cursor down to the bottom of the screen and type LIST to see that the comma has been added to line 10.

4. Use the technique you just learned to change PORPOISE to PURPOSE in line 20. Remember, you must use the forward arrow <→> to copy the line, starting on the 2. When you get to the first O in PORPOISE, type a U instead. Then when the cursor is positioned on the I in PURPOISE, avoid copying it by typing < ESC > K to move the cursor to the right one space. Then press the < SPACE > bar to get back to copying, and use <→> for the rest of the line.

5. Add a period at the end of the word EVERYTHING in line 30. Notice that when you copy to the end of a line on the screen, the cursor automatically goes on to the beginning of the next line. Type LIST 30 to see the results. The jumble you probably see on the screen results from copying all the spaces that the computer puts in the line in order to make it look nice when it is LISTed. You can avoid copying these spaces by using < ESC > and then repeated K's to pass over the extra spaces at the end of each line; then press the < SPACE > bar and continue with the <→> on the next line. Try it and see if you can get line 30 to look right.

6. *Challenge:* Add the word REALLY to line 10 so that it reads:

```
10 PRINT "A REALLY CRAZY PROGRAM,"
```

You may recopy, but not retype, CRAZY PROGRAM,".

IBM

1. Type the following program into the computer:

```
10 PRINT "A CRAZY PROGRAM"
20 PRINT "THE PORPOISE OF WHICH"
30 PRINT "IS TO ILLUSTRATE EDITING"
40 END
```

2. As you know, you can change a line in a program simply by retyping it using the same line number, making the necessary corrections as you type. Another easier method is to use the EDIT command. For example, suppose you want to add a comma to the end of the string in line 10, so that it reads this way: 10 PRINT "A CRAZY PROGRAM,".

   To do this, first type: EDIT 10. Line 10 will then appear on the screen with the cursor positioned beneath the number 1. Use the forward-arrow key <→> to move the cursor to the right until it is under the last quotation mark in the line. If the cursor goes too far, you can back it up using the back arrow <←>. Now type the comma and another quotation mark. Then press the < ENTER > key to record the change you made in the line. LIST the program to see if the comma has been added to line 10.

3. Now change PORPOISE in line 20 to PURPOSE. Type EDIT 20, and use the forward arrow <→> to position the cursor under the first O of

PORPOISE. Then type the correct letter (U). Now move the cursor to the position under the I in PURPOISE and *delete* it by pressing the < DEL > key. When you are done, press < RETURN >. LIST the program to verify that the changes have been made.

4. *Insert* the word REALLY (use the < INS > key) in line 10 so that it reads like this: 10 PRINT "A REALLY CRAZY PROGRAM,".

TRS-80

1. Type the following program into the computer:

```
10 PRINT "A CRAZY PROGRAM"
20 PRINT "THE PORPOISE OF WHICH"
30 PRINT "IS TO ILLUSTRATE EDITING"
40 END
```

2. As you know, you can change a line in a program simply by retyping it using the same line number, making the necessary corrections as you type. Another method is to use the EDIT command. For example, suppose you want to add a comma to the end of the string in line 10, so that it reads this way: 10 PRINT "A CRAZY PROGRAM,".

To do this, first type: EDIT 10. This will cause the number 10 to appear on the screen, with the cursor located one space after the line number. Type L (but do *not* press < ENTER >) to *list* the statement in line 10. Now press the < SPACE > bar repeatedly to move the cursor forward so that it is positioned immediately after the letter M. If the cursor moves too far, you can back it up using the back arrow <←>. To insert the comma at the position of the cursor, type I (for *insert*), then type the comma. Now press the < SHIFT > and up-arrow < ↑ > keys at the same time to cancel inserting. Press < ENTER > to record the change you made in the line. The line should appear on the screen the way you wanted it to. LIST the program to be sure the change has been made.

3. Now change PORPOISE in line 20 to PURPOSE. Type EDIT 20, followed by L to see the line that you are editing. Use the < SPACE > bar to move the cursor to the position immediately after the first P of PORPOISE. Type D (for *delete*) to get rid of the letter O (the letter will appear with exclamation marks (!) on both sides of it). Then type I *(insert)* followed by the correct letter (U). Now, type < SHIFT > ↑ to cancel inserting. Next, move the cursor to the position immediately after the O in PURPOISE. Type D to delete the letter I. When you are done, press < ENTER >. LIST the program to verify that the changes have been made.

4. Insert the word REALLY in line 10 so that it reads like this:

```
10 PRINT "A REALLY CRAZY PROGRAM,"
```

Chapter Summary

A *variable* in BASIC consists of either a single letter, or a letter followed by other letters or the digits 0 to 9. A *string variable* must end with a dollar sign and have a string as its value; a *numeric variable* must have a number value.

The LET statement is used to assign values to variables. String values must be enclosed in quotation marks. The statement LET Z = Y assigns the value of Y to the variable Z. The value of Y does not change.

The statement LET C = C + 1 adds 1 to the present value of *counter* C and stores the new value at the same location. The old value of C is replaced.

The statement INPUT *variable* causes the computer to print a ? and assign the typed number or string to the specified variable. Several variables may be assigned values in the same INPUT statement (for example, INPUT NAM$, AGE, PET$). The variables must be separated by commas.

Messages may be placed within INPUT statements in the following form:

INPUT "message"; *variable*

REM statements are explanatory remarks placed in the program to help the user understand the program. REMs do not affect how a program RUNs.

Program *documentation* should include the purpose of the program, the role of important lines in the program, instructions on how to use the program, and other useful information.

READ . . . DATA statements may be used to assign values to variables. For example, in the program

```
20 READ X, Y$, Z$
30 DATA 10, NICE, NOTICE
40 END
```

the READ statement assigns the number 10 to X, the string NICE to Y$, and the string NOTICE to Z$.

The RESTORE statement allows you to use the same DATA values more than once in a program.

A GOTO statement changes the order in which the lines in a program are executed. For example, the statement 60 GOTO 30 causes the computer to execute line 30 immediately after executing line 60.

Chapter Test

1. Tell whether each of the following is a legal variable name. If not legal, explain why.
   a. X$ **b.** Y2$ **c.** LIST **d.** 2R2D

2. Predict the output of each of the following programs.

a.
```
10 LET X=5
20 LET X=X+2
30 PRINT X
40 LET X=2 * X
50 PRINT X
60 END
```

b.
```
10 INPUT A, B
20 LET C=A+B
30 PRINT "A PLUS B="; C
40 END
?7, 5
```

c.
```
10 READ A1, B$, C2
20 PRINT C2, B$, A1
30 READ D$
40 PRINT A1, D$, C2
50 DATA 7, BOY, 3, GIRL
60 END
```

d.
```
10 READ A$, B$
20 PRINT B$; "  "; A$; "  ";
30 RESTORE
40 READ A$, B$, C$
45 PRINT C$; "  "; A$; "  "; B$
50 DATA WE, TRY, EVEN, HARDER
60 END
```

3. Write a program that INPUTs the lengths of the sides of a triangle, then calculates and PRINTs the perimeter.

4. A library charges a 20¢ fine per day for each overdue book. Write a program that INPUTs the number of books borrowed and the number of days overdue, then calculates and PRINTs the amount of the fine.

5. Write a program using READ . . . DATA statements that has the following output:

   THE COW JUMPED OVER THE MOON

   Use this DATA line: `100 DATA MOON, COW, OVER`

6. Write a program using a loop that has the following output:

```
1 EXAMPLE
2 EXAMPLES
3 EXAMPLES
4 EXAMPLES
5 EXAMPLES
.
.
.
```

Computerized Check-Out

Grocery-Store Computers

Have you been through a check-out counter at a grocery store lately? If you have, you probably have had your purchases "rung up" by a clerk who barely touched any keys on the cash register. At a check-out line that is computer equipped, all the clerk has to do is pass each grocery item over a scanner that is electronically linked to the cash register. The laser-equipped scanner reads the bars and stripes of the Universal Product Code, or UPC, which allows the computer to identify the product. The computer then shows the product name and price on a visual display for the customer to see, and prints the same information on the customer's receipt.

The early scanners often missed the UPC on oddly-shaped packages or those held at an improper angle, so the clerk had to repeatedly pass the

Electronic check-out scanner

Universal Product Codes of grocery items

package over the scanner until the UPC was detected. Now an improved reader has been introduced that is capable of "seeing" the bottom and sides of any item passed over the scanner window, at almost any angle. Beneath the scanner window, a laser beam is bounced off a scanning disk that contains a holographic (3-dimensional) image of the item. The beam is then reflected from the UPC marked on the item to a detector that converts the optical signals to electrical pulses. A computer checks these signals against what is stored in its memory for the product's name, size (weight), and price, and then prints that information on the receipt.

Advantages of Computer

The computer at the core of the scanning system provides versatility for the store manager, who can easily program changes for special sales or daily price fluctuations. The computer also remembers each item that has passed over the scanner. If, for example, you buy two small bottles of fruit juice priced at two for 99 cents, the computer will charge 50 cents for the first bottle that crosses the scanner. Then, no matter how many other different items have been handled in between, when the second bottle of juice passes across the scanner the computer will ring up only 49 cents. In handling produce that must be weighed, the computer reads the UPC from the plastic bag containing the produce, or the clerk presses the key with the name of the fruit or vegetable. When the bag is placed on the scale, the computer (programmed with the price per pound) calculates and prints the cost.

While the computer is calculating and printing prices, it is also keeping track of the store's inventory list, warning the manager when a product must be reordered. This saves the store time and money. Since most grocery stores operate on a very small profit margin, the savings that the computerized check-out system provide can be substantial.

The information gathered by the store's computer can also be used by marketing experts. Advertising agencies can analyze the data collected to confirm which products are selling best and to decide where to target their advertising. The store manager can also use the information to gauge the effectiveness of store displays and the store's own advertising in local newspapers.

The next time you go to the grocery store and are standing in a check-out line, take note of how the computer is changing the grocery business. The computerized check-out system allows the clerk to quickly and accurately check the groceries, provides the manager with flexibility to change prices and a constant update of the inventory, and saves the store time and money.

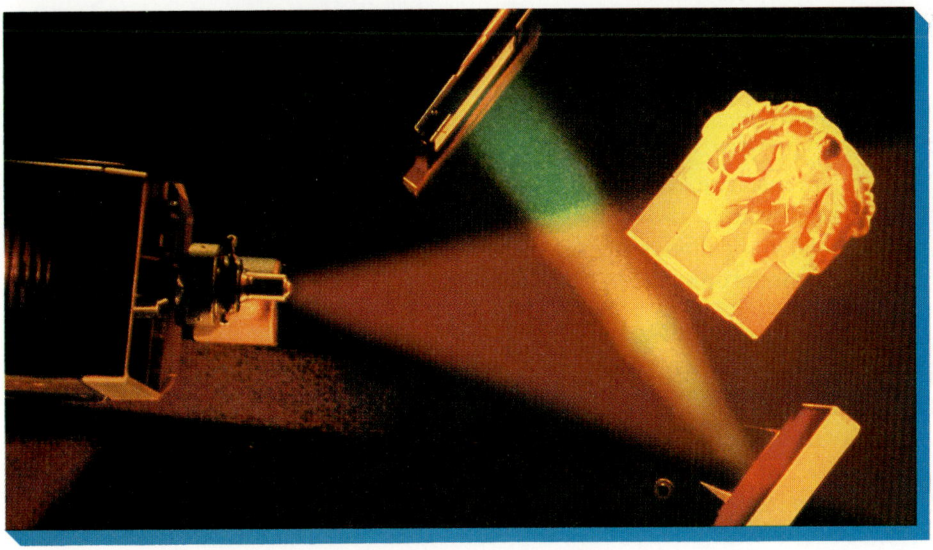

Holographic image being created of miniaturized statue of Abraham Lincoln

The computer language Logo is noted for its *turtle graphics.* Historically, the development of Logo began in the late 1960's and gained momentum in 1970 when the project was moved to the artificial intelligence laboratory at the Massachusetts Institute of Technology. The Logo Group at MIT, under the direction of Seymour Papert, designed Logo as an "object to think with," a means by which to establish "powerful ideas," and a tool that could be used even by young children to control the computer.

The turtle graphics aspect of the computer language Logo is an incredibly rich area for exploration and discovery. The turtle was inspired by developments in robotics. The first turtle developed by MIT was a three-dimensional turtle robot that responded to computer commands directing its movements in specified directions around the floor. The programming language Logo provided an environment in which a two-dimensional version of the turtle robot could exist. The turtle is simulated on the computer screen in high resolution graphics as a small shape, usually a triangle.

Logo turtle robot

The turtle has a limited vocabulary of primitive commands: RIGHT, LEFT, FORWARD, BACK, PENUP, and PENDOWN to name just a few. The command RIGHT 90, for instance, commands the turtle to rotate or turn 90 degrees in a clockwise direction, and FORWARD 50 commands the turtle to move 50 points (dots) in the direction it is facing. LEFT and BACK commands result in turtle movements opposite to RIGHT and FORWARD.

The turtle also has a pen attached to it, which it can lower with the command PENDOWN or raise with the command PENUP. If the pen is down, the turtle draws a line tracing its path as it is directed to move around the screen. If the pen is up, the turtle can move around the screen without leaving a path.

Once communication has been established with the turtle, the primitive commands can be used to direct it about the screen, tracing a path of interesting and unusual graphic designs. The turtle can also extend its vocabulary by learning new words, called *procedures.* A *procedure* begins with the word TO and ends with the word END. The *body* of the following procedure, called TRIANGLE, lists instructions for the turtle to draw an equilateral triangle. Once the procedure is set up, the turtle will respond to the new command word TRIANGLE.

```
TO TRIANGLE
FORWARD 40
RIGHT 120
FORWARD 40
RIGHT 120
FORWARD 40
RIGHT 120
END
```

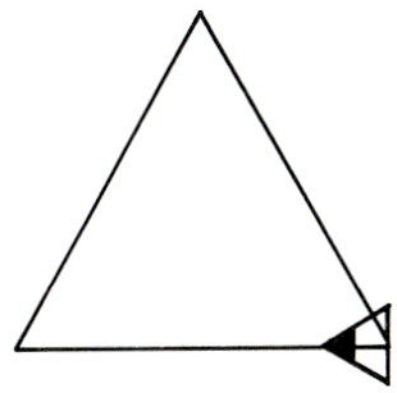

In Logo, when steps within a procedure need to be repeated, the command REPEAT can be used. The previous procedure would then contain only these three lines:

```
TO TRIANGLE
REPEAT 3 [FORWARD 40 RIGHT 120]
END
```

In a procedural language like Logo, one procedure can use another procedure, known as a subprocedure, to do part of its work. Logo is also a *recursive* language, which means that a procedure can be a subprocedure of itself. This recursive property allows very large problems to be stated in very compact form.

Logo is a relatively easy language to learn and to use. With turtle graphics, beginners can create designs the first time they use a computer. The control structures in Logo (like REPEAT) make it possible to describe rather complicated procedures with a few words. Also, the use of abbreviations in commands simplifies typing — a feature that is particularly helpful to young children.

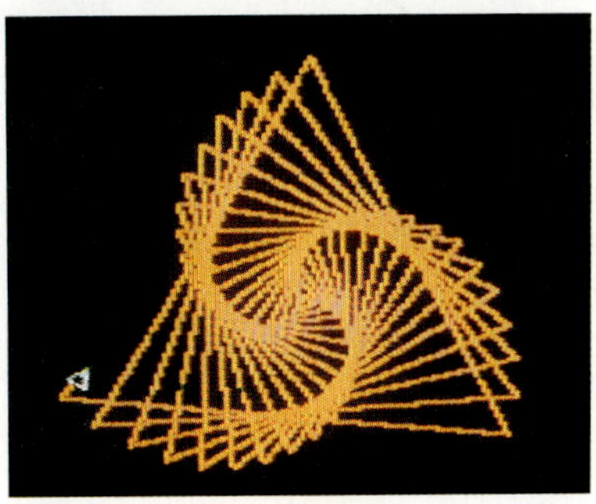

Logo-generated graphics

CHAPTER

4 Branching

The image above is from a computer-generated driving simulation. Using a driving simulator, engineers can test vehicles and study critical driving situations without endangering human life.

Introduction

As you learn more about BASIC, you will write increasingly complicated programs. In order to make such programs understandable to you, the programmer, as well as to other people, it is important to have a systematic approach to *designing* computer programs.

One successful approach, which will be followed in this book, is called *top-down design.* (It is referred to by other names as well: *structured programming* or *high-level design,* for example.) You will be introduced to this approach in the first section of this chapter. The remainder of the chapter is concerned with *branching,* which is a way of making the computer perform different tasks under different conditions. As you will see, branching techniques are essential for writing flexible, powerful programs.

4-1 Top-down Design

Essentially, the top-down approach requires you to have a thorough understanding of what a program is supposed to do before any of it is written in BASIC. This is accomplished by focusing attention on the *inputs* and *outputs* of the program. Once these are specified in detail, a general outline is made of the steps the program must follow to get from the inputs to the desired outputs. This list of steps that the program follows is called the *algorithm.* After an outline of the algorithm is completed, each step is broken down and more detail given. Finally, the detailed algorithm is *coded* into the computer language being used (BASIC in this book) and is *tested* thoroughly and corrected *(debugged).*

At first glance, the process described above may seem unnecessarily complicated for many simple problems you will encounter. But for more difficult problems, it is very important to have the thorough and detailed understanding required by the top-down approach before you write even a single line of BASIC.

Example 1

Any step-by-step process may be described using part of the top-down approach. An outline and a detailed algorithm can be given, at least. Consider, for example, the process of planting a tree. One possible outline is as follows:

Step 1 Prepare hole.
Step 2 Put tree in hole.
Step 3 Finish up.

This outline covers the main steps without getting involved with too many details. The next thing to do is to elaborate each step. For example:

Step 1 Prepare hole.
- **a.** Select location.
- **b.** Dig hole.
- **c.** Add fertilizer and peat moss.

Step 2 Put tree in hole.
- **a.** Check and adjust depth of hole.
- **b.** Remove burlap sack and drop tree in hole.
- **c.** Adjust position of tree.

Step 3 Finish up.
- **a.** Fill hole around tree and pack down soil.
- **b.** Water tree.
- **c.** Take a shower.

Each sub-step of this more detailed outline can be further elaborated. How much detail to give depends on the purpose of the description (or "program"); an experienced gardener needs less explicit instructions than a beginner. In writing an algorithm for a program, the outline must be detailed enough to be easily translated into BASIC, as in the following example.

Example 2

Suppose you have a combination lock that is opened by dialing three numbers, each between 0 and 36. Imagine that you know the three numbers, at least you have a pretty good idea of what they are, but you are unsure of their order. Have the computer print out all possible orderings of the three numbers, used once each.

Inputs: Since you are not certain of the three numbers, it makes sense to have the program INPUT them. You should decide now on variables; let N1, N2, and N3 represent the numbers.

Outputs: The results should be all possible orderings of the three numbers. Here is a sample output for the numbers 2, 16, and 25:

```
2-16-25
2-25-16
16-2-25
16-25-2
25-2-16
25-16-2
```

Outline of Program (the Algorithm):

Step 1 INPUT the three numbers.

Step 2 PRINT the numbers in all possible orders.

More Detail:

1. Step 1 need not be elaborated further; that is, it can easily be coded into BASIC.
2. Step 2 needs some thought. You might think of several possible algorithms for producing the lock combinations. One method is to put N1 first, followed by all possible orderings of N2 and N3 (there are only 2); then N2 first, followed by all possible orderings of N1 and N3; then N3 first, followed by all possible orderings of N1 and N2. This results in the following list:

```
N1  N2  N3
N1  N3  N2
N2  N1  N3
N2  N3  N1
N3  N1  N2
N3  N2  N1
```

Coding: The detailed algorithm can now be translated easily into this BASIC program:

```
10 PRINT "LOCK COMBINATIONS"
15 PRINT
20 INPUT "TYPE THE 3 NUMBERS:  "; N1, N2, N3
30 PRINT "POSSIBLE ORDERINGS:"
40 PRINT N1; "  —  "; N2; "  —  "; N3
50 PRINT N1; "  —  "; N3; "  —  "; N2
60 PRINT N2; "  —  "; N1; "  —  "; N3
70 PRINT N2; "  —  "; N3; "  —  "; N1
80 PRINT N3; "  —  "; N1; "  —  "; N2
90 PRINT N3; "  —  "; N2; "  —  "; N1
100 END
```

Testing and Debugging: You should test the program by typing values for which the correct result is known (2, 16, and 25 in our example). Then compare the computer's result with the known result to see if the program works properly. Other choices of the three numbers should also be tested, including as many "special cases" as possible. Can you think of any? What if two (or all three) of the numbers are the same? Will the program produce correct or desired results in that case? Can you accept the program as is, should you change the code, or must you go back to the outline of the algorithm and redesign the entire program? The answers to these questions depend on the context in which the problem was posed. For example, you might be more relaxed about a program intended for your own use than about a program to be used by someone (an employer, perhaps) who knows nothing at all about computers.

Avoiding Pitfalls

Beginning programmers sometimes start to write code before a problem or its solution is completely understood. This results in a confusing program in which the statements do not lead logically from one to another. Following the top-down approach will help you to structure your programs clearly and concisely.

Summary

The *top-down approach* to designing a program consists of the following steps:

1. Deciding on the exact form of *inputs* and *outputs,* including variable names.
2. Outlining the *algorithm,* that is, the steps to be followed by the program.
3. Completing all the *details* in each step of the algorithm.
4. *Coding* the detailed algorithm into BASIC.
5. *Testing* and *debugging* the program.

Exercises 4-1

In Exercises 1–3, divide the steps in each algorithm into several sub-steps.

A 1. Getting up in the morning:
Step 1 Turn off alarm. (*Hint:* What are some steps you go through to turn off the alarm?)
Step 2 Get out of bed.
Step 3 Get dressed.

2. Eating lunch:
Step 1 Decide what to eat.
Step 2 Prepare food.
Step 3 Eat food.
Step 4 Clean up.

3. Playing a nine-inning baseball game:
Step 1 Visiting team is at bat for 1/2 inning. (*Hint:* What are the major steps involved in playing an inning?)
Step 2 If visiting team has been up to bat 9 or more times and home team is ahead, then quit. Otherwise, home team gets to bat for 1/2 inning.
Step 3 If home team has been up 9 or more times and either team is ahead, then quit. Otherwise, go to Step 1.

In Exercises 4–7, write algorithms for each of the given activities.

4. Baking a cake.

5. Washing a dog.

6. Catching a fish.

7. Changing an automobile tire.

8. Predict the output of the program in Example 2 if a user types 3, 26, and 26 as the three numbers.

9. Using an extension of the algorithm of Example 2, page 130, list all the possible lock combinations for four numbers represented by N1, N2, N3, and N4. How many lines of BASIC code are needed to PRINT out all such orderings?

B 10. Write a program (use top-down design and outline an algorithm first) that INPUTs three letters from A to Z, then PRINTs all the possible orderings of the three INPUT letters. For example, if the INPUT letters are D, J, and R, then the output should be DJR, DRJ, JDR, and so on.

11. Three girls and three boys are to be paired on a blind date. Write a program (use top-down design and outline an algorithm first) that INPUTs the three girls' names and the three boys' names, and then PRINTs all the possible pairings of the three girls' names with the three boys' names. (*Hint:* One way to do this is to keep the girls' names in the same order all of the time. Assign the boys' names to each girl's name in as many different ways as possible.)

12. Two of the four members of a dance-planning committee are to be selected to hire a band. Write a program (use top-down design and outline an algorithm first) that PRINTs all possible ways this subcommittee selection can be made. Assign the four INPUT names to the variables N1$, N2$, N3$, and N4$. (The order in which the numbers are selected does not matter; in other words, N3$; " AND "; N2$ should not be PRINTed if N2$; " AND "; N3$ has already been PRINTed.)

13. Write a program (use top-down design and outline an algorithm first) that INPUTs values for three numbers N1, N2, and N3. Then have the program PRINT the values of the expressions N1 * (N2 + N3) and N1 * N2 + N1 * N3 to verify the well-known fact (called the *Distributive Law*) that these two expressions are always equal. The program should PRINT the two expressions with the three numbers in all possible orders:

```
N2 * (N1 + N3), N2 * N1 + N2 * N3
N3 * (N1 + N2), N3 * N1 + N3 * N2
.
.
.
```

4-2 Making Decisions: IF . . . THEN

Suppose we want to write a program to INPUT a user's age, then PRINT how much older he or she is than a certain 13-year old pet animal. Designing the program using the top-down approach, we need a variable for the user's age, say AGE, and a variable for the difference of the ages, say, OLDER. An outline of the steps in the algorithm might be as follows:

Step 1 Ask for the user's AGE.

Step 2 Compute the difference of the ages (OLDER = AGE − 13).

Step 3 PRINT the result with a message.

This algorithm is easily translated into a BASIC program, as you can see in Program 1 below.

Program 1

Statement

```
10  INPUT "HOW OLD ARE YOU:  "; AGE
15  PRINT
20  LET OLDER = AGE — 13
30  PRINT "GOLLY, YOU ARE  "; OLDER; "  YEARS OLDER THAN MY PET SKUNK."
40  END
```

Output

```
HOW OLD ARE YOU:  ? 15

GOLLY, YOU ARE 2 YEARS OLDER THAN MY PET SKUNK.

RUN
HOW OLD ARE YOU:  ? 11

GOLLY, YOU ARE —2 YEARS OLDER THAN MY PET SKUNK.
```

If you type 15 as your age in response to the INPUT in line 10, then the value of OLDER is 2 (OLDER = 15 − 13 = 2) and the program will PRINT a message that you are 2 years older than the pet skunk. If, however, you type 11 as your age, then the value of OLDER is −2 (OLDER = 11 − 13 = −2) and the program will PRINT this message:

```
GOLLY, YOU ARE —2 YEARS OLDER THAN MY PET SKUNK.
```

Obviously, we need to revise the algorithm so that the program will PRINT a more appropriate message in this case. A possible outline of the revised algorithm is at the top of the next page.

Step 1 Ask for the user's AGE.

Step 2 If AGE is greater than 13, then PRINT a message that you are AGE − 13 years older.

Step 3 If AGE equals 13, then PRINT a message that you are the same age.

Step 4 If AGE is less than 13, then PRINT a message that you are 13 − AGE years younger.

This algorithm may be coded into BASIC using a new instruction: IF . . . THEN.

Program 2*

Statement

```
10  INPUT "HOW OLD ARE YOU:   "; AGE
15  PRINT
20  IF AGE > 13 THEN PRINT "GOLLY, YOU ARE   "; AGE — 13; "   YEARS OLDER THAN
      MY PET SKUNK."
30  IF AGE = 13 THEN PRINT "GOLLY, YOU ARE THE SAME AGE AS MY PET SKUNK."
40  IF AGE < 13 THEN PRINT "GOLLY, YOU ARE   "; 13 — AGE; "   YEARS YOUNGER THAN
      MY PET SKUNK."
50  END
```

Output

```
HOW OLD ARE YOU:   ? 15

GOLLY, YOU ARE 2 YEARS OLDER THAN MY PET SKUNK.

RUN
HOW OLD ARE YOU:   ? 11

GOLLY, YOU ARE 2 YEARS YOUNGER THAN MY PET SKUNK.
```

Now suppose you type 15 as your age. Then in line 20 it is *true* that AGE is greater than 13 (AGE > 13), so the rest of line 20 will be executed; the computer will PRINT:

GOLLY, YOU ARE 2 YEARS OLDER THAN MY PET SKUNK.

Furthermore, in line 30, the condition AGE = 13 is *false* (since AGE is still equal to 15), so that the message in line 30 will *not* be PRINTed. Similarly, in line 40 it is *false* that AGE is less than 13 (AGE < 13), so the computer will not execute the rest of line 40 either.

* The programs in this book are printed in a way that will make them clear and easy to read. The programs may look different on your screen, depending upon how many characters your computer prints on one line.

In an IF . . . THEN statement, the *condition* (the expression right after the IF) may be any comparison of two BASIC numerical expressions. (In the next section you will see how to make comparisons between strings.) The following BASIC symbols may be used in *conditions:*

Symbol		Example	
<	less than	−5<2	(This condition is true.)
>	greater than	X+1>X	(This condition is always true.)
=	equals	Y=X	(This condition depends on the values of X and Y.)
<=	less than or equal to	2.3<=−1+2	(This condition is false.)
>=	greater than or equal to	1.5>=1.5	(This condition is true.)
<>	not equal to	3.2<>3.2	(This condition is false.)

In an IF . . . THEN statement, the *action* (the expression right after THEN) may be any BASIC instruction that causes the computer to *do* something. For example:

```
IF X < 5 THEN GOTO 40
IF A + 3 <> B THEN LET A = B
IF A + C = 5 THEN READ X
IF X > 10 THEN PRINT "DONE"
```

The statement IF A = 2 THEN DATA 7, 6, however, does not make sense, since DATA is not an *action* instruction. (So far, DATA and REM are the only instructions you have learned that are *not* action instructions.)

Here is an example of a program that uses IF . . . THEN statements to reject unwanted INPUT values. (This process is called *error trapping*.) The program INPUTs the coordinates of a point to be plotted on the graphics screen. Any point that is located near the top left corner of the screen is plotted; any other point is rejected. The program must be stopped manually.

Program 3

Statement | **Remark**

```
10  REM * PLOTTING POINTS
20  REM * PLOT POINTS ONLY IN TOP LEFT CORNER
30  INPUT "TYPE X, Y COORDINATES (BETWEEN 0
      AND 20):  "; X, Y
```

```
40  IF X < 0 THEN GOTO 30                    Error trap.
50  IF X > 20 THEN GOTO 30
60  IF Y < 0 THEN GOTO 30
70  IF Y > 20 THEN GOTO 30
 .  (Instructions to clear the screen
 .    and do graphics on your
 .    computer. See Section 2-5, page 45.)
100 (Instruction to plot the point X, Y on
      your computer.)
110 GOTO 30                                  Get another point.
120 END
```

Output

```
TYPE X, Y COORDINATES (BETWEEN 0 AND 20):  ? 18, 16
```

(Screen clears, then (18, 16) is plotted.)

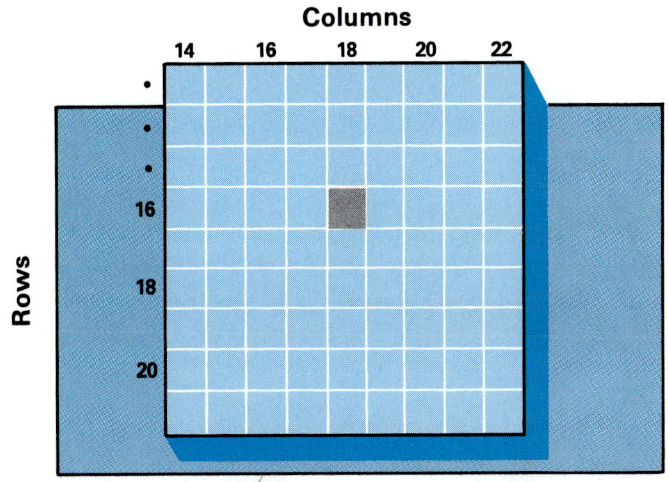

(*Note:* On *IBM* and *TRS-80* computers, the GOTO 30 instruction in line 110 may cause the message in line 30 to print over the plotted point before you have a chance to see it. On these machines, change line 110 to the following: 110 GOTO 110. This "empty" loop will stall the program and prevent the message in line 30 (or anything at all) from interfering with the plotted point. With this technique, the program must be stopped manually, then RUN again to plot another point.)

Notice in lines 40–70 of Program 3 that a point will not be plotted if either of its coordinates is less than 0 or greater than 20. The action GOTO 30 in each of these lines allows the user to try another point.

Avoiding Pitfalls

Even if the *condition* of an IF . . . THEN statement is *true,* the computer *always* executes the next line after the IF . . . THEN statement (unless the *action* is a GOTO instruction). For example, in the program

```
10 INPUT X
20 IF X=5 THEN PRINT "FIVE"
30 PRINT "SIX"
40 END
```

the computer always PRINTs the message SIX, even if the INPUT value of X is 5. However, if you change line 20 to

```
20 IF X=5 THEN GOTO 40
```

then the computer will not PRINT the message SIX (or anything at all) if you type 5 for the value of X.

Summary

An IF . . . THEN statement has this form:

IF *condition* THEN *action*

If the condition is *true,* then the action is performed, and the computer goes to the next program line (unless the action is a GOTO instruction). If the condition is *false,* then the action is *not* performed and the computer goes directly to the next line in the program.

The *condition* may be any comparison of two BASIC numerical expressions using the following symbols:

<	less than
>	greater than
=	equals
<=	less than or equal to
>=	greater than or equal to
<>	not equal to

The *action* may be any BASIC instruction that causes the computer to *do* something.

Error trapping in a program is the use of IF . . . THEN statements to reject any INPUT values that are unwanted.

Exercises 4-2

A **1.** Tell whether each condition is true or false.

a. 5 <= 7

b. X + 1 <> X + 1

c. −2.4 >= −2.4

d. −6.2 < −6.0

e. (X + 2) ↑ 2 < 6, when X = 1

f. 2 * X − 4 < 7 * Y, when X = 4 and Y = 1

2. Tell whether each of the following instructions makes sense in BASIC. Explain your answer.

a. IF X < 3 THEN GOTO 370

b. IF READ Y THEN PRINT X

c. IF X + 3 <> 0 THEN PRINT X

d. IF X > 3 THEN LET X > 2

e. IF (X + 3) * 2 = 7 THEN END

f. IF A = B THEN READ A = A + 1

g. IF 6 <> 2 THEN REM WHY NOT

h. IF Y = 2 THEN INPUT Z

3. Predict the output of each of the following programs.

a.
```
10 LET X=4
20 IF X<>3 THEN GOTO 40
30 PRINT "NICE"
40 PRINT "NASTY"
50 END
```

b.
```
10 READ A, B
20 IF A+B<36 THEN PRINT A
30 IF A+B>10 THEN PRINT B
40 DATA 5, 6, 30, 8
50 END
```

c.
```
10 LET X=2
20 PRINT X
30 IF X>5 THEN GOTO 60
40 LET X=X+1
45 PRINT X
50 GOTO 30
60 END
```

d.
```
10 READ A, B
20 IF A+B<36 THEN LET A=2
30 IF A+B>10 THEN PRINT B
35 GOTO 10
40 DATA 5, 6, 30, 8
50 END
```

e.
```
10 READ A, B
20 IF A+B<36 THEN PRINT A
25 PRINT B
30 IF A+B>10 THEN PRINT B
33 PRINT A
35 GOTO 10
40 DATA 5, 6, 30, 8
50 END
```

f.
```
10 LET A=3
20 LET B=4
30 IF A=1 THEN GOTO 80
40 IF A+B<=6 THEN PRINT "OK"
50 PRINT B
60 LET A=A-1
70 GOTO 30
80 END
```

4. The following program is supposed to PRINT one message for INPUT numbers that are 90 or larger, and another for numbers less than 90. Change line 30 so that the program works correctly.

```
10 INPUT "ENTER GRADE:  "; G
20 IF G >= 90 THEN PRINT "EXCELLENT"
30 PRINT "NOT EXCELLENT"
40 END
```

5. The following program is supposed to INPUT two students' names and their weights, then PRINT the name of the student who weighs less. Change the program so that it works correctly.

```
10 INPUT "FIRST NAME, WEIGHT:   "; N1$, W1
20 INPUT "SECOND NAME, WEIGHT:   "; N2$, W2
30 IF W1 < W2 THEN PRINT N1$; "  WEIGHS LESS"
40 IF W1 > W2 THEN PRINT N2$; "  WEIGHS LESS"
50 PRINT "YOU WEIGH THE SAME"
60 END
```

6. **a.** The following program is supposed to PRINT the English word corresponding to the digit 0, 1, or 2, typed by a user. Change the program so that it works correctly.

```
10 PRINT "DIGITS"
20 INPUT "TYPE DIGIT:  "; DIG
30 IF DIG = 0 THEN PRINT "ZERO"
40 IF DIG = 1 THEN PRINT "ONE"
50 PRINT "TWO"
100 END
```

   b. Change the program so that it also PRINTs the word THREE if the number 3 is typed.
   c. Add the line 90 GOTO 20 to the program in (b). Change this new version of the program so that it will PRINT the message TOO BIG if the digit typed is greater than 3.
   d. Change the program in (c) so that it will END if a user types a negative number.

7. **a.** Modify Program 2 so that it PRINTs a grammatically correct message if you type 12 as your age. (*Hint:* Add another statement that begins IF AGE = 12 THEN . . . .)
   b. Change the program so that it PRINTs a grammatically correct message when you type 14 as your age.

8. Complete Program 3 with the instructions for your computer. Change the program so that it will reject any INPUT point having an X- or Y-coordinate that is off your screen. (Be sure to change lines 20 and 30.)

9. Change Program 3 so that the message POINT OUT OF BOUNDS is PRINTed if the INPUT point is rejected.

B 10. Write a program that PRINTs one of three messages depending on whether a user types 1, 2, or 3. Use this outline:

```
10 INPUT "WHICH MESSAGE? "; M
20 IF M=1 THEN PRINT " . . .
30 IF M=2 THEN PRINT " . . .
40 . . .
 .
 .
 .
```

11. a. Write a program that calculates a day's wages for a bus driver who earns \$10 per hour for the first 8 hours (or less) and \$15 per hour (overtime) after that. Have the program INPUT the number of hours, then PRINT the wages. For the overtime use this statement:

```
IF HRS > 8 THEN LET WAGES = 8 * 10 + (HRS -8) * 15
```

b. Predict the output of the program in (a) if −5 is typed as the number of hours worked. Add a line to the program that will reject any negative number of hours typed by the user.

c. Suppose each bus driver is allowed to work a maximum of 4 hours overtime per day. Modify the program so that it will not calculate wages for more than a 12-hour workday.

12. a. Complete the RUN chart for the following program assuming that the numbers 5, −2, and 6 are typed as the values of A, B, and C, respectively.

```
10 INPUT "THREE NUMBERS: "; A, B, C
20 IF A < B THEN LET LEAST = A
30 IF A >= B THEN LET LEAST = B
40 IF C < LEAST THEN LET LEAST = C
50 PRINT LEAST
60 END
```

LINE	CONDITION	A	B	C	LEAST	OUTPUT
10		5	−2	6		
20	false					
30	true				−2	
40	false					
50						
60						

A new column called *condition* has been added to the RUN chart. The condition column should be filled in with *true* or *false* whenever an IF . . . THEN statement is encountered in a program.

b. Construct a RUN chart for the program, assuming that the numbers 2, 5, and 3 are typed as the values of A, B, and C, respectively.

c. Describe what the program does with any three INPUT numbers.

d. Change the program so that it PRINTs the smallest of any four INPUT numbers.

13. Construct a RUN chart (see Exercise 12) for each of the following programs.

a.
```
10 READ X
20 IF X < 0 THEN GOTO 60
30 IF X > 6 THEN PRINT X — 1
40 GOTO 10
50 DATA 7, 6, 10, —1
60 END
```

b.
```
10 LET X = 4
20 IF X <> 3 THEN PRINT "OOPS"
30 LET X = X — 1
40 IF X > 0 THEN GOTO 20
50 END
```

14. a. Write a program that will calculate a taxicab fare, given that the rate is $2.00 for the first quarter of a mile (or less) traveled and $.75 for each additional quarter of a mile. The program should INPUT the total number of quarter-miles traveled and PRINT the resulting fare.

b. Rewrite the program to give the correct fare if the distance traveled is INPUT in *miles,* rather than in quarter-miles.

15. (Graphics) Write a program that INPUTs the X- and Y-coordinates of a point on the graphics screen, and also INPUTs a shape number (1 or 2). The program should plot a short vertical line segment starting at the position (X, Y) if the shape number is 1, and a horizontal line segment if the shape number is 2. Have the program ask again for the shape number if the user types any number other than 1 or 2.

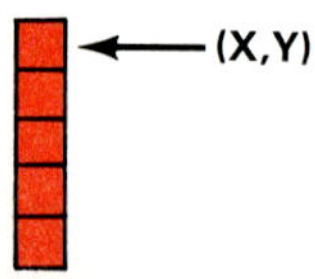

Shape number 1

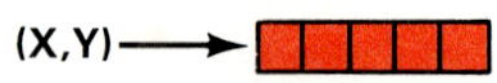

Shape number 2

C **16.** (Graphics) Write a program that INPUTs the X- and Y-coordinates of a point on the graphics screen, then plots the figure shown at the right.

Add one or more IF . . . THEN statements that will reject any INPUT point having an X- or Y-coordinate that will make any part of the figure go off the screen.

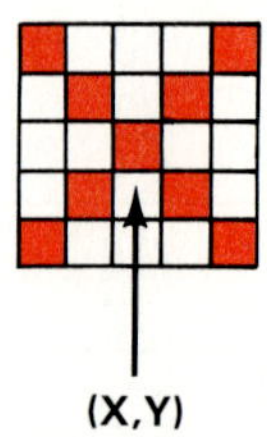

17. a. Write a short addition quiz for second-grade students. Have the program READ two one-digit numbers, ask the student for the sum, then tell the young aspiring mathematician whether the answer is correct or not. The program should ask for at least 5 sums.

b. *Challenge:* Try to modify the program in (a) so that it will END without an OUT OF DATA error message.

Lab Activity

Comparing Strings

The comparison symbols <, >, <=, >=, =, <> all have meaning in comparing strings as well as numbers. In this activity, you can discover how strings are compared. Type the following program into the computer, then do the problems below.

```
10  PRINT "STRING EQUALS"
20  LET A$ = "CC"
30  LET B$ = "DD"
40  IF A$ = B$ THEN PRINT A$; "  =  "; B$
50  IF A$ <> B$ THEN PRINT A$; "  <>  "; B$
60  END
```

Problems

1. RUN the program. Is it true that the string CC is equal to the string DD?

2. Change line 30 to:

```
30  LET B$ = "CC"
```

Verify that A$ = B$ is true.

3. Change line 30 to assign the string C■C to B$ (there is a space between the C's). Are the strings CC and C■C equal? Do spaces in the middle of a string affect equality?

4. Change line 30 to:

```
30  LET B$ = "■CC"
```

RUN the program. Does A$ = B$? Now change line 30 to:

```
30  LET B$ = "CC■"
```

Are the strings CC and CC■ equal?

5. **a.** Change lines 20 and 30 so that the program INPUTs the strings typed for A$ and B$. Determine if spaces at the beginning, middle, or end of a string make a difference now. (Compare string CC with ■CC, then with C■C, then with CC■.) As you can see, the INPUT instruction ignores spaces in certain positions when a string is entered. What position(s) exactly?

b. Try enclosing the INPUT strings in part (a) in quotation marks when you type them. Do the quotes make a difference?

Here is a program that can help you discover the meaning of < when applied to strings:

```
10 PRINT "STRING LESS THAN"
15 PRINT
20 LET A$ = "C"
30 LET B$ = "D"
40 IF A$ < B$ THEN PRINT A$; "  <  "; B$
50 IF A$ > B$ THEN PRINT A$; "  >  "; B$
60 IF A$ = B$ THEN PRINT A$; "  =  "; B$
70 END
```

6. a. RUN the program above. Is it true that the string C is "less than" the string D?

b. Change line 20 to:

```
20 LET A$ = "F"
```

RUN the program again. Is it true that the string F is "less than" the string D?

c. Change line 20 to:

```
20 LET A$ = "DA"
```

Run the program again. Is it true that the string DA is "less than" the string D?

d. Can you explain what < does when used to compare strings? Experiment with other strings (including some containing more than one letter) in lines 20 and 30 to verify your prediction.

7. *Challenge:* By experimenting further, determine more complete rules for <. For example, what effect do leading and trailing spaces in strings have with <? Are punctuation marks "less than" letters? Can you think of a reason why a programmer might want to use < to compare strings?

4-3 IF . . . THEN with Strings

In the last section you used the comparison symbols

=, <>, <, >, <=, and >=

with numerical expressions to form conditions in IF . . . THEN statements. Each of these symbols can be used to compare strings as well as numerical expressions.

The simplest comparisons between strings involve the = and <> symbols. Two strings are *equal* if they are identical, character for character. Otherwise, of course, they are *not equal*. Some examples are included in the table on the next page.

Comparison	Truth Value
"A" = "A"	true
"MY" = "MY"	true
"MY" = "MYA"	false — (The strings are not the same length.)
"MYA" <> "MYB"	true
"M Y" = "MY"	false — (Spaces count as characters.)
"M4" <> "M5"	true
"13" = "13.0"	false — (The numbers 13 and 13.0 are equal, but the strings are not identical.)

As you can see from the list of comparisons in the table, when strings are used with comparison symbols they must be enclosed in quotation marks.

Here is a program that compares strings using the = symbol.

Program 1

Statement

```
10  PRINT "WHAT'S IN A NAME?"
20  INPUT "TYPE YOUR NAME, PLEASE:   "; N$
30  IF N$ = "ROMEO" THEN PRINT "WHEREFORE?"
40  IF N$ = "JULIET" THEN PRINT "SIGH!!"
50  END
```

Output

```
WHAT'S IN A NAME?
TYPE YOUR NAME, PLEASE:   ? ROMEO
WHEREFORE?

RUN
WHAT'S IN A NAME?
TYPE YOUR NAME, PLEASE:   ? JULIET
SIGH!!
```

The program is quite simple. If you type ROMEO as your name, then the program gives you the message in line 30; if you type JULIET, then you get the message in line 40. The program PRINTs only the introductory messages in lines 10 and 20 if you type any string other than ROMEO or JULIET.

Suppose we want the program to PRINT the message GET OUT OF MY PLAY! when a string other than ROMEO or JULIET is typed. There are several ways to do this. Program 2 makes use of the < > symbol.

Program 2

Statement

```
10  PRINT "WHAT'S IN A NAME, PART 2"
20  INPUT "TYPE YOUR NAME, PLEASE:   "; N$
30  IF N$ <> "ROMEO" THEN GOTO 40
33  PRINT "WHEREFORE?"
37  GOTO 50
40  IF N$ <> "JULIET" THEN GOTO 48
43  PRINT "SIGH!!"
45  GOTO 50
48  PRINT "GET OUT OF MY PLAY!"
50  END
```

Output

```
WHAT'S IN A NAME, PART 2
TYPE YOUR NAME, PLEASE:   ? BILLY
GET OUT OF MY PLAY!
```

If you type BILLY for the value of N$ in line 20, then the condition in line 30 is true, so the computer executes line 40 next. The condition in line 40 is also true, so the computer goes to line 48. This line PRINTs the message GET OUT OF MY PLAY!, as you can see in the output above.

You have seen how the = and < > symbols can be used to compare strings. The other comparisons between strings are defined in terms of alphabetical order (like in a dictionary):

A$ < B$	is true if the string (assigned to) A$ comes *before* the string B$ in alphabetical order.
A$ > B$	is true if the string A$ comes *after* the string B$ in alphabetical order.
A$ <= B$	is true if the string A$ comes before the string B$, or the two strings are identical.
A$ >= B$	is true if the string A$ comes after the string B$, or the two strings are identical.

Here are some examples:

Comparison	*Truth Value*
"A" < "B"	true (A comes before B in alphabetical order.)
"AC" > "AD"	false (AC comes before AD in alphabetical order.)

Comparison	*Truth Value*
"ABC" < "DEF"	true (ABC comes before DEF in alphabetical order.)
"ABC" > "ABCD"	false (ABC comes before ABCD in alphabetical order.)
"AB" <= "ABCD"	true (AB comes before ABCD in alphabetical order.)
"ABC" <= "ABC"	true (The two strings are identical.)
"ABC" >= "AA"	true (ABC comes after AA in alphabetical order.)

There are special rules for ordering when comparing strings containing spaces, numbers, or punctuation marks. Spaces are considered as coming before all other symbols in alphabetical order, most punctuation marks come next, then the digits 0, 1, . . . , 9 (in order), then the letters of the alphabet (in order). More detail, including the order of different punctuation marks and the effect of lower and upper case (if your computer has lower case), will be given in Chapter 8.

Here is a program that INPUTs two names, then PRINTs the name that comes first in alphabetical order.

Program 3

Statement

```
10  PRINT "ALPHABETIZE"
20  INPUT "TYPE TWO NAMES, PLEASE:  "; N1$, N2$
30  IF N1$ < N2$ THEN LET FIRST$ = N1$
40  IF N1$ > N2$ THEN LET FIRST$ = N2$
50  PRINT FIRST$; "  IS FIRST IN ALPHABETICAL ORDER."
60  END
```

Output

```
ALPHABETIZE
TYPE TWO NAMES, PLEASE:   ? RIVERS, RICHARDS
RICHARDS IS FIRST IN ALPHABETICAL ORDER.
```

If you type RIVERS and RICHARDS for the values of N1$ and N2$, respectively (in line 20), then the condition N1$ < N2$ in line 30 is false, so the computer goes on to line 40. There the condition "RIVERS" > "RICHARDS" is true so the rest of the line is executed; the value of N2$ (RICHARDS) is assigned to FIRST$. Finally, the message in line 50 is PRINTed, as in the output above. What will be the output of the program if the INPUT names are identical? How can you change the program so that it will consider this possibility?

Avoiding Pitfalls

1. Any spaces at the beginning of an INPUT string are ignored by the computer. However, on many computers (including *Apple* and *TRS-80*, but not *IBM*), spaces at the end of an INPUT string are considered part of the string. This can lead to a problem if a user presses the space bar after typing a string. For example, in the program

```
10 INPUT "SMALL INSECT, 3 LETTERS:  "; W$
20 IF W$ = "ANT" THEN PRINT "CORRECT"
30 END
```

   a user might type ANT■ and the program would consider the answer to be incorrect.

2. If you try to compare a string with a number in a condition (for example, IF "CATS" = 9 THEN . . .), a message such as TYPE MISMATCH ERROR will result. (See page 658 for the exact form of the message given on your computer.)

Summary

A$ = B$ is true if the strings assigned to A$ and B$ are identical (same length, same characters, and same order); otherwise, A$ <> B$ is true.

A$ < B$ is true if the string assigned to A$ comes before the string assigned to B$ in alphabetical order. The conditions A$ > B$, A$ >= B$, and A$ <= B$ are defined similarly.

In BASIC, spaces come before all other symbols in alphabetical order, most punctuation marks come next (see the Lab Activity), followed by the digits 0 through 9 (in order), followed by the letters of the alphabet (in order).

Exercises 4-3

A 1. Tell whether each of the following conditions is true or false.

a. "CAT" = "CAT"
b. "DOG" <> "DOG"
c. "CA T" = "CAT"
d. "90" <> "090"
e. "QUIT" < "END"
f. "FIRST" < "LAST"
g. "13N" > "13A"
h. "AT" <= "B"
i. "BE MINE" > "BEE LINE"
j. "303" > "330"

2. Predict the output of the following program for each of the INPUTs given below.

```
10 INPUT A$, B$
20 IF A$ < B$ THEN PRINT A$
30 PRINT B$
40 END
```

a. A$: CAR
   B$: DOG

b. A$: CAT
   B$: CAR

c. A$: PAT
   B$: PAN

d. A$: PRO
   B$: PRY

e. A$: PONG
   B$: PON

f. A$: P4
   B$: PA

3. a. Predict the output of the following program.

```
10 LET A$ = "ORANGE"
20 LET B$ = "JUICE"
30 IF A$ = B$ THEN GOTO 70
40 IF A$ <= B$ THEN GOTO 60
50 PRINT A$, B$
55 GOTO 70
60 PRINT B$, A$
70 PRINT "THAT'S ALL"
80 END
```

b. Predict the output if line 10 is changed to:

```
10 LET A$ = "GRAPEFRUIT"
```

4. a. Predict the output of the following program.

```
10 READ X, Y
20 READ A$, B$
30 IF X <= Y THEN GOTO 60
40 IF A$ > B$ THEN PRINT A$
50 GOTO 80
60 IF A$ > B$ THEN PRINT B$
70 DATA 3, 5, MY DOG, HAS FLEAS
80 END
```

b. Predict the output if line 70 is changed to:

```
70 DATA 7, —1, MY CAT, MY DOG
```

5. Predict the output of the following program.

```
10 READ C$, D$
20 IF C$ < D$ THEN GOTO 10
30 IF C$ > D$ THEN GOTO 60
40 PRINT "SAME"
50 GOTO 80
60 PRINT D$; "  IS FIRST"
70 DATA DO, RE, MI, FA, SO, SO
80 END
```

6. Complete the RUN chart for each of the following programs. (See Exercise 12, page 141, for an explanation of the *condition* column.)

a.
```
10 LET A$ = "ALPHA"
20 LET B$ = "BETA"
30 IF A$ = B$ THEN PRINT A$
40 PRINT "DONE"
50 END
```

LINE	CONDITION	A$	B$	OUTPUT
10		ALPHA		
20			BETA	
30	false			
. . .				

b.
```
10 LET A$ = "ALPHA"
20 LET B$ = "BETA"
30 IF A$ = B$ THEN PRINT A$
40 IF A$ < B$ THEN GOTO 60
50 PRINT B$
60 PRINT "DONE"
65 PRINT "BYE"
70 END
```

LINE	CONDITION	A$	B$	OUTPUT
10		ALPHA		
20			BETA	
. . .				

c.
```
10 READ WRD$
20 IF WRD$ <= "M" THEN PRINT WRD$
30 IF WRD$ = "A" THEN GOTO 60
40 GOTO 10
50 DATA ME, YOU, I, A, THEM
60 END
```

LINE	CONDITION	WRD$	OUTPUT
10		ME	
20			
30			
40			
. . .			

d.
```
10 LET NUM = 0
20 READ WRD$
30 IF WRD$ < "B" THEN GOTO 50
40 IF WRD$ < "C" THEN LET NUM = NUM + 1
50 IF WRD$ >= "A" THEN GOTO 20
60 DATA A, BEE, CAN, BE, 9, B
70 END
```

LINE	CONDITION	WRD$	NUM	OUTPUT
10			0	
20		A		
30	true			
50	true			
20		BEE		
30				
. . .				

By studying the RUN chart above can you determine the purpose of the program?

7. Change Program 3 so that it PRINTs the message NAMES ARE THE SAME if N1$ and N2$ are identical strings.

8. Change Program 3 so that it PRINTs *both* names in alphabetical order.

9. Here is a program that simulates what a gas station attendant might say to the driver of an older-model car.

```
10  REM * GAS STATION ATTENDANT
20  INPUT "FILL IT UP?  "; ANS$
30  IF ANS$ = "YES" THEN GOTO 90
40  IF ANS$ = "NO" THEN GOTO 70
50  PRINT "WHAT DID YOU SAY?"
60  GOTO 20
70  INPUT "HOW MANY GALLONS?  "; GALL
80  IF GALL = 0 THEN GOTO 150
90  INPUT "REGULAR OR PREMIUM?  "; KIND$
100  IF KIND$ = "PREMIUM" THEN GOTO 140
110  IF KIND$ = "REGULAR" THEN GOTO 170
120  PRINT "WHAT?"
130  GOTO 90
140  PRINT "WE'RE OUT OF PREMIUM"
150  PRINT "GOODBYE"
160  GOTO 180
170  PRINT "HEY, WHERE'S THE GAS TANK ON THIS"
175  PRINT "RATTLETRAP?"
180  END
```

a. Explain what the program will do if you answer MAYBE to the question in line 20.
b. Explain what the program will do if you do not want your gas tank filled.
c. Explain what the program will do if you want REGULAR gas.
d. Explain what the program will do if you want PREMIUM gas.
e. Change the program so that if you ask for PREMIUM gas, the attendant will say YOU'RE WASTING YOUR MONEY BUYING EXPENSIVE GAS FOR THIS JALOPY.

B **10.** Write a program that INPUTs a word, then PRINTs the message FIRST PART OF ALPHABET if the word comes before the letter M in alphabetical order. Otherwise, the program should PRINT the message LAST PART OF THE ALPHABET.

11. Write a program that INPUTs a person's name, then PRINTs the message WHAT A PRETTY NAME if the name is MELISSA, the message WHAT AN UNUSUAL NAME if the name is PTGRSK, and the message YOUR MOTHER CALLED YOU THAT? if the name is FRANKENSTEIN.

12. Write a program that INPUTs a word, then PRINTs the word only if it starts with the letter C. (*Hint:* A word starts with the letter C if and only if the word is < "D" and >= "C".)

13. Write a program that INPUTs two numbers and one of the operations "+", "−", "*", "/". The program then should perform the operation on the two INPUT numbers and PRINT the result. For example, if 3 and 7 are the two numbers, and "*" is the operation, the output should be 3 * 7 = 21.

14. Write a program that simulates a short conversation between a jogger and a shoe salesperson (use Exercise 9 as a model).

C 15. a. Using Program 3 as a model, write a program that INPUTs three names, then PRINTs the name that comes first in alphabetical order.
b. Modify the program in (a) so that it PRINTs all three names in alphabetical order.

Lab Activity

"Alphabetical" Order of Non-alphabetic Characters

Type the following program into your computer:

```
10 PRINT "ORDERING"
20 INPUT "TYPE ANY 2 KEYS:  "; K1$, K2$
30 IF K1$ < K2$ THEN LET FIRST$ = K1$
40 IF K2$ <= K1$ THEN LET FIRST$ = K2$
50 PRINT FIRST$; "  IS FIRST IN ALPHABETICAL ORDER."
60 GOTO 20
70 END
```

Problems

1. RUN the program and experiment with different pairs of keys to try to determine exactly the "alphabetical" order for punctuation marks, single digits, operation symbols, lower-case letters (if your computer has them), and other characters on your keyboard. (To use the program with commas or colons, enclose the comma or colon in quotation marks. The alphabetical order of the quote character ("), however, cannot be investigated in this way.)

2. There is a special numbering of all available characters that is called the ASCII (pronounced "ask'ee") code. To find the ASCII code of, say, the letter "Q", simply type the immediate mode command:

```
PRINT ASC("Q")
```

The computer will PRINT the number 81. An alternative is to give two commands:

```
LET A$ = "Q"
PRINT ASC(A$)
```

Suppose you want to determine if the exclamation point (!) comes before or after the letter Q in "alphabetical" order. If you PRINT ASC("!"), then the result is 33. Since 33 comes before 81 in numerical order (33 < 81 is true), the exclamation point (!) must come before Q in "alphabetical" order.

Verify by typing PRINT commands with ASC that the "alphabetical" order you found in Problem 1 corresponds exactly to the numerical order of the ASCII codes given by ASC. That is, A$ < B$ is true exactly when ASC(A$) < ASC(B$), where A$ and B$ represent single characters.

3. *Challenge:* Can you determine the ASCII code of the quote character (") by the process of elimination?

4-4 Ending INPUT and DATA: Trailer Values

The first program of this section could serve as a short telephone directory.

Program 1

Statement	Remark
10 PRINT "TELEPHONE DIRECTORY PROGRAM"	
20 INPUT "TYPE NAME DESIRED: "; WANT$	*Ask for the name user wants.*
30 READ NAM$	*READ name.*
40 READ TELNO$	*READ telephone number.*
50 IF NAM$ <> WANT$ THEN GOTO 30	*If name doesn't match, go back to 30.*
60 PRINT NAM$; " 'S TELEPHONE NUMBER IS: ";	
70 PRINT TELNO$	
80 DATA LAURIE, 443-2679, HEATHER, 236-6686	
85 DATA BRIAN, 299-9198	
90 END	

Output

```
TELEPHONE DIRECTORY PROGRAM
TYPE NAME DESIRED:   ? HEATHER
HEATHER'S TELEPHONE NUMBER IS:   236-6686
```

After asking you the name of the person whose telephone number you want, the program keeps READing (lines 30 and 40) the DATA values until it finds the name requested (HEATHER, for example, as shown above). At this point NAM$ does equal WANT$, so the condition in line 50 is false, and the computer goes on to lines 60 and 70 and PRINTs the name and telephone number.

What happens, though, if you type a name that is not on the list? The program will READ all the names on the DATA line without finding a match, and then print an OUT OF DATA error message and stop. For this particular program, the OUT OF DATA error might be acceptable, but it would certainly be more helpful for the program to give a more meaningful message, such as SORRY, THAT NAME IS NOT ON THE LIST. (Moreover, you will soon be writing programs that contain instructions to be executed after all of the DATA values have been READ. Thus you need to learn how to avoid having the program stop because of an OUT OF DATA error.)

One way to avoid an OUT OF DATA error is to put a *trailer value* on the DATA list. The trailer value is a special number or string that signals the end of the DATA list. Any number or string that has no meaning in the program, and thus will not be confused with the real data, can be used as a trailer value. For example, in Program 1, ZZZZ is a sufficiently rare name that no one is likely to ask for his or her telephone number. Thus we can use ZZZZ for a trailer value, as in this new version of the program.

Program 2

Statement	Remark
10 PRINT "TELEPHONE DIRECTORY, PART 2"	
20 INPUT "TYPE NAME DESIRED: "; WANT$	
30 READ NAM$	*READ name.*
35 IF NAM$ = "ZZZZ" THEN GOTO 77	*ZZZZ is the trailer value.*
40 READ TELNO$	*READ telephone number.*
50 IF NAM$ <> WANT$ THEN GOTO 30	*If name doesn't match, go back to 30.*
60 PRINT NAM$; " 'S TELEPHONE NUMBER IS: ";	
70 PRINT TELNO$	
75 GOTO 90	
77 PRINT "SORRY, THAT NAME IS NOT ON THE LIST."	*PRINT the new message.*
80 DATA LAURIE, 443-2679, HEATHER, 236-6686	
85 DATA BRIAN, 299-9198, ZZZZ	
90 END	

Output

```
TELEPHONE DIRECTORY, PART 2
TYPE NAME DESIRED:   ? BENJAMIN
SORRY, THAT NAME IS NOT ON THE LIST.
```

If WANT$ is a name that is on the DATA list, the program works the same as before. However, if WANT$ is not on the list, eventually the string ZZZZ will be READ and assigned to NAM$. Then the condition NAM$ = "ZZZZ" in line 35 will be true, causing the computer to GOTO line 77 and PRINT the new message shown in the output. Notice that line 75 was added to the revised program. What would happen if you were to ask for a name that is on the list and line 75 were not there?

It might have occurred to you to combine lines 30 and 40 in Program 2:

```
30  READ NAM$, TELNO$
```

In that case, two trailer values would be required — one for NAM$ and another for TELNO$. Otherwise, if WANT$ were not on the list, our new line 30 could assign ZZZZ to NAM$, but would find no value left in the DATA list to assign to TELNO$. An OUT OF DATA error would occur. Here is a third version of the program, using a multiple READ statement and a double trailer value.

Program 3

Statement	Remark
10 PRINT "TELEPHONE DIRECTORY, PART 2"	
20 INPUT "TYPE NAME DESIRED: "; WANT$	
30 READ NAM$, TELNO$	*READ name, telephone number.*
35 IF NAM$ = "ZZZZ" THEN GOTO 77	*ZZZZ is the trailer value.*
50 IF NAM$ <> WANT$ THEN GOTO 30	*If name doesn't match, go back to 30.*
60 PRINT NAM$; " 'S TELEPHONE NUMBER IS: ";	
70 PRINT TELNO$	
75 GOTO 90	
77 PRINT "SORRY, THAT NAME IS NOT ON THE LIST."	*PRINT the new message.*
80 DATA LAURIE, 443-2679, HEATHER, 236-6686	
85 DATA BRIAN, 299-9198, ZZZZ, 000-0000	
90 END	

Output

```
TELEPHONE DIRECTORY, PART 2
TYPE NAME DESIRED:  ? BENJAMIN
SORRY, THAT NAME IS NOT ON THE LIST.
```

Let's consider another example of the use of a trailer value, this time using INPUT rather than READ . . . DATA. The problem is to PRINT the largest number of a sequence of positive numbers typed by the user. Since the numbers typed are supposed to be positive, −999 would be a safe choice for a trailer value (it could not be mistaken for meaningful data).

Following the top-down approach to program design, we first specify the inputs. They will be the numbers typed by the user; we will assign them to the variable NUM. The output is to be the largest number typed; call it LARGEST. A first outline of the algorithm might be this:

Step 1 Get number (NUM) from the user.

Step 2 If NUM = −999 (the trailer value), then GOTO Step 5.

Step 3 If NUM <> −999, then determine if NUM is the largest number so far. If it is, store it in LARGEST.

Step 4 Go back to Step 1.

Step 5 PRINT LARGEST, then END.

Step 3 needs some elaboration. How can the program decide if NUM is the largest number entered so far? This can be easily done: If NUM > LARGEST is true, then NUM is the largest so far, and the program should assign a new value to LARGEST (that is, LET LARGEST = NUM). Only one difficulty remains — LARGEST has to be given an initial value. Otherwise, the first comparison NUM > LARGEST won't make any sense. The simplest solution is to LET LARGEST = 0 before Step 1. Since each number (NUM) typed is supposed to be positive, this means that LARGEST will surely be made equal to the first value of NUM in Step 3. (Actually, as you learned in Chapter 3, all numeric variables are assigned the value 0 the instant the program is RUN. But it is a good practice always to *initialize* each numeric variable, that is, give it a starting value, at the beginning of a program.)

The revised algorithm, suitably renumbered, is as follows:

Step 1 LET LARGEST = 0.

Step 2 Get number (NUM) from the user.

Step 3 If NUM = −999 then GOTO Step 6.

Step 4 Otherwise (if NUM <> −999), if NUM > LARGEST, then LET LARGEST = NUM.

Step 5 GOTO Step 2.

Step 6 PRINT LARGEST, then END.

Here is the detailed algorithm translated into BASIC code:

Program 4

Statement

```
10 PRINT "FINDING THE LARGEST VALUE"
20 LET LARGEST = 0
30 INPUT "TYPE A POS. NUM. (OR -999 TO QUIT):  "; NUM
40 IF NUM = -999 THEN GOTO 70
```

Program continued on next page.

```
50  IF NUM > LARGEST THEN LET LARGEST = NUM
60  GOTO 30
70  PRINT "LARGEST =  "; LARGEST
80  END
```

Output

```
FINDING THE LARGEST VALUE
TYPE A POS. NUM. (OR -999 TO QUIT):  ? 56
TYPE A POS. NUM. (OR -999 TO QUIT):  ? 48
TYPE A POS. NUM. (OR -999 TO QUIT):  ? -999
LARGEST =  56
```

Notice that there is no instruction IF NUM < > −999 THEN . . . , as you might expect from Step 3 of the original algorithm. Such a test is unnecessary as the program is written; because of the condition in line 40, the computer cannot reach line 50 unless NUM < > −999 is true. Trace through the program (use a RUN chart) for the INPUTs shown above to see that the program works correctly.

Avoiding Pitfalls

1. Be careful not to initialize a variable more than once. For example, if line 60 in Program 3 had been 60 GOTO 20, then LARGEST would have been set equal to 0 before each new number was typed. As a result, in line 50 LARGEST would store the number just INPUT rather than the largest number INPUT so far.
2. To avoid having a program include the trailer value as meaningful data, the IF . . . THEN test usually should come immediately after the INPUT or READ statement that assigns values to the variable(s).
3. Be sure the number of trailer values in the DATA list matches the number of variables to be READ. Otherwise, an OUT OF DATA error may occur.

Summary

A *trailer value* is a special string or number that signals the end of a DATA list or the end of a sequence of INPUTs. An IF . . . THEN statement is used to test whether the trailer value has been reached.

Be sure to check all variables in your program to see if they need to be *initialized* (given a starting value).

Exercises 4-4

A **1.** Explain why the string FRANCES would not be a good choice for a trailer value in Program 2. Give three good choices for a trailer value other than the string ZZZZ.

2. Explain why ZZZZ cannot be used for a trailer value in Program 4.

3. Explain why the number 38 would not be a good choice for a trailer value in Program 4. Give three good choices for a trailer value other than the number −999.

4. **a.** Predict the output of the following program.

```
10  LET F$ = "NOT FOUND"
20  READ A$
30  IF A$ = "NEVER" THEN GOTO 60
40  IF A$ = "ALWAYS" THEN LET F$ = "FOUND"
50  GOTO 20
60  PRINT F$
70  DATA PLEASE, USE, BACK, STAIRWAY
75  DATA ALWAYS, NEVER
80  END
```

b. Predict the output if line 70 is changed to:

```
70  DATA PLEASE, NEVER, USE, THE, WINDOW
```

c. Predict the output if line 50 is changed to:

```
50  GOTO 10
```

(Line 70 stays the same as in (b).)

5. Predict the output for the INPUTs given below each program.

a.

```
10  LET C = 0
20  INPUT ADJ$
30  IF ADJ$ = "XXX"  THEN GOTO 55
40  LET C = C + 1
50  GOTO 20
55  PRINT "ADJECTIVES:  "; C
60  END
? BRAVE
? COURAGEOUS
? BOLD
? XXX
```

b.

```
10  INPUT A$
20  READ B$
30  IF B$ = "QQQ" THEN GOTO 60
40  IF B$ > A$ THEN LET A$ = B$
50  GOTO 20
60  PRINT A$, B$
65  DATA BAT, BOP, BAN, QQQ
70  END
? BEG
```

6. Predict the output of each of the following programs. If necessary, construct a RUN chart.

a.
```
5  PRINT "X", "X SQUARED"
10 READ X
20 IF X=-1 THEN GOTO 50
30 PRINT X, X ↑ 2
40 GOTO 10
50 PRINT "DONE"
60 DATA 10, 20, 30, -1
70 END
```

b.
```
10 PRINT "ITEM NO.", "ITEM"
12 LET I=0
15 READ ITEM$
20 IF ITEM$="$$" THEN GOTO 40
25 LET I=I+1
30 PRINT I, ITEM$
35 GOTO 15
40 PRINT "NO. OF ITEMS:  "; I
50 DATA HAT, COAT, GLOVES, $$
55 END
```

7. In Program 2, suppose line 35 is renumbered as line 45 (so that line 35 is deleted, and line 45 is IF NAM$ = "ZZZZ" THEN GOTO 77). What will this revised program do if you type a name not on the DATA list?

8. In Program 4, what will be the output if a user types only −999?

9. Change Program 4 so that it READs the numbers from a DATA statement rather than using an INPUT statement.

10. Change Program 4 to do both of the following:
    a. Reject any negative number other than the trailer value −999.
    b. Reject any number larger than 100.

11. In Program 4, change line 60 to 60 GOTO 20. Assume that a user types the numbers 7, 6, and −999. What is the output? Does the program work correctly? Explain.

12. The following program is supposed to look for an INPUT positive number on a DATA list. Add a trailer value and have the program PRINT the message CAN'T BE FOUND if the INPUT number is not on the list.

```
10 INPUT "NUMBER:  "; LOOK
20 READ NUM
30 IF NUM=LOOK THEN GOTO 50
40 GOTO 20
50 PRINT LOOK; "  IS ON THE LIST"
60 DATA 5, 3, 0, 6, 38
70 END
```

B 13. Write a program that determines whether the first string on a DATA list occurs later on in the list. If the string does appear again, have the program PRINT the message FIRST STRING REPEATS.

14. Write a program that has a DATA list of names and telephone numbers. If a name is INPUT that is on the list, the corresponding telephone number should be PRINTed. If a telephone number is INPUT that is on the list, then the corresponding name should be PRINTed. If the INPUT name or telephone number is not on the list, the message SORRY, NOT ON THE LIST should be PRINTed.

15. (Graphics) Write a program to draw your initials in graphics mode. Use one or more DATA statements to give the X- and Y-coordinates of each point to be plotted, and use a trailer value to avoid the OUT OF DATA error.

16. (Graphics) Write a program that uses a DATA statement to give the X- and Y-coordinates of 5 points located in different areas of the graphics screen. At each point, have the program draw the same X-shaped figure.

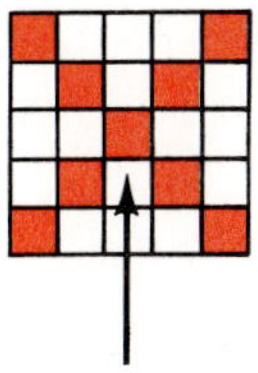

Use a trailer value to signal the end of the list and *error trapping* to reject any values that would make any part of the figure go off the screen.

C **17. a.** Write a program that PRINTs the smallest positive number of a sequence of positive numbers typed by a user. (*Hint:* Use Program 4 as a model. Change the variable LARGEST to SMALLEST. Unfortunately, the initial value SMALLEST = 0 will not work. (Why not?) In fact, no choice of initial value of SMALLEST will work every time. Instead, use two INPUT statements. Have the program assign the first INPUT number to SMALLEST, and all subsequent INPUT numbers to NUM, which can then be compared with SMALLEST.)

b. Modify the program in (a) so that it PRINTs the largest number of a sequence of numbers, regardless of whether the numbers typed are positive or negative. (The number −999 used as the trailer value in Program 4 would be a poor choice here, since −999 might be one of the numbers the user types in the sequence. Instead, you could add another INPUT statement that includes the message ANY MORE NUMBERS?, then PRINT the largest number in the sequence when NO is typed.)

18. *Challenge:* Write a program that determines whether or not a DATA list of strings is in alphabetical order. Use ZZZZ for a trailer value and PRINT the message LIST IS OK if the strings are in alphabetical order. Otherwise, PRINT the message NOT IN ORDER.

Lab Activity

Flowcharts

In Section 4–1, you were introduced to the top-down technique of approaching programming problems. A somewhat different approach, in which all of the details of an algorithm are given right from the beginning, has been followed successfully by many programmers. These programmers organize their solution to a programming problem by drawing a diagram called a *flowchart.* Here is a flowchart for Program 2 of this section.

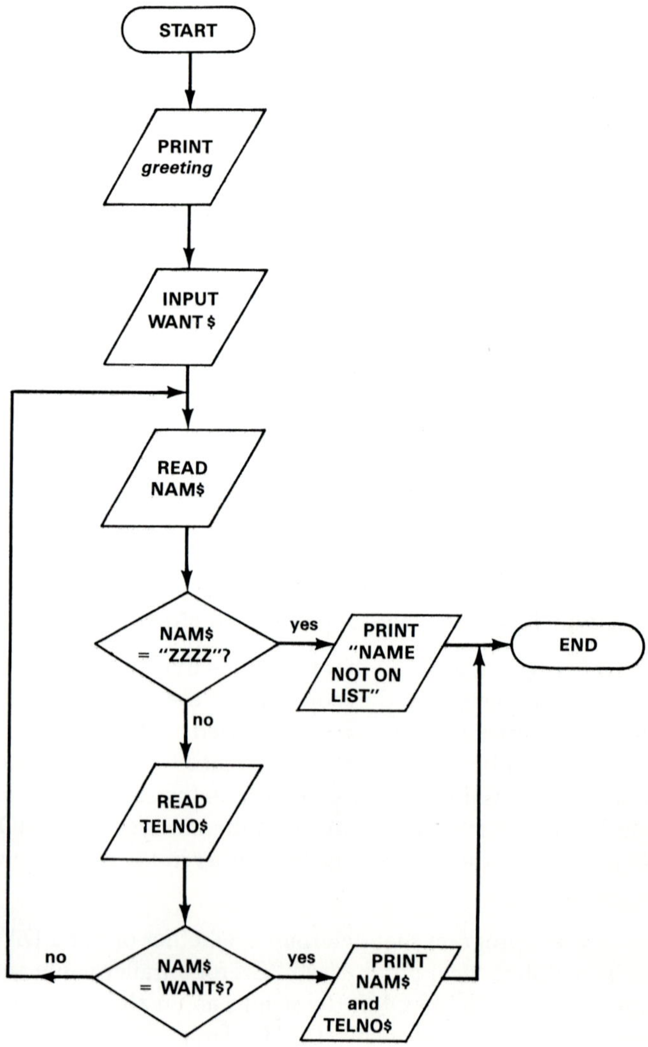

A flowchart uses box-like shapes and connecting arrows to indicate the actions that the program will carry out, and the decisions it must make. Each shape has its own meaning. Ovals ⬭ are used to indicate the beginning and end of the program. Parallelograms ▱ are used to describe input (INPUT, READ) and output (PRINT). Diamonds ◇ are used for decisions (IF . . . THEN). In addition, rectangles ▭ are used to describe any processing of numbers and strings (LET). Study the flowchart given on the preceding page, along with Program 2 of this section, to see how they both express the same algorithm.

Here is a flowchart for Program 3 of this section:

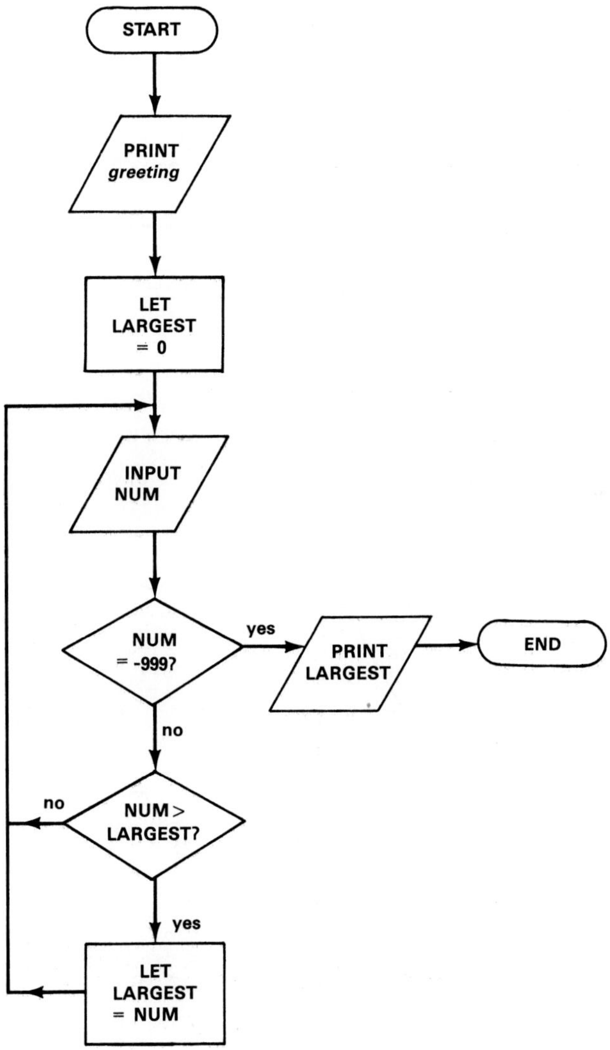

Again, study the flowchart along with Program 3 and notice that they both express the same algorithm.

Problems

In Problems 1–3, write a BASIC program for the given flowchart.

1.

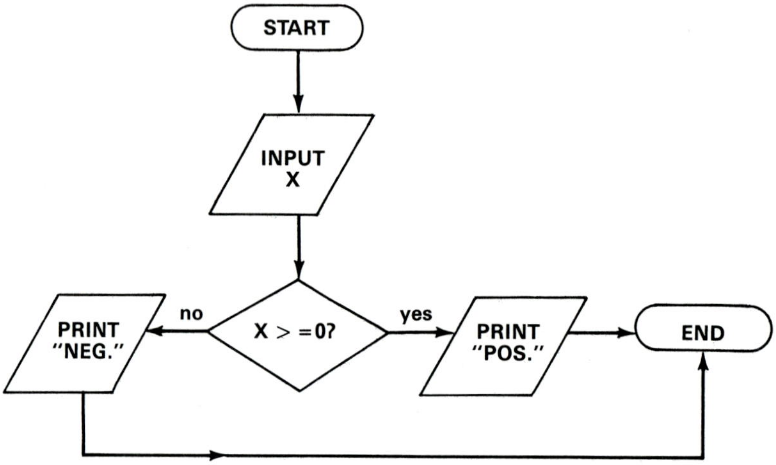

2.

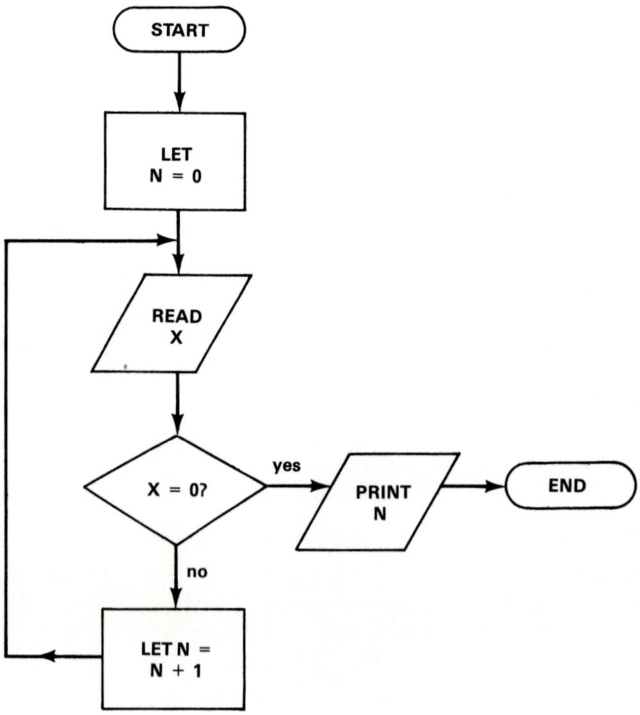

3.

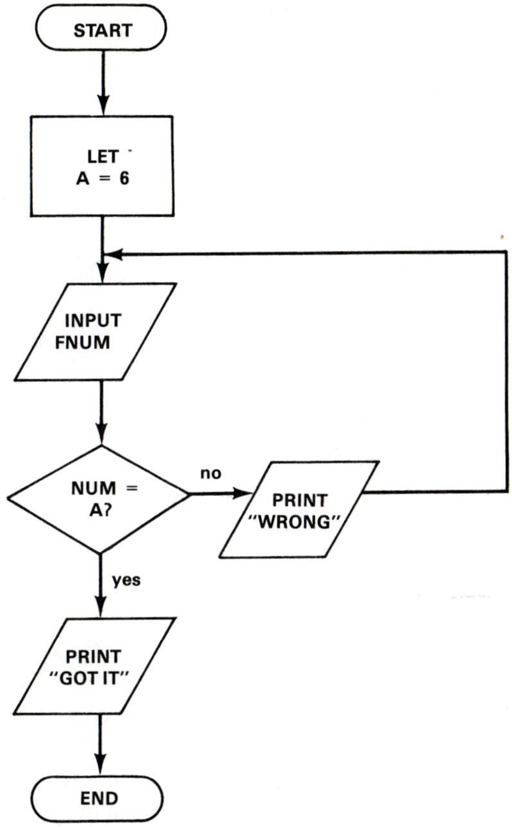

In Problems 4–7, draw a flowchart for the program in the given exercise.

4. Exercise 4(a) of this section.

5. Exercise 5(a) of this section.

6. Exercise 6(a) of this section.

7. Exercise 6(b) of this section.

4-5 Complex Conditions with IF . . . THEN

The condition in an IF . . . THEN statement of the form

IF *condition* THEN *action*

may be made more complicated than the simple comparisons used in the previous sections of this chapter. Comparisons may be combined using the conjunctions AND and OR, or they may be modified using NOT, in much the same way complex English sentences are constructed using these words. For example, the program on the next page uses *complex conditions* in a natural way to convert number grades into letter grades.

Program 1

Statement

```
10  PRINT "CONVERTING TO LETTER GRADES"
20  INPUT "TYPE YOUR NUMBER GRADE (0-100):  "; NUM
30  PRINT "YOUR LETTER GRADE IS:  ";
40  IF (NUM < 60) THEN PRINT "E"
50  IF (60 <= NUM) AND (NUM < 70) THEN PRINT "D"
60  IF (70 <= NUM) AND (NUM < 80) THEN PRINT "C"
70  IF (80 <= NUM) AND (NUM < 90) THEN PRINT "B"
80  IF (90 <= NUM) THEN PRINT "A"
90  END
```

Output

```
CONVERTING TO LETTER GRADES
TYPE YOUR NUMBER GRADE (0-100):  ? 82
YOUR LETTER GRADE IS:  B
```

In line 50, the first instance of a complex condition, the action PRINT "D" will be executed only if *both* of the comparisons 60 <= NUM and NUM < 70 are true; it will not be executed if either comparison is false. A similar explanation can be made for lines 60 and 70. If you type 82 for your number grade, as shown above, then none of the actions in lines 40, 50, and 60 will be executed (why?). When the computer reaches line 70, however, the comparisons 80 <= 82 and 82 < 90 are both true, so the computer executes the action PRINT "B". (The parentheses around the conditions in lines 40 to 80 are optional, but are often used to make the meaning clear.)

Conditions in IF . . . THEN statements may also be combined using the word OR. For example, in the statement

```
IF (NUM < 0) OR (NUM > 100) THEN PRINT "ILLEGAL NUMBER"
```

the message ILLEGAL NUMBER will be printed if *either* comparison is true, or if *both* are true. Of course, it is impossible for both of the comparisons in this example to be true at the same time. But consider this statement:

```
IF (A < 0) OR (B > 100) THEN GOTO 50
```

In this case, the action GOTO 50 will be executed if A < 0 is true, or if B > 100 is true, or if both A < 0 and B > 100 are true (which is quite possible).

Complex conditions can make programs shorter and easier to read. For example, here is a revised version of the point plotting program (Program 3, page 136), which introduced error trapping.

Program 2

Statement

```
10  REM * PLOTTING POINTS, PART 2
20  REM * PLOT POINTS ONLY IN TOP LEFT CORNER
30  INPUT "TYPE X, Y COORDINATES (BETWEEN 0 AND 20):  "; X, Y
40  IF (X < 0) OR (X > 20) OR (Y < 0) OR (Y > 20) THEN GOTO 30
 .  (Instructions to clear the screen
 .     and do graphics on your
 .     computer. See Section 2–5, page 45.)
70  (Instruction to plot the point X, Y on your computer.)
80  GOTO 30
90  END
```

(*Note:* On *IBM* and *TRS-80*, change line 80 to 80 GOTO 80. See page 137.)

Output

```
TYPE X, Y COORDINATES (BETWEEN 0 AND 20): ? 18, 16
```

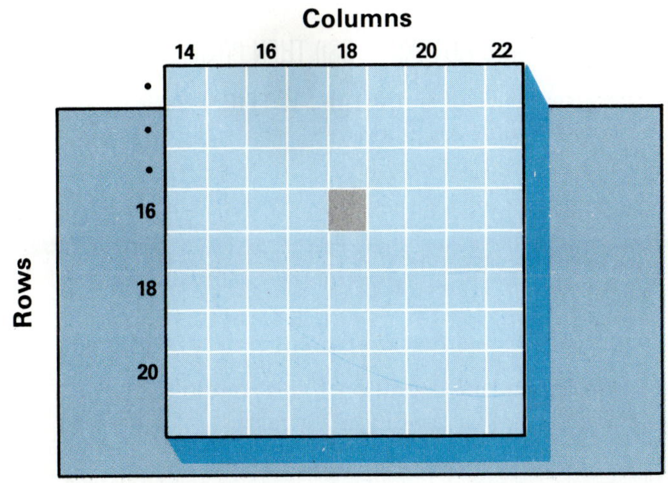

The comparisons in line 40 do all of the error trapping in one statement. If any one of the four comparisons is true for an INPUT point, then the instruction GOTO 30 will be executed and the point will not be plotted.

Conditions may also be modified by using the word NOT, which has its usual English meaning. In the statement

```
IF NOT (A < 10) THEN PRINT "HICCUP"
```

the condition NOT (A < 10) will be true if (A < 10) is false; NOT (A < 10) will be false if (A < 10) is true.

Avoiding Pitfalls

1. Inequalities cannot be combined in the short-hand way that they sometimes are in mathematics. For example, if you write a statement such as IF (4 < X < 8) THEN PRINT D, the computer ignores the condition and always PRINTs the value of D. To test if 4 < X < 8, use

```
IF (4 < X) AND (X < 8) THEN PRINT D.
```

   Of course, you could write X > 4 instead of 4 < X and 8 > X instead of X < 8.

2. If comparisons are combined, they must be complete comparisons. The statement IF (A < 6 AND > 7) THEN PRINT "NO GOOD" is not valid because > 7 is not a complete comparison. The programmer probably intended this:

```
IF (A < 6) AND (A > 7) THEN PRINT "NO GOOD"
```

   Similarly, (A NOT > 4) is not valid; the correct form is NOT (A > 4).

3. Conditions can sometimes become so complicated that they are difficult to understand. For example:

```
IF (A > 3) OR NOT ((C$ = "ME") AND NOT (X$ = B$)) THEN PRINT "YECCCH!"
```

   It is usually better to use a sequence of simpler IF . . . THEN statements to express extremely complex conditions.

Summary

In the statement

IF *(condition 1)* AND *(condition 2)* THEN . . .

the complex condition is true only if *both* condition 1 and condition 2 are true; it is false if either condition 1 or condition 2 is false.

In the statement

IF *(condition 1)* OR *(condition 2)* THEN . . .

the complex condition is true if *either* condition is true (or both are true); it is false if both condition 1 and condition 2 are false.

In the statement

IF NOT *(condition 1)* THEN . . .

the condition NOT *(condition 1)* will be true if condition 1 is false; it will be false if condition 1 is true.

Exercises 4-5

A

1. If X = 5, Y = 3, A$ = "ME", and B$ = "YOU", determine whether each of the following conditions is true or false.
   - **a.** X > Y
   - **b.** A$ > B$
   - **c.** (X > Y) AND (A$ > B$)
   - **d.** (X > Y) OR (A$ > B$)
   - **e.** NOT (X > Y)
   - **f.** NOT (A$ = B$)
   - **g.** (X = Y) OR (A$ = B$)
   - **h.** (2 < 7) OR (3 > 8)
   - **i.** ("NAUGHTY" <= "NICE") AND (A$ = "ME")
   - **j.** (7 < X * Y) OR NOT (X + Y < 7)
   - **k.** NOT ((A$ = "ME") AND (B$ = "US"))
   - **l.** NOT (A$ = "ME") OR NOT (B$ = "US")

2. Tell whether each of the following is a valid BASIC statement.
   - **a.** IF (X >= 3) OR (Y < 15 * X) THEN GOTO 100
   - **b.** IF ("MY DEAR" = A$) AND (B$ = "AUNT SALLY") THEN GOTO 100
   - **c.** IF ("IT IS SNOWING") OR ("IT IS RAINING") THEN PRINT "GET THE UMBRELLA"
   - **d.** IF (X > 46) OR (X >= −58) THEN GOTO 100
   - **e.** IF NOT (M$ = "PLEASE EXCUSE") THEN PRINT "ALGEBRA"
   - **f.** IF (−45 < X <= 37) THEN PRINT "JUST RIGHT"
   - **g.** IF (A > 3 OR < −6) THEN GOTO 103
   - **h.** IF (A NOT = 7) THEN PRINT "NOT"

3. For each statement in Exercise 2 that is not valid, give a possible correction. Try to imagine what the programmer intended.

4. Predict the output of each of the following programs.

   a.
```
10 LET X = 17
20 IF (X < 3) OR (X > 18) THEN PRINT "YES"
30 PRINT "I DON'T KNOW"
40 END
```
   b.
```
10 LET X = 17
20 IF (X >= 3) OR (X < 0) THEN PRINT "YES"
30 PRINT "NO"
40 END
```
   c.
```
10 LET X = 17
20 IF NOT (X > 36) THEN GOTO 50
30 PRINT "NOT"
40 GOTO 60
50 PRINT "KNOT"
60 END
```

d.
```
10 LET X = 17
20 IF (X < 7) AND (3 <= X) THEN PRINT "PUG"
30 PRINT "MILL"
40 END
```

e.
```
10 LET A$ = "PURPLISH"
20 IF (A$ > "GREENISH") AND ("GREEN QUICHE" <= A$) THEN PRINT "RADISH"
30 PRINT "NADA"
40 END
```

f.
```
10 LET X = 4
20 LET Y = 7
30 IF (X >= Y) AND (Y <= 9) THEN PRINT "OUCH"
40 IF (X + 1 > 3) OR (Y * X < 15) THEN PRINT "LESS"
50 IF NOT (X + Y = 11) THEN PRINT "CURE"
60 END
```

g.
```
10 READ G$, Y$, F$
20 IF (G$ <= Y$) OR (NOT (Y$ = F$)) THEN PRINT G$; Y$
30 IF (Y$ >= "APPLESAUCE") AND (G$ < "EEEE") THEN PRINT Y$; F$
40 DATA ANKLE, DEEP, MUD
50 END
```

5. For each pair of programs below, determine whether they will both have the same output for every possible INPUT. If not, give an example of an INPUT value that will cause the two programs to have different output.

a.
```
10 INPUT A, B
20 IF (A < 5) THEN GOTO 50
30 IF (B >= 4) THEN GOTO 50
40 PRINT "NO"
45 GOTO 60
50 PRINT "YES"
60 END
```

```
10 INPUT A, B
20 IF (A < 5) AND (B >= 4) THEN GOTO 50
40 PRINT "NO"
45 GOTO 60
50 PRINT "YES"
60 END
```

b.
```
10 INPUT A, B
20 IF (A < 5) THEN GOTO 50
```

```
30 IF (B >= 4) THEN GOTO 50
40 PRINT "NO"
45 GOTO 60
50 PRINT "YES"
60 END
```

```
10 INPUT A, B
20 IF (A < 5) OR (B >= 4) THEN GOTO 50
40 PRINT "NO"
45 GOTO 60
50 PRINT "YES"
60 END
```

c.

```
10 INPUT A, B
20 IF (A < 5) THEN GOTO 40
30 GOTO 50
40 IF (B >= 4) THEN GOTO 70
50 PRINT "NO"
60 GOTO 80
70 PRINT "YES"
80 END
```

```
10 INPUT A, B
20 IF (A < 5) AND (B >= 4) THEN GOTO 70
30 PRINT "NO"
40 GOTO 80
70 PRINT "YES"
80 END
```

d.

```
10 INPUT A, B
20 IF NOT (A < 5) THEN GOTO 60
30 IF NOT (B >= 4) THEN GOTO 60
40 PRINT "YES"
50 GOTO 70
60 PRINT "NO"
70 END
```

```
10 INPUT A, B
20 IF (A < 5) AND (B >= 4) THEN GOTO 40
30 PRINT "NO"
35 GOTO 50
40 PRINT "YES"
50 END
```

e.
```
10  INPUT A
20  IF (A >= -6) THEN PRINT "YELLOW"
30  PRINT "BLOSSOMS"
40  END
```

```
10  INPUT A
20  IF (A > -6) AND (A = -6) THEN PRINT "YELLOW"
30  PRINT "BLOSSOMS"
40  END
```

f.
```
10  INPUT A
20  IF NOT (A > 6) THEN PRINT "YELLOW"
30  PRINT "ROSE"
40  END
```

```
10  INPUT A
20  IF (A <= 6) THEN PRINT "YELLOW"
30  PRINT "ROSE"
40  END
```

g.
```
10  INPUT X$, C$, A
20  IF (A > 3) OR NOT ((C$ = "ME") AND NOT (X$ = B$)) THEN PRINT "YECCH!"
30  PRINT "OK"
40  END
```

```
10  INPUT X$, C$, A
20  IF (A > 3) THEN GOTO 100
30  IF (X$ = B$) THEN GOTO 100
40  IF NOT (C$ = "ME") THEN GOTO 100
50  PRINT "OK"
60  GOTO 120
100  PRINT "YECCH!"
120  END
```

6. Change Program 1 to do all of the following:

a. PRINT the message ALL DONE if a user types −99 for a trailer value.

b. Reject any number grades that are less than 0 or greater than 100. (Have the user try again if such a number is typed.)

c. PRINT plus (+) and minus (−) grades. For example, in the B range have 80 to 82 be a B−, 83 to 86 be a straight B, and 87 to 89 be a B+.

7. Change Program 2 so that it ENDs when a user types the number −999 as the X-coordinate for the point to be INPUT.

B **8.** **a.** Write a program that calculates a baby sitter's fee if the charge is $1.25 per hour from 8:00 P.M. to 10:00 P.M., $1.75 per hour from 10:00 P.M. to 11:00 P.M., and $2.75 per hour after 11:00 P.M. Have the program INPUT the number of hours, assuming that the baby sitter starts at 8:00 P.M.

b. Modify the program in (a) to calculate the fee if the baby sitter's starting time remains at 8:00 P.M., but the ending time is INPUT (assume to the nearest hour). Be sure to consider the possibility that the baby sitter may work after midnight.

9. Write a program that INPUTs three strings. Have the program PRINT the message

NOT ALIKE

if the three strings are all different from one another. Otherwise, PRINT the message MATCH.

10. Write a program that INPUTs three strings. Have the program PRINT the following messages:
IN ORDER, if the strings are in alphabetical order; BACKWARDS, if the strings are in the reverse order from alphabetical order; and MIXED UP otherwise.

11. Write a program that INPUTs four single-letter strings (say A$, B$, C$, and D$). The program then should test whether the "word" consisting of the four letters in the order they were typed (A$–B$–C$–D$) is the same as the "word" spelled backwards (D$–C$–B$–A$). Such a word, "DEED" and "TOOT" are examples, is called a *palindrome.*

12. Write a program that INPUTs values for three numbers X, Y, and Z, then PRINTs whichever of the three is between the other two. For example, if a user types 7, −3, and 9, the program should PRINT this message:

7 IS IN THE MIDDLE

13. Write a program that INPUTs four strings, then PRINTs the message

FIRST IS OK

if the first string typed comes first in alphabetical order. Otherwise, PRINT the message REARRANGE.

C **14.** (Graphics) Write a program that INPUTs the X- and Y-coordinates of a point on the graphics screen. The program then should draw a block letter C in the top left quarter of the screen if (X, Y) is located there, a block letter A in the top right quarter of the screen if (X, Y) is located there, a block letter K if (X, Y) is in the bottom left quarter, and a block letter E if (X, Y) is in the bottom right quarter. Use −999 as a trailer value for the X-coordinate to end the program.

Lab Activity

Exploring Logical Equivalence

Let *p*, *q*, and *r* represent *logical propositions* — that is, statements that can be determined to be true or false. For example, the conditions we have used in IF . . . THEN statements are all logical propositions since the computer can determine if they are true or false. Mathematical statements such as "The sum of the angles of a triangle is 180°" are logical propositions. Even some everyday statements of verifiable fact, such as "It is raining in Albuquerque", are logical propositions. The truth or falsity of a logical proposition is called its *truth value.*

Just as we may combine conditions using AND, OR, and NOT, any number of logical propositions may be combined using these same *logical connectives.* The truth value of the combined proposition depends both on the truth value of each of the propositions it is made of, and also on the particular connectives being used. For example, if *p* is a true logical proposition and *q* is a false one, then *p* OR *q* is a *true* logical proposition. On the other hand, if *p* is false and *q* is false, then *p* OR *q* is *false.* A complete summary of all the possibilities for the logical connective OR looks like this (T stands for true and F stands for false):

p	*q*	*p* OR *q*
T	T	T
T	F	T
F	T	T
F	F	F

This chart is called the *truth table* for *p* OR *q*. As you can see, *p* OR *q* is true if either *p* is true, or *q* is true, or both are true. This corresponds exactly with how the computer decides whether a complex condition consisting of two comparisons connected by OR is true or false.

We can use the computer to obtain truth values and then construct a truth table. Consider this program:

```
10 PRINT "P OR Q"
20 INPUT "TRUTH VALUE FOR P (TYPE T OR F):  "; P$
30 INPUT "TRUTH VALUE FOR Q (TYPE T OR F):  "; Q$
40 IF (P$ = "T") OR (Q$ = "T") THEN GOTO 70
```

```
50 PRINT "TRUTH VALUE OF (P OR Q) IS F"
55 PRINT
60 GOTO 20
70 PRINT "TRUTH VALUE OF (P OR Q) IS T"
75 PRINT
80 GOTO 20
90 END
```

In line 40, the condition P$ = "T" stands for the logical proposition *p*. If you type T as the truth value for *p*, then P$ = "T" will be *true*, but if you type F, then P$ = "T" will be *false*. The same explanation holds for *q* as well.

Problems

1. Use the program to verify the truth table for *p* OR *q* given previously. (*Note:* The program must be stopped manually. You may want to add a trailer value.)

2. Change the "OR" to "AND" in line 40 and then find the truth values for *p* AND *q*. Use these values to construct a truth table for *p* AND *q*. It should look like this:

p	*q*	*p* AND *q*
T	T	T
T	F	F
F	T	F
F	F	F

Notice that *p* AND *q* is true only if both *p* and *q* are true. It is false otherwise.

3. Change the program to find truth values for NOT (*p* AND *q*). Change line 40 to

```
40 IF NOT ((P$ = "T") AND (Q$ = "T")) THEN GOTO 70
```

and be sure to make the appropriate changes in lines 10, 50, and 70. Use the truth values to construct the truth table for the complex proposition NOT (*p* AND *q*).

4. Change the program to find truth values for (NOT *p*) OR (NOT *q*). Construct the truth table for (NOT *p*) OR (NOT *q*). You should find that the truth table for (NOT *p*) OR (NOT *q*) is identical to that of NOT (*p* AND *q*) in Problem 3. Two complex propositions like these with the same truth table are said to be *logically equivalent*. They are completely interchangeable in any logical argument or in any IF . . . THEN condition.

5. Change the program to INPUT three truth values (*p*, *q*, and *r*) and then complete the truth table below for *p* AND (*q* OR *r*). Note that there are 8 possible combinations of truth values for three logical propositions.

p	*q*	*r*	*p* AND (*q* OR *r*)
T	T	T	
T	T	F	
T	F	T	
T	F	F	
F	T	T	
F	T	F	
F	F	T	
F	F	F	

6. Change the program to find the truth values for (*p* AND *q*) OR (*p* AND *r*). Construct a truth table for this combined proposition. Compare the result with the truth table in Problem 5. Is the proposition *p* AND (*q* OR *r*) logically equivalent to (*p* AND *q*) OR (*p* AND *r*)?

7. Based on your results from Problems 5 and 6, try to predict a proposition that might be logically equivalent to *p* OR (*q* AND *r*). Use the program, suitably modified, to verify your prediction.

4-6 Multiple Actions with IF . . . THEN

On most microcomputers, it is possible to have more than one *action* follow from the *condition* (or complex condition) in an IF . . . THEN statement. This often allows for shorter and more easily understood programs. For example, here is a third version of the WHAT'S IN A NAME program of Section 4–3. Compare it with the two previous versions (Program 1, page 145, and Program 2, page 146).

Program 1

Statement

```
10  PRINT "WHAT'S IN A NAME, PART 3"
20  INPUT "TYPE YOUR NAME, PLEASE:  "; N$
30  IF N$ = "ROMEO" THEN PRINT "WHEREFORE?": GOTO 60
40  IF N$ = "JULIET" THEN PRINT "SIGH!!": GOTO 60
50  PRINT "GET OUT OF MY PLAY!"
60  END
```

Output

```
WHAT'S IN A NAME, PART 3
TYPE YOUR NAME, PLEASE:   ? JULIET
SIGH!!
```

If there are two or more actions in an IF . . . THEN statement, as in lines 30 and 40, then they must be separated by colons. If the condition is *true,* then *all* of the actions in that line are executed. If the condition is *false,* then *none* of the actions in that line are executed. For example, if the name JULIET is typed as shown above, the condition in line 30 is false and the computer goes on to line 40. There the condition N$ = "JULIET" is true, so both actions are executed; the message SIGH!! is PRINTed and the GOTO 60 instruction causes the program to END. Notice that line 50 will never be reached if you type in ROMEO or JULIET as the name, since in both cases a GOTO 60 instruction is executed (causing the computer to skip line 50).

Here is another example of a program using the technique of *multiple actions* in an IF . . . THEN statement. This program has the computer perform simple numerical operations like a calculator.

Program 2

Statement

```
10  INPUT "TYPE TWO NUMBERS (—999, —999 TO QUIT):  "; X, Y
15  IF X=—999 THEN GOTO 70
20  INPUT "TYPE AN OPERATION ( + OR * ):  "; OP$
30  IF OP$ = " * " THEN LET Z=X * Y: PRINT "THE PRODUCT IS:  "; Z: GOTO 10
40  IF OP$ = " + " THEN LET Z=X + Y: PRINT "THE SUM IS:  "; Z: GOTO 10
50  PRINT "SORRY, THAT OPERATION IS NOT ALLOWED."
60  GOTO 10
70  END
```

Output

```
TYPE TWO NUMBERS (—999, —999 TO QUIT):  ? 20, 30
TYPE AN OPERATION (+ OR * ):  ? +
THE SUM IS:  50
TYPE TWO NUMBERS (—999, —999 TO QUIT):  ? —999, —999
```

The IF . . . THEN statements in lines 30 and 40 contain three actions. If a user types two numbers, say 20 and 30 as shown above, and + for the operation, then in line 40 all three actions will be executed: the computer will assign 50 to Z, PRINT a message along with the value of Z, and loop back to line 10. The user can then type two more numbers.

The final program in this section INPUTs the X- and Y-coordinates of a point on the graphics screen. The program then plots a single point if X < 10, two points if X ≥ 10 and X < 20, and three points if X ≥ 20 and X < 30.

Program 3

Statement

```
10 REM * MORE PLOTTING
20 INPUT "TYPE X, Y COORDINATES:  "; X, Y
 .  (Instructions to clear the screen
 .     and do graphics on your
 .     computer. See Section 2-5, page 45.)
60 IF (X < 10) THEN plot the point X, Y: GOTO 90
70 IF (X < 20) THEN plot the point X, Y: plot the point X, Y + 1: GOTO 90
80 IF (X < 30) THEN plot the point X, Y: plot the point X, Y + 1: plot the point X, Y + 2
90 END
```

Output

```
TYPE X, Y COORDINATES:  ? 15, 12
```

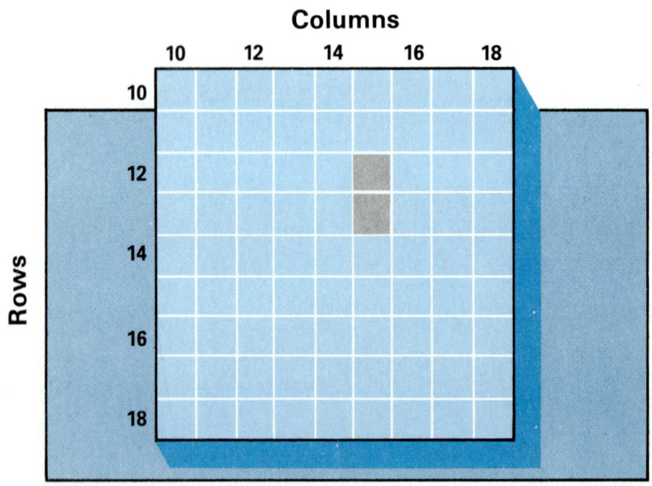

(*Note:* On *IBM* and *TRS-80* computers, change line 90 to 90 GOTO 90. This change will prevent the cursor and OK or READY prompts from interfering with the plotted points. The program will then have to be stopped manually.)

Notice that in line 70 it was not necessary to write

```
IF (X >= 10) AND (X < 20) THEN ...
```

because the computer can never reach line 70 if X is less than 10 — line 60 guarantees that a GOTO 90 instruction will be executed in that case.

Avoiding Pitfalls

1. Multiple actions in an IF . . . THEN statement must be separated by colons. If the colons are left out, or if punctuation other than a colon is used, errors will occur.
2. Multiple actions in an IF . . . THEN statement can lead to errors if you forget that the actions in the line are executed *only* if the condition is *true.*

Summary

Multiple actions in an IF . . . THEN statement have this form:

IF *condition* THEN *action 1: action 2: action 3: . . .*

All of the actions are executed if the condition is *true,* and *none* of them is executed if the condition is *false.*

Exercises 4-6

A 1. Tell whether each of the following is a valid BASIC statement. Give a possible correction for any errors that you find.

a.
```
IF (X > 3) THEN PRINT X: PRINT "CRAZY"
```
b.
```
IF (X <= 3) OR (X > 5) THEN PRINT X: "IS WILD.": GOTO 46
```
c.
```
IF (X <= -3) OR (X > 5) THEN PRINT "WHY NOT?"; GOTO 48
```
d.
```
IF A$ = "YES" THEN PRINT A$: READ A$: PRINT A$
```
e.
```
IF X=3 THEN PRINT "WOW!" PRINT "FIRST ODD PRIME"
```

2. Predict the output of each of the following programs.

a.
```
10  LET X=2
20  IF X < 3 THEN PRINT X: LET X=X+2
30  PRINT X-1
40  END
```
b.
```
10  READ A$
20  IF A$ < "PERFUME" THEN PRINT A$: PRINT "SMELL" : GOTO 10
30  DATA ONIONS
35  DATA GARLIC CLOVES
40  DATA ROSES
50  END
```

c.
```
10 LET X = 5
20 IF X < 7 THEN PRINT X: PRINT X + 1: LET X = X + 2: GOTO 40
30 GOTO 50
40 PRINT "FINAL VALUE IS:  "; X
50 END
```

d.
```
10 LET A$ = "GONE"
20 IF A$ < "WIND" THEN LET B$ = "WITH": GOTO 40
30 LET B$ = "THE"
40 PRINT A$; "  "; B$
50 END
```

e.
```
10 READ X
20 IF X = 1 THEN PRINT "UNO": GOTO 10
30 IF X = 2 THEN PRINT "DOS": GOTO 10
40 PRINT "NOT ENOUGH FINGERS"
50 DATA 1, 2, 2, 5, 1
60 END
```

f.
```
10 READ X
20 IF X < 5 THEN PRINT X: GOTO 10
30 IF X <> 5 THEN GOTO 10
40 DATA 3, 8, 7, 5, -2, 19
50 END
```

3. Construct a RUN chart for each of the following programs.

a.
```
10 LET ZZ$ = "UNDO"
20 IF ZZ$ = "NE" THEN PRINT "UNDO"; ZZ$: PRINT "THAT'S ALL": GOTO 50
30 PRINT ZZ$: LET ZZ$ = "NE"
40 GOTO 20
50 END
```

b.
```
10 READ A$
20 IF A$ = "FINISH" THEN PRINT "GOODBYE": GOTO 100
30 IF A$ < "BETAFISH" THEN PRINT A$: READ A$
40 GOTO 10
50 DATA APE, ZORE, GLOC, FINISH, STUFF
100 END
```

c.
```
10 LET X = 5
20 IF X < 2 THEN PRINT X + 1: GOTO 50
30 LET X = X - 1
40 IF X = 0 THEN GOTO 70
```

```
50 IF X < 2 THEN PRINT X
60 GOTO 30
70 END
```

4. For each pair of programs below, determine whether they will both have the same output for every possible INPUT. If not, give an example of an INPUT value that will cause the two programs to have different output.

a.

```
10 INPUT X
20 IF X < 5 THEN PRINT X: GOTO 40
30 IF X > 9 THEN PRINT X
40 END
```

```
10 INPUT X
20 IF X < 5 THEN PRINT X
25 GOTO 40
30 IF X > 9 THEN PRINT X
40 END
```

b.

```
10 INPUT S$
20 IF S$ < "MMM" THEN PRINT S$; S$: LET S$ = "XXX"
30 PRINT S$
40 END
```

```
10 INPUT S$
20 IF S$ < "MMM" THEN PRINT S$; S$
25 LET S$ = "XXX"
30 PRINT S$
40 END
```

c.

```
10 INPUT A, B
20 IF (A < B) OR (B < 6) THEN PRINT "GOT IT": LET A = B: GOTO 40
30 PRINT "NO WAY"
40 PRINT A, B
50 END
```

```
10 INPUT A, B
20 IF (A < B) OR (B < 6) THEN GOTO 35
30 PRINT "NO WAY"
32 GOTO 40
35 PRINT "GOT IT"
37 LET A = B
40 PRINT A, B
50 END
```

5. a. In Program 1, delete ": GOTO 60 " from lines 30 and 40. Then predict the output for each of these three INPUTs:

   ROMEO, JULIET, MARGIE

   b. Predict the output if ": GOTO 60" is deleted only from line 30. (Use the same INPUTs as in (a).)

6. Change Program 2 so that a user can choose to do division and subtraction as well as multiplication and addition.

7. Change Program 3 so that it continues plotting points until a suitable trailer value is typed. Also, add error trapping to reject INPUT X- and Y-coordinates that are off your graphics screen.

8. Rewrite each of the following programs using IF . . . THEN statements with multiple actions.

   a.

```
10  INPUT "HOW MANY DOGS DO YOU HAVE?  "; NDOGS
20  IF NDOGS = 0 THEN GOTO 100
30  IF NDOGS = 1 THEN GOTO 150
40  IF NDOGS = 2 THEN GOTO 200
50  PRINT "THAT'S A LOT OF DOGS."
60  PRINT "WHERE DO YOU KEEP THEM?"
70  GOTO 300
100  PRINT "TOO BAD, ANY CATS?"
110  GOTO 300
150  PRINT "THAT'S NICE."
160  GOTO 300
200  PRINT "WELL, WELL"
300  END
```

   b.

```
10  INPUT "FAVORITE ANIMAL:  "; ANML$
20  IF ANML$ <> "SKUNK" THEN GOTO 60
30  PRINT "PRETTY STINKY!"
40  PRINT "I WON'T HAVE IT IN MY PROGRAM."
50  GOTO 10
60  IF ANML$ <> "GRIZZLY" THEN GOTO 100
70  PRINT "PRETTY FIERCE!"
80  PRINT "I CAN'T BEAR TO THINK OF IT."
90  GOTO 10
100  PRINT "THAT ANIMAL IS OKAY, I GUESS,"
110  PRINT "BUT I PREFER SPINY ANTEATERS!"
115  PRINT "WEIRD"
120  END
```

9. Rewrite the following program *without* using multiple actions in the IF . . . THEN statements.

```
10  INPUT "HOW OLD ARE YOU:   "; AGE
20  IF AGE < 16 THEN PRINT "TOO YOUNG TO DRIVE": GOTO 50
30  IF AGE = 16 THEN PRINT "YOU'LL BE DRIVING SOON, I GUESS": GOTO 50
40  PRINT "WATCH OUT FOR HIDDEN DRIVEWAYS!"
50  END
```

B 10. Write a program that INPUTs a user's age (to the nearest year), then PRINTs how many years the user must wait before obtaining a driver's permit. Assume the legal age is 16. If the user is already old enough, PRINT the message OK TO APPLY.

11. Write a program that simulates a conversation (see Exercise 9, page 152, for an example that can now be written much more efficiently) of a teacher discussing with a student the quality of his or her work. The teacher should ask questions having simple answers, and respond in different ways to different answers.

12. Write a program that simulates a conversation of a manager at a restaurant interviewing you for a part-time job. (See Exercise 9, page 152.)

13. (Graphics) Write (or rewrite — see Exercise 15, page 161) a program to draw your initials in graphics mode starting at any position on the screen a user specifies. Use an INPUT statement to get the starting point (A, B), and error trapping to reject values of A and B that will make any part of your initials go off the screen. Use DATA statements to give the X- and Y-coordinates of the points to be plotted and a trailer value to signal the end of the list. (*Hint:* The values in the DATA statements should not be the actual coordinates of the points; they should be the coordinates relative to the starting point (A, B), INPUT from the user.)

14. (Graphics) Write a program that will draw either an X-shaped figure or a Y-shaped figure on the graphics screen. INPUT a string or number that the program can use to determine which shape a user wants to draw. Then INPUT the coordinates (I, J) of the center point, as shown below:

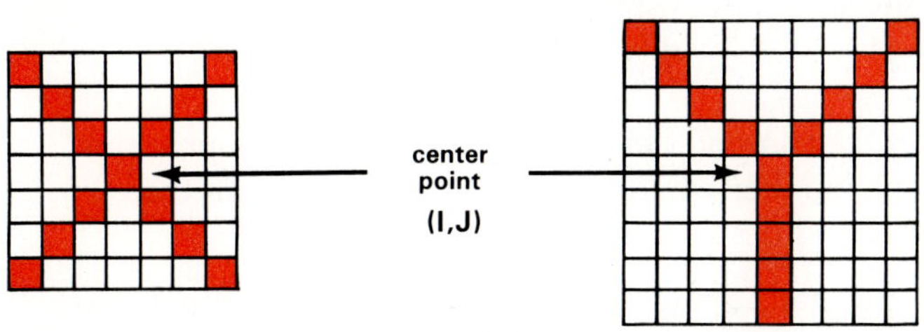

Add a trailer value and use error trapping to reject INPUT values of I and J that will make any part of either figure go off the screen.

Lab Activity

Debugging Techniques: STOP and TRACE

The process of finding errors *(bugs)* in programs and correcting them is called *debugging.* If you have written a program that does not work correctly, first read the LISTing carefully, one line at a time, to see if you can find where you made the mistake(s). Construct a RUN chart, being careful not to skip any steps — this process will often reveal your errors.

Another very useful debugging technique is to insert extra PRINT statements into the program to keep track of the changing values of the variables. For example, the following program is supposed to count to 20, but when it is RUN, nothing seems to happen.

```
10  LET C = 0
20  LET C = C + 1
30  GOTO 10
40  IF C = 20 THEN PRINT "DONE"
50  END
```

Problems

1. Type and RUN the program. Interrupt it manually.
2. Probably you can see what is wrong with the program as it is written. Insert the line

   ```
   25  PRINT "C =   "; C
   ```

   to display the value of the variable each time line 20 is executed. RUN the new version and describe the output.
3. To avoid the repetitious output in Problem 2, insert this line:

   ```
   27 STOP
   ```

   This instruction causes the computer to halt the execution of the program and to give you the line number where the STOP occurred (27 in this case). RUN the program and describe the output.
4. When a STOP instruction halts a program, you can cause the computer to resume execution of the program from the line where it left off by typing CONT (which is an abbreviation of CONTinue). RUN the program and try using CONT.

While a program is STOPped, you can type immediate mode commands to examine current values of the variables (using PRINT), to assign new values (using LET), or to do other calculations. As long as you do not make changes to any line in the program, CONT will cause the program to continue; any changes you make in the values of variables while the program is STOPped will be incorporated.

5. RUN the program again. Try typing LET C = 5, then type CONT. Why is the value of C still equal to 1? The problem, of course, is that line 30 sends the computer back to line 10, which assigns the value 0 to C each time through the loop.

6. Change line 30 to the following:

```
30 GOTO 20
```

RUN the program and try CONT now. What happens? Type RUN, then CONT several times, to verify that the value of C is increasing each time. While the program is STOPped, type

```
LET C = -8,
```

then CONT. Does the output reflect the change you made in the value of C?

7. Another powerful debugging tool is TRACE (on *Apple* computers) or TRON (on *IBM* and *TRS-80* computers). Delete the STOP line from the program, then type TRACE or TRON, and then RUN. Interrupt the program manually after a short time. What you see on the screen is a list of the line numbers of the program in the order they were executed by the computer. Compare this list with the program itself (LIST the current version) to see that the order of execution is what you expect. To turn tracing off, type NOTRACE (*Apple*) or TROFF (*IBM* and *TRS-80*). Now RUN will work the way it normally does.

8. As written, the program never ENDs because the variable C is never compared with the number 20; that is, the computer never gets to line 40. (Look at your TRACE output to make sure.) Change the program to the following version:

```
10 LET C=0
20 LET C=C+1
25 PRINT "C=  "; C
40 IF C=20 THEN PRINT "DONE"
45 GOTO 20
50 END
```

Run the program again. The program still has a bug; it does not stop counting when C arrives at the value 20. Correct this error so the program works properly.

Chapter Summary

The *top-down approach* to designing a program consists of the following steps:

1. Deciding on the exact form of *inputs* and *outputs,* including variable names.
2. Outlining the *algorithm,* that is, the steps to be followed by the program.
3. Completing all the *details* in each step of the algorithm.
4. *Coding* the detailed algorithm into BASIC.
5. *Testing* and *debugging* the program.

An IF . . . THEN statement has this form:

IF *condition* THEN *action*

If the condition is *true,* then the action is performed, and the computer goes to the next line (unless the action is a GOTO instruction). If the condition is *false,* then the action is not performed and the computer goes directly to the next line in the program.

Error trapping in a program is the use of IF . . . THEN statements to reject any INPUT values that are unwanted.

A$ = B$ is true if the strings assigned to A$ and B$ are identical (same length, same characters, and same order); otherwise, A$ <> B$ is true.

A$ < B$ is true if the string assigned to A$ comes before the string assigned to B$ in alphabetical order. Each of the conditions A$ > B$, A$ > = B$, and A$ < = B$ is defined similarly.

A *trailer value* is a special string or number that signals the end of a DATA list or the end of a sequence of INPUTS.

In the statement IF *(condition 1)* AND *(condition 2)* THEN . . . , the complex condition is true only if *both* condition 1 and condition 2 are true.

In the statement IF *(condition 1)* OR *(condition 2)* THEN . . . , the complex condition is true if *either* condition is true (or both are true).

In the statement IF NOT *(condition 1)* THEN . . . , the condition NOT *(condition 1)* will be true if condition 1 is false.

Multiple actions in an IF . . . THEN statement have this form:

IF *condition* THEN *action 1:action 2:action 3:* . . .

All of the actions are executed if the condition is *true,* and *none* of them is executed if the condition is *false.*

Chapter Test

1. Add error trapping to the program below to reject INPUT values of J for which there is no message.

```
10  INPUT "TYPE A NUMBER FROM 1 TO 3:  "; J
20  IF J = 1 THEN PRINT "YOU PICKED ONE."
30  IF J = 2 THEN PRINT "YOU CHOSE TWO."
40  IF J = 3 THEN PRINT "WHY DID YOU CHOOSE THREE?"
50  END
```

2. Predict the output of the following program.

```
10  READ A$, B$
20  IF A$ < B$ THEN PRINT "SQUASH"
30  IF B$ < "S" THEN GOTO 60
40  PRINT B$; A$
50  DATA SUMMER, YELLOW
60  END
```

3. Write a program that calculates a week's salary for an automobile mechanic who earns \$9 per hour for the first 40 hours (or less) and \$13.50 per hour (overtime) after that. Have the program INPUT the number of hours worked, then PRINT the week's salary.

4. Write a program that INPUTs a number, then PRINTs the message LESS THAN if the number is less than 100, BIGGER THAN if the number is over 100, and EQUAL if the number is 100.

5. Write a program that READs the seven days of the week from a DATA list. Have the program PRINT the message WEEKEND if the day READ is SATURDAY or SUNDAY. Otherwise, PRINT the message WEEKDAY. Use XXX for the trailer value and PRINT the message DAYS OF THE WEEK after all the values in the DATA list have been READ.

6. (Graphics) Write a program that INPUTs the X- and Y-coordinates of a point on the graphics screen, then draws the square shown in the diagram at the right. Add error trapping so that the program rejects INPUT values of X and Y that will cause any part of the square to go off the screen.

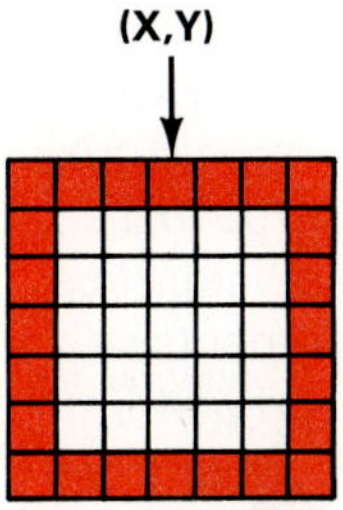

Computer Applications

Computers in Sports

Strike Three!

It's the bottom of the ninth, the bases are loaded, and there is a 3-ball and 2-strike count on the batter. The manager signals the umpire to call time, but instead of walking to the pitcher's mound, the manager types the name of the batter into a microcomputer. On the screen, the computer prints the weaknesses of the batter. The manager notices that the batter will usually swing at a high inside fastball in this situation. The manager signals this information to the catcher, and the pitcher delivers the pitch to the correct location. As predicted by past performance, the batter swings and misses, and the game is over. This may seem like a futuristic scene, but nowadays the use of computers by professional baseball teams is almost commonplace. Computers are also being used today by other professional teams, college teams, individual performers, and by candidates for the U.S. Olympic teams as well.

Uses of Computers

How are computers being used today by sports teams? Most apply them in the following ways: to correlate data on potential new players, to store scouting reports and personnel records, to keep players' statistics, and to monitor improvements in players' conditioning and performance. Another way computers can be used was demonstrated recently by one of the major league baseball teams. When the 1982 season was over, each player's past performance data was run through a computer. After interpreting the results, the team management decided to move the location of home plate forward eight feet. The computer had indicated that with the team's current personnel, this move would give them more of an advantage than the opposition in producing home runs.

Professional football teams are using computers to find "sleepers" in the draft of college players, to devise new formations and plays, to find weaknesses in opposing teams defenses, and to monitor each player's physical condition.

Individual athletes have recently begun to use the computer to analyze performance and suggest improved training techniques. For example, the computer can devise specific exercises keyed to an individual athlete's muscular system. The computer can also monitor diet and heart rates so that athletes such as bicyclists, marathon runners, and swimmers may know their ideal weight and how to pace themselves properly during tests of endurance.

Computers are used extensively at the U.S. Olympic Training Center in Colorado Springs to help athletes get into

Computer monitoring breathing of athlete on a treadmill

condition, train properly, and maximize performance. Many of the Olympic events require speed, power, and endurance, all of which involve strength. At the training center, strength is measured by having an athlete push hard against a resistance device. Data about the force of the exertion is then fed into a computer. The computer analyzes the data and provides an accurate picture of the athlete's muscular strengths and weaknesses. With this information, the athlete and trainer can devise training techniques to tone up weak areas. The computer is also used to analyze the athlete's ability to use oxygen efficiently, and thus improve aerobic fitness.

Biomechanics

The Olympic Training Center uses computer graphics to study the actual movements that an athlete makes in performing a sport. The study of an athlete's movements is called *biomechanics*. To analyze an athlete's form, a film or videotape is made of the athlete in action. The image is displayed on a screen and information about the position of various body points is fed into the computer. The computer then produces a replica stick-figure of the athlete in motion.

By examining the stick-figure, athletes and coaches can analyze the form and make slight adjustments that may trim seconds from a marathoner's running time, add inches to a high jumper's ability, or dramatically improve a gymnast's techniques. The computers at the center are also being used to redesign athletic equipment for better safety and durability.

The advancement of modern computers has had a great impact in nearly all sports. Not only can today's computers improve an athlete's performance, but they can also improve the organization of a team. As a result, computers may be called the "assistant coaches" of the future.

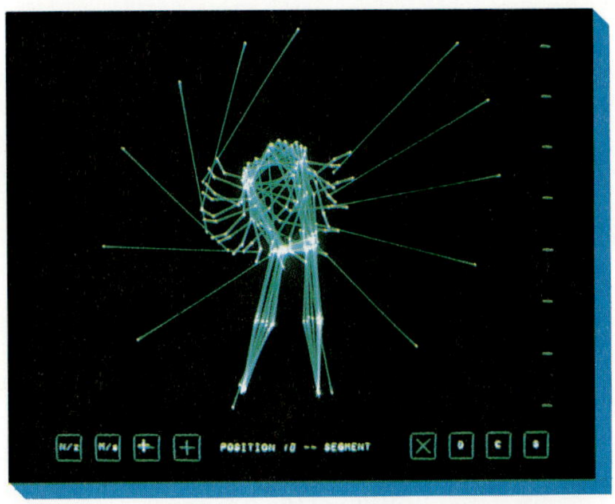

Computer graphics stick-figure showing movements of a golfer's swing

Charles Moore had a goal to make himself a more productive programmer. During the 1960's he developed his own personal programming tool to help himself accomplish that goal. This tool was the programming language Forth. Moore had worked with computers of the 1960's and hoped that his language would come *forth* as one widely-used with computers of the 1970's. For this reason, along with the fact that his system would allow name identifiers of no more than five letters, he named his language Forth — a name with five letters.

In the early 1970's, Moore wrote a Forth program to control the movements of the thirty-six foot radio telescope at Kitt Peak National Observatory in Arizona. As a result of the work, astronomers were the first group to enthusiastically promote this new language. By the mid-1970's, Forth user groups had formed in the United States and in Europe. International standards for the language were developed in 1979 and the Forth-79 standards have been incorporated into the more recent versions of Forth.

Kitt Peak Observatory

The language Forth relies heavily on the use of a *stack* and *reverse notation.* A *stack* is an area of computer memory organized like a stack of cafeteria trays, so that the first item put on the stack is the last one removed. In *reverse notation,* the mathematical or logical operation symbols follow the numbers to which they apply. For instance, the expression $7 + 3 \times 5$ would be written this way:

```
3 5 * 7 + .
```

Here are the steps the computer follows in doing Forth computations:

Step 1 When the computer needs a number, it "pushes" that number onto the top of the stack.

Step 2 When it reads an operation symbol like * or +, it "pops" the top two numbers off the stack.

Step 3 It then performs the operation and "pushes" the result back onto the top of the stack.

Therefore, the Forth expression 3 5 * 7 + results in the number 22 on top. Forth just 'pushes' and 'pops' numbers from the stack as needed. The stack actually resides in the computer's random-access memory (RAM), where data can be manipulated easily using calls.

The programmer must keep track of where items are on the stack. Needless to say, a beginning programmer can have a difficult time learning Forth; however, an experienced programmer usually likes the power, speed, and creativity possible with Forth.

Even beyond basic computation, the syntax of Forth can be rather involved and obscure-looking. Here is an example of a definition (statement) in Forth:

```
: ? @ . ;
```

A definition in Forth, which can be a complete program, begins with a colon and ends with a semicolon. The colon indicates the beginning of a definition (or program) and the semicolon the end. Some Forth programs seem very similar to those written in other programming languages. The following program, for example, averages three numbers:

```
: AVERAGE CR
." Enter the first number and press return " #IN CR
." Enter the second number " #IN CR
." Enter the third number " #IN CR
." Your numbers are " OVER OVER OVER . . . CR
." The average is " + 3 / , ;
```

Forth has been customized to meet the needs of a wide variety of applications. It has been used around the world for tasks involving astronomical telescopes and observations, where real-time control tasks are a necessity. It has also been used for controlling portable heart monitors, running remote cameras, graphics applications, electronic filing, database management, word processing, and a variety of complex financial calculations, as well as other real-time control tasks.

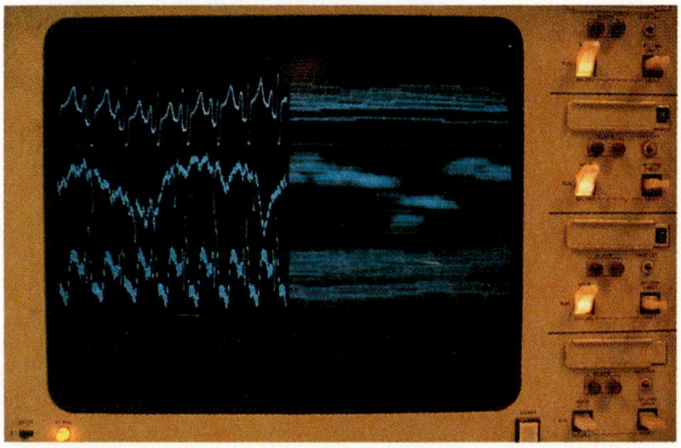

Computerized heart monitoring is often controlled by programs written in Forth.

CHAPTER

5 Looping

Robots are becoming commonplace in a number of fields, including entertainment, medicine, tool and die casting, and the automotive and steel industries.

Introduction

If you have simple calculations to do, it is usually easier to use a calculator or immediate mode commands on your computer than it is to write a program. Similarly, most people find it easier to write down a single name and phone number than to write a program to record such information. Computers become overwhelmingly useful when simple tasks are repeated over and over, for example, when many calculations must be made, or when a great deal of information must be handled. In this chapter, you will learn how to make computers repeat calculations and other processes in controlled ways.

5-1 Finite Loops: Counters and GOTO

Using the GOTO statement, you can easily write programs that repeat an action or sequence of actions over and over again — programs that *loop*. For example, the following program PRINTs a tongue twister repeatedly.

Program 1

Statement

```
10 PRINT "TONGUE TWISTER"
20 READ A$
30 PRINT A$
40 GOTO 30
50 DATA RUBBER BABY BUGGY BUMPERS
60 END
```

Output

```
TONGUE TWISTER
RUBBER BABY BUGGY BUMPERS
RUBBER BABY BUGGY BUMPERS
RUBBER BABY BUGGY BUMPERS
.
.
.
```

The loop in Program 1 is *infinite* (it never ends unless you stop it manually). How can we make a *finite* loop (one that comes to an end by itself)? Suppose, for example, that we want the program to PRINT the string in line 50 only five times, and then END? This could be accomplished without a loop by repeating the statement PRINT A$ five times in the program, but that is not a very practical idea. It would not work very well if we wanted 1000 repetitions, for example.

A more general solution is to use a *counter* that is increased each time the computer goes through the loop. Then, instead of a simple GOTO at the end of the loop, we can use an IF . . . THEN GOTO . . . , repeating the loop only as long as the comparison used to test the counter remains true. Program 2 uses this method to PRINT the tongue twister in line 80 exactly 4 times.

Program 2

Statement	Remark
10 PRINT "TONGUE TWISTER, PART 2"	
20 READ A$	
30 LET I=1	*Give the counter its initial value.*
40 PRINT A$	*Body of the loop.*
50 LET I=I+1	*Increment the counter.*
60 IF I<=4 THEN GOTO 40	*Test the counter.*
70 PRINT "SEE — NO MISTAKES"	*Smart Aleck.*
80 DATA PETER PIPER PICKED A PECK OF PICKLED PEPPERS	
90 END	

Output

```
TONGUE TWISTER, PART 2
PETER PIPER PICKED A PECK OF PICKLED PEPPERS
PETER PIPER PICKED A PECK OF PICKLED PEPPERS
PETER PIPER PICKED A PECK OF PICKLED PEPPERS
PETER PIPER PICKED A PECK OF PICKLED PEPPERS
SEE — NO MISTAKES
```

Note the remark for line 40. By *body of the loop* we mean all the instructions we want repeated. In line 50, where 1 is added to the counter I, we say that I is *incremented* by 1. Line 60 causes the computer to repeat the PRINTing and incrementing until I = 5, at which point the loop ends and the message in line 70 is PRINTed.

Program 2 can be written other ways. For example, the variable I can start with the value 0 and end with 3, or the statements in lines 40 and 50 can be interchanged using these new first and last counter values. Fundamentally, however, a finite loop such as the one in Program 2 has this form:

Step 1 Initialize counter (give it a starting value).
Step 2 Body of the loop (all the instructions to be repeated).
Step 3 Increment counter (add 1 or some other number).
Step 4 Test counter (GOTO start of body of loop if a certain condition is true).

Note that the incrementing of the counter in Step 3 is considered to be a separate step, and not part of the body of the loop.

Program 3 is another example of a finite loop that uses a counter. It PRINTs all the odd numbers from 1 to 101.

Program 3

Statement	Remark
10 PRINT "ODD NUMBERS"	
20 LET NUM = 1	*Initialize the counter.*
30 PRINT NUM	*Body of the loop.*
40 LET NUM = NUM + 2	*Increment the counter.*
50 IF NUM <= 101 THEN GOTO 30	*Test the counter.*
60 END	

Output

```
ODD NUMBERS
1
3
5
.
.
.
101
```

One difference between this program and Program 2 is that the counter is incremented by 2 each time through the loop (why?). Line 50 causes the computer to repeat the PRINTing and incrementing until NUM = 103, at which point the loop is exited and the program ENDs.

The final example of this section is a program in which the computer increment is negative. (A negative increment is sometimes called a *decrement*.)

Program 4

Statement	Remark
10 PRINT "COUNTDOWN"	
20 LET SEC = 10	*Initialize the counter.*
30 PRINT SEC	*Body of the loop.*
40 LET SEC = SEC − 1	*Increment the counter.*

Program continued on next page.

```
50  IF SEC >= 0 THEN GOTO 30
60  PRINT
70  PRINT "BLAST OFF!!"
80  END
```

Test the counter.

Output

```
COUNTDOWN
10
9
8
.
.
.
0
BLAST OFF!!
```

In line 50 the test of the counter uses the >= symbol, which is the reverse of the inequality symbol in line 50 of Program 3. Since SEC is *decreasing,* we want to repeat the loop as long as SEC remains nonnegative.

Avoiding Pitfalls

In using counters, it is sometimes difficult to determine what the first and last values should be. Be sure that the *initial* counter value is the first number you want, and that the test at the end of the loop uses a comparison that repeats the loop the desired number of times. Go through the loop by hand (use a RUN chart if necessary), paying particular attention to the first and last counter values.

Summary

A *standard finite loop* using GOTO and a counter has this form:

Step 1	*Initialize* the counter.	(LET I = *initial value*)
Step 2	Body of the loop.	(PRINT . . . LET . . . READ . . . . . .)
Step 3	*Increment* the counter.	(LET I = I + *increment*)
Step 4	*Test* the counter.	(If I <= *final value* THEN GOTO Step 2)

(*Note:* If the increment is negative, then the counter test uses ">=.")

Exercises 5-1

In Exercises 1–6, do each of the following:

- **a.** Identify the counter.
- **b.** State the line where the counter is initialized.
- **c.** State the line(s) in the body of the loop.
- **d.** State the line where the counter is incremented.
- **e.** State the line where the counter is tested.
- **f.** Predict the output.

A

1.
```
10 LET I=1
20 PRINT "JOSEPHINE"
30 LET I=I+1
40 IF I<=5 THEN GOTO 20
50 END
```

2.
```
10 LET I=0
20 PRINT "NAPOLEON"
30 LET I=I+1
40 IF I<=4 THEN GOTO 20
50 END
```

3.
```
10 LET J=-3
20 PRINT J+2
30 PRINT "ABC"
40 LET J=J+1
50 IF J<=1 THEN GOTO 20
60 END
```

4.
```
10 LET K=0
20 PRINT K
30 PRINT "CBA"
40 LET K=K-1
50 IF K>=-4 THEN GOTO 20
60 END
```

5.
```
10 LET PE=2
20 PRINT PE, PE * PE
30 LET PE=PE+2
40 IF PE<8 THEN GOTO 20
50 END
```

6.
```
10 LET CRAZY=12
20 LET NUTS=CRAZY * 5-1
30 PRINT 2 * NUTS
40 LET CRAZY=CRAZY-1
50 IF CRAZY>9 THEN GOTO 20
60 END
```

7. The following program PRINTs your name 7 times:

```
10 INPUT "TYPE YOUR NAME, PLEASE:  "; NME$
20 LET N=1
30 PRINT NME$
40 LET N=N+1
50 IF N<=7 THEN GOTO 30
60 END
```

Change the program to do each of the following:

- **a.** PRINT your name 12 times.
- **b.** PRINT your name 78 times.
- **c.** INPUT the number of times you want to PRINT your name.
- **d.** READ your name and the number of repetitions you want from a DATA line.

8. Change Program 2 to do each of the following:
   a. PRINT the given tongue twister 40 times.
   b. INPUT the particular tongue twister you want to PRINT and the number of times you want to PRINT it.

9. Predict the output if line 40 of Program 1 is changed to: 40 GOTO 20.

10. Predict the output of Program 2 if the "<=" in line 60 is changed to each of the following:
   a. <
   b. >=

11. Change Program 3 to do each of the following:
   a. PRINT all the odd numbers from 1 to 223.
   b. PRINT all the odd numbers from 103 to 615.
   c. PRINT the squares of all the even numbers from 50 to 100.
   d. INPUT values for the variables FIRST and LAST, then PRINT all the odd numbers from FIRST to LAST. Have the program tell the user to type an odd number for FIRST.

12. Change Program 4 to PRINT the numbers from:
   a. 100 down to 0
   b. 20 down to 2
   c. 20 down to 2 by decrements of two

13. Predict the output of Program 4 if the ">=" in line 50 is changed to each of the following:
   a. <
   b. >

14. Complete the RUN chart for each of the following programs.

a.
```
10 LET X=1
20 PRINT X
30 LET X=X+3
40 IF X<10 THEN GOTO 20
50 END
```

b.
```
10 LET X=13
20 PRINT X-6
30 LET X=X-2
40 IF X>7 THEN GOTO 20
50 PRINT X
60 END
```

LINE	CONDITION	X	OUTPUT
10		1	
20			1
30		4	
40	true		
⋮			

LINE	CONDITION	X	OUTPUT
10		13	
20			7
30		11	
40	true		
⋮			

15. Construct a RUN chart for each of the following programs.

a.
```
5  PRINT "RUN CHART 1"
10 LET A = 1
20 PRINT A, 2 * A - 1
30 LET A = A + 1
40 IF A <= 3 THEN GOTO 20
50 END
```

b.
```
5  PRINT "RUN CHART 2"
10 LET A = 1
20 IF A > 3 THEN GOTO 60
30 PRINT A, 2 * A - 1
40 LET A = A + 1
50 GOTO 20
60 END
```

c.
```
5  PRINT "RUN CHART 3"
10 LET I = 2
20 PRINT I - 1
30 LET I = I * I
40 IF I < 12 THEN GOTO 20
50 END
```

d.
```
5  PRINT "RUN CHART 4"
10 LET I = 2
20 LET I = I + 2
30 PRINT I - 1
40 IF I < 10 THEN GOTO 20
50 END
```

B **16.** There are structures for finite loops other than that given in this section. They work just as well, although they tend to be more difficult to understand. Rewrite each of the following programs using the structure given in this section: *initialization, body, increment, test.*

a.
```
10 INPUT NUM
20 LET COUNT = 1
30 IF COUNT > NUM THEN GOTO 70
40 PRINT COUNT * NUM
50 LET COUNT = COUNT + 1
60 GOTO 30
70 PRINT "EASY"
80 END
```

(This program has the form: *initialization, test, body, increment.*)

b.
```
10 INPUT P
20 LET J = 27
30 LET J = J - 1
40 IF J < P THEN GOTO 70
50 PRINT J; "   PINATAS"
60 GOTO 30
70 PRINT "DIFFERENT"
80 END
```

(This program has the form: *initialization, increment, test, body.*)

c.
```
10 INPUT ZZ
20 LET Q=0
30 PRINT Q, Q * Q
40 IF Q > ZZ THEN GOTO 70
50 LET Q=Q+1
60 GOTO 30
70 END
```

(This program has the form: *initialization, body, test, increment.*)

17. Write a program using the finite loop structure given in this section to do each of the following:
a. PRINT the numbers from 1 to 50.
b. PRINT the odd numbers from 1 to 50.
c. PRINT the even numbers from 1 to 50.
d. PRINT the multiples of 5 from 5 to 50.

18. a. Write a program that uses a finite loop to PRINT exactly the following:

```
1. HELLO
2. HELLO
3. HELLO
GOODBYE
```

b. Change the program to INPUT the number of HELLO's to PRINT.

19. a. Write a program that uses a finite loop to PRINT exactly the following:

```
ONE
ONE
ONE
TWO
```

b. Change the program to PRINT the pattern infinitely many times.
c. Change the program to PRINT the pattern exactly 6 times.
d. *Challenge:* Change the program to INPUT the number of times to PRINT "ONE" in each pattern and also the number of times to repeat the entire pattern. (*Hint:* You need to use one finite loop within another finite loop in (b) and (c).)

20. Rewrite the telephone directory program (Program 2, Section 4–4, page 155) so that it does not use a trailer value to avoid the OUT OF DATA error message. Instead have the program READ, as the first item of DATA, the number of names on the list, then use a finite loop to READ all the names and phone numbers on the DATA list.

21. Write a program that will help you sketch an accurate graph of $y = x^3 - 2x + 4$. Have the program PRINT a table of y-values for the x-values $-2, -1.8, -1.6, \ldots, 2$.

Lab Activity

Graphing Patterns

Problems

1. Complete the following program by filling in the appropriate instructions for your computer.

```
10 (Instructions to clear the screen
20    and do graphics on your
.     computer.)
.
.
40 LET X=0
50 LET Y=0
60 (Instruction to plot the point at X, Y.)
70 LET X=X+1
80 IF X<=(the largest X-value on your screen) THEN GOTO 60
90 END
```

(*Note:* On *IBM* and *TRS-80* computers, change line 90 to 90 GOTO 90 to avoid having the prompt and cursor interfere with the output. The program will then have to be stopped manually.)

RUN the program. What figure does it draw?

2. Change the program so that it draws a horizontal line at Y = 20 (change line 50).

3. Change the program so that it draws a vertical line at the left side of the screen. (Change X to Y in lines 70 and 80 and change line 50 back to its original form.)

4. Change the program so that it draws a vertical line at the right side of the screen.

5. By incrementing *both* X and Y, you can draw a diagonal line. Make these changes in the original program:

```
75 LET Y=Y+1
80 IF (X<=____) AND (Y<=____) THEN GOTO 60
```

(Fill in the blanks in line 80 with the largest X- and Y-values on your screen.)

6. Draw a steeper line than in Problem 5 by changing the Y-increment in line 75.

7. Change the program so that it draws a diagonal from the lower left corner to the upper right corner of your screen.

8. Rewrite the program in Problem 5 so that it INPUTs the value of a variable START, which is the starting position of a diagonal line at the left side of the screen. (Line 40 remains the same, but change line 50 as follows: 50 LET Y = START.) RUN the program and draw several diagonals with different starting positions.

9. Change the program in Problem 8 so that START is not INPUT, but rather given an initial value 0. Then each time a diagonal is drawn, increase START by 2, until it reaches the largest Y-value on your screen. If your computer has color, try to change the color of the diagonals as they fill the screen.

5-2 Counting and Summing

Counters, used in the previous section to control finite loops, can also be used — as their name implies — to count things. For example, the following program counts the number of words on a DATA list. The string 999 is used as the trailer value.

Program 1

Statement	Remark
10 PRINT "COUNTING DATA"	
20 LET COUNT = 0	*Initialize the counter.*
30 READ A$	
40 IF A$ = "999" THEN GOTO 70	*Exit the loop.*
50 LET COUNT = COUNT + 1	*Increment the counter.*
60 GOTO 30	
70 PRINT "THERE ARE "; COUNT; " WORDS."	
80 DATA APE, APRICOT, ZOO, BIO, 999	
90 END	

Output

```
COUNTING DATA
THERE ARE 4 WORDS.
```

The trailer value 999 is not counted as a word on the DATA list because the exit from the loop occurs *before* the counter is incremented. (Why are the quotes necessary in line 40?) As is true of finite loops in general, counting loops such as the one in Program 1 can be written in many different ways. Some other possibilities are explored in the exercises.

As a variation of Program 1, the next example counts the number of times a user types in the word THE in a sequence of words. A period is used as the trailer value.

Program 2

Statement	Remark
10 PRINT "COUNTING THE'S"	
20 LET NUM = 0	*Initialize the counter.*
30 INPUT "TYPE A WORD: "; WRD$	
40 IF WRD$ = " . " THEN GOTO 70	*Exit the loop.*
50 IF WRD$ = "THE" THEN LET NUM = NUM + 1	*Increment the counter.*
60 GOTO 30	
70 PRINT "YOU USED 'THE' "; NUM; " TIMES."	
80 END	

Output

```
COUNTING THE'S
TYPE A WORD:  ? THE
TYPE A WORD:  ? AN
TYPE A WORD:  ? THE
TYPE A WORD:  ? .
YOU USED 'THE' 2 TIMES.
```

This program differs from Program 1 in that the counter in line 50 is incremented only part of the time — only when the word THE is INPUT. (Why do single quotes enclose THE in line 70 rather than the usual quotation marks?)

An important feature of computers is their ability to work with lists of numbers. Program 3, for example, adds the numbers on a DATA list. It uses a variable called a *summing variable,* or more simply, a *summer.* The number 0 is used as the trailer value.

Program 3

Statement	Remark
10 PRINT "SUMMING DATA"	
20 LET SUM = 0	*Initialize the summer.*
30 READ NUM	
40 IF NUM = 0 THEN GOTO 70	*Exit the loop.*
50 LET SUM = SUM + NUM	*Add to the summer.*

Program continued on next page.

```
60 GOTO 30
70 PRINT "SUM=  "; SUM
80 DATA 14, 78, 32, 0
90 END
```

The essential arithmetical step in the program is line 50, in which the current value of NUM, read from the DATA list, is added to the summer SUM. Study the following RUN chart to see how this summing is done each time the computer goes through the loop.

LINE	CONDITION	NUM	SUM	OUTPUT
10				SUMMING DATA
20			0	
30		14		
40	NUM = 0 is false			
50			(0 + 14) = 14	
30		78		
40	NUM = 0 is false			
50			(14 + 78) = 92	
30		32		
40	NUM = 0 is false			
50			(92 + 32) = 124	
30		0		
40	NUM = 0 is true			
70				SUM = 124

Avoiding Pitfalls

1. The most common error in writing counting and summing loops is to include the counter (or summer) initialization step in the loop, so that the counter (or summer) is set to its initial value every time through the loop. For example, in Program 2, it would be incorrect to have: 60 GOTO 20. The final value of NUM would be 0 if this line were in the program.

2. Another common error in writing counting and summing loops is to include the trailer value in the sum or to count it as a meaningful DATA value. For example, in Program 1, if the statements in lines 40 and 50 were interchanged, then 999 would be counted as a word on the DATA list.

Summary

A standard counting (or summing) loop using READ or INPUT has this form:

Step 1 *Initialize* the counter (or summer).

Step 2 READ or INPUT a *value* (string or number).

Step 3 If *value* = *trailer value,* then GOTO step 6 (exit the loop).

Step 4 *Increment* the counter (or add value to summer). This step may or may not be subject to some condition.

Step 5 GOTO Step 2.

Step 6 PRINT the results or do other necessary processing.

Exercises 5-2

A **1.** Predict the output of each of the following programs. If necessary construct a RUN chart.

a.
```
5  PRINT "COUNTING"
10 LET COUNT = 1
20 READ X$
30 IF X$ = "007" THEN GOTO 60
40 LET COUNT = COUNT + 1
50 GOTO 20
60 PRINT "THERE ARE  "; COUNT; "  WORDS."
70 DATA BOND, SECRET
75 DATA AGENT, 007
80 END
```

b.
```
5  PRINT "SUMMING"
10 LET SUM = 0
20 READ TEST
30 IF TEST = -1 THEN GOTO 60
40 LET SUM = SUM + TEST
50 GOTO 20
60 PRINT "AVERAGE =  "; SUM / 4
70 DATA 86, 74, 91, 70
75 DATA -1
80 END
```

c.
```
10 LET I=0
20 READ N
30 IF N=−7 THEN GOTO 80
40 LET I=I+N
50 PRINT N, I
60 GOTO 20
70 DATA 1, 3, −7
80 END
```

d.
```
10 LET P=1
20 READ N
30 IF N=0 THEN PRINT P: GOTO 70
40 LET P=P*N
50 GOTO 20
60 DATA 5, 7, −3, 0
70 END
```

e.
```
10 LET C=0
20 READ A$
30 IF A$="FINE" THEN PRINT
      "DONE": GOTO 60
40 LET C=C+1
50 GOTO 20
60 PRINT C
70 DATA TWO, ONE, FINE
80 END
```

f.
```
10 LET C=0
20 LET S=0
30 READ N
40 IF N<0 THEN GOTO 80
50 LET C=C+1
60 LET S=S+N
70 GOTO 30
80 PRINT "C= "; C, "S= "; S
90 DATA 7, 6, −1
100 END
```

g.
```
10 LET I=0
20 READ A$
30 LET I=I+1
40 PRINT I, A$
50 IF A$="ZAP" THEN GOTO 80
60 GOTO 20
70 DATA TURBID, −6, ZAP, FROG
80 END
```

h.
```
10 LET T=0
20 READ X
30 IF X<0 THEN GOTO 60
40 IF X=2 THEN LET T=T+1
50 GOTO 20
60 PRINT "TWO DOES NOT EQUAL "; T
70 DATA 3, 2, 1, 2, −1, 6
80 END
```

2. Predict the output of the following program for the INPUTs shown.

```
10 LET SUM=0
20 INPUT X
30 IF X=0 THEN GOTO 60
40 LET SUM=SUM+X
50 GOTO 20
60 PRINT "SUM= "; SUM
70 END
?80
?60
?70
?0
```

3. Predict the output of the following program for the INPUTs shown.

```
10 LET COUNT = 0
20 INPUT "WORD:  "; WRD$
30 IF WRD$ = "QUIT" THEN GOTO 60
40 LET COUNT = COUNT + 1
50 GOTO 20
60 PRINT "YOU TYPED  "; COUNT;
65 PRINT "  WORDS."
70 END
WORD:  ? FRONT
WORD:  ? BACK
WORD:  ? MIDDLE
WORD:  ? SIDE
WORD:  ? QUIT
```

4. Change Program 1 so that it counts the number of words INPUT from a user (continue to use 999 as the trailer value).

5. Predict the output of Program 2 if the statements in lines 20 and 30 are interchanged. (If necessary, construct a RUN chart.)

6. Change Program 2 so that the word to be counted is first INPUT from a user (be sure to change the message in line 70).

7. Change Program 2 so that it counts the number of AN's as well as the number of THE's.

8. Change Program 2 so that it counts the total number of words INPUT as well as the number of THE's. Have the program calculate and PRINT the percent of the total words that are the word THE.

$$(\text{percent} = \frac{\text{number of THE's}}{\text{total words}} * 100)$$

9. Change Program 2 so that the message in line 70 is grammatically correct when NUM = 1 (in this case, TIMES should be changed to the singular form).

10. Change Program 3 so that it counts how many numbers are on the DATA list as well as finds their sum. Have the program PRINT the average of the numbers.

11. Change Program 3 so that it calculates and PRINTs the average of all the numbers on the DATA list that are 30 or above.

12. Change Program 3 so that it PRINTs how many numbers on the DATA list are between 1 and 20, how many are between 21 and 40, between 41 and 80, and between 81 and 100.

13. a. Change Program 2 so that it counts the number of INPUT words that begin with the letter B. (*Hint:* Such words must be >= "B" and < what letter?)
    b. Modify the program in (a) to calculate and PRINT the percent of the total words INPUT that begin with the letter B.

14. Verify by constructing RUN charts that each of the following programs counts how many numbers over 100 are on the DATA list. Which program has the structure presented in this section?

    a.
```
10 LET COUNT=0
20 READ X
30 IF X=0 THEN GOTO 60
40 IF X>100 THEN LET COUNT=COUNT+1
50 GOTO 20
60 PRINT "ANSWER=  "; COUNT
70 DATA 20, 151, 75, 102, 0
80 END
```
    b.
```
10 LET COUNT=0
20 READ X
30 LET COUNT=COUNT+1
35 IF X=0 THEN GOTO 60
40 IF X<=100 THEN LET COUNT=COUNT-1
50 GOTO 20
60 PRINT "ANSWER=  "; COUNT-1
70 DATA 20, 151, 75, 102, 0
80 END
```
    c.
```
10 LET COUNT=-1
20 LET COUNT=COUNT+1
30 READ X
40 IF X=0 THEN GOTO 70
50 IF X<=100 THEN GOTO 30
60 GOTO 20
70 PRINT "ANSWER=  "; COUNT
80 DATA 20, 151, 75, 102, 0
90 END
```

15. Rewrite Program 1 using the following test in the condition in line 40:

```
40 IF A$<>"999" THEN . . .
```

(*Hint:* Use multiple actions in the IF . . . THEN statement in line 40.)

B **16.** Write a program that finds the sum of the squares of the numbers on a DATA list. Use 0 as the trailer value.

17. Write a program to find the product of the positive numbers on a DATA list. Use 0 as the trailer value. (*Hint:* What initial value is needed for the product?)

18. **a.** Write a program to find the sum of the integers from 1 to 100 without using a DATA list. (*Hint:* To get the integers, use a finite loop with a counter that goes from 1 to 100. In the body of the loop, add the counter to a summer.)
b. Modify the program in (a) so that it finds the sum from 1 to N, where N is a positive integer INPUT from a user.

19. Write a program without using a DATA list to do each of the following:
a. Count and PRINT the number of even integers from 54 to 104.
b. Count and PRINT the number of multiples of 3 from 3 to 39.
(*Hint:* Two counters are needed in (a) and (b).)

20. **a.** Write a program without using a DATA list to find the sum of the odd integers from 509 to 731.
b. Modify the program in (a) so that it also counts how many odd integers there are from 509 to 731.

21. Write a program to find the product of the integers from 1 to N, where N is a positive integer INPUT from a user.

Lab Activity

Round-Off Error

Suppose you add $\frac{1}{10}$ to itself 10 times. What should the sum be? Here is a program to verify that your answer is correct. It may also reveal a limitation of your computer.

```
10 INPUT "TYPE A NUMBER:  "; N
20 LET SUM = 0
30 LET I = 1
40 LET SUM = SUM + (1 / N)
50 LET I = I + 1
60 IF I <= N THEN GOTO 40
70 PRINT "RESULT:  "; SUM
80 END
```

Problems

1. Study the program to see that it adds $\frac{1}{N}$ to itself N times, so that the result should always be

$$N * \left(\frac{1}{N}\right) = 1.$$

RUN the program to see that the result is correct for N = 10.

2. RUN the program with N = 40. What is the result? On most microcomputers you will probably not get a SUM exactly equal to 1. The reason is that the computer retains only a certain number of decimal places when it does arithmetic. (You can see how many places by looking at the result for N = 40.) Results of arithmetic operations are necessarily rounded off, and therefore are not always exactly correct.

3. Use long division to find the decimal equivalent of $\frac{1}{40}$. How many places are there after the decimal point in the answer? Since your computer uses many more decimal places than that, it appears unlikely that any round-off error should occur when N = 40. However, as you may know from the Computer Language feature on page 64, the computer uses *binary* representation of numbers, and the binary representation of $\frac{1}{40}$ has a repeating pattern that must be rounded off so that the computer can handle it.

4. Use trial and error to find other numbers that give inaccurate results with the program. Find some numbers that give results greater than 1. What number can you find that gives the most inaccurate result? To obtain results more quickly, you may want to add this line:

```
75 GOTO 10
```

Another example of an arithmetic procedure that should give exact answers, but doesn't always on the computer, is the square root operation. In BASIC, the square root of X is denoted SQR(X). If you square the square root of a positive number, the result should be the number you started with. For example, $\sqrt{9} = 3$, and $3^2 = 9$. In BASIC then, we should have

```
SQR(X) ↑ 2 = X.
```

5. Write a program that will square the square root of any positive number that is INPUT. RUN the program. Is the result always exactly correct? What number can you find that gives the most inaccurate result? (Add a GOTO statement to obtain results more quickly.)

5-3 FOR . . . NEXT Loops

Consider a standard finite loop of the form:

```
        .
        .
        .
        100  LET I = 1
     ┌  110 ┐
     │   .  │
     │   .  ├   body of the loop
loop │   .  │
     │  290 ┘
     │  300  LET I = I + 1
     └  310  IF I <= 26 THEN GOTO 110
        320 ┐
         .  │
         .  ├   rest of program
         .  ┘
```

This loop is executed 26 times, as you learned in Section 5–1. Such loops are so common and useful in programming that BASIC has included special instructions — FOR and NEXT — for constructing them. In terms of these new instructions, the loop above may be written this way:

```
         .
         .
         .
      ┌  100  FOR I = 1 TO 26
      │  110 ┐
      │   .  │
loop* │   .  ├   body of the loop
      │   .  │
      │  290 ┘
      └  310  NEXT I
         320 ┐
          .  │
          .  ├   rest of program
          .  ┘
```

* In the examples in this book, FOR . . . NEXT loops are identified by brackets.

The purpose, then, of the FOR statement at the beginning of the loop is to name the counter and give its initial and final values. The NEXT statement indicates the end of the loop, increments the counter, and then tests the counter. If the counter is less than or equal to 26 in line 310, then the program goes to the statement immediately following the FOR statement (line 110 in the example). If the counter is greater than 26 in line 310, then the loop ends and the program continues on to the line following the NEXT statement (line 320 in the example).

Note: Some computers test the counter at the FOR line rather than the NEXT line, but that makes no real difference at this point. We will assume in this book that the test is done at the NEXT line, since it is likely your computer works this way.

To illustrate FOR . . . NEXT loops, here is the tongue twister program again (see Program 2, page 194). Study the old program and the new version below to see how the finite loop has been translated into FOR . . . NEXT form. Notice, in particular, that the NEXT statement *both* increments and tests the counter.

Program 1

Statement	Remark
10 PRINT "TONGUE TWISTER, PART 3"	
20 READ A$	
30 FOR I = 1 TO 4	*Name the counter, give its initial and final values.*
40 PRINT A$	*Body of the loop.*
50 NEXT I	*Increment and test the counter.*
80 DATA SHE SELLS SEA SHELLS BY THE SEA SHORE	
90 END	

Output

```
TONGUE TWISTER, PART 3
SHE SELLS SEA SHELLS BY THE SEA SHORE
SHE SELLS SEA SHELLS BY THE SEA SHORE
SHE SELLS SEA SHELLS BY THE SEA SHORE
SHE SELLS SEA SHELLS BY THE SEA SHORE
```

As another simple example, suppose you want to PRINT the numbers from 5 to 17. If you think of the FOR . . . NEXT loop as making a counter go from the initial value to the final value in increments of 1, this is straightforward, as you can see in Program 2 at the top of the next page.

Program 2

Statement	Remark
10 PRINT "COUNT UP"	
20 FOR COUNT = 5 TO 17	*Initialize the counter COUNT.*
30 PRINT COUNT	*Body of the loop.*
40 NEXT COUNT	*Increment and test the counter.*
50 PRINT "WE DID IT"	
60 END	

Output

```
COUNT UP
5
6
7
.
.
.
17
WE DID IT
```

The final example of this section uses a FOR . . . NEXT loop to find the sum of a DATA list of numbers. We did this in the last section (Program 3, page 203) using a trailer value to signal the end of the list. This time, in the program below, the number of values on the DATA list is placed at the beginning of the list.

Program 3

Statement	Remark
10 PRINT "SUMMING DATA, PART 2"	
20 LET SUM = 0	*Initialize the summer.*
30 READ N	*Get number of DATA values to add.*
40 FOR ITEM = 1 TO N	*The counter ITEM starts with 1, ends with N.*
50 READ NUM	
60 LET SUM = SUM + NUM	*NUM is added to SUM.*
70 NEXT ITEM	*Increment and test the counter ITEM.*
80 PRINT "SUM = "; SUM	
90 DATA 4, 160, 83, 20, 27	*4 is number of DATA values to add.*
100 END	

Output

SUMMING DATA, PART 2
SUM = 290

Notice that a variable (N) is used as the final counter value in line 40. In general, the initial and final values in a FOR statement may be numbers, variables (whose values have been previously assigned using LET, READ, or INPUT), or BASIC numerical expressions (such as 5 * S − T). Only a simple numeric variable may be used as the counter name immediately after the words FOR and NEXT, however.

Avoiding Pitfalls

1. Be sure every FOR statement is paired with a NEXT statement and every NEXT statement is paired with a FOR statement. The variable in the NEXT statement must match the simple numeric variable named as the counter in the FOR statement.

2. It is legal and sometimes necessary to use a GOTO (or IF . . . THEN GOTO . . .) instruction *within* a FOR . . . NEXT loop:

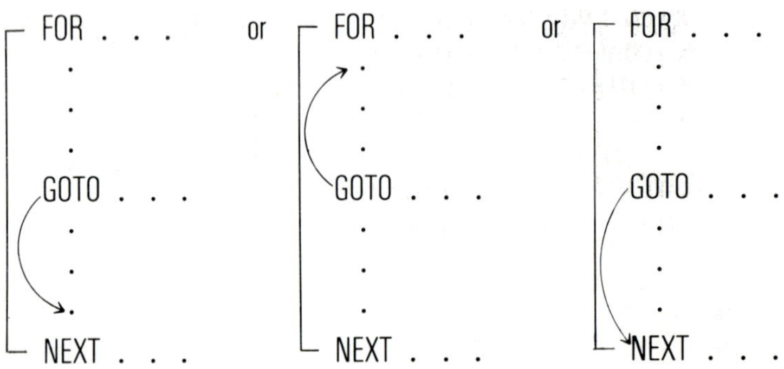

However, it is *not* legal to use a GOTO (or IF . . . THEN GOTO . . .) instruction to jump into the body of a FOR . . . NEXT loop from a line outside the loop.

The illegal jumps diagrammed on the bottom of the preceding page result in a NEXT WITHOUT FOR error message.

3. It is possible to use a GOTO (or IF . . . THEN GOTO . . .) instruction to jump to a line *outside* of a FOR . . . NEXT loop, but this should be avoided. Transferring from a FOR . . . NEXT loop early leaves information in the computer's memory that would be cleared out by a completed FOR . . . NEXT loop. If enough of this information is left on the *stack* (see the Lab Activity for Section 5–6, page 250), as this portion of the computer's memory is called, an OUT OF MEMORY error can occur.

4. It is possible to use a GOTO (or IF . . . THEN GOTO . . .) instruction to jump to the FOR line from any line in the program. However, this always gives the counter its initial value again, which may not be your intention.

5. Changing the value of the counter within a FOR . . . NEXT loop (using LET, READ, or INPUT) easily leads to error and negates the most important reason for using FOR . . . NEXT loops: they are easy to construct and easy to understand.

Summary

The purpose of the FOR statement at the beginning of a FOR . . . NEXT loop is to *name* the counter and give its *initial* and *final* values. The NEXT statement indicates the *end* of the loop, *increments* the counter, and then *tests* the counter (on most computers).

A standard FOR . . . NEXT loop has this form:

```
 .
 .
 .
┌100  FOR counter = initial value TO final value
│110 ┐
│ .  │
│ .  ├     body of the loop
│ .  │
│160 ┘
└170  NEXT counter
 .
 .
 .
```

The initial and final counter values in a FOR statement may be numbers, variables (whose values have been previously assigned), or BASIC numerical expressions. The variable in the NEXT statement must match the simple numeric variable named as the counter in the FOR statement.

Exercises 5-3

A **1.** State whether each of the following is a legal BASIC statement.

a. `20 FOR I = 1 TO 64`
b. `20 FOR 6 = I TO J`
c. `20 LET X = 3 TO 17`
d. `20 FOR AB = K + J TO M`
e. `20 FOR I = 1, 36`
f. `20 FOR X + Y = J TO K`
g. `20 FOR J = 36 TO K + 5 * M`
h. `20 NEXT PLUM`
i. `20 NEXT 56`
j. `20 NEXT X + Y`

2. Predict the output of each of the following programs.

a.
```
10 FOR I = 1 TO 5
20 PRINT I, 2 * I
30 NEXT I
40 END
```

b.
```
10 FOR J = 1 TO 4
20 PRINT " **** "
30 NEXT J
40 END
```

c.
```
10 READ NUM
20 FOR I = 1 TO NUM
30 READ X
40 PRINT X
50 NEXT I
60 DATA 5, 2, 5, -1, 6, 9
70 END
```

d.
```
10 LET FRST = -2
20 LET LST = 1
30 FOR BE = FRST TO LST
40 PRINT BE
50 NEXT BE
60 END
```

3. a. Write a program using a FOR . . . NEXT loop to PRINT the message HI, KID eleven times.

b. Change the program so that it first INPUTs both the message and the number of times it should be PRINTed.

4. a. Write a program using a FOR . . . NEXT loop to PRINT the numbers from 16 to 31.

b. Modify the program so that it also calculates and PRINTs the sum of the numbers from 16 to 31.

c. Modify the program so that two variables FIRST and LAST are INPUT from a user, then have the program calculate and PRINT the sum of the numbers from FIRST to LAST.

5. Write a program using a FOR . . . NEXT loop to PRINT the following:

```
HELLO #1
HELLO #2
   .
   .
   .
HELLO #12
```

6. a. Write a program using a FOR . . . NEXT loop to PRINT exactly the following output:

```
I HAVE 2 MARBLES.
I HAVE 3 MARBLES.
I HAVE 4 MARBLES.
    .
    .
    .
I HAVE 9 MARBLES.
I HAVE LOST MY MARBLES.
```

b. Change the program so that it first PRINTs:

```
I HAVE 1 MARBLE.
```

7. Write a program using a FOR . . . NEXT loop to PRINT exactly the following output:

```
I 1 A SKUNK.
I 2 A SKUNK.
I 3 A SKUNK.
    .
    .
    .
I 8 A SKUNK.
PHEWW!
```

8. Rewrite each of the following programs using a FOR . . . NEXT loop.

a.
```
10 LET I=1
20 PRINT 2*I+1
30 LET I=I+1
40 IF I<=17 THEN GOTO 20
50 PRINT "DONE"
60 END
```

b.
```
10 LET AB=1
20 PRINT AB, AB ↑ 2
30 LET AB=AB+1
40 IF AB<=10 THEN GOTO 20
50 PRINT "SQUARES ARE DONE"
60 END
```

c.
```
10 LET X=0
20 LET I=1
30 LET X=X+I
40 LET I=I+1
50 IF I<=31 THEN GOTO 30
60 PRINT X
65 PRINT "WITH EASE"
70 END
```

d.
```
10 LET X=3
20 LET J=2
30 LET X=X*2
40 LET J=J+1
50 IF J<=5 THEN GOTO 30
60 PRINT X
65 PRINT "STOP"
70 END
```

9. Rewrite each of the following programs without using a FOR . . . NEXT loop.

a.
```
10 FOR JX=1 TO 18
20 PRINT 18-JX
30 NEXT JX
35 PRINT "ALL RIGHT"
40 END
```

b.
```
10 FOR J=1 TO 5
20 READ X$
30 PRINT X$
40 NEXT J
50 DATA FOR, NEXT, LOOPS
55 DATA ARE, EASIER
60 END
```

c.
```
10 INPUT N$
20 INPUT TTL
30 FOR I=1 TO TTL
40 PRINT N$; "  HAS  "; TTL;
45 PRINT "  EYES."
50 NEXT I
60 PRINT "RIGHT?"
70 END
```

d.
```
10 LET N=3
20 LET K=2
30 FOR I=K-1 TO N+1
40 LET X=I*K
50 PRINT X; "  INCORRIGIBLE DIRIGIBLES"
60 NEXT I
70 END
```

10. Predict the output, or give the ERROR message, for each of the following programs.

a.
```
10 FOR I=1 TO 4
20 IF I=2 THEN GOTO 40
30 PRINT I
40 NEXT I
50 END
```

b.
```
10 FOR K=2 TO 5
20 PRINT K
30 IF K=4 THEN GOTO 10
40 NEXT K
50 END
```

c.
```
10 LET X=3
20 IF X<5 THEN GOTO 50
30 FOR I=1 TO 3
40 PRINT I
50 NEXT I
60 END
```

d.
```
10 READ X
20 IF X<3 THEN GOTO 50
30 GOTO 80
40 FOR I=1 TO 5
50 PRINT I
60 NEXT I
70 PRINT X
80 DATA 2, 8, -2
90 END
```

11. Change Program 3 so that it finds the average of the numbers on the DATA list. Continue to use the FOR . . . NEXT loop.

12. Change Program 3 so that it counts how many numbers on the DATA list are greater than or equal to 80. Use a FOR . . . NEXT loop and an additional counter.

B **13.** Complete the RUN chart for the following program to verify that it PRINTs the even numbers from 18 to 22.

```
10 FOR K=9 TO 11
20 PRINT 2 * K
30 NEXT K
40 END
```

LINE	CONDITION	K	OUTPUT
10		9	
20			18
30		10	
30	(K <= 11) is true		
20			

(*Note:* The NEXT instruction in line 30 involves two steps — an increment and a test — so that it needs two lines in the RUN chart. If the condition *counter <= final value* is true, then the program goes to the line directly after the FOR instruction.)

14. a. Modify the program in Exercise 13 so that it PRINTs the even numbers from −8 to 40. (Change line 10.)

b. Modify the program so that it PRINTs the multiples of 3 from 3 to 45.

c. Modify the program so that it PRINTs the numbers 5, 8, 11, . . . , 47. (*Hint:* What must you add to the multiples from 3 to 45 in (b) to get the given sequence of numbers from 5 to 47?)

d. Modify the program so that it PRINTs the odd numbers from 7 to 31.

15. Construct a RUN chart (see the note in Exercise 13) for the following:

a.
```
10 FOR I=1 TO 5
20 PRINT I
30 IF I=2 THEN PRINT I+1
40 NEXT I
50 END
```

b.
```
10 FOR I=1 TO 5
20 IF I=3 THEN GOTO 40
30 PRINT I
40 NEXT I
50 END
```

16. a. Construct a RUN chart (see the note in Exercise 13) to verify that the following program PRINTs the numbers from 20 down to 17.

```
10 FOR I=0 TO 3
20 PRINT 20-I
30 NEXT I
40 END
```

b. Modify the program to PRINT the numbers from 30 down to 5.

c. Modify the program to PRINT the numbers from 6 down to −7.

17. Write a program using a FOR . . . NEXT loop to PRINT the even numbers from 20 down to 0. (*Hint:* See Exercises 13, 14, and 16.)

18. Write a program that INPUTs 10 strings from a user (use a FOR . . . NEXT loop), then PRINTs the number of times the user typed the string LULU.

19. Write a program that INPUTs 15 positive numbers from a user, then calculates and PRINTs their sum and average.

20. Write a program that PRINTs a large block letter L, composed of asterisks, as shown in the figure at the right. Use two FOR . . . NEXT loops.

```
**
**
**
**
**
******
******
```

You can use a FOR . . . NEXT loop to draw a vertical or horizontal line (segment) in graphics mode. For example, the sample program below will draw a horizontal line segment from (10, 30) to (25, 30).

Sample

```
10 (Instructions to clear the screen
20    and do graphics on your
30    computer.)
40 FOR X = 10 TO 25
50 (Instruction to plot the point at X, 30.)
60 NEXT X
70 END
```

In Exercises 21–25, use the sample program as a guide in drawing the required line segments.

21. (Graphics) Write a program that INPUTs the left and right endpoint and the Y-coordinate of a horizontal line segment, then draws (using a FOR . . . NEXT loop) the line segment in graphics mode. Have the program reject any INPUT values too big for the screen.

22. (Graphics) Modify the program in Exercise 21 so that it draws a vertical line segment of the same length through the middle (approximately) of the horizontal line segment.

23. (Graphics) Write a program that INPUTs the length and width of a rectangle, then draws the rectangle with the given dimensions in graphics mode. Have the program reject any INPUT values too big for the screen.

24. (Graphics) Rewrite the program of Exercise 20 so that it draws the letter L in graphics mode.

C 25. (Graphics) Rewrite the programs in the Lab Activity for Section 5–1, page 201, using FOR . . . NEXT loops to draw the lines.

Lab Activity

Time-Delay Loops

Finite loops, and particularly easy-to-write and understand FOR . . . NEXT loops, can be used to introduce time delays into your programs. You might, for example, want to PRINT a message on the screen, wait a few seconds, then clear the screen and draw a picture in graphics mode.

The standard time-delay loop is simply a FOR . . . NEXT loop with nothing in the body of the loop between the FOR and the NEXT statements. Here is a program using such a loop. You can type the number of times the loop should be executed.

```
10 INPUT "TYPE NO. OF TIMES:  "; N
20 FOR I = 1 TO N
30 NEXT I
40 PRINT "STOP"
50 END
```

Problems

1. Carefully time how long it takes for your computer to go through the time-delay loop 10,000 times. One way to do this is: Type RUN, then 10000 (but do not press the < RETURN > or < ENTER > key). When the second display on your watch or clock is at a convenient place, press the < RETURN > or < ENTER > key. Keep one eye on the clock or watch and one on the screen (good luck!). When STOP appears on the screen, write down the time elapsed.

2. Based on your result in Problem 1, approximately how many seconds (what decimal part of a second) does it take for the computer to go through the loop once? (Divide by 10,000.)

3. RUN the program again and time how long it takes the computer to go through the loop 20,000 times. This should be approximately twice as long as it took to do it 10,000 times, naturally. Why is your answer (probably) not *exactly* twice what you timed in Problem 1?

4. Time how long it takes the computer to go through the loop 30,000 times. Is this answer approximately consistent with your answers in Problems 1 and 3? What is your best estimate of the time it takes the computer to go through the loop once?

5. By experimenting with the time-delay loop, you can find out approximately how long it takes for the computer to perform arithmetic operations. For example, add the line 25 LET X = 12 + 9 and RUN the program with N = 20000, timing carefully as before. Calculate the amount of time it now takes to go through the loop once. The difference between the time it took to go through the empty loop once, and the time it takes to go through the loop *and* add 12 + 9, should give the time it takes the computer to add the numbers. How long does the addition take?

6. Use the same technique as in Problem 5 to determine how long it takes the computer to multiply 12 * 9. (*Note:* The speed of arithmetic computations depends on the type of computer and on the language being used. Machine language, for example, is much faster than BASIC.)

5-4 Different Increments: The STEP Instruction

BASIC has a special feature — the STEP instruction — that makes constructions of FOR . . . NEXT loops even easier and more useful. In the FOR . . . NEXT loops of the last section, the counter was always incremented by 1 at the NEXT statement. It is possible, however, to make the increment any number desired by using the word STEP at the end of the FOR statement. For example, Program 1 below PRINTs the even numbers from 10 to 20 by using the STEP instruction to specify increments of 2.

Program 1

Statement	Remark
10 PRINT "EVEN NUMBERS"	
20 FOR C = 10 TO 20 STEP 2	*Name counter, give its initial and final values, and specify increment.*
30 PRINT C	*Body of the loop.*
40 NEXT C	*Increment by 2 and test the counter.*
50 END	

Output

```
EVEN NUMBERS
10
12
14
16
18
20
```

To make it clear exactly how the STEP instruction works in Program 1, here is a version without a FOR . . . NEXT loop. Compare the two programs and note that the STEP instruction does not change the structure of the loop, since the counter is still incremented and tested at the NEXT line (on most computers).

Program 2

Statement	Remark
10 PRINT "EVEN NUMBERS, NO FOR . . . NEXT"	
20 LET C = 10	*Initialize the counter.*
30 PRINT C	*Body of the loop.*
40 LET C = C + 2	*Increment the counter.*
45 IF C <= 20 THEN GOTO 30	*Test the counter.*
50 END	

The value of the increment specified by STEP may be negative, but then the initial value of the counter should be larger than the final value. For example, this next program uses the STEP instruction to specify increments (actually, decrements) of −3.

Program 3

Statement

```
10 PRINT "NEGATIVE INCREMENT"
20 FOR C = 21 TO 0 STEP -3
30 PRINT C
40 NEXT C
45 PRINT "BACKWARDS"
50 END
```

Output

```
NEGATIVE INCREMENT
21
18
15
12
9
6
3
0
BACKWARDS
```

In Program 3, the NEXT instruction in line 40 *subtracts* 3 from the counter and compares the new value of the counter with the final value 0. The loop is repeated as long as the condition C >= 0 is *true*. (The direction of this inequality symbol is the reverse of that in line 45 of Program 2 because the counter C is *decreasing* rather than *increasing*.) What would be PRINTed if the final counter value of C in line 20 were changed to −1?

As is true of the initial and final counter values, the increment specified by the STEP instruction in a FOR statement may be a number, a variable (whose value has been previously assigned), or a BASIC numerical expression. Here is a program that uses a decimal increment to calculate the simple interest for one year on money invested at each of the interest rates 7%, 7.5%, 8%, 8.5%, and 9%. It uses the formula:

$$\text{Interest} = \text{Principal} * \text{Rate}$$

Program 4

Statement

```
10 PRINT "SIMPLE INTEREST"
20 INPUT "PRINCIPAL:  "; P
30 FOR R = 7 TO 9 STEP .5
40 LET I = P * R / 100
50 PRINT "INTEREST AT  "; R; "% IS  "; I
60 NEXT R
70 END
```

Output

```
SIMPLE INTEREST
PRINCIPAL:  ? 500
INTEREST AT 7% IS 35
INTEREST AT 7.5% IS 37.5
INTEREST AT 8% IS 40
INTEREST AT 8.5% IS 42.5
INTEREST AT 9% IS 45
```

Notice that the interest rates are necessarily converted to their decimal form in line 40, but are PRINTed as percents in line 50.

The increment specified by the STEP instruction may of course be 1, but then STEP is not needed at all: the statement

```
FOR I = 1 TO 10 STEP 1
```

is the same statement as FOR I = 1 TO 10.

Avoiding Pitfalls

1. Remember that a FOR . . . NEXT loop with *positive* increment is executed repeatedly until the counter becomes *larger* than the final value. If the increment is *negative,* then the loop is executed until the counter becomes *smaller* than the final value. In using negative increments, therefore, it is important to make the initial value greater than the final value.

2. When the test of the counter is at the NEXT statement (see the Lab Activity to determine how your computer works), a FOR . . . NEXT loop is always executed at least once, even though the initial value of the counter may be too large (for positive increments) or too small (for negative increments). For example, consider this program:

```
  10 INPUT START
┌ 20 FOR I = START TO 5
│ 30 PRINT I
└ 40 NEXT I
  50 END
```

If you type 4 for START in line 10, then the computer will PRINT 4 and 5 when the program is RUN. If you type 5, the output will be 5 alone. If you type 6, the output will be 6 (on most computers), since the loop is executed once in any case. To avoid this situation, you could add this line: 15 IF START > 5 THEN GOTO 50.

Summary

A FOR . . . NEXT loop with increment other than 1 has this form:

```
   .
   .
   .
┌100  FOR counter = initial value TO final value STEP increment
│110 ┐
│ .  │
│ .  }      body of the loop
│ .  │
│160 ┘
└170  NEXT counter
   .
   .
   .
```

In line 100, the initial value, final value, and increment may be numbers, variables, or BASIC numerical expressions.

Exercises 5-4

A **1.** State whether each of the following is a valid BASIC statement.

a. `10 FOR I = 1 TO 5 STEP 6`
b. `10 FOR CD = -3 TO 5 STEP .3`
c. `10 FOR N = 2 TO B STEP -A + 2`
d. `10 FOR X - 3 = 7 TO D STEP - .01`
e. `10 FOR X = STEP TO NEXT`
f. `10 FOR A = 1 TO B STEP 1`
g. `10 FOR B = 7 TO 3 STEP - 2`
h. `10 FOR J = A TO B + 2 STEP - K`
i. `10 FOR AB = 1 TO 5 STEP X * X`
j. `10 NEXT A + 2`
k. `10 NEXT STEP`
l. `10 NEXT X ↑ 2`

2. Predict the output of each of the following programs.

a.
```
10 FOR I = 2 TO 12 STEP 2
20 PRINT I
30 NEXT I
40 END
```

b.
```
10 FOR I = 2 TO 12 STEP 4
20 PRINT I
30 NEXT I
40 END
```

c.
```
10 FOR I = 12 TO 8 STEP -3
20 PRINT 2 * I
30 NEXT I
40 END
```

d.
```
10 FOR J = -3 TO -3 STEP -3
20 PRINT J ↑ 2
30 NEXT J
40 END
```

e.
```
10 LET K = 3
15 PRINT K
20 FOR K = 1 TO 3 STEP 1
30 PRINT K
40 NEXT K
50 END
```

f.
```
10 LET X = 3
20 FOR I = 2 * X TO 3 * X STEP X
30 PRINT I
40 NEXT I
50 END
```

3. The output of each of the following programs varies from computer to computer (see the Lab Activity). Predict the output for your computer.

a.
```
10 FOR J = 2 TO 1 STEP 2
20 PRINT J
30 NEXT J
40 END
```

b.
```
10 FOR J = 1 TO 3 STEP -1
20 PRINT J
30 NEXT J
40 END
```

4. Correct the following program so that it PRINTs the squares of the even numbers between 10 and 20.

```
10 FOR N = 10 TO 20
20 PRINT N * N
30 PRINT "THAT'S ALL"
40 END
```

5. Rewrite Program 3, page 223, without using a FOR . . . NEXT loop.

6. Rewrite Program 4, page 224, so that it calculates the simple interest for one year on money invested at each of the following rates: 3.8%, 3.9%, 4.0%, and so on up to 4.6%.

7. Change Program 1, page 222, so that it INPUTs the initial and final values of the counter, and the increment. The program should reject values that are not appropriate; that is, it should require that the initial value be less than or equal to the final value if the increment is positive, and the reverse if the increment is negative. An increment of 0 should be excluded.

B 8. Write a program using STEP to add the even numbers from 2 to 100.

9. Write a program using STEP to calculate each of the following sums:

a. $3 + 6 + 9 + \ldots + 303$

b. $4 + 8 + 12 + \ldots + 408$

c. $\frac{1}{2} + \frac{1}{4} + \frac{1}{6} + \ldots + \frac{1}{94}$

d. the multiples of 5 from 5 to 500

10. Write a program using STEP to find each of the following products:

a. $2 * 6 * 10 * \ldots * 58$

b. $\frac{1}{3} * \frac{1}{6} * \frac{1}{9} * \ldots * \frac{1}{60}$

11. Write a program using STEP to find this product:

$$\frac{3}{5} * \frac{6}{8} * \frac{9}{11} * \ldots * \frac{72}{74}.$$

12. (Graphics) Write a program to draw dashed horizontal lines in graphics mode. Use FOR X = 0 TO *largest X-value on your screen* STEP 2 (or 3 or 4 or . . .). Have your program draw the dashed horizontal lines at any INPUT Y-value (in any INPUT color, if your computer has color).

13. (Graphics) Write a program in graphics mode to draw the following pattern across the top of your screen:

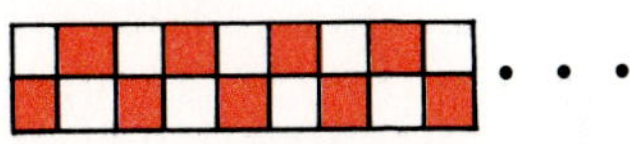

(*Hint:* Use two FOR . . . NEXT loops — see Exercise 12.)

C 14. a. (Graphics) Change the program in Exercise 13 so that it draws the 2-row pattern across the screen at any INPUT Y-value.

b. (Graphics) Change the program in (a) so that it draws the 2-row pattern across the screen repeatedly (this will fill the screen with a checkerboard pattern). Rather than using INPUT to get a particular Y-value, use a FOR . . . NEXT loop that draws the pattern at every other Y-value from 0 to the largest Y-value on your screen. (*Hint:* The loops in the program in (a) should be *inside* the FOR . . . NEXT loop you are constructing in (b).)

Lab Activity

Exploring FOR . . . NEXT

Computers interpret FOR . . . NEXT loops, such as the one in Program 1 below, in one of two ways.

Program 1

```
10  FOR K=1 TO 4
20  PRINT K
30  NEXT K
40  END
```

The most common interpretation is to test the counter at the NEXT line, as explained in Section 5–3 and as illustrated in this version of Program 1 that uses a finite loop with GOTO:

Program 2

```
10  LET K=1
20  PRINT K
30  LET K=K+1               }
35  IF K<=4 THEN GOTO 20    } <------ test counter (NEXT K)
40  END
```

Some computers, however, test the counter at the FOR line, as in this version of Program 1:

Program 3

```
10  LET K=1                 }
15  IF K>4 THEN GOTO 40     } <------ test counter (FOR K=1 TO 4)
20  PRINT K
30  LET K=K+1
35  GOTO 15
40  END
```

Convince yourself that all three programs have the same output. But now suppose that you change the 4 to 0 in each of the programs. In Program 2 the loop will be executed once, and the output will be 1. In Program 3 the loop will not be executed at all (since the condition $K > 0$ in line 15 is true immediately), and there will be no output.

Problems

1. RUN Program 1 with 0 in place of 4 and determine whether the counter is tested at the FOR line (no output) or at the NEXT line (output 1) on your computer.

2. To investigate other aspects of FOR . . . NEXT loops, type this more general program into your computer.

```
10 INPUT "INITIAL VALUE:  "; START
20 INPUT "FINAL VALUE:  "; FINISH
30 INPUT "INCREMENT:  "; INCR
40 FOR COUNT = START TO FINISH STEP INCR
50 PRINT COUNT
60 NEXT COUNT
70 END
```

   RUN the program with initial value 1, final value 0, and increment 1 to verify the result you obtained in Problem 1.

3. What do you predict for the output of the program in Problem 2 if the INPUT increment is negative and the initial value is less than the final value? RUN the program and explain the result.

4. What do you predict for the output of the program in Problem 2 if the increment is 0? RUN the program with INCR = 0 and the initial value greater than the final value. RUN the program again with the initial value less than the final value. Do the results verify your prediction?

5. Add a line to the program in Problem 2 that will PRINT the value of the counter *after* the loop is ended (line 65). Try several different values of START, FINISH, and INCR. Summarize your results when the initial value is greater (or less) than the final value and the increment is positive (or negative).

6. Delete line 65 in Problem 5 and add this line:

```
55 LET START = START + 17
```

   Does this line have any effect on the output? Can you explain?

7. By changing line 55 in Problem 6, investigate whether changing the value of FINISH or INCR within the body of the loop has any effect on the output. Summarize your results.

8. Change line 55 in Problem 6 to: 55 LET COUNT = COUNT + 2. RUN the program with the initial value less than the final value and positive increment. Does changing the counter in the body of a loop have any effect on the output?

5-5 Loops within Loops: Nested FOR . . . NEXT

Suppose that we want to write a program with output as follows:

```
THE SKY
THE SKY
THE SKY
THE SKY
IS AN ONION.
THE SKY
THE SKY
THE SKY
THE SKY
IS AN ONION.
THE SKY
THE SKY
THE SKY
THE SKY
IS AN ONION.
```

One way to look at this problem is to think of the program producing the following pattern three times:

```
THE SKY
THE SKY
THE SKY
THE SKY
IS AN ONION.
```

This repetition of the pattern can be translated into BASIC by writing a simple FOR . . . NEXT loop:

```
┌20  FOR I = 1 TO 3
│30 ┐
│ .  │
│ .  ├ (statements to produce the pattern)
│ .  │
│60 ┘
└70  NEXT I
```

It remains to write the BASIC statements to produce the pattern itself; that involves the repetition of one message (THE SKY) four times, followed by a second message (IS AN ONION.) just once. This can be done using the statements at the top of the next page.

```
30 FOR J = 1 TO 4
40 PRINT "THE SKY"
50 NEXT J
60 PRINT "IS AN ONION."
```

By combining the preceding statements, we get this program:

Program 1

Statement

```
10 PRINT "POETRY?"
20 FOR I = 1 TO 3
30 FOR J = 1 TO 4
40 PRINT "THE SKY"
50 NEXT J
60 PRINT "IS AN ONION."
70 NEXT I
80 END
```

Program 1 uses *nested loops* — one loop (the inner loop of lines 30 to 50) completely enclosed within another loop (the outer loop of lines 20 to 70). Each time the computer executes the outer loop once, the inner loop is repeated from the beginning (that is, the counter J is given its initial value again).

Often nested loops may be most easily understood (and written) by thinking of the outer loop as causing a repetition of some sequence of actions whose details at first are left undeveloped. Then, once the statements for the outer loop are outlined, the body of the outer loop is developed. In this case, the body of the loop itself involves a repetitive procedure — another loop.

The next example is another program using nested FOR . . . NEXT loops. We will analyze it by constructing a RUN chart.

Program 2

Statement

```
10 REM * NESTED COUNTING
20 FOR K = 1 TO 2
30 FOR J = 3 TO 4
40 PRINT K, J
50 NEXT J
60 NEXT K
70 END
```

Study each step in the RUN chart to see how nested loops work. Recall that NEXT statements, which both increment and test the counter, need two lines in the RUN chart.

LINE	CONDITION	K	J	OUTPUT	REMARK
10					
20		1			
30			3		
40				1 3	
50			4		
50	(J <= 4) is true				GOTO the beginning of the body of the J loop.
40				1 4	
50			5		
50	(J <= 4) is false				GOTO next line.
60		2			
60	(K <= 2) is true				GOTO top of body of K loop.
30			3		J is initialized again.
40				2 3	
50			4		
50	(J <= 4) is true				
40				2 4	
50			5		
50	(J <= 4) is false				
60		3			
60	(K <= 2) is false				
70					Program ends.

The output, then, of Program 2 is:

```
1          3
1          4
2          3
2          4
```

This output can also be predicted by thinking of the nested FOR . . . NEXT loops as working this way: For *each* of the K values 1 and 2, the counter J goes from 3 to 4.

Two, three, four or more FOR . . . NEXT loops may be nested. Legal ways of nesting three FOR . . . NEXT loops are diagrammed on page 238.

Avoiding Pitfalls

1. In nested loops, the counters for the inner and outer loops must not be the same (a NEXT WITHOUT FOR error will occur if they are the same).

2. In nested loops, the NEXT statement for the inner loop must occur *before* the NEXT statement for the outer loop. (That is, the inner loop must be completely enclosed by the outer loop.) The proper structure is as follows:

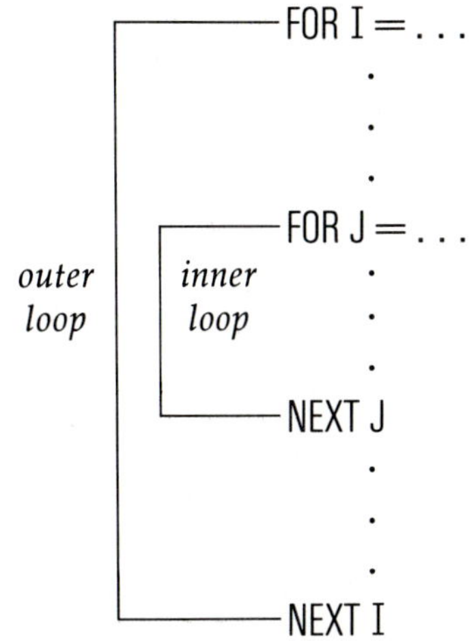

Overlapping arrangements such as the following are *not legal* and will lead to a NEXT WITHOUT FOR error.

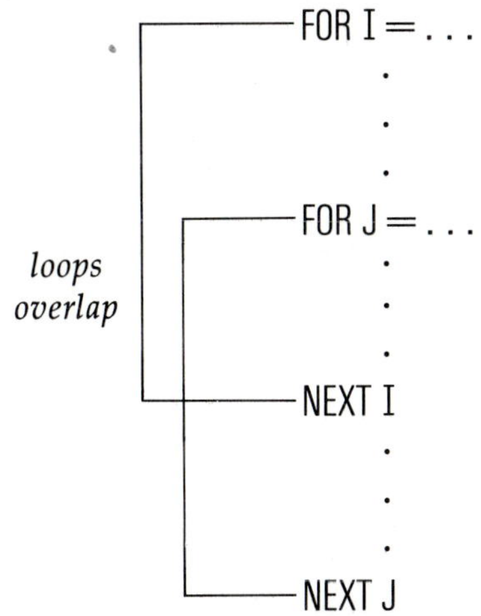

(*Note:* The brackets used to indicate each FOR . . . NEXT loop must *not* overlap.)

Summary

Nested FOR . . . NEXT loops involve one FOR . . . NEXT loop (the inner loop) completely enclosed in another FOR . . . NEXT loop (the outer loop). Each time the computer executes the outer loop once, the inner loop is repeated from the beginning.

Exercises 5-5

A **1.** Predict the output of the following programs. Construct a RUN chart.

a.
```
10 FOR I = 1 TO 2
20 FOR J = 2 TO 3
30 PRINT I, J
40 NEXT J
50 NEXT I
60 END
```

b.
```
10 FOR P = 1 TO 3
20 FOR Q = -1 TO 2
30 PRINT P, Q
40 NEXT Q
50 NEXT P
60 END
```

c.
```
10 FOR C = 2 TO 0 STEP -1
20 PRINT "KNEE";
30 FOR D = 0 TO 1
40 PRINT "DEEP  ";
50 NEXT D
60 PRINT
70 NEXT C
80 END
```

d.
```
10 FOR X = 1 TO 3
20 PRINT "YES"
30 FOR Y = 1 TO 4
40 PRINT "OR NO"
50 NEXT Y
60 NEXT X
70 END
```

e.
```
10 FOR I = 3 TO 6
20 PRINT I
30 FOR J = 8 TO 10
40 PRINT I * J
50 NEXT J
60 NEXT I
70 END
```

f.
```
10 FOR I = 1 TO 3
20 FOR J = 1 TO I
30 PRINT I
40 NEXT J
50 NEXT I
60 END
```

2. a. Modify Program 1 so that it repeats THE SKY eleven times within each pattern.

b. Modify the program in (a) so that it repeats IS AN ONION four times within each pattern.

c. Change the program so that it INPUTs the number of times THE SKY and IS AN ONION are to be repeated in each pattern, and also INPUTs the number of times the pattern as a whole is to be repeated.

3. Find the errors, if any, in each of the following programs. Give possible corrections. (First study the diagrams following Exercise 8 that show legal ways of nesting three FOR . . . NEXT loops.)

a.
```
10 FOR K=27 TO 33
20 PRINT K
30 FOR L=-1 TO 6
40 PRINT L
50 NEXT K
60 NEXT L
70 END
```

b.
```
10 FOR I=2 TO 4
20 PRINT "RAH"
30 FOR I=-1 TO 1
40 PRINT "RAH-RAH"
50 NEXT I
60 NEXT I
70 END
```

c.
```
10 FOR COUNT=7 TO -6 STEP -2
20 FOR IP=3 TO 8 STEP 3
30 PRINT "ME"
40 NEXT IP
50 PRINT "YOU"
70 NEXT COUNT
80 PRINT "DONE"
90 END
```

d.
```
10 FOR KPL=1 TO 6
20 PRINT "HI"
30 FOR KPL=2 TO 5
40 PRINT "LO"
50 NEXT KPL
60 PRINT "FORGET IT"
70 NEXT KPL
80 END
```

e.
```
10 FOR I=1 TO 5
20 PRINT I
30 NEXT I
40 FOR I=6 TO 10
50 PRINT 10-I
60 NEXT I
70 END
```

f.
```
10 FOR I=1 TO 4
20 FOR J=5 TO 7
30 FOR K=-2 TO 0
40 PRINT I, J, K
50 NEXT K
60 NEXT J
70 NEXT I
80 END
```

g.
```
10 FOR I=1 TO 4
20 PRINT I
30 FOR J=-6 TO 2
40 PRINT "PEANUT"
50 FOR K=1 TO 2
60 PRINT J, K
70 NEXT J
80 PRINT "BUTTER"
90 NEXT K
100 NEXT I
110 END
```

h.
```
10 FOR I=1 TO 5
20 PRINT I
30 FOR J=2 TO 7
40 PRINT I, J
50 NEXT J
60 FOR K=2 TO 6
70 PRINT I, K
80 NEXT K
90 PRINT
100 NEXT I
110 END
```

4. Change Program 2 so that its output is as follows:

a.
```
1    4
1    5
2    4
2    5
```

b.
```
4    1
5    1
4    2
5    2
```

c.
```
1    5
1    6
2    5
2    6
3    5
3    6
```

d.
```
1    1
1    2
1    3
2    1
2    2
2    3
```

e.
```
-1    0
-1    0
-1    0
 1    1
 1    1
 1    1
```

f.
```
5    2
5    5
5    8
9    2
9    5
9    8
```

B 5. Write a program using nested FOR . . . NEXT loops to produce the following output:

```
1. MESSAGE #1
2. MESSAGE #1
3. MESSAGE #1
1. MESSAGE #2
2. MESSAGE #2
3. MESSAGE #2
1. MESSAGE #3
2. MESSAGE #3
3. MESSAGE #3
```

6. (Graphics)
   - **a.** Write a program using a FOR . . . NEXT loop to draw a horizontal line (segment) in graphics mode at a Y-value assigned in a LET statement.
   - **b.** Change the program to draw five horizontal lines from Y = 14 to Y = 18. (*Hint:* Delete the line with LET Y = . . . , then use nested loops.)
   - **c.** Change the program to fill the entire screen with horizontal lines (in any INPUT color, if your computer has color).

7. (Graphics)
   - **a.** Write a program to produce the following pattern

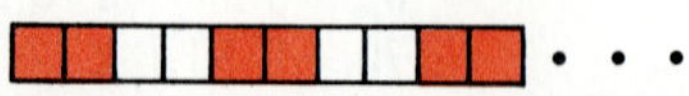

in graphics mode across the screen at any Y-value INPUT from a user. (*Hint:* Use FOR X = 0 TO *largest X-value on your screen* STEP 4. Within the loop, plot two points: X, Y and X + 1, Y.)

b. Write a program to produce this checkerboard pattern across the top of your screen:

(*Hint:* Use separate nested loops to produce the top two rows and the bottom two rows.)

c. Modify the program in (b) to fill the entire screen with the checkerboard pattern.

d. Modify the program in (c) to fill the entire screen with this checkerboard pattern:

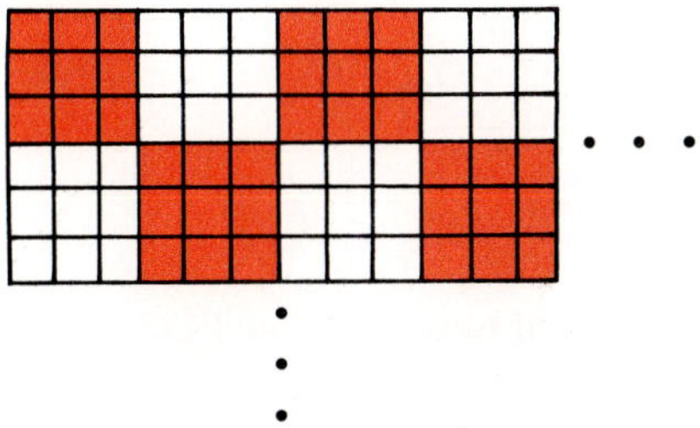

e. *Challenge:* Modify the program so that it INPUTS the "size" of the squares in the checkerboard. (*Note:* In (b) the size of the squares is 2, in (d) the size is 3.)

8. (Graphics)

a. Complete the outline of the following program to draw a triangular pattern in graphics mode:

```
10  (Instructions to clear the screen
20     and do graphics on your
30     computer.)
100  FOR Y=1 TO 15
110  FOR X=1 TO Y
120  (Instruction to plot the point at X, Y.)
130  NEXT X
140  NEXT Y
150  END
```

The program above uses nested FOR . . . NEXT loops. The key to plotting the triangular pattern is that when Y = 1, X goes from initial value 1 to final value 1 (only one point is plotted). When Y = 2, X goes from initial value 1 to final value 2 (two points are plotted), and so on.

b. Change line 110 to: FOR X = 1 TO 16 − Y. Use a RUN chart to predict the resulting pattern. RUN the program and verify your prediction.

c. Change the program in (b) to plot the pattern shown below:

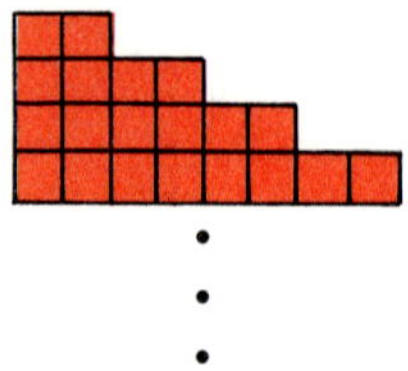

(*Hint:* In row Y, how many points are plotted?)

d. *Challenge:* Change the program in (c) to plot the pattern shown below:

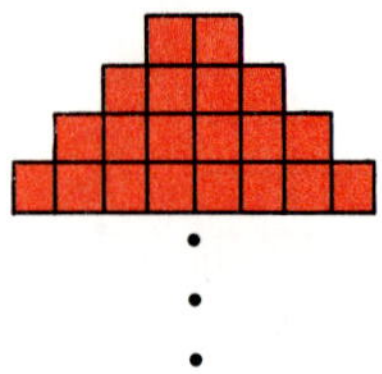

The diagrams below show legal ways of nesting three FOR . . . NEXT loops:

```
FOR I  = . . .
   .
   .
   .
FOR J  = . . .
   .
   .
   .
FOR K = . . .
   .
   .
   .
NEXT K
   .
   .
   .
NEXT J
   .
   .
   .
NEXT I
```

```
FOR I  = . . .
   .
   .
   .
FOR J  = . . .
   .
   .
   .
NEXT J
   .
   .
   .
FOR K = . . .
   .
   .
   .
NEXT K
   .
   .
   .
NEXT I
```

When three FOR . . . NEXT loops are nested, the counter in the *first* FOR statement must match the counter in the *last* NEXT statement.

9. In each of the following programs three FOR . . . NEXT loops are nested. Predict the output. If necessary, construct a RUN chart.

a.
```
10  FOR I = 1 TO 2
20  FOR J = 1 TO 3
30  PRINT "MARYBELLE"
40  NEXT J
50  PRINT "AND PINCUS"
60  FOR K = 1 TO 4
70  PRINT "FLOWERS"
80  NEXT K
90  NEXT I
100  END
```

b.
```
10  FOR I = 1 TO 2
20  FOR J = 3 TO 4
30  FOR K = -1 TO -2 STEP -1
40  PRINT I, J, K
50  NEXT K
60  NEXT J
70  NEXT I
80  END
```

10. Write a program using nested FOR . . . NEXT loops to PRINT a 9 × 9 multiplication table. Use spaces inside quotation marks to try to get the columns to align properly.

*	0	1	2	3	. . .	9
0	0	0	0	0	. . .	
1	0	1	2	3	. . .	
2	0	2	4	6	. . .	
3	0	3	6	9	. . .	
.	.	.	.	.		
.	.	.	.	.		
.	.	.	.	.		
9						

11. According to the converse of the *Pythagorean theorem,* the triangle shown here is a *right triangle* if $a^2 + b^2 = c^2$. A triangle with sides of length 3, 4, and 5, for example, is a right triangle because $3^2 + 4^2 = 5^2$. Write a program to find all right triangles whose sides are integers less than 50. (*Hint:* Use three nested FOR . . . NEXT loops to test triples of integers A, B, and C, each between 1 and 50, to see if A ↑ 2 + B ↑ 2 = C ↑ 2. Try to make the program RUN faster by leaving out unnecessary tests.)

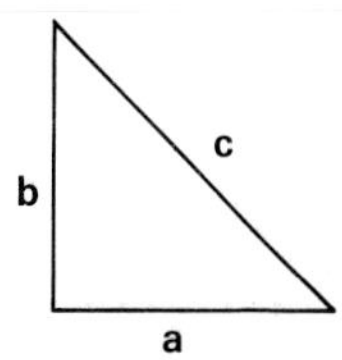

C **12. a.** Write a program using nested FOR . . . NEXT loops to calculate and PRINT the amount in a savings account at the end of each of 4 years. Assume that the account initially contains $100 (the principal) and the interest rate is 10% compounded quarterly. (*Hint:* Use the inner loop to calculate the interest earned each quarter. Recall the formula: interest = principal * rate.)

b. *Challenge:* Modify the program in (a) so that it calculates the amount in the savings account at the three rates 8%, 10%, and 12%, each compounded quarterly. PRINT the output in a table as follows:

```
RATE      YEAR 1      YEAR 2      YEAR 3      YEAR 4
8%
10%
12%
```

(*Hint:* Use three nested FOR . . . NEXT loops.)

Lab Activity

Plotting Patterns

A rather efficient graphics plotting program can be constructed using nested FOR . . . NEXT loops. Suppose, for example, that you want a program to plot the pattern below (or a more complex pattern):

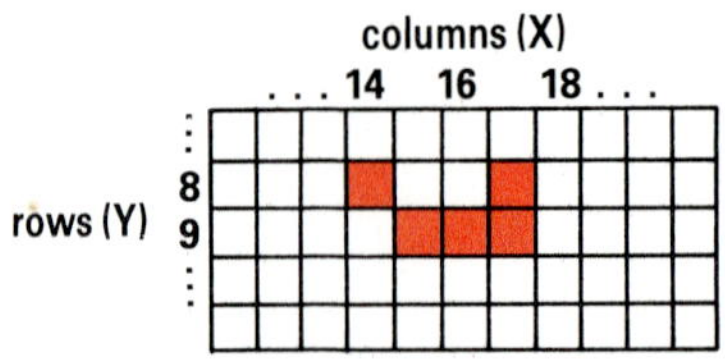

One way to encode this pattern is to place the coordinates of each point in a DATA statement. This method works well for simple shapes. A more general method, which is more efficient for complex patterns, can be outlined as follows:

1. Write down the number of rows in the pattern (2 in the example above).
2. For each row in the pattern:
   - **a.** Give the Y-coordinate of that row.
   - **b.** Give the number of columns to be plotted in that row.
   - **c.** For each column to be plotted, give its X-coordinate.
3. Write the numbers in order in a DATA statement.

For the pattern given above, for example, the outline looks like this:

1. Number of rows in the pattern = 2.
2. **a.** Y-coordinate of first row = 8.
   - **b.** Number of columns to be plotted in eighth row = 2.
   - **c.** X-coordinates of columns to be plotted in eighth row = 14, 17.

a. Y-coordinate of second row = 9.
b. Number of columns to be plotted in ninth row = 3.
c. X-coordinates of columns to be plotted in ninth row = 15, 16, 17.

3. Placing these numbers in order on a DATA list, we get the following statement:

```
400  DATA 2, 8, 2, 14, 17, 9, 3, 15, 16, 17
```

An algorithm for our program can be written as follows:

Step 1 Instructions to clear the screen and go into graphics mode.

Step 2 READ the number of rows (NROWS).

Step 3 For each ROW:
- **a.** READ the Y-coordinate (Y).
- **b.** READ the number of columns to be plotted (NCOL).
- **c.** For each column to be plotted:
  - **i.** READ the X-coordinate (X).
  - **ii.** Plot the point with coordinates X, Y.

Here is an outline of the plotting program that shows the nested loops implied in Step 3 of the algorithm:

```
10  REM * NESTED LOOP PLOTTING PROGRAM
20  (Instructions to clear the screen and
30      do graphics on your
40      computer.)
    .
    .
    .
100  FOR ROW = 1 TO NROWS
    .
    .
    .
200  FOR COL = 1 TO NCOL
    .
    .
    .
300  NEXT COL
310  NEXT ROW
400  DATA . . .
500  END
```

Problems

1. Complete the program, based on the algorithm and outline given. Test the program by drawing the pattern coded in the DATA statement of our example.
2. Draw your initials on a grid for your screen (or on graph paper), write a DATA statement coding the pattern, and then RUN the program.
3. Repeat Problem 2 with an interesting pattern of your own creation.
4. Change the program so that it can draw several different patterns, possibly overlapping. (*Hint:* A new first DATA value should be the number of shapes. Enclose the outer loop in lines 100 to 310 within another FOR . . . NEXT loop such as:

```
┌─90   FOR SHAPE = 1 TO NSHAPES
│   .
│   .
│   .
└─320  NEXT SHAPE
```

   Test your program on two or three simple patterns.)
5. If your computer has color, add DATA values to code the color of each pattern drawn. Change the program to set a new color for each shape.

5-6 Subroutines: GOSUB . . . RETURN

Loops can be thought of as *structural blocks* out of which programs can be built. Many programs are constructed by placing one loop after another, or in the case of nested loops, inside one another. Besides loops, there are other extremely important program building blocks called *subroutines.* A *subroutine* is a short program (subprogram) that performs a relatively small task. It is part of a main program (or *routine*) and can be used by the main program wherever it is needed. The following program, which PRINTs names in a fancy format, illustrates the use of subroutines.

Program 1

Statement	Remark
10 PRINT "NAMES WITH FANFARES"	
20 GOSUB 1000: REM * GET N$	*Go to the subroutine at line 1000.*
30 GOSUB 1500: REM * PRINT FANCY	*Go to the subroutine at line 1500.*
40 GOTO 20	

```
999  REM ** SUBROUTINE TO INPUT NAME AND
            TEST FOR TRAILER VALUE **
1000 INPUT "NAME, PLEASE (ZZZZ TO END):  "; N$
1010 IF N$ = "ZZZZ" THEN GOTO 2000
1020 RETURN                                      Subroutine ends, go to line 30.
1499 REM ** SUBROUTINE FOR FANCY FORMAT **
1500 PRINT
1510 PRINT "TA DA!"
1520 PRINT
1530 PRINT "************************"
1540 PRINT "************************"
1550 PRINT N$
1560 PRINT "************************"
1570 PRINT "************************"
1580 PRINT
1590 RETURN                                      Subroutine ends, go to line 40.
2000 END
```

Output

```
NAMES WITH FANFARES
NAME, PLEASE (ZZZZ TO END):   ? BALTHAZAR

TA DA!

************************
************************
BALTHAZAR
************************
************************

NAME, PLEASE (ZZZZ TO END):   ? ZZZZ
```

When the computer executes line 20, it immediately goes to the subroutine at line 1000. (GOSUB 1000 is an abbreviation for "GOto the SUBroutine at line 1000.") There it INPUTs and tests N$. If the trailer value ZZZZ has not been typed, then the RETURN instruction in line 1020 ends the subroutine and causes the computer to go to the line immediately following the instruction GOSUB 1000, namely to line 30. There the instruction GOSUB 1500 begins a similar sequence for the subroutine at line 1500.

Subroutines may occur anywhere within a program, but the program will usually be easier to understand if they are placed at the end.

Of course, Program 1 need not be written with subroutines at all, but the main routine (lines 10–40) is shorter and easier to read if the INPUTing and PRINTing are not done there. The REMs in lines 20 and 30 are particularly useful in making the main routine clear. A REM statement at the end of a line is separated from the rest of the line by a colon.

In addition to making programs easier to understand (and to write), the use of subroutines can save typing time and debugging effort when used to handle tasks that occur repeatedly in a program. For example, the following program uses the fancy PRINT subroutine of Program 1 (lines 1500–1590) in two different places. Without the subroutine, all of these lines would have to be typed twice.

Program 2

Statement	Remark
10 PRINT "GUESS MY NAME"	
20 INPUT "YOUR GUESS: "; GUESS$	
30 PRINT "YOUR GUESS IS:"	
40 LET N$ = GUESS$	*Assigns guess to N$.*
50 GOSUB 1500: REM * PRINT GUESS	*Computer goes to the subroutine at line 1500, PRINTs the name guessed.*
60 IF GUESS$ = "RUMPELSTILTSKIN" THEN PRINT "CURSES, FOILED AGAIN": GOTO 200	*IF guess is correct, PRINT message and END.*
70 PRINT "ACTUALLY, MY NAME IS:"	
80 LET N$ = "RUMPELSTILTSKIN"	*Assigns real name to N$.*
90 GOSUB 1500: REM * PRINT REAL NAME	*Computer goes to the subroutine at line 1500, PRINTs the real name.*
100 PRINT "TOO BAD, I KEEP THE KID."	
200 END	
1499 REM ** SUBROUTINE FOR FANCY FORMAT **	
1500 PRINT	
1510 PRINT "TA DA!"	
1520 PRINT	
1530 PRINT "*************************"	
1540 PRINT "*************************"	
1550 PRINT N$	
1560 PRINT "*************************"	
1570 PRINT "*************************"	
1580 PRINT	
1590 RETURN	*Computer goes to the line following the last GOSUB instruction executed.*

Output

```
GUESS MY NAME
YOUR GUESS:   ? CASPAR
YOUR GUESS IS:

TA DA!

************************

************************
CASPAR
************************

************************

ACTUALLY, MY NAME IS:

TA DA!

************************

************************
RUMPLESTILTSKIN
************************

************************

TOO BAD, I KEEP THE KID.
```

By assigning two different strings to the variable N$ (in lines 40 and 80), we had the subroutine at line 1500 perform two slightly different tasks. Notice that the END statement (line 200) occurs at the end of the main routine, rather than after the subroutines. If this statement were missing, then after executing line 100 the computer would continue on to line 1490, and enter the subroutine at line 1500 (causing an ERROR message — see Pitfalls 1 and 4).

Avoiding Pitfalls

1. If the computer enters a subroutine without having executed a GOSUB statement, it will not know which line to go to when it arrives at the RETURN statement — a RETURN WITHOUT GOSUB error will occur. (See page 658 for the message given on your computer.)
2. Every subroutine must end with a RETURN statement.
3. Variables that are assigned values within a subroutine retain those values after the computer RETURNs to the main routine. If you use the same counting variable in a subroutine as in the main routine, then errors can develop that are hard to find. Consider, for example, the program at the top of the next page:

```
10 FOR I=1 TO 5
20 GOSUB 500
30 NEXT I
40 END
500 FOR I=1 TO 3
510 PRINT "EXO"
520 NEXT I
530 PRINT
540 RETURN
```

This program might be expected to PRINT five groups of three EXO's each. But that does not happen because the value of the counter I is changed within the subroutine. (How many groups of EXO's do you predict in the output?)

4. Remember to place an END statement (or a GOTO an END statement) at the end of the main routine *before* the subroutines. Otherwise, the computer will simply start executing the first subroutine after finishing the main routine — a RETURN WITHOUT GOSUB error will occur.

Summary

The instruction GOSUB 2600 causes the computer to go to the *subroutine* at line 2600 and start executing lines until a RETURN instruction is encountered. The RETURN instruction causes the computer to go to the statement immediately following the instruction GOSUB 2600.

A REM statement may be added at the end of any line, preceded by a colon. It is particularly important to use a REM with a GOSUB instruction to make clear the task that the subroutine will handle.

Exercises 5-6

A 1. Find the errors, if any, in each of the following programs. Give possible corrections and then predict the output.

a.
```
10 GOSUB 150
20 GOSUB 200
150 PRINT "IPSO"
160 RETURN
170 PRINT "FACTO"
180 RETURN
```

b.
```
10 GOSUB 100
20 PRINT "FICTION"
30 END
100 PRINT "FACT"
110 RETURN
```

c.
```
10 LET N = 5
20 GOSUB 500
30 PRINT "NOW"
40 GOSUB 500
50 END
500 FOR I = 1 TO N
510 PRINT "JOY"
520 NEXT I
530 END
```

d.
```
10 FOR I = 1 TO 5
20 GOSUB 400
30 PRINT "IS LOST"
40 END
400 LET I = 2
410 PRINT "ATLANTIS"
420 RETURN
```

2. Predict the output of each program.

a.
```
10 LET I = 3
20 GOSUB 100
30 LET I = 5
40 GOSUB 100
50 PRINT I
60 END
100 PRINT I * I
110 RETURN
```

b.
```
10 LET I = 2
20 GOSUB 100
30 PRINT I
40 GOSUB 100
50 PRINT I
60 END
100 LET I = 2 * I
110 RETURN
```

c.
```
10 FOR K = 1 TO 3
20 GOSUB 500
30 GOSUB 700
40 NEXT K
50 END
500 LET I = 2 * K
510 RETURN
700 PRINT I + K
710 PRINT "CORRECT"
720 RETURN
```

d.
```
10 READ D$
20 FOR J = 1 TO 3
30 FOR K = 1 TO 2
40 GOSUB 200
50 NEXT K
60 NEXT J
70 END
200 PRINT D$
210 RETURN
300 DATA GIVE ME A BREAK
```

e.
```
10 READ X
20 GOSUB 100
30 END
100 READ Y
110 GOSUB 200
120 PRINT Z
130 RETURN
200 LET Z = X - Y
210 RETURN
220 DATA 6, 3
```

f.
```
10 READ A$
20 GOSUB 500
30 READ A$
40 GOSUB 520
50 END
500 PRINT A$
510 PRINT "*****"
520 PRINT "WEARS COMBAT BOOTS"
530 RETURN
600 DATA G.I. JOE, HUMPTY DUMPTY
```

3. Change Program 1 by writing a subroutine at line 1700 that PRINTs two lines of asterisks (as in lines 1530 and 1540). Replace lines 1530 and 1540 with a GOSUB 1700, and do the same for lines 1560 and 1570. Construct a RUN chart to verify that the output is the same as Program 1.

4. Rewrite each of the following programs without using subroutines. Predict the output.

a.
```
10 LET A$="CURLY AND WAVY"
20 LET N=3
30 GOSUB 1000
40 LET A$="STRINGY AND STRAIGHT"
50 LET N=5
60 GOSUB 1000
70 END
999 REM ** SUBROUTINE **
1000 FOR I=1 TO N
1010 PRINT A$
1020 NEXT I
1030 RETURN
```

b.
```
10 FOR I=1 TO 5
20 GOSUB 1000
30 PRINT X
40 NEXT I
50 LET I=-3
60 GOSUB 1000
70 PRINT X
80 END
999 REM ** SUBROUTINE **
1000 LET X=I*(3-I)
1010 RETURN
```

5. **a.** Write a subroutine to calculate the average (AVG) of two numbers X and Y. Write a main routine that INPUTs X and Y, then PRINTs the average using the subroutine.
b. Modify the program in (a) to INPUT five numbers and find their average.

B 6. **a.** Write a subroutine starting at line 1000 that PRINTs five stars on a single line: *****
b. Write another subroutine starting at line 2000 that PRINTs one star on each of three lines:
```
*
*
*
```

c. Write a main routine that uses subroutines 1000 and 2000 to PRINT a block letter E:

```
*****
*
*
*
*****
*
*
*
*****
```

7. a. Change the program in Problem 6 so that it PRINTs a large block letter F.

b. Add a subroutine so that the program can PRINT block letters H and P.

8. (Graphics) Write a subroutine to plot the following shape at any point (X, Y) on the graphics screen:

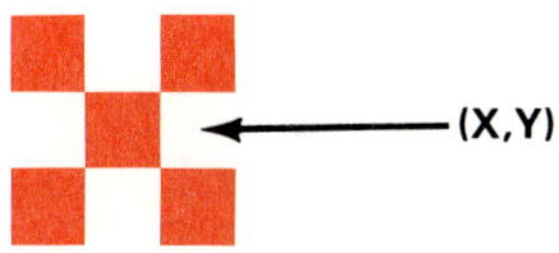

Write another subroutine to plot this shape:

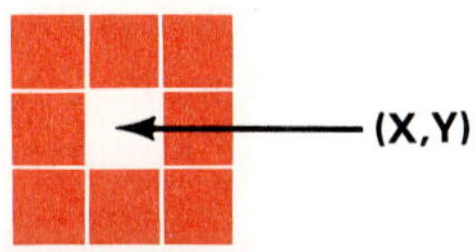

Finally, write a main routine that INPUTs a letter corresponding to the shape desired and the coordinates of (X, Y), then plots the shape at that location.

9. (Graphics) Write a program to draw a 10-by-10 square in graphics mode. Do this as follows:

a. Write a subroutine that plots a horizontal line segment point by point (use a FOR . . . NEXT loop) from the point (10, Y) to the point (19, Y), where Y is a variable. (The value of Y will be assigned later in the main routine.)

b. Write a similar subroutine that plots a vertical line segment from the point (X, 10) to (X, 19).

c. Write a main routine that assigns the values of X and Y needed in the two subroutines to draw the square. (If necessary, sketch the square on graph paper.)

10. (Graphics) Use the subroutines in Problem 9 to write a program to draw each of the letters E, H, and T in graphics mode. What other letters can be drawn with these subroutines?

Lab Activity

Recursion and Memory Limitations

A subroutine that contains a GOSUB to itself is said to be *recursive*, or to use *recursion.* As you will see, recursion is not a very useful technique in BASIC, although it is a very important part of programming in several other languages, such as LOGO and Pascal. Nevertheless, experimenting with recursion can reveal something interesting about the internal workings of your computer. Here is an example of a program using recursion:

```
10  LET I=1
20  GOSUB 100
30  END
100  PRINT I
110  LET I=I+1
120  GOSUB 100
130  RETURN
```

As you can see, the subroutine (lines 100–130) GOSUBs to itself in line 120. Can you predict the output? Well, when the computer first goes to line 100 (after executing the GOSUB statement in line 20), 1 is PRINTed and I is made equal to 2. Then the computer goes to line 100 again, 2 is PRINTed, and I is made equal to 3. This process continues without apparent end.

Problems

1. RUN the program to determine the output. (Be patient.) Eventually something surprising happens; you should get an OUT OF MEMORY error message. (Write down the final value of I that is PRINTed prior to the error message.) The reason is that every time GOSUB is executed, the computer must save the location to go to when RETURN is encountered. This takes up memory in the computer, and soon none is left. (Actually, much more memory is available for other purposes, but the particular segment of memory reserved for saving RETURN addresses is limited.)

2. Type this program:

```
10  LET I=1
20  GOSUB 100
30  LET I=I+1
40  GOTO 20
100  PRINT I
130  RETURN
```

Since the program just typed also uses the same subroutine over and over, you might expect the same OUT OF MEMORY error message. RUN the program for a while and see. The difference in this case is that a RETURN address is saved only until the RETURN instruction is encountered; then the memory space being used for that address is released for other uses (in particular, the next RETURN address). Such a use of memory, in which items are added to memory, then taken off when no longer needed, is called a *stack*.

3. Change the program back to its original form (as in Problem 1) and add this line (be sure to include the parentheses):

```
115  LET X=(1+1)
```

RUN the program. How many times does the subroutine GOSUB to itself (notice I's final value) before memory is used up? Compare the result with I's final value in Problem 1. It appears that the stack is used for purposes other than saving RETURN addresses.

4. Change line 115 to the following:

```
115  LET X=(1+(1+1))
```

RUN the program again. Does this change affect the remaining capacity in the stack more rapidly than you discovered in Problem 3? (Compare the final I-values.)

5. Experiment with other arithmetic expressions in line 115. See how much stack space you can fill (that is, how few times the subroutine can GOSUB to itself before the OUT OF MEMORY message occurs). (*Hint:* Increase the number of nested parentheses in the expression in line 115.)

6. It is possible to have recursion only finitely many times and avoid the OUT OF MEMORY error by adding an exit condition to a subroutine. For example, add this line to the original program:

```
105  IF I=5 THEN GOTO 130
```

RUN the program. The fifth time through the subroutine, this new line will cause the computer to RETURN to the statement immediately following the last GOSUB 100, namely to itself in line 130. This in turn causes another RETURN to line 130. These RETURNs to 130 continue until the only remaining GOSUB 100 is at line 20. Then the computer goes to line 30 and the program ENDs.

(*Note:* This Lab Activity gives no particular insight into what use recursion has in other computer languages. A detailed answer cannot be given here, but it has been found that many algorithms are most simply stated in recursive terms. Several languages have more powerful and flexible subroutine structures than BASIC and lend themselves more readily to recursion.)

Chapter Summary

A *standard finite loop* using GOTO and a counter has this form:

Step 1 *Initialize* the counter (give it a starting value).
Step 2 Body of the loop (all the instructions to be repeated).
Step 3 *Increment* the counter (add 1 or some other number).
Step 4 *Test* the counter (GOTO start of body of loop if a certain condition is true).

A standard *counting* (or *summing*) *loop* using READ or INPUT has this form:

Step 1 *Initialize* the counter (or summer).
Step 2 READ or INPUT a *value* (string or number).
Step 3 If *value* = *trailer value,* then GOTO Step 6 (exit the loop).
Step 4 *Increment* the counter (or add value to summer). This step may or may not be subject to some condition.
Step 5 GOTO Step 2.
Step 6 PRINT the results or do other necessary processing.

A FOR . . . NEXT loop with STEP has this form:

```
  .
  .
  .
┌100  FOR counter = initial value TO final value STEP increment
│110┐
│ . │
│ . ├   body of the loop
│ . │
│160┘
└170  NEXT counter
  .
  .
  .
```

Nested FOR . . . NEXT loops involve one FOR . . . NEXT loop (the inner loop) completely enclosed in another FOR . . . NEXT loop (the outer loop). Each time the computer executes the outer loop once, the inner loop is repeated from the beginning.

The instruction GOSUB 2000 causes the computer to go to the *subroutine* at line 2000 and start executing lines until a RETURN instruction is encountered. The RETURN instruction causes the computer to go to the statement immediately following the instruction GOSUB 2000.

A REM statement may be added at the end of any line, preceded by a colon.

Chapter Test

1. Rewrite the following program using a FOR . . . NEXT loop.

```
10 LET K=8
20 PRINT "CANINE"
30 LET K=K+1
40 IF K<=14 THEN GOTO 20
50 PRINT "DONE"
60 END
```

2. Predict the output of each of the following programs.

a.
```
10 LET K=5
20 PRINT K
30 LET K=K+1
40 PRINT K-1
50 IF K<10 THEN GOTO 20
60 END
```

b.
```
10 FOR J=1 TO 4
20 FOR K=1 TO J
30 PRINT "PREDICT  ";
40 NEXT K
50 PRINT
60 NEXT J
70 END
```

3. Write a program that uses a standard finite loop to PRINT exactly:

```
1. WAKE UP
2. WAKE UP
3. WAKE UP
GO TO SLEEP
```

4. Write a program that uses a standard finite loop to sum the even integers from 100 to 200. Do not use a DATA list.

5. Write a program using a FOR . . . NEXT loop and STEP to do each of the following:
   a. PRINT the even integers from 8 to 40.
   b. PRINT the integers from 85 to 50 in descending order.

6. Write a program using nested FOR . . . NEXT loops to PRINT exactly:

```
2     3
2     4
3     3
3     4
```

7. Write a subroutine to calculate the product (PROD) of two numbers A and B. Write a main routine that INPUTs A and B, then PRINTs the product using the subroutine.

Computer Applications *Computers that Speak and Listen*

Recent Advances

When you hear the word computer, you probably think of a silent machine that performs programmed tasks. Recently, however, advances in microchip technologies have enabled computers to "speak" and "listen." Since 1978, when the learning aid *Speak and Spell* was introduced, computers that talk and listen have been appearing in increasing numbers in factories, offices, and homes. The applications for these types of computers are so numerous that computer companies are investing large sums to produce better and better speech-synthesis chips (to allow computers to speak) and voice-recognition chips (to allow computers to listen).

Computers that Speak

Wherever there is a need for a person to read instruments, speaking computers can be used. For example, truck drivers, airplane pilots, and train engineers can be relieved of the need

Computerized instrument panel in airplane

"Talking" electronic teller

to watch gauges and meters continuously, since speaking computers can give verbal warnings of potential malfunctions. Computers that speak are already being used in newer-model automobiles to give safety warnings, or to warn of low fuel or the need for part maintenance. Some other applications that are being developed include elevators that announce floor numbers and the merchandise located on each floor, automatic banking terminals that give verbal instructions about deposit and withdrawal procedures, exit signs that broadcast emergency procedures in three different languages, and teaching machines that instruct students verbally.

How does a computer produce speech? Basically, it translates a word stored in its memory into digital signals. Then it electronically interprets the signals back into sound. The quality of the sound depends on the speech-synthesizer chip. Newer speech-synthesis chips produce much more intelligible speech than did older ones that output speech sounding hollow and mechanical.

Many computers today use the Sound Interface Device chip (SID, for short). The SID and other similar chips can control pitch, rate, frequency, and amplitude (range) to achieve quite lifelike speech.

Computers that Listen

The SID chip and others like it have helped researchers overcome the main obstacles in developing a machine that can reproduce a human voice. The next major hurdle is to develop a machine that will be able to listen and ''comprehend'' a human voice. One company is developing a dictating machine that will allow an office worker to speak to the machine, which will then convert the spoken words into printed text and display the results on the screen. With a push of a button, the office worker could have a copy of the information on paper. Certain automobile companies have already developed cars for the handicapped that use voice recognition to adjust the position of the driver's seat and to turn on the windshield wipers, lights, and radio.

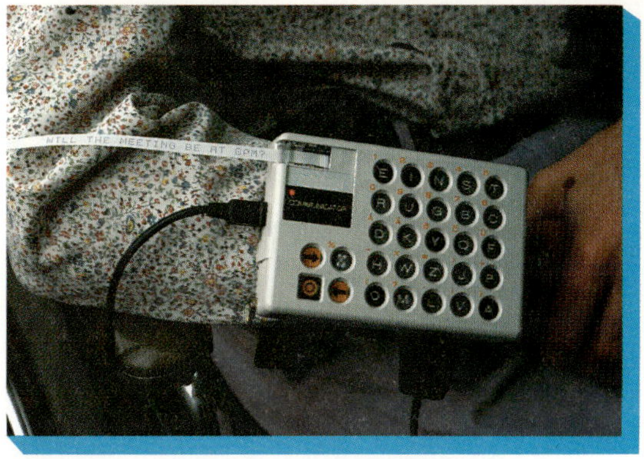

Computerized communication device for speech- and hearing-impaired people

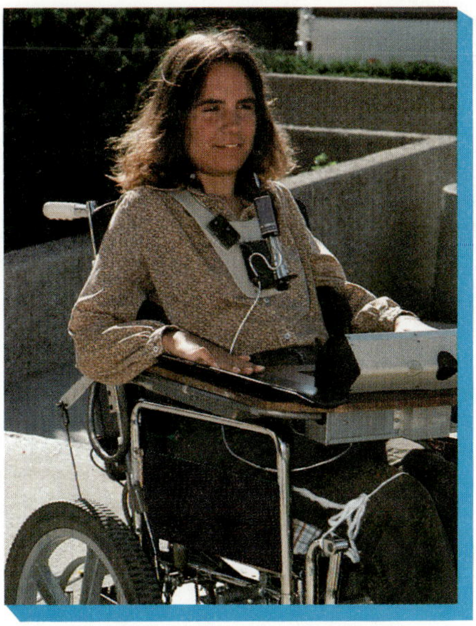

Voice-controlled computerized wheelchair

Though voice-recognition machines have an almost unlimited potential, researchers say they must first overcome some difficult technological problems to make a better chip. In order to understand a spoken word, a computer must first change the word to numbers, then it must compare the result with speech patterns already stored in its memory. If the person speaking uses a word outside the computer's limited vocabulary, the machine can easily stop ''listening.''

With technology constantly improving speech-synthesis and voice-recognition devices, it is possible that before long we may be able to carry on a ''conversation'' with a robot or understand a ''conversation'' between two machines.

Computer Languages FORTRAN

FORTRAN is a high-level computer language that was developed and introduced during the mid-1950's. Designed primarily for dealing with scientific applications and problems related to mathematics and engineering, this first widely-used computer language derives its name from FORmula TRANslator. The syntax, symbols, and rules used with FORTRAN are quite similar to those used in mathematics.

Engineers use FORTRAN in designing dams.

A FORTRAN program usually consists of three parts: a *header* statement (naming the program), *specification* statements (explaining the purpose of the program), and *executable* statements (like LET, and READ in BASIC). The letter C typed in column 1 indicates that a remark follows, just as a REM statement does in BASIC. The C is used when giving the header and specification statements as well as when other documentation is needed. Line numbers are needed only to direct branching or looping, and as a specific part of the format for input and output statements that require the reading and writing of data. Here is a FORTRAN program that calculates the amount earned when $100 is invested at 12% interest for four years.

```
C       VALUE OF AN INVESTMENT
C
C  THIS PROGRAM WILL CALCULATE THE VALUE OF YOUR INVESTMENT
C  OVER A FOUR YEAR PERIOD AT A RATE OF INTEREST OF 12%
C
        WRITE(*, 1)
      1 FORMAT('ENTER THE AMOUNT YOU WISH TO INVEST FOR A PERIOD
        OF FOUR YEARS')
        READ(*, 2)
C  FULL DOLLAR AMOUNTS UP TO SIX DIGITS WILL BE ALLOWED
      2 FORMAT(F6.0)
C
        WRITE(*, 3)
      3 FORMAT('YEAR     INTEREST      TOTAL VALUE')
```

```
C
        DO 100 I = 1, 4
        AINT = .12 * AMT
        AMT = AMT + AINT
C
        WRITE(*, 4) I, AINT, AMT
      4 FORMAT(I4, F13.2, F16.2)
    100 CONTINUE
        STOP
        END
```

Notice the similarity of a DO . . . CONTINUE loop to a BASIC FOR . . . NEXT loop. FORTRAN is a compiled computer language, as are the programming languages COBOL and Pascal. A FORTRAN compiler translates all program statements to machine language instructions and then produces a *compiled,* or *object* program. It is this object program that is then executed by the computer. (BASIC, on the other hand, is usually an *interpreted* language. This means that a BASIC interpreter converts each program statement, line by line, to machine language instructions as the program is being executed.) Most programmers prefer a compiled language because faster execution is possible. Both the original program and the compiled object program can be saved on a disk. The compiled object program can be run the next time it is needed, thus eliminating the need to translate the original program to machine language instructions each time.

As a computer programming language, FORTRAN has many advantages. The language has been in use for over 30 years, and implemented on almost every type of computer. There has been extensive sharing of information, which has made available to FORTRAN users a huge library of mathematical routines. This huge library and the language's ability to deal easily with the most complex of mathematical formulas will help keep FORTRAN a prominent programming language in the future.

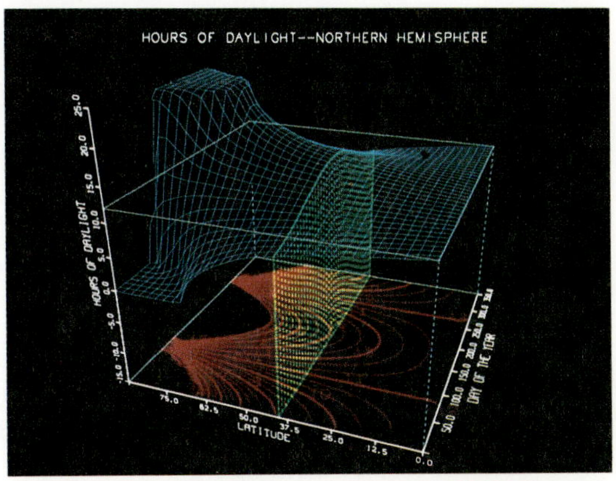

Three-dimensional graphics made using FORTRAN.

Projects

A computer project should contain more than just the programming statements to accomplish a specific task. It should also contain a title screen, a description or instruction screen, a menu screen (if necessary), an option to run the program again, and a good-by message.

The title screen can be presented using either text or graphics. It should contain the name of the project program, the programmer's name, and the date. A description screen is used to tell the user what the program is about, and an instruction screen guides the user on how to respond to the program. A menu screen offers a choice of several options related to the program. These options can be controlled internally by using several IF . . . THEN statements or subroutines.

Once the program is RUN and completed, the user should be offered the option to RUN it again. If the user answers "no" to this option, a friendly good-by message should be displayed on the screen, and the program should END.

The project should be a complete package, that is, one complete program that is user-friendly and well-documented. Here are several possibilities for computer projects:

1. Write an arithmetic-quiz program. Use a menu to offer a choice of different operations. Each quiz should contain 10 questions. A score should be given at the conclusion of the quiz, and a congratulatory (or encouraging) message should be PRINTed.
2. Write a vocabulary-drill program. Relate it to a subject of your choice. A multiple-choice format can be used. Limit the drill to 10 questions. Give the score at the end of the drill.
3. Write a program to PRINT how much change a customer would receive from a $1, $5, or $10 bill. The user should INPUT the cost of an item and the value of the bill. The output should contain the total amount of change, and the quantity of each coin (exclude half dollars) and bill needed to make the correct change.
4. Write a program that converts numbers to different bases. Use a menu to offer several choices. For example, one choice could be changing a base-ten number to a base-two number, and another choice could be changing a base-two number to a base-ten number. (*Hint:* INPUT the digits one at a time.)

5. Write a scrambled-word program that PRINTs a word with its letters all mixed up. The user should have one or two tries to guess the correct word. If the guess is correct, PRINT a congratulatory message; otherwise, PRINT the unscrambled word. (Another possibility is to have the game set up for two players.)

6. Write a treasure-hunting program in which the user searches for a treasure by typing possible screen coordinates for its location. Allow six guesses before PRINTing the treasure's name and its exact location. The game can be played several times in a row if the information (that is, treasure's name and screen coordinates) is READ from a DATA list.

7. Write a program to simulate a savings account. Have the user type the amount of the initial deposit, the annual rate of interest, and the length of time involved (6 months, 1 year, and so on). Have the program PRINT the total amount accumulated in the savings account at the end of the specified time period. If you do not know the formula for compounding interest, look it up in your school library.

8. Write a program that simulates the game of NIM. If you are not familiar with how the game is played, do some research in your school library.

9. Write a program that PRINTs form letters announcing upcoming road races. The user should be able to enter each runner's name, the date of the race, the location, the distance, a courteous closing remark, and the name of the sponsor of the race.

10. Write a program to help your teacher calculate class averages. The teacher should be able to type a student's name, the number of test scores, and the actual scores. The output should be the average of the grades, PRINTed along with an appropriate message (A = "EXCELLENT", D = "WORK HARDER", and so forth).

11. How much do you sleep each night? How much of your life have you spent sleeping? Write a program that INPUTs the average number of hours the user sleeps per night, then PRINTs the number of hours the user sleeps in a week, a 30-day month, and a year. The program then should INPUT the user's age (to the nearest year), and PRINT how many years, months, and days the user has spent sleeping.

Projects

12. Write a zodiac program in which the user types a day and month of birth, then the program PRINTs the name of the user's zodiac sign (and possibly a picture using graphics), plus a description of that sign's characteristics.

13. Write a temperature-conversion program that will convert degrees Celsius to degrees Fahrenheit, and vice versa. Use a menu to offer a choice to the user. Along with the conversion output, also tell the user how much above or below freezing the INPUT temperature is, and the corresponding wind-chill temperature.

14. Write a program to keep track of the payments of an automobile loan. The user should type the amount of money borrowed and the annual rate of interest, then the program should PRINT the amount of each monthly payment for the loan over a period of 24, 36, 48, and 60 months.

15. Write a program to find the areas and perimeters of several different geometric figures, such as a triangle, a square, a parallelogram, or a trapezoid. Have the user select a geometric figure from the menu, and then type the figure's dimensions. Have the program draw the figure (use graphics) and PRINT the results on the screen.

16. Suppose that to inherit two million dollars, you must first give away a million dollars. How long will it take you to distribute the money? Write a program that asks the user to select the amount to be given away every minute ($1, $5, $10, $20, $50, or $100). The program should then ask the user to guess how long it would take (more than a day or less than a day, more than a week or less than a week, . . ., more than a year or less than a year, and so on). PRINT the actual amount of time necessary, along with an appropriate message relating to the accuracy of the user's guess.

17. Write a program to calculate the yearly cost of giving a monthly present to a young stamp collector. A grandparent has set up a fund to begin in January and run for one year (12 months total). The fund will allow the user to purchase a plate block of stamps the first month, two plate blocks the second month, and so on. Since postal rates fluctuate periodically, the user should type the cost of a plate block of stamps. The output should PRINT how many plate blocks could be purchased over the one-year period, and the total cost to the grandparent.

18. Write a program to determine the amount of money a person can earn per week, per month, and per year, when the total number of hours worked and the hourly pay are INPUT (assume there is no overtime). If possible, have the program determine the deductions for federal income tax, state income tax, and Social Security. Then PRINT the net "take-home" pay. You may need to go to your school library for a table of tax rates.

19. Write a program to produce an itemized bill to a customer at a restaurant. Have the program PRINT a menu that allows the choice of an appetizer, a main course, a beverage, and a dessert. The program should PRINT at least three items in each category. The bill should list the items chosen, their cost, the subtotal, a 7% tax, a 15% tip, and the final total.

20. Create a menu similar to the one in Project 19. Have the program determine and PRINT the calories consumed when one item is selected from each of the categories. Display a chart listing the items and the calories associated with each, the total number of calories, and the number of miles a person would have to jog to use up all of the calories. Assume that a person must jog one mile to use up approximately 110 calories.

21. Write a quiz program consisting of 10 questions related to one of the following topics:

a) geography
b) sports, in general
c) a specific sport, basketball or baseball, for example
d) movies
e) music groups
f) specific types of music, classical or rock, for example
g) famous people in history
h) computer history — facts and people

Once the quiz has been completed, PRINT the score and an appropriate message based on the number of questions answered correctly. (10 correct = "EXCELLENT"; 5 correct = "FAIR"; and 0 correct = "TRY ANOTHER TOPIC".) The quiz format could be multiple-choice, true-false, or fill in the blank, and should allow for one or two players.

CHAPTER

6 Formatting; Graphics

This abstract image, named "Awesome Rainbow," was created by a program that plots random points and then draws lines connecting the points. The program can move the random points to produce different images.

Introduction

In Chapter 2 you learned how commas and semicolons can be used in PRINT statements to control where output will appear on the screen. Most computers provide additional ways of positioning output, which you can use to make your output clear and attractive. You will learn some of these methods in this chapter. In addition, you will explore graphics further.

6-1 The PRINT TAB Statement

BASIC provides a statement — PRINT TAB — that lets you specify where output will begin on the line being printed. Here's a simple example:

Program 1

Statement	Remark
10 PRINT "TAB PROGRAM"	
20 PRINT	*Blank line.*
30 PRINT TAB(7); "YELLOW"	*Start at column number 7.*
40 PRINT	*Blank line.*
50 PRINT TAB(13); "VIOLET"	*Start at column number 13*
60 END	

To visualize where the output of this program will appear, imagine that the columns on your screen are numbered across the top. (Of course, these numbers do not actually appear on the screen.) Then the output will be PRINTed as shown below.

Output

```
(1 2 3 4 5 6 7 8 9 10 11 12 13 14 15 16 17 18 . . . ←—— column numbers)
 T A B   P R O G R A M

             Y E L L O W

                         V I O L E T
```

The TAB instruction in line 30 causes the string YELLOW to be PRINTed starting in column number 7. Similarly, the TAB in line 50 causes VIOLET to be PRINTed starting in column number 13. (*Note:* On some computers the column at the left edge of the screen is numbered 0 instead of 1. On these machines, YELLOW still would be PRINTed starting in column number 7, but that column would be 8 spaces in from the left edge of the screen; similarly, VIOLET would be PRINTed starting in column number 13, but that would be 14 spaces in from the left.)

The PRINT TAB statement has this form:

PRINT TAB(X); *any string or expression allowed with PRINT*

X may be a number, a numeric variable, or a BASIC numerical expression. (See the Lab Activity to experiment with large and small values of X with PRINT TAB.)

Multiple TAB Instructions

More than one TAB instruction can be given on the same program line as long as semicolons separate the TAB instructions from the strings or expressions to be PRINTed. For example:

Program 2

Statement

```
5  REM * MULTIPLE TABS
10  LET A=4
20  LET B=6
30  PRINT TAB(A); B; TAB(A+5); B ↑ 2
40  END
```

Output

(1 2 3 4 5 6 7 8 9 10 . . . ⟵ column numbers)

```
      6      36
```

Note that the exact location of numerical output depends on whether your computer leaves a space in front of a number for a possible minus sign (as do *IBM* and *TRS-80* computers, but not *Apple*).

The next example of a program with TAB illustrates one of its more common uses — PRINTing output in table form. You learned one way to do this with commas in Chapter 2; TAB is more flexible since you can put the columns wherever you like. The program calculates a sales tax of 5% on a few familiar items and PRINTs the total cost of each item.

Program 3

Statement

```
10  REM * TABLE HEADINGS
20  PRINT "ITEM"; TAB(11); "COST"; TAB(21); "SALES"; TAB(31); "TOTAL"
30  PRINT TAB(21); "TAX"; TAB(31); "COST"
35  PRINT
```

```
40  LET S = .05: REM * 5% SALES TAX
45  READ ITEM$, CST
50  IF ITEM$ = "ZZZZ" THEN GOTO 90
55  LET TAX = CST * S
60  PRINT ITEM$; TAB(11); CST; TAB(21); TAX; TAB(31); CST + TAX
70  GOTO 45
80  DATA RECORD, 7.40, TAPE, 10, RADIO, 29.60
85  DATA ZZZZ, —1
90  END
```

Output

```
ITEM      COST      SALES     TOTAL
                    TAX       COST

RECORD    7.4       .37       7.77
TAPE      10        .5        10.5
RADIO     29.6      1.48      31.08
```

The values in the TAB instructions in line 60 are the same as the TAB values in line 20. This ensures that the strings and numbers to be PRINTed in line 60 "line up" beneath the table headings. Of course, in BASIC, numbers are not automatically PRINTed in correct dollars and cents form. You will learn some techniques later to do that. Notice that the trailer value ZZZZ ends the program (line 50), but the last DATA value in line 85 is —1 (why is this value needed?).

TAB instructions can be used to draw shapes with PRINTed characters; block letters and simple geometric figures are particularly easy. Program 4 below shows one way of drawing a triangle with text characters.

Program 4

Statement	Remark
10 REM * DRAW WITH TAB	
20 PRINT	
30 PRINT TAB(10); " * "	*PRINTs the * at the top of △.*
40 FOR X = 1 TO 4	
50 PRINT TAB(10 — X); " * "; TAB(10 + X); " * "	*PRINTs the two sides of the triangle.*
60 NEXT X	
70 PRINT TAB(5); " * * * * * * * * * * * "	*PRINTs the base of the △.*
75 PRINT "TRIANGLE"	
80 END	

Output

```
          *
        *   *
      *       *
    *           *
  *               *
* * * * * * * * * * *
T R I A N G L E
```

Trace through the FOR . . . NEXT loop in lines 40–60 to see how the instruction PRINT TAB(10 − X); " * "; TAB(10 + X); " * " causes the two sides of the triangle to be drawn.

Avoiding Pitfalls

1. The TAB instruction can move the cursor only from left to right. Be careful that a program line does not contain a TAB instruction to PRINT a string or number at a location that the cursor has already passed. (See the Lab Activity for this section to determine what happens when the values in the TAB instructions in a program line are given in decreasing order.)
2. Be careful not to use a value in a TAB instruction that is larger or smaller than that allowed on your computer. (See the Lab Activity for this section to experiment and discover the largest and smallest value allowed.)

Summary

The PRINT TAB statement, which has the form

PRINT TAB(X); *any string or expression allowed with PRINT*

moves the cursor to the right to column number X before PRINTing the string or expression after it. X may be a number, a numeric variable, or a BASIC numerical expression.

Multiple TAB instructions can be given on the same program line (using only one PRINT) as long as semicolons separate the TAB instructions from the strings or numbers to be PRINTed.

Exercises 6-1

In Exercises 1–10, predict the exact output of each program, with the key columns labeled.

A

1.
```
10 PRINT TAB(12); "THE"
20 PRINT TAB(13); "END"
30 END
```

2.
```
10 LET A = 20
20 PRINT A; TAB(A); A
30 END
```

3.
```
10 PRINT TAB(15); "A = ";
20 PRINT TAB(20); 10
30 PRINT
40 PRINT TAB(15); "THAT'S IT"
50 END
```

4.
```
10 LET X = -2
20 PRINT TAB(20); X
30 LET X = X + 2
40 PRINT TAB(X + 20); X
50 END
```

5.
```
10 PRINT TAB(5); "NUMBER"; TAB(19); "SQUARE"; TAB(33); "CUBE"
20 PRINT
30 LET X = 1
40 PRINT TAB(8); X; TAB(22); X * X; TAB(34); X * X * X
50 LET X = X + 2
60 IF X <= 9 THEN GOTO 40
70 END
```

6.
```
10 FOR I = 10 TO 12
20 PRINT TAB(I); "X"; TAB(26 - I); "X"
30 NEXT I
40 LET I = 13
50 FOR J = 1 TO 5
60 PRINT TAB(I); "X"
70 NEXT J
80 PRINT
90 PRINT TAB(18 - I); "LETTERS ARE EASY!"
100 END
```

7.
```
10 FOR T = 1 TO 3
15 PRINT TAB(17); "TTTTTTTTT"
20 NEXT T
25 FOR N = 1 TO 6
30 PRINT TAB(20); "TTT"
35 NEXT N
40 END
```

8.
```
10 PRINT TAB(8); "%%%%%"
20 FOR I = 1 TO 3
30 PRINT TAB(I + 8); "%";
     TAB(I + 12); "%"
40 NEXT I
50 PRINT TAB(12); "%%%%%"
60 END
```

9.
```
10  READ A
20  IF A = 999 THEN GOTO 50
30  PRINT TAB(A + 15); A
40  GOTO 10
50  PRINT
60  PRINT TAB(10); "BLAST OFF!!"
70  DATA 10, 9, 8, 7, 6, 5, 4, 3, 2, 1
75  DATA 0, 999
80  END
```

10.
```
10  GOSUB 100
20  GOSUB 200
30  GOSUB 100
40  END
100  PRINT TAB(18); " * * * * * *"
110  RETURN
200  FOR X = 1 TO 3
205  PRINT TAB(18); " * "
210  NEXT X
220  RETURN
```

In Exercises 11–14, write a program using TABs that will draw each design starting at the center column on your screen. Whenever possible, use FOR . . . NEXT loops.

B 11.
```
      A
     B
    C
   D
  E
 F
G
```

12.
```
3     3
 4   4
  5 5
   6
   7
   8
   9
```

13.
```
     *
    * *
   *   *
  *     *
 *       *
***********
    * *
    * *
    * *
```

14.
```
IIIIIIIIII
IIIIIIIIII
IIIIIIIIII
   IIII
   IIII
   IIII
   IIII
   IIII
IIIIIIIIII
IIIIIIIIII
IIIIIIIIII
```

15. Write a program that will PRINT (use TABs) your initials in large block letters. Use FOR . . . NEXT loops and subroutines whenever possible.

16. Write a program that will calculate the diameter and area of circles with different radii. (*Remember:* diameter = 2 * radius; area = pi * r^2.) Use PI = 3.14 and READ the values of the radii from a DATA statement. The output should be PRINTed (use TABs) with headings, in a form similar to the following:

CIRCLES

RADIUS	DIAMETER	AREA
3	6	28.26
4	8	50.24
5	10	78.5
6	12	113.04
7	14	153.86
8	16	803.84

17. Write a program using TABs that will PRINT the rectangle shown here at the lower left part of your screen. (*Hint:* PRINT blank lines to move the cursor down to the lower part of the screen.)

```
? ? ? ? ? ? ? ? ? ?
?                 ?
?                 ?
? ? ? ? ? ? ? ? ? ?
```

18. Write a program using TABs and a FOR . . . NEXT loop to PRINT the triangle shown here at the lower right part of your screen. (See the hint for Exercise 17.)

```
@ @ @ @ @ @ @ @
  @           @
    @         @
      @       @
        @     @
          @   @
            @ @
              @
```

C 19. *Challenge:* Write a program using TABs that will PRINT the tree shown here at the center of your screen. Use nested FOR . . . NEXT loops.

```
          *
        * * *
      * * * * *
    * * * * * * *
  * * * * * * * * *
* * * * * * * * * * *
        * * *
        * * *
        * * *
```

20. *Challenge:* Write a program using TABs that will PRINT a rectangle (consisting of asterisks) whose length L and width W are INPUT from a user. Beneath the rectangle, PRINT the rectangle's length, width, perimeter (P = 2 * L + 2 * W), and area (A = L * W), with appropriate labels. For example, if the INPUT values of L and W are 10 and 5, respectively, then beneath the rectangle PRINT the following:

L: 10   W: 5   P: 30   A: 50

Lab Activity

Experimenting with TAB

Problems

1. Type the following program into your computer:

```
10 INPUT "TYPE A VALUE FOR X IN TAB(X):  "; X
20 PRINT "!"; TAB(X); "!"
30 END
```

RUN the program several times and answer the following:

a. What is the maximum value of X in TAB(X) that keeps the cursor on the same line as the original "!"?

b. What happens when the value of X is greater than the maximum value you determined in (a)?

c. Is there a maximum value of X that your computer accepts in TAB(X)?

2. Type the following program into your computer:

```
10 PRINT " * "
20 PRINT TAB(—1); " * "
30 PRINT TAB(0); " * "
40 PRINT TAB(1); " * "
50 PRINT TAB(2); " * "
60 END
```

a. RUN the program. What is the number of the column at the left edge of your computer's screen?

b. What happens if the number in the parentheses in a TAB instruction is less than the number of the first column?

3. Type this program into your computer:

```
10 PRINT TAB(30); "WOW"; TAB(10); "THIS"
20 PRINT TAB(30); "IS"; TAB(10); "DIFFERENT"
30 END
```

(Notice that the TAB values are in decreasing order in lines 10 and 20.)

a. RUN the program. Study the output. Summarize what your computer does when a program line contains a TAB instruction to PRINT at a location the cursor has already passed.

b. Change the values in the TAB instructions so the message reads the way you think the programmer intended.

6-2 Positioning the Cursor

Thus far, you have learned to control the placement of output by using PRINT with commas and semicolons, blank PRINTs, strings consisting of spaces, and PRINT TAB. Most computers provide additional ways of positioning the cursor so that output can be placed *anywhere* on the screen. This section will explore the instructions HTAB and VTAB for *Apple* computers, PRINT @ ("print at") for *TRS-80,* and LOCATE for *IBM*.

Apple: HTAB and VTAB

In Chapter 2 (see the Lab Activity on page 20), you determined the size of the *Apple* text screen. You learned that the screen accommodates up to 24 lines, or *rows,* of print; each row contains 40 character spaces, or columns. The rows and columns are shown on the grid below. (*Note:* Some *Apple* computers have "80-column cards" that allow them to display 80 columns on their text screen; we won't discuss the use of 80 columns on the *Apple*.)

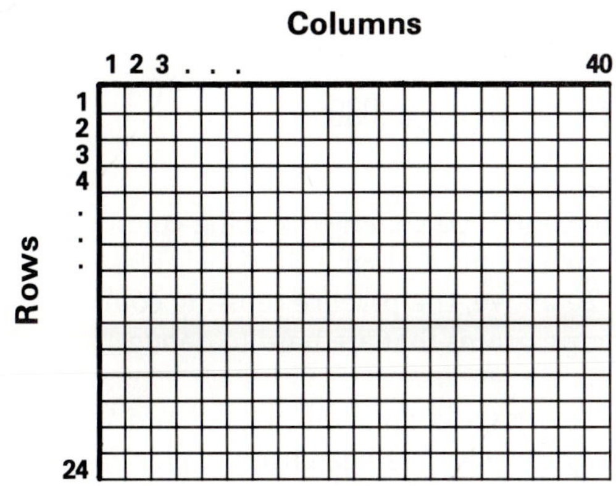

The Commodore is like the Apple but use the commands COL=▢:LINE=▢ instead of HTab and VTAB

The HTAB and VTAB statements can be used to position the cursor at any location on the screen where you want to PRINT output. HTAB specifies the column number and VTAB the row number, as Program 1 illustrates.

Program 1

Statement	Remark
10 HOME	*Erase screen.*
20 HTAB 10	*Move cursor to column 10.*
30 VTAB 4	*Move cursor to row 4.*
40 PRINT "MOVE THE CURSOR"	*PRINTs at row 4, column 10.*
50 END	

Output

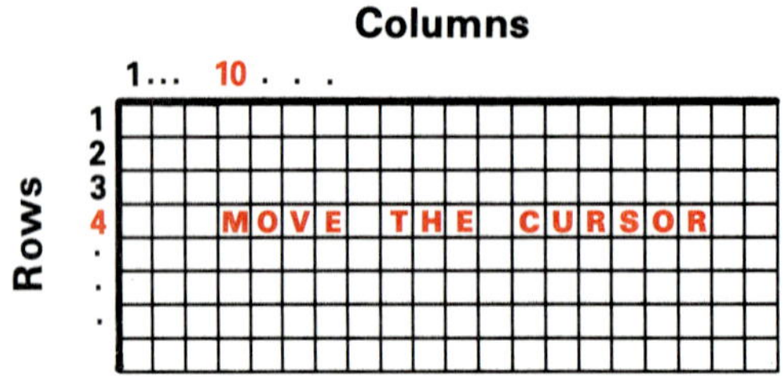

Note that HTAB and VTAB, unlike TAB, are not used inside a PRINT statement and do not require parentheses around the column or row numbers.

Colons can be used to combine HTAB, VTAB, and a PRINT instruction on one program line. The following program has the same output as Program 1.

Program 2

Statement

```
10  HOME
20  HTAB 10: VTAB 4: PRINT "MOVE THE CURSOR"
30  END
```

(*Note:* Previously, you have seen combined statements using colons with multiple actions in IF . . . THEN statements and with REMs. However, except for simple cases such as in line 20 above, the practice of using combined statements can lead to confusing programs that are hard to debug.)

Planning output on a grid sheet can make coding with HTAB and VTAB relatively simple. For example, the grid below has been used to plan the location for the title of what the author hopes will be an interesting book.

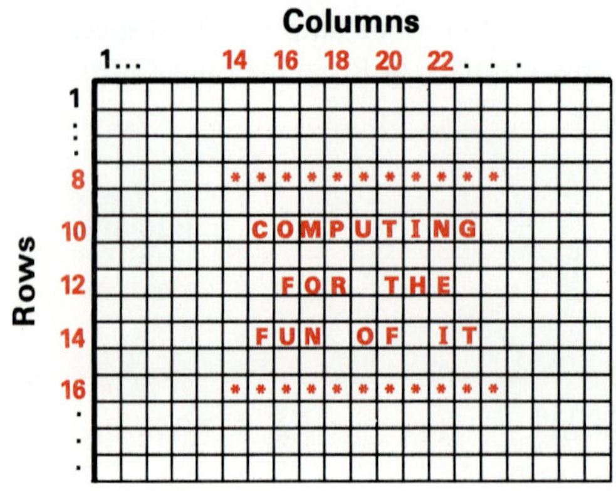

Here is the BASIC program to PRINT the title, with the column and row numbers from the grid sheet inserted in the HTAB and VTAB instructions:

Program 3

Statement

```
10  HOME
20  HTAB 14: VTAB 8: PRINT "* * * * * * * * * * *"
30  HTAB 15: VTAB 10: PRINT "COMPUTING"
40  HTAB 16: VTAB 12: PRINT "FOR THE"
50  HTAB 15: VTAB 14: PRINT "FUN OF IT"
60  HTAB 14: VTAB 16: PRINT "* * * * * * * * * * *"
70  END
```

The most important feature of HTAB and VTAB is that they can move the cursor anywhere on the screen — left, right, up, or down — not just to the right as with TAB.

The column and row numbers in HTAB and VTAB statements may be represented by BASIC numerical expressions, as in this program:

Program 4

Statement

```
   10  HOME
┌─ 20  FOR I = 1 TO 5
│  30  HTAB 2 * I: VTAB I + 1: PRINT "S L I P P I N G"
└─ 40  NEXT I
   50  END
```

Output

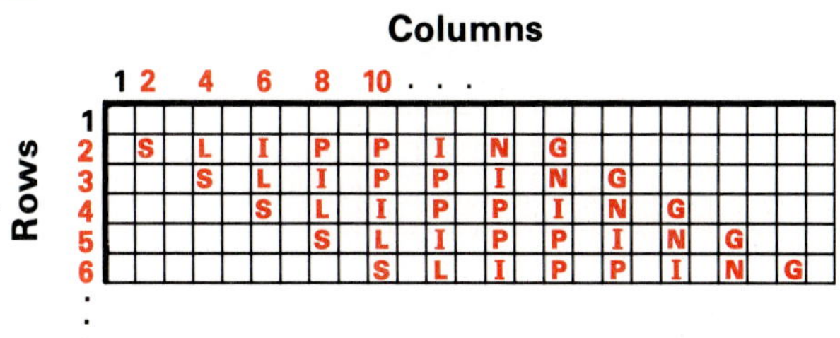

Trace through the FOR . . . NEXT loop in lines 20–40 to verify the HTAB and VTAB positions shown in the grid.

Avoiding Pitfalls

1. An instruction such as PRINT HTAB 5 will cause a SYNTAX error message. HTAB and VTAB are not used inside a PRINT statement.
2. If you specify a number greater than 255 (or < 0) with HTAB, or a number greater than 24 (or < 1) with VTAB, an ILLEGAL QUANTITY ERROR will result.

Summary for Apple

HTAB and VTAB statements can be used to position the cursor anywhere on the screen that you want to PRINT output.

The statement HTAB X moves the cursor to *column* X.

The statement VTAB Y moves the cursor to *row* Y.

(Exercises 6–2 are on page 280.)

TRS-80: PRINT @

In Chapter 2 (see the Lab Activity for Section 2–1, page 20), you discovered the size of the *TRS-80* screen. You learned that the screen holds up to 16 lines, or *rows,* of print; each row contains 64 character spaces, or *columns.* This means that there is a total of $16 \times 64 = 1024$ possible positions to which you can move the cursor to PRINT output. The 1024 positions are numbered from 0 to 1023, as you can see on the grid below.

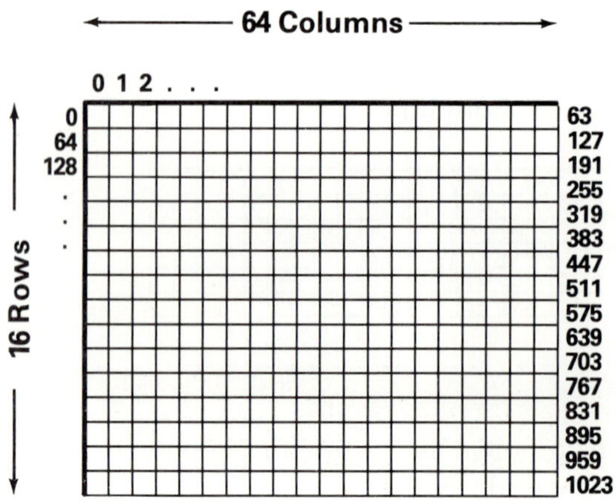

You can specify any one of the 1024 positions by using the instruction PRINT @, either as a program statement or an immediate mode command. The PRINT @ instruction has this form:

PRINT @ *position number, any string or expression allowed with PRINT*

Here is a short program using PRINT @:

Program 1

Statement

```
10  CLS
20  PRINT @ 145, "MOVE THE CURSOR"
30  END
```

Output

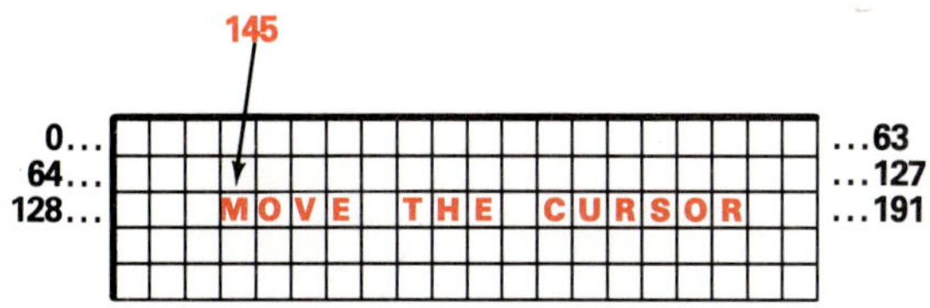

Note that the PRINT @ instruction, unlike PRINT TAB, requires no parentheses around the position number. (A SYNTAX ERROR will result if parentheses are used.)

Multiple PRINT @ instructions can be given on one program line, without repeating the PRINT, as in the following program.

Program 2

Statement

```
10  CLS
20  PRINT @ 9, "MOVE"; @ 81, "ANYWHERE"; @ 134, "YOU"; @ 203, "WANT"
30  END
```

Output

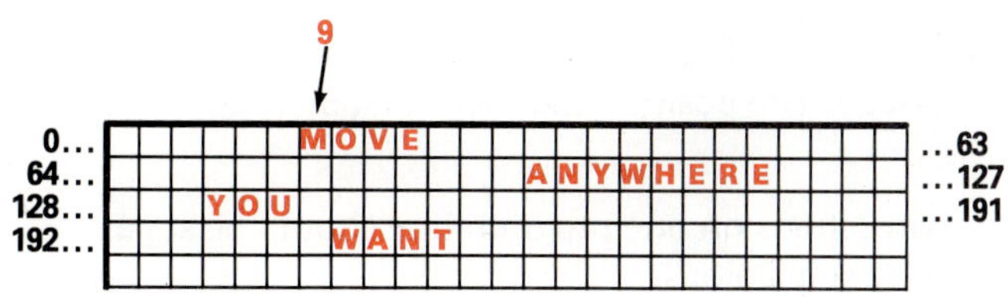

Multiple PRINT @ instructions must be separated from each other by semicolons as in line 20. The position numbers in a program line can be given in any order. For example, if line 20 were changed to

```
20 PRINT @ 81, "ANYWHERE"; @ 134, "YOU"; @ 9, "MOVE"; @ 203, "WANT"
```

the output of the program would still be the same. The most important feature of the PRINT @ instruction is that it can move the cursor anywhere on the screen — left, right, up, or down — not just to the right as with TAB.

The position numbers in PRINT @ instructions may be represented by BASIC numerical expressions, as in this program:

Program 3

Statement

```
10 CLS
20 FOR I = 1 TO 4
30 PRINT @ 70 * I, "BOUNCING"
40 NEXT I
50 END
```

Output

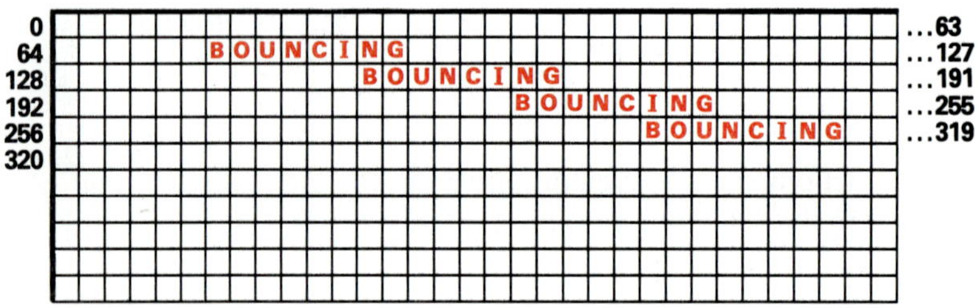

The PRINT @ 70 * I instruction in line 30 causes the string BOUNCING to appear at the position numbers 70 * 1 = 70, 70 * 2 = 140, . . . , and 70 * 4 = 280, as you can see in the grid above.

Avoiding Pitfalls

1. A PRINT @ instruction such as PRINT @ 68; "BYE" will cause a SYNTAX ERROR message. The position number must be followed by a comma.
2. Multiple PRINT @ instructions on one program line should be separated from each other by semicolons.

3. If the position number specified in a PRINT @ instruction is off the screen (that is, it is greater than 1023 or less than 0), then the computer will print an ILLEGAL FUNCTION CALL error message and your program will stop.

Summary for TRS-80

The PRINT @ instruction can be used to position the cursor at any location where you want to PRINT output. The PRINT @ instruction has the following form:

PRINT @ *position number, any string or expression allowed with PRINT*

The position numbers may range from 0 to 1023.

(Exercises 6–2 are on page 280.)

IBM: LOCATE

In Chapter 2 (see the Lab Activity for Section 2–1, page 20), you discovered the size of the *IBM* text screen. You learned that the screen accommodates up to 25 lines, or *rows,* of print; each row contains 80 character spaces, or *columns.* The rows and columns are shown on the grid below.

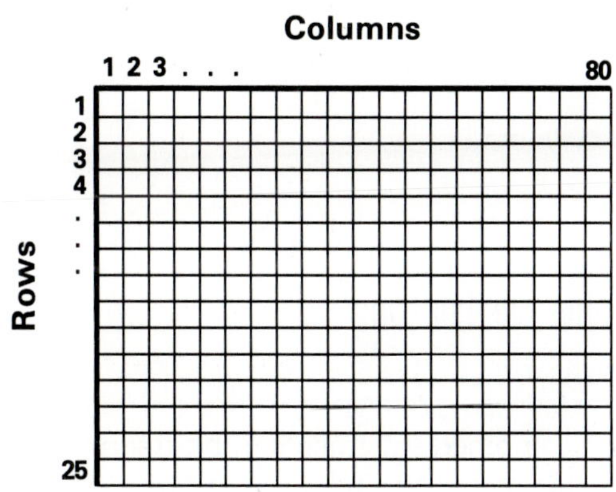

The LOCATE instruction can be used to position the cursor at any location on the screen where you want to PRINT output. The row and column numbers are specified this way:

LOCATE *row number, column number*

LOCATE can be used either as an immediate mode command or as a program statement. There is a short program illustrating the use of LOCATE at the top of the next page.

Program 1

Statement	Remark
10 CLS	
20 LOCATE 4, 6	*Row 4, column 6.*
30 PRINT "MOVE THE CURSOR"	
40 END	

Output

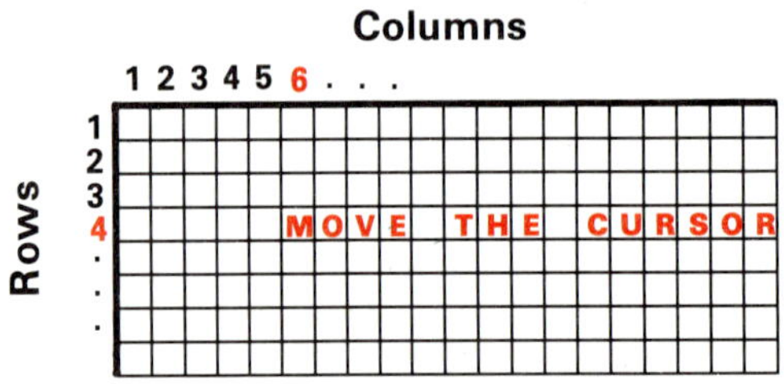

Note that LOCATE, unlike TAB, requires no parentheses around the row and column numbers.

A colon can be used to combine a LOCATE instruction and a PRINT instruction on the same program line. The following program has the same output as Program 1.

Program 2

Statement

```
10  CLS
20  LOCATE 4, 6: PRINT "MOVE THE CURSOR"
30  END
```

(*Note:* Previously, you have seen combined statements using colons with multiple actions in IF . . . THEN statements and with REMs. On most machines, BASIC allows virtually any statements to be combined on a single program line. However, except for simple cases such as in line 20 above, the practice of using combined statements can lead to confusing programs that are hard to debug.)

Planning the output of a program on a grid sheet can make the coding of LOCATE instructions relatively simple. For example, the grid sheet at the top of the next page has been used to plan the location for the title of what the author hopes will be an interesting book.

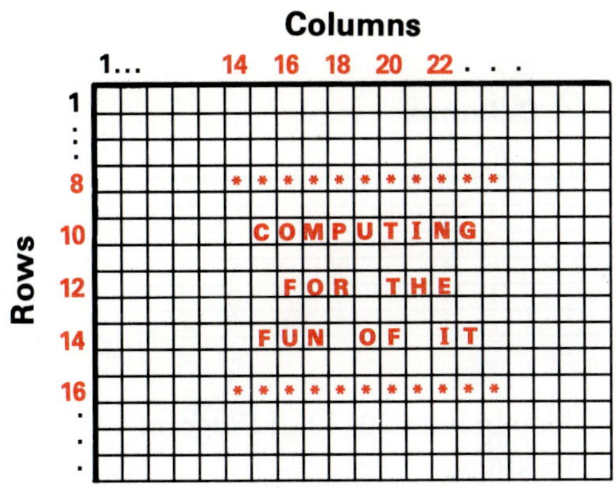

Here is the BASIC program to PRINT the title, with the row and column numbers from the grid sheet inserted in the LOCATE instructions:

Program 3

Statement

```
5  REM * GRID-SHEET CODING
10 CLS
20 LOCATE 8, 14: PRINT "***********"
30 LOCATE 10, 15: PRINT "COMPUTING"
40 LOCATE 12, 16: PRINT "FOR THE"
50 LOCATE 14, 15: PRINT "FUN OF IT"
60 LOCATE 16, 14: PRINT "***********"
70 END
```

The important feature to note with LOCATE is that it can move the cursor anywhere on the screen — left, right, up, or down — not just to the right as with TAB.

The row and column numbers in LOCATE instructions may be represented by BASIC numerical expressions, as in this next program:

Program 4

Statement

```
10 CLS
20 FOR I = 1 TO 5
30 LOCATE I + 1, 2 * I: PRINT "S L I P P I N G"
40 NEXT I
50 END
```

Output

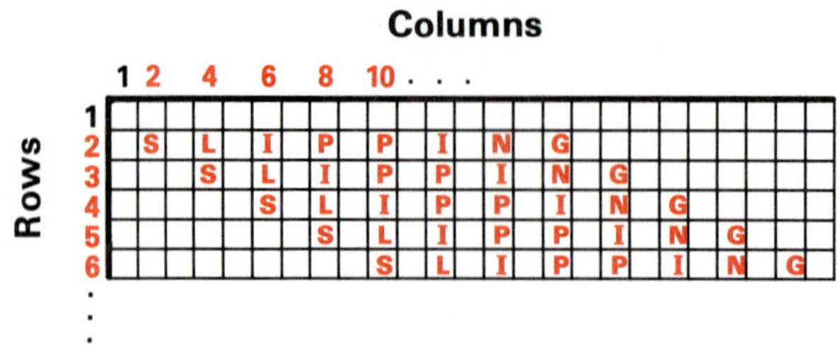

Trace through the FOR . . . NEXT loop in lines 20–40 of Program 4 to verify the LOCATE positions shown in the grid.

Avoiding Pitfalls

1. Be careful when using LOCATE that you do not enclose the row and column numbers in parentheses (or a SYNTAX ERROR will result).
2. In a LOCATE instruction, do not specify a row number greater than 25, or a column number greater than 80, or an ILLEGAL FUNCTION CALL error will result.

Summary for IBM

The LOCATE instruction can be used to position the cursor anywhere on the screen that you want to PRINT output. The statement has this form:

LOCATE *row number, column number*

Exercises 6-2

A **1.** Using the grid on a piece of graph paper to help you, predict the exact location of the output of each program listed for your computer. Label the grid with numbers as was done in the examples in this section.

Apple

a.
```
10 HOME
20 HTAB 5
30 VTAB 8
40 PRINT "SAYINGS"
50 END
```

b.
```
10 HOME
20 HTAB 15: VTAB 10
30 PRINT "SALUTATIONS"
40 HTAB 14: VTAB 7
50 PRINT "GREETINGS AND"
60 END
```

c.
```
10 HOME
20 LET M = 4
30 HTAB M: VTAB M
40 PRINT "NOTHING VENTURED"
50 HTAB M + 2: VTAB M + 6
60 PRINT "NOTHING GAINED"
70 END
```

d.
```
10 HOME
20 FOR X = 1 TO 5
30 HTAB 2 * X: VTAB X
40 PRINT X
45 NEXT X
50 END
```

TRS-80

a.
```
10 CLS
20 PRINT @ 260, "FANTASY"
30 END
```

b.
```
10 CLS
20 PRINT @ 140, "SOMETHING"
30 PRINT @ 151, "SPECIAL"
40 END
```

c.
```
10 CLS
20 LET X = 365
30 PRINT @ X, "NOTHING"
40 PRINT @ X + 64, "FANCY"
50 END
```

d.
```
10 CLS
20 FOR I = 1 TO 5
30 PRINT @ I * 10, "GOING"
40 NEXT I
50 END
```

IBM

a.
```
10 CLS
20 LOCATE 8, 25
30 PRINT "TAKE A LOOK"
40 END
```

b.
```
10 CLS
20 LOCATE 20, 10: PRINT "DOWN"
30 LOCATE 10, 20: PRINT "UPSIDE"
35 PRINT "UPSIDE DOWN"
40 END
```

c.
```
10 CLS
20 LET X = 5
30 LET Y = X * 4
40 LOCATE X, Y: PRINT "VARIETY
     ADDS SPICE"
50 END
```

d.
```
10 CLS
20 FOR I = 15 TO 20
30 LOCATE I, 40 - I
40 PRINT "I KNEW IT"
50 END
```

B **2.** For each of the outputs in (a)–(e), write a program to produce the output shown. Whenever possible, use FOR . . . NEXT loops.

a.

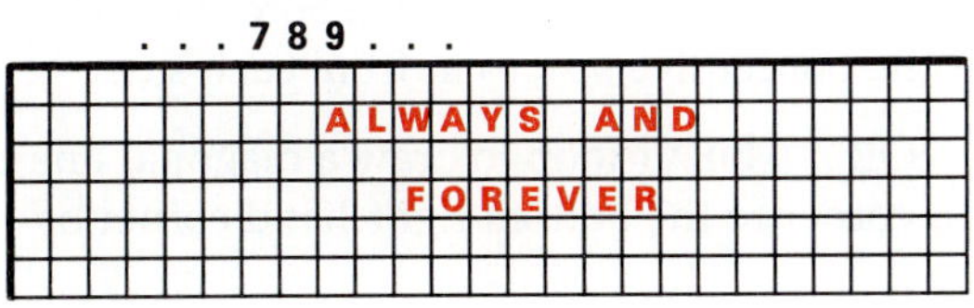

b.

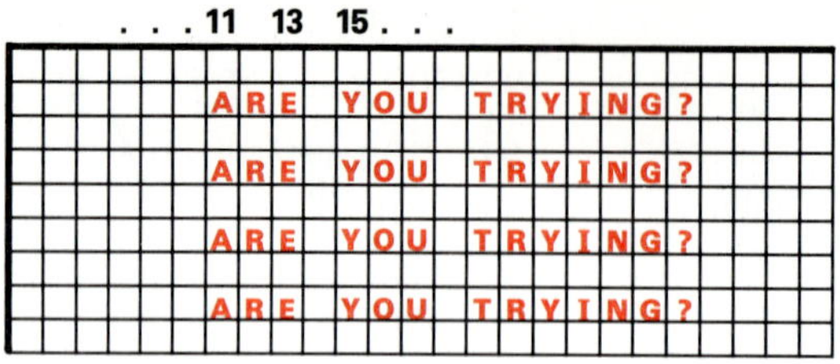

c.

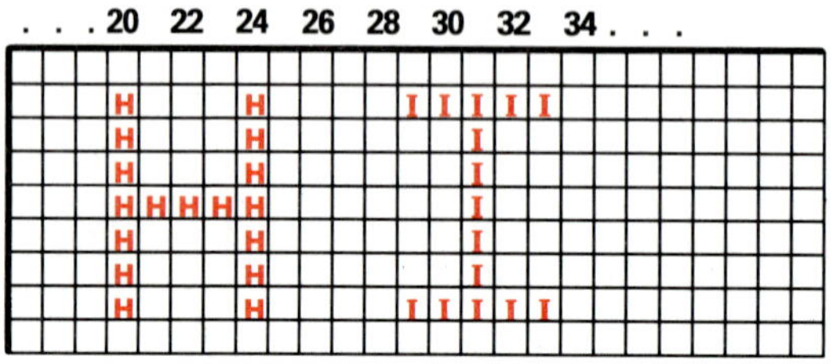

(In part (c), use subroutines to PRINT the vertical and horizontal parts of each blockletter.)

d.

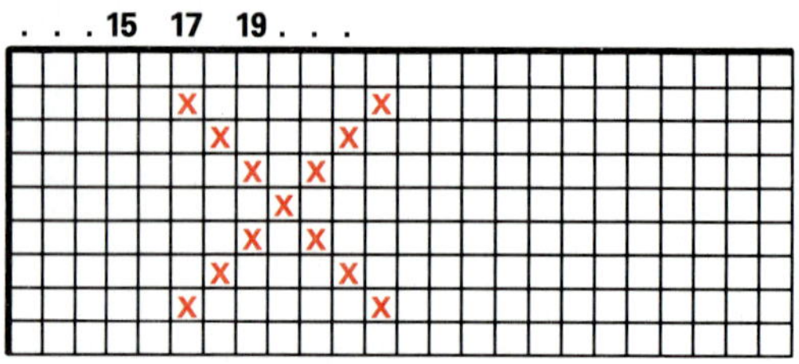

e. *Challenge:*

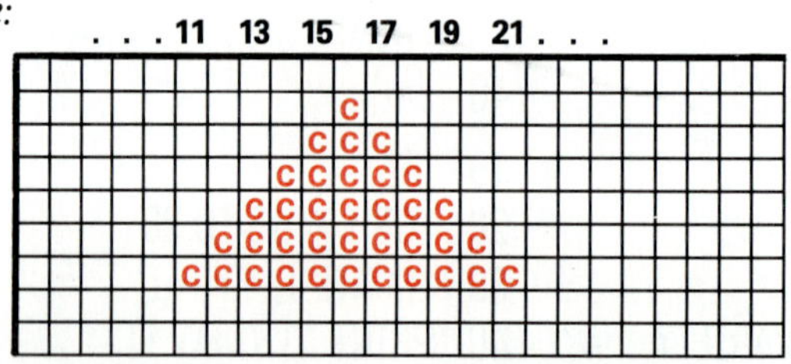

In Exercises 3–8, use LOCATE *(IBM)*, PRINT @ *(TRS-80)*, or HTAB and VTAB *(Apple)*.

3. Write a program that PRINTs your initials in block letters made up of $'s at the center of the screen.

4. Write a program using FOR . . . NEXT loops to display a border of *'s around the screen. Position the border five spaces in from each side.

5. a. Write a program using a FOR . . . NEXT loop to draw a diagonal line of ?'s from the top left-hand corner to the bottom right-hand corner of the screen.

b. Add to the program in (a) so that it also draws a diagonal line of ?'s from the top right-hand corner to the bottom left-hand corner.

6. a. Write a program to display the message ON YOUR MARK . . . at the center of the screen. Have the program erase the message (PRINT a string of blank spaces) and display the message GET SET . . . at the same location.

b. Modify the program in (a) so that each message is displayed for only a few seconds and is then erased. (Use a FOR . . . NEXT time-delay loop. See the Lab Activity for Section 5–3, page 221.) After GET SET . . . is erased, display the message GO at the same location.

7. Write a program with an INPUT statement that has GET IT? as the message. Display the message on the next to last line of your screen. Have the program PRINT the message GOOD at the center of the screen if the user types GOT IT in response to the INPUT statement. END the program if the user types NO. If any message other than GOT IT or NO is typed, that message should be erased (PRINT a string of blank spaces). The user then should be allowed to respond again to the GET IT? prompt.

8. Write a program that PRINTs the number 0 at the center of the screen. If the user presses the < RETURN > or < ENTER > key, have the program change the 0 to a 1 and PRINT it at the same location. Next time the user presses < RETURN > or < ENTER >, the 1 should be replaced by a 2, and so forth. If anything other than < RETURN > or < ENTER > is typed, have the user try again. END the program when DONE is typed. (*Hint:* Use INPUT to detect a < RETURN > or < ENTER > key press.)

Lab Activity

Dynamic Printing

Using the precise cursor control introduced in this section, some very pleasing text displays can be designed. Type the following program. (Some lines vary for different computers; choose the version for your machine.)

Apple

Statement

```
10 REM * DYNAMIC PRINTING
20 HOME
30 LET VCNTR = 12: REM * VERTICAL CENTER OF SCREEN
40 LET HCNTR = 20: REM * HORIZONTAL CENTER OF SCREEN
```

Program continued on next page.

```
50  FOR NUM = 0 TO 11
60  LET CH$ = " * ": REM * CHARACTER TO BE PRINTED
70  GOSUB 500: REM * PRINT SQUARE NUM SPACES OUT FROM CENTER
80  NEXT NUM
90  GOTO 90: REM * TO AVOID CURSOR
100  END
490  REM ** SUBROUTINE TO PRINT SQUARE **
500  LET VSTRT = VCNTR — NUM: REM * START NUM SPACES UP FROM CENTER
510  LET HSTRT = HCNTR — NUM: REM * START NUM SPACES TO THE LEFT
520  LET VFIN = VCNTR + NUM: REM * STOP NUM SPACES BELOW CENTER
530  LET HFIN = HCNTR + NUM: REM * STOP NUM SPACES TO RIGHT
540  REM ** PRINT TOP AND BOTTOM ROWS **
550  FOR H = HSTRT TO HFIN
560  LET V = VSTRT
570  GOSUB 700: REM * PRINT CH$ AT H, V
580  LET V = VFIN
590  GOSUB 700
600  NEXT H
610  REM ** PRINT LEFT AND RIGHT COLUMNS **
620  FOR V = VSTRT TO VFIN
630  LET H = HSTRT
640  GOSUB 700: REM * PRINT CH$ AT H, V
650  LET H = HFIN
660  GOSUB 700
670  NEXT V
680  RETURN
690  REM ** SUBROUTINE TO PRINT CH$ AT H, V **
700  HTAB H: VTAB V
710  PRINT CH$;
720  RETURN
```

TRS-80

Here are the changes for *TRS-80* computers:

```
20  CLS
30  LET VCNTR = 8
40  LET HCNTR = 32
50  FOR NUM = 0 TO 7
700  PRINT @ 64 * (V — 1) + H, CH$;
710  ←— delete
```

IBM

Here are the changes for *IBM* computers:

```
20  CLS
40  LET HCNTR = 40
700  LOCATE V, H
```

(Also, you need to change the REM statements in lines 570, 640, and 690 to read: REM * PRINT CH$ at V, H.)

Problems

1. RUN the program. You will need to interrupt the program manually because of the infinite loop in line 90. What figure is displayed on the screen?

2. Change line 50 so that the first square drawn is the biggest one rather than the small one in the middle. (*Hint:* Use STEP.)

3. Change the program in Problem 2 so that after each square is drawn, it is immediately erased before the next (smaller) square is drawn. (*Hint:* Have the program GOSUB 500 again, but with CH$ = " ".)

4. Restore the program to its original form. Change subroutine 500 so that the program PRINTs only the top and bottom rows of each square and therefore produces an "hour-glass" figure that looks similar to figure (a) at the right.

a.
```
* * * * * * * * *
  * * * * * * *
    * * * * *
      * * *
        *
      * * *
    * * * * *
  * * * * * * *
* * * * * * * * *
```

5. Change the program in Problem 4 so that only the corners of the squares are PRINTed, thus producing an "X" shape similar to that shown in figure (b). (*Hint:* Add a STEP instruction in line 550 so that only the two endpoints of the top and bottom rows are PRINTed.)

b.
```
*               *
  *           *
    *       *
      *   *
        *
      *   *
    *       *
  *           *
*               *
```

6. *Challenge:* Change the program in Problem 5 so that the X shape "flashes" slowly on the screen. (*Hint:* First draw the shape, then erase it, then redraw it, and so forth. Use a time-delay loop to slow the rate of flashing.)

c.
```
*       *       *
  *     *     *
    *   *   *
      * * *
* * * * * * * * *
      * * *
    *   *   *
  *     *     *
*       *       *
```

7. *Challenge:* Make a couple of changes to the program in Problem 6 to produce a flashing "star" that looks similar to the one shown in figure (c).

IBM and TRS-80

6-3 PRINT USING

At times you may want to display the output of your program in a special format. Many computers (including *IBM* and *TRS-80,* but not *Apple*) provide a PRINT USING statement, which allows you to specify more exactly than with PRINT how numbers should appear in the output. (Special techniques that will help determine the precise format of *Apple* output will be presented in Chapter 8.) A statement such as

```
30 PRINT USING "###.##"; Y
```

will PRINT the value of Y with two digits after the decimal point. The expression ###.## is called a *formatting string;* each # reserves space for one digit. The formatting string in line 30 above reserves space for up to five digits, three digits to the left of the decimal point and two digits to the right.

For example, if Y = 454.58

then the output from line 30 will be

454.58.

For another example, if Y = 54.58

then the output will be 54.58.

Note that the computer does not fill unused reserved spaces in front of the decimal point with zeros. For unused reserved spaces after the decimal point, however, just the opposite is true, as Program 1 illustrates.

Program 1

Statement

```
10 PRINT USING "##.##"; 52.5
20 END
```

Output

```
52.50
```

Ordinarily, the 0 in 52.50 would not be printed in BASIC (that is, the output of the instruction PRINT 52.50 is 52.5). However, it is convenient to have the zero PRINTed at the end when the program is printing amounts of money or is printing columns of numbers in a table.

The formatting string in a PRINT USING statement may be represented by a string variable, as in the program at the top of the next page.

Program 2

Statement

```
10 LET A$ = "###.#"
20 PRINT USING A$; 25.87
30 END
```

Output

```
25.9
```

Look at the output. Since the formatting string in line 10 reserves space for only one digit after the decimal point, the computer rounds off .87 to .9. As you can see, PRINT USING provides a simple way of PRINTing decimals rounded off to any desired number of places.

Single variables or more complicated BASIC numerical expressions may be used in a PRINT USING statement as long as the variables or expressions are separated from each other by commas, as in Program 3.

Program 3

Statement

```
10 PRINT "SPECIAL FORMAT"
20 READ A, B
30 IF A = -1 THEN GOTO 70
40 PRINT USING "###       ###.##"; A, B
50 GOTO 20
60 DATA 20, 152.45, 155, 98.966, 200, 58.5, -1, -1
70 END
```

Output

```
SPECIAL FORMAT
 20      152.45
155       98.97
200       58.50
```

The formatting string in line 40 reserves space for up to three digits for the values of A, and five digits for B (three in front of the decimal point and two after). The spaces inserted in the formatting string between ### and ###.## create the space between the columns shown in the output. Note that PRINT USING provides a way to align decimal points when numbers are to be output in a column. The comma in line 40 does *not* cause the values of A and B to appear in the first two PRINT zones, as would be the case in an ordinary PRINT statement containing commas.

When the numbers in a program represent amounts of money, it is often desirable to print a dollar sign ($) in the output. A statement of the form 50 PRINT USING "$$###.##"; Y will put a single $ in front of the value of Y. For example, if Y is 356.84, then the output from line 50 will be $356.84. Two $'s are needed in the formatting string to tell the computer to move, or float, the $ to the position immediately in front of the leftmost digit whenever any of the reserved spaces in front of the decimal point are unused.

The PRINT USING statement is particularly useful when you want to display output in a table, with numbers in columns lined up beneath headings, and all decimal points aligned. One easy way to do this is first to write a PRINT statement that displays the headings and then, directly underneath, a statement that assigns the formatting string. By lining up (approximately) the #'s in the formatting string beneath the appropriate headings, you can produce the table, as in this revised version of Program 4.

Program 4

Statement

```
10 PRINT "SPECIAL TABLE FORMAT"
20 PRINT "ITEMS           COST          TOTAL"
30 LET A$ = "###           $$###.##      $$#####.##"
40 READ A, B
50 IF A = -1 THEN GOTO 90
60 PRINT USING A$; A, B, A * B
70 GOTO 40
80 DATA 20, 152.45, 155, 98.966, 200, 58.5, -1, -1
90 END
```

Output

```
SPECIAL TABLE FORMAT
ITEMS       COST       TOTAL
 20       $152.45    $3049.00
155        $98.97   $15339.73
200        $58.50   $11700.00
```

There are other formats that may be used in a PRINT USING statement, involving symbols other than ., $, and #. The location of commas within a string of #'s can be specified, and numbers can be displayed with + (plus) or − (minus) signs, or in exponential notation. There are also symbols to output any specified number of characters in a string or to insert a string in a specified location in the output. Refer to your computer's manual for a complete list of formatting rules.

Avoiding Pitfalls

1. Remember that the formatting string in a PRINT USING statement must be followed by a semicolon, then one or more simple variables or BASIC numerical expressions, separated by commas.

2. If the number to be PRINTed is larger than the number of spaces reserved in the formatting string of a PRINT USING statement, then the computer will PRINT the number with a % symbol in front. For example, the statement

```
50 PRINT USING "##.#"; 300.5
```

will have %300.5 as its output. The % symbol tells the programmer that not enough spaces have been reserved.

Summary

The PRINT USING statement can be used to specify exactly how digits of a number should appear in the output of a program. For example, the statement

```
40 PRINT USING "$$###.##"; 52.468
```

has $52.47 as its output, since the formatting string rounds 52.468 to two decimal places.

Exercises 6-3

A 1. Predict the output of each of the programs in (a)–(j).

a.
```
10 PRINT USING "####"; 320
20 END
```

b.
```
5 LET X = 87.5
10 PRINT USING "####.#"; X
20 END
```

c.
```
10 LET X = 25
20 LET A$ = "###"
30 PRINT USING A$; X
40 END
```

d.
```
10 LET X = 5
20 LET A$ = "##.##"
30 PRINT USING A$; X
40 END
```

e.
```
10 LET X = 18.9
20 LET A$ = "###.##"
30 PRINT USING A$; X
40 END
```

f.
```
10 LET Y = 74.368
20 LET A$ = "##.##"
30 PRINT USING A$; Y
40 END
```

g.
```
10 LET K = 23.4
20 LET X$ = "$$###.##"
30 PRINT USING X$; K
40 PRINT "NICE"
50 END
```

h.
```
10 FOR I = 1 TO 5
20 READ X
30 PRINT USING "##.##"; X
40 NEXT I
50 DATA 32, 96.4, .87
55 DATA 5.66, 1.765
60 END
```

i.
```
10 LET Y = 2 * 2 * 3.1416
20 LET B$ = "##.###"
30 PRINT USING B$; Y
40 END
```

j.
```
10 LET A$ = "##.##"
20 FOR J = 1 TO 3
30 PRINT USING A$; J * 1.5
40 NEXT J
50 END
```

2. Complete the formatting string in line 20 to produce each output shown below.

```
10 LET X = 6.753
20 LET A$ = ". . .
30 PRINT USING A$; X
40 END
```

a. 6.75 **b.** $6.75 **c.** 6.7530 **d.** 6.8

3. Predict the output of Program 3 if line 60 is changed to read:

```
60 DATA 5, 23.6, 100, 4, 12, 8.333, −1, −1
```

4. Modify Program 4 of Section 5–4 (page 224) so that the output is PRINTed in table form, with decimal points aligned and $'s included, as follows:

```
SIMPLE INTEREST
PRINCIPAL:  ? 500
RATE            INTEREST
7.0             $35.00
7.5             $37.50
8.0             $40.00
8.5             $42.50
9.0             $45.00
```

B **5.** An automobile salesperson usually earns a *commission* based on a percentage of total sales (*commission = rate of commission × total sales*). Write a program that INPUTs the total sales and the rate of commission, then PRINTs the amount of the salesperson's commission in dollars and cents, with a $ included.

6. Write a program that calculates the weekly wage of a computer operator who earns $6.20 per hour for the first 35 hours (or less) and time and a half per hour (1.5 * 6.20) for overtime. Have the program INPUT the number of hours worked, then calculate and PRINT the operator's weekly wage in dollars and cents, with a $ included.

7. Write a program to convert meters to decimeters, centimeters, and millimeters (1 m = 10 dm = 100 cm = 1000 mm). Have the program READ the number of meters from a DATA list. PRINT the results in table form, with numbers and decimal points aligned, similar to this:

METERS	DECI-	CENTI-	MILLI-
3.40	34.0	340	3400
0.60	6.0	60	600
0.55	5.5	55	550
1.80	18.0	180	1800

8. a. Write a program to help fourth-grade students learn decimal addition. Have the program READ two decimals from a DATA line and PRINT them one beneath the other with decimal points aligned. Ask the student for the sum, then PRINT whether the answer is correct or incorrect. Use the following list of DATA values (—1, —1 is the double trailer value):

```
DATA 25.53, 10.5, 4.62, 50.2, 100.23, 64.6, 500.20, 9.99, —1, —1
```

b. Modify the program in (a) so that it keeps track of the number of correct and incorrect answers. PRINT the results for the student before ending the program.

C 9. *Challenge:* Write a program that keeps track of the balance in a checking account. Have the program READ positive numbers (deposits) and negative numbers (withdrawals) from a DATA list. Start with $200 in the account and PRINT the results in a table similar to the following:

DEPOSITS	WITHDRAWALS	BALANCE
34.50		234.50
	—50.00	184.50
	—25.25	159.25
.	.	.
.	.	.
.	.	.

The DATA statement should have at least eight values. (*Hint:* Use two formatting strings — one for positive numbers, the other for negative numbers. For the negative numbers, you can use a formatting string like this: "— ##.##".)

Lab Activity

Displaying Characters: INVERSE, FLASH, and NORMAL

(for use with *Apple* computers)

Apple computers can display three different forms of each character on the screen: normal, flashing, and inverse (black on white). These different types of character display are turned on by the respective commands

NORMAL, FLASH, and INVERSE.

Problems

1. Type the following program into the computer:

```
5  REM * DISPLAYING CHARACTERS
10 PRINT "USUAL"
20 FLASH
30 PRINT "CRAZY"
40 INVERSE
50 PRINT "WILD"
60 NORMAL
70 END
```

   RUN the program. Describe the effect of FLASH (line 20) and INVERSE (line 40).

2. What do you think will happen if you delete line 60 from the program? Try it. Now type LIST. Does the computer invert strings that *you* type (look at LIST to see)? How about strings that the computer itself sends to the screen?

3. Experiment to see whether the INVERSE and FLASH instructions are turned off if < CTRL > < RESET > is pressed. What happens if < CTRL > C is pressed? What happens if TEXT is typed?

4. Write a program that PRINTs your name at the middle of the screen, then INPUTs a one-letter string (move the cursor back HOME to 1, 1 so that the INPUT string is typed at the top of the screen). If the letter typed is N, have the program PRINT your name in NORMAL at the middle of the screen; if the letter typed is I, then PRINT your name in INVERSE, and if it is F, PRINT your name so that it is FLASHing. Stop the program when the user types Q.

Lab Activity

Exploring IF . . . THEN . . . ELSE

(for use with *IBM* and *TRS-80* computers)

The *IBM* and *TRS-80* microcomputers have an extension of the IF . . . THEN instruction that can be quite convenient. In this Lab Activity, you can discover the properties of IF . . . THEN . . . ELSE.

The following sets of statements from two programs are equivalent.

```
100 IF X = 3 THEN PRINT "THREE" ELSE PRINT "NOT"
110 . . .
```

```
100 IF X = 3 THEN PRINT "THREE": GOTO 110
105 PRINT "NOT"
110 . . .
```

Problems

1. Add the lines

```
10 REM * IF . . . THEN . . . ELSE
20 INPUT "TYPE A NUMBER:  "; X
110 END
```

to each version above. Use the computer to verify that both programs have exactly the same output for any value of X that you type. (Of course, be sure to try X = 3.)

2. Write the shortest version of the following program that you can, using an IF . . . THEN . . . ELSE statement. Use the computer to verify that both programs have exactly the same output.

```
10 REM * IF . . . THEN . . . ELSE
20 INPUT "TYPE A NAME:  "; N$
25 IF N$ = "ANN" THEN GOTO 50
30 PRINT "TOO BAD"
40 GOTO 60
50 PRINT "HI"
60 END
```

3. Predict the output of the following program. Verify your prediction by RUNning the program for several different values of X.

```
10  INPUT "TYPE A NUMBER:  "; X
20  IF X=7 THEN PRINT X ELSE PRINT "NO GOOD": GOTO 10
30  END
```

Based on the output from this program, does a statement of the form

IF *condition one* THEN *action one* ELSE *action two: action three*

perform action 3 if condition 1 is true or if condition 1 is false?

4. A "chain" of IF . . . THEN . . . ELSE statements can be formed to replace what would otherwise be several lines of BASIC code. For instance, the following program PRINTs the English word corresponding to the digit 1, 2, or 3, typed by a user.

```
10  REM * CHAINING IF . . . THEN . . . ELSE
20  INPUT "TYPE AN INTEGER (—999 TO END):  "; I
25  IF I=—999 THEN GOTO 40
30  IF I=1 THEN PRINT "ONE" ELSE IF I=2 THEN PRINT "TWO" ELSE IF
      I=3 THEN PRINT "THREE" ELSE PRINT "MISTAKE"
35  GOTO 20
40  END
```

RUN the program. Does it work correctly for all INPUT values of I? Write an equivalent version of the program that does not use ELSE.

APPLE AND IBM

6-4 Advanced Graphics

In Chapter 2 you learned how to draw simple shapes by plotting points one at a time on the graphics screen. Most microcomputers have additional commands that will let you draw lines and display more finely detailed graphics output. In this section we will present some advanced graphing techniques for *Apple* and *IBM* microcomputers. Special techniques for *TRS-80* microcomputers will be presented in Chapter 8.

Apple: Drawing Lines

Until now, if you wanted to plot either a horizontal or vertical line (segment) using *Apple* low resolution graphics, you probably used a FOR . . . NEXT loop similar to the one in Program 1 at the top of the next page.

Program 1

Statement	Remark
10 HOME	*Clear screen.*
20 GR	*Low resolution graphics mode.*
30 COLOR = 9	*Orange.*
40 FOR X = 10 TO 16	*Loop draws an orange horizontal*
50 PLOT X, 15	*line from column 10 to column 16*
60 NEXT X	*at row 15.*
70 END	

Output

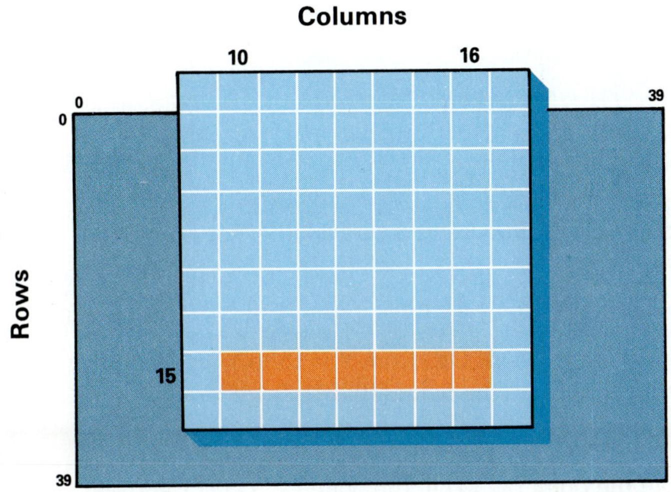

There are two convenient commands that make drawing horizontal and vertical line segments much easier: HLIN and VLIN.

HLIN

The statement

```
50 HLIN 10, 16 AT 15
```

will draw a horizontal line from X = 10 to X = 16 along Y = 15; that is, from the point (10, 15) to the point (16, 15). The line will be drawn in the current COLOR. This one statement can replace the FOR . . . NEXT loop in lines 40 to 60 of Program 1.

The general form of the HLIN statement is as follows:

```
HLIN X1, X2 AT Y
```

The statement HLIN X1, X2 AT Y will draw a horizontal line from the point (X1, Y) to the point (X2, Y). It is helpful to remember that X1 and X2 specify the columns at the beginning and end of the horizontal line, and the Y-value indicates the row at which the line will be plotted. Note that X1 can be greater than or even equal to X2.

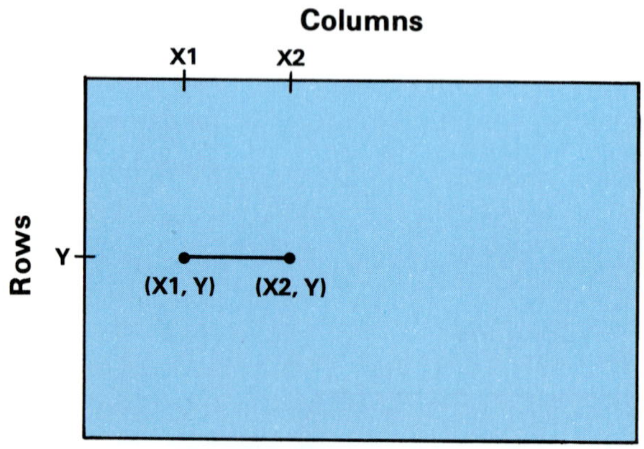

VLIN

The VLIN statement works like HLIN, but draws a vertical line. For example, the statement

```
60  VLIN 15, 24 AT 10
```

will draw a vertical line (in the current COLOR) from Y = 15 to Y = 24 at X = 10; that is, from the point (10, 15) to the point (10, 24). In general,

```
VLIN Y1, Y2 AT X
```

will draw a vertical line from the point (X, Y1) to the point (X, Y2). Y1 and Y2 specify the rows at the top and bottom of the vertical line (not necessarily in that order), and the X-value indicates the column at which the line will be plotted.

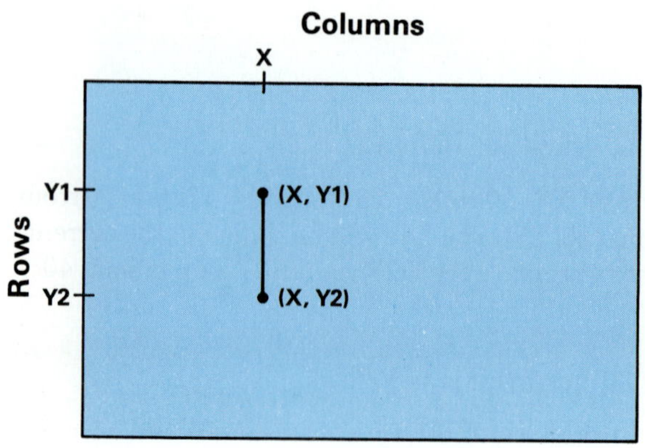

Here is a program that draws a square using HLIN and VLIN:

Program 2

Statement	Remark
10 HOME	
20 GR	
30 COLOR = 13	*Yellow.*
40 HLIN 10, 16 AT 15	*Horizontal line from (10, 15) to (16, 15).*
50 HLIN 10, 16 AT 21	*Horizontal line from (10, 21) to (16, 21).*
60 VLIN 15, 21 AT 10	*Vertical line from (10, 15) to (10, 21).*
70 VLIN 15, 21 AT 16	*Vertical line from (16, 15) to (16, 21).*
80 END	

Output

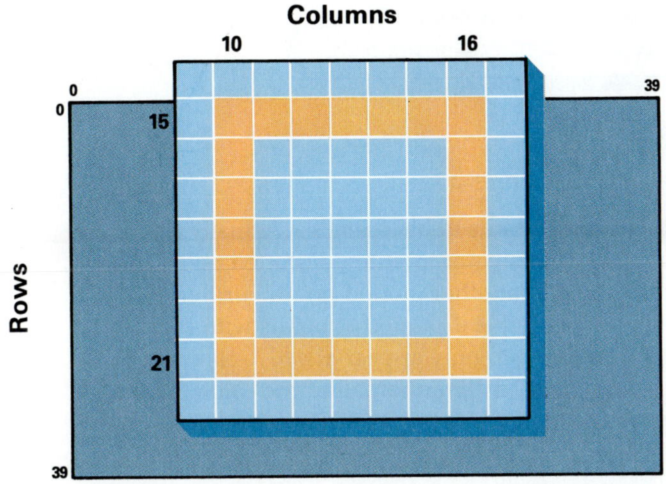

Lines that are neither horizontal nor vertical can be drawn on the low resolution graphics screen, but not with a single statement like HLIN or VLIN.

Apple: High Resolution Graphics

High resolution graphics mode allows you to draw more finely detailed shapes than those drawn on the low resolution graphics screen. The plotted dots are much smaller in high resolution graphics and there are many more of them.

HGR

To draw shapes or pictures using high resolution graphics, you must first give the instruction HGR. HGR can be either an immediate mode command or a program statement. HGR clears the screen to black and sets up an invisible graphics display grid with 160 rows and 280 columns. As in low resolution graphics, the bottom four lines on the screen are reserved for text; to put any text you want below your drawing use VTAB and PRINT.

The entire screen can be used for drawing if the instruction HGR2 rather than HGR is given. HGR2 sets up an invisible display grid with 192 rows and 280 columns.

HCOLOR

The HCOLOR statement is used in high resolution graphics to designate the color of plotted points. Here are the available colors and their numbers:

High Resolution Colors

0 = Black1	4 = Black2
1 = Green	5 = Orange
2 = Violet	6 = Blue
3 = White1	7 = White2

As an example, the statement

HCOLOR = 3

will cause all subsequent plotting of points to be in white. (Actually, it's a little more complicated than that: On a color monitor, a plotted point will look white only if it is plotted next to another plotted point. Furthermore, blue and purple points will only be visible if plotted at points with *even* X-coordinates; green and orange points can only appear at *odd* X-coordinates. On a black and white (or black and green) monitor, all of the colors in the table above except the two blacks look white (or green). See the Lab Activity for more details.)

HPLOT

The HPLOT statement is used in high resolution graphics for plotting both points and lines. A statement of the form

HPLOT X, Y

will plot a single point at coordinates (X, Y). The value of X in this statement may range from 0 to 279, and the value of Y from 0 to 191 (although ordinarily, only with the HGR2 instruction will points with Y-values between 160 and 191 be visible).

The short program

```
10 HGR
20 HCOLOR = 5
30 HPLOT 120, 70
40 END
```

will plot a single orange point at coordinates (120, 70), as shown below.

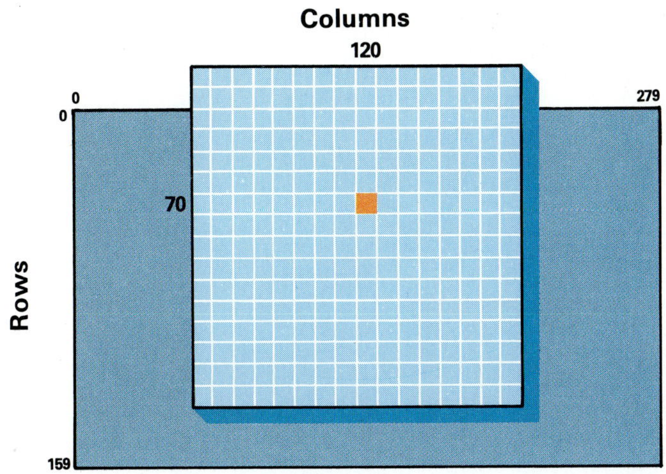

The HPLOT statement can also be used to draw a line connecting *any* two points on the screen. A statement of the form

```
HPLOT X1, Y1 TO X2, Y2
```

will draw a line from the point (X1, Y1) to (X2, Y2), in the current color.

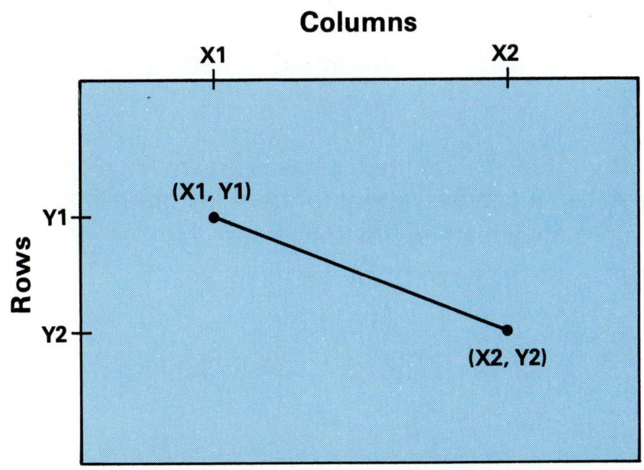

The HPLOT statement can be extended to draw several connected lines, as illustrated in the rectangle-drawing program at the top of the next page.

Program 3

Statement

```
5  REM * HI-RES RECTANGLE
10  HOME
20  HGR
30  HCOLOR = 3
40  HPLOT 10, 15 TO 20, 15 TO 20, 24 TO 10, 24 TO 10, 15
50  END
```

Output

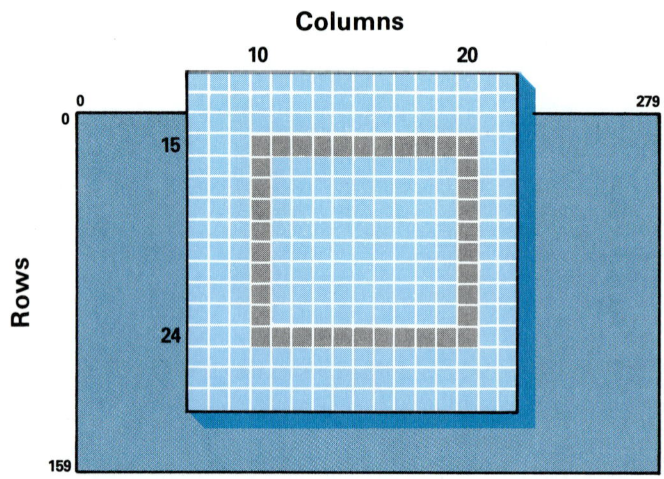

Line 40 instructs the computer to draw a line from (10, 15) to (20, 15), then one from (20, 15) to (20, 24), one from (20, 24) to (10, 24), and so forth. Thus, line 40 draws lines connecting the four points at the corners of the rectangle shown above.

If the first set of coordinates after HPLOT is omitted, a line is drawn from the last point plotted by a previous HPLOT statement to the point specified after the word TO. With this alternative method, the statement

```
40  HPLOT 10, 15 TO 20, 15 TO 20, 24 TO 10, 24 TO 10, 15
```

can be rewritten using these statements:

```
40  HPLOT 10, 15
42  HPLOT TO 20, 15
44  HPLOT TO 20, 24
46  HPLOT TO 10, 24
48  HPLOT TO 10, 15
```

Avoiding Pitfalls

1. Remember that HLIN and VLIN are used in the low resolution graphics mode; HPLOT is available only with high resolution graphics.
2. In low or high resolution graphics, if you specify coordinates that are off the screen, an ILLEGAL QUANTITY ERROR will result.
3. Be sure to set HCOLOR to a number between 1 and 7 for high resolution graphics, or the points you try to HPLOT will be invisible. (See the Lab Activity for further restrictions on colors.)
4. If you use parentheses with HPLOT, for example HPLOT (100, 80), you will get a SYNTAX ERROR message.

Summary for Apple

HLIN X1, X2 AT Y will draw a horizontal line segment from the point (X1, Y) to the point (X2, Y) on the low resolution screen. For example, the statement 70 HLIN 15, 25 AT 10 will draw a horizontal line from the point (15, 10) to the point (25, 10).

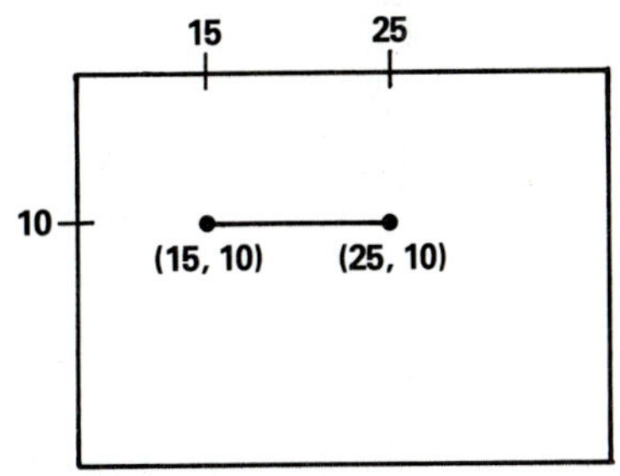

VLIN Y1, Y2 AT X will draw a vertical line segment from the point (X, Y1) to the point (X, Y2) on the low resolution screen. For example, the statement 50 VLIN 15, 25 AT 10 will draw a vertical line from the point (10, 15) to the point (10, 25).

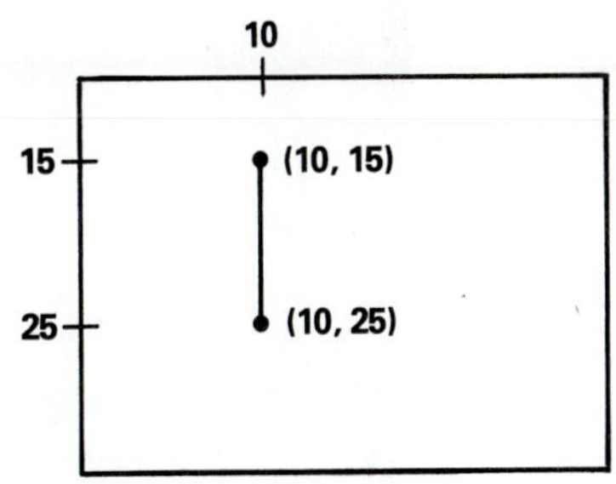

HGR clears the screen to black and sets up an invisible high resolution graphics display grid with 160 rows and 280 columns.

HCOLOR = N causes subsequent points to be plotted in color number N.

HPLOT X1, Y1 TO X2, Y2 TO X3, Y3 will draw a line from the point (X1, Y1) to the point (X2, Y2) and another line from the point (X2, Y2) to the point (X3, Y3).

(Exercises 6–4 are on page 307.)

IBM: Drawing Lines

(A Color/Graphics Monitor is needed.)

Until now, if you wanted to plot horizontal and vertical lines (segments) using medium resolution graphics, you probably used a FOR . . . NEXT loop similar to the one in the following program:

Program 1

Statement	Remark
10 CLS	*Clear screen.*
20 SCREEN 1, 0	*Medium resolution graphics, with color.*
30 COLOR 0, 0	*Black background, Palette 0.*
40 FOR X = 50 TO 80	*Loop draws a red horizontal line*
50 PSET(X, 30), 2	*from column 50 to column 80 at*
60 NEXT X	*row 30.*
70 END	

Output

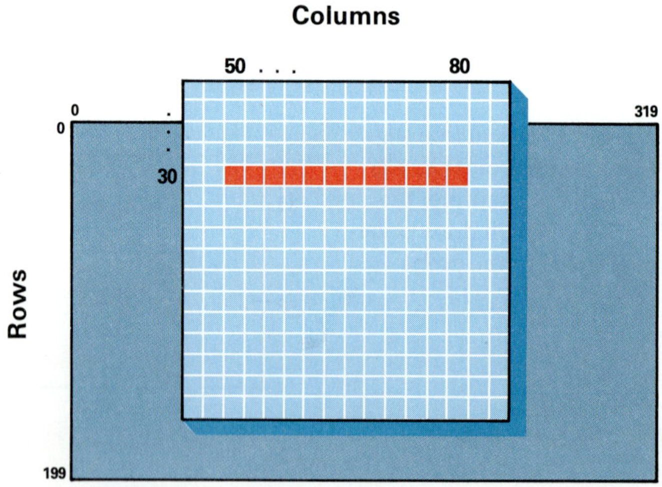

LINE

There is a convenient instruction in medium resolution graphics for drawing not only horizontal and vertical lines but also lines connecting *any* two points: LINE. The LINE statement has this form:

LINE (X1, Y1) – (X2, Y2), *color*

The statement at the bottom of the preceding page will draw a line from the point (X1, Y1) to the point (X2, Y2), using the *color* chosen from the palette previously selected in the COLOR statement. For your reference, the 16 available background colors and the possible choices of color for each palette are listed below:

Background Color Table

0 Black	8 Gray
1 Blue	9 Light Blue
2 Green	10 Light Green
3 Cyan	11 Light Cyan
4 Red	12 Light Red
5 Magenta	13 Light Magenta
6 Brown	14 Yellow
7 White	15 Bright White

PSET and LINE Colors

Palette 0	Palette 1
Green (1)	Cyan (1)
Red (2)	Magenta (2)
Brown (3)	White (3)

Here is a program using a single LINE instruction to produce the same output as Program 1.

Program 2

Statement

```
5  REM * USING LINE
10 CLS
20 SCREEN 1, 0
30 COLOR 0, 0
40 LINE (50, 30) - (80, 30), 2
50 END
```

As in Program 1, the COLOR statement in line 30 selects a black background and palette 0. On palette 0, color number 2 is red, so in line 40 the horizontal line drawn from the point (50, 30) to the point (80, 30) will be drawn in red on a black background. Notice that the single program line 40 replaces the FOR . . . NEXT loop in lines 40 to 60 of Program 1.

IBM: High Resolution Graphics

High resolution graphics mode allows you to draw more finely detailed shapes than those possible on the medium resolution graphics screen. In each row on the high resolution screen, you can plot twice the number of points that are available in medium resolution. A slightly different SCREEN instruction must be given to do high resolution graphics.

SCREEN 2

To draw shapes or pictures using high resolution graphics on an *IBM* computer, you must first give the computer the instruction SCREEN 2 (rather than SCREEN 1, 0), which can be either an immediate mode command or a program statement. The SCREEN 2 instruction sets up an invisible graphics display grid with 200 rows and 640 columns on a black screen. SCREEN 2 does not clear the screen (except the first time you use it), so you will usually want to use CLS as a first step in drawing a design. In high resolution graphics the COLOR statement is not available; shapes may be drawn only in black and white.

The PSET and LINE statements are used in high resolution graphics to draw points and lines. These statements have the same form as in medium resolution graphics except that the number 1 at the end of either statement indicates a white point or line, and the number 0 a black point or line. Of course, a black point or line will be invisible on a black screen. Nevertheless, plotting in black is useful, as you will see in the next section.

Program 3

Statement	Remark
10 CLS	
20 SCREEN 2	*High resolution graphics mode.*
30 PSET(80, 90), 1	*Plot a white point at (80, 90).*
40 LINE (80, 120) – (150, 120), 1	*Draw a white horizontal line from (80, 120) to (150, 120).*
50 END	

Output

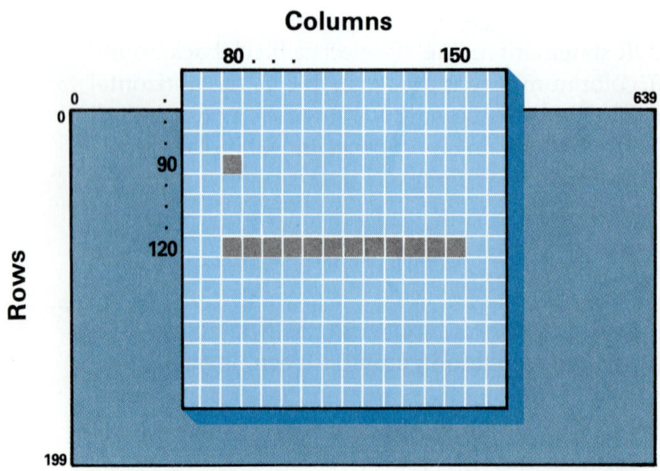

When you want to leave high resolution graphics, type SCREEN 0, 0. This command will return you to an 80-column text screen for typing, LISTing, and RUNning other programs.

Here is a program that uses LINE instructions to draw a triangle in high resolution graphics mode:

Program 4

Statement

```
5  REM * HI-RES TRIANGLE
10 CLS
20 SCREEN 2
30 LINE (50, 20) - (80, 60), 1
40 LINE - (20, 60), 1
50 LINE - (50, 20), 1
60 END
```

Output

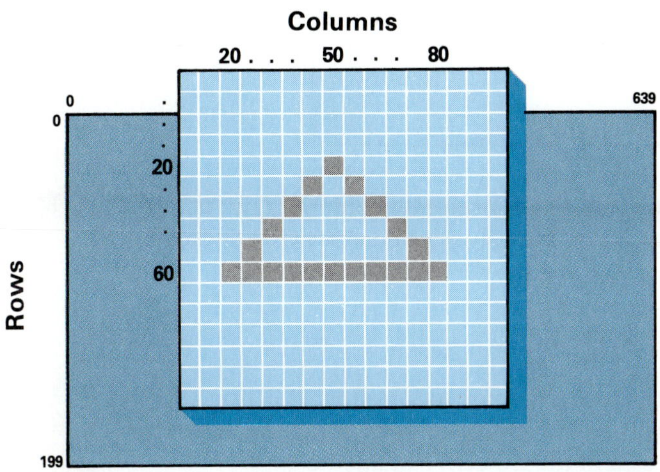

Notice lines 40 and 50. If the first pair of coordinates is missing in a LINE statement (either in high or medium resolution graphics), then the line is drawn from the last point plotted (by either PSET or LINE) to the point immediately after the dash. Since the last point plotted in line 30 is the point (80, 60), the line drawn by the instruction in line 40 goes from the point (80, 60) to the point (20, 60). Similarly, the last point plotted in line 40 is (20, 60), so the line drawn in line 50 goes from the point (20, 60) to the point (50, 20). Of course, the LINE statements in lines 40 and 50 could have been written so that they specify both endpoints of the lines to be drawn.

Avoiding Pitfalls

1. Be sure that the coordinates of the points specified in a LINE statement are enclosed in parentheses.
2. Remember that the COLOR statement is available only in medium resolution graphics.

Summary for IBM

The LINE statement can be used to draw a line connecting any two points on the medium or high resolution screens (but without COLOR in high resolution). The statement LINE (X1, Y1) – (X2, Y2), *color*

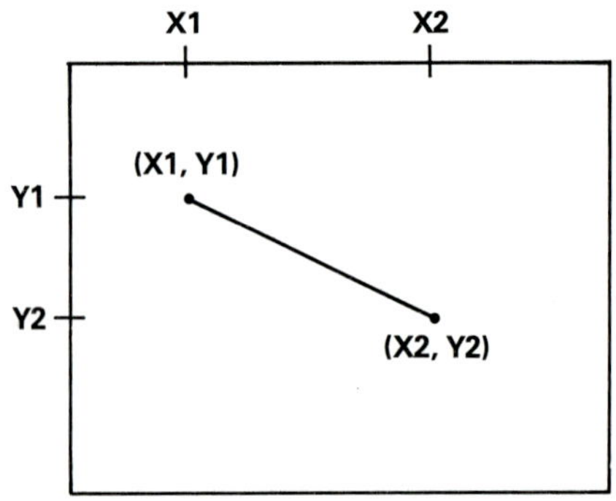

will draw a line from the point (X1, Y1) to the point (X2, Y2), using the *color* chosen from the palette previously selected in the COLOR statement.

A statement of the form

LINE – (X, Y), *color*

will draw a line from the last point plotted (by either PSET or LINE) to the point immediately after the dash, using the *color* chosen from the palette previously selected in the COLOR statement.

The instruction SCREEN 2 sets up a high resolution graphics display grid with 200 rows (numbered 0 to 199) and 640 columns (numbered 0 to 639).

The COLOR statement is not available in high resolution graphics mode; points and lines may be drawn only in black or white. In high resolution graphics, a PSET or LINE instruction followed by the number 1 will plot a white point or line; the number 0 after these instructions will cause a black point or line to be plotted.

Exercises 6-4

A **1.** Using the grid on a piece of graph paper to help you, predict the output of each program listed beneath your computer's name. Label the appropriate row and column numbers and give the color of each line drawn.

Apple

a.
```
10 HOME
20 GR
30 COLOR = 5
40 HLIN 5, 10 AT 4
50 END
```

b.
```
10 HOME
20 GR
30 COLOR = 8
40 VLIN 6, 16 AT 20
50 END
```

c.
```
10 HOME
20 GR
30 COLOR = 9
40 VLIN 1, 5 AT 2
50 HLIN 2, 8 AT 5
60 END
```

d.
```
10 HOME
20 HGR
30 HCOLOR = 2
40 HPLOT 6, 9 TO 16, 9
50 END
```

e.
```
10 HOME
20 HGR
30 HCOLOR = 3
40 HPLOT 19, 20 TO 19, 60
50 END
```

f.
```
10 HOME
20 HGR
30 HCOLOR = 3
40 HPLOT 20, 20 TO 30, 30 TO 40, 20 TO 20, 20
50 END
```

g.
```
10 HOME
20 HGR
30 HCOLOR = 3
40 HPLOT 15, 20
50 HPLOT TO 20, 15
60 HPLOT TO 15, 15
70 HPLOT TO 15, 20
80 END
```

h.
```
10 HOME
20 HGR
30 HCOLOR = 3
40 HPLOT 10, 20 TO 30, 20 TO 30, 30
50 HPLOT TO 10, 20
60 HPLOT TO 10, 30
70 HPLOT TO 30, 30
80 END
```

IBM

a.
```
10 CLS
20 SCREEN 1, 0
30 COLOR 8, 0
40 LINE (25, 65) - (25, 100), 2
50 END
```

b.
```
10 CLS
20 SCREEN 1, 0
30 COLOR 0, 1
40 LINE (20, 20) - (45, 20), 1
50 END
```

c.
```
10 CLS
20 SCREEN 1, 0
30 COLOR 9, 0
40 LINE (40, 20) – (40, 50), 3
50 LINE – (60, 50), 3
60 LINE – (60, 80), 3
65 LINE – (50, 50), 3
70 LINE – (40, 20), 3
80 END
```

d.
```
10 CLS
20 SCREEN 1, 0
30 COLOR 6, 1
40 LINE (10, 10) – (10, 80), 3
50 LINE (50, 10) – (50, 80), 3
60 LINE (10, 80) – (50, 10), 3
70 END
```

e.
```
10 CLS
20 SCREEN 2
30 LINE (300, 100) – (400, 150), 1
40 LINE (300, 100) – (350, 50), 1
50 LINE (300, 100) – (200, 50), 1
60 END
```

f.
```
10 CLS
20 SCREEN 2
30 LINE (20, 20) – (100, 20), 1
40 LINE – (100, 100), 1
50 LINE – (20, 100), 1
60 LINE – (20, 20), 1
70 END
```

B **2.** Write a program using HLIN or VLIN *(Apple)*, or LINE *(IBM* medium resolution graphics), to draw each of the following shapes in the color of your choice.

a.

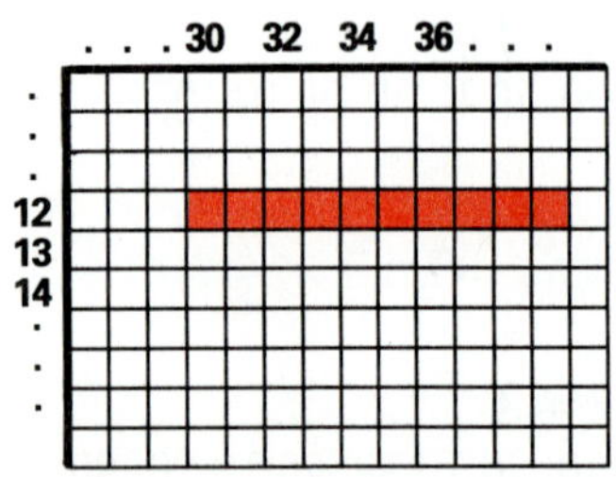

b.

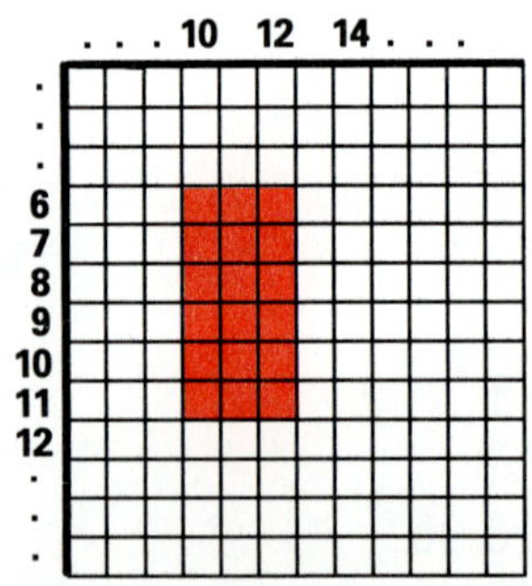

c.

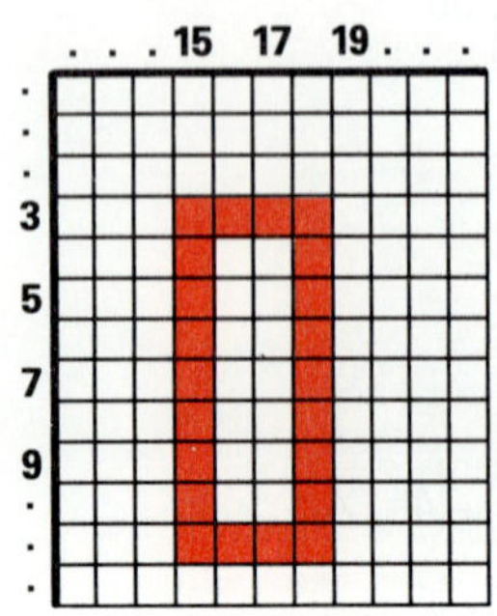

d.

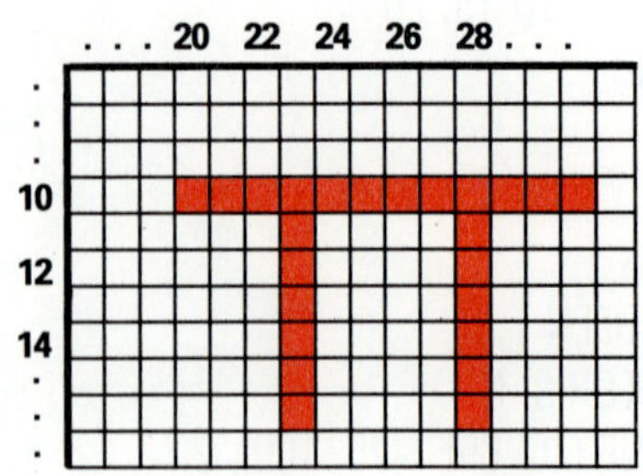

3. Write a program in high resolution graphics using HPLOT *(Apple)* or LINE *(IBM)* to draw each of the following shapes.

a.

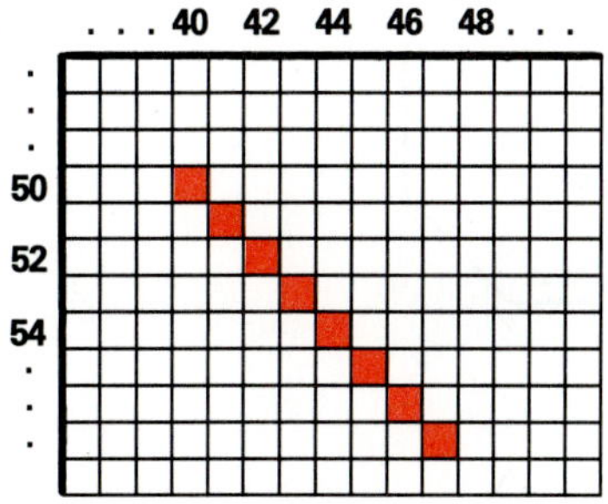

b.

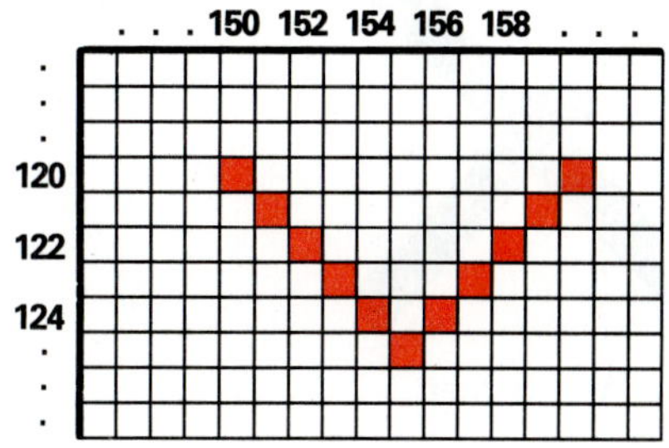

c.

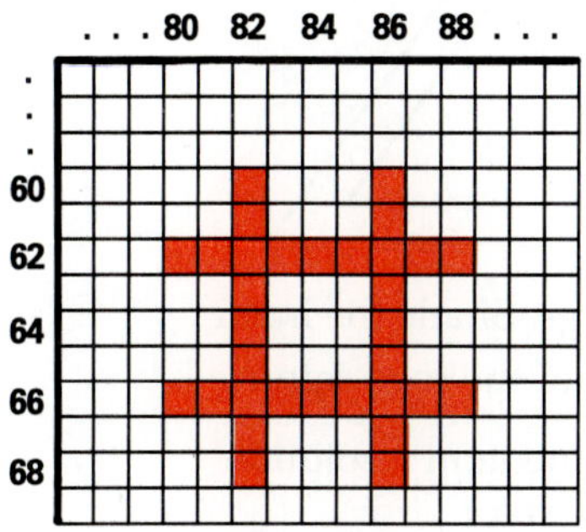

d.

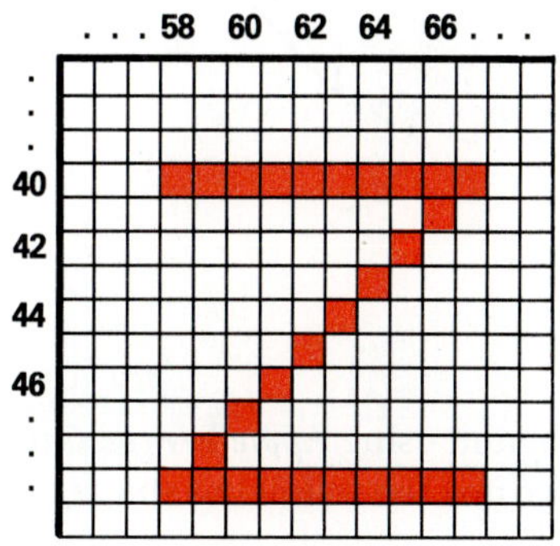

4. a. Write a program using high resolution graphics to draw a right triangle at the center of the screen. One side should be 10 dots long, and the other 20, as shown in the diagram at the right.

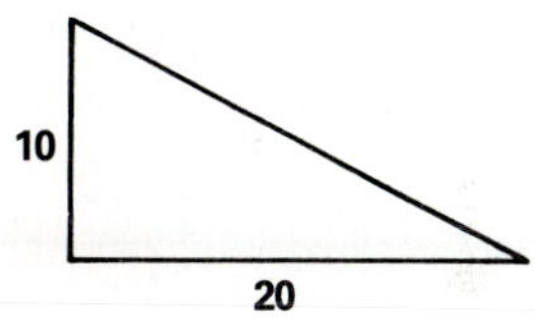

   b. Modify the program in (a) so that the lengths of the sides are INPUT from the user.

5. Write a program using graphics of your choice to draw the word WOW in large block letters at the center of the screen.

6. a. Write a program using high resolution graphics and HPLOT *(Apple)* or LINE *(IBM)* to draw the word EXIT in large block letters on the screen.
   b. Modify the program in (a) so that the letters are drawn and erased (use HOME or CLS) to produce a "flashing" effect. (*Hint:* Add a time-delay loop to slow the rate of flashing.)

7. Write a program using high resolution graphics and HPLOT *(Apple)* or LINE *(IBM)* to shade the left half of the screen white. (*Hint:* Use a FOR . . . NEXT loop.)

C 8. Write a program using high resolution graphics to draw each of the road-sign shapes at the top of the next page. Display the shapes at the center of the screen. (Use the grid on a piece of graph paper to help you.)

a. Railroad Crossing:

b. Stop Sign:

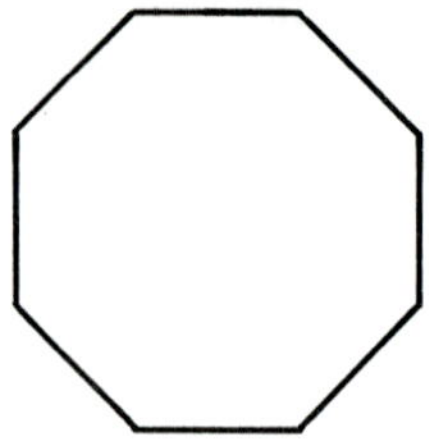

c. One Way Street:

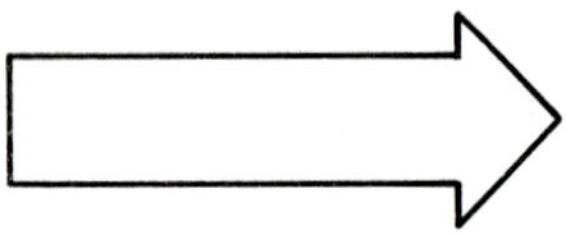

d. DANGER:

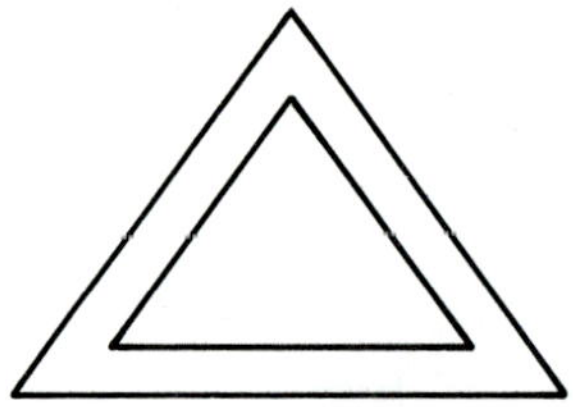

(*Challenge:* Shade the inner triangle of the road sign.)

9. Write a program using *Apple* low resolution or *IBM* medium resolution graphics to draw the following shape, in any INPUT color.

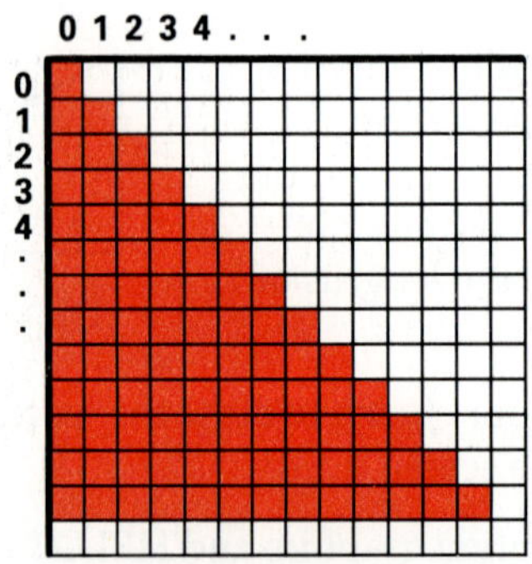

Lab Activity

Exploring High Resolution Colors

(for use with *Apple* computers)

In this Lab Activity, you will use the simple plotting program on the next page to explore some of the peculiarities of the *Apple's* high resolution colors. You will need a color monitor to benefit fully from this experiment.

```
10 REM * HIGH RESOLUTION COLORS
20 HGR
30 HOME: VTAB 24: REM * PUT CURSOR AT BOTTOM
40 INPUT "TYPE COLOR NUMBER (—1 TO CLEAR SCREEN):  "; CLR
50 IF CLR = —1 THEN GOTO 20
60 INPUT "TYPE STARTING POINT X, Y:  "; XST, YST
70 INPUT "TYPE ENDING POINT X, Y:  "; XND, YND
80 HCOLOR = CLR
90 HPLOT XST, YST TO XND, YND
100 GOTO 40
110 END
```

For your reference, here is the table of high resolution colors:

0 = Black1	4 = Black2
1 = Green	5 = Orange
2 = Violet	6 = Blue
3 = White1	7 = White2

Problems

1. RUN the program and draw a long horizontal orange (CLR = 5) line segment (make both Y-values the same in lines 60 and 70). Then draw a long horizontal green (CLR = 1) segment. Adjust the color on your monitor, if necessary, so that these colors are as true as you can get them.

2. Clear the screen (CLR = −1) and then draw nearly vertical line segments from (0, 150) to (5, 0) in white1 (CLR = 3), and from (42, 150) to (47, 0) in white2 (CLR = 7). What colors result from the two versions of white? (If you are uncertain, draw a few short horizontal segments in each of the colors in the table and compare with the vertical segments.)

3. Without erasing the segments from Problem 2, draw a vertical segment from (1, 150) to (6, 0) in white1 and a vertical segment from (43, 150) to (48, 0) in white2 (these are right next to the two vertical segments from Problem 2). Describe the results.

4. Clear the screen and again draw a segment from (0, 150) to (5, 0) in white1. Now draw a purple (CLR = 2) segment from (10, 150) to (15, 0). Notice the missing parts of the purple segment. Guess the X-coordinates of the missing points. Use the program to draw short vertical purple segments at X = 30, at X = 41, at X = 50, and at X = 153. Which of these segments are invisible? Purple dots only appear at points with *even* X-coordinates.

5. Clear the screen and experiment with vertical segments (with plenty of space between them) to determine at which X-coordinates orange dots (CLR = 5) will appear on the screen (odd or even?). Do the same for green (CLR = 1) and blue (CLR = 6) dots. (Sometimes orange dots will come out brown when they are plotted at a point (X, Y) where X divided by 7 gives a remainder of 6. Try it.)

6. The dots that appear on your graphics screen (and the characters that appear on your text screen) are represented in the computer's memory by numbers (see the Computer Language feature on page 64). In high resolution graphics, each number represents seven dots that are lined up next to each other horizontally. The complicated way this is done (we'll leave out the details here) has the consequence that the color of a dot can influence the color of some of its neighbors.

   For example, for any given Y-value, the seven dots with X-coordinates 0 through 6 can influence each other in this way, as can the next seven dots (X = 7 through X = 13), and so forth. To see this work, clear the screen and draw a purple segment from (0, 150) to (0, 50). Then draw a blue segment from (5, 150) to (5, 100). What happens to the purple? Now redraw the purple segment from (0, 150) to (0, 100). What happens to the blue segment? Now draw a blue segment from (5, 110) to (5, 130). What happens to the purple? You see that a point can influence the color of its neighbors even though it is itself invisible.

7. Write a program to shade the high resolution graphics screen green (draw horizontal green line segments from (0, Y) to (279, Y) at each Y from 0 to 159). Then have the program draw a diagonal line segment in blue from (0, 0) to (279, 159). Explain why the little orange rectangles appear (see Problem 6).

Lab Activity

Circles

(for use with *IBM* computers with BASICA loaded)

IBM computers have a built-in command that will draw circles (see Section 7–5, Program 2, page 382, for how to draw circles on *Apple* and *TRS-80* computers). In medium resolution graphics, the instruction

```
CIRCLE (X, Y), R, C
```

will draw a circle of radius R, with center at (X, Y), in the color C (selected from the palette previously chosen in the COLOR statement).

Problems

1. Write a short program using medium resolution graphics to draw a circle of radius 50 with center at (75, 85). Use this instruction: CIRCLE (75, 85), 50, 2.

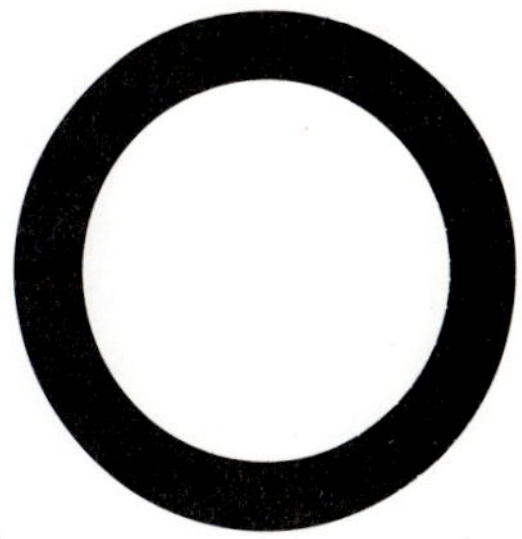

2. Add to the program in Problem 1 so that it draws a thick ring like the one shown at the right. (*Hint:* Draw several circles of slightly different radii, all with center at (75, 85).)

3. Write a program to produce a figure that looks like this:

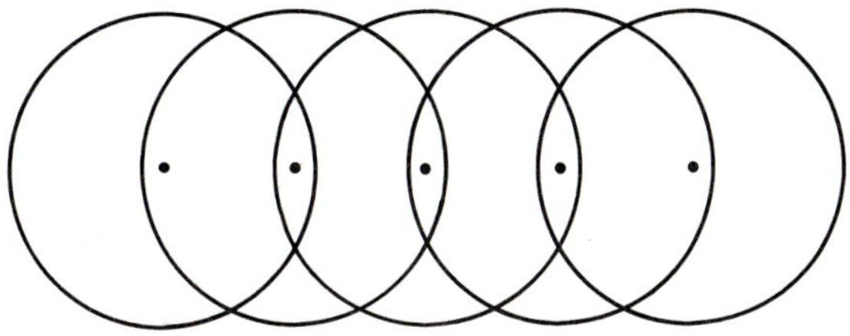

   (*Hint:* Use STEP with a FOR . . . NEXT loop to repeat the circle.)

4. Write a simple program that sets up medium resolution graphics, chooses a background color and palette, and contains this instruction:

```
CIRCLE (150, 100), 50, 2, 0, 1
```

   RUN the program and describe the output. Clear the screen, and change the CIRCLE instruction to CIRCLE (150, 100), 50, 2, 0, 2. How does this affect the output? Experiment with the last number in the CIRCLE instruction to find which value produces a semicircle. What is the *smallest* value of the last number that produces a complete circle?

5. Try this instruction in your program in Problem 4: CIRCLE (150, 100), 50, 2, , , 0.5. What does it do? Try changing the last number in the CIRCLE instruction to 0.1, to 2.0, and to 6. Describe the results.

6-5 Moving Shapes: Animation

Imagine writing a program that draws a shape on your computer's screen, then erases it, then immediately redraws it at a nearby position, then erases it again, and so forth, repeating the entire sequence rapidly and changing the position of the shape steadily in a single direction. If the position changes rapidly enough, you will see the shape moving across the screen. This idea of rapidly viewing a sequence of images, each slightly changed from the previous one, is the basis of movies and cartoons. When the images are drawn rather than photographed from life, the process is called *animation.*

Animating a Point

Let's design a program to move a point horizontally across the screen, say from column 10 to column 100, using the idea of drawing, then erasing, redrawing, and so forth. Following the top-down approach, we first specify the *inputs.* In this case, we will have the user type the number of the row in which the point will move across the screen; we will assign this row number to the variable ROW. The *output* will be the point moving across the screen from column 10 to column 100 at row number ROW. An outline of the *algorithm* might be this:

Step 1 Get row number (ROW) from the user.
Step 2 If ROW is off the graphics screen, then have the user try again.
Step 3 Enter graphics mode.
Step 4 From column X = 10 to 100, plot the point (X, ROW), erase the point (X, ROW).

Step 4 needs some elaboration. How can the point at (X, ROW) be erased? This is done quite simply by plotting the point (X, ROW) over again, but in a color that *matches* the background color of the screen. Then it will look as if the point has been erased, since the point will be invisible. One other difficulty remains — the plotting and erasing of the points in Step 4 may happen so quickly that the illusion of motion may be lost. A time-delay loop such as

```
FOR T = 1 TO 40: NEXT T*
```

may be added to slow the rate at which the point moves across the screen.

Here is the algorithm translated into BASIC code for the *Apple, IBM,* and *TRS-80* microcomputers. For simplicity, only black and white points are plotted. The programs for the *Apple* and *IBM* computers can easily be modified to do animation in color.

Apple

Program 1

Statement	Remark
10 PRINT "MOVING A POINT"	
15 INPUT "TYPE A ROW (FROM 0 TO 159): "; ROW	
20 IF ROW < 0 OR ROW > 159 THEN PRINT "TRY AGAIN": GOTO 15	*Error trap.*
30 HOME	

* See the note on page 272 concerning combined statements with colons.

Statement	Remark
40 HGR	*High-res graphics, black screen.*
50 FOR X = 10 TO 100	*Column 10 to column 100.*
60 HCOLOR = 3	*Set color to white.*
70 HPLOT X, ROW	*Plot a white point on a black background at (X, ROW).*
80 FOR T = 1 TO 40: NEXT T	*Time-delay loop.*
90 HCOLOR = 0	*Set color to black.*
100 HPLOT X, ROW	*Plot a black point on a black background at (X, ROW).*
110 NEXT X	
120 END	

IBM

Program 1

Statement	Remark
10 PRINT "MOVING A POINT"	
15 INPUT "TYPE A ROW (FROM 0 TO 199): "; ROW	
20 IF ROW < 0 OR ROW > 199 THEN PRINT "TRY AGAIN": GOTO 15	
30 CLS	
40 SCREEN 2	*High resolution graphics mode, black screen.*
50 FOR X = 10 TO 100	*Column 10 to column 100.*
60 PSET(X, ROW), 1	*Plot a white point at (X, ROW).*
70 FOR T = 1 TO 50: NEXT T	*Time-delay loop.*
80 PSET(X, ROW), 0	*Plot a black point at (X, ROW).*
90 NEXT X	
100 END	

Note the 0 at the end of the PSET statement in line 80. Recall that in high resolution graphics a color value of 0 with PSET causes the specified point to be plotted in black. In medium resolution graphics, however, a color value of 0 with PSET causes the point to be plotted in the background color selected in the COLOR statement, no matter which palette is chosen. For example, the statements

```
300  SCREEN 1, 0
310  COLOR 1, 0
320  PSET(20, 50), 0
```

will plot a blue point at coordinates (20, 50) on a blue background (making the point invisible).

TRS-80

Program 1

Statement	Remark
10 PRINT "MOVING A POINT"	
15 INPUT "TYPE A ROW (FROM 0 TO 47): "; ROW	
20 IF ROW < 0 OR ROW > 47 THEN PRINT "TRY AGAIN": GOTO 15	
30 CLS	*Clear screen.*
40 FOR X = 10 TO 100	*Column 10 to column 100.*
50 SET(X, ROW)	*Plots white point at (X, ROW).*
60 FOR T = 1 TO 40: NEXT T	*Time-delay loop.*
70 RESET(X, ROW)	*Plot a black point at (X, ROW).*
80 NEXT X	
90 END	

A new statement — RESET — is used in line 70. RESET works the same way as SET, except RESET draws a black point at the specified coordinates (erasing the point).

Animating a Line

Moving a line (segment) horizontally across the screen from left to right is somewhat more difficult than moving a point, but creating the motion again involves the plotting and erasing of points. You could just draw the line, erase it, draw it again at a new location, erase it again, and so forth. This makes the line blink, which detracts from the illusion of motion. A smoother animation results if after the line is initially drawn, only the left endpoint is erased, and the right is extended by one dot (rather like an earthworm crawling along the ground). Here is a diagram showing the progression of a small line segment across the screen:

 initial position (plot first line)

 1st movement (erase left point, plot new right point)

 2nd movement (erase left point, plot new right point)

Let's use the top-down approach again to design a program to move a horizontal line segment (say, eight dots long) from the left edge of the screen to the right edge. As before, the number of the row (ROW) in which the line will move across the screen will be INPUT from the user. The *output* will be the moving line segment. There is a possible outline for the *algorithm* at the top of the next page.

Step 1 Get row number (ROW) from the user.
Step 2 If ROW is off the graphics screen, then have the user try again.
Step 3 Enter graphics mode.
Step 4 Draw the line segment at the left side of the screen.
Step 5 Erase the left endpoint and plot a new right endpoint. Continue until the right edge of the screen is reached.

In Steps 4 and 5, we can let the left endpoint coordinate be X. Then X should go from 0 to 8 less than the maximum column number on your screen, so that the 8-dots-long segment won't go off the screen.

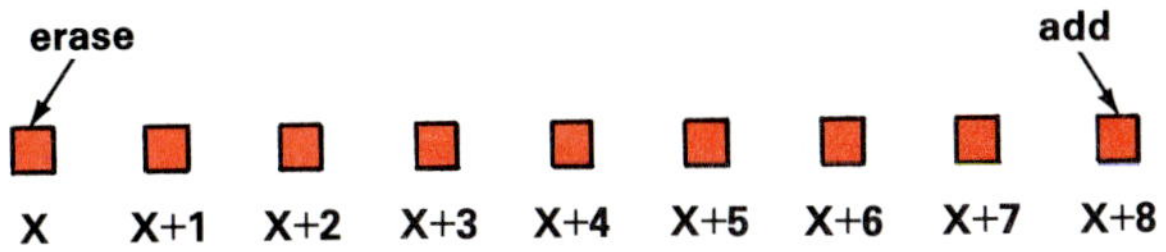

At any moment, the point to be erased at the left end is (X, ROW) and the point to be added is (X + 8, ROW). Again, we will need a time-delay loop.

A similar process can be used to move a horizontal line segment across the screen from right to left (erase the *right* endpoint and add a new point to the *left* end each time), or move a vertical line segment from the top of the screen to the bottom of the screen (erase the point at the *top* and add a point to the *bottom* each time).

Translating the algorithm into BASIC code for the *Apple, IBM,* and *TRS-80* microcomputers, we get the following:

Apple

Program 2

Statement	Remark
10 PRINT "MOVING A LINE"	
15 INPUT "TYPE A ROW (FROM 0 TO 39): "; ROW	
20 IF ROW < 0 OR ROW > 39 THEN PRINT "TRY AGAIN": GOTO 15	
30 HOME	
40 GR	*Low resolution graphics mode, black screen.*
45 COLOR = 3	
50 HLIN 0, 7 AT ROW	*Draw initial segment at left side of screen.*

Program continued on next page.

60 FOR X = 0 TO 31	*31 + 8 = 39 = maximum column number on the low resolution screen.*
70 FOR T = 1 TO 40: NEXT T	*Time-delay loop.*
75 COLOR = 0	*Set color to black.*
80 PLOT X, ROW	*Plot black point (erase on the left).*
85 COLOR = 3	*Set color to white.*
90 PLOT X + 8, ROW	*Plot new point.*
100 NEXT X	*Move to next column.*
110 END	

IBM

Program 2

Statement	Remark
10 PRINT "MOVING A LINE"	
15 INPUT "TYPE A ROW (FROM 0 TO 199): "; ROW	
20 IF ROW < 0 OR ROW > 199 THEN PRINT "TRY AGAIN": GOTO 15	
30 CLS	
40 SCREEN 2	*High resolution mode, black screen.*
50 LINE (0, ROW) – (7, ROW), 1	*Draw initial white segment.*
60 FOR X = 0 TO 631	*631 + 8 = 639 = maximum column number on high-res screen.*
70 FOR T = 1 TO 50: NEXT T	*Time-delay loop.*
80 PSET(X, ROW), 0	*Plot black point (erase on the left).*
90 PSET(X + 8, ROW), 1	*Add new point to right end.*
100 NEXT X	*Move to the next column.*
110 END	

TRS-80

Program 2

Statement	Remark
10 PRINT "MOVING A LINE"	
15 INPUT "TYPE A ROW (FROM 0 TO 47): "; ROW	
20 IF ROW < 0 OR ROW > 47 THEN PRINT "TRY AGAIN": GOTO 15	
30 CLS	

40 FOR A = 0 TO 7	*Draw initial segment at left edge of screen.*
50 SET(A, ROW)	
55 NEXT A	
60 FOR X = 0 TO 119	*119 + 8 = 127 = maximum column number on graphics screen.*
70 FOR T = 1 TO 40: NEXT T	*Time-delay loop.*
80 RESET(X, ROW)	*Erase the line's left point.*
90 SET(X + 8, ROW)	*Add point to right end of segment.*
100 NEXT X	*Move to the next column.*
110 END	

Animating a Shape

Moving a more complex shape across the screen involves a similar technique of plotting and erasing points. Let's move a shape that looks a little like a ship. If we label the point at the top of the ship (X, Y), then all the other points can be labeled according to their position relative to (X, Y):

		X, Y		
	X-1, Y+1	X, Y+1	X+1,Y+1	
X-2, Y+2	X-1, Y+2	X, Y+2	X+1,Y+2	X+2,Y+2

How can we move the ship horizontally across the screen from left to right? Well, notice that the shape consists of a single point at the top, a line segment three points long across the middle, and a line segment five points long at the bottom. The single point and the two lines can be moved using the method of plotting and erasing explained previously.

Program 3 will move the ship across the screen for *Apple, IBM,* and *TRS-80* microcomputers. Three subroutines are used:

- Subroutine 500 draws the ship.
- Subroutine 600 erases the point at the top of the ship and the left endpoint of each line segment.
- Subroutine 700 draws a new point at the top of the ship and at the right end of each of the line segments.

The location of the row (Y) where the top of the ship is to appear is INPUT from the user.

Apple

Program 3

Statement	Remark
10 PRINT "MOVING A SHAPE"	
15 INPUT "TYPE A ROW (FROM 0 TO 37): "; Y	
20 IF Y < 0 OR Y > 37 THEN PRINT "TRY AGAIN": GOTO 15	
30 HOME	
40 GR	
45 GOSUB 500: REM * DRAW SHIP	
50 FOR X = 2 TO 36	*Move shape from left to right.*
60 FOR T = 1 TO 40: NEXT T	
70 GOSUB 600: REM * ERASE POINTS	
75 GOSUB 700: REM * ADD NEW POINTS	
80 NEXT X	*Move to the next column.*
90 END	
490 REM * * SUBROUTINE TO DRAW SHIP * *	
500 COLOR = 3	*Set color to white.*
510 PLOT 2, Y	*Plot point at top of shape.*
520 HLIN 1, 3 AT Y + 1	*Draw middle line of shape.*
530 HLIN 0, 4 AT Y + 2	*Draw bottom line of shape.*
540 RETURN	
590 REM * * SUBROUTINE TO ERASE POINTS * *	
600 COLOR = 0	*Set color to black.*
610 PLOT X, Y	*Erase top point.*
620 PLOT X − 1, Y + 1	*Erase left endpoint of middle line.*
630 PLOT X − 2, Y + 2	*Erase left endpoint of bottom line.*
640 RETURN	
690 REM * * SUBROUTINE TO ADD POINTS * *	
700 COLOR = 3	*Set color to white.*
710 PLOT X + 1, Y	*Plot point at top of shape.*
720 PLOT X + 2, Y + 1	*Add point to right end of middle line.*
730 PLOT X + 3, Y + 2	*Add point to right end of bottom line.*
740 RETURN	

In the complex condition in line 20, row numbers less than 0 and greater than 37 are rejected to ensure that the top or bottom of the shape does not go off the graphics screen.

IBM

Program 3

Statement	Remark
10 PRINT "MOVING A SHAPE"	
15 INPUT "TYPE A ROW (FROM 0 TO 197): "; Y	
20 IF Y < 0 OR Y > 197 THEN PRINT "TRY AGAIN": GOTO 15	
30 CLS	
40 SCREEN 1, 1	*Medium resolution graphics, no color.*
45 GOSUB 500: REM * DRAW SHIP	
50 FOR X = 2 TO 316	*Move shape from left to right.*
60 GOSUB 600: REM * ERASE POINTS	
70 GOSUB 700: REM * ADD NEW POINTS	
80 NEXT X	*Move to the next column.*
90 END	
490 REM * * SUBROUTINE TO DRAW SHIP * *	
500 PSET(2, Y), 1	*Plot point at top of shape.*
510 LINE (1, Y + 1) - (3, Y + 1), 1	*Draw middle line of shape.*
520 LINE (0, Y + 2) - (4, Y + 2), 1	*Draw bottom line of shape.*
530 FOR T = 1 TO 50: NEXT T	
540 RETURN	
590 REM * * SUBROUTINE TO ERASE POINTS * *	
600 PSET(X, Y), 0	*Erase top point.*
610 PSET(X − 1, Y + 1), 0	*Erase left endpoint of middle line.*
620 PSET(X − 2, Y + 2), 0	*Erase left endpoint of bottom line.*
630 RETURN	
690 REM * * SUBROUTINE TO ADD POINTS * *	
700 PSET(X + 1, Y), 1	*Plot point at top of shape.*
710 PSET(X + 2, Y + 1), 1	*Add point to right end of middle line.*
720 PSET(X + 3, Y + 2), 1	*Add point to right end of bottom line.*
730 RETURN	

In the complex condition in line 20, row numbers less than 0 or greater than 197 are rejected to ensure that the top or bottom of the shape does not go off the graphics screen. Why are the numbers 2 and 316 used as the counter values in line 50 rather than 0 and 319?

TRS-80

Program 3

Statement	Remark
10 PRINT "MOVING A SHAPE"	
15 INPUT "TYPE A ROW (FROM 0 TO 45): "; Y	
20 IF Y < 0 OR Y > 45 THEN PRINT "TRY AGAIN": GOTO 15	
30 CLS	
40 GOSUB 500: REM * DRAW SHIP	
50 FOR X = 2 TO 124	*Move shape from left to right.*
55 FOR T = 1 TO 40: NEXT T	
60 GOSUB 600: REM * ERASE POINTS	
70 GOSUB 700: REM * ADD NEW POINTS	
80 NEXT X	*Move to the next column.*
90 END	
490 REM * * SUBROUTINE TO DRAW SHIP * *	
500 SET(2, Y)	*Plot point at top of shape.*
510 FOR A = 1 TO 3	*Draw middle line of shape.*
520 SET(A, Y + 1)	
530 NEXT A	
540 FOR B = 0 TO 4	*Draw bottom line of shape.*
550 SET(B, Y + 2)	
560 NEXT B	
570 RETURN	
590 REM * * SUBROUTINE TO ERASE POINTS * *	
600 RESET(X, Y)	*Erase top point.*
610 RESET(X − 1, Y + 1)	*Erase left endpoint of middle line.*
620 RESET(X − 2, Y + 2)	*Erase left endpoint of bottom line.*
630 RETURN	
690 REM * * SUBROUTINE TO ADD POINTS * *	
700 SET(X + 1, Y)	*Plot point at top of shape.*
710 SET(X + 2, Y + 1)	*Add point to right end of middle line.*
720 SET(X + 3, Y + 2)	*Add point to right end of bottom line.*
730 RETURN	

In the complex condition in line 20, row numbers less than 0 or greater than 45 are rejected to ensure that the top or bottom of the shape does not go off the screen. Why are the numbers 2 and 124 used as the counter values in line 50 rather than 0 and 127?

In this section we have moved points, line segments, and shapes only in one direction, across the screen from left to right. With careful planning and the use of top-down design, you can write programs to move shapes anywhere about the screen by erasing trailing points and plotting leading points. Some possibilities are explored in the exercises. Unfortunately, BASIC runs too slowly to allow realistic animation of any but the simplest shapes, but the principles you have seen here apply to more complicated situations. Other computer languages you may learn in the future can be used to make your programs more fun.

Avoiding Pitfalls

1. Remember that careful planning is needed to animate shapes. Draw your shape first and label one of the points with general coordinates, say (X, Y). Next label all the other points according to their position relative to (X, Y). Then use top-down design and outline an algorithm. Finally, translate the algorithm into BASIC code.

2. Be sure to include error trapping in animation programs to prevent the shape from going off the screen.

Summary

When working with graphics you can make shapes appear to move by using the technique of plotting and erasing points. This process is called *animation.*

A point or line can be erased by plotting it over again in the background color:

On *Apple* computers, use COLOR = 0 or HCOLOR = 0;
On *IBM* computers, use PSET(X, Y), 0 or LINE (X1, Y1) – (X2, Y2), 0;
On *TRS-80* computers, use RESET(X, Y).

Exercises 6-5

A

1. Modify Program 1 for your machine so that the point moves horizontally across the screen from the column at the right edge to the column at the left edge, at the INPUT row.

2. Modify Program 2 for your machine so that the line moves horizontally across the screen from the column at the right edge to the column at the left edge, at the INPUT row.

3. Modify Program 3 for your machine so that the ship moves horizontally across the screen from the column at the right edge to the column at the left edge at the INPUT row. (*Hint:* Study the diagram on page 319 to determine which points should be erased and which should be added.)

B 4. a. Write a subroutine that will draw the following shape:

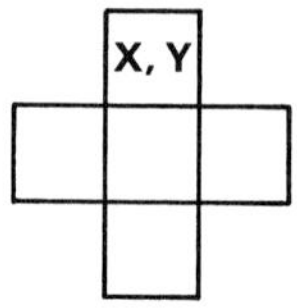

b. Write subroutines to erase and add the proper points if the shape is to move horizontally across the screen from left to right.

c. Using the subroutines from (a) and (b), write a program to move the shape horizontally across the graphics screen from the left edge to the right edge, at any INPUT row.

5. Repeat Exercise 4 for this figure:

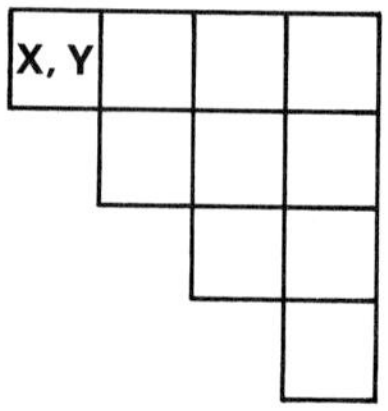

6. a. Write a program to move a point vertically from the top row to the bottom row of your graphics screen, at any INPUT column. If possible, use color.

b. Add to the program in (a) so that the point returns along the same column back to the top of the screen.

7. a. Write a program to move a six-point vertical line segment from the top row to the bottom row of your graphics screen, at any INPUT column. If possible, use color.

b. Add to the program in (a) so that the line segment returns to the top of the screen along the same column.

8. a. Write a program to move the ship-like shape (diagrammed on page 319) vertically from the top row to the bottom row of your graphics screen, at any INPUT column. If possible, use color.

b. Add to the program in (a) so that the ship moves horizontally to the right edge of the screen after it reaches the bottom row.

9. Write a program to move a point diagonally from the top left corner to the bottom right corner of your graphics screen. (*Hint:* Add 1 to both the X-coordinate and Y-coordinate each time the point is redrawn.)

C **10.** *Challenge:* Write a program to create the illusion of a bird flying from left to right across your screen. Have the wings move as realistically as you can. (*Hint:* Keep the shape simple.)

Lab Activity

A General Animation Program

The animation techniques explored in this section work fairly well if one or only a very few shapes are moving across the screen in a systematic way. If you want to have a figure changing shape or moving on a more haphazard path, another approach is necessary.

The program presented in this Lab Activity is a general animation program; it will work for any shapes and for any kind of motion. As you will see, however, it has serious limitations. First, it is very slow, so that you must squint your eyes and use a lot of imagination to see the motion that is the whole purpose of animation. This problem could be overcome by using a computer language that will run much faster; machine language (see the Computer Language feature on page 64), for example, would work very well with this kind of program.

Another limitation of the program is that it uses DATA statements to give the coordinates of all the points used to make the shapes. It is tedious to type all the coordinates. This typing problem could be overcome by writing another (much more complicated) program that would let the user draw the shapes using the keyboard, a joystick, a light pen, or a graphics tablet.

Despite its limitations, the program illustrates an important principle; pictures — even moving pictures — can be coded into numbers, but it takes an enormous amount of data to encode even a very simple sequence of pictures. In this program, pictures are drawn as follows: In line 210, the program goes to subroutine 1000 where it plots white dots at points whose coordinates are given in the first DATA line (4000). The coordinates are given *relative to the center of the screen;* thus (0, 0) refers to the center of the screen, (2, −3) refers to the point 2 to the right and 3 down from the center, and so forth. (Thus, the GOSUB 1000 in line 210 plots the points at the center (0, 0), one up from the center (0, 1), one to the right of the center (1, 0), and one to the right and one up (1, 1).) The pair 1000, 1000 at the end of each DATA line is a double trailer value that tells the subroutine when to stop. Line 230 calls subroutine 1000 again, which adds 8 points to the shape (their relative coordinates are (−1, 0), (−1, 1), and so forth, see line 4010).

Subroutine 1000 (2000 on *TRS-80*), which the program calls again in line 260, erases points by plotting invisible black points on a black screen. The process of adding and then erasing points is repeated until the final double trailer value 2000, 2000 is reached in line 4130. (Some program lines vary for different computers; choose the version for your machine.)

Apple

```
10  REM * * GENERAL ANIMATION PROGRAM * *
100  HGR
200  HCOLOR = 3
210  GOSUB 1000: REM * DRAW INITIAL PICTURE
220  HCOLOR = 3
230  GOSUB 1000: REM * ADD POINTS
240  IF X = 2000 THEN GOTO 280: REM * IF END OF PROGRAM
250  HCOLOR = 0
260  GOSUB 1000: REM * ERASE POINTS
270  IF X <> 2000 THEN GOTO 220
280  END
999  REM * * SUBROUTINE TO PLOT POINTS * *
1000  READ X, Y
1010  IF X = 1000 OR X = 2000 THEN GOTO 1040: REM * TRAILER VALUES
1020  HPLOT 140 + X, 96 — Y: REM * X AND Y ARE RELATIVE TO CENTER OF SCREEN
1030  GOTO 1000
1040  RETURN
4000  DATA 0, 0, 0, 1, 1, 0, 1, 1, 1000, 1000
4010  DATA —1, 0, —1, 1, —1, 2, 0, 2, 1, 2, 2, 2, 2, 1, 2, 0, 1000, 1000
4020  DATA 1000,1000
4030  DATA —2, 3, —2, 4, —1, 3, —1, 4, 0, 3, 0, 4, 1, 3, 1, 4, 2, 3, 2, 4, 3, 3, 3, 4, 1000, 1000
4040  DATA 1000, 1000
4050  DATA —2, 5, —2, 6, —1, 5, —1, 6, 0, 5, 0, 6, 1, 5, 1, 6, 2, 5, 2, 6, 3, 5, 3, 6, 1000, 1000
4060  DATA —2, 3, 3, 3, 1000, 1000
4070  DATA —3, 5, —3, 6, —3, 7, —2, 7, —1, 7, 0, 7, 1, 7, 2, 7, 3, 7, 4, 7, 4, 6, 4, 5, 1000, 1000
4080  DATA —2, 4, 3, 4, 1000, 1000
4090  DATA —4, 6, —4, 7, —4, 8, —4, 9, —3, 8, —3, 9, —2, 8, —2, 9, —1, 8, —1, 9, 0, 8, 0,
        9, 1, 8, 1, 9, 2, 8, 2, 9, 3, 8, 3, 9, 4, 8, 4, 9, 5, 8, 5, 9, 5, 7, 5, 6, 1000, 1000
4100  DATA —3, 5, —2, 5, 3, 5, 4, 5, 1000, 1000
4110  DATA —5, 7, —5, 8, —5, 9, —5, 10, —4, 10, —3, 10, —2, 10, —1, 10, 0, 10, 1, 10, 2,
        10, 3, 10, 4, 10, 5, 10, 6, 10, 6, 9, 6, 8, 6, 7, 1000, 1000
4120  DATA —2, 6, —3, 6, —4, 6, 3, 6, 4, 6, 5, 6, 1000, 1000
4130  DATA 2000, 2000
```

TRS-80

Here are the changes for *TRS-80* computers:

```
100   CLS
200, 220, 250 ←— delete
260   GOSUB 2000: REM * ERASE POINTS
270   IF X <> 2000 THEN GOTO 230
1020  SET(64 + X, 24 − Y): REM * X AND Y ARE RELATIVE
          TO CENTER OF SCREEN
2000  READ X, Y: REM * POINTS TO BE ERASED
2010  IF X = 1000 OR X = 2000 THEN GOTO 2040
2020  RESET(64 + X, 24 − Y)
2030  GOTO 2000
2040  RETURN
```

IBM

Here are the changes for *IBM* computers:

```
100   SCREEN 1, 1: REM * MEDIUM RESOLUTION GRAPHICS
          WITHOUT COLOR
110   CLS
200   LET C = 1
220   LET C = 1
250   LET C = 0
1020  PSET(160 + X, 100 − Y), C
```

Problems

1. Type and RUN the version of the program for your computer. If you have typed the program lines correctly you should see a "T" shape growing out of a small blob.

2. Add DATA lines to the end of the program (replace line 4130, which tells the program to END) that will make the T grow larger, or will make it start to fly away at an angle, or will make it fall over, or explode.

To do this, use a grid sheet to determine the exact location of all the points in the shape when the original program ENDs. (Trace through the program, adding and erasing points as the program would.) Then determine the coordinates of the points you need to add and to erase (a few at a time) to make the shape do what you want. Don't forget to add the double trailer value 1000, 1000 at the end of each DATA line, and the final 2000, 2000 to END the program.

Chapter Summary

The PRINT TAB statement, which has the form

PRINT TAB(X); *any string or expression allowed with PRINT*

moves the cursor to the right to column number X before PRINTing the string or expression after it. X may be a number, a numeric variable, or a BASIC numerical expression.

Multiple TAB instructions can be given on the same program line (using only one PRINT) as long as semicolons separate the TAB instructions from the expressions or strings to be PRINTed.

The PRINT USING statement (*TRS-80* and *IBM*) uses a *formatting string* to specify exactly how digits of a number are to appear in the output of a program.

POSITIONING THE CURSOR

Apple

The statement HTAB X moves the cursor to *column* X.

The statement VTAB Y moves the cursor to *row* Y.

TRS-80

The PRINT @ instruction can be used to position the cursor at any one of 1024 locations on the *TRS-80* screen. (The position numbers may range from 0 to 1023.) The instruction has this form:

PRINT @ *position number, any string or expression allowed with PRINT*

IBM

The instruction LOCATE R, C moves the cursor to *row* R, *column* C.

ADVANCED GRAPHICS

Apple

See the summary on page 301.

IBM

See the summary on page 306.

When working with graphics you can make shapes appear to move by using the technique of plotting and erasing points. This process is called *animation.* A point can be erased by plotting it in the background color.

Chapter Test

1. Predict the output of each of the following programs. Use a grid sheet.

   a.
   ```
   10 PRINT TAB(7); "BIGFOOT WEARS
        A SIZE";
   20 PRINT TAB(28); 12; TAB(34);
        "SHOE"
   30 PRINT TAB(10); "WOW"
   40 END
   ```

   b.
   ```
   10 FOR T = 1 TO 5
   20 READ K
   30 PRINT TAB(K + 5); K
   40 NEXT T
   45 DATA 10, −2, 21, 30, 0
   50 END
   ```

2. Write a program that has the following output. Position the cursor initially at column 8 and row 4. (Use subroutines.)

   ```
   EEEE    TTTTT
   E         T
   E         T
   EEEE      T
   E         T
   E         T
   EEEE      T
   ```

3. Write a program that has the following output. Position the cursor initially at column 16 and row 5. (Use a FOR . . . NEXT loop.)

   ```
   YOU WILL SUCCEED!
    YOU WILL SUCCEED!
     YOU WILL SUCCEED!
   ```

4. (*IBM* and *TRS-80*) Predict the output of the following program.

   ```
   10 FOR A = 1 TO 5
   20 READ B
   30 PRINT USING "$$##.##"; B
   40 NEXT A
   50 DATA 29, 18.6, 74.904, 3.88, 2.177
   60 END
   ```

5. Write a program (in high resolution graphics, if available) that draws the letter M in the lower right portion of the screen.

6. Write a program using animation to move a block of six points vertically from the top of the screen to the bottom of the screen, at any INPUT column.

Computer-related Careers

The Technological Revolution

From your study of American history, you are probably familiar with the Industrial Revolution of the late 1800's and the changes it brought to society. Many sociologists today say that the invention of the computer in the 1940's signaled the beginning of a "technological revolution." This ongoing revolution has created an economy in which more and more jobs are related to computer technology and the services computers help provide.

People in today's society having basic computing skills can better compete for the jobs they want. Computer applications are extensive, regardless of the field of interest. People who work in food production, in health-care facilities, in schools, banks, and businesses use computers daily. Computers play a role in nearly every occupation, but there are some careers that are directly related to computers.

Workers in businesses use computers.

Programmers

The role of a *computer programmer* is to develop, test, implement, and update computer programs. *Applications programmers* design programs for specific tasks in such fields as business, government, science, and engineering. Applications programmers may need special knowledge of a subject area. For instance, a programmer who wants to design a program to simulate how the stock market works probably would want a business background. *Systems programmers* write programs that control the operations of the computer, or serve as tools for applications programmers to use. Programmers always include *documentation* for completed programs and are usually capable of programming in several different computer languages. Many programmers are college graduates who have majored in computer science.

Systems Analysts

Another computer-related job is that of computer *systems analyst.* A systems analyst works with a company to develop an overall plan for how computers can be used most effectively by the company. After the systems analyst has made a thorough study of the company's problem areas, several suggestions are offered to management. The plans usually specify what kind of computer(s) to buy, where they should be located, what tasks they should perform, and what type of

Computer operators

software should be purchased. A systems analyst is usually a college graduate and has had experience with several computer languages and various "software packages."

Operators

Computer operations is another type of computer-related occupation. Computer operations personnel are collectively responsible for preparing and inputting data, for monitoring computer operations, and for supplying output to users. Operations personnel work with many different peripheral devices such as keypunch machines, high-speed printers, sorting machines, and optical scanners. Some of the jobs associated with computer operations are computer terminal operator, data control clerk, keypunch operator, operations supervisor, and computer systems operator.

Engineers and Technicians

Two other occupations that require working with computer hardware are those of *computer engineer* and *computer technician.* Computer engineers design entire computer systems, including the central processing unit (CPU), and all input and output devices. They often use a computer to help them design circuits to be used in a new computer. Computer engineers should have a strong background in electrical engineering as well as in computer science. After a computer is designed, it must be assembled and thoroughly tested. This job is performed by the *computer technician.* Technicians are also responsible for tracing and correcting malfunctions.

Many job forecasters predict that there will be a need in the near future for *robot technicians.* As the manufacture and use of robots becomes more widespread, technicians will be needed to program the robots and to fix them when they break down.

Many new careers have resulted from the continuing development of computers. If you have an interest in a computer-related career, investigate what preparation may be necessary to enable you to pursue it.

Computer technician with circuit boards

Computer Languages

C

Developed by Dennis Ritchie at Bell Laboratories in the early 1970's, C is a structured programming language, sometimes referred to as a middle-level language and also as a portable assembly language. C is a compact, general-purpose language with about 30 reserved words. Like Forth and Lisp, its vocabulary can be extended by adding more complicated commands to existing ones. The syntax of C is very suitable for structured programming (like the *top-down* approach you are familiar with from BASIC).

Users of C believe it is easier to learn than assembly language, while offering most of the advantages of that low-level language. Moreover, C provides a standard support library of over one hundred functions. It places few restraints on programmers, allowing them to pursue goals not so easily attainable with other computer languages.

The syntax of C is independent of any specific computer operating system. Programs are written in block form, which makes them easier to read and debug. The main body of the program is usually short, and the functions are called by name from within the program in which they are defined, or from the library of subroutines. C also uses many low-level operations that correspond to the notation of machine language, such as: shift left (<<), decrease (--), increase (++), AND (&) and OR (|). Also, input and output (I/O) routines are not defined in the main body of a C program. They are called from the standard library and, thus, are easy to modify. The various features of C enhance the writing of "portable" programs, since C programs will run on different computers with minimal modifications.

Here is a short program written in C:

```
/ * This program prints the message "This is an example of a C program" * /
main( )
{
   printf ("This is an example of a C program \ n");
}
```

Notice that line numbers are not used in C. A comment statement, which requires a REM instruction in BASIC, must begin with the symbols / * and end with the symbols * /. The instruction *main* is used to indicate the beginning of the main routine (or module) the program will perform. The parentheses that follow *main* are used to enclose any arguments or values that the program would use. In this program, values and arguments are not used and, therefore, the parentheses are empty. The braces, { and }, are used to indicate the beginning and end of the body of a program. *Print formatted* is the meaning of the function *printf,* which is in the C library of routines. Any information in parentheses after this function will be processed and printed. Since the message above is a string, it is enclosed in quotes. The \ n characters at the end of a string indicate a new line or carriage return. As in Pascal, each program statement must end with a semicolon.

Since its development, C has been closely associated with the UNIX operating system, which was developed at Bell Laboratories. UNIX, written in the C language, was created for the time-sharing computer systems of the 1970's. It supports multiprocessing, which means that it can handle and tell the difference between files of several users and their applications all at the same time.

UNIX and C were initially very popular in universities and industry. Now they are being used for a wide variety of applications, including many major development projects within the computer software industry. The special effects of C's powerful graphic capabilities can be viewed in such movies as *Star Trek II*, *Tron,* and *Return of the Jedi.*

Movie still from the motion picture Tron showing computer-generated graphics

CHAPTER

7 Numeric Functions

Computer-enhanced visualizations such as the one above of spiral galaxy NGC 1097 assist astronomers in their studies of outer space. The vibrant colors were produced using color graphics.

Introduction

Most programming languages, BASIC included, have *built-in functions.* You may have studied functions in mathematics class; in programming, a function is a routine that takes a value (string or number) as an input, and produces a single (usually different) value as output.

input value ⟶ [function routine] ⟶ output value

In this chapter you will learn about BASIC *numeric* functions; that is, functions in which the input and output values are numbers. *String* functions will be explored in Chapter 8.

7-1 The INT Function

Probably the most useful built-in numeric function in BASIC is the function called INT (short for INTeger). INT *rounds down* any input number to the nearest integer. The result of applying the INT function to a number X is written INT(X), and is read "INT of X." For example, if you round X = 3.8 down to the nearest integer, you get 3; thus INT(3.8) = 3. Similarly,

INT(4) = 4	INT(3.46) = 3
INT(.41) = 0	INT(−2) = −2
INT(−2.4) = −3	INT(−.001456) = −1

The instruction PRINT INT (4.6) has output 4.

The instruction LET X = INT(1.3) assigns the value 1 to X.

Notice that if N is an integer, then INT(N) = N. The negative numbers might give you difficulty; remember that *rounding down* means moving to the *left* on the number line. In Example 1, two of the INT instructions from above are graphed on a number line:

Example 1

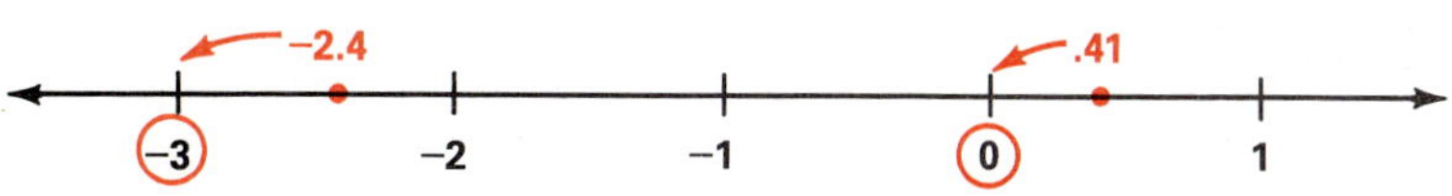

Program 1 on the next page shows a common use of INT — error trapping to test whether an INPUT number is an integer. The program is based on the observation that INT(N) = N exactly if N is an integer.

Program 1

Statement

```
10  PRINT "ERROR TRAPPING"
20  INPUT "TYPE AN INTEGER:   "; N
30  IF N <> INT(N) THEN PRINT "TRY AGAIN": GOTO 20
40  PRINT N; "  IS AN INTEGER"
50  END
```

Output

```
ERROR TRAPPING
TYPE AN INTEGER:   ? 4.5
TRY AGAIN
TYPE AN INTEGER:   ? 50
50 IS AN INTEGER
```

If 4.5 is typed for the value of N, then in line 20 the condition N <> INT(N) is true (4.5 <> INT (4.5) = 4), so the user is asked again to type an integer.

In addition to numbers and variables, BASIC numerical expressions may be used in the parentheses that follow INT. For example, if

$$X = 2.1 \text{ and } Y = -3.8,$$

then

$$\begin{aligned} \text{INT}(X + 2 * Y) &= \text{INT}(2.1 - 7.6) \\ &= \text{INT}(-5.5) \\ &= -6 \end{aligned}$$

Rounding to the Nearest Integer

You have seen how the INT function rounds down. But what if you want to round off to the *nearest* integer? For example, if you want to round 2.6 to the nearest integer, the result should be 3 (since the tenths digit 6 is greater than 5), and not INT (2.6) = 2. To make this happen, you add .5 to the number in parentheses. This ensures that rounding will be to the nearest integer:

$$\text{INT}(2.6 + .5) = \text{INT}(3.1) = 3$$

Here are some other examples using INT to round numbers to the nearest integer:

$X = 2.3;\quad \text{INT}(X + .5) = \text{INT}(2.3 + .5) = \text{INT}(2.8) = 2$

$X = 4.55;\quad \text{INT}(X + .5) = \text{INT}(4.55 + .5) = \text{INT}(5.05) = 5$

$X = -2.7;\quad \text{INT}(X + .5) = \text{INT}(-2.7 + .5) = \text{INT}(-2.2) = -3$

$X = -2.1;\quad \text{INT}(X + .5) = \text{INT}(-2.1 + .5) = \text{INT}(-1.6) = -2$

Try some other values of X and convince yourself that INT(X + .5) always rounds X to the nearest integer. (*Note:* On *IBM* computers, you do not have to use this technique; you can use the built-in function CINT to round numbers to the nearest integer.)

Rounding to a Specified Number of Decimal Places

The INT function can also be used to round off numbers to a specified number of decimal places, rather than just to the nearest integer. Suppose you want to round results to the nearest hundredth, which is commonly done in programs involving money. The idea is to move the decimal point two places to the right (multiply by 100), then round to the nearest integer (add .5 and apply INT), then move the decimal point back two places to the left (divide by 100). This procedure leads to the following expression:

$$\text{INT}(X * 100 + .5) / 100$$

For example, if $X = 4.687$, then

$$\begin{aligned}\text{INT}(X * 100 + .5) / 100 &= \text{INT}(4.687 * 100 + .5) / 100 \\ &= \text{INT}(468.7 + .5) / 100 \\ &= \text{INT}(469.2) / 100 \\ &= 469 / 100 = 4.69\end{aligned}$$

If you want to round to three decimal places, use 1000 rather than 100 in both places in the expression. For example, if $X = 28.2653$, then

$$\begin{aligned}\text{INT}(X * 1000 + .5) / 1000 &= \text{INT}(28.2653 * 1000 + .5) / 1000 \\ &= \text{INT}(28265.3 + .5) / 1000 \\ &= \text{INT}(28265.8) / 1000 \\ &= 28265 / 1000 = 28.265\end{aligned}$$

Program 2 below uses the rounding-off technique to calculate to the nearest cent the unit price (cost per pound) of a box of detergent.

Program 2

Statement	Remark
10 PRINT "UNIT PRICING"	
20 INPUT "TYPE NAME, COST: "; NME$, CST	
30 INPUT "NO. POUNDS PER BOX: "; NUM	
40 LET UP = CST / NUM	*Calculate cost per pound.*
45 LET R = INT(UP * 100 + .5) / 100	*Round to nearest cent.*
50 PRINT "UNIT PRICE IS: $"; R	
60 END	

Output

```
UNIT PRICING
TYPE NAME, COST:   ? WHIZZO, 6.24
NO. POUNDS PER BOX:   ? 13
UNIT PRICE IS:   $.48
```

Avoiding Pitfalls

1. Remember that the INT function rounds a number *down* to the integer immediately to its left on the number line. If you want to round a number to the *nearest* integer, be sure to add .5 inside the parentheses. For example:

   $$\text{INT}(4.6) = 4, \text{ but INT}(4.6 + .5) = 5$$

2. The INT function and all the other built-in functions you will learn about are expressions that yield values; they are not variables. Thus, the statement LET INT(X) = 4 is *not* legal.

Summary

INT(X) rounds a decimal number X *down* to the nearest integer to its left on the number line.

If N is an integer, INT(N) = N.

INT(X + .5) rounds X to the *nearest* integer.

INT(X * 10 ↑ D + .5) / 10 ↑ D rounds X to D decimal places. For example, if D = 2, 10 ↑ D = 100, and INT(X * 100 + .5) / 100 rounds X to 2 decimal places.

Exercises 7-1

A 1. Give the output of each of the following commands.

a. PRINT INT(8.2)	**b.** PRINT INT(6.7)
c. PRINT INT(5.0)	**d.** PRINT INT(—4.5)
e. PRINT INT(—6)	**f.** PRINT INT(.3)
g. PRINT INT(—1.2)	**h.** PRINT INT(—.3)
i. PRINT INT(—3.6)	**j.** PRINT INT(.95)

2. Give the output of each of the following commands if J = 2 and K = 5.

   a. PRINT INT(J * 1.25)
   b. PRINT INT(—.5 * K)
   c. PRINT INT(9 / J)
   d. PRINT INT(J / K)
   e. PRINT INT(J — K)
   f. PRINT INT(—1 / K)

3. Tell whether each of the following conditions is true or false:

   a. INT(5) = 5
   b. INT(7/ 2) <> 7/ 2
   c. INT(X) = X (when X = 3.4)
   d. INT(X + .5) = 3 (when X = 2.6)
   e. INT(X + .5) = —2 (when X = —2.9)
   f. INT(X + .5) <> 0 (when X = .3)

4. Write a BASIC statement that will round a decimal number Y to:

   a. the nearest integer
   b. two decimal places
   c. four decimal places

5. Give the output of each of the following commands.

   a. PRINT INT(2.65 * 10 + .5) / 10
   b. PRINT INT(8.462 * 100 + .5) / 100
   c. PRINT INT(9.333 * 100 + .5) / 100
   d. PRINT INT(—1.25 * 10 + .5) / 10
   e. PRINT INT(2 / 3 * 10 + .5) / 10
   f. PRINT INT(—8.44 * 10 + .5) / 10
   g. PRINT INT(.875 * 10 + .5) / 10
   h. PRINT INT(8 / 3 * 1000 + .5) / 1000
   i. PRINT INT(—.7964 * 100 + .5) / 100
   j. PRINT INT(5 / 8 * 100 + .5) / 100
   k. PRINT INT(62.74 * .1 + .5) / .1
   l. PRINT INT(367.5 * .01 + .5) / .01

6. Predict the output of the following program for each of the INPUTs shown below. Construct a run chart, if necessary.

```
10 INPUT "TYPE THE NUMERATOR:  "; NUM
20 INPUT "TYPE THE DENOMINATOR:  "; DEN
30 LET Q = INT(NUM / DEN)
40 LET R = NUM — DEN * Q
50 PRINT "QUOTIENT =  "; Q
60 PRINT "REMAINDER =  "; R
70 END
```

   a. NUM = 8
DEN = 4
   b. NUM = 15
DEN = 3
   c. NUM = 9
DEN = 2
   d. NUM = 22
DEN = 4
   e. NUM = 8
DEN = 3
   f. NUM = 43
DEN = 7

7. Determine whether each of the following is true or false by substituting several well-chosen decimal values for X and Y.

a. INT(X + Y) = INT(X) + INT(Y)
b. INT(X * Y) = INT(X) * INT(Y)
c. INT(X * Y) = X * INT(Y)

8. Substitute several values of X in the subroutine below:

```
1000 REM ** SUBROUTINE TO ? **
1010 LET Y = INT(X)
1020 IF X - Y > .5 THEN LET Y = Y + 1
1030 RETURN
```

What is the purpose of the subroutine? Compare this method to the one illustrated in this section. Which seems better? Why?

B 9. Write a program to ask a person how many goldfish he or she owns. If a number other than a positive integer is typed, have the program ask repeatedly until the correct form of response is given.

10. Write a program that rounds an INPUT number to the nearest multiple of 10. For example, if 21 is entered, the output should be 20. If 146 is entered, the output should be 150. (*Hint:* See Exercise 5(k).)

11. Write a program that INPUTs a worker's weekly salary before taxes (*gross pay*). Have the program calculate the worker's *net pay* by subtracting the amount paid for Social Security taxes, and for state and federal income taxes. These amounts should be rounded to the nearest cent. Assume that 16% of a worker's salary goes to federal taxes, $5\frac{1}{2}$% to state taxes, and $7\frac{1}{4}$% to Social Security taxes. The output should be similar to this:

```
GROSS PAY: $366
FED. TAX: $58.56
STATE TAX: $20.13
SOC. SEC. TAX: $26.54
NET PAY: $260.77
```

12. Write a program that calculates the *commission* earned by an automobile salesperson (*commission = total sales * rate of commission*). Have the program INPUT the salesperson's total sales for one month, then calculate a 3% rate of commission on the first \$15,000 of total sales, and a $5\frac{3}{4}$% rate of commission on the amount of total sales over \$15,000. The program should PRINT the commission earned by the salesperson to the nearest dollar.

13. Write a subroutine that rounds a decimal number X *up* to the nearest integer Y. Write a main routine that INPUTs the value of X, GOSUBs to the subroutine, and then PRINTs Y.

14. Some computers have a built-in function ROUND that rounds an input number to the *nearest* integer (indeed, the IBM PC has CINT that does this). Suppose your computer has ROUND but not INT. Write an expression for INT(X) in terms of ROUND. (*Hint:* See the rounding-off expression discussed on page 337.)

15. Some computers have a built-in function TRUNC that merely drops (TRUNCates) everything after the decimal point of an input number. For example, TRUNC(45.834) = 45, TRUNC(−4.59) = −4. How does TRUNC differ from INT? Write a subroutine that will simulate TRUNC; take a number X, delete everything after the decimal, and call the resulting integer Y.

16. a. (A computer is needed for this exercise.) Write a program that INPUTs two numbers (not necessarily integers), rounds them *down* to the nearest integer, then plots the point with the resulting coordinates on the graphics screen. Have the computer then plot the point with the original (non-integer) coordinates. Are the points identical?
    b. Change the program in (a) to round the INPUT coordinates to the *nearest* integer, then plot the points with the original and with the rounded-off coordinates. Are these identical?
    c. What does your computer do to points with non-integer coordinates?

17. (Graphics) Write a program that INPUTs the coordinates of two points on your graphics screen, then calculates the midpoint between the two points (the average of the X-values, the average of the Y-values). The program should round each of the coordinates of the midpoint to the nearest integer, then plot the midpoint and the original two points.

C 18. (Graphics) Write a program that INPUTs the coordinates of two points on your graphics screen, then plots the line segment connecting the two points and another line segment that lies on the perpendicular bisector. (*Hint:* Calculate the midpoint between the two INPUT points (see Exercise 17). Then find another point, which when joined to the midpoint, forms a line segment perpendicular to the line segment connecting the two original points. Remember that perpendicular lines have negative reciprocal slopes. (*TRS-80* users should see the Lab Activity for a line–drawing routine.)

19. a. *Challenge: Without using* INT, write a subroutine starting, say, at line 1000, that takes a positive number X and rounds it down to the nearest integer Y. Write a main routine that INPUTs X, GOSUBs to the subroutine, and then PRINTs the resulting integer Y.
    b. Extend your subroutine to work for negative values of X as well.

Lab Activity

A Line Routine and Moire Patterns

The *IBM* and *Apple* (high resolution) graphics have built-in line-drawing procedures (see Section 6–4). The *TRS-80* does not — you have to write your own subroutine to draw a line from one point (XBEG, YBEG) to another (XND, YND). The subroutine given below, if suitably modified, will work on any of these machines. It would be instructive for you to study and understand how it works, whichever computer you are using.

Subroutine

Statement	Remark
5000 REM * SUBROUTINE TO PLOT LINE FROM (XBEG, YBEG) TO (XND, YND) *	
5010 IF YBEG <= YND THEN LET YSTP = 1: GOTO 5030	*Y increases from YBEG to YND.*
5020 LET YSTP = −1	*Y decreases from YBEG to YND.*
5030 IF XBEG = XND THEN FOR Y = YBEG TO YND STEP YSTP: SET(XBEG, Y): NEXT Y: RETURN	*Draw vertical line.*
5040 IF XBEG < XND THEN LET XSTP = 1: GOTO 5060	*X increases from XBEG to XND.*
5050 LET XSTP = −1	*X decreases from XBEG to XND.*
5060 LET M = (YND − YBEG) / (XND − XBEG)	*M is slope of the line.*
5070 LET B = YBEG − M * XBEG	*B is Y-intercept of line.*
5080 LET YOLD = YBEG	*Start of vertical segment.*
5085 SET(XBEG, YBEG)	*Plot beginning point.*
5090 FOR X = XBEG TO XND STEP XSTP	*Loop plots vertical seg. at every X.*
5100 LET YNU = INT(M * X + B + .5)	*True Y-value on line, rounded off.*
5110 IF YOLD = YNU THEN SET(X, YNU): GOTO 5160	*If vertical segment is only a single dot, plot it.*
5120 FOR Y = YOLD + YSTP TO YNU STEP YSTP	*Loop plots vertical segment.*
5130 SET(X, Y)	
5140 NEXT Y	
5150 LET YOLD = YNU	*Start of next vertical segment.*
5160 NEXT X	
5170 RETURN	

Lines in computer graphics are necessarily jagged; they consist of short vertical segments as in the diagram at the right (in a horizontal line, all the vertical "segments" are one dot high).

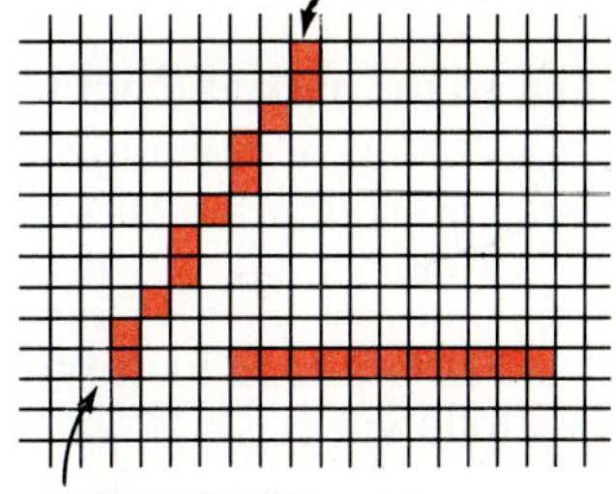

Here is how the line-drawing subroutine works: If the line segment is vertical (that is, XBEG = XND), then it is plotted right away by the instructions in line 5030. (YSTP will be explained in a moment.) Any nonvertical line has a slope and a y-intercept; they are calculated in lines 5060 and 5070. Then, at each X-value between XBEG and XND, the corresponding "true" y-value on the line, called YNU (line 5100), is calculated using the slope-intercept formula $y = mx + b$; YNU is rounded off to the nearest integer. Then the short vertical segment is plotted at that X, from the end of the last segment (YOLD) to YNU (lines 5120–5140).

You will notice that every FOR statement has a STEP XSTP or STEP YSTP attached to it. This is done to take into account the possibility that X or Y in these FOR statements can either *increase* (STEP 1) or *decrease* (STEP −1). For example, in line 5090, we do not know whether XBEG < XND (in which case the computer should add +1 to X every time through the loop), or XBEG > XND (in which case it should add −1 every time). Both possibilities are taken care of at the same time by defining XSTP in line 5040 to be either +1 or −1, whichever is appropriate. The same explanation applies to the variable YSTP.

Problems

1. Add a main routine to the program that will INPUT the coordinates XBEG, YBEG, XND, and YND, will set up graphics, and then GOSUB 5000 to draw the line. (Users of computers other than the *TRS-80* should change SET(X, Y) to the instruction on their computer to plot the point (X, Y).) Test the program thoroughly by drawing vertical, horizontal, and diagonal lines of various slopes.

2. You may have noticed that the loop in lines 5120–5140 does not simply plot a vertical segment from YOLD to YNU; instead, it goes from YOLD + YSTP to YNU. What do you predict will happen if you eliminate STEP YSTP from line 5120? Run the program and see if your prediction is correct. (Be sure to try both YND > YBEG and YBEG > YND.) Are lines that are not horizontal or vertical as pleasing as originally? Explain the difference.

MOIRE PATTERNS

Have you ever noticed the dark and light patterns that you see when you look through two superimposed window screens? Similar effects can be achieved by drawing on your graphics screen a sequence of closely-spaced lines with slightly varying slopes.

3. Change subroutine 5000 back to its original form, and replace the main routine with the following:

```
10  INPUT "TYPE FIXED POINT:  "; XBEG, YBEG
20  (Instructions to clear the screen
 .     and do graphics (in white)
 .     on your computer.)
 .
50  FOR XND = 0 TO ____ STEP 4
60  LET YND = 0
70  GOSUB 5000: REM * DRAW LINE
80  NEXT XND
90  END
```

[Fill in biggest horizontal coordinate on your screen.]

[*Apple* and *IBM* users can substitute built-in line-drawing command.]

RUN this program, typing the coordinates of a point toward the bottom of the screen for (XBEG, YBEG). Can you explain what causes the effect you see? If you were to draw those same lines on paper with a pencil and ruler, your picture would not look at all like that. What is different about lines on the computer?

4. Change the program so that the lines are drawn to every other point (that is, to every point with even horizontal coordinates) on the top line. RUN the program. Experiment with different STEP values in line 50 to find the most pleasing effect.

5. Change the program again so that it INPUTs two fixed points (X1, Y1) and (X2, Y2), and a STEP value S. Then have the program draw lines from both (X1, Y1) and (X2, Y2) to every Sth point along the top of the screen. Experiment with different STEP values to get the most pleasing effect. (S should probably be bigger than 4.)

7–2 More Built-in Functions: ABS, SQR, SGN

In addition to the INT function discussed in the previous section, there are a number of other functions that occur frequently in mathematics, science, and other fields, and have been included as built-in functions in BASIC. Three of these functions are explored in this section.

ABS

You may already be familiar with the *absolute-value function* from your mathematics courses. The absolute value of a number X is denoted by $|X|$ and is defined as follows:

$$\text{If } X >= 0, \text{ then } |X| = X$$
$$\text{If } X < 0, \text{ then } |X| = -X$$

For example $|5| = 5$, $|-2| = -(-2) = 2$, $|0| = 0$, and $|5.2| = 5.2$

If you wanted to have the computer calculate absolute values, you could write a program similar to the following:

Program 1

Statement

```
10  PRINT "FINDING ABSOLUTE VALUES"
20  INPUT "TYPE A NUMBER:  "; X
30  IF X >= 0 THEN PRINT "ABSOLUTE VALUE IS:  "; X
40  IF X < 0 THEN PRINT "ABSOLUTE VALUE IS:  "; - X
50  END
```

Output

```
FINDING ABSOLUTE VALUES
TYPE A NUMBER:  ? -2
ABSOLUTE VALUE IS:  2
```

Program 1 can be simplified by using the BASIC built-in function ABS. Here is the revised program:

Program 2

Statement

```
10  PRINT "ABSOLUTE VALUE USING ABS"
20  INPUT "TYPE A NUMBER:  "; X
30  PRINT "ABSOLUTE VALUE IS:  "; ABS(X)
40  END
```

Output

```
ABSOLUTE VALUE USING ABS
TYPE A NUMBER:  ? -2
ABSOLUTE VALUE IS:  2
```

Notice how easy it is to calculate absolute values directly using ABS, rather than setting up conditions as in Program 1. Of course, the computer calculates ABS(X) using an algorithm related to that of Program 1, but it is written in machine language (see the Computer Language feature on page 64).

SQR

Another function that you are probably familiar with from mathematics is the *square-root function,* denoted by the symbol $\sqrt{\ }$. In BASIC, this function is written SQR. If X is a nonnegative real number, SQR(X) is the principal (nonnegative) square root of X. That is, SQR(X) is the nonnegative number which, when multiplied by itself, yields X. For example,

SQR(9) = 3, because 3 * 3 = 9.

Also, in BASIC SQR(2) = 1.41421356 because 1.41421356 * 1.41421356 = 2 (approximately). Note that SQR(−3) will cause an error, because negative numbers cannot have real-number square roots (any real number times itself must be nonnegative).

As an example of a program using SQR, we can design a program that tests an INPUT integer N to see whether it is a *perfect square.* The number N = 36, for example, is a perfect square because its principal square root is an integer, namely, 6. The algorithm seems straightforward: the program should take the square root of N, then test whether it is an integer.

Program 3

Statement	Remark
10 PRINT "TEST FOR PERFECT SQUARES"	
20 INPUT "TYPE A POSITIVE INTEGER: "; N	
25 IF N < 0 OR INT(N) < > N THEN PRINT "TRY AGAIN": GOTO 20	*Error trap.*
30 LET S = SQR(N)	*S is the square root.*
40 PRINT "SQUARE ROOT IS: "; S	
50 IF INT(S) = S THEN PRINT "IT'S A PERFECT SQUARE"	*PRINT message if S is an integer.*
60 END	

Output

```
TEST FOR PERFECT SQUARES
TYPE A POSITIVE INTEGER:  ? 64
SQUARE ROOT IS:  8
IT'S A PERFECT SQUARE
```

```
RUN
TEST FOR PERFECT SQUARES
TYPE A POSITIVE INTEGER:  ? 16
SQUARE ROOT IS:  4
IT'S A PERFECT SQUARE

RUN
TEST FOR PERFECT SQUARES
TYPE A POSITIVE INTEGER:  ? 39
SQUARE ROOT IS:  6.244998

RUN
TEST FOR PERFECT SQUARES
TYPE A POSITIVE INTEGER:  ? 25
SQUARE ROOT IS:  5
```

The output from the first three RUNs should not be surprising, but the program seems to have missed the fact that 25 is a perfect square. In other words, it failed to recognize that S = SQR(25) is an integer. The problem is round-off error (see the Lab Activity for Section 5–2, page 209); because the computer uses only a few decimal places, it must round off all the partial results in any calculation. This can lead to errors. Thus, the number that the computer calculated as the square root of 25 was not exactly 5, although it appeared as 5 when it was rounded off to be displayed on the screen. Since the internal representation of S was not exactly equal to 5, the computer decided that INT(S) was not equal to S.

One way to solve this round-off problem, which arises often when making comparisons between decimals calculated by the computer, is to change the condition in line 50. Rather than demanding that INT(S) and S be exactly equal, we can require only that their values be very close. This is easily done. Observe that the distance between two numbers X and Y on the number line can be expressed by ABS(X − Y). For example, the distance from X = 3 to Y = −2 is

$$\text{ABS}(3 - (-2)) = \text{ABS}(5) = 5.$$

If we require that S and INT(S) be within, say, .00001 of each other (which is rather close), we can change line 50 of Program 3 to read:

```
50  IF ABS(S – INT(S)) < .00001 THEN PRINT "IT'S A PERFECT SQUARE"
```

The program works correctly with this change.

If the computer is adding, subtracting, and multiplying relatively small *integers,* integers that are not automatically converted to exponential form, then round-off errors *cannot* occur.

SGN

A number can be tested to see if it is negative by comparing it to zero or by using ABS (see Exercise 2). Another way is to use the *sign* function: SGN. The SGN function indicates the sign (+ or −) of a number and is defined by:

$$\text{If } X > 0, \text{ then SGN}(X) = 1$$
$$\text{If } X = 0, \text{ then SGN}(X) = 0$$
$$\text{If } X < 0, \text{ then SGN}(X) = -1$$

In Program 3, you could change line 25 to

```
25  IF SGN(N) = −1 OR . . .
```

in order to error trap for negative INPUT values (although it is just as easy to use IF N < 0 OR . . .).

A more substantial use of the SGN function is illustrated in the next program, which counts from the INPUT integer A to the INPUT integer B. The program counts *up* by adding +1 if A < B, and it counts *down* by adding −1 if A > B.

Program 4

Statement | **Remark**

```
10  REM * COUNTING UP OR DOWN
20  INPUT "FIRST INTEGER:  "; A
30  IF INT(A) <> A THEN PRINT "NOT AN
       INTEGER": GOTO 20
40  INPUT "SECOND INTEGER:  "; B
50  IF INT(B) <> B THEN PRINT "NOT AN
       INTEGER": GOTO 40
60  PRINT "COUNTING FROM  "; A; "  TO  "; B
70  IF A = B THEN PRINT A: GOTO 120          Special case.
80  FOR I = A TO B STEP SGN(B − A)           Step 1 or step −1.
90  PRINT I; "  ";
100  NEXT I
110  PRINT
120  END
```

Output

```
FIRST INTEGER:  ? 7
SECOND INTEGER:  ? −2
COUNTING FROM 7 TO −2
7 6 5 4 3 2 1 0 −1 −2
```

```
RUN
FIRST INTEGER:  ? —2
SECOND INTEGER:  ? 7
COUNTING FROM —2 TO 7
—2 —1 0 1 2 3 4 5 6 7
```

The key to Program 4 is line 80: If A = 7 and B = −2, then

$$B - A = -2 - 7 = -9, \text{ so } SGN(B - A) = SGN(-9) = -1.$$

Thus, the counting goes *down* (STEP −1) from 7 to −2. What will happen if A = 3 and B = 9? What will happen if A = B = −6?

It should be mentioned that all the usual BASIC (numeric) built-in functions have the same form: a three-letter name, followed by parentheses enclosing a number, a variable, or a BASIC numerical expression.

Avoiding Pitfalls

1. Be sure to error trap for negative numbers before using the SQR function. Otherwise, an ILLEGAL QUANTITY (or ILLEGAL FUNCTION CALL) error message will result.
2. To avoid round-off error when making comparisons between two decimal numbers calculated by the computer, replace comparisons of the form IF X = Y with IF ABS(X − Y) < D, where D is a small decimal such as .00001.

Summary

ABS(X) calculates the *absolute value* of a number X. For example,

$$ABS(-6.2) = 6.2, ABS(8) = 8, \text{ and } ABS(0) = 0.$$

ABS(X − Y) calculates the distance between the numbers X and Y on the number line.

SQR(X) calculates the nonnegative *square root* of a nonnegative number X. For example,

$$SQR(9) = 3, SQR(0) = 0, \text{ and } SQR(28.09) = 5.3.$$

SGN(X) gives the *sign* (+, −, or 0) of the number X. For example,

$$SGN(-3.2) = -1, SGN(0) = 0, \text{ and } SGN(5) = 1.$$

Exercises 7-2

A **1.** Predict the output of each of the following.

a. PRINT SGN(—5.4)
b. PRINT ABS(4)
c. PRINT ABS(0)
d. PRINT SQR(81)
e. PRINT SGN(0)
f. PRINT SQR(1.44)
g. PRINT SQR(1)
h. PRINT ABS(—3.2)
i. PRINT SGN(—1.6)
j. PRINT ABS(6 — 8)
k. PRINT SQR(SGN(6))
l. PRINT SQR(ABS(—64))

2. Predict the output of the following program.

```
10 REM * ABSOLUTE VALUE AND SIGNS
20 PRINT "SGN(X)", "ABS(X) / X"
25 PRINT
30 FOR I = 1 TO 8
40 READ X
50 PRINT SGN(X), ABS(X) / X
60 NEXT I
70 DATA 9.6, 8.3, 1, —5, —6.8, —12.4, —1, 0
80 END
```

Is ABS(X) / X always equal to SGN(X)?

3. Predict the output of the following program for each of the X- and Y-values shown below.

```
10 REM * SIGNS
20 INPUT X
30 INPUT Y
40 IF SGN(X) = SGN(Y) THEN PRINT "PRODUCT IS POSITIVE": GOTO 70
50 IF SGN(X) = 0 OR SGN(Y) = 0 THEN PRINT "PRODUCT IS ZERO": GOTO 70
60 PRINT "PRODUCT IS NEGATIVE"
70 END
```

a. X = —5, Y = 4 **b.** X = —23, Y = —6.5 **c.** X = 0, Y = 45 **d.** X = 27, Y = 113

4. Show how ABS can be used to test whether a number X is positive or negative. (*Hint:* See Exercise 2.)

5. a. Write a subroutine to simulate the function SGN; if X is any number, have the subroutine produce a number Y that equals +1 if X > 0, 0 if X = 0, and —1 if X < 0.

b. Rewrite Program 4 without using SGN; use a subroutine similar to the one in part (a).

6. There is another way to fix the bug (round-off error) in the original version of Program 3: After finding the square root S, round S off to the nearest integer I, then multiply I * I. If I * I = N, then N must be a perfect square (and N can be a perfect square only if it equals I * I). Change Program 3 to reflect this algorithm.

B **7.** Write a program that INPUTs 10 numbers, then PRINTs both the sum of the numbers and the sum of their absolute values.

8. Write a program that INPUTs a positive integer N, then calculates the product P of the integers N, N + 1, N + 2, and N + 3. Have the program then test whether P + 1 is a perfect square (it always is).

9. Write a program that INPUTs a positive odd integer M, then calculates the sum S of all the odd integers from 1 to M. Have the program then test the sum S to see if it is a perfect square (it always is). What number, expressed in terms of M, is the square root of the sum?

10. According to the *triangle inequality*, the sum of the lengths of any two sides of a triangle is always greater than the length of the third side. Write a program that INPUTs the lengths x, y, and z of three line segments, then determines if they could form the sides of a triangle.

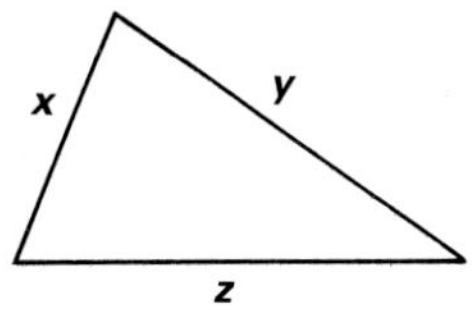

11. **a.** The area of a triangle may be calculated using *Hero's formula:*

$$\text{Area} = \sqrt{s(s-x)(s-y)(s-z)}$$

where x, y, and z are the lengths of the sides of the triangle and

$$s = \frac{x+y+z}{2}.$$

Write a program that INPUTs the lengths x, y, and z of the sides of a triangle, then calculates the area using Hero's formula.

b. Modify the program in (a), using the *triangle inequality* discussed in Exercise 10 to test whether the lengths x, y, and z form the sides of a triangle.

12. According to the *Pythagorean theorem*, if the triangle shown at the right is a *right triangle*, then $a^2 + b^2 = c^2$. Write a program using SQR that INPUTs the lengths a and b, then calculates the length c of the *hypotenuse*. (The hypotenuse is the longest side and is opposite the right angle.) Use error trapping to reject INPUT values less than or equal to 0.

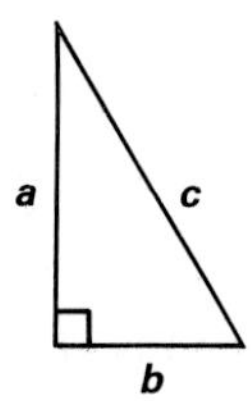

13. The distance between two points with coordinates (X1, Y1) and (X2, Y2) can be calculated by using the *distance formula:*

$$\text{distance} = \sqrt{(X2 - X1)^2 + (Y2 - Y1)^2}$$

Write a program that INPUTs the coordinates of the points (X1, Y1) and (X2, Y2), then calculates the distance between them.

14. The *converse of the Pythagorean theorem* says that if the square of one side of a triangle is equal to the sum of the squares of the other two sides, then the triangle is a *right triangle.* Write a program that INPUTs the coordinates of three points, then determines whether the triangle with vertices at those three points is a right triangle. If the triangle is a right triangle, have the program PRINT the length of the hypotenuse (the longest side). (*Hint:* Use the distance formula (see Exercise 13) to calculate the lengths of the sides.)

15. Write a program that will play a number-guessing game with the user. Have the program READ an integer between 1 and 100 from a DATA list, then INPUT guesses of the number from the user. After each guess the distance between the guess and the actual number should be PRINTed. When the user guesses correctly, the program should PRINT a congratulatory message, then END. (This game will be more interesting after the next section, where you will learn how to make the computer choose a *random* number.)

16. You may have learned an algorithm for calculating approximate square roots that works like this: To find the square root of 5,

    Step 1 Make a guess (let's guess 2).

    Step 2 Divide the original number by the guess: 5 / 2 = 2.5.

    Step 3 Find the average of the current guess and the number obtained in Step 2. This is the new guess: (2 + 2.5) / 2 = 2.25.

    Step 4 If the new guess and the previous guess are sufficiently close to each other (say, within .0001), then output the new guess as the answer. Otherwise, go back to Step 2 (divide the original number by the new guess).

    Write a program that utilizes this algorithm to calculate the square root of any INPUT nonnegative number. Have the program also PRINT the square root as calculated by the built-in function SQR.

C 17. (A computer is needed for this exercise.) Discover instances in which your computer makes round-off errors in doing multiplication; write a program to INPUT three numbers A, B, and PROD. Then have the program PRINT "EQUAL" if A * B = PROD and "NOT EQUAL" otherwise. RUN the program until you find several instances in which the computer makes a mistake. (Be sure to try simple decimals.) Change the condition A * B = PROD to

```
ABS(A * B - PROD) < .00001
```

and verify that this takes care of most of the difficulty. However, can you now discover three numbers A, B, and PROD for which A * B really isn't equal to PROD, but for which the modified program will output EQUAL?

18. *Challenge:* Design an algorithm and write a program to calculate an approximate cube root of any INPUT positive number. (*Hint:* Do not try to imitate the algorithm in Exercise 16 — it won't work. Rather, try to think of how you could find a cube root with just pencil and paper by guessing and then modifying your guess.)

Lab Activity

Graphing Functions

A computer can obviously be very useful in mathematics; one of its most attractive uses is in graphing functions. This lab activity shows you how to do this. It assumes that you have studied graphs in your mathematics class. You should recall, for example, that the graph of the equation $y = x^2$ consists of all the points (x, y) that satisfy the equation, as shown in the diagram at the right.

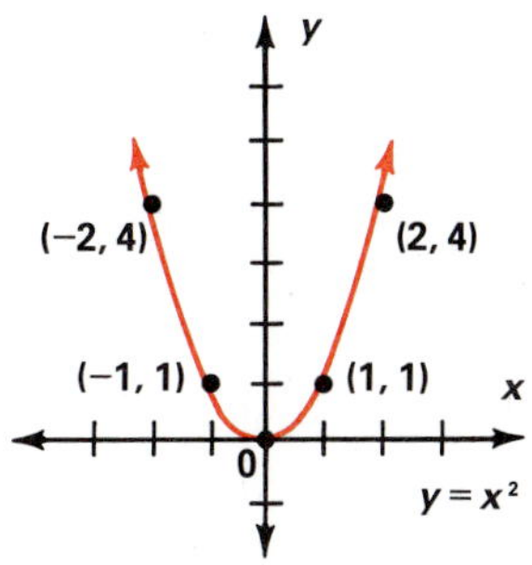

Since your computer has a graphics screen with horizontal and vertical coordinates, it is essentially a simple matter to plot the points of a graph. The only difficulty is that the coordinates on your screen are not convenient for most mathematical graphing. First of all, the vertical coordinates increase from top to bottom, which is the opposite direction from the usual mathematical way of doing things. Furthermore, (0, 0) is in the upper left-hand corner (on most computers), rather than in the center of your screen. Finally, screen coordinates have only integer values, and become much too large for practical graphing of most expressions. All of these problems can be solved using short but somewhat complicated formulas, as you will see.

For the purposes of explanation, suppose that the horizontal coordinates on your screen go from 0 to 59. You want 10 screen spaces (dots) to correspond to a "real" interval of length 1, and you want the "real" X = 0 to occur in the middle of the screen, which ought to be located at screen coordinate 59 / 2 = 29.4. Since this is not an integer, we'll round down; the center will be located at INT(59 / 2) = 29 as illustrated in the diagram at the top of the next page.

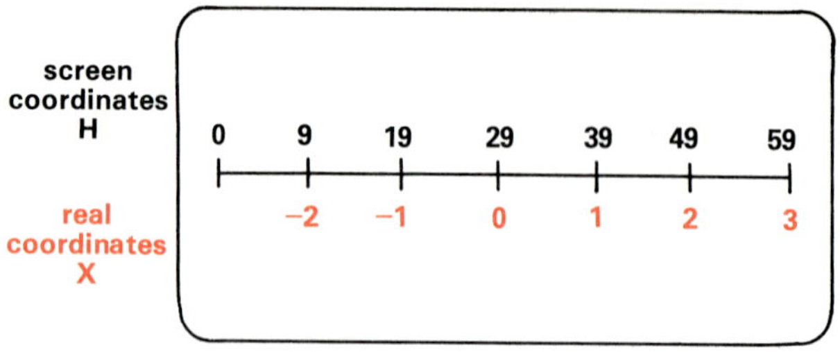

From the diagram, we can construct the following table of "real" X-coordinates and their corresponding horizontal screen coordinates, say H:

Real coordinates	Screen coordinates
X	H
−2	9
−1	19
0	29
1	39
2	49
3	59

Clearly, each change of 1 in the value of X corresponds to a change of 10 in the value of H. Also, $X = 0$ corresponds to $H = 29$. A formula that reflects these facts is

$$H = 10 * X + 29.$$

Try the formula for several values of X. (Do you remember the straight line equation $y = mx + b$?)

Now, your computer is unlikely to have the screen coordinates used in this example. In order to write a graphing program for all computers at once, we'll use variables for the different screen sizes and derive general formulas. Suppose that the horizontal coordinates on your screen go from 0 to GH (short for *greatest horizontal*). Then the center will have horizontal coordinate CH (short for *center horizontal*) equal to INT(GH / 2).

In the example given above, 10 screen spaces corresponded to a real interval of length 1. We'll allow this factor to vary by calling HS the number of *horizontal spaces* on the screen in a real interval of length 1. The formula in the example will translate in the general case into

$$H = HS * X + CH$$

or, solving for X,

$$X = (H - CH) / HS.$$

Similarly, replacing all the H's (horizontal) with V's (vertical), and replacing X with Y, we get

$$V = CV - VS * Y$$

or, solving for Y,

$$Y = (CV - V) / VS.$$

The reason for the differences in sign in the H and V formulas is the upside-down way that vertical coordinates work on most computers.

The graphing program given below assigns values (in lines 40–70) to the screen variables explained above and sets up graphics (subroutine 500); it then draws the axes and puts marks on them at every "real" integer value (subroutines 600 and 800). To plot the graph, the program takes each horizontal screen position H from 0 to GH, and calculates the corresponding real X-value by the formula given above (line 1020), and also the value of Y for that X (subroutine 2000). Then it calculates the corresponding vertical screen coordinate V (line 1040), and finally plots the screen point (H, V) in line 1060.

Here is the program. Using the diagram of a computer screen shown below to assist you, fill in all the details.

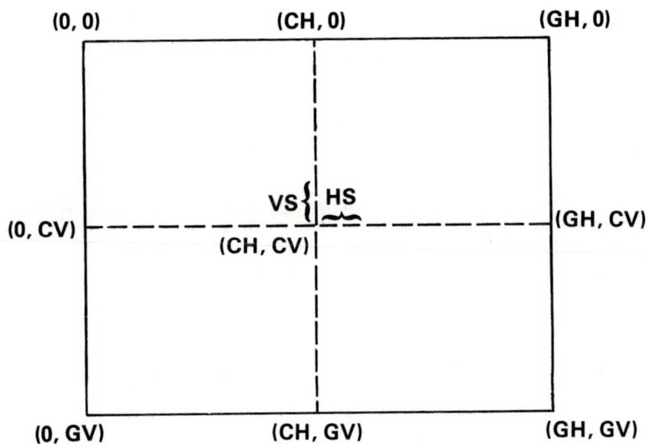

Statement	Remark
10 REM ** GRAPHING PROGRAM **	
20 LET HS = 10	*HS is number of horizontal spaces per unit interval.*
30 LET GH = *(Fill in greatest horizontal screen coordinate.)*	
40 LET CH = INT(GH / 2)	*CH is horizontal screen coordinate of center.*
50 LET VS = 6	

Statement	Remark
60 LET GV = *(Fill in greatest vertical screen coordinate.)*	
70 LET CV = INT(GV / 2)	CV is vertical screen coordinate of center.
75 REM ** SUBROUTINES **	
100 GOSUB 500	Set up graphics screen.
110 GOSUB 600	Draw horizontal axis and mark it.
120 GOSUB 800	Draw vertical axis and mark it.
130 GOSUB 1000	Graph the function defined in subroutine 2000.
135 *(Instruction to locate cursor near bottom of screen.)*	
140 END	
500 REM ** SUBROUTINE TO SET UP THE GRAPHICS SCREEN **	
510 *(Instructions to clear the screen and do* 520 *graphics, high resolution if possible, in* 530 *color—white is probably best.)* . . .	
590 RETURN	
600 REM ** SUBROUTINE TO DRAW THE HORIZONTAL AXIS AND MARK IT **	
610 *(Instruction(s) to draw line from 0, CV to GH, CV.)* . . .	
650 LET XMAX = INT(CH / HS)	XMAX is number of horizontal unit intervals between center and edge of screen.
660 FOR X = −XMAX TO XMAX	Go from least horizontal integer to the greatest.
670 LET H = HS * X + CH	Convert X to screen coordinate.
680 *(Instructions to plot the points H, CV −1 and* 690 *H, CV + 1.)*	Mark the horizontal axis.
700 NEXT X	
710 RETURN	

Statement	Remark
800 REM ** SUBROUTINE TO DRAW VERTICAL AXIS AND MARK IT **	
810 *(Instruction(s) to draw line from CH, 0 to CH, GV.)*	
.	
.	
.	
850 LET YMAX = INT(CV / VS)	*YMAX is number of vertical unit intervals between center and edge of screen.*
860 FOR Y = −YMAX TO YMAX	*Go from least vertical integer to the greatest.*
870 LET V = CV − VS * Y	*Convert Y to screen coordinate.*
880 *(Instructions to plot the points CH − 1, V and*	*Mark the vertical axis.*
890 *CH + 1, V.)*	
900 NEXT Y	
910 RETURN	
1000 REM ** SUBROUTINE TO GRAPH FUNCTION **	
1010 FOR H = 0 TO GH	*Go from least horizontal screen dot to the greatest.*
1020 LET X = (H − CH) / HS	*Convert to real X-value.*
1030 GOSUB 2000	*Calculate Y-value.*
1040 LET V = CV − VS * Y	*Convert to vertical screen coordinate.*
1050 IF (V > GV) OR (V < 0) THEN GOTO 1070	*Don't plot if off screen.*
1060 *(Instruction to plot the point H, V.)*	
1070 NEXT H	
1080 RETURN	
2000 REM ** SUBROUTINE TO CALCULATE THE Y-VALUE FOR A GIVEN X **	
2010 LET Y = X * X	
2020 RETURN	

Problems

1. Complete the program for your computer. Use high resolution graphics, if possible. If you have color, you may find that white on black works best. RUN the program (be patient) and compare the graph shown on the screen to that of $y = x^2$, diagrammed on page 353, to verify that the program works correctly.

2. RUN the program several times and experiment with different values of HS and VS to vary the scales on the vertical and horizontal axes.

3. Change subroutine 2000 to graph each of the following functions (sketch each graph to verify that the program works accurately).

   a. Y = X * X + X − 6
   b. Y = ABS(X)
   c. Y = ABS(X + 3)
   d. Y = ABS(X − 2)
   e. Y = SGN(X)
   f. Y = SQR(ABS(X))
   g. Y = INT(X)
   h. Y = INT(2 * X)
   i. Y = −INT(X)

4. Change subroutine 2000 to graph each of the following functions.

   a. Y = SGN(ABS(X))
   b. Y = INT(ABS(X))
   c. Y = (X − 2) ↑ 2 − 1
   d. Y = X ↑ 3 − 2 * X

7-3 Random Numbers: RND

Many events in real life are *random* — they happen in a fundamentally unpredictable way, governed entirely by chance. In flipping a fair coin, for example, there is no way to predict whether a head or a tail will come up; it is a random event. Slightly more predictable occurrences, such as meeting a friend unexpectedly at the grocery store, are partly random. Even though you may both live close to the store and so are rather likely to run into each other, it is seemingly by chance that you both arrive at the same moment.

Random Decimals

Computers can be used to simulate random processes such as coin tosses by generating random numbers. BASIC has a built-in function — RND — that generates these random numbers. On most computers (including *Apple* and *IBM* — but not *TRS-80*), the expression RND(1) will produce a random decimal from 0 to .999999999. The number of digits in the random decimal depends on the computer. (*Note:* On *TRS-80* computers, RND(0) is used instead of RND(1) as the random number generator.) The 1 (or 0) inside the parentheses following RND has no particular significance — it's just always used. Here is a program that uses RND to generate seven random decimals.

Program 1

Statement

```
10 PRINT "RANDOM NUMBERS"
20 FOR X = 1 TO 7
30 PRINT RND(1)
40 NEXT X
50 END
```

One possible output for the program might be the following seven random numbers:

```
RANDOM NUMBERS
.234510091
.816332743
.014231859
.387623212
.901992785
.461472876
.720041552
```

Each time line 30 is executed a different decimal is PRINTed, even though the same expression RND(1) is used. On some computers (*Apple*, for instance), if you were to RUN the program again, a different list of random decimals would be PRINTed. Other computers, however, require a statement such as RANDOM *(TRS-80)* or RANDOMIZE *(IBM)* at the beginning of the program to cause a different sequence to be generated each time the program is RUN. (See the Lab Activity for this section.)

Random Integers

Random decimals can be awkward to work with. For example, if we want to write a program to simulate a coin toss, it would be helpful to generate randomly one of two possible values — say 1 or 2 — to represent a head or a tail. How can this be done? To change a decimal to an integer, of course we could use INT. However, INT(RND(1)) will always equal 0. (Do you see why?) To get two different values from INT(X), the X will have to have a larger range than that of RND(1), which is just from 0 to .999999999. One way to give it a larger range is to multiply by two. Then the expression 2 * RND(1) will go from

$$2 * 0 = 0 \quad \text{to} \quad 2 * (.999999999) = 1.999999998.$$

Then INT(2 * RND(1)) will give the integers 0 and 1:

$$\text{INT}(0) = 0 \quad \text{and} \quad \text{INT}(1.999999998) = 1.$$

Similarly, INT(5 * RND(1)) will give an integer from

$$\text{INT}(5 * 0) = 0 \quad \text{to} \quad \text{INT}(5 * .999999999) = \text{INT}(4.999999995) = 4.$$

In other words, INT(5 * RND(1)) will equal 0, 1, 2, 3, or 4. Suppose you want 1, 2, 3, 4, or 5 instead? Simply use INT(5 * RND(1)) + 1. (*Note:* On *TRS-80* computers, RND(5) will produce a random integer among 1, 2, 3, 4, or 5.)

Program 2 on the next page uses INT and RND to generate 20 random integers between 1 and 10, inclusive.

Program 2

Statement

```
10 PRINT "RANDOM INTEGERS"
20 FOR X = 1 TO 20
30 PRINT INT(10 * RND(1)) + 1;"  ";
40 NEXT X
50 END
```

Here is a possible output for the program:

```
RANDOM INTEGERS
3 1 5 6 8 8 7 2 4 10 5 9 1 9 3 8 2 4 1 6
```

Let's return to writing the coin-tossing program. We will have the program generate randomly a 1 (representing a head) or a 2 (representing a tail) to simulate flipping the coin 100 times. Two counters will be used to tally the results.

Program 3

Statement

```
10 PRINT "TOSSING COINS"
14 LET HEADS = 0
18 LET TAILS = 0
20 FOR X = 1 TO 100
30 LET FLIP = INT(2 * RND(1)) + 1
40 IF FLIP = 1 THEN LET HEADS = HEADS + 1
50 IF FLIP = 2 THEN LET TAILS = TAILS + 1
60 NEXT X
70 PRINT "NUMBER OF HEADS:  "; HEADS
80 PRINT "NUMBER OF TAILS:  "; TAILS
90 END
```

Output

```
TOSSING COINS
NUMBER OF HEADS:  46
NUMBER OF TAILS:  54

RUN
TOSSING COINS
NUMBER OF HEADS:  55
NUMBER OF TAILS:  45
```

Another example of using random numbers is a graphical simulation of the path followed by a rather dim-witted beetle in search of food. Suppose that the beetle, to be represented on the screen by a dot, travels in one of only four directions — North (up), West (left), South (down), or East (right). At any instant, the direction of the next step is completely random — a choice among the four possible directions.

(A path resulting from such random choices of direction is called a "random walk." The study of random walks is a serious mathematical pursuit and has important applications, particularly in studying the motion of small particles suspended in a fluid.)

To simulate our poor insect, we'll start the dot at the middle of the screen, then repeatedly choose a random integer from 1 to 4. The number chosen will determine the direction of the next step. The number 3, for example, means East (or right), so that 1 is added to the X-coordinate of the beetle's position (line 160). Since the program contains an infinite loop, it must be stopped manually.

Program 4

Statement	Remark
10 REM * THE BEETLE'S PROGRESS	
20 *(Instructions to clear the screen*	
. *and do graphics*	
. *on your computer.)*	
.	
100 LET X = *(X-coordinate of center of your screen)*	
110 LET Y = *(Y-coordinate of center of your screen)*	
120 LET DIR = INT(4 * RND(1)) + 1	*Random integers from 1 to 4.*
130 IF DIR = 1 THEN LET Y = Y − 1	*Go up.*
140 IF DIR = 2 THEN LET X = X − 1	*Go left.*
150 IF DIR = 3 THEN LET Y = Y + 1	*Go down.*
160 IF DIR = 4 THEN LET X = X + 1	*Go right.*
170 *(Instruction to plot the point X, Y*	
on your computer.)	
180 GOTO 120	

At times you may want to generate random integers starting with a number other than 0 or 1. For example, suppose you want to get random integers between 25 and 50, inclusive. Notice that there are 26 possible integers from 25 to 50 (remember, you have to count the endpoints). You know that the expression INT(26 * RND(1)) will produce a random integer from 0 to 25.

Thus, INT(26 * RND(1)) + 25 will produce a random integer from 25 to 50. Similarly, the expression

```
INT(31 * RND(1)) + 40
      ↑              ↑
31 integers      starting
between 40       point
and 70
```

will produce a random integer between 40 and 70, inclusive.

In general, the expression

```
INT((B + 1) * RND(1)) + A
```

will produce a random integer between A and A + B, inclusive. (*Note:* On *TRS-80* computers, random integers from A to B can be produced by using RND(B − A + 1) + A − 1.)

Avoiding Pitfalls

Remember that an expression such as INT(5 * RND(1)) will produce a random integer from 0 to 4. If you intend to produce a random integer from 1 to 5, use INT(5 * RND(1)) + 1.

Summary

RND(1) will produce a random decimal from 0 to .999999999. (On *TRS-80* computers, RND(0) is used instead of RND(1).)

INT(N * RND(1)) will produce a random integer between 0 and N − 1, inclusive.

INT((B + 1) * RND(1)) + A will produce a random integer between A and A + B, inclusive. (On *TRS-80* computers, RND(B), for B > 1, yields a random integer between 1 and B, inclusive.)

Exercises 7-3

A **1.** Tell all the possible values that may be assigned to X in each of the following LET statements. (*TRS-80* users should replace RND(1) with RND(0).)

a. LET X = INT(8 * RND(1))

b. LET X = INT(24 * RND(1)) + 1

c. LET X = INT(5 * RND(1)) + 5

d. LET X = INT(10 * RND(1)) + 15

2. Write a statement that will produce a random integer from:

a. 0 to 9 b. 1 to 52

c. 20 to 40 d. J to K

3. a. Complete Program 4 and add error trapping so that the beetle will not go off the screen. Have the beetle stay where it is if a particular choice of direction will make it leave the screen.

b. Change the program in part (a) so that rather than stopping when it is about to go off the screen, the beetle will disappear and then reappear at the opposite point on the opposite border of the screen.

4. Change Program 4 so that the beetle does not leave a trail of previously plotted dots (points); a dot should appear only at its present position. Add error trapping so that the beetle will not go off the screen.

5. Change Program 4 so that the beetle has a twin whose motion mirrors its motion. If the beetle is currently at point (X, Y), its mirror image will be at (MAX — X, Y), where MAX is the largest X-coordinate on the screen. At each step, plot the position of both beetles. Add error trapping so that neither beetle moves if either one goes off the screen.

B 6. a. Write a program to generate 12 random integers from 10 to 30.

b. Change the program in (a) to allow a user to specify the number of random integers to be generated.

7. Write a program that INPUTs two integers A and B, then generates 10 random integers between A and B, inclusive. Use error trapping to ensure that A < B.

8. a. Write a program to simulate rolling one die 100 times. Have the program tally the number of 1's, 2's, . . . , and 6's that are rolled and PRINT the results.

b. Rewrite the program in part (a) so that it simulates the rolling of two dice and finds their sum. Have the program tally the number of 2's, 3's, . . . , and 12's that occur and PRINT the results.
(*Hint:* Have the program generate two random numbers, say D1 and D2.)

9. a. Write a program to simulate tossing two coins a total of 10 times each. The output should be a list of abbreviations such as HH (if 2 heads occur), TT (2 tails), HT (1 head and 1 tail), and TH (1 tail and 1 head). (*Hint:* Have the program generate two random numbers, say C1 and C2.)

b. Modify the program in (a) to simulate tossing three coins 10 times each. The output should be a list of abbreviations such as HHH, HHT, HTH, and so on.

10. Write a program in which the user tries to guess a randomly generated number (integer) from 1 to 100. Have the program PRINT appropriate messages such as TOO HIGH, TOO LOW, or GOT IT after each guess. Also, have the program PRINT the number of guesses it takes the user to get the number.

11. Write a program that randomly selects one of five colors from a DATA list. (*Hint:* Generate a random number (integer) from 1 to 5. Then if the number is, say 3, use a FOR . . . NEXT loop to READ the first three colors, but PRINT only the third color, ignoring the first two.)

12. Write a program that contains a DATA list of 10 names. Have the program choose two different names randomly (see Exercise 11), then PRINT a flattering message from the first person to the second. (*Hint:* Remember the RESTORE statement?)

13. (Graphics)
   a. Write a program that plots points randomly on your graphics screen. Use an infinite loop so that the screen will gradually turn white. (If your computer has COLOR, shade the screen the color of your choice.)
   b. Modify the program in (a) so that it erases each point after it is plotted, causing a blinking effect.

14. (Graphics) Write a program to produce random short line segments on your graphics screen (high resolution, if available) by choosing random endpoints. (*TRS-80* users: See the Lab Activity for Section 7–1, page 342, for a line-drawing subroutine.)

15. (Graphics) Write a program to produce randomly placed and random-sized rectangles on your graphics screen. Fill in the rectangles with random colors (if COLOR is available).

C 16. (Graphics) Write a program that plays a point-guessing game with the user. The program should choose a random point on the graphics screen (but not plot it) and ask the user to guess its coordinates. After each guess, the distance between the guess and the actual point should be PRINTed (see Exercise 13, page 352). When the guess is correct, or within a radius of 5 from the target point, the program should PRINT a congratulatory message and tell the user how many guesses were required to find the point.

17. (Graphics) Write a program that simulates a race between a turtle and a hare. Have the turtle and hare shapes (or dots) start at the left side of the screen. Have the program choose randomly the integer 1 or 2. The lucky animal whose number is chosen should move a short distance to the right. The race continues until either the turtle or hare crosses the finish line set up near the right side of the screen. Have the program declare the winner.

Lab Activity

Randomizing

When the computer is given an RND command, it performs a complicated computation to produce the next "random" number. The calculation involves manipulating a number stored in the computer's memory. This number, called the "seed," is operated on and then put out as the new random number. The new random number then becomes the seed for the next RND calculation. Where does the first seed number come from? The computer has a built-in seed that it provides when it is first turned on — and it is always the same seed.

Problems

1. Show that your computer gives the random number generator (as RND is sometimes known) the same seed every time it is turned on by following these steps:

Step 1 Turn on the computer.

Step 2 Type PRINT RND(1), RND(1), RND(1) and record the output. [*TRS-80* users should type RND(0) instead of RND(1).]

Step 3 Turn off the computer.

Step 4 Repeat Steps 1 to 3 a few more times.

2. Find out whether your computer gives a new seed to the random number generator every time a program is RUN. Use the following simple program to test:

```
90  REM * TESTING
100  PRINT RND(1), RND(1), RND(1)
200  END
```

Some computers will give the same output every time this program is RUN. Does yours? Such computers provide a seed (the same one) every time RUN is typed. Other computers will give different output every time (unless they are turned off in the meantime), because the random number generator is not re-seeded when a program is RUN.

SEEDING RND: YOUR CHOICE

On some computers, it is possible to give the random number generator a seed of your own choosing. This is sometimes an advantage, particularly when you are debugging a troublesome program that uses random numbers.

Apple

On *Apple* computers, the statement LET X = RND(−5) will provide the seed 5 (the X can be any numeric variable). Subsequent RND(1)'s can be used as usual. The statement LET X = RND(−12) will provide an entirely different seed and will generate an entirely different sequence of RND(1) values. In other words, different negative numbers inside the parentheses provide different seeds.

IBM

On *IBM* computers, the instruction RANDOMIZE 5 provides the random number generator with the seed 5. Subsequent RND(1)'s will give an entirely different sequence of numbers than if the seed 12 had been supplied by the instruction RANDOMIZE 12.

TRS-80

There is no simple way to generate a seed of your own choosing for the random number generator on the *TRS-80*.

3. If you are using an *Apple* or *IBM* computer, RUN the program below to show the following:

a. Every time 5 is provided as the seed, the same random numbers are generated.
b. If some other seed is provided, a different sequence of random numbers occurs.

```
   10  INPUT "TYPE SEED (A POSITIVE INTEGER):  "; SEED
   20  LET X = RND(—SEED): REM * APPLE
or 20  RANDOMIZE SEED: REM * IBM
   30  PRINT RND(1), RND(1), RND(1)
   40  GOTO 10
   50  END
```

(The program must be stopped manually.)

SEEDING RND: THE COMPUTER'S CHOICE

If you want the results of your program to be really unpredictable, then you will not want the computer to provide the same random number generator seed every time your program is RUN or every time the machine is turned on. For the same reason, you will not want your *program* to provide the same seed every time. On all computers, it is possible to make the computer give a random seed to the random number generator. This will make all of the "random" numbers really unpredictable.

TRS-80

On *TRS-80* computers, all you have to do is include the instruction

```
RANDOM
```

early in the program.

IBM

On *IBM* computers, there is an internal clock that starts up when the computer is turned on with the DOS diskette inserted. The seconds that show on the clock at the moment the program is RUN will be fairly unpredictable, and can be used as a seed by including the statement

```
RANDOMIZE VAL(MID$(TIME$, 7, 2))
```

early in the program. (This statement will make a lot more sense after you have studied Chapter 8; just use it in your program as a magical instruction for now.)

Apple

On *Apple* computers there is a crude kind of internal timer, although it is ticking away only while the computer is waiting for you to type something (which is quite often). The output of this timer can be used as a seed by including this statement:

```
LET X = RND(— PEEK(78) — 256 * PEEK(79))
```

As before, X can be any numeric variable. (Don't worry too much about what this statement means; basically, it uses the contents of the internal "clock" as a seed. You will learn about the PEEK and POKE instructions later in the book in the Lab Activity for Section 11–1, page 592.)

4. RUN the following program several times to show that you get a different sequence of random numbers whenever it is RUN. (Actually, you could get the same sequence twice in a row, just as you could get 100 heads in a row if you were flipping a coin, but that would be very unlikely.) Try turning off the computer between RUNs, as in Problem 1. Do you get different random numbers output each time?

```
      10 RANDOM: REM * TRS-80
or    10 RANDOMIZE VAL(MID$(TIME$, 7, 2)): REM * IBM
or    10 LET X = RND(— PEEK(78) — 256 * PEEK(79)): REM * APPLE
     ┌20 FOR I = 1 TO 5
     │30 PRINT RND(1): REM * ON TRS-80 USE RND(0)
     └40 NEXT I
      50 END
```

YOUR OWN RANDOM NUMBER GENERATOR

You need not rely on the random number generator built into your computer, although it is fast and has been thoroughly tested; you can write your own. A standard algorithm is to take the seed X (a decimal from 0 to .999999999), multiply it by some outrageous number like 417.83, add a crazy decimal like .361428913, then discard anything to the left of the decimal point. The resulting number is the output — the new seed.

5. The program below implements the algorithm outlined above. RUN the program. Observe that it gives the same sequence each time a given seed is INPUT, but that different seeds give different (and apparently unpredictable) sequences of "random" numbers.

Statement	Remark
10 REM * YOUR OWN RANDOM NUMBER GENERATOR	
20 INPUT "TYPE SEED (A DECIMAL BETWEEN 0 AND .999999999): "; X	
25 PRINT	
30 FOR I = 1 TO 5	
40 LET X = 417.83 * X + .361428913	
50 LET X = X − INT(X)	*Discard integer part.*
60 PRINT X	*X is the new seed in line 40.*
70 NEXT I	
75 PRINT	
80 GOTO 20	
90 END	

(The program must be stopped manually.)

7-4 More About INT: Integer Division and Finding Factors

Suppose that a farmer has 57 strawberry plants that are to be planted in rows of 6 plants each. How many rows will the farmer need, and how many plants will be left over? To solve this problem, of course, you divide 57 by 6 to obtain the quotient (the number of rows) and the remainder (the number of plants left over).

```
             9 <—— Quotient
Divisor ——> 6)57
             54
              3 <—— Remainder
```

How can we get the computer to do this calculation for us? You have probably noticed that the quotient is INT(57 / 6) = INT(9.5) = 9. What about the remainder? If you examine the calculation shown above, you will see that the remainder R is obtained by subtracting the quotient (9) times the divisor (6) from the total number of plants (57); that is,

$$\text{Remainder} = R = 57 - 9 * 6 = 3.$$

In general, when you divide an integer N by an integer D, the (integer) quotient is

$$Q = INT(N / D)$$

and the remainder is

$$\begin{aligned} R &= N - D * Q \\ &= N - D * INT(N / D). \end{aligned}$$

Here is a program that solves any similar problem our farmer might have:

Program 1

Statement	Remark
10 PRINT "SPRING PLANTING"	
20 INPUT "TYPE NUMBER OF PLANTS: "; PLANTS	
30 IF (PLANTS < 1) OR (INT(PLANTS) < > PLANTS) THEN PRINT "TRY AGAIN": GOTO 20	
40 INPUT "TYPE NUMBER OF ROWS: "; ROWS	
50 IF (ROWS < 1) OR (INT(ROWS) < > ROWS) THEN PRINT "TRY AGAIN": GOTO 40	
60 LET PPROW = INT(PLANTS / ROWS)	*Quotient = plants per row.*
70 LET LFT = PLANTS − PPROW * ROWS	*Remainder = no. left over.*
80 PRINT "THERE SHOULD BE "; PPROW;	
85 PRINT " PLANTS PER ROW,"	
90 PRINT "WITH "; LFT; " PLANTS LEFT TO FEED YOUR PIG."	
100 END	

Output

```
SPRING PLANTING
TYPE NUMBER OF PLANTS:  ? 57
TYPE NUMBER OF ROWS:  ? 6
THERE SHOULD BE 9 PLANTS PER ROW,
WITH 3 PLANTS LEFT TO FEED YOUR PIG.
```

A special case of integer division occurs when the remainder is 0. For example, 15 / 3 = 5 with zero remainder, and 16 / 4 = 4 with zero remainder. When N / D gives a zero remainder, then D is said to be a *factor* or a *divisor* of N. (We also say that N is *divisible* by D.) Thus, 3 is a factor of 15, and 4 is a factor of 16. The fact that the remainder is 0 in this case provides a condition the computer can use to test for factors: D is a divisor of N when the remainder R is 0. That is, if

$$R = N - D * INT(N / D) = 0$$

or

$$N = D * INT(N / D).$$

It is usual to divide both sides of this condition by D:

$$N / D = INT(N / D)$$

This should look familiar; in Section 7–1, it was noted that a number X is an integer exactly if X = INT(X). The condition N / D = INT(N / D) is therefore true exactly if N / D is an integer. This makes sense: 5 (D) is a factor of 30 (N) because N / D = 30 / 5 = 6 is an integer, but 7 (D) is not a factor of 30 (N) because N / D = 30 / 7 ≈ 4.29 is not an integer.

Here is a program that uses the special case of D = 2 to determine whether an INPUT integer is even or odd.

Program 2

Statement	Remark
10 PRINT "EVEN OR ODD?"	
20 INPUT "TYPE AN INTEGER: "; N	
30 IF N <> INT(N) THEN PRINT "NO GOOD": GOTO 20	*Error trap.*
40 IF N / 2 = INT(N / 2) THEN PRINT "EVEN": GOTO 60	*If 2 is a divisor of N, then N must be even.*
50 PRINT "ODD"	
60 END	

Output

```
EVEN OR ODD?
TYPE AN INTEGER:   ? 10
EVEN
```

If an even number is typed for the value of N, then 2 is a divisor of N (the condition in line 40 is true) and the message EVEN is PRINTed. If an odd number is typed, the condition in line 40 is false, so the message ODD is PRINTed in line 50.

Program 1 tests only whether an INPUT number has 2 as a factor. Let's design a program using the top-down approach to determine *all* the factors of any positive integer N that is INPUT from a user. The output should be all the factors of N. One possible outline of an algorithm is on the next page.

Step 1 Get a number (N) from the user.
Step 2 Error trap: Accept only positive integer values of N.
Step 3 Test each integer D from 1 to N to see if it is a divisor of N.

Here is the algorithm translated into BASIC code:

Program 3

Statement	Remark
10 PRINT "FACTORS"	
20 INPUT "TYPE A POSITIVE INTEGER: "; N	
30 IF N <> INT(N) OR N < 1 THEN PRINT "NO GOOD": GOTO 20	
40 LET D = 1	*Start at 1.*
50 IF N / D = INT(N / D) THEN PRINT D; " IS A FACTOR OF "; N	
60 LET D = D + 1	
70 IF D <= N THEN GOTO 50	*Test up to N.*
80 END	

Output

```
FACTORS
TYPE A POSITIVE INTEGER:   ? 8
1 IS A FACTOR OF 8
2 IS A FACTOR OF 8
4 IS A FACTOR OF 8
8 IS A FACTOR OF 8

RUN
FACTORS
TYPE A POSITIVE INTEGER:   ? 23
1 IS A FACTOR OF 23
23 IS A FACTOR OF 23
```

Notice that the only factors of 23 are 1 and 23. An integer greater than 1 that has no factors other than itself and 1 is called a *prime* number (note that 1 is not considered prime). The first several prime numbers are as follows:

2, 3, 5, 7, 11, 13, 17, 19, 23, . . .

Let's revise Program 3 so that it PRINTs either the message PRIME or the message NOT PRIME, whichever one applies to the INPUT value of N. To do this we note that an integer N is a prime if $N > 1$ and none of the numbers 2, 3, 4, . . . , or $N - 1$ is a factor of N.

Here is the revised program:

Program 4

Statement	Remark
10 PRINT "PRIME CHECK"	
15 PRINT	
20 INPUT "TYPE AN INTEGER (BIGGER THAN 1): "; N	
30 IF N < > INT(N) OR N < 2 THEN PRINT "NO GOOD": GOTO 20	
40 LET D = 2	*Start at 2.*
50 IF N / D = INT(N / D) THEN PRINT N; " IS NOT PRIME": GOTO 80	
60 LET D = D + 1	
70 IF D < N THEN GOTO 50	*Test up to N − 1.*
75 PRINT N; " IS PRIME"	
80 END	

Output

```
PRIME CHECK

TYPE AN INTEGER (BIGGER THAN 1):  ? 12

12 IS NOT PRIME

RUN
PRIME CHECK
TYPE AN INTEGER (BIGGER THAN 1):  ? 19
19 IS PRIME
```

The careful reader may have noticed there is a bug in the program. What if N = 2? In that case, the condition in line 50 would be true, so the program would PRINT incorrectly: 2 IS NOT PRIME. To ensure that this mistake does not occur, we can treat 2 as a special case and add this line:

```
35  IF N = 2 THEN GOTO 75
```

Avoiding Pitfalls

When designing an algorithm for a BASIC program to test whether an integer is prime, be sure to consider whether the number 2 must be treated as a special case.

Summary

If the condition N / D = INT(N / D) is true, then the integer D is a *divisor,* or *factor,* of the integer N.

If a positive integer N is divided by a positive integer D, then the (integer) quotient is Q = INT(N / D) and the remainder is R = N − D * Q = N − D * INT(N / D).

Exercises 7-4

A

1. Tell whether the condition N / D = INT(N / D) is true or false for each of the following values of N and D.

   a. N = 4, D = 2 **b.** N = 18, D = 3
   c. N = 7, D = 5 **d.** N = 16, D = 2
   e. N = 42, D = 7 **f.** N = 2, D = 6
   g. N = 63, D = 8 **h.** N = 125, D = 26

2. Calculate the value of R = N − D * INT(N / D) for each of the following values of N and D.

   a. N = 3, D = 2 **b.** N = 8, D = 5
   c. N = 7, D = 7 **d.** N = 15, D = 3
   e. N = 19, D = 4 **f.** N = 20, D = 6
   g. N = 21, D = 3 **h.** N = 41, D = 8

3. Predict the output of the following program for each of the INPUTs shown below.

```
10  INPUT N1
20  INPUT N2
30  LET Q = INT(N1 / N2)
40  LET R = N1 − N2 * Q
50  IF R = 0 THEN PRINT "GCF IS:  "; N2: GOTO 90
60  LET N1 = N2
70  LET N2 = R
80  GOTO 30
90  END
```

   a. N1 = 18, N2 = 12 **b.** N1 = 25, N2 = 4 **c.** N1 = 144, N2 = 36 **d.** N1 = 1024, N2 = 80

Note: The program above follows the *Euclidean Algorithm* to find the *greatest common factor* (GCF) of two INPUT integers. (The GCF is the largest integer that is a factor of two given integers.)

4. Predict the output of the following program for each of the INPUTs shown below.

```
10 INPUT N, D
20 FOR F = D TO 1 STEP -1
30 IF N / F <> INT(N / F) THEN GOTO 60
40 IF D / F <> INT(D / F) THEN GOTO 60
50 PRINT "GCF IS:  "; F: GOTO 70
60 NEXT F
70 END
```

a. N = 20 D = 10 **b.** N = 12 D = 9 **c.** N = 18 D = 7 **d.** N = 36 D = 24

The program above is another way to find the *greatest common factor* (GCF) of two INPUT integers. (See the note in Exercise 3.)

5. a. Predict the output of the following program.

```
10 PRINT "SUMMING"
15 LET S = 0
20 FOR X = 1 TO 15
30 IF X / 3 = INT(X / 3) THEN LET S = S + X
35 NEXT X
40 PRINT "SUM IS:  "; S
50 END
```

b. Do you see an easier way to write a program to accomplish what the program in (a) does? (*Hint:* Use STEP.)

6. Change Program 2 so that it INPUTs 15 integers. In addition to PRINTing the message EVEN or ODD, the program should keep track of the number of INPUT integers that are even and the number that are odd, and then PRINT the final result.

7. Change Program 3 so that it uses a FOR . . . NEXT loop rather than a finite loop in lines 40–70.

B **8. a.** Write a program that INPUTs a positive integer N, then determines if N has 5 as a divisor.

b. Change the program in (a) so that it determines if N has 6 as a divisor.

9. Write a program that INPUTs the number of peanuts you have in a bag and the number of elephants you have to feed. Then have the program PRINT the number of peanuts each elephant will get (if the peanuts are divided as evenly as possible), and the number of peanuts left over for you.

10. a. Change Program 3 so that it PRINTs a positive integer N as a product of its factors. For example, if N = 8, the output of the program should look like this:

```
FACTORS
TYPE A POSITIVE INTEGER:  ? 8
1 * 8 = 8
2 * 4 = 8
4 * 2 = 8
8 * 1 = 8
```

b. Modify the program in (a) so that each pair of factors is PRINTed only once. For example, in the output shown in (a), 4 * 2 and 2 * 4 are the same pair; only one of them should be PRINTed. (*Hint:* Is it necessary to test values of D all the way up to N in line 50 of Program 3?)

11. a. In Program 4, it may have occurred to you that it was not necessary to test all of the numbers up to N − 1 to see if they were factors of N. Factors of N always come in pairs. For example, since 2 is a factor of 38, so is 38 / 2 = 19. Therefore, it is only necessary to check half of the possible factors of N. Since the operation involved here is multiplication, "half way" means "up to the square root of N." Of any pair of factors whose product is N, one of them must be less than or equal to SQR(N) and the other must be greater than or equal to SQR(N). (If both were *less* than SQR(N), then their product, which is N, would be less than SQR(N) * SQR(N) = N. That's impossible!)

Change Program 4 to check factors only up to INT(SQR(N) + .5). (You need to round SQR(N) to the nearest integer to avoid problems with round-off errors.)

b. Add another time-saving strategy to your program: Do not test any even numbers other than 2 as factors. (Why will this work?)

12. Write a program that will convert an INPUT integer number of minutes into hours and minutes. For example, if 258 minutes is INPUT, the output should be 4 HOURS, 18 MINUTES.

13. Write a program that will convert an INPUT integer number of inches into yards, feet, and inches. For example, if 284 inches is INPUT, the output should be 7 YARDS, 2 FEET, 8 INCHES. (*Hint:* First make the number of YARDS as great as possible (divide by 36), then the number of FEET left over as great as possible.)

14. If the minute hand of a clock is at 14 minutes past the hour, then 168 minutes later it will be at 2 minutes past the hour, since we have 168 min + 14 min = 182 min = 3 hr 2 min. Write a program that INPUTs an initial position of the minute hand and the number of elapsed minutes, and then outputs the final position of the minute hand.

15. a. Write a program that will convert any amount of money INPUT in cents to the correct number of dollars, quarters, dimes, nickels, and pennies. (*Hint:* First make the number of dollars as great as possible, then the number of quarters as great as possible, and so on.)

    b. Change the program in (a) so that it will INPUT the amount of a purchase and the amount of money given to the cashier, then will compute the change in dollars, quarters, dimes, nickels, and pennies.

16. Write a program to generate 50 random integers, each between 1 and 50. Have the program count the number of even integers and the number of odd integers produced, then PRINT the results.

17. a. Write a program that will PRINT a list of 100 random integers, each between 1 and 50. Have the program stop at every twentieth integer in the listing (the number of integers PRINTed at that time should be divisible by 20) and wait until the user presses the < RETURN > or < ENTER > key before continuing (use INPUT).

    b. Change the program in (a) so that it adds the random numbers and PRINTs the current value of the sum at every twentieth integer.

18. An integer is said to be *perfect* if it is equal to the sum of all its factors that are less than itself. For example, the factors of 6 are 1, 2, 3, and 6. The sum of those less than 6 is equal to $1 + 2 + 3 = 6$, so that 6 is perfect. Write a program that INPUTs a positive integer and then tests whether it is perfect. (There are very few small perfect numbers. The numbers 28 and 496 are two that you can test.)

19. a. Write a program to determine and PRINT all the prime numbers from 100 to 200. (*Hint:* Use nested FOR . . . NEXT loops. Try to avoid unnecessary tests. See Exercise 11.)

    b. Modify the program in (a) to INPUT two positive integers J and K, then PRINT all the prime numbers from J to K, inclusive. Use error trapping to ensure that $J < K$.

20. Write a program that INPUTs a positive integer N greater than 1, then PRINTs only the prime factors of N. (*Hint:* Use nested FOR . . . NEXT loops. Try to avoid unnecessary tests. See Exercise 11.)

21. A fraction N / D can be reduced to lowest terms by dividing both N and D by the *greatest common factor* (GCF) of N and D. For example, the fraction $8 / 12 = 2 / 3$ because the GCF of 8 and 12 is 4 and if you divide 8 and 12 by 4, you get 2 and 3, respectively. Write a program that INPUTs positive integers N and D, then reduces the fraction N / D to lowest terms. (*Hint:* Modify the program in Exercise 4.)

22. Write a program that finds the *least common multiple* of two INPUT integers J and K. (The *least common multiple* is the smallest positive integer that has both J and K as factors.)

23. Write a program that INPUTs the numerators (say, integers N1 and N2) and denominators (say, integers D1 and D2) of two fractions, then finds the numerator and denominator of their sum, reduced to lowest terms. (See Exercises 21 and 22.)

C 24. *Challenge:* To convert a base-10 integer like 22 to binary (base-2) form, the following algorithm may be used:

Step 1 Divide the integer by 2 repeatedly, as shown below for 22.

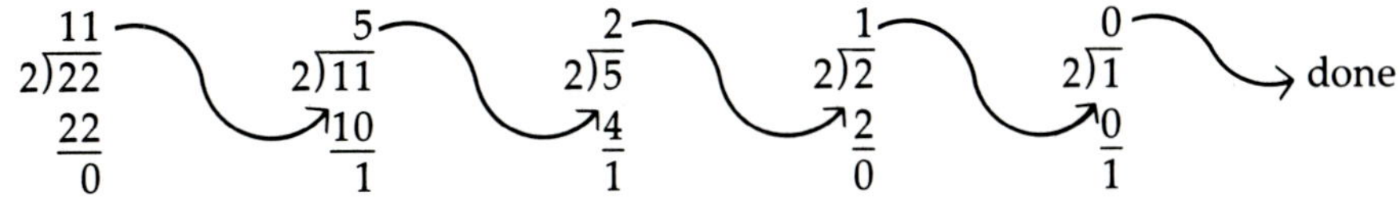

Step 2 The binary form of the integer is obtained by taking the remainders from the division in Step 1 in the opposite order in which they appear. For 22, the resulting binary form is: 10110.

Write a program to convert an INPUT positive integer into binary form. (See the Lab Activity for more information and hints.)

25. (Graphics) Suppose that you want to distribute N horizontal line segments, each L dots long, on a single horizontal line across the middle of your graphics screen. You want to make the spaces between segments as even as possible and the first and last segments touch the edges of the screen:

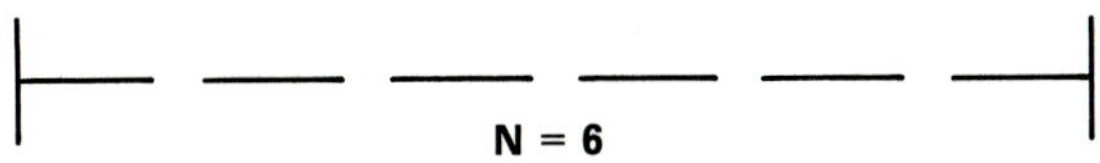

Write a program that INPUTs N and L, then plots the segments, evenly distributed.

Lab Activity

Isolating Digits; Palindromic Numbers

In this section you learned how to do integer division using INT; the integer quotient you get from dividing N by D is Q = INT(N / D), and the remainder is R = N − D * Q. In the special case of D = 10, the remainder R is the *ones* digit of the original number N. For example, 378 / 10 = 37 with a remainder of 8; in BASIC terms,

```
Q = INT(378 / 10) = 37
```

and

```
R = N - 10 * Q = 378 - 10 * 37 = 8.
```

To get the *tens* digit, we can simply find the ones digit of the quotient; that is, let N = Q = 37, and then repeat the process to obtain

Q = INT(37 / 10) = 3

and R = 37 − 10 * 3 = 7.

To extract all of the digits, one at a time, the process can be repeated until Q becomes equal to zero. Here is a program that accomplishes this isolation of the digits of an INPUT integer.

Statement	Remark
10 REM * ISOLATING DIGITS	
20 INPUT "TYPE A POSITIVE INTEGER: "; N	
30 LET Q = INT(N / 10)	
40 LET R = N − 10 * Q	*R is the ones digit of the current value of N.*
50 PRINT "DIGIT: "; R	
60 IF Q = 0 THEN GOTO 90	*Done when Q becomes 0.*
70 LET N = Q	
80 GOTO 30	*Repeat the process.*
90 END	

Problems

1. Test the program with several different positive integers.

2. Does the program work with negative INPUT integers?

3. What happens when you type a decimal, such as 23.68?

In your mathematics class, you may have encountered word problems that involved reversing the digits of a positive integer. For example, the reverse of 467 is 764. We can change the program to accomplish this. Notice that the program produces the digits of the original integer in reverse order (from right to left). We just have to put them back together from left to right. Suppose that you want to put together the digits 7 and 6 to make the number 76. All you need to do is multiply the 7 by 10 and then add 6, as follows:

76 = 7 * 10 + 6

If you then want to add a 4 to the right end to make 764, you can multiply the 76 by 10 and then add the 4:

764 = 76 * 10 + 4

In general, if you have an integer REV (for "reverse") and want to add the digit R to its right end, you can use this statement:

```
LET REV = REV * 10 + R
```

4. Change the program by adding these lines:

```
25  LET REV = 0      (initialize the reverse integer)
100 END
```

Then change lines 50 and 90 to read:

```
50  LET REV = REV * 10 + R
90  PRINT "REVERSE:  "; REV
```

Check the program thoroughly. What happens when you type in an integer ending in one or more zeros? What happens when you type in a really big integer, like 6897896432?

PALINDROMES

An integer that is unchanged when its digits are reversed is called a "palindrome." (The same word is applied to strings that are the same when reversed.) For example, 727 and 4664 are palindromes, but 7684 is not.

5. Do you see how to change the program in Problem 4 to test whether the INPUT number is a palindrome? You might think of changing line 90 to this:

```
90  IF REV = N THEN PRINT "PALINDROME"
```

RUN the program and see if it PRINTs that 4664 is a palindrome.

6. You probably found that the change in Problem 5 doesn't work; by the time the program gets to line 90, N is no longer equal to its original value. (What value is it equal to?) You need another variable to save the original integer. Change N to SVE in lines 20 and 90 of the program in Problem 5 and add this line: 22 LET N = SVE. Test the program by typing 4664.

7. Make the following changes and additions to the program in Problem 6:

```
28  LET SVE = SVE + REV
100 IF SVE <> REV THEN PRINT SVE; "  +  "; REV; "  =  ";
      SVE + REV : GOTO 22
110 END
```

RUN this program and type 67 as the integer. Can you see what is happening? The program adds the INPUT integer to its reverse (67 + 76 = 143), then repeats the exact same process with the resulting integer (143 + 341 = 484), until a palindrome occurs (in this case, 484). It is a remarkable fact that most integers eventually produce palindromes if this process is applied to them. Try the program on several two-digit positive integers. What happens if you type a palindrome for the initial integer? Try to find two-digit integers that make the program repeat the reversing and adding process many times. What's the largest number of repetitions you can produce? (*Hint:* Notice that the program will repeat the process the same number of times for 74 as for 47. Can you tell why?)

7-5 The Trigonometric Functions; Logarithms and the Exponential Function (Optional)

There are a number of specialized functions that occur frequently in mathematics and science which, as a programming convenience, are included as built-in functions in BASIC. This section explores the sine, cosine, and tangent functions of trigonometry, and the exponential and logarithmic functions (two functions usually studied in advanced algebra).

SIN, COS, and TAN

Many problems in trigonometry can be solved on the computer using the built-in trigonometric functions. In BASIC, the functions SIN(X), COS(X), and TAN(X) will calculate the values of the sine, cosine, and tangent for an angle of X *radians.* Since π radians = 180 degrees, to convert an angle from degrees to radians, you multiply the angle by $\pi \approx 3.14159265$ and then divide by 180.

Here is a type of problem you may be familiar with that can be solved using trigonometry:
If an observer on the ground at point A sees an airplane 26° above the horizon, and the airplane is directly over a building that is 3.1 km from point A, then how high is the plane above the ground?

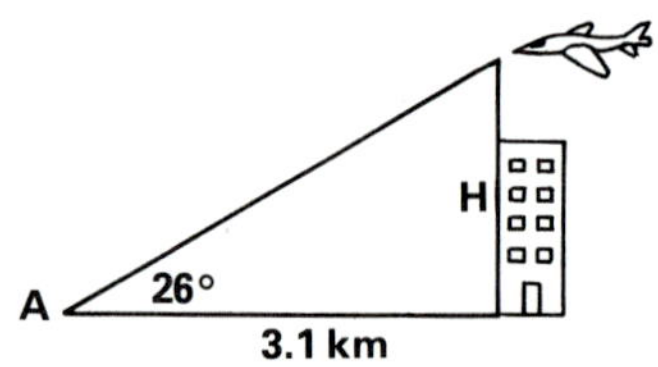

Here is a program that uses the built-in TAN function to calculate the solution to problems of this type.

Program 1

Statement	Remark
10 PRINT "PLANE PROBLEM"	
20 INPUT "TYPE THE ANGLE OF ELEVATION (IN DEGREES): "; A	*∠A is the angle of elevation.*
30 LET RAD = A * 3.14159265 / 180	*Convert from degrees to radians.*
40 INPUT "TYPE DISTANCE FROM OBSERVER TO BUILDING: "; D	
50 LET H = D * TAN(RAD)	*tan A = H / D; H = D * tan A.*
60 PRINT "PLANE'S HEIGHT IS "; H ; " KM"	
70 END	

Output

```
PLANE PROBLEM
TYPE ANGLE OF ELEVATION (IN DEGREES):  ? 26
TYPE DISTANCE FROM OBSERVER TO BUILDING:  ? 3.1
PLANE'S HEIGHT IS 1.511971 KM
```

You may have seen trigonometric functions defined in terms of points on a circle. We can use the relationship between trigonometric functions and circles to write a program to draw circles.

Consider a circle of radius R with center at the origin. Given any point (X, Y) on the circle, if A is the angle between the positive X-axis and the radius drawn from the center to (X, Y), then

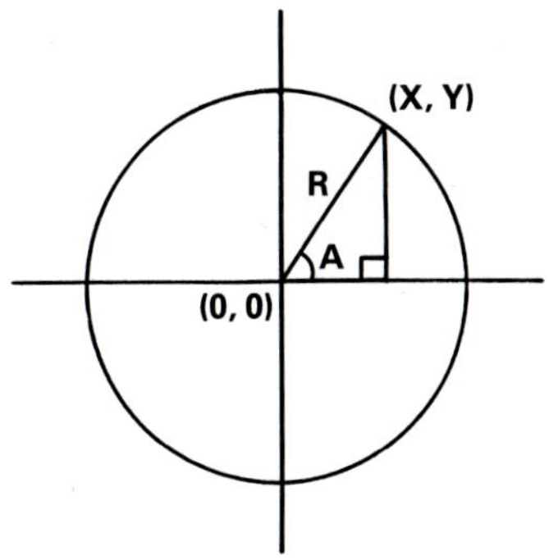

$$SIN(A) = Y / R$$

$$\text{or} \quad Y = R * SIN(A)$$

and

$$COS(A) = X / R$$

$$\text{or} \quad X = R * COS(A).$$

These equations are true for *any* angle A, not just an angle in the first quadrant (as illustrated in the diagram).

These observations lead to an easy method of drawing circles on your graphics screen: Given a radius R, plot the point

$$(X, Y) = (R * COS(A), R * SIN(A))$$

as A goes from 0 to 2π radians by some small increment (such as 0.1).

One complication; we do not want all circles to be centered at (0, 0), since on the computer such circles would be mostly off the screen. To position the center of the circle at the point (XC, YC), as shown in the diagram at the right, we can simply add XC and YC to the respective X- and Y-coordinates of the circle points derived earlier. Thus, we will plot the point

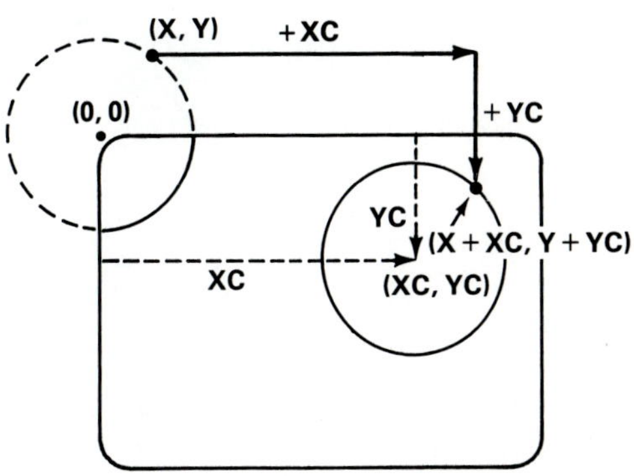

$$(XC + R * COS(A), YC + R * SIN(A))$$

as A goes from 0 to 2π radians by some small increment.

Here is the circle-drawing program:

Program 2

Statement

```
10   REM * CIRCLE-DRAWING PROGRAM
20   INPUT "TYPE CENTER (X, Y):   "; XC, YC
30   INPUT "TYPE RADIUS:   "; R
35   (Instruction(s) for error trapping.)
40   (Instructions to clear screen
 .        and do graphics on
 .        your computer.)
 .
100   GOSUB 1000: REM * DRAW CIRCLE, RADIUS R,
          CENTER (XC, YC)
130   END
1000   REM ** SUBROUTINE TO DRAW CIRCLE **
1010   FOR A = 0 TO 6.28 STEP 0.1: REM * 6.28 = 2 * PI (APPROX.)
1020   (Instruction to plot the point XC + R * COS(A), YC + R * SIN(A)
          on your computer.)
1030   NEXT A
1040   RETURN
```

Output

```
TYPE CENTER (X, Y):   ? 60, 50
TYPE RADIUS:   ? 40
```

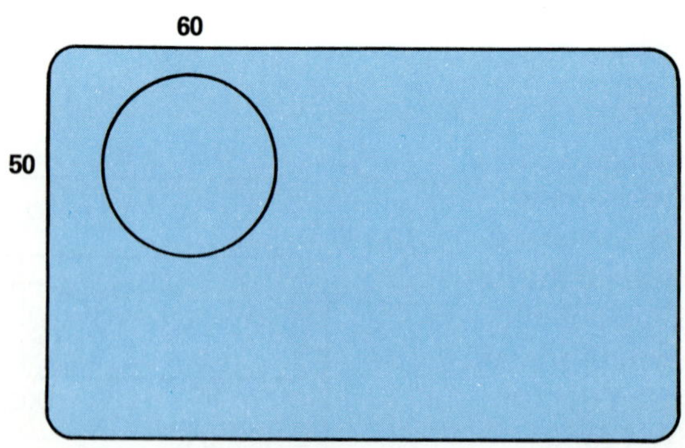

On some computers, the circle in the output will be distorted on the screen because screen dots are taller than they are wide. In the exercises, you will explore how to make the circles rounder. (*Note: IBM* computers have a built-in circle-drawing command. See the Lab Activity for Section 6–4, page 312.)

LOG and EXP

In BASIC, the built-in function EXP(X) is used to find values of the exponential function e^x, where e is a special constant with the approximate value 2.71828. If you have studied logarithms, you probably know that e is the base of natural logarithms (usually $\log_e$ is denoted ln). In BASIC, the built-in logarithm function base e is written LOG. If X is a positive number, LOG(X) will calculate the natural logarithm of X.

Logarithms and exponential functions have many applications, as you may have seen in your mathematics courses and will see in the exercises in this section. These functions are very important in the operations of computers, because they form the basis of *all* calculations involving exponents. The following properties of logarithms are used in these calculations:

1. $a^{\log_a b} = b$

   Special case: $e^{\log_e b} = b$, which is expressed in BASIC by

   EXP(LOG(B)) = B.

2. $\log_a b^c = c \log_a b$

   Special case: $\log_e b^c = c \log_e b$, which translates into BASIC as

   LOG(B ↑ C) = C * LOG(B).

It follows from these two properties that

3. $a^{c \log_a b} = a^{\log_a b^c} = b^c$

   Special case: $e^{c \log_e b}$, or

   EXP(C * LOG(B)) = B ↑ C.

To calculate B ↑ C, then, the computer does the equivalent of finding LOG(B), multiplying by C, then taking EXP of the result, as in (3) above. The following program will verify that these calculations are identical:

Program 3

Statement

```
10  PRINT "EXPONENTIAL CALCULATIONS"
20  INPUT "TYPE BASE:  "; B
30  INPUT "TYPE EXPONENT:  "; C
40  PRINT "B ↑ C=   "; B ↑ C
50  PRINT "EXP(C * LOG(B)) =   "; EXP(C * LOG(B))
60  END
```

Output

```
EXPONENTIAL CALCULATIONS
TYPE BASE:  ? 12.8
TYPE EXPONENT:  ? 3.8
B ↑ C = 16121.2193
EXP(C * LOG(B)) = 16121.2193
```

If you type very large numbers for B and C in this program, then an error occurs, as in the following output:

```
RUN
EXPONENTIAL CALCULATIONS
TYPE BASE:  ? 416
TYPE EXPONENT:  ? 439.8
OVERFLOW ERROR IN 40
```

← ***Error messages vary. See page 658 for the form given on your computer.***

The problem here is that 416 ↑ 439.8 is too large a number for the computer to handle. We can use the ideas discussed earlier to write a program that will calculate such big numbers in scientific notation. Before proceeding, we need two more properties of logarithms and exponents:

4. *Change-of-base formula:* $\log_a b = \dfrac{\log_c b}{\log_c a}$

For our purposes, we will use $a = 10$, and $c = e$, so that the formula will take the form

$$\log_{10} \mathrm{B} = \mathrm{LOG(B)\ /\ LOG(10)}.$$

5. $a^{b+c} = a^b * a^c$

We will use the form $10^{\mathrm{D}+\mathrm{N}} = 10^{\mathrm{D}} * 10^{\mathrm{N}}$.

In calculating an enormous number like 416 ↑ 439.8, the program will make this computation:

$$\begin{aligned} \log_{10}(416 \uparrow 439.8) &= 439.8 * \log_{10}(416) && \text{[by property (2)]} \\ &= 439.8 * (\mathrm{LOG}(416)\ /\ \mathrm{LOG}(10)) && \text{[by property (4)]} \\ &\approx 1151.877 \end{aligned}$$

Then, by property (1),

$$\begin{aligned} 416 \uparrow 439.8 &= 10^{\log_{10}(416 \uparrow 439.8)} \\ &\approx 10^{1151.877} && \text{[by substitution from the calculation above]} \\ &\approx 10^{.877} * 10^{1151} && \text{[by property (5)]} \\ &\approx 7.534 * 10^{1151} \end{aligned}$$

The program for large calculations is on the next page.

Program 4

Statement	Remark
10 PRINT "LARGE CALCULATIONS"	
20 INPUT "TYPE BASE: "; B	
30 INPUT "TYPE EXPONENT: "; C	
40 LET L = C * LOG(B) / LOG(10)	*Assigns $\log_{10} B^C$ to L.*
50 LET N = INT(L)	*Assigns integer part of log to N.*
60 LET D = L − N	*Assigns decimal part of log to D.*
70 PRINT "B ↑ C = "; 10 ↑ D; " * 10 ↑ "; N	
80 END	

Output

```
LARGE CALCULATIONS
TYPE BASE:  ? 416
TYPE EXPONENT:  ? 439.8
B ↑ C = 7.53783899 * 10 ↑ 1151
```

Avoiding Pitfalls

1. Be sure X in SIN(X), COS(X), and TAN(X), is in *radian* measure.
2. Remember that LOG(X) calculates the *natural logarithm* of X, that is, the logarithm base *e*. If you want to calculate the *common logarithm* of X, that is, the logarithm base 10, use the change-of-base formula:

$$\log_{10} X = \text{LOG(X) / LOG(10)}$$

3. Parentheses are required in all BASIC functions; you cannot type LET X = SIN A as is conventional in mathematics.

Summary

The built-in functions SIN(X), COS(X), and TAN(X) will calculate the values of the sine, cosine, and tangent of the angle X, where X is measured in radians. (Another common built-in function is the arctangent function: ATN(X). See Exercise 11.)

The built-in function EXP(X) is used to find values of the exponential function e^x, where e has the approximate value 2.71828.

The built-in function LOG(X) will calculate the natural logarithm of X (that is, the logarithm base e). X must be a positive number.

Exercises 7-5

A 1. Write a LET statement representing each of the following formulas.

a. $y = \sin^2 x + \cos^2 x$

b. $y = \sqrt{\dfrac{1 + \cos x}{1 - \cos x}}$

c. $A = Pe^{rt}$

d. $y = e^{-\frac{1}{2}\ln x}$

2. a. Write a program to PRINT a table of values for SIN(X) and COS(X), for values of X between 0 and 3.1, in increments of 0.1. Round the values to four decimal places. Have the output look similar to this:

```
X      SIN(X)     COS(X)
0      0          1
.1     .0998      .995
.2     .1987      .9801
.      .          .
.      .          .
.      .          .
```

b. Modify the program in (a) so that each value in the column labeled X is PRINTed as an angle in degree measure, and the functions are calculated at every five degrees from 0 to 90.

3. Write a program that calculates and PRINTs the value of $\sin^2 x + \cos^2 x$ for values of x between 0 and 1, in increments of 0.1. (The result should always equal what number?)

4. Write a program to verify the identity $\dfrac{\sin x \cos x}{1 - \sin^2 x} = \tan x$, for values of x between 0 and 3.1, in increments of 0.1. Have the program PRINT the value of each side of the identity at every value of X.

5. Write a program that verifies the identity LOG(EXP(X)) = X by PRINTing the value of each side of the identity for any INPUT real number X.

6. Write a program that calculates EXP(B ↑ C) and C * EXP(B) for any INPUT real numbers B and C. How are these expressions related?

B 7. (A computer is needed for this exercise.)

a. Complete Program 2 and try RUNning it. Make the dots on the circle closer together by changing the STEP value in line 1010 to .02.

b. Make the circle into an *ellipse* by having the program INPUT two positive numbers R1 and R2 instead of a single radius R, then plot in line 1020 the point (XC + R1 * COS(A), YC + R2 * SIN(A)). RUN the program with different values of R1 and R2.

8. Using subroutine 1000 of Program 2, write a program that will draw the International Olympic Logo, as shown in the diagram at the right.

9. Using the ideas in Program 2, write a program that INPUTS the center and radius of a circle, and also the beginning (BEGANG) and ending (NDANG) angle for an arc of the circle. Then the program should draw the arc on the graphics screen.

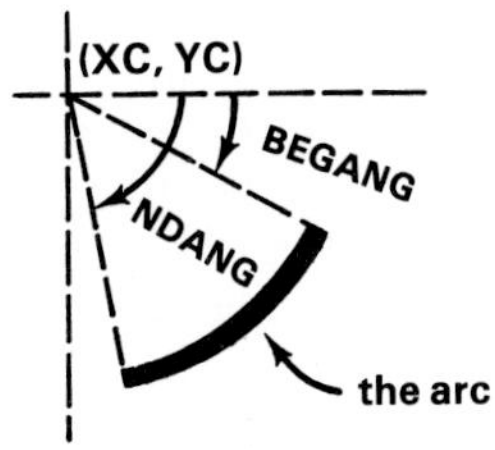

10. a. A 22–foot ladder, leaning against the side of a house, is positioned in such a way that it forms a 75° angle with the ground (see the diagram). Write a program to calculate and PRINT how high (H) the top of the ladder is above the ground. Have the program round the result to two decimal places.

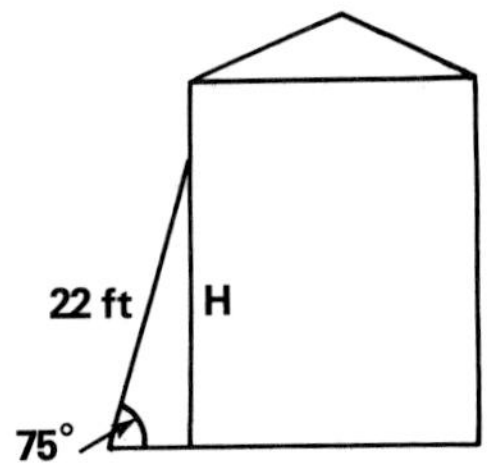

b. Modify the program in (a) to calculate how far the base of the ladder is from the side of the house. Allow the user to type the measure of the angle formed by the ladder and the ground (in degrees). Have the program round the result X to two decimal places.

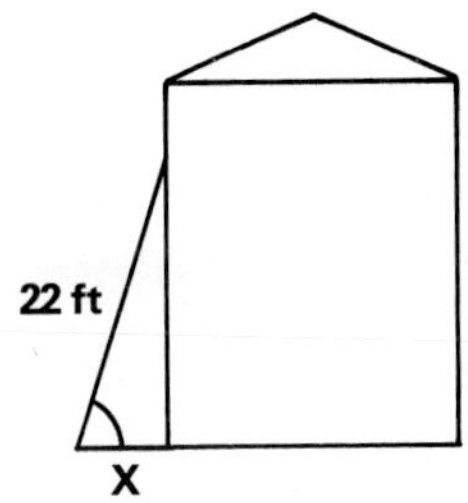

11. A support cable for a television transmitting tower 117 meters high is anchored in the ground 18 meters from the base of the tower. Write a program to calculate and PRINT the measure (in degrees) of the angle A that the cable makes with the ground, rounded to two decimal places. (Use the built-in inverse trigonometric function ATN. ATN(X) is the arctangent of X: the angle in radians between $-\frac{\pi}{2}$ and $\frac{\pi}{2}$ whose tangent is X.)

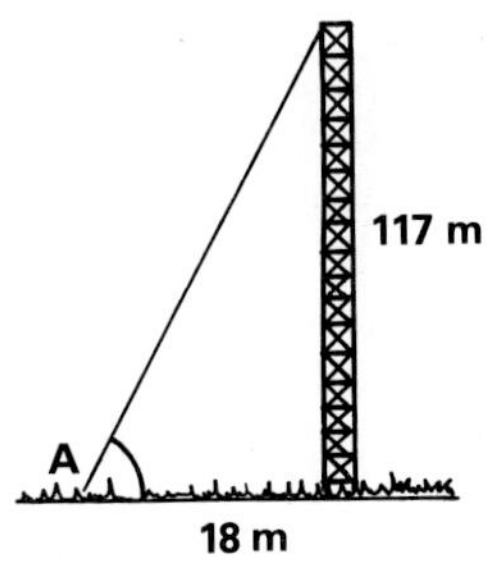

12. For the triangle shown at the right, the *Law of Cosines* gives the following relationship:

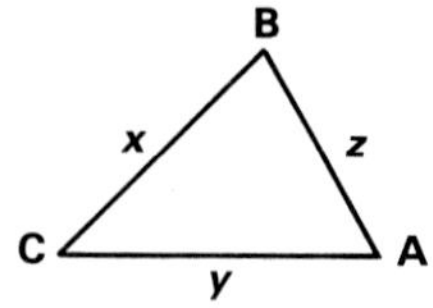

$$z^2 = x^2 + y^2 - 2xy \cos C$$

Write a program that INPUTs the measure of angle C (in degrees) and the lengths of sides x and y, then calculates and PRINTs the length of side z, rounded to two decimal places.

13. For the triangle shown at the right, the *Law of Sines* gives the following relationship:

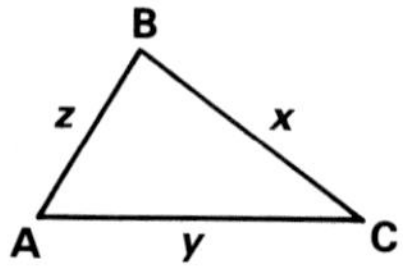

$$\frac{\sin A}{x} = \frac{\sin B}{y} = \frac{\sin C}{z}$$

Write a program that INPUTs the measure of angles A and B (in degrees) and the length of side z, then calculates and PRINTs the measure of angle C (in degrees) and the lengths of sides y and x. Round all results to two decimal places.

14. The *pH* of a solution measures how acidic or alkaline it is. By definition,

$$pH = -\log_{10} ([H^+]),$$

where $[H^+]$ is the concentration of hydrogen ions in the solution, in moles per liter. Pure water, which has a *pH* of 7, is considered neutral. A *pH* less than 7 is acidic; a *pH* more than 7 is alkaline. Write a program to PRINT *pH* values when the concentration of $[H^+]$ ions in a given solution is INPUT.

15. (A computer is needed for this exercise.) The amount of money in a savings account that earns interest at the rate r (written as a decimal) per year, compounded yearly, is given by

$$A = P(1 + r)^t,$$

where P is the *principal* (the amount initially invested) and t is the number of years.

a. Write a program that INPUTs P, r, and t and then PRINTs A. Use the program to estimate how long it takes an account to double if it is invested at 8% compounded yearly. (Make guesses, and modify your guesses on the basis of the output of the program.)

b. Theoretically, the time it takes to double the amount in an account is given by:

$$\text{doubling time} = \log_2 (1 + r)$$

Verify the result you obtained in (a) by having the computer calculate this value for $r = .08$.

16. a. Some banks compound interest *continuously* using the formula

$$A = Pe^{rt}$$

where P represents the *principal* (the amount initially invested), r the rate of interest (written as a decimal), t the time in years, and A the amount in the account at the end of t years. Write a program using the built-in function EXP to calculate the amount in an account after 3 years if the initial deposit is \$500, the rate of interest is $r = .11$, and the interest is compounded continuously.

b. Modify the program in (a) so that the values of P, r, and t are INPUT from the user.

17. (A computer is needed for this exercise.) Use the GRAPHING FUNCTIONS program in the Lab Activity of Section 7–2, page 353, to graph each of the following functions. Sketch each graph to verify that the program works accurately.

a. Y = SIN(X)
b. Y = COS(X)
c. Y = TAN(X)
d. Y = EXP(X)
e. Y = 3 * SIN(X) ↑ 2
f. Y = LOG(X), X > 0
g. Y = LOG(EXP(X))
h. Y = ABS(SIN(X))

18. Stereo photographs, which were very popular about the turn of the century, were produced by taking pictures of the same object with two different cameras. The cameras were placed side by side, but a little distance apart. If the two resulting photographs were viewed separately by a person's two eyes, an illusion of three-dimensional depth resulted. Suppose that an object was photographed by two side-by-side cameras 2 feet apart and that one of the cameras was aimed 2° inward from parallel, as in the illustration. How far away from the cameras was the object? Write a program that will INPUT the angle (in degrees) and that will output the distance d to the object.

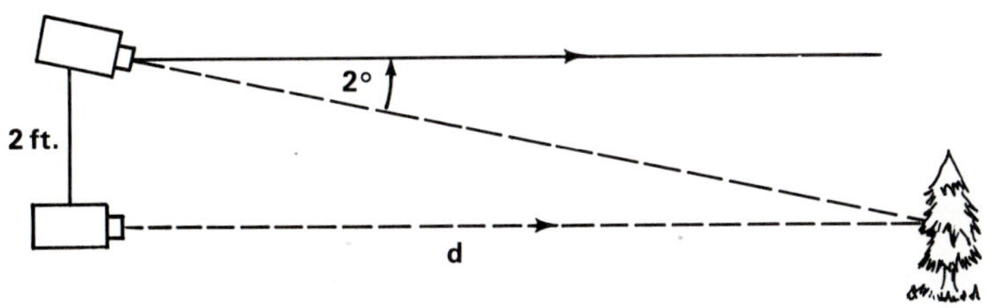

C **19.** The computer calculates the trigonometric functions by using infinite series. In advanced mathematics one learns, for example, that if x is in radians, then

$$\sin(x) = x - \frac{x^3}{3*2*1} + \frac{x^5}{5*4*3*2*1} - \frac{x^7}{7*6*5*4*3*2*1} + \cdots$$

For a particular value of x, $\sin(x)$ can be approximated to any desired degree of accuracy by combining enough of the terms on the right side of this equation.

a. Write a program that INPUTs X, then combines four terms of the series above and PRINTs the result. Have the program also PRINT the value of the built-in function SIN(X) for comparison. (*Hint:* You can write out separate LET statements for the four terms and then combine them.)

b. *Challenge:* Change the program in (a) so that it INPUTs the number of terms in the series that should be calculated. (*Hint:* Use a FOR . . . NEXT loop.)

Lab Activity

Applying Trigonometry to Write a Computer Game

In this Lab Activity, we will write a simple computer game that makes use of trigonometric ratios. Imagine that you are playing golf and you want to hit the ball so that it will land on the green. Assuming that your ball will go straight toward the green and that you hit it equally hard every time, you must choose how much "lift" to put on the ball (golfers do this by choosing the right club); that is, you must determine the angle between the ground and the path of the ball.

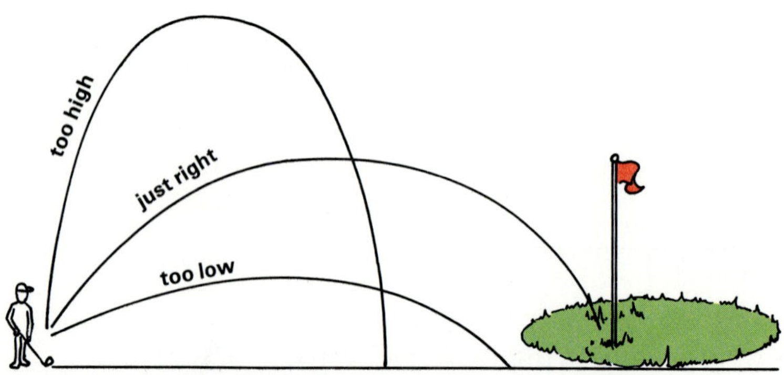

If you hit the ball too high by choosing too large an angle, it will land near you (watch out for straight up!). If you aim too low, it will not reach the green. There must be some angle in between the two that will get the ball to the green, assuming it's not too far away.

Where does trigonometry come into the problem? Well, suppose you hit the ball with speed SPD, measured in meters per second, at an angle ANG with the horizon. Then you can think of the velocity (speed and direction) of the ball as being composed of a horizontal component HRZ and a vertical component VERT, as shown in the diagram at the right. By right-triangle trigonometry,

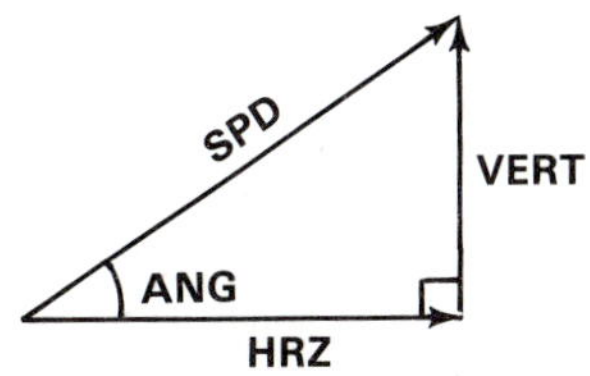

COS(ANG) = HRZ / SPD, or HRZ = SPD * COS(ANG),

and

SIN(ANG) = VERT / SPD, or VERT = SPD * SIN(ANG).

Now in the first tenth of a second, the ball will travel .1 * HRZ meters to the right toward the green and *about* .1 * VERT units upward. We say "about" because something else happens in that time; VERT decreases by a certain amount (we'll call this amount G) because gravity is pulling the ball downward. (HRZ does not change at all if we neglect air resistance, which we will do to keep things simple.)

As the small intervals of time go by, the ball will continue to move upward and to the right toward the green. After a while, VERT will become equal to zero because G will have been subtracted so many times that the original vertical component of the velocity will be completely canceled out. The ball will continue to travel to the right, but will no longer be climbing.

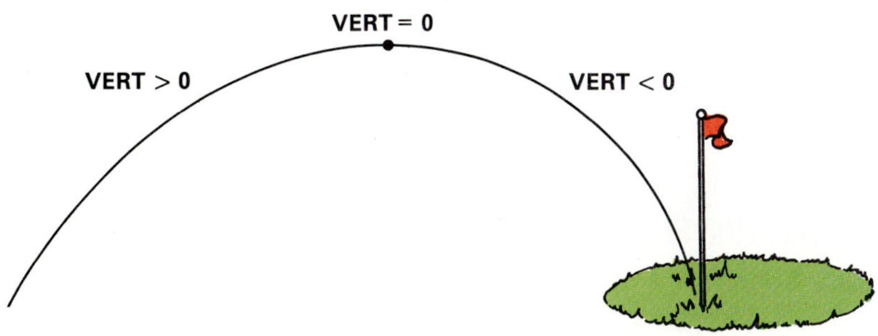

Then, as G continues to be subtracted from VERT, the vertical velocity will become negative and the ball will start coming down, until eventually it reaches the ground again. If the position of the ball when it reaches the ground is on the green, the player wins the game.

Here is the program. You will have to supply the details.

Statement	Remark
10 REM * PITCHING TO THE GREEN	
20 LET G = *(Use trial and error to determine.)*	*G is effect of gravity on VERT.*
30 LET SPD = *(Use trial and error to determine.)*	*SPD is initial speed of the ball.*
40 LET XI = 0	
50 LET YI = *(Fill in vertical coordinate of ball's initial position.)*	
60 GOSUB 1000	*Draw ball and green.*
70 GOSUB 1200	*INPUT angle (lift).*
80 GOSUB 1400	*Draw flight of ball.*
90 GOSUB 1600	*Test whether ball lands on green.*
100 END	
999 REM ** SUBROUTINE TO DRAW BALL AND GREEN **	
1000 *(Instructions to clear screen*	
1010 *and do graphics (in color)*	
1020 *on your computer.)*	
.	
.	
.	
1050 *(Instruction(s) to draw a short horizontal*	
1060 *line segment (the target) on the right at the bottom of screen.)*	
.	
.	
.	
1100 *(Instruction to plot the point (the ball) at XI, YI.)*	
1110 RETURN	
1199 REM ** SUBROUTINE TO INPUT ANGLE **	
1200 *(Instruction to move cursor to an appropriate place for PRINTing.)*	
1210 INPUT "TYPE ANGLE OF SHOT (IN DEGREES BETWEEN 0 AND 90): "; ANG	
1230 LET RAD = ANG * 3.14159265 / 180	*Convert to radians.*
1240 LET HRZ = SPD * COS(RAD)	*HRZ is horizontal velocity.*
1250 LET VERT = SPD * SIN(RAD)	*VERT is vertical velocity.*
1260 RETURN	

Statement	Remark
1399 REM ** SUB. TO DRAW FLIGHT OF BALL **	
1400 LET X = XI + .1 * HRZ	*Move .1 * HRZ units to the right.*
1410 LET Y = YI − .1 * VERT	*Move .1 * VERT units up. (VERT is subtracted because Y increases from top to bottom of screen.)*
1420 LET VERT = VERT − G	*Subtract effect of gravity.*
1430 IF YI >= 0 THEN *(Instruction to erase point at XI, YI.)*	*Erase point if it's on the screen.*
1440 IF X > *(biggest horiz. coordinate)* AND Y > *(biggest vert. coordinate)* THEN RETURN	*Go back if (X, Y) is off screen.*
1450 IF Y >= 0 THEN *(Instruction to plot the point at X, Y.)*	*Plot (X, Y), the new ball position, if it's on screen.*
1460 LET XI = X	*New point becomes old point for next instant of time.*
1470 LET YI = Y	
1480 *(Instructions for a delay loop, if needed.)*	
1490 GOTO 1400	
1599 REM ** SUB. TO TEST IF BALL IS ON GREEN **	
1600 IF X >= *(left endpoint of green)* AND X <= *(right endpoint of green)* THEN PRINT "YOU HIT IT" : RETURN	
1610 PRINT "MISSED THE GREEN"	
1620 RETURN	

Problems

1. Complete the program for your computer, filling in all lines except for lines 20 and 30. (Use high resolution graphics, if available.)
2. RUN the program several times and use trial and error to determine values of G (line 20), SPD (line 30), and ANG (line 1210) that will get the ball to the green. (*Hint:* Try values of G between 0 and 2, values of SPD between 10 and 100, and values of ANG between 0 and 90.)
3. Using the values of G and SPD you obtained in Problem 2, try to hit the green with two completely different choices of angles (ANG) in line 1210.
4. Change the program so that the player will get more than one chance to hit the green. Have the program keep track of the number of guesses.
5. Modify the program so that the position of the green is chosen randomly.
6. *Challenge:* There are many possible improvements to this game, such as drawing a small circle for the ball and a larger one for the green, as well as many others. See what you can do to make it more interesting.

7-6 User-defined Functions: DEF FN

Besides providing the built-in functions, BASIC has the statement DEF FN that lets you define your own functions. One of the advantages of a *user-defined function* is that once the function is defined it may be used anywhere in the program, in the same way that subroutines or the built-in functions are used. Another advantage is that a user-defined function can easily be changed to another function.

The following DEF FN statement defines a function that sums the square of a number and three times the number:

DEF FNS(X) = X * X + 3 * X

Here, S is the function name, X is the variable (referred to as a "dummy" variable because it is only used to define what the function should do with any number that is substituted for it), and X * X + 3 * X is the BASIC numerical expression that defines the function. As in the f(x) notation you may be familiar with from mathematics, FNS(6) is the result of calculating FNS(X) with X = 6. Thus, for the function defined above,

FNS(6) = 6 * 6 + 3 * 6 = 54
FNS(9) = 9 * 9 + 3 * 9 = 108
and FNS(A) = A * A + 3 * A = 10, if A = 2.

The DEF FN statement has the following form:

DEF FN*function name* (variable) = *any BASIC numerical expression*

The *function name* following DEF FN (short for DEFine FuNction) may be any legal numeric variable (such as G, F, PR, G2, and so forth). The "dummy" variable in the parentheses following the function name may also be any legal (usually different) numeric variable. Usually this variable occurs in the numerical expression on the other side of the equals sign as well.

The DEF FN statement may appear at various places in a program, but a function must be defined by DEF FN *before* it is used in the program. The following program calculates several more values of the function

FNS(X) = X * X + 3 * X.

Program 1

Statement	Remark
10 PRINT "USER-DEFINED FUNCTIONS"	
20 DEF FNS(X) = X * X + 3 * X	*Define function S.*
30 PRINT "X", "FNS(X)"	

```
40 FOR Y = 1 TO 4
50 PRINT Y, FNS(Y)
60 NEXT Y
70 LET Z = INT(15 * RND(1)) + 10
80 PRINT "THE VALUE OF FNS("; Z ;") IS:  "; FNS(Z)
90 END
```

Function S is calculated with the current value of Y substituted for X.

Z is a random number from 10 to 24. [On TRS-80 computers, use RND(0).]

Output

```
USER-DEFINED FUNCTIONS
X              FNS(X)
1              4
2              10
3              18
4              28
THE VALUE OF FNS(16) IS:  304
```

If the DEF FN statement were not used, the BASIC numerical expression in line 20 would have to be typed twice (in lines 50 and 80). Notice that this program can be easily modified to calculate values of other functions by simply changing the DEF FN statement.

The DEF FN statement in Program 1 could have been replaced by a subroutine, as in this version:

Program 2

Statement

```
10 PRINT "SUBROUTINE VERSION"
30 PRINT "X", "FNS(X)"
40 FOR Y = 1 TO 4
50 GOSUB 200 : REM * CALCULATE S FROM Y
55 PRINT Y, S
60 NEXT Y
70 LET Y = INT(15 * RND(1)) + 10
75 GOSUB 200
80 PRINT "THE VALUE OF FNS("; Y; ") IS:  "; S
90 END
190 REM ** SUBROUTINE TO CALCULATE S **
200 LET S = Y * Y + 3 * Y
210 RETURN
```

You can see from Program 2 the advantage of using DEF FN rather than a subroutine; a shorter, more readable program can result. Of course, DEF FN cannot be used in place of most subroutines — only those that compute a single value in a single line.

Here are some more examples of user-defined functions:

DEF FNA(R) = 3.14159 * R ↑ 2	Calculates approximate area of circle with radius R. ($\pi \approx 3.14159$)
DEF FNB(Y) = INT(10 * Y + .5) / 10	Rounds the value of Y to the nearest tenth.
DEF FNP(A) = INT(A * RND(1)) + 1	Calculates a random integer from 1 to A (if A is an integer greater than 1).

The next program simulates the rolling of two standard 6-sided dice. The function D in line 20 chooses a random integer between 1 and N (N = 6 in line 50). This random integer corresponds to rolling one of the numbers on the face of a die.

Program 3

Statement

```
10 PRINT "DICE ROLL"
20 DEF FND(N) = INT(N * RND(1)) + 1
30 INPUT "HOW MANY ROLLS:  "; K
40 FOR I = 1 TO K
50 LET SUM = FND(6) + FND(6) : REM * SUM THE 2 FACES ROLLED
60 PRINT "ROLL  "; I; "  IS:  "; SUM
70 NEXT I
80 END
```

Output

```
DICE ROLL
HOW MANY ROLLS:  ?4
ROLL 1 IS:  5
ROLL 2 IS:  7
ROLL 3 IS:  11
ROLL 4 IS:  6
```

Can you explain why, in line 50, the two numbers that are added together are not necessarily equal?

Functions of Two Variables

On some computers (including *IBM* and *TRS-80,* but *not Apple*), the DEF FN statement may have more than one variable in the parentheses following the function name. (See your computer's manual for the exact number allowed.) For example, the statement

DEF FNA(L, W) = L * W

defines a function that could be used to calculate the area of a rectangle of length L and width W. If L is 5 units and W is 12 units, then

FNA(5, 12) = 5 * 12 = 60.

Here are some other examples of user-defined functions of more than one variable:

```
DEF FNP(X, Y) = SQR(X ↑ 2 + Y ↑ 2)
DEF FNB(L, W) = 2 * (L + W)
DEF FNA(H, B1, B2) = H / 2 * (B1 + B2)
```

Do you know the purpose of any of these functions?

Avoiding Pitfalls

1. Be sure to locate the DEF FN statement that defines a function so that it is executed before any program statement that uses the function.
2. When calculating the value of a function in a program, be sure the variable you place in the parentheses following the function name is the one you want, or unintended results can occur. For example, in the program

```
10  DEF FNP(X) = X ↑ 2
20  INPUT Y
30  PRINT FNP(X)
40  END
```

the output will always be 0, no matter what value of Y is INPUT, since X is automatically assigned the value 0 when the program is RUN and FNP(0) = 0. The programmer probably intended line 30 to read: 30 PRINT FNP(Y).

Summary

The DEF FN statement may be used to define your own function. In the statement DEF FNG(X) = X ↑ 3 − 5 * X + 1 the function name is G, X is the variable, and X ↑ 3 − 5 * X + 1 is the BASIC numerical expression that defines the function.

Exercises 7-6

A **1.** Find the error in each of the following programs. Give a possible correction.

a.
```
10 DEF FN(X)=X ↑ 2
20 LET Y=3
30 PRINT FN(Y)
40 END
```

b.
```
10 INPUT Q
20 PRINT FND(Q)
30 DEF FND(Q)=Q * 5
40 END
```

c.
```
10 FNS(Y)=Y * 2+3
20 LET Z=-1
30 PRINT FNS(Z)
40 END
```

d.
```
10 DEF FN1(X)=X ↑ 3+1
20 INPUT P
30 PRINT FN1(P)
40 END
```

2. Predict the output of the following program for each of the INPUTs shown below.

```
10 REM * FUNCTION PROGRAM
20 DEF FNP(X)=X ↑ 2+2 * X-3
30 INPUT Y
40 PRINT FNP(Y)
50 END
```

a. Y=1 **b.** Y=-2 **c.** Y=3 **d.** Y=0

3. Predict the output of each of the following programs.

a.
```
10 PRINT "POINTS ON A LINE"
20 DEF FNS(J)=2 * J-3
25 PRINT"K", "FNS(K)"
30 FOR K=1 TO 5
40 PRINT K, FNS(K)
50 NEXT K
60 END
```

b.
```
10 PRINT "POINTS ON A SEMICIRCLE"
20 DEF FNS(Z)=SQR(9-Z * Z)
30 PRINT "Z", "FNS(Z)"
40 FOR Y=-3 TO 3
50 PRINT Y, FNS(Y)
60 NEXT Y
70 END
```

4. Translate each of the following expressions into a DEF FN statement defining a function.

a. y^2+4y **b.** $|3x-2|$
c. $\sqrt{16-z^2}$ **d.** y^3-y^2-y+1

5. Write a DEF FN statement defining a function that will do each of the following.
a. Round a number to the nearest integer.
b. Find the square root of the absolute value of a number.
c. Produce a random integer between 70 and 90.

6. Functions may be defined in terms of one another, as in this portion of a program:

```
90  DEF FNA(X)  = SQR(X)
100  DEF FNB(X) = X * X - 2
110  DEF FNC(X) = FNA(X) - 3 * FNB(X)
120  DEF FND(X) = FNB(FNA(X + 2))
```

For example: FND(—1) = FNB(FNA(—1 + 2)) = FNB(FNA(1)) = FNB(1) = —1

Find the output of each of the following program lines:

a. 150 PRINT FND(7)
b. 160 PRINT FND(—2)
c. 170 PRINT FNC(4)
d. 180 PRINT FND(FNC(1))

7. A function definition may contain variables other than the "dummy" variable named on the left side of the equals sign. Their current values are used to evaluate the function. For example, in the following portion of a program

```
70  DEF FNCRAZY(PLUS) = A * PLUS - ABS(PLUS)
80  LET A = 3
90  PRINT FNCRAZY(4)
```

the output of line 90 will be FNCRAZY(4) = 3 * 4 – ABS(4) = 8, since A has the current value 3 and PLUS the value 4.

Find the output of the following lines from the same program:

```
100  PRINT FNCRAZY(-2)
110  LET A = FNCRAZY(1)
120  PRINT FNCRAZY(1)
```

8. (For *IBM* and *TRS-80* computer users.) Suppose that a function MAX is defined by this statement:

DEF FNMAX(X, Y) = (X + Y + SGN(X — Y) * (X — Y)) / 2

For example, FNMAX(1, 6) = (1 + 6 + SGN(1 — 6) * (1 — 6)) / 2
= (7 + (—1) * (—5)) / 2
= 12 / 2
= 6

Find the output of each of the following commands.

a. PRINT FNMAX(4, 3)
b. PRINT FNMAX(–1, 5)
c. PRINT FNMAX(5, –1)
d. PRINT FNMAX(2, –9.3)
e. Explain what the function MAX does.
f. Define a function MIN of two variables X and Y that has as its value the minimum of X and Y.

9. Define a function RTEN of a single variable BOTT that produces a random integer between BOTT and BOTT + 10.

B 10. (For *IBM* and *TRS-80* users.) Write a program to INPUT four values A, B, C, and D, then PRINT the larger of INT(A + B) and INT(C + D). Use a DEF FN statement to define a function G(X, Y) = INT(X + Y).

11. Write a program that offers the option of converting an INPUT number from degrees Fahrenheit F to degrees Celsius C, or vice versa. Use DEF FN statements to define functions for the conversion formulas

$$F = \frac{9}{5}C + 32 \qquad \text{and} \qquad C = \frac{5}{9}(F - 32).$$

12. Write a program to PRINT values of the function F(X) = ABS(X − 5), for values of X between −5 and 5. Have the output look like this:

```
X    F(X)
-5   10
-4   9
-3   8
 .    .
 .    .
 .    .
```

Lab Activity

Boolean Values and Complex Function Definitions

Problems

1. Type PRINT 5 > 2 as an immediate mode command. On an *Apple* computer, you should get output 1, and on a *TRS-80* or *IBM* you should get −1.

2. Type PRINT 5 < 2 as an immediate mode command. This should produce 0 as output on any of these machines.

The results from the commands in Problems 1 and 2 are called *Boolean* values, named after George Boole, a nineteenth-century logician. When the computer encounters a condition like 5 > 2 in a statement, it determines whether the condition is true or false. To "remember" the result of the evaluation, it assigns a numerical value (a Boolean value, to be precise) to the expression and stores it in memory. As you saw in Problem 1, *Apple* computers encode *true* by 1, and *TRS-80* and *IBM* computers encode *true* by −1. All three machines assign 0 to signify *false*.

3. Predict the output of each of the following commands. Verify your predictions on the computer.

   a. PRINT 5 = 6 b. PRINT 3 < 7.6

   c. PRINT ABS(3 < 7.6) d. PRINT (3 > 5) OR (7 <= 9)

   In executing PRINT ABS(X < Y), all three machines output 1 if X < Y is true, and 0 if it is false. We will use this principle later.

Boolean values allow you to give neatly-expressed definitions of rather complicated functions. For example, suppose that a worker makes $7 per hour for the first 40 hours worked each week, and $10 for each hour after that. If you needed a function that expresses the worker's hourly rate for any specific hour, say T, you would want something like this:

$$\text{RTE(T)} = \begin{cases} 7, \text{ if } T <= 40 \\ 10, \text{ if } T > 40 \end{cases}$$

For example, RTE(5) = 7 since T = 5 is less than or equal to 40. Therefore, the rate for the fifth hour is $7.

The function RTE could be defined in a subroutine using IF . . . THEN, but then the advantages of DEF FN would be lost. Here is a way to define it using DEF FN and Boolean values:

DEF FN RTE(T) = ABS(T <= 40) * 7 + ABS(T > 40) * 10

The reason this function works is that if T <= 40 is true, then

ABS(T <= 40) = 1 and ABS(T > 40) = 0,

so that RTE(T) = 1 * 7 + 0 * 10 = 7.

If T > 40 is true, then

ABS(T <= 40) = 0 and ABS(T > 40) = 1,

so that RTE(T) = 0 * 7 + 1 * 10 = 10.

4. Write a program using the definition of RTE above that INPUTs values for T and then PRINTs the value of RTE(T). Test the program.

5. Change the program in Problem 4 so that it defines and tests this function:

$$G(X) = \begin{cases} 2 * X + 1, \text{ if } X < 4 \\ 4 * X + 8, \text{ if } X >= 4 \end{cases}$$

6. Suppose that our worker is paid $7 for each of the first 30 hours worked, then $9 for each of the next 12 hours, and then $12 for each hour after that. Define and test a new RTE function for these rates.

7. Write a program using a function that will find the *total* pay (say, PAY(T)) for the worker in Problem 6, where T is the total number of hours worked in a week. For example, if T = 38, then the worker earns

   30 * 7 + 8 * 9 = 210 + 72 = 282 dollars.

Chapter Summary

The BASIC language has several built-in numeric functions:

INT(X) rounds a decimal number *down* to the nearest integer. For example,

$$\text{INT}(4.6) = 4 \qquad \text{INT}(3) = 3 \qquad \text{INT}(-1.6) = -2$$

INT(X + .5) rounds X to the *nearest* integer.

INT(X * 10 ↑ D + .5) / 10 ↑ D rounds X to D decimal places.

ABS(X) calculates the *absolute value* of a number X, where

$$\text{ABS}(X) = \begin{cases} X \text{ if } X >= 0 \\ -X \text{ if } X < 0 \end{cases}$$

SQR(X) calculates the nonnegative *square root* of a nonnegative number.

SGN(X) gives the *sign* (+, −, or 0) of the number X, where

$$\text{SGN}(X) = \begin{cases} 0 \text{ if } X = 0 \\ 1 \text{ if } X > 0 \\ -1 \text{ if } X < 0 \end{cases}$$

RND(1) [*Apple* and *IBM*] or RND(0) [*TRS-80*] will produce a random decimal between 0 and .999999999, inclusive.

INT(N * RND(1)) + 1 produces a random number between 1 and N, inclusive.

INT ((B + 1) * RND(1)) + A produces a random number between A and A + B, inclusive.

If the condition N / D = INT(N / D) is true for integers N and D, then D is a *divisor* or *factor* of N.

If N and D are positive integers, then the integer quotient is Q = INT(N / D) and the remainder is R = N − D * Q.

SIN(X), COS(X), and TAN(X) will calculate the values of the *sine*, *cosine*, and *tangent* of angle X (respectively), where X is measured in radians.

EXP(X) is used to find values of the *exponential function* e^x, where *e* is approximately equal to 2.71828.

LOG(X) will calculate the *natural logarithm* of X. X must be a positive number.

The DEF FN statement may be used to define your own function.

Chapter Test

1. Predict the output of each of the following commands:

   a. PRINT INT(3.62)
   b. PRINT INT(—5.8)
   c. PRINT INT(2.6 + .5)
   d. PRINT INT(—1.4 + .5)
   e. PRINT INT(8.3 * 10 + .5) / 10
   f. PRINT ABS(4)
   g. PRINT SGN(0)
   h. PRINT SQR(121)
   i. PRINT ABS(SGN(—4))
   j. PRINT SQR(ABS(—9))

2. Write a BASIC statement that will produce the following:

   a. A random integer between 0 and 8, inclusive.
   b. A random integer between 3 and 15, inclusive.

3. Write a DEF FN statement defining a function to do each of the following:

   a. Subtract 2 from the square of a number.
   b. Round a number to 3 decimal places.

4. For parents' night at your school, you have been recruited to set up some tables and chairs. Six people will sit around each table. Write a program that INPUTs the number of people that will attend, then PRINTs the exact number of tables needed and also how many people will be seated at the last table.

5. Write a program that simulates tossing two coins 100 times. Have the program PRINT the number of times two heads occur, the number of times two tails occur, and the number of times a head and a tail (not necessarily in that order) occur.

6. Write a program that determines if an INPUT positive integer N is a prime number.

7. Write a program that generates 20 random integers, each between 50 and 150, inclusive. Have the program PRINT the number of random integers produced that are divisible by 5.

8. (Optional) A ramp from the ground to the back of a truck is 10.5 ft long. The ramp makes an angle of 26° with the ground. Write a program using trigonometry to calculate and PRINT the height of the floor of the truck above the ground.

Computer Applications

Computer-Aided Design

Electronic Drafting

Computer graphics may be the biggest boon to architects and interior designers since the invention of the drafting pencil. Imagine taking a tour of a new house or business structure while it is still being designed! All you need to do is visit a construction firm and talk with an architect who designs aided by a computer. You can tell the architect details that you have in mind for the building, then in a short time see the architect's design displayed on a computer screen, somewhat like a sketch. This sketch, however, can be viewed in two or three dimensions and has mobile parts. You can look at the design from several angles and zoom in for a closeup of any room. At the press of a button, changes can be made in the building's walls, doors, windows, and even furnishings! In addition, you can quickly check alternatives such as how each room would look if the ceilings were made higher, if the windows were made larger or smaller or were spaced differently, or if more doors were included.

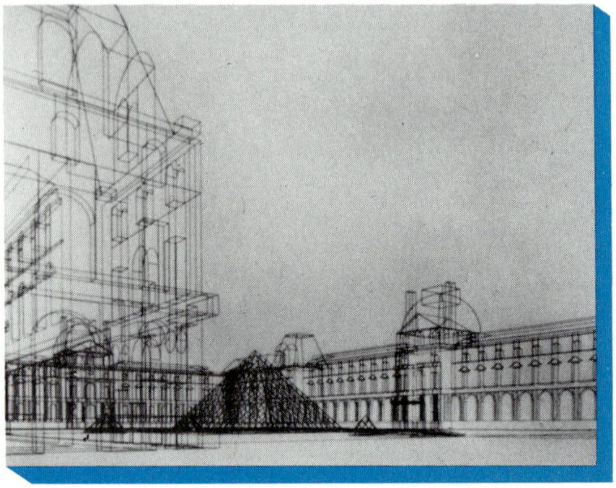

CAD image of the structure of the Louvre in Paris, France

CAD image of all-terrain vehicle

The CAD System

The secret to this electronic drafting is a computer system referred to as CAD (which stands for *Computer-Aided Design*). With CAD, an architect "draws" by pointing a stylus at the computer screen at the location where a line, a circle, or a predesigned unit (such as a door or window) already stored in the computer's memory is to be drawn. By moving the stylus, the architect can move these shapes anywhere in the design. At the touch of a button, the design can be viewed from different angles, or printed out on paper using a device called a *plotter*.

A CAD system can make it easier for architects to coordinate the work of engineers, contractors, and other specialists. The computer can help lay out a building's plumbing and electrical systems, screen out weaknesses in the structural plans, determine heat gain and loss, analyze active and passive solar design possibilities, and determine insulation requirements.

With a CAD system, architects are able to design buildings many times faster than is possible drawing by hand. Time can also be saved by having the computer print copies of construction specifications (type and size of lumber, and so on) and also "blueprints" to be used during the actual construction phase. The computer has enabled many architects to reduce their design fee and increase their profit margins at the same time. As a result, projects that once were considered too small and time-consuming by many architectural firms can now be designed economically with the use of a CAD system.

CAD image of a contour map

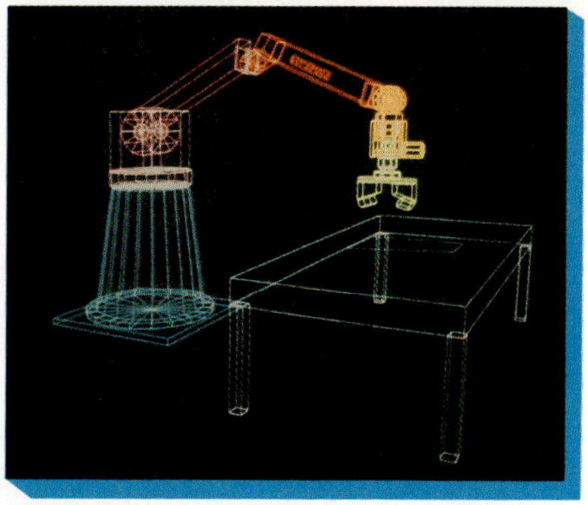

CAD image of a robot arm

Applications of CAD

CAD is also moving architectural firms into entirely new businesses. CAD can be used to build complex three-dimensional contour maps that show the best locations for roadways, buildings, and factories. CAD can also be used to construct drawings of oil fields based on geological data that has been input into the computer. CAD can even be used to simulate the impact of hurricanes and snowstorms on buildings, and to determine the exact wind force that will cause a building to collapse.

CAD systems are used in a number of fields in addition to architecture. For example, design engineers commonly use CAD in the automotive and aircraft industries.

Critics of the use of CAD systems are concerned that architects' creativity will be hampered. But advocates of CAD respond that design engineers do not abandon their talent to the computer; instead, they use the computer as a tool. This tool allows designers to sketch in a very different medium, one that is quick and versatile.

Computer Languages

COBOL

In 1959, a group of people interested in developing a high-level computer language that could process data for businesses met in Washington, D.C. The group, composed of people from business, education, government, and the computer industry, wanted a language that would be close to the standard English vocabulary normally used within the business environment, and that would also be independent of any specific computer system. As a result of this meeting, COBOL (short for COmmon Business-Oriented Language) was developed in the early 1960's.

Business applications programs are written in COBOL.

Prior to this time, most computer languages had been developed for, and by, mathematicians and scientists. COBOL was the first high-level computer language suitable for handling large amounts of data related to payroll, credit and debit accounts, inventory, and a variety of other business applications.

Even though COBOL was originally developed before there was an emphasis on structured programming, the techniques of structured programming can easily be applied to it. A typical COBOL program is made up of four different parts or sections, called *divisions.*

1. The *Identification Division* is used to identify the program's name, the author, the date, and a variety of other business details. This division contains the type of *documentation* that might be found in the initial REM or PRINT statements of a BASIC program.
2. The *Environment Division* is used to identify the equipment needed for both the input and output of data.
3. The *Data Division* is used by the programmer to name and define the variables, files, and records that will be used in the program.
4. The *Procedure Division* is used to specify the steps (the *algorithm*) that the computer must follow to obtain the desired results.

On the next page, you can study the procedure division of a COBOL program that asks the user to type 10 numbers and then finds the largest of them.

```
PROCEDURE DIVISION.
000-MAIN-SECTION.
    DISPLAY "ENTER TEN NUMBERS" UPON CONSOLE.
    MOVE 1 TO COUNTER.
    PERFORM 010-GET-ENTRY UNTIL COUNTER > 10.
    MOVE GREATEST-VAL TO DISPLAY-ANSWER.
    DISPLAY "GREATEST NUMBER ENTERED WAS " DISPLAY-ANSWER.
    STOP RUN.
010-GET-ENTRY.
    DISPLAY "TYPE NUMBER " UPON CONSOLE.
    ACCEPT ENTERED-VAL FROM CONSOLE.
    IF ENTERED-VAL > GREATEST-VAL
      MOVE ENTERED-VAL TO GREATEST-VAL
    ELSE
      NEXT SENTENCE.
    ADD 1 TO COUNTER.
```

COBOL programs usually are very long due to the English phrases that are used and the descriptive detail of the format, but the COBOL system is an asset for the maintenance of a program. It is much easier to fix bugs, alter routines, or change data when a program is written in an outline style using common business phrases.

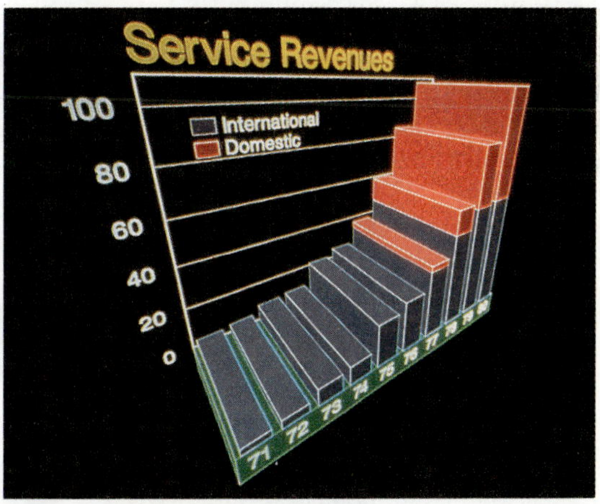

Computer-generated business chart

COBOL is an easy-to-learn language studied by many college students majoring in business. COBOL's handling of records and files gives most students better insight into problems related to data processing than they might otherwise obtain from studying other languages. One disadvantage of COBOL is that at the present time its availability for microcomputers is limited. Of course, students also are sometimes dismayed by the amount of typing required for even a simple COBOL program.

CHAPTER 8 String Functions

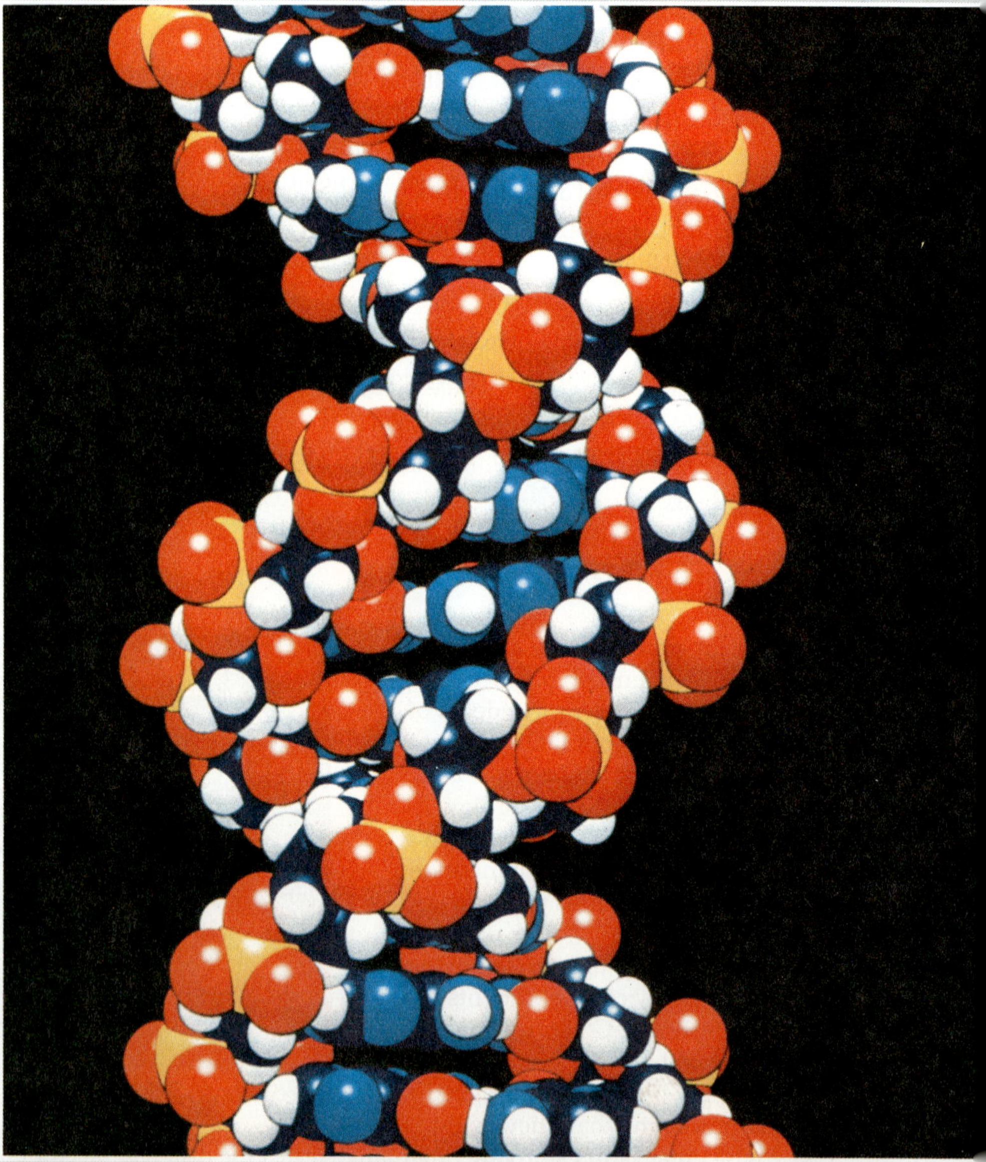

This is a computer model of a 20-base pairs B DNA molecule. Nitrogen atoms are light blue, hydrogen are white, oxygen are red, phosphorus are yellow, and carbon are dark blue.

Introduction

The last chapter showed you how to manipulate numbers using the built-in functions of BASIC, or by defining your own functions. Many computer applications today involve manipulations of ordinary language — of strings. BASIC has several built-in functions to take strings apart, change the parts, then put them back together, as you will see in this chapter.

8-1 Taking Strings Apart: LEN, LEFT$, and RIGHT$

LEN

The first requirement in manipulating a string is to know how many characters it contains; the BASIC built-in function LEN accomplishes this, as Program 1 illustrates.

Program 1

Statement

```
10 PRINT "DEMONSTRATION OF LEN FUNCTION"
15 PRINT
20 FOR I = 1 TO 3
30 READ A$
40 PRINT A$, LEN(A$)
50 NEXT I
60 PRINT "GOODBYE", LEN("GOOD RIDDANCE")
70 DATA BLEATING, LIKE A, SHEEP
80 END
```

Output

```
DEMONSTRATION OF LEN FUNCTION

BLEATING      8
LIKE A        6
SHEEP         5
GOODBYE       13
```

As you can see, the value of LEN(A$) is an integer — the number of characters in the string A$, including spaces. Note that the LEN function works with string variables [as in LEN(A$)] and also with strings inside quotes [such as LEN("GOOD RIDDANCE")].

LEFT$ and RIGHT$

There are two built-in functions that alter a string by extracting a portion from the beginning or end of it. LEFT$(A$, N) is the string you get from A$ by taking the first (leftmost) N characters. For example:

LEFT$("GOODBYE", 3) is the string GOO.

IF B$ = "FORGET IT", then LEFT$(B$, 5) is the string FORGE.

LEFT$("BE", 3) is the string BE (since there are not 3 characters available, the entire string is taken).

Naturally, there is a function RIGHT$(A$, N), which represents the string you get from A$ by taking the last (rightmost) N characters. For example:

RIGHT$("GOODBYE", 3) is the string BYE.

IF B$ = "FORGET IT", then RIGHT$(B$, 5) is the string ET IT.

RIGHT$("BE", 4) is the string BE (since there are not 4 characters available, the entire string is taken).

LEFT$, RIGHT$, and LEN may be used in LET statements. Since LEN(A$) represents a number, it may be assigned to a numeric variable. For example, if A$ is the string FAREWELL, then the statement

```
20  LET L = LEN(A$)
```

assigns the number 8 to L. On the other hand, LEFT$ and RIGHT$ represent strings, so that if they are to be assigned to a variable, then it must be a string variable. For example, if A$ still has the value FAREWELL, the statements

```
110  LET FRST$ = LEFT$(A$, 4)
120  LET LST$ = RIGHT$(A$, 4)
```

assign the strings FARE and WELL to FRST$ and LST$, respectively. Here is a program that uses the functions LEN and LEFT$ to PRINT a string in an unusual format.

Program 2

Statement

```
10  PRINT "TRIANGULAR PRINTING"
20  LET A$ = "TRIANGLE"
30  FOR I = 1 TO LEN(A$)
40  PRINT LEFT$(A$, I)
50  NEXT I
60  END
```

Output

```
TRIANGULAR PRINTING
T
TR
TRI
TRIA
TRIAN
TRIANG
TRIANGL
TRIANGLE
```

Study the loop to see how the program works: if I is 1, then LEFT$(A$, 1) is the string T, which is PRINTed in line 40. When I = 2, the first two letters, TR, are PRINTed in line 40, and so forth. Finally, when I = LEN(A$), all eight of the letters of A$ are PRINTed.

Avoiding Pitfalls

1. Remember that LEN has no $ after it, since it yields a number; the results of LEFT$ and RIGHT$ are strings, however, so that a $ is required.
2. The LEN function can be used only to find the lengths of strings, not of numbers. A statement such as 50 LET B = LEN(X) is not legal and will result in an error message such as TYPE MISMATCH.
3. Be sure when you use expressions of the form LEFT$(A$, N) and RIGHT$(A$, N) that the string A$ comes first and the integer N comes second.
4. Remember that the functions LEN, LEFT$, and RIGHT$ always count spaces in strings. For example, the value of LEN("NO NO") is 5 and LEFT$("NO NO", 4) gives the string NO N.

Summary

LEN(A$) is the number of characters in the string A$.

LEFT$(A$, N) is the string consisting of the leftmost N characters of A$. If N >= LEN(A$), then LEFT$(A$, N) = A$.

RIGHT$(A$, N) is the string consisting of the rightmost N characters of A$. If N >= LEN(A$), then RIGHT$(A$, N) = A$.

Exercises 8-1

A **1.** Why is a \$ included at the end of the functions LEFT\$ and RIGHT\$, but not after the LEN function?

2. Give the output of each of the following instructions.

a. PRINT LEN("CHICKEN")

b. PRINT LEN("CHICKEN SOUP")

c. PRINT LEN ("***")

d. PRINT LEN (" ")

3. Find the errors, if any, in each of the following instructions. Give a possible correction.

a. PRINT LEN(B\$)

b. PRINT LEFT\$("WALRUSES", 6)

c. PRINT LEN(RIGHT(44.68, 9))

d. PRINT LEFT\$(LENTILS, 4)

e. LET A = RIGHT\$(A\$, 4)

f. LET LEN(A\$) = P

g. PRINT LEFT\$("MYSOUP", 5)

h. LET B\$ = LEN("SEA LIONS")

4. Give the output of each instruction if A\$ = "ABBRA", B\$ = "SESAME", and N = 3.

a. PRINT LEN(A\$)

b. PRINT LEFT\$(A\$, N)

c. PRINT RIGHT\$(B\$, N)

d. PRINT LEFT\$(B\$, N + 2)

e. PRINT RIGHT\$(A\$, 16)

f. PRINT RIGHT\$(B\$, LEN(B\$) − 1)

g. PRINT LEFT\$(A\$, LEN(A\$) − 2)

h. PRINT LEN(LEFT\$(B\$, 8))

i. PRINT LEFT\$(RIGHT\$(A\$, 4), 2)
(*Hint:* First evaluate RIGHT\$(A\$, 4).)

j. PRINT RIGHT\$(LEFT\$(B\$, 3), 1)

5. a. Repeat Exercise 4 with A\$ = "FLOWERS", B\$ = "DANDELION", and N = 5.

b. Repeat Exercise 4 with A\$ = "SOAP SUDS", B\$ = "LAUNDRY", and N = 4.

6. Change Program 2 so that its output is as follows:

a.
```
TRIANGULAR PRINTING
TRIANGLE
TRIANGL
TRIANG
TRIAN
TRIA
TRI
TR
T
```

b.
```
TRIANGULAR PRINTING
TRIANGLE

TRIANG

TRIA

TR
```
(*Hint:* Use STEP.)

7. Change Program 2 so that its output is as follows:

a.
```
TRIANGULAR PRINTING
E
LE
GLE
NGLE
ANGLE
IANGLE
RIANGLE
TRIANGLE
```

b.
```
TRIANGULAR PRINTING
       E
      LE
     GLE
    NGLE
   ANGLE
  IANGLE
 RIANGLE
TRIANGLE
```
(*Hint:* Use TAB.)

B 8. Write a program that INPUTs a person's first and last names into separate variables, then PRINTs the person's first and last initials with a friendly message.

9. Write a program that INPUTs a person's first and last names into a single variable (say A$). If the number of characters (including spaces) in A$ is greater than 20, have the program PRINT the message

```
LIMIT YOUR NAME TO 20 CHARACTERS, PLEASE
```

and have the user try again; otherwise, PRINT the person's name centered on the screen.

10. Write a program that INPUTs four strings, then PRINTs them in a column *right-justified* on the screen (that is, with the last character of each string aligned along the last column on the screen).

11. Write a program that READs a list of words from a DATA list, then counts and PRINTs how many of the words start with the letter C.

12. **a.** Write a program that INPUTs a string, then PRINTs a message telling whether the string ends with the letter S.
    b. Modify the program in (a) so that it also PRINTs a message telling whether the string ends with the letters ING.

13. **a.** Show by giving examples that LEFT$(A$, LEN(A$) − 1) is the string you get from A$ by deleting the last (rightmost) letter.
    b. Write a program that READs strings from a DATA list, then PRINTs them out with their last letter deleted. Will your program work with strings having only one letter?
    c. Change the program so that it deletes the first (leftmost) two letters of each string it READs.
    d. Change the original program so that it deletes the first and last letters of each string READ.

14. Write a program that INPUTs a word, then PRINTs the first and last letters of the word in their appropriate positions, but replaces the rest of the letters with *'s. For example, if the INPUT word is WORLD, then the output should be W * * * D.

15. Write a program that INPUTs a string, then deletes all *'s at the right end of the string and PRINTs the result. For example, if the INPUT string is A * B * *, then the output should be A * B.

Lab Activity

The Null String and Invisible Characters

(for use with *Apple* computers)

Most programmers have had the following very perplexing thing happen to them at least once; they type a line in a program that appears to be absolutely correct, only to get a SYNTAX ERROR message when the program is RUN. Usually, if they retype the line, the program works perfectly. The reason is this: a character that is invisible on the screen has been typed by mistake. In this activity, you will type some invisible characters into strings on purpose.

Problems

1. Use the following program to show that there is an empty string containing no characters at all (called, as you probably know, the *null string*):

```
10 INPUT "TYPE A STRING:  "; S$
20 PRINT S$, LEN(S$)
30 PRINT
40 END
```

   RUN the program and just press the <RETURN> key when you are prompted to type a string. The resulting string S$ has no characters, and its length is 0, as you can see in the output.

2. RUN the program again, and type "" (with no space between the quotation marks). Again, S$ is the null string. (In fact, this suggests how you can assign the null string to a string variable: LET A$ = "".)

3. RUN the program again; when you are prompted to type a string, press and hold the CONTROL key <CTRL> and at the same time type A. Where S$ should be PRINTed on the screen, you will see nothing (the character <CTRL> A is invisible). Nevertheless, S$ has length 1; it contains a character, although the character does not show on the screen.

4. RUN the program again, typing < CTRL > G several times before you press the < RETURN > key. What happens? Is LEN(S$) equal to the number of times you typed < CTRL > G?

5. The < CTRL > key does not affect all of the keys on the keyboard. The "7" key, for example, appears the same on the screen with or without < CTRL > being pressed, and has length 1. Use the program to verify this fact.

6. Experiment with the program (you may want to add the instruction 35 GOTO 10) to determine which keys the < CTRL > key affects. Make as complete a list as you can of the characters on your computer keyboard that are invisible on the screen.

7. RUN the program and type in an ordinary word with some invisible characters contained in it. Does the LEN function count the invisible characters?

8. Write a short program that will determine whether a word with invisible characters contained in it is considered by the computer to be equal to the same word with the invisible characters deleted. For example, is it true that APE = A< CTRL >BPE?

9. Write a program (see the Lab Activity for Section 4–3, page 153) to determine where in the "alphabetical" ordering of keyboard characters the invisible characters fall. For example, is it true that < CTRL > A is less than (<) the letter A?

8-2 More Dissection of Strings: MID$

In the last section, you learned how to extract the first or last part of a string using LEFT$ or RIGHT$. Another BASIC built-in string function, MID$, allows you to select any part of a string:

> MID$(S$, WHERE, N) gives N characters of the string S$, starting with the character in position WHERE.

Here are some examples:

> MID$("I LEFT MY HEART", 3, 4) is the string LEFT.
> (Starting at the 3rd position, take 4 characters.)
>
> MID$("IN ALBUQUERQUE", 5, 8) is the string LBUQUERQ.
> (Starting at the 5th position, take 8 characters.)
>
> MID$(A$, 4, 1) is the 4th character of the string A$.
>
> MID$("SURPRISING", 9, 4) is the string NG.
> (Starting at the 9th position, there are only 2 characters left.)

The next to last example on the preceding page, MID$(A$, 4, 1), shows how to examine one character of a string at a time. Using this idea, we can write a program to PRINT any INPUT string backwards.

Program 1

Statement	Remark
10 PRINT "BACKWARDS ECHO"	
20 INPUT "TYPE A STRING: "; S$	
30 PRINT	
40 PRINT "HERE IS THE STRING BACKWARDS:"	
50 FOR I = LEN(S$) TO 1 STEP −1	*Start with the last character, go down to the first.*
60 PRINT MID$(S$, I, 1);	*Print the Ith character.*
70 NEXT I	
80 PRINT	
90 END	

Output

```
BACKWARDS ECHO
TYPE A STRING:   ? PLUG

HERE IS THE STRING BACKWARDS:
GULP
```

As a second example of the use of MID$, here is a program that determines whether one string is a *substring* of another string. What a substring is, can best be explained by an example: SUB is a substring of SUBSTRING and also of MY SUBWAY, but not of SIT UP BRIGHTLY.

Program 2

Statement	Remark
10 PRINT "FINDING SUBSTRINGS"	
20 INPUT "BIG STRING: "; ST$	
30 INPUT "POSSIBLE SUBSTRING: "; SUB$	
40 LET LBIG = LEN(ST$)	*LBIG is the length of big string.*
50 LET LSUB = LEN(SUB$)	*LSUB is the length of possible substring.*
60 FOR WHERE = 1 TO LBIG	*Check all possible starting positions.*
70 IF SUB$ = MID$(ST$, WHERE, LSUB) THEN GOTO 200	
80 NEXT WHERE	

```
90  PRINT SUB$;"  IS NOT A SUBSTRING OF  "; ST$
100  GOTO 210
200  PRINT SUB$; "  IS A SUBSTRING OF  "; ST$
210  END
```

Output

```
FINDING SUBSTRINGS
BIG STRING:  ? SLIPPERY
POSSIBLE SUBSTRING:  ? LIP
LIP IS A SUBSTRING OF SLIPPERY
```

The key step in the program is line 70, in which the possible substring SUB$ is compared with the actual substring of ST$ that starts at the WHEREth character and has the same length as SUB$. For example, if ST$ = SLIPPERY and SUB$ = LIP, then the first time through the loop the computer compares LIP to MID$(ST$, 1, 3) = SLI. The second time through the loop the computer compares LIP to MID$(ST$, 2, 3) = LIP, so the condition is true and the computer goes to line 200 and PRINTs the message shown there.

MID$ has another form: The variable N in MID$(S$, WHERE, N) can be left out. Then MID$(S$, WHERE) gives *all* the characters of S$, starting at the WHEREth position. (Do you see the difference between this use of MID$ and the function RIGHT$?) For example:

MID$("SOMETHING", 4) is the string ETHING.

RIGHT$("SOMETHING", 4) is the string HING.

MID$("IT", 2) is the string T.

MID$("IT", 3) is the null string (since IT has only 2 characters).

Avoiding Pitfalls

1. Be sure that you have the correct order inside the parentheses in MID$(S$, WHERE, N). First comes the string, then the starting position, then the number of characters.
2. Remember that if S$ has fewer than N characters remaining when you start at the WHEREth position, then MID$(S$, WHERE, N) is the same as MID$(S$, WHERE). For example,

   MID$("YIPES", 3, 4) = "PES" = MID$("YIPES", 3).

   Similarly, if WHERE > LEN(S$), then MID$(S$, WHERE) is the null string. (See the last example preceding Avoiding Pitfalls.)

Summary

MID$(A$, WHERE, N) is the string obtained by taking N characters of A$ (or as many as A$ has), starting at position WHERE.

MID$(A$, WHERE) is the string obtained by taking all of the rest of the characters of A$, starting at position WHERE.

The *null string* is the string containing no characters at all. It can be assigned to the variable ST$ by this instruction: LET ST$ = "".

Exercises 8-2

A

1. Give the output of each statement if A$ = "LEFT HAND".
   a. PRINT MID$(A$, 3, 4)
   b. PRINT MID$(A$, 4, 1)
   c. PRINT MID$(A$, 6, 6)
   d. PRINT MID$(A$, 4)
   e. PRINT RIGHT$(A$, 4)
   f. PRINT MID$(A$, 1)
   g. PRINT LEN(MID$(A$, 2, 5))
   h. PRINT LEN(MID$(A$, 5, 7))
   i. PRINT LEFT$(MID$(A$, 2, 3), 2)
   j. PRINT MID$(RIGHT$(A$, 6), 3, 2)
2. If B$ = "RIGHT FOOT" in (a) through (h), fill in the blanks with numbers that will produce the substring on the right side of the equals sign.
   a. MID$(B$, ?, ?) = "IGHT"
   b. MID$(B$, ?, ?) = "FOOT"
   c. MID$(B$, ?) = "FOOT"
   d. RIGHT$(B$, ?) = "FOOT"
   e. MID$(B$, ?, ?) = "RIGHT"
   f. LEFT$(B$, ?) = "RIGHT"
   g. MID$(B$, ?, ?) = "H"
   h. MID$(B$, ?, ?) = "F"
3. Explain whether Program 2 will work correctly in each of the following cases.
   a. If SUB$ and ST$ are the same length.
   b. If SUB$ is longer than ST$.

4. Change Program 2 so that if SUB$ is a substring of ST$, then its starting position in ST$ will be PRINTed. For example, the starting position of SUB in MY SUBWAY is 4.

5. Predict the output of the following program for each of these INPUTs:

   a. S$ = "LAUGH" **b.** S$ = "HA HA" **c.** S$ = "FUN TIME"

```
10 PRINT "MYSTERY"
20 INPUT "STRING:  "; S$
30 FOR I = 1 TO LEN(S$)
40 LET L$ = MID$(S$, I, 1)
50 IF L$ <> "  " THEN PRINT L$;
60 NEXT I
70 PRINT
80 END
```

   Can you explain the purpose of the program?

B

6. Write a program that PRINTs every other character of an INPUT string, starting with the first one. For example, if FEATS OF SKILL is INPUT, the output should be FASO   KL.

7. Write a program that INPUTs a string, then counts and PRINTs the number of times the letter T occurs in the string.

8. Write a program to count and PRINT the number of times the substring TH occurs in an INPUT string.

9. Write a program that INPUTs a string, then PRINTs each character of the string five times on a single line. For example, if FETED is INPUT, then the output should be this:

```
FFFFF
EEEEE
TTTTT
EEEEE
DDDDD
```

10. Write a program that INPUTs a string, then PRINTs the string with all the letter E's changed to *'s. For example, if the INPUT string is FEET UP!, then the output should be F * * T UP!.

11. A company's mailing list includes some women's names that accidentally were preceded by the title "MR." rather than "MS.". Write a program to change the title MR. of an INPUT name to MS., then PRINT the result. (For example, if the INPUT name is MR. ROBERTS, then the output should be MS. ROBERTS. Note that you cannot just change every R to S — that would give the incorrect output MS. SOBESTS.)

C **12.** *Challenge:* Write a program that READs a word randomly from a DATA list of 10 words. Have the program PRINT the length of the chosen word and then ask the user to guess the word. If the guess is correct, PRINT the message CONGRATULATIONS; otherwise, have the program compare each letter of the guess to all the letters of the random word, then PRINT any correct letters. Allow the user only five guesses. (See the *hint* in Exercise 11, Section 7-3, page 364, for a method of choosing words randomly from a DATA list.)

13. *Challenge:* Write a program that asks the user to type a long message (not to exceed 255 characters). Have the program PRINT the message on several lines if necessary, breaking the message at the nearest space that occurs before the end of each line.

Lab Activity

PRINTing in Curves

In this activity, you will PRINT messages in formats that are themselves attractive designs. Here is a program that PRINTs a message on a diagonal line, for example.

Statement	Remark
10 REM * PRINTING IN CURVES	
20 READ MESS$	
30 FOR LNE = 1 TO 16	
40 LET WHERE = LNE	*WHERE is the starting position of PRINTed substring.*
50 LET N = 1	*N is the number of characters to be printed.*
60 PRINT TAB(WHERE); MID$(MESS$, WHERE, N)	*PRINT the substring.*
70 NEXT LNE	
80 DATA GOODDAYBONJOURBUENOSDIASBUON GIORNOGUTENTAG	
90 END	

Problems

1. Trace through the program. Then RUN it to see that it works as expected.
2. Change the program so that it PRINTs four letters of the string on each line, as shown at the top of the next page.

```
GOOD
 OODD
  ODDA
   .
   .
   .
```

3. Change the program in Problem 2 so that it PRINTs one letter on the first line, two on the second, three on the third, and so forth.

4. Change all program lines back to their original form, then change line 30 so that the string is PRINTed on the opposite diagonal — the one going from the lower left-hand corner to the upper right-hand corner.

5. To have the string PRINTed on a curve (a *parabola*) change line 30 back to its original form, then type:

```
40  LET WHERE = LNE * (17 - LNE) / 3
```

RUN the program to see the curve.

6. Now change line 50 of the program in Problem 5 to:

```
50  LET N = 39 - WHERE
```

This change should cause the side of the screen to the right of the curve to fill in with substrings of the big string.

7. Change the program in Problem 6 so that the substrings are PRINTed on the side of the screen to the left of the curve, rather than to the right. (*Hint:* Change line 60.)

8. In the program in Problem 7, change lines 50 and 60 to their original form, then type:

```
40  LET WHERE = 10 * SIN(LNE / 3) + 15
```

(If you have never heard of the SIN function, that's okay. RUN the program and describe what it does.) For a better effect, change line 30 to 30 FOR LNE = 1 TO 50 and RUN the program again.

9. RUN the program in Problem 8 several times, changing each of the numbers in the new line 40, one at a time. Describe what happens to the shape for each number you change.

10. To display the string between two SINuous curves, change line 40 back to what it was originally in Problem 8, then change line 30 back to 30 FOR LNE = 1 TO 16, and then type:

```
50  LET N = (8 * SIN(LNE / 2) + 31) - WHERE
```

RUN the program. Experiment by changing the numbers in lines 40 and 50 and describe what happens to the curves.

8-3 Putting Strings Together: Concatenation

Two or more strings may be joined to form a new string by means of the + symbol. A$ + B$ is the string you get by putting the string B$ immediately after the string A$. This process of linking strings is called *concatenation*. Here are some examples:

"MY" + "RA" is the string "MYRA".

"MY" + " " + "RAH" is the string "MY RAH".

"" + A$ is just A$, since the first string is the null string (containing no characters).

The instruction PRINT "DELI" + "CIOUS" will give the result DELICIOUS (the concatenated string is formed, then PRINTed).

The instructions

```
100  LET A$ = "DELI" + "CIOUS"
110  PRINT A$
```

also will give the result DELICIOUS, but the assignment in the LET statement in line 100 will cause the concatenated string to be stored in the variable A$.

As an example of the use of string concatenation, here is a program that INPUTs an adjective and adverb from a user, then checks to see if the roots of the two words are the same (that is, if the adverb was formed from the adjective). The program does the checking by adding "LY" to the end of the adjective, then testing to see if the extended word is the same as the adverb. (Will this algorithm work correctly for all adjectives?)

Program 1

Statement

```
10  PRINT "ADJECTIVE / ADVERB"
15  PRINT
20  INPUT "TYPE THE ADJECTIVE (OR Q TO END):  "; ADJ$
25  IF ADJ$ = "Q" THEN GOTO 80
30  INPUT "TYPE THE ADVERB:  "; AVRB$
40  LET V$ = ADJ$ + "LY": REM * FORM RELATED ADVERB FROM ADJECTIVE
50  IF V$ = AVRB$ THEN PRINT "SAME ROOT": GOTO 15
60  PRINT "SOMETHING'S WRONG"
70  GOTO 15
80  END
```

Output

```
ADJECTIVE / ADVERB

TYPE THE ADJECTIVE (OR Q TO END):   ? SAD
TYPE THE ADVERB:   ? SADLY
SAME ROOT

TYPE THE ADJECTIVE (OR Q TO END):   ? HAPPY
TYPE THE ADVERB:   ? HAPPILY
SOMETHING'S WRONG

TYPE THE ADJECTIVE (OR Q TO END):   ? Q
```

Notice that the program does not correctly handle adjectives ending in "Y" (such as HAPPY). Can you think of other adjective endings for which the program needs modification? (See Exercise 2.)

The next example is another version of the program in the previous section that PRINTed strings backwards (Program 1, page 416). This version stores the backwards string in the variable B$, then PRINTs it.

Program 2

Statement	Remark
10 PRINT "BACKWARDS ECHO, PART 2"	
15 PRINT	
20 INPUT "TYPE A STRING: "; S$	
30 LET B$ = ""	*Start with the null string.*
40 FOR I = 1 TO LEN(S$)	*Do one character at a time.*
50 LET B$ = MID$(S$, I, 1) + B$	*Add Ith letter of S$ to B$.*
60 NEXT I	
70 PRINT "THE BACKWARDS STRING IS: "; B$	
80 END	

Output

```
BACKWARDS ECHO, PART 2

TYPE A STRING:   ? GAB
THE BACKWARDS STRING IS:   BAG
```

The statement in line 50 causes the characters in B$ (BAG) to be in the reverse order from the characters in S$ (GAB). The first time the computer reaches line 50, B$ is assigned the letter G:

B$ = MID$("GAB", 1, 1) + B$ = "G" + "" = "G"

The next time through the FOR . . . NEXT loop, the computer changes B$ to:

B$ = MID$("GAB", 2, 1) + B$ = "A" + "G" = "AG"

Then, the final time through the loop,

B$ = MID$("GAB", 3, 1) + B$ = "B" + "AG" = "BAG".

Avoiding Pitfalls

1. Adding numbers is completely different from concatenating strings, even though the same symbol (+) is used in both cases. Note that 323 + 6 = 329, but "323" + "6" = "3236".
2. An expression such as A$ − B$ is not allowed in BASIC. Use LEFT$, RIGHT$, or MID$ to delete part of a string.
3. Remember the importance of order when concatenating strings; A$ + B$ is not the same as B$ + A$.

Summary

Concatenation is the process of linking strings: A$ + B$ + C$ + . . . is the string obtained by taking, in order, all the characters of A$, followed by all the characters of B$, followed by all the characters of C$, ...

Exercises 8-3

A 1. Predict the result of the following instructions or sets of instructions.

a. PRINT "APRIL" + "SHOWERS"

b. PRINT "APRIL" + " SHOWERS"

c.
```
100  LET A$ = "APRIL" + "  " + "SHOWERS"
110  PRINT A$
```

d.
```
100  LET A$ = LEFT$("APRIL", 1) + RIGHT$("SHOWERS", 2)
110  PRINT A$ + A$
```

e.
```
100  LET A$ = RIGHT$("MAYPOLE", 1) + LEFT$("MAYPOLE", 6)
110  PRINT A$
```

f.
```
100  LET A$ = "DANCE"
110  FOR I = 1 TO 5
120  LET A$ = MID$(A$, 2) + LEFT$(A$, 1)
130  PRINT A$
140  NEXT I
```

g.
```
100 LET A$="AB"
110 FOR I=1 TO 3
120 LET A$=A$+A$
130 PRINT A$
140 NEXT I
```
h. `PRINT 36+12+10`

i. `PRINT "36"+"12"+"10"`

2. As mentioned earlier, Program 1 does not correctly handle many of the adjectives in the English language. Change the program so that it works properly in both of these cases:
   a. For INPUT adjectives ending in Y (for example, the adverb formed from SLEEPY is SLEEPILY).
   b. For INPUT adjectives ending in IC (for example, HEROIC becomes HEROICALLY).

3. Rewrite Program 1 so that it deletes the last two letters of the adverb, then compares the result with the adjective.

4. If line 40 of Program 2 is changed to

   `40 FOR I=LEN(S$) TO 1 STEP −1,`

   then how should the statement in line 50 be changed so that the program will still work correctly?

B 5. Write a program that INPUTs as three separate strings a person's first name, middle name, and last name, then constructs and PRINTs the string consisting of the first letter of each name (that is, PRINTs the person's initials).

6. Write a program that INPUTs a string A$, then deletes all spaces from A$ (assigning the resulting string to, say, B$), then PRINTs the result B$. (*Hint:* Start with B$ = "". As the program checks each character of A$, it should add a character to B$ only if it is not a space.)

7. a. A "palindrome" is a string that looks the same whether it is written forwards or backwards. For example, OTTO is a palindrome, as is ABLE WAS I ERE I SAW ELBA. Write a program that PRINTs whether an INPUT string is a palindrome.
   (*Hint:* Use Program 2 as a guide and write a subroutine that reverses the INPUT string. Then test to see if the INPUT string is the same as its reverse.)
   b. If you ignore spaces and punctuation, then many more strings become palindromes. For example, "MADAM, I'M ADAM" is a palindrome if you leave out the comma, the apostrophe, and the two spaces. Change the program you wrote in (a) so that it PRINTs whether an

INPUT string is this kind of palindrome. (*Hint:* First eliminate all spaces, commas, semicolons, colons, and apostrophes. See Exercise 6.)

8. Write a program that INPUTs a single string consisting of a person's first, middle, and last names, then constructs and PRINTs the string consisting of the person's initials. (*Hint:* In the original string, what precedes both the middle and last names?)

C **9.** Words are translated from English to pig Latin in the following way:
   i. If the word begins with A, E, I, O, or U, then add AY to the end of the word (for example, APPLE becomes APPLEAY).
   ii. Otherwise, the first letter of the word is put at the end of the word, and AY is added to the end (for example, SAND becomes ANDSAY).

   a. Write a program that INPUTs a word, then constructs and PRINTs its pig Latin translation.
   b. In pig Latin 2, we learn that PRUNE is translated into UNEPRAY, not RUNEPAY, as rule (ii) above would require. Modify the program to work correctly with words (like PRUNE) that start with a double consonant.

10. *Challenge:* Write a program that INPUTs a message (not to exceed the number of characters that fit on one line). Have the program PRINT the message *fully-justified* on the screen; that is, with the first character in the first column of the screen and the last character in the last column. (*Hint:* Add enough extra spaces so that the message is evenly-spaced across the screen.)

Lab Activity

INSTR: A Special Instruction for IBM and TRS-80

Some versions of BASIC, including those used by the *IBM* and *TRS-80* computers (but not *Apple*), have a function that is useful for searching a string for substrings. Here is a program that will help you to discover its features.

```
5  REM * SUBSTRING SEARCH
10 INPUT "TYPE STARTING NUMBER:  "; START
20 INPUT "TYPE BIG STRING:  "; BIG$
30 INPUT "TYPE LITTLE STRING:  "; LITTLE$
40 LET I = INSTR(START, BIG$, LITTLE$)
50 PRINT "INSTR("; START; ",  "; BIG; ",  "; LITTLE$;  ")  =  "; I
60 PRINT
70 END
```

Problems

1. RUN the program, typing 1 for the starting number, ALPHABET for the big string, and PHAB for the little string. What is the result?

2. RUN the program again and find INSTR(1, "ALPHABET", "ABE"). Type 1 as the starting number, ALPHABET as the big string, and ABE as the little string.

3. Predict the value of INSTR(1, "MOTHER", "OTHER"). Verify your prediction using the program.

4. To see what happens when the "little" string is not a substring of the "big" string, find

   ```
                INSTR(1, "SON", "ONION")
   and then     INSTR(1, "CRAMP", "ROMP").
   ```

5. Predict the values of each of the following.

   ```
   INSTR(1, "PEOPLE", "EOP")
   INSTR(1, "PEOPLE", "EOPLE")
   INSTR(1, "PEOPLE", "P")
   INSTR(1, "PEOPLE", "E")
   INSTR(1, "PEOPLE", "EPE")
   ```

   Verify your predictions by using the program. What happens when the little string occurs twice or more as a substring of the big string?

6. You are no doubt wondering about the role of the number START in INSTR(START, BIG$, LITTLE$). Experiment with the program by typing starting numbers bigger than 1 in several examples. Describe what START does. If you need help, try finding the value of each of the following:

   ```
   INSTR(2, "PEOPLE", "E")
   INSTR(3, "PEOPLE", "E")
   INSTR(2, "AAPABPAB", "PA")
   INSTR(5, "AAPABPAB", "PA")
   ```

8-4 Character Coding: ASC and CHR$

Computer memory devices cannot handle entire strings — or even single characters or numbers — directly. Everything that the computer is to store must be converted into sequences of 0's and 1's. Numbers are represented in *binary,* or base 2, form. (See the Computer Language feature on page 64.)

Strings must be converted, one character at a time, into numbers. Most computers use a special code to convert characters into numbers called the *A*merican *S*tandard *C*ode for *I*nformation *I*nterchange — ASCII for short (pronounced "ask'ee"). Here is a table of the code numbers for most of the standard characters you ordinarily use in text or programs.

Table of ASCII Codes

Character	Code	Character	Code
(space)	32	>	62
!	33	?	63
"	34	@	64
#	35	A	65
$	36	B	66
%	37	C	67
&	38	D	68
'	39	E	69
(	40	F	70
)	41	G	71
*	42	H	72
+	43	I	73
,	44	J	74
—	45	K	75
.	46	L	76
/	47	M	77
0	48	N	78
1	49	O	79
2	50	P	80
3	51	Q	81
4	52	R	82
5	53	S	83
6	54	T	84
7	55	U	85
8	56	V	86
9	57	W	87
:	58	X	88
;	59	Y	89
<	60	Z	90
=	61		

From the table you can see that the computer converts, for example, the letters in the string MAD into this sequence of numbers: 77, 65, 68. These numbers, in turn, are converted automatically into the binary numbers 01001101, 01000001, and 01000100. (We will not be concerned with this final conversion any further.)

Notice that the digits 0 to 9 have their own ASCII codes; thus, the *string* "46" has this ASCII code: 52, 54. In BASIC, strings are always enclosed in quotation marks or assigned to variables with a $ at the end, so the computer always knows whether to interpret the contents of a memory location as a number (to be added, say, to another number) or as the code for a character in a string.

You probably have noticed that the codes 0 to 31 are missing from the table. These ASCII codes are used primarily for characters in conjunction with the CONTROL < CTRL > key, but vary from computer to computer. There are also many codes missing from the other end of the table (most machines have ASCII codes up to 255). These codes represent graphics characters, lower-case letters, or other special symbols, but they also differ from machine to machine. You can explore these ASCII codes in the Lab Activity for this section.

ASC and CHR$

Occasionally, you may want to use the ASCII codes directly in a BASIC program. There is a built-in function that gives the codes: ASC(A$) gives the ASCII code for the *first character* of the string A$. For example, the instruction PRINT ASC("A") gives output 65. Here are some other examples:

PRINT ASC("M") gives output 77.

PRINT ASC("!") gives output 33.

PRINT ASC ("YOU") gives output 89 (since Y is the first character of the string.)

LET B = ASC("9") assigns the number 57 to B.

There is also a built-in function in BASIC that gives you the character corresponding to any ASCII code number: CHR$(N) gives the character (a string of length 1) whose ASCII code is the number N. For example:

PRINT CHR$(65) gives output A.

PRINT CHR$(41) gives output).

PRINT CHR$(60); CHR$(58); CHR$(63) gives output <:? .

LET D$ = CHR$(70) assigns the string F to D$.

Here is a short program that uses CHR$ to PRINT the letters of the alphabet.

Program 1

Statement

```
 10 PRINT "ALPHABET"
 15 PRINT
┌20 FOR Y = 65 TO 90
│30 PRINT CHR$(Y);
└40 NEXT Y
 45 PRINT
 50 INPUT "DO YOU WANT TO SEE THE ALPHABET AGAIN:  "; Y$
 60 IF ASC(Y$) = 89 THEN PRINT: GOTO 10
 70 END
```

Output

```
ALPHABET

ABCDEFGHIJKLMNOPQRSTUVWXYZ
DO YOU WANT TO SEE THE ALPHABET AGAIN:  ? YES

ALPHABET

ABCDEFGHIJKLMNOPQRSTUVWXYZ
DO YOU WANT TO SEE THE ALPHABET AGAIN:  ? NO
```

Notice that ASC is used to test the first character of Y$ in line 60. This technique ensures that the action (GOTO 10) will be executed even if the user makes a mistake typing the second or third characters of the string YES. (Do you see how the same test can be done using LEFT$?) What would happen to the output if the PRINT instruction in line 45 were omitted?

In this computer age, many banks, businesses, and other organizations need to keep stored or transmitted computerized information secret. To accomplish this, they often encode the information. One of the simplest techniques for encoding messages involves substituting a particular letter for every "A" in the message, another letter for every "B" in the message, and so forth.

Program 2 on the next page makes the substitution of

B for A, C for B, D for C, . . . , Z for Y, and A for Z.

This substitution is done by changing each character into its ASCII code (line 60), adding 1 to the code (line 70), and then converting the resulting code into its corresponding character (line 90). The letter Z is treated as a special case (line 80).

Program 2

Statement	Remark
10 PRINT "CODING"	
20 INPUT "TYPE MESSAGE: "; MESS$	
30 LET CODE$ = ""	*Start with null coded message.*
40 FOR I = 1 TO LEN(MESS$)	
50 LET C$ = MID$(MESS$, I, 1)	*C$ is the Ith character of MESS$.*
60 LET N = ASC(C$)	*N is the ASCII code of Ith character.*
70 LET N = N + 1	*Get ASCII code of next character alphabetically.*
80 IF N = 91 THEN LET N = 65	*If character is Z, make it an A.*
90 LET D$ = CHR$(N)	*D$ is the substituted character.*
100 LET CODE$ = CODE$ + D$	*Add substituted character to coded message.*
110 NEXT I	
120 PRINT "CODED MESSAGE IS: "; CODE$	
130 END	

Output

```
CODING
TYPE MESSAGE:   ? NEW PASSWORD IS JP23MA
CODED MESSAGE IS:   OFX!QBTTXPSE!JT!KQ34NB
```

You can refer to the table of ASCII codes on page 428 to see why the exclamation points are substituted for the spaces in the coded message shown in the output above. It should be pointed out that this coding technique is too simple for practical use; the code is easily broken by anyone with some experience.

Another rather specialized use of CHR$ is to introduce quotation marks into PRINT statements. The output of the statement

```
PRINT "MY DOG SAID "BOWSIE WOWSIE" "
```

will not be as expected, because the quotation marks before BOWSIE close the quotes around MY DOG SAID. The computer will interpret that BOWSIE is not in quotes at all, and will consider it a numeric variable. It is possible to produce the output

```
MY DOG SAID "BOWSIE WOWSIE"
```

by using the fact that the ASCII code of the quotation mark character is 34. Here is the corrected statement:

```
PRINT "MY DOG SAID   "; CHR$(34); "BOWSIE WOWSIE"; CHR$(34)
```

Avoiding Pitfalls

When you are working with the ASC and CHR$ functions, remember the following:

1. ASC has no $ after it (it yields a number) and is defined only for strings. For example, ASC("Z") = 90.
2. CHR$ has a $ after it (it yields a one-character string) and is defined only for numbers. For example, CHR$(42) = " * ".
3. ASC(A$) gives the ASCII code only of the *first* character of A$. For example, ASC("WAKE UP") = 87. To get the ASCII code of any other character of a string, you have to use ASC along with MID$; for example, ASC(MID$("WAKE UP", 3, 1)) = 75, the code for the third character (K) of the string.

Summary

The ASCII code is used by the computer to convert strings into numbers, character by character, for internal storage.

ASC(A$) gives the ASCII code of the first character in the string A$.

CHR$(N) gives the character, if any, whose ASCII code is the number N.

Exercises 8-4

A

1. Why is there a need for a code such as ASCII?
2. Using the table on page 428, find the sequence of numbers representing the ASCII codes of each of the following strings.
   a. MY
   b. (2 + 3) < 5
   c. 23 SKID
   d. P.O. #43
   e. SHE SAID "DON'T GO!"
3. Using the table on page 428, find the string represented by each sequence of ASCII codes given below.
   a. 68, 85, 77, 66
   b. 66, 85, 78, 78, 89
   c. 50, 32, 43, 32, 50, 61, 51
   d. 87, 82, 79, 78, 71, 33, 33
   e. 66, 79, 78, 75, 69, 82, 83, 63

4. Give the output of each instruction in (a) through (h).

a. PRINT ASC("Q")
b. PRINT ASC(".")
c. PRINT ASC("QPERIOD")
d. PRINT ASC(" ")
e. PRINT CHR$(38)
f. PRINT CHR$(77); CHR$(79); "B"
g. PRINT "MO"B" "
h. PRINT "MO"; CHR$(34); "B"; CHR$(34)

5. Predict the output of each of the following programs.

a.
```
10 LET A$ = "ITS"
20 FOR I = 1 TO LEN(A$)
30 PRINT ASC(MID$(A$, I, 1))
40 NEXT I
50 END
```

b.
```
10 FOR I = 1 TO 3
20 READ C
30 PRINT CHR$(C);
40 NEXT I
50 DATA 65, 67, 69
60 END
```

6. Change Program 1 to PRINT the alphabet backwards.

7. Change Program 2 so that the program makes the following substitutions in the coded message: A becomes C, B becomes D, . . . , X becomes Z, Y becomes A, and Z becomes B.

8. Change Program 2 so that it rejects (with an appropriate message) any INPUT string containing characters other than the letters A to Z.

9. Change Program 2 so that it makes substitutions only for the letters A to Z in the INPUT string, leaving other characters, including punctuation, as they were. For example, the INPUT string BE GONE! should become CF HPOF! .

B **10.** **a.** Write a program to produce the Table of ASCII Codes shown on page 428 in a two-column format, with appropriate headings.
b. Modify the program in (a) using TAB to produce the table in a four-column format.

11. Write a program that generates 10 random numbers each between 33 and 90, then PRINTs the characters corresponding to the ASCII codes of the random numbers.

12. Write a program that INPUTs a string, then determines whether the string represents a positive integer. (*Hint:* Take each character in the string one at a time and use ASC to see if it is a digit from 0 to 9.)

13. Write a program that will *decode* any coded message created by Program 2.

Lab Activity

The Other ASCII Codes

Here is a program that will help you to discover the ASCII codes of most of the characters you can type on your keyboard.

```
5  REM * ASCII CODES
10 INPUT "TYPE ANY KEY (—1 TO END):  "; A$
15 IF A$ = "—1" THEN GOTO 50
20 PRINT ASC(A$)
30 PRINT
40 GOTO 10
50 END
```

Problems

1. RUN the program and verify that the Table of ASCII Codes is correct.
2. Experiment and try to discover any keys on your keyboard that have ASCII codes between 0 and 31, or 91 and 255. (On *Apple* computers, press and hold the CONTROL key < CTRL > while typing other keys to see if CONTROL characters fill in some of the gaps in the ASCII codes.)

Some of the ASCII codes cannot be generated by keys on your keyboard. You can discover the characters many of them represent by using the following program:

```
5  REM * ASCII CODES
10 INPUT "TYPE A NUMBER (—1 TO END):  "; X
15 IF X = —1 THEN GOTO 50
20 PRINT CHR$(X)
30 PRINT
40 GOTO 10
50 END
```

3. RUN the program, typing numbers between 32 and 90 to verify again the Table of ASCII Codes.
4. Experiment with the program and type numbers between 0 and 31, or 91 and 255, to see what characters they generate on your machine. (Some of the characters may be invisible — see the Lab Activity for Section 8–1, page 414 — but perhaps you can discover what they are by looking at any pattern that develops.)

5. (Do this problem only if you have a *TRS-80* computer.) If you are using this machine, you will have discovered the graphics characters, which have ASCII codes 128 through 191. There is a pattern to these characters. Each is the size of a normal PRINTed character, and consists of six cells; each cell can be either on (lighted) or off (not lighted). Here is a diagram of the six cells:

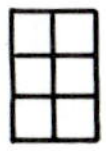

a. Use the second program above to verify that the first several graphic characters, with their ASCII codes, are as follows:

128 129 130 131 132 133 134

These graphic characters just represent *binary*, or base 2, numbers (see the Computer Language feature on page 64). This will be clearer if we rearrange the diagrams:

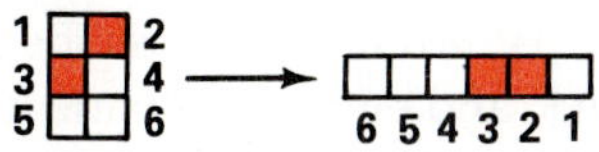

The binary number corresponding to the pattern

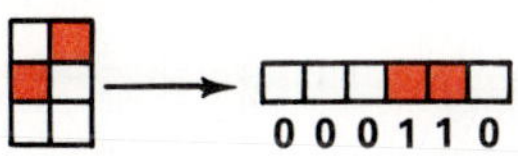

is $0 * 32 + 0 * 16 + 0 * 8 + 1 * 4 + 1 * 2 + 0 * 1$, which equals 6. The ASCII code is obtained by adding

$$128 + 6 = 134.$$

For another example, consider the pattern

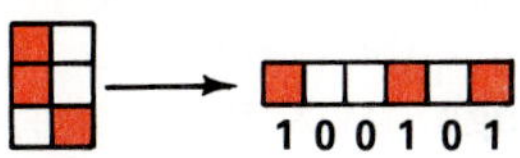

Its ASCII code is:

$$128 + (1 * 32 + 0 * 16 + 0 * 8 + 1 * 4 + 0 * 2 + 1 * 1) = 165.$$

b. Use the same program to verify that CHR$(165) looks like the pattern given above.

c. Figure out the ASCII code for the character that looks like this:

Use the program to see if your answer is correct.

d. Several graphics characters can be combined using concatenation. For example, the extended pattern

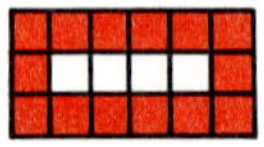

consists of the three characters with ASCII codes 183, 179, and 187, respectively. You can PRINT the pattern on the screen by RUNning this simple program.

```
10  LET A$ = CHR$(183) + CHR$(179) + CHR$(187)
20  PRINT A$
30  END
```

Try it.

e. Add to the program in (d) to have the pattern move across the screen. Replace line 20 with 20 PRINT @ I, A$, and enclose this line in a FOR . . . NEXT loop using the counter I = 0 to 1023. To prevent the pattern from leaving a trail, include a CLS instruction inside the loop.

8-5 Number and String Conversions: VAL and STR$

At times you may find it useful to manipulate numbers using the built-in string functions described in this chapter, but to do so the numbers must first be converted to strings. To convert a specific number, say 846, to string form, ordinarily all you need to do is enclose it in quotation marks: "846". If the number has been stored in a variable though, say X, then using quotation marks no longer works; certainly "X" is a string, but it has no relationship to the number 846 that is the value of X. Fortunately, BASIC has a built-in function — STR$ — that converts numbers to strings. Here are some examples:

STR$(36.8) is the string "36.8".
STR$(−.0001) is the string "−.0001".
LET B$ = LEFT$(STR$(893), 1) assigns the string "8" to B$.
PRINT MID$(STR$(84869), 3, 2) has the string "86" as its output.

There is also an easy way in BASIC — using the built-in function VAL — to convert a string representing a number back to the number itself. VAL(S$) is the number that the string S$ represents. For example:

> VAL("36.8") is the number 36.8.
> VAL("−2.64") is the number −2.64.
> LET Y = VAL("3" + "8") assigns the number 38 to Y.
> PRINT VAL("3") + VAL("8") has the number 11 as its output.

If a string S$ contains characters that cannot occur in a number, then VAL(S$) is the number represented by the first part of S$ — up to the first non-numerical character. For example,

> VAL("23SKIDOO") is the number 23.
> VAL("ANTELOPE") is the number 0.

To illustrate the use of STR$ and VAL, let's first write a program to add the digits of any INPUT positive integer. For example, if the integer is 846, then the output should be 8 + 4 + 6 = 18. (This is the first step of the process called "casting out nines" in arithmetic. See Exercise 3.) The program can be written using an entirely arithmetical approach, as in the following version.

Program 1

Statement	Remark
10 PRINT "ADD DIGITS"	
20 INPUT "TYPE A POSITIVE INTEGER: "; N	
25 IF N < > INT(N) OR N < 1 THEN GOTO 20	*Error trap.*
30 LET SUM = 0	
40 LET DIG = N − 10 * INT(N / 10)	*Extract rightmost digit of N.*
50 LET SUM = SUM + DIG	
60 LET N = INT(N / 10)	*Assign integer with last digit removed to N.*
70 IF N > 0 THEN GOTO 40	
80 PRINT "SUM OF DIGITS = "; SUM	
90 END	

Output

```
ADD DIGITS
TYPE A POSITIVE INTEGER:   ? 846
SUM OF DIGITS  =  18
```

The key arithmetical steps in the program occur in lines 40 and 60. The statement in line 40

```
LET DIG = N − 10 * INT(N / 10)
```

extracts one digit at a time from the integer N. For example, if N = 846, then

```
DIG = 846 — 10 * INT(846 / 10)
    = 846 — 10 * INT(84.6)
    = 846 — 10 * 84
    = 6
```

(Calculate the value of DIG, using the formula in line 40, for other values of N and convince yourself that it always gives the last (rightmost) digit of N.) The statement in line 60

```
LET N = INT(N / 10)
```

then assigns to N the integer that results from removing the last digit from N:

```
N = INT(846 / 10)
  = INT(84.6)
  = 84
```

This process of extracting digits from N and then adding them to SUM continues as long as N > 0 is true (line 70).

Another approach to this problem of adding digits uses the string form of the INPUT integer, and uses techniques that have become familiar to you in this chapter.

Program 2

Statement	Remark
`10 PRINT "ADD DIGITS, STRING APPROACH"`	
`20 INPUT "TYPE A POSITIVE INTEGER:  "; N`	
`30 IF N <> INT(N) OR N < 1 THEN GOTO 20`	
`40 LET N$ = STR$(N)`	*N$ is string form of integer.*
`50 LET SUM = 0`	
`60 FOR I = 1 TO LEN(N$)`	
`70 LET SUM = SUM + VAL(MID$(N$, I, 1))`	*Add the Ith digit of N$.*
`80 NEXT I`	
`90 PRINT "SUM OF DIGITS  =  "; SUM`	
`95 END`	

Output

```
ADD DIGITS, STRING APPROACH
TYPE A POSITIVE INTEGER:  ? 342
SUM OF DIGITS  =  9
```

Notice the use of VAL in line 70. The expression MID$(N$, I, 1) represents the Ith character (digit) of N$ in string form, so it must be converted to a number before it can be added to SUM.

Avoiding Pitfalls

When you are working with the functions VAL and STR$, remember the following:

1. VAL has no $ after it (it yields a number), and is defined only for strings. For example, if X$ = "28.4", then VAL(X$) is the number 28.4.
2. STR$ must have a $ (it yields a string), and is defined only for numbers. For example, STR$(.083) is the string ".083".

Summary

VAL(S$) is the number represented by the first part of the string S$, starting at the first character of S$ and continuing until the first non-numerical character is reached. For example, VAL("123GO") is the number 123.

STR$(X) is the string form of the number X.

Exercises 8-5

A 1. Give the output for each of the following instructions or set of instructions if X = 18 and Y$ = "68".

a. PRINT VAL("33.88")
b. PRINT STR$(−6.03)
c. PRINT VAL(STR$(46.3))
d. PRINT VAL(Y$ + "2")
e. PRINT VAL("2" + Y$)
f. PRINT VAL("2") + VAL(Y$)
g. PRINT VAL(Y$ + "YELL")
h. PRINT VAL(Y$ + Y$)
i. PRINT VAL(Y$) + VAL(Y$)
j. PRINT X + VAL(Y$)
k. PRINT STR$(X + X)
l. PRINT LEFT$(STR$(369), 2)
m. PRINT VAL(MID$(Y$ + "32", 3, 1))
n.
```
110  FOR I = 1 TO 3
120  PRINT MID$(STR$(8569), I)
130  NEXT I
```

2. Find the errors, if any, in each of the following instructions. Give a possible correction.

a. PRINT VAL(A)
b. PRINT VAL$(A$)
c. LET X$ = VAL(A$)
d. LET Y$ = STR$(A)
e. PRINT STR$(A) + "OUCH"
f. LET X = STR$(A + 2)
g. PRINT VAL(A$ + "OUCH")
h. READ STR$(2)

3. In "casting out nines", you first add the digits of a given integer. If the result is bigger than 9, you add the digits of the result. This process is continued until a one-digit sum is obtained. If the one-digit sum is 9, then the original number is divisible by 9. For example, $684 \longrightarrow 6 + 8 + 4 = 18 \longrightarrow 1 + 8 = 9$, so 684 is divisible by 9. Change Program 2 so that it casts out nines from any INPUT positive integer, then PRINTs a message telling whether the integer is divisible by 9.

B 4. Write a program that INPUTs an integer, then PRINTs the integer obtained by changing each digit D to the digit 9 − D. For example, if 756 is INPUT, then the output should be 243. The number 243 is called the "nines complement" of the number 756. If you want to subtract a number X from a larger number Y, you can find the sum of Y and the nines complement of X, then make a simple change in the answer. Can you discover how this works?

5. Write a program that INPUTs an integer, then PRINTs the integer obtained by repeating each of the original digits. For example, if the INPUT integer is 346, then the output should be 334466.

6. a. Write a program that uses VAL and STR$ to simulate the INT function for INPUT positive numbers. For example, if the INPUT number is 36.85, then the output should be 36. (*Hint:* Convert the number to a string. Find the decimal point, if any, then delete the decimal point and all the characters to its right.)
   b. You know that you can round a number X to the nearest integer by using the expression INT(X + .5). Modify the program in (a) so that it rounds the INPUT number to the nearest integer using STR$ and VAL rather than INT.

7. Write a program that INPUTs the number of cents that a grocery item costs, then PRINTs the cost in dollars and cents. Use string functions only to ensure that the output always has exactly two places after the decimal point. For example, if the INPUT number is 360, then the output should be $3.60 — not $3.6.

8. Write a program using ASCII codes to PRINT the numerical value of an INPUT string, without using VAL. Assume that the INPUT string contains no characters other than the digits 0 to 9. (*Hint:* The digit 0 has ASCII code 48, the digit 1 has ASCII code $49 = 48 + 1, \ldots,$ and the digit 9 has ASCII code $57 = 48 + 9$.)

C 9. a. Write a program that PRINTs the string form of an INPUT positive integer N, without using STR$. (*Hint:* Find the digits of X in order from right to left, as in Program 1, then convert the digits to strings using CHR$.)
   b. Modify the program in (a) so that it also works for negative INPUT integers.

Lab Activity

VAL(STR$(X)) and STR$(VAL(X$))

If you start with a number represented by a variable X, convert it to a string using STR$(X), then convert back to a number value using VAL(STR$(X)), it seems reasonable to expect that you will get back to the number X you started with.

Problems

1. RUN the following program five or more times, typing different positive values for X to see if VAL(STR$(X)) is always equal to X.

```
10 INPUT "NUMBER:  "; X
20 LET Y = VAL(STR$(X))
30 PRINT "VAL(STR$(X)) =  "; Y
40 END
```

2. RUN the program, typing the number 1234567891234567891 for the value of X. Is VAL(STR$(X)) equal to X for this large value of X?

3. Experiment with the program to find the smallest positive integer for which X is not equal to VAL(STR$(X)).

4. RUN the program several more times, putting a decimal point in various places in the number you found in Problem 3. Does the location of the decimal point affect the inequality?

5. Add several zeros to the (rightmost) end of the integer you found in Problem 3. Do the zeros affect the inequality?

6. Add a decimal point and place several zeros between the decimal point and the first digit of the integer you found in Problem 3. Does this change affect the inequality?

Now let's do the conversion the other way: If you start with a string X$ that represents a number, convert X$ to its numerical value using VAL(X$), then convert back to a string using STR$(VAL(X$)), ordinarily you would expect to get back to X$ again.

7. Write a program similar to the one in Problem 1 to investigate under what circumstances X$ = STR$(VAL(X$)). Experiment to see that this equality is true for moderately large numbers.

8. RUN the program several times, typing some very large numbers with

lots of zeros at the end (like 1230000000000). Is X$ = STR$(VAL(X$)) for these large numbers? Explain the difference between the result here for large numbers and the one in Problem 2.

9. RUN the program several times, typing some very small numbers (like .00000000000123). Is X$ = STR$(VAL(X$)) for these small numbers? Can you explain why or why not?

8-6 One-Character Input: GET or INKEY$

There are many programs in which the user must give simple commands or answers to questions over and over again. The INPUT statement can be awkward to use in such programs, since the statement requires pressing the < RETURN > or < ENTER > key each time something is typed. Most computers have an instruction that will input a single character and assign it as a one-character string to a string variable (without the < RETURN > key or < ENTER > key being pressed). The instruction varies from computer to computer. This section explains the GET instruction for *Apple* computers, and the INKEY$ instruction for *TRS-80* and *IBM* computers.

Apple: GET

On Apple computers, an instruction of the form

GET *string variable*

puts a blinking cursor on the screen and causes the computer to wait until a single key is pressed. That keyboard character is then assigned to the string variable. For example, if a program contains the statement 100 GET A$ and the user types an * after the blinking cursor (the * will not appear on the screen), then the computer assigns the string * to A$.

TRS-80 and IBM: INKEY$

On these computers there is a string function INKEY$ that is used for one-character input. The instructions needed are of this form:

```
98 LET A$ = INKEY$
99 IF A$ = "" THEN GOTO 98   (A$ is the null string.)
```

These statements will cause the computer to keep examining INKEY$ until it contains a character. When a key is pressed (the typed character will not appear on the screen), INKEY$ takes on the value of the key, and this value is assigned to A$ in line 98.

Using GET or INKEY$

As an example of the use of this one-character input technique, here is a program that allows you to draw pictures in graphics mode by moving a point around the screen using these keys: U (up), D (down), R (right), and L (left). If Q is pressed, the program will stop.

Program 1

Statement	Remark
10 PRINT "DOODLE"	
20 GOSUB 1000	*Set up graphics mode.*
30 GOSUB 1200	*Initialize point (X, Y) to coordinates at center of screen.*
40 *(Instruction to plot the point X, Y on your computer.)*	
50 GET A$ or 50 LET A$ = INKEY$ 51 IF A$ = "" THEN GOTO 50	
55 IF A$ = "Q" THEN GOTO 110	
60 IF A$ = "U" THEN LET Y = Y − 1: GOTO 40	*This moves the point up.*
70 IF A$ = "D" THEN LET Y = Y + 1: GOTO 40	*This moves the point down.*
80 IF A$ = "L" THEN LET X = X − 1: GOTO 40	*This moves the point to the left.*
90 IF A$ = "R" THEN LET X = X + 1: GOTO 40	*This moves the point to the right.*
100 GOTO 50	
110 END	
990 REM * * SUBROUTINE TO SET UP GRAPHICS MODE * *	
1000 *(Instructions to clear the screen and do graphics on your computer.)* · · ·	
1030 RETURN	
1190 REM * * SUBROUTINE TO INITIALIZE POINT (X, Y) TO COORDINATES AT CENTER OF SCREEN * *	
1200 LET X = (*Apple:* 140 *TRS-80:* 64 *IBM:* 320)	
1210 LET Y = (*Apple:* 80 *TRS-80:* 24 *IBM:* 100)	
1220 RETURN	

The instructions in line 50 (or 50 and 51) cause the computer to wait until a key is pressed, then assign that key to the string variable A$. What will happen if an inappropriate key (like "P") is pressed? Why is GET (or INKEY$) a more convenient instruction than INPUT to use in this program?

The GET (or INKEY$) instruction is also useful when a program presents directions to the user that fill more than one screen. To prevent the instructions from scrolling off the screen, you can PRINT a message such as PRESS ANY KEY TO CONTINUE on the bottom line of the first screen of directions. Then by using GET (or INKEY$), you can allow the user to control when the next screen is PRINTed by simply typing a single key.

Avoiding Pitfalls

1. With *Apple* computers, be sure to use GET A$ rather than LET A$ = INKEY$. To an *Apple* computer, INKEY$ is just another string variable, so that LET A$ = INKEY$ will assign its current value to A$.
2. On *TRS-80* and *IBM* computers, be sure to use LET A$ = INKEY$ rather than GET A$. On these computers, the GET instruction is used for other purposes (as you will see in Chapter 11).

Summary

The instructions

```
90 GET A$
```
Apple or

```
90 LET A$ = INKEY$
91 IF A$ = "" THEN GOTO 90
```
TRS-80 and *IBM*

cause the computer to wait until a key is pressed. That key is then assigned, as a one-character string, to the variable A$.

Exercises 8-6

A 1. Change Program 1 so that it will not allow the point (X, Y) to go off the screen.

2. Write a program (using GET or INKEY$) that PRINTs the integers from 1 to 100, then pauses to ask the user for a one-key command that indicates whether to continue the program or END it. If the command is to continue, the program should PRINT the next 100 integers, then pause and ask again whether to continue, and so forth.

3. Write a program (using GET or INKEY$) to input single characters. For each character typed, have the program fill an entire line with the PRINTed character. The program should END when the < RETURN > or < ENTER > key is pressed. Since the ASCII code of < RETURN > or < ENTER > is 13, you can use a comparison like this:
   IF ASC(A$) = 13 THEN . . . or IF A$ = CHR$(13) THEN . . .

B **4.** Write a program (using GET or INKEY$) that begins by PRINTing the number 0 (assigned, say, to the variable N). If the user types "+" as the one-key command, have the program add 1 to N and PRINT the new value. If "−" is typed, have the program subtract 1 from N and PRINT the new value. The program should continue adding and subtracting until "Q" is typed. All of the numbers should be PRINTed at the same location on the screen.

5. The GET (or INKEY$) instruction can be used in place of INPUT if desired; you can type any string into the computer one character at a time and use concatenation to assign the entire string to a variable.

a. Write a subroutine that inputs a string one character at a time, continuing until the <RETURN> or <ENTER> key (ASCII code 13) is pressed by the user.

b. Modify Program 2 of Section 8–3, page 423, to use the subroutine instead of the INPUT statement in line 20. What advantages does INPUT have? What advantages does the subroutine approach have?

6. Program 1 plots every point (X, Y) as it changes position in response to the user's one-key commands. Change the program so that if the user types M (move), then from then on, when the user types D, L, R, or U, the old point is erased before the new point is plotted. (No trail is left on the screen.) When a P (plot) is typed, old points are left on the screen. (*Hint:* Use a variable that has a value of 1 when points are to remain on the screen, and a value of 0 when they are not.)

C **7.** Write a program that PRINTs the string

ABC * DE

centered on the screen. Have the program move the * to the left if L is typed (the new string is AB * CDE), or to the right if R is typed (the new string is ABCD * E). END the program if Q is typed.

8. (Graphics — for *Apple* computer users only)
Write a program using the following method to shade the screen with the color specified by the user: The color number is to be the ones digit of the ASCII code of the key pressed by the user in response to a GET instruction. For example, if "C" is pressed, the screen should fill with the color represented by the number 7, since ASC("C") = 67. (*Hint:* See the method of Program 1, page 437, that uses the INT function to isolate the ones digit.)

9. (The ideas presented in the Lab Activity for this section are needed in this exercise.)
Challenge: Using Program 1 as a guide, write a doodle program in which the point (X, Y) keeps moving slowly (use a FOR . . . NEXT time-delay loop) to the left, right, up, or down, until the user types a key changing the direction. Do not allow the point to go off the screen.

Lab Activity

Has a Key Been Pressed?

The GET B$ (*Apple*) instruction and the instructions

```
98  LET B$ = INKEY$
99  IF B$ = ""  THEN GOTO 98
```

TRS-80 and *IBM*

cause a program to stop and wait until the user presses a key. Sometimes it is useful to have the program *continue* with what it is doing until a key is actually pressed.

TRS-80 and IBM

This is easily accomplished on machines that use INKEY$. INKEY$ is equal to the null string unless a key has been pressed. If at any instant INKEY$ is null, then the program can continue with what it is doing. If INKEY$ is not null, then the program will respond to the user's command. Here is a simple program using this idea. It counts until the user types a key, at which point it PRINTs the value of the counter, and then continues counting.

```
10  PRINT "COUNTING"
20  LET N = 0: REM * INITIALIZE COUNTER
30  LET B$ = INKEY$
40  IF B$ <> "" THEN PRINT N: REM * PRINT IF KEY PRESSED
50  LET N = N + 1
60  GOTO 30
70  END
```

for the commodore line 30 should be 30 Get B$

Apple

The procedure is trickier using the GET instruction on *Apple* computers. First, here is some necessary background: Every memory location in your computer has a numerical address associated with it. The particular memory location we will be concerned with has address 49152. This location (and every other location as well) always contains a number between 0 and 255 (recorded in binary form). This number is less than 128 if no key has been pressed since the last INPUT, RUN, or GET instruction. If a key has been pressed, then the number in location 49152 is greater than or equal to 128 (in fact, the number is equal to 128 plus the ASCII code of the key that was pressed). Any of the instructions GET, INPUT, or RUN makes the number in location 49152 go back below 128. Therefore, the *Apple* version of the preceding program need only compare the contents of location 49152 with the number 128 to see if a key has been pressed. The contents of any memory location can be determined by using the function PEEK; in particular, PEEK(49152) is the number that is in location 49152. Here then is the *Apple* version of the program.

```
10  PRINT "COUNTING ON APPLE"
20  LET N = 0: REM * INITIALIZE COUNTER
30  IF PEEK(49152) >= 128 THEN GET B$: PRINT N
50  LET N = N + 1
60  GOTO 30
70  END
```

The purpose of the GET B$ instruction in line 30 is to cancel the key that was pressed; that is, to make the number in location 49152 go below 128 once more, so that the next key press can be detected. In some programs, it is important to know which key was pressed; GET B$ assigns the key's character to B$.

Problems

1. RUN the version of the program for your computer a couple of times and verify that it PRINTs the value of the counter only if a key has been pressed.

2. Change the program so that the value of the counter is PRINTed only if "P" is pressed, the program ENDs if "Q" is pressed, and the program continues uninterrupted if any other key is pressed.

3. Write a program that will fill the text screen with *'s (use PRINT "*";), until it is interrupted by a one-key command. Have the program skip a space (PRINT " ";) whenever the one-key command is a press of the space bar (ASCII code 32). Put in a FOR . . . NEXT time-delay loop so that the PRINTing will be slow enough to control. See if you can draw a recognizable picture by pressing the space bar at the appropriate times. If the one-key command is "Q", have the program stop.

4. Will your computer "remember" a key that was pressed earlier in the program, or does it only detect a key that is being held down at the instant that LET B$ = INKEY$ or PEEK(49152) is executed? To determine the answer, write a program that starts with a long time-delay loop (during which you can press a key). Then have the program PRINT one of two different messages, depending on whether or not a key press was detected. Experiment with the program to determine which key the computer remembers if you type two different characters during the initial time delay. Does it remember the first one or the second one?

Chapter Summary

There are several built-in string functions in BASIC:

LEN(A$) gives the number of characters in the string A$. For example, if A$ = "UNREAL", then LEN(A$) = 6.

LEFT$(A$, N) gives the string consisting of the leftmost N characters of A$. If N >= LEN(A$), then LEFT$(A$, N) = A$.

RIGHT$(A$, N) gives the string consisting of the rightmost N characters of A$. If N >= LEN(A$), then RIGHT$(A$, N) = A$.

MID$(A$, WHERE, N) gives the string consisting of N characters of A$, beginning at position WHERE. MID$(A$, WHERE) gives the string consisting of all the characters of A$, beginning at position WHERE.

ASC(A$) gives the ASCII code of the first character of the string A$. For example, if A$ = "YOU", then ASC(A$) = 89.

CHR$(N) gives the character, if any, whose ASCII code is the number N. For example, if N = 66, then CHR$(N) is the letter B.

VAL(S$) gives the number represented by the first part of the string S$, starting at the very first character of S$ and continuing until the first non-numerical character is reached. For example, if the string S$ = "442ABCD", then VAL(S$) = 442.

STR$(X) gives the string form of the number X. For example, if X = 385, then STR$(X) = "385".

The *null string* is the string containing no characters at all. The statement LET B$ = "" assigns the null string to B$.

Concatenation is the process of linking strings: A$ + B$ + C$ + . . . is the string obtained by taking — in order — all the characters of A$, followed by all the characters of B$, followed by all the characters of C$, and so forth.

The instructions

```
90 GET A$
```
Apple or

```
90 LET A$ = INKEY$
91 IF A$ = "" THEN GOTO 90
```
TRS-80 and *IBM*

cause the computer to wait until a key is pressed. That key is then assigned, as a one-character string, to the variable A$.

Chapter Test

1. Give the output of each of the following instructions.

   a. PRINT LEN("NO DEAL")
   b. PRINT LEFT$("TECHNICAL", 4)
   c. PRINT RIGHT$("NATURAL", 3)
   d. PRINT MID$("DIALING", 3, 4)
   e. PRINT "GRAPH" + "ICS"
   f. PRINT LEFT$("MANAGE", 2) + MID$("FILL", 2, 2)
   g. PRINT VAL("68" + "22")
   h. PRINT VAL("34") + VAL("18")

2. Give the output of each of the following instructions if R$ = "STARFISH", T$ = "OYSTER", and X = 2.

   a. PRINT LEN(T$) + LEN(R$)
   b. PRINT RIGHT$(R$, LEN(R$) − 1)
   c. PRINT MID$(RIGHT$(R$, 4), 2, 2)
   d. PRINT MID$(R$, X + 1)

3. Predict the output of the following program for each of the values of W shown below.

```
10  INPUT W
20  LET W$ = STR$(W)
30  LET R = VAL(RIGHT$(W$, 2))
40  IF R / 4 = INT(R / 4) THEN PRINT "IS"
50  IF R / 4 <> INT(R / 4) THEN PRINT "IS NOT"
60  END
```

   a. W = 316
   b. W = 451
   c. W = 7365

4. Write a program that INPUTs a string and then PRINTs the first and last letters of the string.

5. Write a program to produce the following output:

   COUNTER
   COUNTE
   COUNT
   COUN
   COU
   CO
   C

6. a. Write a program that INPUTs a string, then deletes from the string all occurrences of the letter T, and then PRINTs the result.
   b. Modify the program in (a) so that strings with a length less than 3 characters or greater than 20 characters are rejected.

7. Write a program using GET or INKEY$ that accepts numbers only, then adds them until the < RETURN > or < ENTER > key (ASCII code 13) is pressed. The program should PRINT the resulting sum.

Purpose of Simulation

Computers can help us make decisions by simulating (that is, imitating) real-life situations. First we must create a *model* of the situation we want to investigate. This model might consist of equations and numerical data that describe the important characteristics of the situation. We can then write a computer program that contains these equations and data. By varying the information that we input into the computer, we can explore what might happen under different conditions. Observing the results of the simulation helps us predict what will happen in the real-life situation. Simulations are particularly useful when the situation under consideration is difficult, impossible, or very costly to observe directly. Suppose, for example, that an architect wants to test whether the structural design of a newly-planned building can withstand the powerful tremors of an earthquake. A computer simulation can be developed that allows the architect to test the building's tolerance to earthquakes of varying intensity, and to investigate the effect of different design modifications.

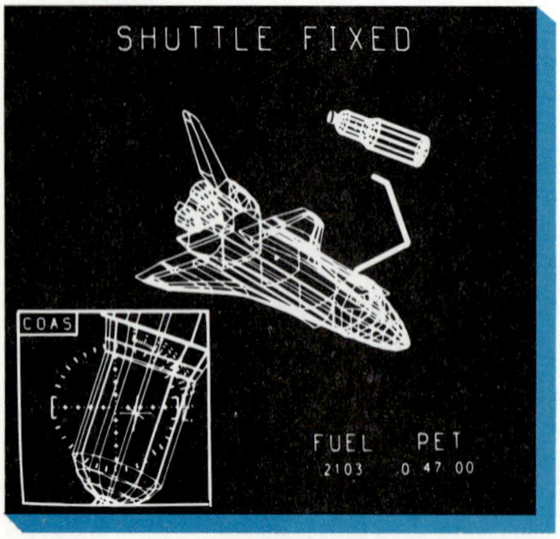
Space-shuttle simulation

Wind-tunnel simulation

Some Examples

Simulation techniques are currently used in a wide range of fields, including consumer-buying patterns, financial forecasting, water-resource management, ambulance dispatching, harbor design, and city planning. In each of these fields, simulation is a tool for solving problems. There are many examples from science and technology. Specifically, there are computer simulations that test the behavior of nuclear reactors under different conditions, predict the result of subjecting the human body to environmental stress, determine a bridge's ability to withstand different weight

Automobile-driving simulation

loads, and demonstrate the workings of oil refineries so that gasoline can be processed more economically. The National Aeronautics and Space Agency (NASA) uses computer simulation to test space vehicles and to train astronauts to fly and land space shuttles. Before astronauts ever pilot a spacecraft, they spend hours of practice in a *simulator,* a mock-up of the real spacecraft.

Simulations are useful in education. For instance, a computer simulation can be used to help students learn how to operate a business. Typically, students must decide which products to manufacture and in what quantities, the selling price of each product, and the number of employees that are needed. The simulation can present surprise conditions such as a workers' strike, an economic recession, an oil embargo, or increased foreign competition to complicate running the business, and thus test the students' ability to manage effectively. The important features of this simulation are that students can be placed in decision-making roles they would not be in otherwise, and that mistakes can be made without disastrous results.

Importance of Model

Failure to understand the limitations of a model can result in real-world difficulties. The Tacoma Narrows Bridge, despite successful simulated 100-mph wind tunnel tests, was destroyed in a 40-mph wind. The design failed to take into account that the span would develop self-destructive vibrations at lower wind speeds. The success of a computer simulation depends on the accuracy of the model. All relevant factors must be considered, but it is a waste of time to create a very elaborate model when a simple one — focusing, perhaps, on a single aspect of the situation — can give adequate approximation. Computer simulations, when used carefully and with full awareness of their limitations, are an important tool for solving real-life problems.

Tacoma Narrows bridge being destroyed

Pascal

The computer language Pascal, named after the French mathematician and scientist Blaise Pascal (1623–1662), was designed by Niklaus Wirth of Zurich, Switzerland, about 1970.

At first, the language was compatible only with large mainframe computers. However, through the efforts of Kenneth Bowles and a group of people at the University of California at San Diego, a version of Pascal known as UCSD Pascal was developed and has been adapted for use with various microcomputer systems. Pascal is a very powerful general-purpose programming language used in many university undergraduate programs.

Blaise Pascal

Pascal was originally intended to be a language used to teach programming concepts using syntax related to a structured form of programming (such as *top-down design*). With a structured program, it is important to think through a programming problem carefully before writing any program statements. Always start by writing a detailed outline (an *algorithm*) of the steps a program is to follow. Then translate the outline into programming code.

Chemists use Pascal programs.

Any structured-language program, regardless of size, is made up of subprograms (like subroutines in BASIC), each of which is itself a structured program. There are three basic sections to a program written in Pascal: a *heading*, *declarations*, and *statements*. The *heading* is used to name the program. The *declaration* section can be used to specify such elements of a program as labels, variable names, constants, data types, and subroutines. The *statement* section contains the actual program instructions that tell the computer how to reach the desired result.

Here is a simple Pascal program that calculates the area of a rectangle, and then prints the result.

```
PROGRAM AREA;
VAR LENGTH, WIDTH, AREA: REAL;
BEGIN
   WRITELN ('ENTER THE LENGTH OF THE RECTANGLE');
   READ (LENGTH);
   WRITELN ('ENTER THE WIDTH OF THE RECTANGLE');
   READ (WIDTH);
   AREA: = LENGTH * WIDTH;
   WRITELN ('THE AREA OF THE RECTANGLE IS ', AREA);
END.
```

Program Analysis

Heading: The word PROGRAM is followed by the program name and a semicolon.

Declaration: The variables (VAR) are descriptively named and separated by a comma. The last variable is followed by a colon and then the numerical type of data to be used (in this case, real numbers).

Statements: The words BEGIN and END indicate the instruction sequence of the program. Only one sequence is shown here. More complicated programs may have many such sequences, each indicated with the words BEGIN and END. A period follows the last END statement in the program.

In Pascal, unlike BASIC, procedures and functions are referred to by name rather than by line number. This improves readability and results in a program easier to modify than a BASIC program. In most cases, Pascal is considered to be a superior language when the problem to be solved is mathematical in nature and requires a large program.

Many microcomputers are capable of processing Pascal programs.

CHAPTER 9 Arrays

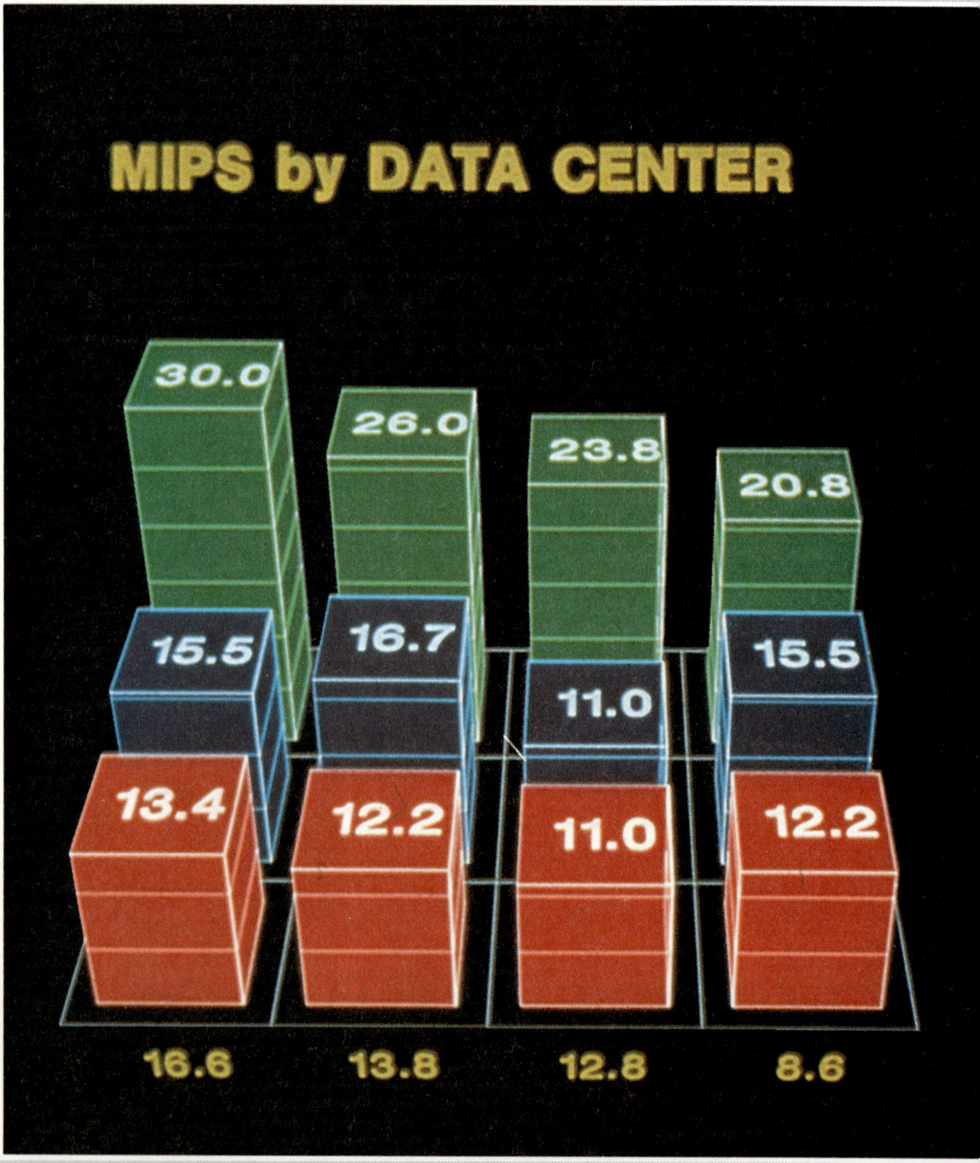

The software package used to create this bar graph contains a library of more than 400 FORTRAN subroutines. The word MIPS at the top of the graph stands for "millions of instructions per second."

Introduction

Imagine how difficult it would be to write a computer program using as many as 50 different variables. Certainly, it would be a tedious task typing 50 different LET, INPUT, or READ statements. To be useful, a computer programming language must provide an easy way to handle situations in which numbers and strings are to be assigned to many different variables. The BASIC language provides such a means — *subscripted variables.* These variables are introduced in the first section below and their uses are illustrated throughout this chapter.

9-1 Subscripted Variables

In the programs you have written so far, you have used *simple variable* names (for example, Y, B1, AB2, NUM, C$, or NME$). BASIC *subscripted variables* are named the same way as simple variables except that they are followed by a *subscript.* The subscript must be either 0 or a positive integer and is *always* enclosed in parentheses. The following are some examples of subscripted variables:

A(5), B$(6), Z(2), CD(10), NEED$(8)

In the first example, A is the variable name and 5 is the subscript. This variable is read "A sub 5." In the next example, B$ is the variable name and 6 is the subscript. This variable is read "B string sub 6." The variables in the rest of the examples are read similarly.

On most microcomputers, the biggest number that may be used as a subscript is 10, unless the computer is given a specific instruction telling it to allow subscripts greater than 10. (You will learn about this instruction in Section 9–3.)

Like simple variables, subscripted variables name locations in the computer's memory. (The locations can be thought of as compartments or "mailboxes," as explained earlier, in Chapter 3.) Each subscripted variable can be used to store one number or string. Note that the variables X1 and X(1) name *different* memory locations — X1 is a simple variable, whereas X(1) is a subscripted variable.

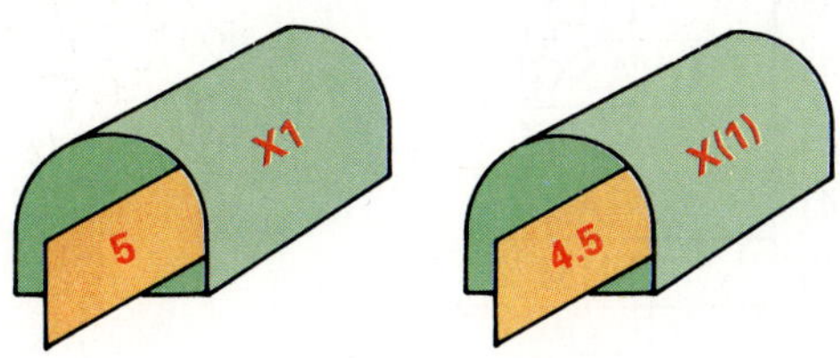

Arrays

An *array* is a collection of subscripted variables with the same variable name. For example, the collection P(0), P(1), . . . , P(7) is an array with the name P. The members, or *elements*, of the array are P(0), P(1), and so on up to P(7). Arrays can be represented in the form of a diagram, as illustrated below:

Array P

P(0)	
P(1)	
P(2)	
P(3)	
P(4)	
P(5)	
P(6)	
P(7)	

Since subscripted variables name memory locations, you can think of the boxes in the diagram as compartments in which the values of the variables are stored. Values are assigned to the subscripted variables by LET, READ, or INPUT. For example, the instruction LET P(3) = 28 assigns the value 28 to the variable P(3).

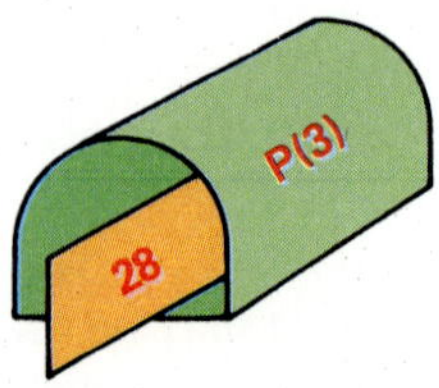

Whenever the computer encounters a subscripted variable — say P(2) — in a program, it automatically reserves 11 memory locations (for variables with subscripts from 0 to 10) for the array P. Thus, for the eight subscripted variables in array P diagrammed above, we can just as easily use subscripts from 1 to 8 (or 2 to 9); the variable P(0) is available, but it need not be used. Here is an example of an array in which the elements have string values:

Array YUM$

YUM$(1)	APPLE
YUM$(2)	ORANGE
YUM$(3)	PEACH
YUM$(4)	PEAR
YUM$(5)	PLUM
YUM$(6)	GRAPE

The name of this array is YUM$. The variable YUM$(3), for example, contains the string PEACH, so the value of YUM$(3) is PEACH. The instruction PRINT YUM$(6) will produce the string GRAPE as output.

Subscripted variables can have numeric variables for subscripts. For example, the subscripted variable R(J) has J as a subscript:

If J = 1, then R(J) is the subscripted variable R(1);
If J = 5, then R(J) is the subscripted variable R(5).

Actually, the subscript can be more complex than a single numeric variable. Any legal BASIC numerical expression having a nonnegative integer value can be used as a subscript. For example, suppose the elements in array R, and the variables A and M, have the following values:

Array R

	Array R
R(1)	3
R(2)	2.4
R(3)	−1
R(4)	6
R(5)	12
R(6)	8

A	M
2	3

Then the subscripted variables below would have these values:

R(A) = R(2) = 2.4
R(M) = R(3) = −1
R(A * M − 5) = R(6 − 5) = R(1) = 3

In particular, notice that

R(A + M) = R(2 + 3) = R(5) = 12

but R(A) + R(M) = R(2) + R(3) = 2.4 + −1 = 1.4

Avoiding Pitfalls

1. The subscript of a subscripted variable should not have a negative or a decimal value.
2. Remember that X2 and X(2) are different variables. X2 is a simple variable, whereas X(2) is one element in an array that may contain many elements.
3. The subscript is part of the variable name and must not be confused with the value of the subscripted variable. For example, in the statement LET A(4) = 6, the subscript is 4 and the value of A(4) is 6.

Summary

A *subscripted variable* in BASIC consists of a variable followed by a set of parentheses containing a nonnegative integer (or a variable or numerical expression whose value is a nonnegative integer). The expression in the parentheses is called the *subscript.*

An *array* is a collection of subscripted variables with the same variable name. For example, FAN$(0), FAN$(1), . . . , FAN$(7) is an 8-element array called FAN$.

Exercises 9-1

A **1.** Tell whether each of the following is a legal variable name.

a. K$ **b.** K1$ **c.** K$(1)
d. 2F(2) **e.** ZZ **f.** ZZ(1)
g. P(4)$ **h.** EM(0) **i.** X(B$)
j. B6$(6) **k.** 1Y(2) **l.** NICE$(4)

2. In Exercise 1, list the legal subscripted variables.

3. Write each of the following as a BASIC subscripted variable.

a. X sub 4 **b.** AB sub 10 **c.** L string sub 8
d. MN sub 0 **e.** MICE string sub 7 **f.** R3 sub 3

B **4.** The student store at BIG High School keeps track of some of the items it sells by storing the name of each item in a string array, called ITEM$. Use this diagram of array ITEM$ to answer (a)–(f) below:

Array ITEM$

ITEM$(0)	NOTEBOOK
ITEM$(1)	PENCIL
ITEM$(2)	JACKET
ITEM$(3)	EMBLEM
ITEM$(4)	RULER
ITEM$(5)	COMPASS
ITEM$(6)	PENNANT

a. PRINT ITEM$(5) **b.** PRINT ITEM$(0)
c. PRINT ITEM$(6) **d.** PRINT ITEM$(1)
e. PRINT LEFT$(ITEM$(4), 4) **f.** PRINT RIGHT$(ITEM$(5), 4)

5. Give the output of each of the commands below if the elements in array NUM have these values:

Array NUM

NUM(1)	5
NUM(2)	2
NUM(3)	17
NUM(4)	9
NUM(5)	25
NUM(6)	0

a. PRINT 5 * NUM(1)
b. PRINT NUM(2) + 3
c. PRINT NUM(2) + NUM(3)
d. PRINT NUM(2 + 3)
e. PRINT NUM(1 * 3)
f. PRINT NUM(1) * 3

6. Give the output of each of the commands below if the elements in array TREE$ and the variables I and K have these values:

Array TREE$

TREE$(0)	MAPLE
TREE$(1)	PALM
TREE$(2)	OAK
TREE$(3)	WILLOW
TREE$(4)	PINE
TREE$(5)	CHESTNUT
TREE$(6)	BIRCH

I	2
K	−1

a. PRINT TREE$(I)
b. PRINT TREE$(K + 6)
c. PRINT TREE$(I + 2)
d. PRINT TREE$(K + 3 * I)
e. PRINT TREE$(4) + " CONE"
f. PRINT "WHITE " + TREE$(6)
g. PRINT MID$(TREE$(3), 2, 3)
h. PRINT TREE$(4) + MID$(TREE$(5), 6, 3)

Lab Activity

Experimenting with Subscripts

Generally, when using subscripted variables, the number in the parentheses should be a nonnegative integer. Some computers, however, allow for other numbers as subscripts. In this lab activity, you will investigate what types of numbers your computer permits. Type the program at the top of the next page into your computer:

```
10 INPUT "TYPE SUBSCRIPT NUMBER:  "; N
20 LET TRY(N) = 99: REM * TRY(N) IS THE SUBSCRIPTED VARIABLE
30 PRINT TRY(N)
40 END
```

Problems

1. RUN the program, typing 0 as the subscript. Does your computer PRINT the number 99 or give an ERROR message? Is 0 allowed as a subscript?
2. RUN the program again and type −6 for the subscript. Does your computer PRINT the number 99 or give an ERROR message? Are negative numbers allowed as subscripts?
3. RUN the program a third time and type 1.4. What is the result? Does your computer accept decimals as subscripts or print an error message?
4. If in Problem 3 your computer PRINTed the number 99 when 1.4 was INPUT as the subscript, then change line 30 to

   ```
   30 PRINT TRY(1)
   ```

   and add this line:

   ```
   35 PRINT TRY(2)
   ```

   RUN the program and type 1.4. What does the computer PRINT?
5. RUN the program again and type 1.9. What does the computer PRINT?
6. Can you state precisely what your computer does to a decimal subscript? Test your conclusion by RUNning the program for each of the values 2.1, 2.7, .5, and −.2.

9-2 Filling and PRINTing an Array

Filling an Array

Strings or numbers may be assigned to the subscripted variables in an array using LET, READ, or INPUT statements. Let's write a program to store the strings shown in the diagram below in array KIT$.

Array KIT$

KIT$(1)	MORRIS
KIT$(2)	FELIX
KIT$(3)	MICKEY
KIT$(4)	SAM
KIT$(5)	GARFIELD

One way to fill this array is illustrated by the READ . . . DATA statements of Program 1 below:

Program 1

Statement

```
10 REM * CATS OR KITTENS?
20 READ KIT$(1), KIT$(2), KIT$(3), KIT$(4), KIT$(5)
30 DATA MORRIS, FELIX, MICKEY
35 DATA SAM, GARFIELD
40 END
```

With this program there does not seem to be a need for subscripted variables. You could use these five simple variables just as well: K1$, K2$, . . . , and K5$. Recall from the previous section, however, that the subscript of a subscripted variable may itself be a variable. Using this idea, Program 1 can be rewritten using a FOR . . . NEXT loop:

Program 2

Statement

```
10 REM * CATS OR KITTENS, VERSION 2
20 FOR I = 1 TO 5
30 READ KIT$(I)
40 NEXT I
50 DATA MORRIS, FELIX, MICKEY
55 DATA SAM, GARFIELD
60 END
```

When this program is RUN, the subscripted variable KIT$(I) successively represents each of the five elements in the array. The first time through the loop, when I = 1, the string MORRIS is assigned to KIT$(1). The second time through the loop, FELIX is assigned to KIT$(2), and so on.

Program 2 does exactly the same thing as Program 1, but is two lines longer. Suppose, however, that the DATA list contained 50 strings rather than 5. Then the technique of using a FOR . . . NEXT loop and subscripted variables to fill the array would save a lot of typing. Using the method of the first program you would need to type 50 different variables: KIT$(1), KIT$(2), . . . , and KIT$(50). The second program, however, is easily adapted to this situation; just change the 5 to 50 in line 20. (The computer must also be instructed that the subscripts will be bigger than 10. You will learn how to do that in the next section.)

An INPUT statement could be used in Program 2 and the DATA statements omitted. Line 30 would be changed to: 30 INPUT KIT$(I). Then the user could type the strings to fill array KIT$.

Printing an Array

Once strings or numbers are stored in an array, the program can manipulate them in many ways. The simplest thing to do is to PRINT them out using a FOR . . . NEXT loop. Here is a program that fills an array with a list of scores earned by a gymnast, and then PRINTs the array.

Program 3

Statement

```
  10  REM * PRINTING AN ARRAY
┌ 20  FOR J = 1 TO 4
│ 30  READ EVENT(J)
└ 40  NEXT J
┌ 50  FOR M = 1 TO 4
│ 60  PRINT "SCORE ON EVENT #"; M; "  =  "; EVENT(M)
└ 70  NEXT M
  80  DATA 9.4, 9.8, 10, 9.6
  90  END
```

Output

```
SCORE ON EVENT #1 = 9.4
SCORE ON EVENT #2 = 9.8
SCORE ON EVENT #3 = 10
SCORE ON EVENT #4 = 9.6
```

In the first FOR . . . NEXT loop of this program, the numbers on the DATA list are assigned in order to the subscripted variables EVENT(1), EVENT(2), EVENT(3), and EVENT(4). Then, since the counter M also goes from 1 to 4 in the second FOR . . . NEXT loop, the values of these subscripted variables are PRINTed in line 60. Notice that we could have used the same counter in both FOR . . . NEXT loops, since the loops do not overlap.

Program 3 is a rather simple program that illustrates filling and PRINTing an array. Practical programs usually involve some processing of the subscripted variables in an array before PRINTing. Suppose, for example, that the gymnast's scores are to be PRINTed on a scoreboard in reverse order. Program 4 is a revised version that will do this elementary processing.

Program 4

Statement

```
10 REM * WORKING WITH ARRAYS
20 FOR J = 1 TO 4
30 READ EVENT(J)
40 NEXT J
50 FOR M = 4 TO 1 STEP -1
60 PRINT "SCORE ON EVENT #"; M; "  =  "; EVENT(M)
70 NEXT M
80 DATA 9.4, 9.8, 10, 9.6
90 END
```

Output

```
SCORE ON EVENT #4 = 9.6
SCORE ON EVENT #3 = 10
SCORE ON EVENT #2 = 9.8
SCORE ON EVENT #1 = 9.4
```

Avoiding Pitfalls

Beginning programmers are sometimes confused when two different variables are used to represent the subscripts for the same array. Remember that if two subscripts (say, J and M) have the same value, then the subscripted variables EVENT(J) and EVENT(M), as in Program 3, refer to the same element of the array.

Summary

LET, READ, or INPUT statements may be used to assign values to the subscripted variables in an array. An easy way to fill an array is to use a subscripted variable with a variable subscript, where the variable subscript is the counter in a FOR . . . NEXT loop. For example,

```
.
.
.
40 FOR I = 1 TO 9
50 READ B(I)
60 NEXT I
```

Exercises 9-2

A **1.** Give the value of each of the elements in arrays X and N$, diagrammed below, if the following programs are RUN:

```
10  FOR T = 1 TO 6
20  READ X(T)
30  NEXT T
40  DATA 100, 200, 250, 600
45  DATA -2, 723, 1
50  END
```

```
10  FOR M = 0 TO 5
20  READ N$(M)
30  NEXT M
40  DATA GOOD, BAD, INDIFFERENT
45  DATA OKAY, BLAH, UGH
50  END
```

X(1)	?
X(2)	?
X(3)	?
X(4)	?
X(5)	?
X(6)	?
X(7)	?

N$(0)	?
N$(1)	?
N$(2)	?
N$(3)	?
N$(4)	?
N$(5)	?

2. Predict the output of each of the following programs.

a.
```
10  FOR T = 0 TO 5
20  READ A(T)
30  NEXT T
40  FOR P = 0 TO 5
50  PRINT A(P)
60  NEXT P
70  DATA -1, -1, 7, -8, 10, 11
80  END
```

b.
```
10  FOR M = 1 TO 6
20  READ K$(M)
30  NEXT M
40  FOR B = 6 TO 1 STEP -1
50  PRINT K$(B); "  ";
60  NEXT B
65  PRINT
70  PRINT "OKAY"
80  DATA YOU, WITH, IT, HAD, HAVE, I
90  END
```

c.
```
10  FOR R = 8 TO 1 STEP -1
20  READ D$(R)
30  NEXT R
40  PRINT D$(3); D$(7); D$(5)
45  PRINT D$(6); D$(7); D$(5)
50  DATA C, O, M, P, U, T, E, R
60  END
```

d.
```
10  FOR F = 1 TO 7
20  LET NUM(F) = F - 1
30  NEXT F
40  FOR G = 1 TO 7
50  PRINT NUM(G)
60  NEXT G
70  END
```

e.
```
10 FOR T=2 TO 4
20 INPUT COUNT(T)
30 NEXT T
40 FOR Y=4 TO 2 STEP -1
50 PRINT Y, COUNT(Y)
60 NEXT Y
70 END
RUN
? 1
? 2
? 3
```

f.
```
10 FOR V=1 TO 3
20 INPUT COUNT$(V)
30 NEXT V
40 FOR E=1 TO 3
50 PRINT COUNT$(E), E
60 NEXT E
70 END
RUN
? ONE
? TWO
? THREE
```

3. Modify Program 2 so that it PRINTs the elements of array KIT$ in reverse order.

4. Modify Program 2 so that it PRINTs only the first, third, and fifth elements of array KIT$.

B

5. Write a program that uses an INPUT statement to fill an array with five names, then PRINTs the array.

6. Write a program that fills an array with five random integers, each between 50 and 100, then PRINTs the array.

7. Write a program that fills an array CLR$ with the strings in this DATA line: 100 DATA BLUE, PURPLE, GREEN, TURQUOISE. Then have the program PRINT a table similar to the following:

```
VARIABLE       VALUE

CLR$(1)        BLUE
CLR$(2)        PURPLE
CLR$(3)        GREEN
CLR$(4)        TURQUOISE
```

8. Write a program that INPUTs a string, then stores the string in array A$ only if the string begins with the letter P. Have the program PRINT the array as soon as it contains eight elements.

9. Write a program that INPUTs an integer, then stores the integer in the array NUM$ only if the number is odd. Have the program PRINT the array when the trailer value −999 is INPUT. (*Hint:* Use a counter to keep track of how many integers are being put into the array.)

10. Write a program that fills an array with the even integers from 20 to 36 (that is, A(1) = 20, A(2) = 22, A(3) = 24, . . .), then PRINTs the sum of the array elements.

C **11.** *Challenge:* Write a program to fill two arrays (say, NOUN$ and VERB$) with English nouns and verbs. Have the program choose randomly a noun, a verb, and then another noun to form random sentences like:

```
DOG BITES CARROT
CARROT THROWS CAT
.
.
.
```

Lab Activity

A Weaving Simulation

(for use with *Apple* computers)

Computers are used by artists and designers to help them visualize their ideas and sometimes even to produce a final product. In this lab activity, you will explore a rather simple but somewhat long program that generates weaving patterns. The program draws horizontal lines at random intervals on the screen, then "weaves" vertical lines alternately "over" and "under" them, just as in real weaving of cloth or baskets. The illusion of one line being "over" another is achieved by plotting the second line right on top of the first, thus erasing the point on the first line where the crossing occurs. Of course, this works only if the lines are relatively thick and are of different colors or textures. (This activity works best on a color monitor, but you can still see the patterns without color.)

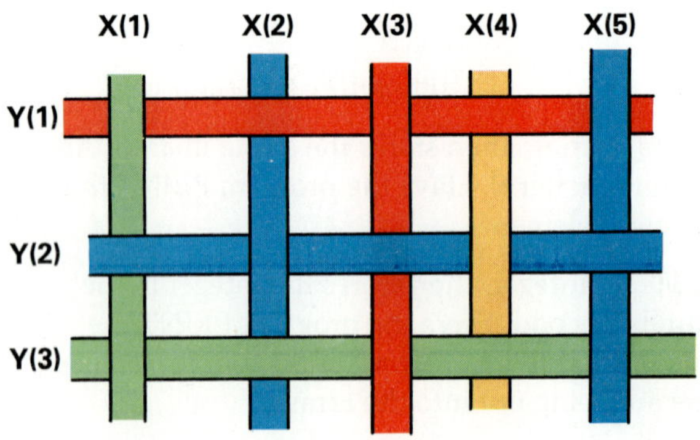

In the program, the variables NY and NX represent the number of horizontal and vertical lines, respectively. Two arrays are used to record the positions of the lines; Y(1) is the vertical coordinate of the first horizontal line, Y(2) is the coordinate of the second horizontal line, and so forth. Similarly, X(1), X(2), . . . , and X(NX) are the horizontal coordinates of the vertical lines. These positions are selected randomly in subroutines 1000 and 1200. The vertical coordinate of the first horizontal line is chosen to be Y(1) = 1 (line 1020); and the horizontal coordinate of the first vertical line is chosen to be X(1) = 1 (line 1220). Then each succeeding line is determined randomly to be between 2 and 7 spaces below or to the right of the preceding one.

Subroutine 1400 draws the horizontal lines in a straightforward way, using a FOR . . . NEXT loop. Subroutine 1500 draws the vertical lines. First, in lines 1530 to 1570, it draws vertical segments from the top of the screen to the point right above the first horizontal line (line 1530), then between each pair of horizontal lines (lines 1540–1560), and finally from below the last line to the bottom of the screen (line 1570). The loop in lines 1580 to 1600 plots the crossovers. If the variable OVER has the value 1, then the loop makes the vertical line being drawn go *over* every second horizontal line starting with the first. If OVER = 2, then the *even* horizontal lines are crossed over. The big loop of subroutine 1500 ends by changing the value of OVER from 1 to 2 or from 2 to 1 (line 1620), so that the next vertical line will cross over the other horizontal lines. (*Note:* The DIM statement in lines 1010 and 1210 tells the computer that subscripts bigger than 10 will be used. DIM will be explained fully in the next section.)

Here is the program.

```
10  REM * WEAVING SIMULATION
20  GR
30  GOSUB 1000: REM * SELECT HORIZONTAL STRIPS
40  GOSUB 1200: REM * SELECT VERTICAL STRIPS
50  GOSUB 1400: REM * DRAW HORIZONTAL STRIPS
60  GOSUB 1500: REM * DRAW VERTICAL STRIPS
70  END
990  REM ** SUBROUTINE TO SELECT Y(1), Y(2), . . . , AND Y(NY), THE
          POSITIONS OF HORIZONTAL STRIPS **
1000  LET NY = 1: REM * NUMBER OF HORIZONTAL STRIPS
1010  DIM Y(39): REM * MAXIMUM NUMBER OF STRIPS
1020  LET Y(1) = 1: REM * TO START THINGS OFF
1030  LET NY = NY + 1: REM * NEXT STRIP
1040  LET Y(NY) = Y(NY - 1) + 2 + INT(5 * RND(1)): REM * MOVE DOWN
        BETWEEN 2 AND 7 ROWS
```

Program continued on next page.

```
1050  IF Y(NY) < 38 THEN GOTO 1030: REM * ROOM REMAINS ON SCREEN
1060  LET NY = NY - 1: REM * ELIMINATE THE LAST STRIP
1070  RETURN
1190  REM ** SUBROUTINE TO SELECT X(1), X(2), . . . , AND X(NX), THE
            POSITIONS OF VERTICAL STRIPS **
1200  LET NX = 1: REM * NUMBER OF VERTICAL STRIPS
1210  DIM X(39): REM * MAXIMUM NUMBER OF STRIPS
1220  LET X(1) = 1: REM * TO START THINGS OFF
1230  LET NX = NX + 1: REM * NEXT STRIP
1240  LET X(NX) = X(NX - 1) + 2 + INT(5 * RND(1)): REM * MOVE OVER
        BETWEEN 2 AND 7 COLUMNS
1250  IF X(NX) < 38 THEN GOTO 1230: REM * ROOM REMAINS ON SCREEN
1260  LET NX = NX - 1: REM * ELIMINATE THE LAST STRIP
1270  RETURN
1390  REM * * SUBROUTINE TO DRAW HORIZONTAL STRIPS **
1400  FOR I = 1 TO NY
1410  COLOR = 1 + INT(15 * RND(1)): REM * COLOR NUMBER FROM 1 TO 15
1420  HLIN 0, 39 AT Y(I)
1430  NEXT I
1440  RETURN

1490  REM ** SUBROUTINE TO DRAW VERTICAL STRIPS **
1500  LET OVER = 1: REM * OVER/UNDER COUNTER
1510  FOR I = 1 TO NX:  REM * FOR EACH VERTICAL STRIP
1520  COLOR = 1 + INT(15 * RND(1)): REM * COLOR NUMBER FROM 1 TO 15
1530  VLIN 0, Y(1) - 1 AT X(I): REM * STRIP FROM TOP TO FIRST
        HORIZONTAL STRIP
1540  FOR J = 1 TO NY - 1: REM * PLOT VERTICAL SEGMENTS BETWEEN
        HORIZONTAL STRIPS
1550  VLIN Y(J) + 1, Y(J + 1) - 1 AT X(I)
1560  NEXT J
1570  VLIN Y(NY) + 1, 39 AT X(I): REM * LAST SEGMENT TO BOTTOM OF SCREEN
1580  FOR J = OVER TO NY STEP 2: REM * NOW PLOT CROSSOVERS EVERY OTHER
        STRIP
1590  PLOT X(I), Y(J)
1600  NEXT J
1610  LET OVER = OVER + 1: REM * CROSS OVER THE OTHER STRIPS NEXT TIME
1620  IF OVER = 3 THEN LET OVER = 1: REM * ALTERNATE BETWEEN 1 AND 2
1630  NEXT I: REM * NEXT VERTICAL STRIP
1640  RETURN
```

Problems

1. RUN the program several times to observe how it works.
2. By changing the statements in lines 1040 and 1240, cause the pattern to be PRINTed closer together (on the average).
3. Change the program so that it makes a *regular* pattern; that is, the spacing between the lines is always the same.
4. Make the pattern even more regular by having the user choose one color for the horizontal strips and another color for the vertical strips.
5. Change the program so that every strip is two screen dots wide.
6. *Challenge:* Change the program so that the strips are of random thickness (between 1 and 3 dots wide) as well as being randomly spaced.

9-3 Big Arrays: DIM

In the two previous sections, we mentioned that the program below needs to be modified before it will RUN correctly.

Program 1

Statement

```
10 REM * CATS OR KITTENS, VERSION 3
20 FOR I = 1 TO 50
30 READ KIT$(I)
40 NEXT I
50 DATA MORRIS, FELIX, . . . (total of 50 DATA values)
60 END
```

Output

```
BAD SUBSCRIPT ERROR IN 30
```

The reason that the BAD SUBSCRIPT ERROR (or SUBSCRIPT OUT OF BOUNDS on some computers) occurs in line 30 is that the computer ordinarily reserves memory space for only 11 elements of an array (with subscripts from 0 to 10). If more elements are needed, you must use a DIM (for DIMension) statement to tell the computer to reserve more space. For example, in Program 1, 50 subscripted variables are needed, so the statement

```
15 DIM KIT$(50)
```

must be included.

When the statement in line 15 is executed, 51 memory locations are reserved for array KIT$ (for subscripts from 0 to 50). The number in the parentheses in a DIM statement tells the computer the biggest subscript that can occur in the array. A DIM statement must be executed before the array is used in the program, so line 15 was chosen as a safe place to DIMension array KIT$ in Program 1.

When writing a program there is no harm in DIMensioning an array with a number larger than the biggest subscript you actually need. When you are not sure how many subscripted variables will be needed, DIMension the array with a big enough number so that the program will RUN. Keep in mind, however, that all computers have a limited amount of memory space, so DIMensions should not be made too large. (See the Lab Activity for this section.) It is a good programming practice to DIMension all arrays, even those in which the subscripts will never exceed 10.

A variable or a BASIC numerical expression whose value is a positive integer may be used in the parentheses in a DIM statement, as Program 2 illustrates.

Program 2

Statement	Remark
10 PRINT "DIMENSIONING ARRAYS"	
20 INPUT "STORE HOW MANY NUMBERS: "; NUM	
30 DIM S(NUM)	*NUM is biggest subscript in array S.*
40 FOR J = 1 TO NUM	
50 INPUT S(J)	
60 NEXT J	
65 PRINT "THE NUMBERS ARE STORED."	
70 END	

Output

```
DIMENSIONING ARRAYS
STORE HOW MANY NUMBERS:   ? 3
? -10
? 1000
? 256
THE NUMBERS ARE STORED.
```

The three numbers −10, 1000, and 256 are now stored in the computer's memory in the locations named S(1), S(2), and S(3). Because the counter J goes from 1 to NUM in line 40, the subscripted variable S(0) of array S is unused.

More than one array may be used in a program. If a program has more than one array to be DIMensioned, this may be done in separate DIM statements or all at one time. For example, in Program 1, if you wanted to store the ages of the cats as well as their names, you could DIMension another array, say AGE, by changing the DIM statement to:

```
15 DIM KIT$(50), AGE(50)
```

Avoiding Pitfalls

1. An array may not be DIMensioned more than once in a program. If two DIM statements for the same array are executed, or if the same DIM statement is executed more than once, a message such as REDIMENSIONED ARRAY ERROR (or DUPLICATE DEFINITION) will result. For example, this error would occur in Program 2 if the DIM statement in line 30 were placed inside the FOR . . . NEXT loop, say at line 45.
2. Be sure that you do not refer in a program to an element of an array with subscript bigger than the array's DIMension. If you do, the computer will PRINT a BAD SUBSCRIPT ERROR message (or SUBSCRIPT OUT OF BOUNDS), and the program will stop.

Summary

If subscripts bigger than 10 are needed in an array in a program, a DIM statement *must* be used. Even if the subscripts in an array will never exceed 10, it is a good programming practice to DIMension the array to save memory space.

A variable or a BASIC numerical expression whose value is a positive integer may be used in the parentheses in a DIM statement.

One or more arrays may be DIMensioned in a single DIM statement.

Exercises 9-3

In Exercises 1–3, write a DIM statement that will reserve enough memory space in the specified array for all the values on the DATA list.

A 1. 100 DATA 36, 42, 25, 18, 19, 18, 37, 26, 40, 40, 28, 23, 33
array: AGE

2. 230 DATA YES, NO, TRUE, FALSE, GOOD, BAD, UP
240 DATA DOWN, LEFT, RIGHT, ACROSS
array: AN$

3. 500 DATA BEANS, CARROTS, CORN, PEPPERS
600 DATA CUCUMBERS, EGGPLANT
array: VEG$

4. Predict the output of each of the following programs.

a.
```
10  DIM A(5), B(5)
20  FOR X = 1 TO 5
30  LET A(X) = X + 8
40  LET B(X) = 3 * X
50  NEXT X
60  PRINT A(X), B(X)
70  END
```

b.
```
10  DIM N(11)
20  FOR Q = 1 TO 11
30  LET N(Q) = Q
40  NEXT Q
50  FOR T = 1 TO 11 STEP 2
60  PRINT N(T)
70  NEXT T
80  END
```

5. For any errors in the following programs, give a possible correction.

a.
```
10  DIM A(14)
20  FOR X = 1 TO 15
30  READ A(X)
40  NEXT X
50  DATA 1, 3, 12, 8, 5, 50, 70, 80
60  DATA -5, 10, -12, 25, 8, 7, 15
70  END
```

b.
```
10  DIM X(12)
20  FOR X = 1 TO 12
30  READ B(X)
40  NEXT X
50  DATA -1, 4, 8, 0, 10, -7
60  DATA 18, 9, -2, 1, 0, 4
70  END
```

c.
```
10  DIM DIR$(11)
20  FOR Y = 1 TO 11
30  INPUT "DIRECTION:  "; DIR$(Y)
40  NEXT Y
50  DIM DIR$(5)
60  FOR Y = 1 TO 5
70  PRINT DIR$(Y)
80  NEXT Y
90  END
```

d.
```
10  DIM XT(20)
20  INPUT "HOW MANY NUMBERS:  "; NUM
30  DIM XT(NUM)
40  FOR J = 1 TO NUM
50  LET XT(J) = J
60  NEXT J
70  END
```

6. Write a single DIM statement that will reserve enough memory space for each of the following arrays:

a. The array EMP$ that will store the names of 56 employees.

b. The arrays REC$ and PRC that will store the names of 100 record albums and their respective prices.

c. The arrays ITEM$ and INV that will store 70 product names and their respective inventory numbers.

B 7. a. Write a program that fills an array with 40 random integers, each between 25 and 60, then PRINTs the array.

b. Change the program in (a) so that it INPUTs the number of random integers to fill the array.

8. a. Write a program using READ . . . DATA to fill an array WRD$ with the English word corresponding to each of the first 15 positive integers (WRD$(1) = "ONE", WRD$(2) = "TWO", and so on). Have the program PRINT the array in reverse order.

b. Change the program in (a) so that it PRINTs the English word corresponding to the number NUM, which is INPUT from a user.

9. Write a program that fills an array with the names of 12 possible vacation sites, then randomly chooses and PRINTs one element of the array.

10. Without using INPUT or READ . . . DATA statements, write a program that fills a 26-element array with the letters of the alphabet, then PRINTs the array in reverse order. (*Hint:* Use ASCII codes and CHR$.)

C 11. *Challenge:* (Graphics) Write a program that fills two arrays X and Y with the horizontal and vertical coordinates, respectively, of points of a figure on the graphics screen. Have the program plot the points. Then when the user types UP, DOWN, LEFT, or RIGHT, the program should erase the screen and then redraw the figure moved 10 points (dots) in the direction specified. (*Hint:* Have the program change the values of the elements of the arrays X and Y before replotting.)

Lab Activity

Big DIMensions

The DIM statement in BASIC causes the computer to reserve space in its memory for arrays. Since the amount of memory space of computers is limited, the number of subscripted variables (that is, the number inside the parentheses in a DIM statement) cannot be made too large without causing the computer to run out of space.

Type the following program that will allow you to investigate the size of your computer's memory.

```
10  INPUT N1
20  DIM BIG(N1)
30  PRINT "OKAY"
40  END
```

Problems

1. RUN the program and type a large number. If the program PRINTs the message OKAY for the output, then the computer accepted the number as a DIMension; otherwise, you will get an error message of some kind. By experimenting, find the biggest number that the computer will accept as a DIMension.

2. Add the following statements to the program:

```
32 LET X = 3 * INT(X / 465) + 10 * BIG(N1)
36 PRINT "MY DOG HAS MEMORY PROBLEMS, TOO"
```

   Now RUN the program and find the largest number the computer will accept as a DIMension. The amount of memory available for the BIG array has decreased because the statements in the new program lines take up some space.

3. Add a second array to the program by deleting lines 32 and 36 and adding the following statements:

```
40 INPUT N2
50 DIM LARGE(N2)
60 PRINT "OKAY AGAIN"
70 END
```

   RUN the program and try different combinations of values for N1 and N2 until the sum of the two is as large as the computer will accept. Is the sum the same as the maximum value you found in Problem 1? What could account for any difference?

4. Rewrite the program to investigate how large a string array can be DIMensioned on your computer.

9-4 Using Arrays: Summing and Tallying

Summing Arrays

Thus far, we have simply filled arrays and then PRINTed them out in order or backwards. Most applications require more complicated manipulations of the data stored in the array. In the following program, for example, the elements of each of two arrays, CAR and TRUCK, are summed. The values in array CAR represent the number of cars sold by the What a Deal automobile company in each of five weeks. The array TRUCK contains the number of trucks sold by the company during each of those same five weeks.

Three subroutines are used in the program: the first one (subroutine 200) fills each array, the second (subroutine 300) sums each array, and the last one (subroutine 500) PRINTs the results.

Here is the program:

Program 1

Statement

```
10  REM * SUMMING ARRAYS
20  DIM CAR(5), TRUCK(5)
30  GOSUB 200: REM * FILL ARRAYS
40  GOSUB 300: REM * SUM ARRAYS
50  GOSUB 500: REM * PRINT RESULTS
60  END
190  REM ** SUBROUTINE TO FILL ARRAYS **
200  FOR J = 1 TO 5
210  READ CAR(J), TRUCK(J)
220  NEXT J
230  RETURN
290  REM ** SUBROUTINE TO SUM ARRAYS **
300  LET S1 = 0
310  LET S2 = 0
320  FOR J = 1 TO 5
330  LET S1 = S1 + CAR(J)
340  LET S2 = S2 + TRUCK(J)
350  NEXT J
360  RETURN
490  REM ** SUBROUTINE TO PRINT RESULTS **
500  PRINT "WEEK"; TAB(10); "CARS"; TAB(20); "TRUCKS"
510  FOR X = 1 TO 5
520  PRINT X; TAB(10); CAR(X); TAB(20); TRUCK(X)
530  NEXT X
540  PRINT "CARS SOLD:  "; S1
550  PRINT "TRUCKS SOLD:  "; S2
560  RETURN
600  DATA 36, 14, 42, 13, 39, 18
610  DATA 33, 14, 40, 15
```

Output

WEEK	CARS	TRUCKS
1	36	14
2	42	13
3	39	18
4	33	14
5	40	15

```
CARS SOLD:  190
TRUCKS SOLD:  74
```

In this program, the filling and summing of the two arrays is done separately (in subroutines 200 and 300). It is possible to omit subroutine 300 and do the summing of the two arrays in the same FOR . . . NEXT loop used to fill the arrays. Subroutine 200 would then need to be changed to:

```
200  LET S1 = 0
210  LET S2 = 0
220  FOR J = 1 TO 5
230  READ CAR(J), TRUCK(J)
240  LET S1 = S1 + CAR(J)
250  LET S2 = S2 + TRUCK(J)
260  NEXT J
270  RETURN
```

Although Program 1 would now be a few lines shorter, it would not necessarily be better. Many programmers prefer to use subroutines for each task, since the resulting structure makes a program that is easier to read, understand, modify, and debug.

Suppose the owner of the What A Deal company also wants to find the total number of cars and trucks sold each week during the five-week period. This is easily done. Simply add a subroutine to Program 1 (the original version) that will fill an array (say TTL, for total) with the sums of the corresponding elements of CAR and TRUCK; namely,

CAR(1) + TRUCK(1), CAR(2) + TRUCK(2), . . .

Here are the statements for the subroutine to be added to the program:

```
45  GOSUB 400: REM * WEEKLY TOTALS
390  REM ** SUBROUTINE TO FIND WEEKLY TOTALS **
400  FOR Y = 1 TO 5
410  LET TTL(Y) = CAR(Y) + TRUCK(Y)
420  NEXT Y
430  RETURN
```

In addition, the statements in lines 20, 500, and 520 need to be changed:

```
20  DIM CAR(5), TRUCK(5), TTL(5)
500  PRINT "WEEK"; TAB(10); "CARS"; TAB(20); "TRUCKS"; TAB(30); "WEEK TOTAL"
520  PRINT X; TAB(10); CAR(X); TAB(20); TRUCK(X); TAB(30); TTL(X)
```

Here is the output of the revised version of Program 1:

```
WEEK       CARS      TRUCKS    WEEK TOTAL
1          36        14        50
2          42        13        55
3          39        18        57
4          33        14        47
5          40        15        55
CARS SOLD:  190
TRUCKS SOLD:  74
```

Tallying

Another important use of arrays involves counting, or *tallying*, the results of simulated or real events. For instance, suppose a survey is taken of some of the students in your school to find out how they rate the lunch program on a scale from 1 ("horrible") to 5 ("fantastic"). The results of this survey could be counted by hand, but it is easy to write a program to do it. Since five different responses need to be counted, you can use a five-element array to tally the number of times each rating occurs. Here is one possible outline of the algorithm:

Step 1 Initialize the elements in the array, say SURVEY, to zero.

Step 2 READ each student's rating, say R, from a DATA list.

Step 3 If R is the trailer value, then GOTO Step 4. Otherwise, add 1 to the element in the array that corresponds to the rating number, then GOTO Step 2.

Step 4 PRINT the results.

Step 3 needs some more detail. If R is not the trailer value, then to which array element should the program add 1? Consider this statement:

```
LET SURVEY(R) = SURVEY(R) + 1
```

If 4, for example, is READ for the value of R, then the statement causes SURVEY(4) to be increased by 1; if 2 is READ, then SURVEY(2) is increased by 1, and so forth. With this statement, each array element is used as a counter.

The algorithm is translated into BASIC code in Program 2 on the next page. Each major task is done in a subroutine. The trailer value is −1.

Program 2

Statement

```
10  PRINT "TALLYING"
20  DIM SURVEY(5)
30  GOSUB 100: REM * INITIALIZE ARRAY
40  GOSUB 200: REM * READ AND TALLY RATINGS
50  GOSUB 300: REM * PRINT RESULTS
60  END
90  REM ** SUBROUTINE TO INITIALIZE ARRAY **
100 FOR J = 1 TO 5
110 LET SURVEY(J) = 0
120 NEXT J
130 RETURN
190 REM ** SUBROUTINE TO READ AND TALLY RATINGS **
200 READ R
210 IF R > 0 THEN LET SURVEY(R) = SURVEY(R) + 1: GOTO 200
220 RETURN: REM * TRAILER VALUE IS NEGATIVE
290 REM ** SUBROUTINE TO PRINT RESULTS **
300 PRINT "RATING", "FREQUENCY"
310 FOR K = 1 TO 5
320 PRINT K, SURVEY(K)
330 NEXT K
340 RETURN
500 DATA 2, 3, 3, 4, 1, 2, 5, 4, 2, 3, 3, 1, 4, 5, 2, 2, 3, 3, 4, 1, 5, 4, 3, 2, 3, -1
```

Output

```
TALLYING
RATING          FREQUENCY
1               3
2               6
3               8
4               5
5               3
```

The data from a tallying program can be represented graphically. For example, the frequency of each rating in the output of Program 2 above may be illustrated by PRINTing a horizontal string of asterisks (or any other text character of your choice), where each asterisk represents one occurrence of a given rating.

The output would then be as follows:

```
TALLYING
RATING                   FREQUENCY
1                        * * *
2                        * * * * * *
3                        * * * * * * * *
4                        * * * * *
5                        * * *
```

A graphical display such as this, representing the frequency with which data occurs, is called a *bar graph* or *histogram.* Here is a subroutine that will PRINT the histogram above for the data in Program 2.

```
55  GOSUB 400: REM * PRINT HISTOGRAM
400 PRINT "TALLYING"
405 PRINT "RATING", "FREQUENCY"
410 FOR T = 1 TO 5
420 PRINT T,
425 IF SURVEY(T) = 0 THEN GOTO 460
430 FOR Q = 1 TO SURVEY(T)
440 PRINT " * ";
450 NEXT Q
460 PRINT
470 NEXT T
480 RETURN
```

The comma at the end of line 420 and the semicolon at the end of line 440 cause the value of T and the asterisks to be PRINTed on the same line. The PRINT instruction in line 460 is needed to move the cursor to the next line before printing the next row.

The tallying technique is very useful in programs that simulate random events. For example, you could write a program to tally the number of times a 1, 2, . . . , or 6 occurs when a die is thrown, or write a program to tally the results of a simulated election. (See Exercises 2 and 5.)

Avoiding Pitfalls

When adding the elements of an array, be sure to initialize the summer to 0. Likewise, when using an array to tally, remember to initialize *all* the array elements to 0 (as was done for elements of the array SURVEY in lines 100–120 of Program 2).

Summary

To find the sum of all the numbers in an array, use a summer in a FOR . . . NEXT loop. For example, if array A has 6 elements, then you can use:

```
   .
   .
   .
50 LET SUM = 0
60 FOR J = 1 TO 6
70 LET SUM = SUM + A(J)
80 NEXT J
   .
   .
   .
```

To fill a third array (say THRD) with the sums of the corresponding elements of two other 8-element arrays (say, FRST and SCND), use a FOR . . . NEXT loop and a statement like the one in line 110 below.

```
    .
    .
    .
100 FOR K = 1 TO 8
110 LET THRD(K) = FRST(K) + SCND(K)
120 NEXT K
    .
    .
    .
```

To use an array (say, TALLY) to tally results, you need a statement such as:

```
LET TALLY(R) = TALLY(R) + 1
```

With this statement, each array element is used as a counter. TALLY(1) counts the number of times that 1 occurs, TALLY(2) the number of 2's, and so forth.

Exercises 9-4

A **1.** Predict the output of each of the programs in (a)–(f).

a.
```
10 DIM A(3)
20 READ A(3), A(2), A(1)
30 FOR K = 1 TO 3
40 PRINT A(K)
50 NEXT K
60 DATA 40, 13, 52
70 END
```

b.
```
10 DIM ST(6)
20 FOR C = 1 TO 6
30 READ ST(C)
40 PRINT ST(C) - 1
50 NEXT C
60 DATA 6, 5, 4, 3, 2, 1
70 END
```

c.
```
10 READ X
20 DIM NM$(X)
30 FOR I = 1 TO X
40 READ NM$(I)
50 NEXT I
60 FOR Y = 1 TO X
70 PRINT NM$(Y)
80 NEXT Y
90 DATA 4, SLOWPOKE, SPURS
95 DATA SADDLE, JEANS
100 END
```

d.
```
10 LET MULT = 1
20 DIM P(4)
30 FOR K = 1 TO 4
40 INPUT P(K)
50 LET MULT = MULT * P(K)
60 NEXT K
70 PRINT MULT
80 END
RUN
? 10
? 5
? 20
? 10
```

e.
```
10 DIM NUM(15)
15 LET SUM = 0
20 FOR J = 1 TO 15
30 READ NUM(J)
40 NEXT J
50 FOR K = 1 TO 15
60 LET SUM = SUM + NUM(K)
70 NEXT K
80 PRINT "SUM IS:  "; SUM
90 DATA 3, 2, 0, 5, 5, 4, 9, 3
100 DATA 1, 7, 6, 1, 4, 0, 2
110 END
```

f.
```
5 DIM X$(3), Y$(3)
10 FOR N = 1 TO 3
20 READ X$(N)
30 NEXT N
40 FOR M = 1 TO 3
50 READ Y$(M)
60 NEXT M
70 FOR P = 1 TO 3
80 PRINT X$(P) + Y$(P)
90 NEXT P
100 DATA SUPER, MEGA
105 DATA EXTRA, DOOPER
110 DATA MAGNIFICENT, ORDINARY
120 END
```

2. Rewrite Program 2 to tally the results of an election between two candidates, I. PROMISE and D. INCUMBENT. Have a 1 on the DATA list represent a vote for D. INCUMBENT, and a 2 represent a vote for I. PROMISE. Then have the program PRINT the total votes received by each candidate and the name of the winning candidate. (Put at least 20 values on the DATA list.)

B 3. a. Write a program that fills an array P with 20 numbers READ from a DATA list, then PRINTs the product of the elements of the array.

b. Change the program in (a) so that it PRINTs the sum of those array elements that are divisible by 3.

c. Change the program in (b) so that it also counts how many of the array elements are divisible by 3.

4. Write a program that fills an array RD with 25 random integers, each between 1 and 100. Have the program calculate and PRINT the average of the integers.

5. a. Write a program that simulates rolling a die 75 times. Have the program use an array to tally the number of times a 1, 2, . . . , or 6 occurs, and then PRINT the results.
   b. Modify the program in (a) so that it also PRINTs a histogram of the results.

6. Write a program that fills an array A$ with the strings in the DATA statements below. Have the program fill a second array B$ with the strings from array A$ that begin with the letter C, then PRINT both arrays.

```
100  DATA COMEDIAN, ACTOR, SINGER, STAGEHAND
110  DATA CAMERA TECHNICIAN, CHOREOGRAPHER
```

7. The Slowpoke Delivery Company bases its delivery rates on zones. The table below shows the cost per pound to ship a package to a particular zone. Write a program that fills an array CST with the numbers listed under COST PER POUND. Have the program INPUT the zone to which a package will be shipped and the weight of the package, and then calculate the total delivery cost. PRINT the output of the program in table form, similar to this:

```
ZONE              COST PER POUND
1                 $1.15
2                 $1.35
3                 $1.45
4                 $1.70
TYPE ZONE, WEIGHT:  ? 3, 5
DELIVERY COST IS:  $7.25
```

8. a. The table below contains the amount of weekly sales and the rate of commission for five salespersons, with employee numbers from 1 to 5. Write a program that fills an array SLE with the numbers listed under SALES and an array RTE with the numbers listed under RATE. Have the program calculate the commission earned by each salesperson, rounded to the nearest cent (commission = sales * rate). PRINT the output of the program in table form, similar to this:

EMPLOYEE	SALES	RATE(%)	COMMISSION
1	435	5.3	$23.06
2	350	6	$21
3	760	4.8	$36.48
4	566	6.2	$35.09
5	310	5	$15.5

b. Modify the program in 8 (a) so that it also sums the elements in array SLE and PRINTs the result.

9. The table below contains the names of seven employees, their employee numbers, and their respective rates of pay per hour. Write a program that fills an array NM$ with the employees' names and an array PAY with their respective rates of pay per hour. Have the program INPUT an employee number and the number of hours worked (not to exceed 40), then PRINT the employee's name and total pay. Have the output PRINT similar to this:

```
EMPLOYEE          NAME             PAY PER HOUR
1                 SUE              $5.25
2                 JOE              $6.80
3                 MARY             $7.25
4                 FRED             $4.95
5                 JILL             $5.15
6                 PETER            $6.50
7                 BETH             $6.75
TYPE EMPLOYEE #, HRS. WORKED:  ? 5, 31
JILL EARNED  $159.65
```

10. Rewrite subroutine 400 (page 479) of Program 2 so that it PRINTs a vertical bar graph, like this:

```
FREQUENCY

                    *
                    *
           *        *
           *        *        *
           *        *        *
  *        *        *        *        *
  *        *        *        *        *
  *        *        *        *        *
  1        2        3        4        5

RATING
```

(*Hint:* Use LOCATE, PRINT @, or VTAB and HTAB.)

11. a. Write a program that uses an array to tally the number of times each letter of the alphabet occurs in an INPUT string (the string is not to exceed 255 characters), then PRINTs the results. (*Hint:* Use ASC.)

b. Modify the program in (a) so that it also PRINTs a histogram of the results.

12. Write a program that uses an array to tally the test grades received by a class of 20 students (the number of A's, B's, C's, and so on), then PRINTs a histogram of the results. Use this DATA statement:

```
200  DATA B, C, E, A, D, C, B, A, C, E, B, B, C, A, A, B, C, D, C, C
```

(*Hint:* Use ASC.)

C 13. Write a program that allows the user to type ten three-digit numbers. Have the program tally and print how many zeros, ones, twos, and so on, appear in the ten numbers. (*Hint:* As a number is INPUT, separate the digits using the INT function. Once a digit has been separated, then add 1 to the appropriate counter in an array.)

14. *Challenge:* Write a program to fill an array with 10 random integers, each between 1 and 50. Then have the program find and PRINT the largest integer.

15. *Challenge:* Write a program to fill an array with scores given by 7 judges during a diving competition (use INPUT). Then have the program discard the highest and lowest scores and PRINT the average of the rest.

Lab Activity

Bar Graphs in Graphics Mode

In this section, you learned how to represent the data in a numerical array in the form of a *bar graph* using text characters. A very effective bar graph display can be produced by using the graphics capability of your computer. Here is a program that loads data into an array using READ . . . DATA and then draws a bar graph. (Choose the version for your computer.)

Apple

```
10  REM ** BAR GRAPHS **
20  GOSUB 1000: REM * FILL ARRAY WITH NUMBERS
30  GOSUB 2000: REM * DISPLAY GRAPH
40  END
990  REM ** SUBROUTINE TO FILL ARRAY NUM **
1000  READ D: REM * DIMENSION
1010  DIM NUM(D)
1020  FOR I = 1 TO D
1030  READ NUM(I)
1040  NEXT I
```

```
1045 RETURN
1990 REM ** SUBROUTINE TO DISPLAY GRAPH **
2000 GR: REM * SET UP GRAPHICS
2010 COLOR = 3: REM * SET COLOR
2020 LET THCK = 3: REM * THICKNESS OF EACH BAR
2030 FOR I = 1 TO D: REM * PLOT EACH BAR
2040 LET X = 5 * I: REM * X-COORDINATE OF VERTICAL BAR
2050 LET Y = NUM(I): REM * LENGTH OF BAR
2055 LET Y = INT(Y + .5): REM * ROUND TO NEAREST INTEGER
2060 GOSUB 2500: REM * PLOT BAR
2070 NEXT I
2080 RETURN
2490 REM ** SUBROUTINE TO PLOT BAR OF LENGTH Y, AT X, WITH THICKNESS THCK **
2500 FOR J = 1 TO THCK: REM * PLOT VERTICAL LINES
2510 VLIN 39, 40 - Y AT X
2520 LET X = X + 1
2530 NEXT J
2540 RETURN
3000 DATA 5
3010 DATA 5, 10, 13, 11, 2
```

TRS-80

Here are the changes for *TRS-80* computers:

```
2000 CLS
2010 ←— delete
2020 LET THCK = 10
2040 LET X = 16 * I
2510 FOR M = 47 TO 48 - Y
2512 SET (X, M)
2515 NEXT M
```

IBM

Here are the changes for *IBM* computers:

```
2000 SCREEN 1, 1
2010 ←— delete
2020 LET THCK = 20
2040 LET X = 25 * I
2510 LINE (X, 199) - (X, 200 - Y)
3010 DATA 25, 50, 65, 55, 10
```

As you can see in subroutine 2500, the program produces vertical bars with thickness THCK. The spacing of the bars is controlled by line 2040 (for each bar, X is the horizontal position and Y is the length). The expression in line 2510 may need some explanation. You must remember that the length of a segment made up of several dots must include both of the endpoints; in the *Apple* version of the program, for example, if Y (length) has the value 3, then the vertical bar will go from 39 to 40 − Y = 40 − 3 = 37, which is 3 dots high.

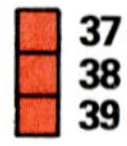

Problems

1. RUN the program and see that it works correctly.
2. Change the DATA so that 8 bars will be produced. Change the thickness of the bars by altering line 2020. RUN the program to see the new results.
3. The display can be made more attractive by spreading it evenly across the screen. If your screen has NH dots available from its left edge to its right edge, and D bars are to be drawn, then each bar and the blank space to its right can use these numbers of dots on the screen:

   ```
   NDOTS = INT((NH − THCK) / (D − 1))
   ```

   There are D − 1 bars that are followed by a blank space. The extra bar at the end takes up THCK dots, so that NH − THCK dots are left to divide up among the first D − 1 bars.

   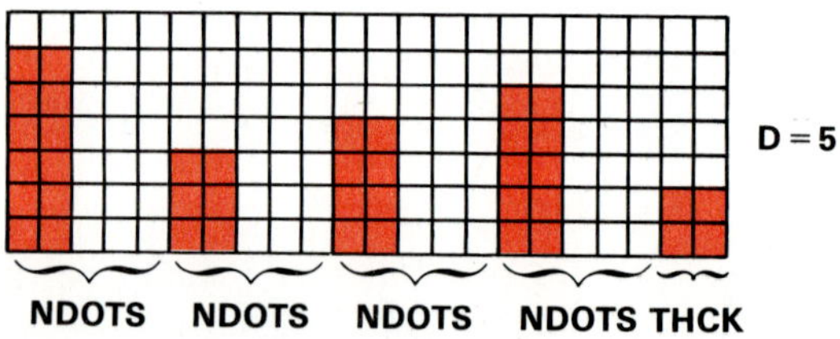

   Add a statement to the program at line 15 to assign NH the appropriate value for your computer. Add a statement at line 2015 to calculate NDOTS according to the formula given above. Finally, change the statement in line 2040 to:

   ```
   2040  LET X = NDOTS * (I − 1)
   ```

   (With this change, the first bar will be at X = NDOTS * 0 = 0, the second will be at X = NDOTS * 1 = NDOTS, and so forth.) RUN the program and verify that it spaces the bars evenly across the screen. RUN the program several times and try different values of D and THCK.

4. If some of the numbers in the NUM array are too large, the corresponding bars will go off the top of the screen. To prevent this, you must scale the bars down to fit. For example, if a hypothetical computer screen is 50 dots high and the biggest number to be graphed is 150, then the height of each bar will have to be made $50/150 = 1/3$ as high as it otherwise would be. In general, if NV is the number of dots from the bottom of your screen to the top, and MAX is the largest number in the NUM array, then the height of the Ith bar will be this:

```
Y = (NV / MAX) * NUM(I)
```

The value of MAX can be found by using the following subroutine:

```
2990 REM ** SUBROUTINE TO FIND MAX VALUE IN NUM ARRAY **
3000 LET MAX = 0
3010 FOR I = 1 TO D
3020 IF NUM(I) > MAX THEN LET MAX = NUM(I)
3030 NEXT I
3040 RETURN
```

The key to this subroutine is line 3020; if an element of the array is found that is bigger than the maximum so far, then a new maximum has been found and it is assigned to MAX. Change the program so that it GOSUBs to 3000 at an appropriate place, defines NV for your computer, and calculates Y in line 2050 according to the formula given above. Test the program thoroughly.

5. Change the program so that it simulates the roll of a single die 400 times. Use the NUM array to tally the results.

9-5 Two-Dimensional Arrays

The location of data in the table below can be described by giving the number of the row in which it appears. For example, 288 is in row 1, 252 is in row 2, and so on.

Students at BIG High School

Rows		
1	Freshmen	288
2	Sophomores	252
3	Juniors	275
4	Seniors	256

You have seen that data such as in the preceding table can be represented by an array S consisting of the subscripted variables S(1) = 288, S(2) = 252, S(3) = 275, and S(4) = 256. (The subscript corresponds to the number of the row in the table.) An array such as S is called a *one-dimensional array* because the location of each element in the array can be described by a single subscript (in this case, the number of the row in which the element appears).

Sometimes two (or more) subscripts are necessary. For example, the table below summarizes the results of a hypothetical poll given to the students at BIG High School concerning a dress code.

Class	In Favor of a Dress Code	Opposed to a Dress Code	No Opinion
Freshmen	158	100	30
Sophomores	131	95	26
Juniors	125	130	30
Seniors	110	124	22

The location of data in this table can be described most conveniently by giving both a row and a column. If we number the table's rows and columns as shown below, then we can describe the location of the number 26, say, as "row 2, column 3."

Rows \ Columns	1	2	3
1	158	100	30
2	131	95	26
3	125	130	20
4	110	124	22

Two-dimensional arrays can be used to store and process data that is arranged in rows and columns. In a two-dimensional array, the location of each element in the array can be described by a subscripted variable having two subscripts. The *first* subscript is the element's *row* number, and the *second* subscript is its *column* number. If we were to store the numbers of the table above in an array D, then the element D(2, 3) would have the value 26. Similarly, the number 130 in the *third* row and *second* column is stored in the *doubly-subscripted variable* D(3, 2).

Since the elements in a two-dimensional array are names of memory locations, the compartment (or "mailbox") idea can be used to illustrate the locations of all the elements in array D, as shown on the next page.

	Col. 1	Col. 2	Col. 3
Row 1	D(1, 1)	D(1, 2)	D(1, 3)
	158	100	30
Row 2	D(2, 1)	D(2, 2)	D(2, 3)
	131	95	26
Row 3	D(3, 1)	D(3, 2)	D(3, 3)
	125	130	20
Row 4	D(4, 1)	D(4, 2)	D(4, 3)
	110	124	22

Two-dimensional arrays are named the same way as one-dimensional arrays, by any legal string or numeric variable. The elements in a two-dimensional array are commonly referred to as *doubly-subscripted variables.*

DIMensioning a Two-Dimensional Array

When a doubly-subscripted variable is used in a program, the largest value allowed for either subscript is 10. However, just as for single-subscripted variables, a DIM statement may be used to specify bigger subscripts. For example, if the data to be assigned to the variables in an array P is arranged in 30 rows and 15 columns, then the statement

```
DIM P(30, 15)
```

can be used. (Actually, this statement reserves memory space for data in 31 rows, numbered 0 to 30, and 16 columns, numbered 0 to 15. When using two-dimensional arrays, however, the number 0 is often avoided as a subscript.) Even though arrays in which the subscripts will never exceed 10 need not be DIMensioned, it is a good programming practice to DIMension all arrays. When more than one array will be used in a program, the arrays may all be DIMensioned in the same statement; for example,

```
DIM LEGUME$(20, 35), FLY(46, 12)
```

Filling and PRINTing Two-Dimensional Arrays

You have already seen that a FOR . . . NEXT loop can be used to fill a one-dimensional array. One method of filling a two-dimensional array is nested FOR . . . NEXT loops.

Let's write a program to fill the array D with the numbers representing the results of the dress code poll. One possible outline of an algorithm is at the top of the next page.

Step 1 Dimension the array D to 4 rows and 3 columns.
Step 2 Arrange the numbers from the table row by row in DATA statements.
Step 3 For each row, READ all the columns.

Steps 2 and 3 need more elaboration. There are many ways the numbers from the table can be arranged in DATA statements, but usually they are typed row by row. With this method, you could type these DATA statements:

```
DATA 158, 100, 30
DATA 131, 95, 26
DATA 125, 130, 20
DATA 110, 124, 22
```

Then in Step 3, to READ all the numbers (columns) across each row, we can have the computer READ the variable D(ROW, COL) in the following order:

```
for ROW = 1
    COL = 1   COL = 2   COL = 3
for ROW = 2
    COL = 1   COL = 2   COL = 3
for ROW = 3
    COL = 1   COL = 2   COL = 3
for ROW = 4
    COL = 1   COL = 2   COL = 3
```

This is exactly the order specified by these nested FOR . . . NEXT loops:

```
FOR ROW = 1 TO 4
FOR COL = 1 TO 3
      .
      .
      .
NEXT COL
NEXT ROW
```

Here is the program:

Program 1

Statement

```
10 PRINT "FILLING A TWO-DIMENSIONAL ARRAY"
20 DIM D(4, 3)
30 FOR ROW = 1 TO 4
40 FOR COL = 1 TO 3
50 READ D(ROW, COL)
60 NEXT COL
70 NEXT ROW
```

```
200  DATA 158, 100, 30
210  DATA 131, 95, 26
220  DATA 125, 130, 20
230  DATA 110, 124, 22
240  END
```

The numbers in the rows do not have to be typed in four statements, as in lines 200–230. The single statement

```
200  DATA 158, 100, 30, 131, 95, 26, 125, 130, 20, 110, 124, 22
```

can be used instead. (Although this single line is more difficult to correct and retype than separate statements.) What is important is the order in which the numbers appear.

Now that array D is filled, let's PRINT the array in table form with row and column numbers. Listed below are the statements that need to be added to the program:

```
80  PRINT "HERE'S THE TABLE:"
90  PRINT "ROW / COL"; TAB(10); "1"; TAB(20); "2"; TAB(30); "3"
100  FOR ROW = 1 TO 4
110  PRINT ROW;
120  FOR COL = 1 TO 3
130  PRINT TAB(10 * COL); D(ROW, COL);
140  NEXT COL
150  PRINT
160  NEXT ROW
```

When Program 1 is RUN with these new statements added, the output looks like this:

Output

```
FILLING A TWO-DIMENSIONAL ARRAY
HERE'S THE TABLE:
ROW / COL       1          2          3
1               158        100        30
2               131        95         26
3               135        130        20
4               110        124        22
```

The instruction PRINT TAB(10 * COL) is used in line 130 to align the output in columns at TAB positions 10, 20, and 30. The blank PRINT statement in line 150 is needed to move the cursor to the next line before printing the next row of output.

Avoiding Pitfalls

1. Remember that the first subscript of a doubly-subscripted variable refers to the row, and the second subscript to the column, in which an array element is located. The variable A(3, 4) is not the same variable as A(4, 3).

2. If a two-dimensional array and a one-dimensional array are both used in the same program, they may not have the same name.

3. Be sure that you do not refer in a program to an element of a two-dimensional array using subscripts bigger than those specified in the DIM statement (or bigger than 10 if there is no DIM statement). If you do, then the computer will print a BAD SUBSCRIPT ERROR message (or SUBSCRIPT OUT OF BOUNDS), and the program will stop.

4. A two-dimensional array may not be DIMensioned more than once in a program. If two DIM statements for the same array are executed, or if the same DIM statement is executed more than once, a message such as REDIMENSIONED ARRAY ERROR (or DUPLICATE DEFINITION) will result.

5. When using nested FOR . . . NEXT loops to fill or PRINT a two-dimensional array, be sure that the loops are nested in the correct order. If you type the strings or numbers from the table into the DATA statements row by row, then the proper order is

```
┌─FOR ROW = . . .
│┌FOR COL = . . .
││       .
││       .
││       .
│└NEXT COL
└─NEXT ROW
```

Summary

A *two-dimensional array* is a collection of *doubly-subscripted* variables having the same variable name. The first subscript of each element refers to the row, and the second subscript to the column, in which the element is located.

If either subscript of a doubly-subscripted variable will be bigger than 10 in a two-dimensional array in a program, then a DIM statement *must* be used. Even when the subscripts will never exceed 10, it is a good programming practice to DIMension all arrays.

Exercises 9-5

A 1. The numbers in the table shown have been stored row by row in the two-dimensional array K. Give the value of the doubly-subscripted variables listed below.

Columns

Rows	1	2	3	4	5	6	7
1	100	104	108	130	170	210	250
2	101	105	109	140	180	220	260
3	102	106	110	150	190	230	270
4	103	107	120	160	200	240	280

a. K(2, 7) **b.** K(3, 4) **c.** K(2, 3)
d. K(4, 2) **e.** K(2, 4) **f.** K(1, 3)
g. K(4, 7) **h.** K(3, 1) **i.** K(3, 6)
j. Write a DIM statement for array K.

2. The letters in the table shown have been stored row by row in the two-dimensional array T$. Fill in the subscripts of each of the doubly-subscripted variables listed below.

Columns

Rows	1	2	3	4	5	6	7	8
1	A	B	C	D	E	F	G	H
2	I	J	K	L	M	N	O	P
3	Q	R	S	T	U	V	W	X

a. T$(?, ?) = "R" **b.** T$(?, ?) = "X" **c.** T$(?, ?) = "K"
d. T$(?, ?) = "E" **e.** T$(?, ?) = "Q" **f.** T$(?, ?) = "I"
g. T$(?, ?) = "B" **h.** T$(?, ?) = "A" **i.** T$(?, ?) = "C"
j. Write a DIM statement for array T$.

3. The characters in the table shown have been stored row by row in the two-dimensional array N$. Predict the output of each of the FOR . . . NEXT loops listed at the top of the next page.

Columns

Rows	1	2	3	4
1	T	O	*	B
2	E	*	O	R
3	N	O	T	*

a.
```
200 FOR Q = 1 TO 4
210 PRINT N$(2, Q);
220 NEXT Q
```

b.
```
300 FOR R = 3 TO 1 STEP -1
310 PRINT N$(R, 2)
320 NEXT R
```

4. Predict the output of each of the following programs.

a.
```
10 DIM D(3, 2)
20 FOR R = 1 TO 3
30 FOR C = 1 TO 2
40 LET D(R, C) = R * C
50 NEXT C
60 NEXT R
70 FOR R = 1 TO 3
80 FOR C = 1 TO 2
90 PRINT D(R, C),
100 NEXT C
110 PRINT
120 NEXT R
130 END
```

b.
```
10 DIM P$(4, 4)
20 FOR I = 1 TO 4
30 FOR J = 1 TO 4
40 IF I < J THEN LET P$(I, J) = "$": GOTO 60
50 LET P$(I, J) = "?"
60 NEXT J
70 NEXT I
80 FOR I = 1 TO 4
90 FOR J = 1 TO 4
100 PRINT P$(I, J);
110 NEXT J
120 PRINT
130 NEXT I
140 END
```

5. Change Program 1, so that it also stores the strings FRESHMEN, SOPHOMORES, JUNIORS, and SENIORS in a one-dimensional array NM$, then PRINTs the output so that it looks like the table on page 488.

B

6. Write a program that fills a two-dimensional array with the strings listed in the table below, then PRINTs the array in table form, with row and column numbers as shown.

ROW / COL	1	2	3	4
1	INSIDE	FRONT	LEFT	UP
2	OUTSIDE	BACK	RIGHT	DOWN

7. a. Write a program that fills a 4-row and 9-column array with random integers, each between 1 and 100, then PRINTs the array in table form with row and column numbers.

b. Change the program in (a) so that it fills the array only with *even* random integers between 1 and 100.

8. The results from a hypothetical election for sheriff are shown in the table at the top of the next page. Write a program that fills a 5-row and 3-column array with the results of the election. Then when the user types a ward number, the program should PRINT the number of votes each candidate received in that ward.

WARD	I.M. TUFFY	B. STRONG	C.D. LIGHT
1	234	123	56
2	126	245	135
3	98	178	256
4	178	122	199
5	200	78	150

9. A small airplane has a seating capacity of 19 rows with 4 seats per row. Write a program using INPUT to fill a two-dimensional array RSV with the location (row, column) of the seat each passenger wants to reserve. If the passenger types a seat location that is already filled, have the program PRINT the message SEAT OCCUPIED. (*Hint:* Initialize each element of RSV to 0. Then when a seat becomes occupied, assign a 1 to the corresponding element of RSV.)

10. A small business having 8 employees keeps a payroll file on each employee. The file contains the following information:

EMPLOYEE NUMBER	HOURS PER WEEK	PAY PER HOUR
11122	38	\$8.50
11123	40	\$7.95
.	.	.
.	.	.
.	.	.

Write a program using INPUT to fill a two-dimensional array PAY with the data on the eight employees (you make up the rest). Have the program PRINT the array in table form with the column headings shown above.

11. **a.** Write a program that fills a 5-row and 10-column array with the numbers from 1 to 50, then PRINTs the array with row and column numbers. The numbers should fill the array row by row. Do not use READ . . . DATA or INPUT.

b. Change the program in (a) so that it fills a 10-row and 5-column array with the numbers from 1 to 50, then PRINTs the array.

12. **a.** Write a program that fills a 9-row and 6-column array with 1's in the first row, 2's in the second row, . . . , and 9's in the ninth row. Have the program PRINT the array in table form with row and column numbers. Do not use READ . . . DATA or INPUT.

b. Change the program in (a) so that instead it fills the array with 1's in the first column, 2's in the second column, . . . , and 6's in the sixth column.

C **13.** *Challenge:* Write a program that fills a 6-row and 6-column array with the numbers shown in the table below. Do not use READ . . . DATA or INPUT.

$$\begin{array}{rrrrrr}
0 & 1 & 1 & 1 & 1 & 1 \\
-1 & 0 & 1 & 1 & 1 & 1 \\
-1 & -1 & 0 & 1 & 1 & 1 \\
-1 & -1 & -1 & 0 & 1 & 1 \\
-1 & -1 & -1 & -1 & 0 & 1 \\
-1 & -1 & -1 & -1 & -1 & 0
\end{array}$$

Lab Activity

Card-Dealing Programs

At some time you may have had an opportunity to play a card game against a computer. In such a game, the program must "deal" out the cards in a random way. In this lab activity, you will see two methods for constructing a program to deal a deck of cards. You could use either of these programs as a subroutine in a program that plays an actual card game.

At first glance, it may seem that card dealing is particularly easy to program; simply choose a suit *(clubs, diamonds, hearts, spades)* and a value *(ace, two, three, . . . , Jack, Queen, King)* at random, and then PRINT the result. The difficulty is that with such a simple algorithm, some cards will undoubtedly be dealt more than once. A card-dealing program must have some way to avoid duplications.

The first card-dealing algorithm uses a two-dimensional array called DEALT to record which cards have already been dealt. The suits are numbered 1 to 4 (arbitrarily in the order *clubs, diamonds, hearts, spades*), and the values are numbered 1 to 13 *(1 = ace, 2 = two, 3 = three, . . . , 11 = Jack, 12 = Queen, 13 = King)*. The columns of array DEALT correspond to the values of the cards, and the rows to the suits, as in the following diagram:

Value

Suit	1	2	3	4	5	6	7	8	9	10	11	12	13
1													
2													
3													
4													

The element of the DEALT array corresponding to a card is either 0 (if the card has not yet been dealt) or 1 (if the card *has* been dealt). For example, DEALT(3, 11) = 1 if the Jack (11) of Hearts (3) has been dealt, and DEALT(2, 4) = 0 if the Four (4) of Diamonds (2) has not yet been dealt.

The algorithm is quite simple:

Step 1 Dimension DEALT to the size 4 by 13.
Step 2 Initialize DEALT to all zeroes (no cards are dealt yet).
Step 3 Deal 52 cards.

Step 3 in the algorithm can be detailed as follows:

Step 3 Deal 52 cards:

a. Select a random number (VLU) between 1 and 13 for the value of the card.
b. Select a random number (SUIT) between 1 and 4 for the suit of the card.
c. If that card has already been dealt (that is, DEALT(SUIT, VLU) = 1), then go back to 3(a). Otherwise, PRINT the suit and value of the card, and then set DEALT(SUIT, VLU) to 1 to indicate that the card has now been dealt.

Here is the program (on *TRS-80* computers, use RND(0) instead of RND(1)):

```
10 PRINT "CARD-DEALING PROGRAM"
20 DIM DEALT(4, 13)
30 GOSUB 1000: REM * INITIALIZE DEALT ARRAY
40 FOR D = 1 TO 52: REM * DO 52 CARDS
50 GOSUB 1500: REM * DEAL ONE CARD
60 NEXT D
70 END
990 REM ** INITIALIZE ALL ELEMENTS OF DEALT TO 0 **
1000 FOR I = 1 TO 4
1010 FOR J = 1 TO 13
1020 LET DEALT(I, J) = 0: REM * NOTHING DEALT YET
1030 NEXT J
1040 NEXT I
1050 RETURN
1490 REM ** SUBROUTINE TO DEAL ONE CARD **
1500 LET VLU = INT(13 * RND(1)) + 1: REM * RANDOM NUMBER FROM 1 TO 13
1510 LET SUIT = INT(4 * RND(1)) + 1: REM * RANDOM NUMBER FROM 1 TO 4
1520 IF DEALT(SUIT, VLU) = 1 THEN GOTO 1500: REM * CARD ALREADY DEALT
1530 PRINT "VALUE:  "; VLU; "  SUIT:  "; SUIT
1540 LET DEALT(SUIT, VLU) = 1: REM * CHECK OFF CARD
1550 RETURN
```

Problems

1. RUN the program. Notice that as the program gets near the end of the deck, it takes longer and longer for each card to be selected. Can you explain why this is so? Time carefully how long it takes this program to deal all 52 cards.

2. Change the program so that it PRINTs the names of cards dealt instead of the numbers. For example, instead of the output

   VALUE: 6 SUIT: 3

   the program should PRINT the output as:

   6 OF HEARTS

   (*Hint:* Set up an array KIND$ that contains the strings ACE, TWO, THREE, . . . , TEN, JACK, QUEEN, KING, and another array TYPE$ that contains the strings CLUBS, DIAMONDS, HEARTS, and SPADES. When VLU and SUIT are chosen, have the program PRINT the appropriate elements of these arrays.) RUN your program and check the results to see that the program works correctly.

There is an algorithm for card dealing that avoids the time-consuming test to see if a card has already been dealt. Instead, a list is stored of all the cards in the order they appear in the deck. A card is chosen at random and its suit and value PRINTed. Then the card dealt is replaced by the bottom card on the deck, and a new card is chosen. (The deck is now missing the last card dealt.) The list of cards in the deck is of course stored in an array — DECK, with dimension 52. Thus, DECK(I) is the code number of the Ith card currently in the deck, as follows:

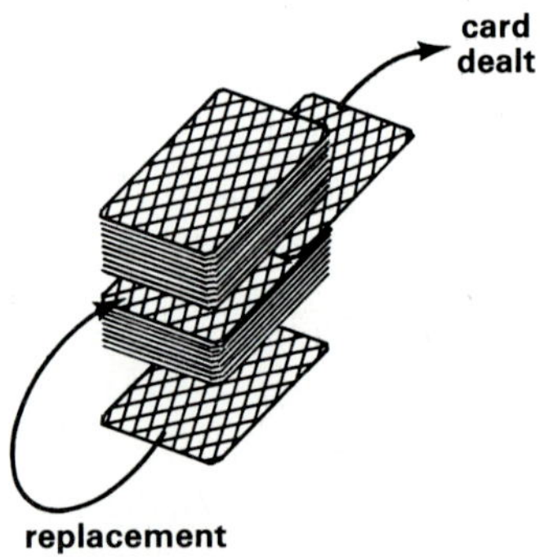

0 = ace of clubs, 1 = two of clubs, . . . , 12 = king of clubs;
13 = ace of diamonds, 14 = two of diamonds, . . . , 25 = king of diamonds;
26 = ace of hearts, 27 = two of hearts, . . . , 38 = king of hearts;
39 = ace of spades, 40 = two of spades, . . . , 51 = king of spades.

This coding allows a simple method of recovering the value and suit from any card number: If you divide the card number by 13, then the integer quotient is 1 less than the number of the suit and the remainder is 1 less than the value. For example, for card number 27, the result of dividing 27 by 13 is integer quotient 2 (add 1 to get 3, which is the number of the Heart suit) and remainder 1 (add 1 to get value 2), so that the card encoded is the TWO OF HEARTS. This process of division is performed in lines 1510 and 1520 of the program on the next page.

```
10  PRINT "CARD- DEALING PROGRAM 2"
20  DIM DECK(52)
30  GOSUB 1000: REM * SET UP DECK ARRAY
40  FOR NUM = 52 TO 1 STEP -1:  REM * NUM = NO. OF CARDS NOW IN DECK
50  GOSUB 1500: REM * DEAL A CARD
60  NEXT NUM
70  END
990  REM ** SUBROUTINE TO PUT CARDS IN DECK IN STANDARD ORDER **
1000  FOR I = 0 TO 51
1010  LET DECK(I) = I
1020  NEXT I
1030  RETURN
1490  REM ** SUBROUTINE TO DEAL ONE CARD **
1500  LET C = INT(NUM * RND(1)):  REM * RANDOM NUMBER FROM 0 TO NUM - 1
1510  LET SUIT = INT(DECK(C) / 13): REM * WHICH SUIT;  NUMBER FROM 0 TO 3
1520  LET VLU = DECK(C) - 13 * SUIT: REM * WHICH CARD;  NUMBER FROM 0 TO 12
1530  PRINT "SUIT:   "; SUIT + 1; "   VALUE:   "; VLU + 1
1540  LET DECK(C) = DECK(NUM): REM * REPLACE DEALT CARD WITH BOTTOM CARD
1550  RETURN
```

3. RUN the second program and carefully time how long it takes to deal the entire deck. Compare it to the result you obtained in Problem 1.

4. Change the program so that it deals 13 cards and PRINTs how many spades have been dealt and how many aces have been dealt.

9-6 Applications of Two-Dimensional Arrays

Suppose the manager of a hardware store wants to use a two-dimensional array (say, INV) to keep track of some of the store's inventory, which is summarized below:

Inventory Part No.	Number of Items	Price per Item
11223	33	1.87
11225	21	.89
11226	87	5.68
10226	13	10.37
10113	117	.23
12687	72	3.45

The manager could fill the array using nested FOR . . . NEXT loops and READ the data row by row, as illustrated in Program 1.

Program 1

Statement

```
10  REM * INVENTORY INFO
20  DIM INV(6, 3)
30  GOSUB 100: REM * FILL ARRAY
90  END
95  REM ** SUBROUTINE TO FILL ARRAY **
100 FOR ROW = 1 TO 6
110 FOR COL = 1 TO 3
120 READ INV(ROW, COL)
130 NEXT COL
140 NEXT ROW
150 RETURN
600 DATA 11223, 33, 1.87, 11225, 21, .89, 11226, 87, 5.68
610 DATA 10226, 13, 10.37, 10113, 117, .23, 12687, 72, 3.45
```

Suppose the manager now wants to add a subroutine to find the total number of items currently in the inventory. This involves summing the elements in the second column of INV: namely,

INV(1, 2) + INV(2, 2) + INV(3, 2) + INV(4, 2) + INV(5, 2) + INV(6, 2).

Notice that the column subscript of each of these elements is always 2, while the row subscript takes on values from 1 to 6. A FOR . . . NEXT loop is clearly called for; the following statements can be added to Program 1 to do the summing:

```
40  GOSUB 200: REM * SUM COLUMN 2
190 REM ** SUBROUTINE TO SUM COLUMN 2 **
200 LET SUM = 0: REM * INITIALIZE SUMMER
210 FOR ROW = 1 TO 6
220 LET SUM = SUM + INV(ROW, 2)
230 NEXT ROW
240 RETURN
```

Do you see how the numbers in the loop in lines 210–230 could be changed to find the sum of the elements in any column of any size array?

Another type of processing the manager might want to do would be to calculate the total dollar value of the inventory. This can be done by adding a third subroutine to Program 1. The algorithm for this subroutine is straightforward. First, have the subroutine calculate the total value for each part. (For example, the total value of the 33 items with part number 11223 is 33 * $1.87 = $61.71.) These values can be assigned to a fourth column of array elements: INV(1, 4), INV(2, 4), . . . , and INV(6, 4). Then, have the subroutine sum these elements to obtain the value of the entire inventory. Here is the algorithm translated into BASIC code. Since the array will now have four columns, the DIM statement must also be changed.

```
20  DIM INV(6, 4)
50  GOSUB 300: REM * FIND TOTAL VALUE FOR EACH PART, THEN SUM
290  REM ** SUBROUTINE TO FIND TOTAL VALUE FOR EACH PART, THEN SUM **
300  LET TTL = 0
310  FOR ROW = 1 TO 6
320  LET INV(ROW, 4) = INV(ROW, 2) * INV(ROW, 3): REM * FILL FOURTH COLUMN
330  NEXT ROW
340  FOR ROW = 1 TO 6
350  LET TTL = TTL + INV(ROW, 4): REM * SUM THE FOURTH COLUMN
360  NEXT ROW
370  RETURN
```

The manager certainly would want to add one more subroutine to the program to PRINT the results. The following subroutine will PRINT the inventory table with the fourth column added, and then will PRINT both the total number of items in the current inventory and the inventory's total value.

```
60  GOSUB 400: REM * PRINT TABLE AND RESULTS
390  REM ** SUBROUTINE TO PRINT TABLE AND RESULTS **
400  PRINT "INVENTORY"; TAB(12); "NUMBER"; TAB(23); "PRICE"; TAB(34); "TOTAL"
410  PRINT "PART NO."; TAB(12); "OF ITEMS"; TAB(23); "PER ITEM";
       TAB(34); "VALUE"
420  FOR ROW = 1 TO 6
425  LET X = 1
430  FOR COL = 1 TO 4
440  PRINT TAB(X); INV(ROW, COL);
450  LET X = X + 11: REM * X IS THE NEXT TAB POSITION
460  NEXT COL
470  PRINT: REM * MOVE CURSOR TO THE NEXT LINE
480  NEXT ROW
485  PRINT
490  PRINT "NO. OF INVENTORY ITEMS:  "; SUM
500  PRINT "INVENTORY IS WORTH:  $"; TTL
510  RETURN
```

Here is the output when the complete program is RUN:

Output

```
INVENTORY      NUMBER      PRICE       TOTAL
PART NO.       OF ITEMS    PER ITEM    VALUE
11223          33          1.87        61.71
11225          21          .89         18.69
11226          87          5.68        494.16
10226          13          10.37       134.81
10113          117         .23         26.91
12687          72          3.45        248.4

NO. OF INVENTORY ITEMS:  343
INVENTORY IS WORTH:  $984.68
```

There are many applications of two-dimensional arrays. Most involve manipulating — adding or multiplying — the elements in the rows or columns, as was done for the array INV in this section. More applications are explored in the exercises.

Avoiding Pitfalls

When adding subroutines to a program involving arrays, be sure to change the original DIM statement if the number of rows or columns in the DIMensioned array(s) changes.

Summary

The statement LET SUM = SUM + P(ROW, COL), placed inside of a FOR . . . NEXT loop, can be used to sum the elements in any row or column of the two-dimensional array P. For example, if P has 3 rows and 5 columns, then you can sum the elements in the *second* row by giving ROW the constant value 2 (assume SUM has been initialized):

```
     .
     .
     .
FOR COL = 1 TO 5
LET SUM = SUM + P(2, COL)
NEXT COL
     .
     .
     .
```

Or, as another example, you can sum the elements in the *fourth* column of P by giving COL the constant value 4:

```
        ⋮
FOR ROW = 1 TO 3
LET SUM = SUM + P(ROW, 4)
NEXT ROW
        ⋮
```

Exercises 9-6

A **1.** The numbers in the table have been stored row by row in the two-dimensional array T. Predict the output of each of the subroutines below.

1	−1	4	−4
2	−2	5	−5
3	−3	6	−6
−3	4	−2	1

a.
```
100 LET SUM = 0
110 FOR Q = 1 TO 4
120 LET SUM = SUM + T(2, Q)
130 NEXT Q
140 PRINT SUM
150 RETURN
```

b.
```
400 LET SUM = 0
410 FOR M = 1 TO 4
420 LET SUM = SUM + T(M, 4)
430 NEXT M
440 PRINT SUM
450 RETURN
```

c.
```
200 LET SUM = 0
210 FOR K = 1 TO 4
220 LET SUM = SUM + T(K, K)
230 NEXT K
240 PRINT SUM
250 RETURN
```

d.
```
300 LET SUM = 0
310 FOR J = 4 TO 1 STEP −1
320 LET SUM = SUM + T(J, 5 − J)
330 NEXT J
340 PRINT SUM
350 RETURN
```

2. The numbers in the table shown have been stored row by row in the two-dimensional array K. In parts (a)–(d) at the top of the next page, write a subroutine to perform the indicated task.

11	12	13	14	15	16
17	18	19	20	21	22
23	24	25	26	27	28

a. Sum the elements in the third column of array K.

b. Sum the elements in the third row of array K.

c. Sum all the elements in array K.

d. Calculate the average of the elements in the second row of array K.

3. Rewrite the program for Exercise 10, page 495, so that it calculates the weekly salary of each of the eight employees, and stores the results in a new fourth column in array PAY. Have the program PRINT the output in table form with column headings similar to this:

EMPLOYEE NUMBER	HOURS PER WEEK	PAY PER HOUR	WEEKLY SALARY
11122	38	8.50	323
11123	40	7.95	318
11124	36	8.25	297
.	.	.	.
.	.	.	.
.	.	.	.

B 4. a. Write a program that will fill a 10-row and 10-column array with the numbers in this multiplication table (do not use READ or INPUT):

*	0	1	2	3	4	5	6	7	8	9
0	0	0	0	0	0	0	0	0	0	0
1	0	1	2	3	4	5	6	7	8	9
2	0	2	4	6	8	10	12	14	16	18
3	0	3	6	9	. . .					27
.										.
.										.
.										.
9	. . .									81

Have the program PRINT the table with row and column numbers as shown, and use TAB instructions to align the columns.

b. Change the program in part (a) so that it PRINTs an 11-row (numbered from 0 to 10) and 11-column (numbered from 0 to 10) multiplication table.

5. a. The data in the table below represents the number of inches of snow that has fallen at three different ski resorts during a recent five-year period:

RESORT/YEAR	1981	1982	1983	1984	1985
SNOWBOWL	106	147	139	153	126
KNEEDEEP	143	151	134	117	139
WAISTHIGH	136	143	130	142	145

Write a program that fills an array with the data in the snowfall table, then calculates and PRINTs the average snowfall for each resort over the five-year period.

b. Change the program in (a) so that it also calculates and PRINTs the average snowfall for all three resorts during each year of the five-year period.

6. Write a program to fill and PRINT a 6-row and 6-column array that looks like this (do not use READ or INPUT):

```
* 0 0 0 0 0
0 * 0 0 0 0
0 0 * 0 0 0
0 0 0 * 0 0
0 0 0 0 * 0
0 0 0 0 0 *
```

7. Write a program that fills a 5-row and 5-column array with random integers, each between 1 and 100. Have the program tally the number of times each multiple of 5 occurs, then PRINT the results in this format:

```
5  OCCURS ____ TIMES
10 OCCURS ____ TIMES
.
.
.
```

8. Write a program that fills two arrays A and B with random integers between 100 and 200. Have the program calculate and PRINT a new array C in which each element is the sum of the two corresponding elements in A and B. For example,

C(1, 1) = A(1, 1) + B(1, 1), C(1, 2) = A(1, 2) + B(1, 2),

and so on.

9. The seating plan for an algebra class at BIG High School is shown below:

ROW/COL	1	2	3
1	PAT	SUE	SCOTT
2	LAURA	MIKE	FRED
3	CINDY	SALLY	TOM
4	WAYNE	CHRIS	BARB

Write a program that fills a two-dimensional string array NM$ with the names in the table, then uses a second two-dimensional array MISS to tally the daily attendance of each student. The program should INPUT the row and column in which the missing student sits. When the double trailer value −1, −1 is typed, the program should PRINT the name of each student and the number of days she or he was absent.

10. A two-dimensional array having the same number of rows and columns is called a *magic square* if the sums of each row, each column, and each diagonal are all equal. Here is an example of a magic square:

$$\begin{array}{ccc} 8 & 1 & 6 \\ 3 & 5 & 7 \\ 4 & 9 & 2 \end{array}$$

The sum of each row, column, and diagonal in this magic square is 15. Write a program to determine if an array W is a magic square. Have the program INPUT the number of rows and columns in W, then use READ . . . DATA to fill the array. The program should then PRINT all row, column, and diagonal sums (properly labeled), and a message telling whether the array is a magic square.

C 11. Write a program that uses a 3-row and 3-column array to represent a tic-tac-toe board. Have the program INPUT the positions (row and column) of three X's on the board, then determine and PRINT whether or not X has won (three in a row horizontally, vertically, or diagonally).

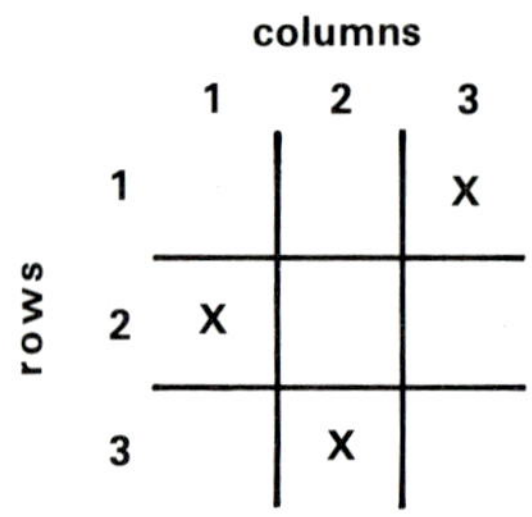

Lab Activity

SNAIL: A Simple Drawing Language

The computer language LOGO (see the Computer Language Feature on page 126) is best known for its "turtlegraphics." Using simple commands, you can write LOGO programs to control an imaginary turtle that draws designs as it crawls around the computer screen. Loops and recursion (see the Lab Activity for Section 5–6, page 250) allow simple programs to produce complex and interesting pictures.

The program in this Lab Activity simulates an extremely small part of turtlegraphics; you control an imaginary snail that leaves a trail on the screen. You can tell the snail to go forward as many dots as you want (with the command FD), or to turn to the right or left as many degrees as you like (with the commands RT or LT, respectively). As you type SNAIL instructions, they are recorded in two arrays — INST$ and AMT. The variable INST$(I) is the Ith instruction (FD, RT, or LT), and AMT(I) is the number of dots the snail is supposed to slide forward or the number of degrees it is supposed to turn.

Since your instructions are saved in the computer, they form a program for the snail to execute. That is, the BASIC program below creates a new (but very limited) computer language that you could call SNAIL. You can write SNAIL programs, add to them, and run them. The SNAIL language cannot handle loops or recursion, so creating complex designs can be tedious; but you should enjoy experimenting with it. Perhaps you can figure out how to change the program so that it will allow you to construct SNAIL loops. (You cannot save your SNAIL programs on a diskette, either, but you will learn how to do this in Chapter 11.)

Before you RUN the program, study it carefully. One new feature is the list of options that is PRINTed in lines 110 through 160. Such a list is called a *menu,* because it is a list of choices just like a menu at a restaurant. When you make your choice (which is called CMND in line 180), the program performs a GOSUB to the subroutine that performs that particular choice. This could have been accomplished by a sequence of IF . . . THEN statements, but the program uses a more efficient method: the ON . . . GOSUB statement in line 200.

It is easy to see how ON . . . GOSUB works: If CMND = 1, then the program GOSUBs to the first subroutine listed, namely subroutine 1000; if CMND = 2, then the GOSUB is to the second subroutine listed, subroutine 2000, and so forth.

The rest of the program should be self-explanatory, except perhaps the statements in lines 3310, 3320, 3500, and 3600. These lines use formulas of trigonometry to move the snail in the proper direction.

Here is the program. Choose the version listed for your computer.

Apple

```
10  REM * SNAIL: A SIMPLE DRAWING LANGUAGE
20  DIM INST$(100), AMT(100)
30  REM * INST$(I) = FD FOR FORWARD, RT FOR RIGHT TURN, LT FOR LEFT TURN
40  REM * AMT(I) = NUMBER OF STEPS OR DEGREES
50  LET NLINES = 0: REM * NUMBER OF LINES IN DRAWING PROGRAM
100  HOME
110  PRINT "MENU:"
120  PRINT
130  PRINT "TYPE 1 TO START NEW SNAIL PROGRAM"
140  PRINT TAB(6); "2 TO LIST YOUR SNAIL PROGRAM"
150  PRINT TAB(6); "3 TO RUN YOUR SNAIL PROGRAM"
160  PRINT TAB(6); "4 TO ADD TO THE END OF PROGRAM"
170  PRINT
```

```
180  INPUT "TYPE YOUR CHOICE:   "; CMND
190  IF CMND < 1 OR CMND > 4 THEN PRINT "INCORRECT RESPONSE": GOTO 170
200  ON CMND GOSUB 1000, 2000, 3000, 4000: REM * 1000 FOR NEW, 2000 FOR
       LIST, 3000 FOR RUN, 4000 FOR ADD
210  GOTO 100

995  REM ** SUBROUTINE TO CREATE NEW PROGRAM **
1000  LET NLINES = 0: REM * NOW NO LINES IN PROGRAM
1010  GOTO 4000: REM * INPUT THE PROGRAM

1995  REM ** SUBROUTINE TO LIST PROGRAM **
2000  HOME
2010  FOR I = 1 TO NLINES
2020  PRINT INST$(I); "   "; AMT(I): REM * INSTRUCTION AND THEN NUMBER
        OF STEPS OR DEGREES
2030  NEXT I
2040  GOSUB 5000: REM * WAIT
2050  RETURN

2995  REM ** SUBROUTINE TO RUN DRAWING PROGRAM **
3000  GOSUB 3200: REM * INITIALIZE GRAPHICS, PUT POINT IN CENTER OF SCREEN
3010  FOR I = 1 TO NLINES: REM * EXECUTE EACH INSTRUCTION
3020  IF INST$(I) = "FD" THEN GOSUB 3300: GOTO 3050: REM * MOVE FORWARD
3030  IF INST$(I) = "RT" THEN GOSUB 3500: GOTO 3050: REM * TURN RIGHT
3040  IF INST$(I) = "LT" THEN GOSUB 3600: REM * TURN LEFT
3050  NEXT I
3060  GOSUB 5000: REM * WAIT
3070  TEXT
3080  RETURN

3195  REM ** SUBROUTINE TO INITIALIZE GRAPHICS **
3200  HOME
3210  HGR
3220  HCOLOR = 3
3230  LET XPT = 140: REM * X-COORDINATE OF PRESENT POINT
3240  LET YPT = 80: REM * Y-COORDINATE OF PRESENT POINT
3250  LET ANG = 0: REM * DIRECTION OF NEXT MOTION
3260  HPLOT INT(XPT + .5), INT(YPT + .5): REM * ROUND POINT OFF TO
        NEAREST INTEGER AND PLOT
3270  RETURN
```

```
3295  REM ** SUBROUTINE TO MOVE FORWARD **
3300  FOR J = 1 TO AMT(I): REM * FORWARD AMT(I) STEPS
3310  LET XPT = XPT + COS(ANG): REM * IN THE DIRECTION ANG
3320  LET YPT = YPT – SIN(ANG): REM * — BECAUSE Y-COORDINATES UPSIDE
        DOWN ON SCREEN
3330  GOSUB 3260: REM * PLOT POINT
3340  NEXT J
3350  RETURN

3495  REM ** SUBROUTINE TO TURN RIGHT **
3500  LET ANG = ANG – AMT(I) * 3.14159 / 180: REM * CONVERT TO RADIANS,
        TURN CLOCKWISE
3510  RETURN

3595  REM ** SUBROUTINE TO TURN LEFT **
3600  LET ANG = ANG + AMT(I) * 3.14159 / 180: REM * CONVERT TO RADIANS,
        TURN COUNTERCLOCKWISE
3610  RETURN

3995  REM ** SUBROUTINE TO ADD NEW INSTRUCTIONS **
4000  HOME
4010  PRINT "INSTRUCTIONS ARE:   FD   RT   LT   END"
4020  PRINT
4030  PRINT
4040  INPUT "TYPE INSTRUCTION:   "; A$
4050  IF (A$ < > "FD") AND (A$ < > "LT") AND (A$ < > "RT") THEN GOTO
        4100: REM * GO IF NOT AN EXECUTABLE INSTRUCTION
4060  LET NLINES = NLINES + 1: REM * ONE MORE LINE IN PROGRAM
4070  LET INST$(NLINES) = A$
4080  INPUT "TYPE AMOUNT:   "; AMT(NLINES): REM * NUMBER OF STEPS OR
        DEGREES
4090  GOTO 4030: REM * NEXT INSTRUCTION
4100  IF A$ < > "END" THEN PRINT "ERROR": GOTO 4030: REM * NOT A
        LEGAL COMMAND
4110  RETURN: REM * END COMMAND WAS TYPED

4995  REM ** SUBROUTINE TO WAIT FOR < RETURN > **
5000  VTAB 23: REM * BOTTOM OF SCREEN
5010  INPUT "PRESS < RETURN > TO CONTINUE:   "; A$
5020  RETURN
```

TRS-80

Here are the changes for *TRS-80* computers.

```
100   CLS
2000  CLS
3070  CLS
3200  CLS
3210  ←—— delete
3220  ←—— delete
3230  LET XPT = 64
3240  LET YPT = 24
3260  SET(INT(XPT + .5), INT(YPT + .5))
4000  CLS
5000  PRINT @ 965,"";
```

IBM

Here are the changes for *IBM* computers.

```
100   CLS
2000  CLS
3070  SCREEN 0: WIDTH 80
3200  CLS
3210  SCREEN 1, 1
3220  ←—— delete
3230  LET XPT = 160
3240  LET YPT = 100
3260  PSET(INT(XPT + .5), INT(YPT + .5)), 1
4000  CLS
5000  LOCATE 1, 24: REM * NEAR BOTTOM OF SCREEN
```

Problems

1. RUN the program for your computer. Choose option 1 (START A NEW SNAIL PROGRAM) and type the following SNAIL program:

```
FD 50   (Type FD when prompted to TYPE INSTRUCTION and
RT 90    type 50 when prompted to TYPE AMOUNT. TRS-80 users
FD 50    should type FD 15 instead of FD 50 throughout.)
RT 90
FD 50
RT 90
FD 50
END
```

If you discover a typing mistake before pressing < RETURN > or < ENTER >, you can erase with the back arrow as usual, but you cannot correct anything after you press < RETURN > or < ENTER >; in that case, you must type END, choose option 1 again, and start over. (However, if you type an instruction other than FD, RT, LT, or END, the program will not accept it; you may then try again.)

After you finish typing in the SNAIL program, choose option 2 (LIST), then option 3 (RUN). What figure do you see? Did the SNAIL follow your instructions correctly?

2. Choose option 1 (START A NEW SNAIL PROGRAM) and type a program to draw an equilateral triangle like the one at right. Use LT 120 to turn and FD 50. (On *TRS-80* computers, use FD 15 instead.)

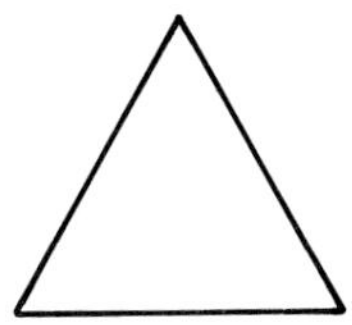

3. Choose option 4 (ADD TO THE END OF PROGRAM) and continue your program from Problem 2 so that the snail will add a square to the bottom of the triangle.

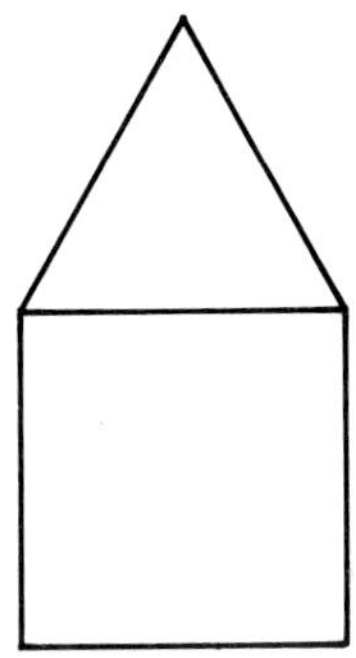

4. Change the BASIC program so that a fifth option is added to the main menu: ERASE THE LAST INSTRUCTION IN THE PROGRAM. (*Hint:* Add a statement at line 165 to PRINT the option, then make the necessary change to line 190, and then add a subroutine 6000 to line 200. Subroutine 6000 need only subtract 1 from NLINES, making the program one line shorter, but make sure that NLINES is not already 0.) Test your new option.

5. Try a SNAIL program that draws a really large figure on the screen. What happens when the unfortunate snail falls off the edge of the screen? Add error trapping to the BASIC program so that such disasters cannot occur.

6. The LOGO turtle is imagined as carrying a pen that is either "down" (leaving a trail) or "up" (leaving no trail). Add two instructions to the SNAIL language, SY *(trail on)* and SF *(trail off)*, which cause the snail to leave a trail or no trail, respectively. You will need to decide what to do about the value of AMT when the instruction is SY or SF, and you will need two new subroutines to handle these instructions.

(*Hint:* You might want to have a variable, say TRAIL, that equals 0 if the trail is currently off, or 1 if the trail is on. Change the point-plotting subroutine (line 3260) so that it plots only if TRAIL has the value 1.)

Chapter Summary

A *subscripted variable* in BASIC consists of a variable followed by a set of parentheses containing a nonnegative integer (or a variable or numerical expression whose value is a nonnegative integer). The expression in the parentheses is called the *subscript.*

An *array* is a collection of subscripted variables with the same variable name. For example,

BIG$(0), BIG$(1), . . . , BIG$(7)

is an 8-element array called BIG$.

If subscripts bigger than 10 are needed in an array in a program, a DIM statement *must* be used. A variable or a BASIC numerical expression whose value is a positive integer may be used as a subscript in a DIM statement. One or more arrays may be DIMensioned in a single DIM statement.

To find the sum of all the numbers in an array, use a summer in a FOR . . . NEXT loop. For example, if array A has 6 elements, then you can use:

```
50  LET SUM = 0
60  FOR J = 1 TO 6
70  LET SUM = SUM + A(J)
80  NEXT J
```

To fill a third array (say THRD) with the sums of the corresponding elements of two other arrays (say, FRST and SCND), use a FOR . . . NEXT loop and a statement like the one in line 110 below. (Assume the arrays have 8 elements.)

```
100  FOR K = 1 TO 8
110  LET THRD(K) = FRST(K) + SCND(K)
120  NEXT K
```

To use an array (say, TALLY) to *tally* results, you need a statement such as:

```
LET TALLY(R) = TALLY(R) + 1
```

With this statement each array element is used as a counter. TALLY(1) counts the number of times that 1 occurs, TALLY(2) the number of 2's, and so forth.

A *two-dimensional array* is a collection of *doubly-subscripted* variables having the same variable name. The first subscript of each element refers to the row, and the second subscript to the column, in which the element is located. If either subscript of a doubly-subscripted variable will be bigger than 10 in a two-dimensional array in a program, then a DIM statement *must* be used.

Chapter Test

1. Give the output of each of the commands below if the elements in array AGE$ have these values:

AGE$(1)	65
AGE$(2)	23
AGE$(3)	99
AGE$(4)	15
AGE$(5)	48

   a. PRINT AGE$(5) – AGE$(2)
   b. PRINT AGE$(4 – 1)
   c. PRINT AGE$(4) – 1
   d. PRINT AGE$(2 + 3) + AGE$(3)

2. Predict the output of each of the following programs:

   a.
```
10  FOR K = 1 TO 5
20  READ TP(K)
30  NEXT K
40  FOR M = 5 TO 1 STEP -1
50  PRINT TP(M) + 1
60  NEXT M
70  DATA  3, -2, 9, 6, 1
80  END
```

   b.
```
10  FOR N = 0 TO 4
20  READ F$(N)
30  NEXT N
40  PRINT F$(2), F$(0), F$(3)
50  DATA BERRY, FRUITY, APPLE,
        MILK, PINEAPPLE
60  END
```

3. Write a program that fills an array with information about the price of tickets for four different seating sections in a theater. The program should INPUT a section number from 1 to 4, then PRINT the cost of a seat in that section. Use this DATA line for the seat prices:

```
100  DATA $18.00, $16.50, $12.50, $10.00
```

4. Write a program that fills an array, say Q, with the odd integers from 7 to 39 (that is, Q(1) = 7, Q(2) = 9, . . .), then PRINTs the sum of the elements.

5. Assume that the letters in the table shown at the right have been previously stored row by row in the two-dimensional array K$. Fill in the subscripts of each of the doubly-subscripted variables listed below.

Rows \ Columns	1	2	3	4	5	6
1	A	B	C	D	Q	R
2	S	T	L	M	N	O
3	F	G	H	W	X	Y

   a. K$(?, ?) = "Q"   b. K$(?, ?) = "T"   c. K$(?, ?) = "Y"   d. K$(?, ?) = "F"

6. Write a program that fills a 10-row and 10-column array with random integers, each between 1 and 25. Have the program use another array to tally and PRINT the number of times each even random number between 2 and 24 occurs.

Computer Applications

Computer Ethics

Information Files

Computers have been used for many different purposes. We have come to expect such computer-related services as direct dialing of long distance phone calls, instant credit-card purchases, and 24-hour electronic banking. Unfortunately, computers have also been misused. One major area of concern is the use of computers to illegally enter data files that belong to others and contain private and personal information.

Computer "data bank"

Today, we live in a world in which "data banks" can store information about millions of individuals. No matter who you are, a computer file probably exists containing information about you. Schools store students' records, doctors maintain files on patients, and credit-reporting agencies keep files on consumer payments. If you have ever filed a tax return, the United States government most likely has a record of it.

Federal income tax form

This same stored information about individuals is important to various organizations. Insurance companies want access to a person's medical records and driving safety record. Employers want information related to a person's past employment and education, and retail stores want consumers' credit ratings.

All of this information is confidential. None of the record-keepers are allowed by law to share the information collected without permission. But how do we protect a person's right to privacy and at the same time allow these organizations the use of files that they deem necessary? Most people agree that records are needed, but they are concerned about the availability of so much information.

Unauthorized use of computerized information can do a great deal of damage. In 1983, a group of computer "hackers" decoded the password and accessed one of the computers at the United States government's Los Alamos National Laboratory in New Mexico. Even though the hackers obtained only non-classified information, imagine the damage they might have caused if they changed any codes related to defense secrets?

Controlling Access

Steps have been taken to solve the problem of unauthorized use of computer data files. The United States Congress in 1974 passed the Privacy Act. This law was an amendment to the Freedom of Information Act and defined and established each citizen's right to privacy. The Privacy Act permits individuals to have access to their records, and prohibits records from being kept on a person's political and religious beliefs.

Today, businesses and organizations use many types of security measures to make entering files difficult for an unauthorized person. Employees are often required to use identification codes such as picture badges, passwords, and signature analysis. Computer hardware may be designed so that it will not run unless an authorized person correctly starts the system. Sometimes the hardware will lock up; other times security guards are notified if the system is used improperly. There are systems to encode data so that it will appear meaningless to people not authorized to use the computer. Unfortunately, none of these security systems are foolproof. Data security still depends on the ethical use of computers by the people who have permission to use them.

Software Copying

The illegal entry of "data banks" is not the only social issue facing the data processing industry. Copying of software is another serious problem. Copying of software is the duplication of software without the written permission of the copyright holder, and is illegal. To counter this illegal copying, software publishers have attempted to include codes in the software to "lock" the programs stored on the disk. This technique has resulted in limited success.

The protection of computer data files and software is a complex problem. Federal and state governments have passed laws in an attempt to solve the problem. Record-keepers have set up elaborate security measures to prevent misuse. But laws and security measures are not all that is needed. We must understand that the right to privacy and the need of organizations to maintain files are social issues and not technological problems. It is the ethical responsibility of each of us as individual programmers and users to prevent abuse.

Employee inserting identification badge

Computer Languages Ada

The U.S. military services have been using computers since the 1940's. At first their programs were written in machine language, then later in assembly language. By the 1970's, they began to use high-level languages for their applications. Since the different services frequently used different computer languages, their systems applications were usually incompatible. Therefore, in the mid-1970's, the Department of Defense decided that a single standardized language should be used by all branches of service. The result, in 1980, was a new high-level structured language named *Ada.*

Charles Babbage

Ada was chosen as the name of this new language to honor a woman who is considered to be one of the first "programmers," Augusta Ada Byron, Countess of Lovelace and daughter of the English poet Lord Byron. Lady Lovelace, as she is also known, was a close friend and colleague of the nineteenth-century computer pioneer Charles Babbage. Her talent in mathematics, and her ability to understand the machines *(difference* and *analytic engines)* that Babbage created, led her to outline sets of instructions that would be needed to get the analytic engine to work as a "computer."

Augusta Ada Byron

The high-level structured language *Pascal* was used as a model for the design development of Ada. Some people now consider Pascal as a subset of the language Ada. Here is a short Ada program:

```
with TEXT_IO; use TEXT_IO;
procedure A_WELCOME is
```

```
<blank line>
begin
put ("Hello!");
put ("This is a minor example of an Ada program.")
end A_WELCOME;
```

The environment in which an Ada program functions is specified prior to the program name. In line 1 of the sample program, the instruction "with TEXT_IO; use TEXT_IO" makes all the special features of the TEXT_IO package available for use by the program. These features include other procedures that have the ability to move data and characters (TEXT) to and from the computer via various input and output (I / O) devices. Every Ada program has a name that follows the keyword *procedure.* All program names must begin with a letter that then may be followed by a combination of letters, numerals, or underscore characters. When a space occurs in a procedure name (like between A and WELCOME), the underscore character *must* be used. The keyword *is* follows the procedure name.

Babbage's analytic engine

A blank line divides this program into two distinct parts. The first two lines, which give the information needed to link the program to its environment, are called the *specification.* The last four lines, which list the actions performed by the program when it is run, are called the *body* of the program.

As in Pascal, the body is indicated by the word *begin.* The *put* statement is actually a procedure contained in TEXT_IO that allows the message in quotes to be displayed via an output device. The output from this program is:

```
Hello!
This is a minor example of an Ada program.
```

To show the end of the body of the program, the statement *end* is used and it must be followed by the program name.

CHAPTER

10 Sorting; Searching

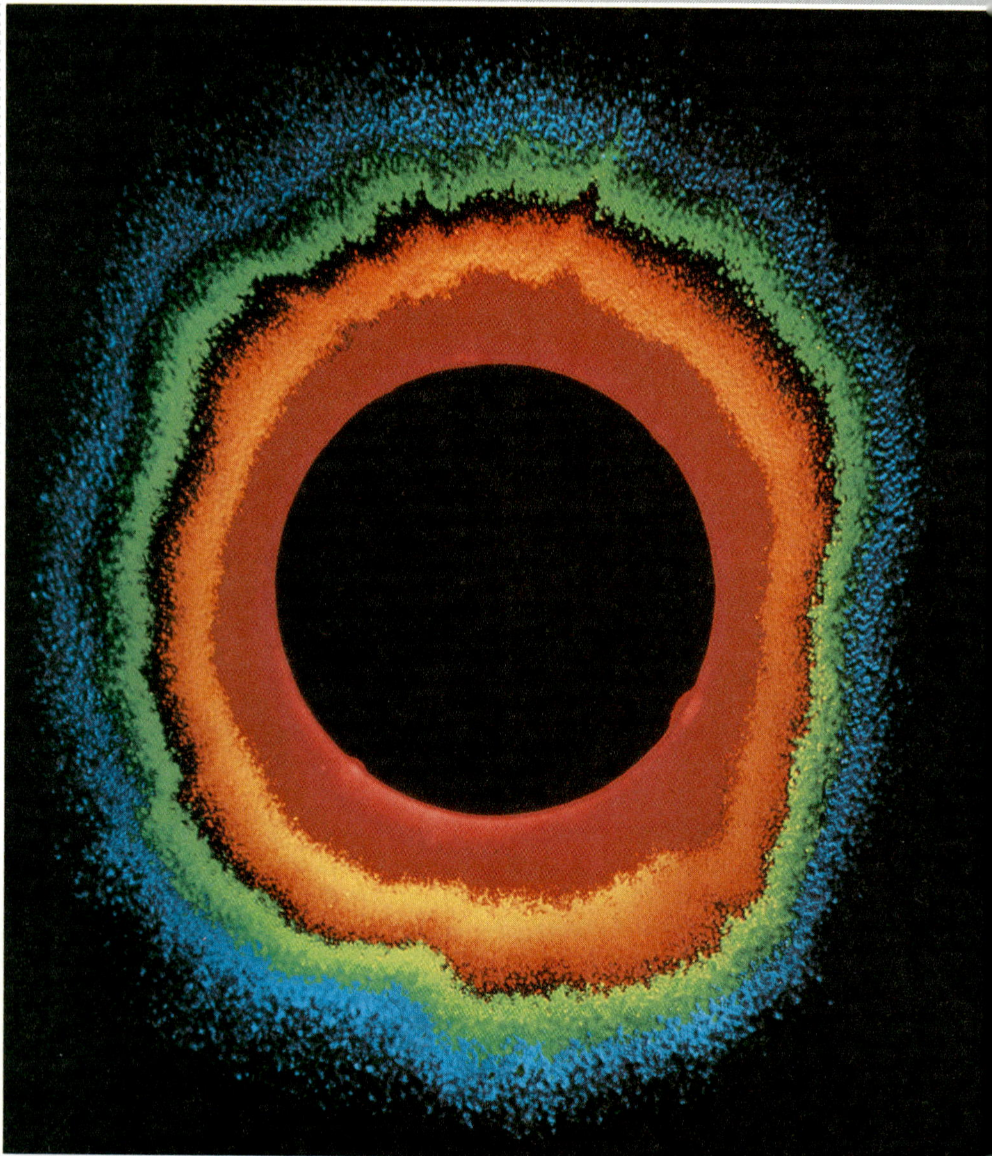

This is a computer-enhanced photo of the total solar eclipse that occurred on February 26, 1979. The dynamic colors are the result of a process called isophote color coding.

Introduction

Almost all businesses in the Western world, except the very smallest, use computers to help carry on their daily activities. Banks use computers to keep track of depositors' account balances, investments, and mortgages. Manufacturers keep computerized files of parts inventories and orders for finished products. Businesses that sell and distribute goods keep files on their orders and those of their customers. Every business and government agency needs to keep information — much of it computerized — on employee wages, taxes, and benefits. These applications of computers — involving large amounts of information (data) that is continually being changed and manipulated — are collectively called *data processing.*

In this chapter and the next, building on your accumulated knowledge of BASIC, you will be introduced to some of the techniques of data processing. The collections of information used will be relatively small; entering large amounts of data into the computer can be very time-consuming. The principles you learn will apply to larger-scale applications in the real world.

10-1 Data Files

Consider the following problem: Write a program to store a list of people's names and their favorite books. Then, have the program INPUT a name and output that person's favorite book (or an appropriate message if the name is not on the list). Suppose that some of the information the program is to use is summarized in the following table:

Name	Favorite Book
Doc	More Healthful Hints
Sleepy	Self-hypnosis in Ten Easy Lessons
Grumpy	My Life and Hates
Sneezy	A Chewy Tale
Snow White	Ten Best Ski Resorts
Prince Charming	Making Sugar from Pure Sap
.	.
.	.
.	.

The information in the table is called a *data file.* The rows are called *records* of the data file. Each record of the data file above consists of a person's name and his or her favorite book. The columns of the data file are called *fields.* In the example, the fields are the name field and the book field. Thus each record consists of one or more fields. If we number the records, we can rewrite our data file as follows:

Fields

	Name	Favorite Book
record #1	Doc	More Healthful Hints
record #2	Sleepy	Self-hypnosis in Ten Easy Lessons
record #3	Grumpy	My Life and Hates
record #4	Sneezy	A Chewy Tale
record #5	Snow White	Ten Best Ski Resorts
record #6	Prince Charming	Making Sugar from Pure Sap
.	.	.
.	.	.
.	.	.

A convenient way to store such a data file in the computer is to use arrays, one for each field. For example, we can use the string arrays NAM$ and BOOK$ and let NAM$(I) represent the string in the name field in record #I, and BOOK$(I) the string in the book field of record #I. (The actual program will be written in the next section.)

As another example of a data file, suppose that your principal wants to keep track of the won-lost records of your school's athletic teams over several years. For each year and each team, the principal wants to record the number of contests won, lost, and tied. The data might be organized like this:

Fields

	Year	Team	Won	Lost	Tied
record #1	1978	Boys' JV Baseball	10	13	0
record #2	1980	Girls' Varsity Soccer	6	5	2
record #3	1984	Freshman Tiddlywinks	0	0	46
.	.	.	.	.	.
.	.	.	.	.	.
.	.	.	.	.	.

Three records of the data file are shown. There are five fields, each of which can be stored in one array. For example, we can use the five arrays YEAR, TEAM$, W, L, and T to represent the fields. How could the data file be used, once it was stored in the computer's memory? The principal can retrieve the won-lost record of any team for any year, or find the overall won-lost record of *all* the teams for a given year. Another possibility would be to compare the won-lost records of a single team over several years. You can probably think of other uses for this data file. In future sections of this chapter and the next, we will develop some of the techniques needed to accomplish these tasks effectively.

Avoiding Pitfalls

Remember that the rows of a data file are the records, and the columns are the fields.

Summary

In computer data processing, information is usually organized into a data file consisting of a list of *records* (rows). All of the records have the same form: they are divided into one or more *fields* (columns), each of which is one small piece of information (number or string). In the computer's memory, each of the separate fields is stored in a separate array.

A Data File

	field A	field B	field C$	field D$
record #1	A(1)	B(1)	C$(1)	D$(1)
record #2	A(2)	B(2)	C$(2)	D$(2)
record #3	A(3)	B(3)	C$(3)	D$(3)

Exercises 10-1

A **1.** Describe how data files might be used by each of the following:
a. a political campaign organization **b.** a city school system

2. Identify the fields and records of each of the data files in (a)–(i). Describe how each file could be stored in a computer (give names of arrays that could be used for the fields).

a.

Name	Favorite color
Yuri	red
Diana	blue
Milton	orange

b.

Student	Class	Lunch Period
Alphie B. Soup	Sophomore	5C
B.K. Bean	Senior	5A
B.R. Sprout	Junior	5B

c. A list of students' names, their ages, and their heights.

d. A list of persons' names, their addresses, and the number of kilowatt hours of electricity they used in the last month.

e. A table giving the per capita consumption of cantaloupes in the United States for each of the last fifty years.

f. The telephone book for Oshkosh, Wisconsin.

g. Your school transcript, giving the subjects you studied and the grades you received for each marking period for the last three years.

h. The summary in the newspaper of yesterday's transactions on the stock exchange.

i. A summary of the results of the weekend college football games.

3. Describe two possible uses of each data file described in Exercise 2.

4. Describe in detail the fields and records in a data file that would keep track of the items on hand at a school store. How could the file be used profitably?

5. Describe in detail the fields and records in a data file that would keep track of the names of books borrowed and overdue from a public library. Describe how the librarian could use the data file.

6. The owner of a small business wants to computerize her payroll operations. Each of her employees has a fixed weekly wage. She must pay money for each employee to Social Security and to a medical insurance plan. She withholds state and federal income taxes from each employee's wages. Describe in detail the fields and records of a data file that would be helpful to her.

7. Suppose that the basketball coach at your school wants to keep track of the names of the starting five players for all the basketball games played by the school in the last five years. Describe in detail the fields and records of a data file that would be helpful to the coach. Give three possible uses of this data file.

8. A citizen's group concerned about the imminent extinction of a certain bird species wants to develop a data file containing the numbers of times the bird has been sighted each month of the last year, in each of the 50 states. Describe the fields and records of such a data file and how it could be used.

B **9.** In certain data files, some of the fields of a given record can be most conveniently represented in the computer by a two-dimensional array. For example, each record of a computerized recipe file might consist of the name of the food to be prepared, followed by a list of ingredients:

Fields

	Food	Ingredients	Amounts
record #1	Fried Watermelon Hearts	watermelon pulp hot vegetable oil allspice	2 pounds 4 tablespoons 1/2 pinch
record #2	Dandelions Au Gratin	dandelions nutmeg fried gratins	4 pounds 3 tablespoons 2 cups

This data file can be represented in the computer by three arrays, say, FOOD$, ING$, and AMT$. The last two will be two-dimensional arrays. Thus, for example,

FOOD$(1) = "FRIED WATERMELON HEARTS"
ING$(1, 1) = "WATERMELON PULP"
AMT$(1, 1) = "2 POUNDS"
ING$(1, 2) = "HOT VEGETABLE OIL"
AMT$(1, 2) = "4 TABLESPOONS"
ING$(1, 3) = "ALLSPICE"
AMT$(1, 3) = "1/2 PINCH"
⋮

Give the values of each of the following:

a. FOOD$(2)
b. ING$(2, 1)
c. AMT$(2, 1)
d. ING$(2, 2)
e. AMT$(2, 2)
f. ING$(2, 3)

10. Describe the fields and records of a data file that could be used to keep track of the subjects being studied by each of the students in your school. Show how a one-dimensional array can be used to store the students' names, and a two-dimensional array can be used to store the subjects' names (see Exercise 9).

11. An administrator at your school wants to computerize a list of the buses used to transport students. Each bus has a number, a regular driver, and a list of students (between 15 and 50 of them) who regularly ride in it. Describe how such a data file could be represented in the computer (see Exercise 9), and give some possible uses of the file.

10-2 The Linear Search

Let's return to the favorite-book problem of the last section. As you will recall, the program is supposed to store the names of people and their favorite books in the arrays NAM$ and BOOK$. Then, for each INPUT name, the program is to PRINT the favorite book of that person, or PRINT the message NAME NOT ON THE LIST if the name is not found. We will have the program repeat the process of retrieving book choices until the user indicates that he or she is finished. One possible outline of an algorithm might be as follows:

Step 1 Fill the arrays.

Step 2 INPUT and process user's request.

Step 3 Ask if user wants to type another name. If yes, go back to Step 2; otherwise, END.

This outline is too general to be translated directly into BASIC. In Step 1, we need to decide how to assign the data to the arrays. As you know, LET, INPUT, or READ . . . DATA can be used. (In the next chapter, you will learn a fourth method.) We'll choose the READ . . . DATA technique. Next, we need to decide how to terminate the data. This could be accomplished by using a trailer value, but we will use a counter going from 1 to the number of records in the file (called NREC).

Step 1 can be made more detailed in this way:

Step 1 Fill the arrays NAM$ and BOOK$.

- **a.** READ NREC (number of records).
- **b.** READ NAM$(I) and BOOK$(I) as I goes from 1 to NREC.

This elaboration of Step 1 is now detailed enough to be translated easily into BASIC code.

Now consider Step 2. Let's assign the name typed by the user to the variable LOOK$. The program should examine each NAM$(I) until a match with LOOK$ is found or until the entire array has been tested. If LOOK$ is different from every name in the array, the message NAME NOT ON THE LIST should be PRINTed. Here is the detailed version of Step 2:

Step 2 Process the user's request:

- **a.** INPUT LOOK$.
- **b.** As I goes from 1 to NREC, test to see if LOOK$ = NAM$(I). If yes, output BOOK$(I) and RETURN.
- **c.** If no match is found, PRINT the message "NAME NOT ON THE LIST" and RETURN.

There is one complication in Step 2(b). It is not a good idea to transfer from the middle of a FOR . . . NEXT loop because doing so leaves information stored in the computer's memory that would be cleared out by a completed FOR . . . NEXT loop. If enough of this information is left on the "stack" (see the Lab Activity for Section 5–6, page 250), as this portion of the computer's memory is called, an OUT OF MEMORY ERROR may occur. Therefore, the loop outlined in (b) will be written as an IF . . . THEN loop in the program (see lines 320–345).

Step 3 is easy to code into BASIC as written. Here is the complete algorithm translated into BASIC code:

Program 1

Statement

```
10 PRINT "FAVORITE BOOKS"
20 GOSUB 200: REM * FILL ARRAYS
30 GOSUB 300: REM * PROCESS USER'S REQUEST
40 PRINT
50 INPUT "DO YOU WANT MORE:  "; ANS$
60 IF ANS$ = "YES" THEN GOTO 30
70 PRINT "BYE"
80 END

190 REM ** SUBROUTINE TO FILL ARRAYS **
200 READ NREC: REM * NREC IS NUMBER OF RECORDS
210 DIM NAM$(NREC), BOOK$(NREC)
220 FOR I = 1 TO NREC
230 READ NAM$(I), BOOK$(I)
240 NEXT I
250 RETURN

290 REM ** SUBROUTINE TO PROCESS REQUEST **
300 PRINT
310 INPUT "TYPE A NAME:  "; LOOK$
320 LET I = 1
330 IF NAM$(I) = LOOK$ THEN PRINT "FAVORITE BOOK:  "; BOOK$(I): GOTO 360
340 LET I = I + 1
345 IF I <= NREC THEN GOTO 330
350 PRINT "NAME NOT ON THE LIST": REM * NO MATCH
360 RETURN
```

Program continued on next page.

```
500 DATA 9, DOC, MORE HEALTHFUL HINTS
505 DATA SLEEPY, SELF-HYPNOSIS IN TEN EASY LESSONS
510 DATA GRUMPY, MY LIFE AND HATES, SNEEZY, A CHEWY TALE
520 DATA SNOW WHITE, TEN BEST SKI RESORTS
530 DATA DOPEY, MY LIFE AND HATES, HAPPY, A CHEWY TALE
540 DATA PRINCE CHARMING, MAKING SUGAR FROM PURE SAP
550 DATA BASHFUL, A CHEWY TALE
```

Output

```
FAVORITE BOOKS

TYPE A NAME:   ? SLEEPY
FAVORITE BOOK:  SELF-HYPNOSIS IN TEN EASY LESSONS

DO YOU WANT MORE:   ? YES

TYPE A NAME:   ? WHISTLER
NAME NOT ON THE LIST

DO YOU WANT MORE:   ? FORGET IT
BYE
```

Program 1 performs what is called a *linear search* of the data file, meaning that it starts at the beginning of the data file and looks at each record (or in this case, at the name field of each record) until the desired information is found or the data is used up. A linear search is a good method to use to recover information from a relatively short data file. If the file contains many records, then a linear search can be very time-consuming.

Think of the inefficiency of looking for a telephone number in a phone book by performing a linear search. If you are searching for your friend John Smith, for example, it would not be smart to start at the beginning of the book, looking at each name in turn; instead, you would skip ahead to that part of the book with last names starting with the letter S. Of course, the reason this strategy works is that the phone book is in alphabetical order; the data file of Program 1 is not. An *efficient* search of a large data file requires that the data file be in some kind of systematic order. Arranging data files in numerical or alphabetical order is called *sorting*. This topic is introduced in the following sections of this chapter.

The Key Field

A search can be made using any of the fields of the data file. The particular field in which a match is being sought is called the *key field*. In Program 1, for example, the name field is the key. We also say that the search is *keyed* on the name field.

Program 1 can easily be changed so that the book field is the key. A librarian, for example, might want to use the data file to find out the names of people who like a certain book. All of the necessary changes occur in subroutine 300. The biggest difference here is that we originally assumed that each name occurred only once in the list, whereas some of the books appear more than once (see lines 500–550). Therefore, if the program is to PRINT the names of *all* the people who prefer a certain book, subroutine 300 should not RETURN after a match is found (line 330). Thus, the program should always go all the way through the final counter value in the finite loop in lines 330–345.

How can the program know whether to PRINT a message about a certain book not appearing on the list, then? One way (different from the method used in Program 1) is to count the number of people who like the book and to output the final value of the counter. Of course, if this final value is 0, then the book does not occur on the list. Here is the new version of subroutine 300. Note that since the program always goes completely through the loop in lines 320 to 340, FOR . . . NEXT is used witout fear of memory problems.

```
290 REM ** SUBROUTINE TO PROCESS REQUEST **
300 PRINT
310 INPUT "TYPE A BOOK:  "; FAVRIT$
315 LET COUNT = 0: REM * COUNT NO. PREFERRING FAVRIT$
320 FOR I = 1 TO NREC
330 IF BOOK$(I) = FAVRIT$ THEN PRINT NAM$(I): LET COUNT = COUNT + 1
340 NEXT I
350 PRINT "NUMBER WHO LIKE  "; FAVRIT$; ":  "; COUNT
360 RETURN
```

Here is a sample output with this new version of subroutine 300:

```
FAVORITE BOOKS

TYPE A BOOK:  ? A CHEWY TALE
SNEEZY
HAPPY
BASHFUL
NUMBER WHO LIKE A CHEWY TALE:  3

DO YOU WANT MORE:  ? YES

TYPE A BOOK:  ? THE FAIREST OF THEM ALL
NUMBER WHO LIKE THE FAIREST OF THEM ALL:  0

DO YOU WANT MORE:  ? NO
BYE
```

Avoiding Pitfalls

1. To avoid errors in data processing programs, it is essential to write a careful outline of the algorithm and to document the program thoroughly with clear REMarks.

2. Transferring from the middle of a FOR . . . NEXT loop to another part of a program (resulting in an unfinished loop) can cause an OUT OF MEMORY error. To avoid this memory problem, use an IF . . . THEN loop rather than a FOR . . . NEXT.

Summary

In a *linear search,* a string or number is INPUT from the user. Then a specific field, called the *key,* is examined in each record to see if it matches the INPUT value. The records are examined in order, starting with the first one in the file.

Exercises 10-2

A 1. The following program uses a data file that contains supermarket names and the price of a head of lettuce at each supermarket. Use the program to answer (a)–(d).

```
10  PRINT "COMPARATIVE SHOPPING"
20  FOR I=1 TO 5
30  READ SUPER$(I), PRICE(I)
40  NEXT I
50  INPUT "TYPE A MARKET:  "; WHICH$
60  FOR I=1 TO 5
70  IF SUPER$(I)=WHICH$ THEN PRINT PRICE(I)
80  NEXT I
100  DATA PETE'S, .79
110  DATA GOLLEY'S, 1.09
120  DATA COLOSSAL COLISEUM, 1.19
130  DATA CROOK'S CASTLE, .89
140  DATA GROSSERIE, .99
200  END
```

a. Predict the output if the user types GOLLEY'S as the name of the market.

b. Predict the output if the user types PRODUCE CITY as the name.

c. Change the program so that it PRINTs the message NO SUCH MARKET if the INPUT name is not in array SUPER$.

d. Change the program so that it INPUTs a price, then PRINTs the names of all the markets whose price for lettuce is lower than that price.

2. Consider this program:

```
10  FOR I=1 TO 8
20  READ K$(I)
30  NEXT I
40  INPUT "TYPE A LETTER:  "; C$
50  LET I=1
60  IF C$=K$(I) THEN PRINT "FOUND": GOTO 100
65  LET I=I+1
70  IF I<=8 THEN GOTO 60
80  PRINT "NOT FOUND"
90  DATA A, B, R, B, R, R, X, Y
100  END
```

a. Predict the output of the program if the user types the letter A for the value of C$.

b. Predict the output for the INPUT letter B.

c. Predict the output for the INPUT letter K.

d. Describe the purpose of the program.

e. Change the program so that it PRINTs the number of times the INPUT letter occurs in the DATA list.

3. Change Program 1 so that another search will be processed if the user's response to the question in line 50 starts with the letter Y, and the program will END if the user's response starts with the letter N. Have the program repeat the question in line 50 if the user types a string starting with any other letter.

4. a. Change Program 1 so that the data file has a third field — the person's age. Make up a list of some ages and add them to the appropriate place in the DATA statements (lines 500–550). Have the program INPUT a person's name, then PRINT that person's age.

b. Change the program in (a) so that it INPUTs an age, then PRINTs the names of all persons of that age (or the message NOBODY IS THAT AGE if it is appropriate).

c. Change the program in (b) so that it INPUTs a book and an age, then PRINTs the names of all persons of that age who like that book (or the message NOBODY LIKES IT when it is appropriate).

B **5. a.** Extend the data file shown below to include seven records (make up four more records). Write a program that will fill three arrays with the fields of the data file. Have the program INPUT a person's name, then PRINT that person's lunch period.

Student	Class	Lunch Period
Alphie B. Soup	Sophomore	5C
B.K. Bean	Senior	5A
B.R. Sprout	Junior	5B
.	.	.
.	.	.
.	.	.

b. Change the program in (a) so that it INPUTs a class, then PRINTs the names of all the students in that class (or the message EMPTY CLASS if it is appropriate).

c. Change the program in (b) so that it INPUTs a lunch period, then PRINTs the names of all the *sophomore* students with that lunch period.

6. a. Create a data file consisting of a list of eight persons' names, their ages, and their heights in inches. Write a program to fill three arrays with the fields of the data file. Have the program INPUT a person's name, then PRINT that person's age and height (or an appropriate message if the name is not on the list).

b. Change the program in (a) so that it INPUTs an age, then PRINTs the number of people who are older than that age, and their names.

c. Change the program in (a) so that it will find and PRINT the name of the tallest person on the list (or all the persons with the greatest height, if there is a tie).

d. Change the program in (a) so that it determines whether the youngest person on the list is also the shortest. Have the program PRINT the message YOUNGEST AND SHORTEST MATCH if that is true; otherwise, the message NO MATCH should be PRINTed. (Assume that there are no ties.)

7. a. Extend the data file of the won-lost records of a school's athletic teams to twelve records (see page 520). Write a program to set up five arrays, YEAR, TEAM$, W, L, and T, with the fields of the data file. Have the program retrieve the won-lost record of any team for any given year; that is, the program should INPUT the year and team name, then PRINT the team's number of wins, losses, and ties.

b. Change the program in (a) for an INPUT year so that it will PRINT the won-lost records (wins, losses, and ties) of *all* the teams for that year.

c. Change the program in (b) so that for an INPUT team it will give its won-lost record for each year that is in the data file.

Lab Activity

A Guessing Game

In this lab activity, you will play a number-guessing game in which one possible — but very inefficient — strategy is a linear search. If you try hard to get the best score you can, you will quickly abandon the linear search approach. Instead, you should develop a search strategy closer to the binary search that will be explained in Section 10–5.

The program below selects a random integer from 1 to 10 (see lines 20 and 40), then asks you to guess the number. The program tells you if your guess is too large or too small, and continues to INPUT guesses until you get the number right.

```
10 PRINT "NUMBER-GUESSING GAME"
20 LET MAX = 10: REM * LARGEST POSSIBLE NUMBER
30 (Fill in randomization instruction for your computer.)
40 LET NUM = INT(MAX * RND(1)) + 1: REM * ON TRS-80 COMPUTERS
     USE RND(0) INSTEAD
50 LET NGUESS = 0: REM * NUMBER OF GUESSES SO FAR
60 PRINT
70 INPUT "TYPE YOUR GUESS:  "; GUESS
80 LET NGUESS = NGUESS + 1
90 IF GUESS < NUM THEN PRINT "TOO LOW": GOTO 60
100 IF GUESS > NUM THEN PRINT "TOO HIGH": GOTO 60
110 PRINT "CORRECT! IT TOOK YOU  "; NGUESS;"  GUESSES"
120 END
```

Problems

1. RUN the game five times, using a linear search. First guess 1, then 2, then 3, and so on, until you get the correct number. Ignore the TOO LOW and TOO HIGH clues. What were your five scores (number of guesses)? What was your average score?

2. RUN the game five more times, using the most reasonable strategy you can think of (try for the lowest score you can). What was your average score? Unless your luck was unusual, you should see a small improvement when you abandon the linear search.

3. Change the value of MAX in line 20 to 100. Over the long term — say, 1000 games — what do you predict the average score would be if you used a linear search?
(*Hint:* Using a linear search, the number of guesses equals the random number (NUM) chosen by the computer. Over the long term, what do you predict would be the average of the random numbers generated between 1 and 100?)

4. RUN the program five to ten more times (with MAX = 100) and try to get your scores as low as possible. What is your average score now? You should see a big difference between this average and the number you predicted for a linear search in Problem 3. Can you describe your strategy in words? If not, play the game a few more times until you can write down how you are approaching the game.

5. A remarkable fact about efficient guessing strategies (search techniques) is that as the number of objects to be guessed (MAX) increases, the number of guesses required increases much more slowly. For example, if MAX = 10, it can be shown that if you follow the best strategy, four guesses will always be enough to find the correct number. If MAX = 100, seven guesses are enough, and if MAX = 1000, then 10 guesses are enough. Thus, as MAX goes from 10 to 1000, a hundredfold increase, the maximum number of guesses required goes from 4 to 10, only two and one-half times as many. RUN the program with MAX = 1000 and see if you can guess the number in 10 tries or less, every time.

10-3 The Bubble Sort

Efficient retrieval of information from a data file requires that the data be in some kind of systematic order. This section will introduce one method for arranging an array of numbers in numerical order (or an array of strings in alphabetical order). This method is called the *bubble sort.*

The *bubble sort* is relatively easily understood and coded into BASIC, but rather unlike any method a person without a computer would use. Sorting algorithms you might use in alphabetizing a list of names by hand are relatively difficult for a computer to work with. A computer can only do one small task at a time, although it can go through a long sequence of simple tasks very quickly. Human beings can manipulate a relatively large amount of information all at once, although we are comparatively slow at it. Computers have been programmed to do human-like things, such as solving word problems, carrying on conversations, or playing chess, but they usually follow algorithms that few humans would be comfortable with.

How the Bubble Sort Works

The bubble sort involves comparisons of adjacent elements in an array. If the two elements being compared are already in the correct order, they are left alone. If they are in the wrong order, they are switched. Then the next pair of elements is examined and is either left alone or switched, whichever is appropriate. If the entire array is passed through enough times in this way, all the elements end up in order.

To illustrate how the bubble sort works, consider the 4-element array A shown in the following diagram:

	Array A
A(1)	4
A(2)	3
A(3)	16
A(4)	2

To arrange the numbers in this array in increasing numerical order (that is, from smallest to largest), the bubble sort technique first compares A(1) with A(2). Since these elements are out of order — A(1) > A(2) — the contents (values) of these two variables must be switched, as illustrated in the *before* and *after* diagrams below:

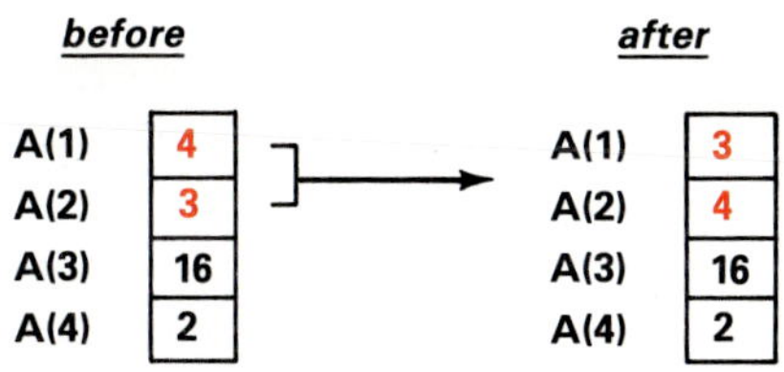

Now the next two elements, A(2) and A(3), are compared. Since they are already in the correct order — A(2) < A(3) — they are not switched, as you can see in the following diagram.

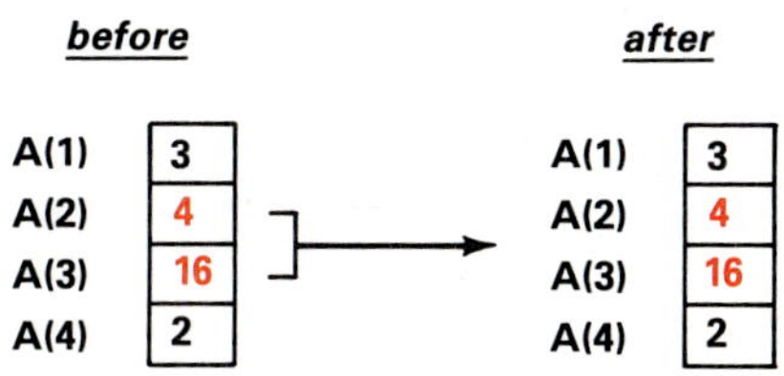

Next, the elements A(3) and A(4) are compared; their contents need to be switched:

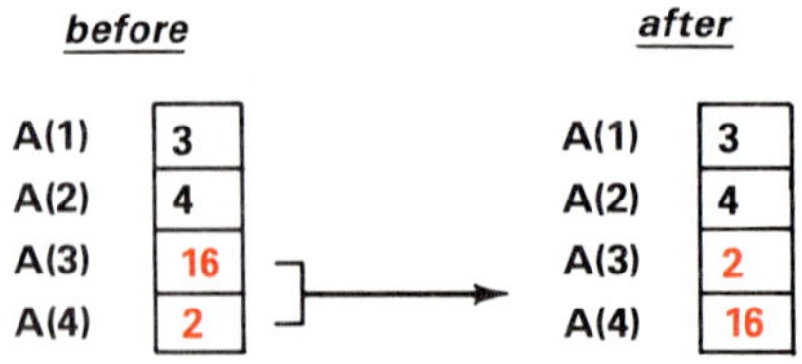

We have gone through the array once. Notice that it is in somewhat better order than it was originally. The biggest number (16) has fallen to the bottom of the list, and smaller numbers have started to "bubble" upward like air bubbles in a fish tank.

Now we go through array A again. Study carefully these diagrams for the second pass through the array:

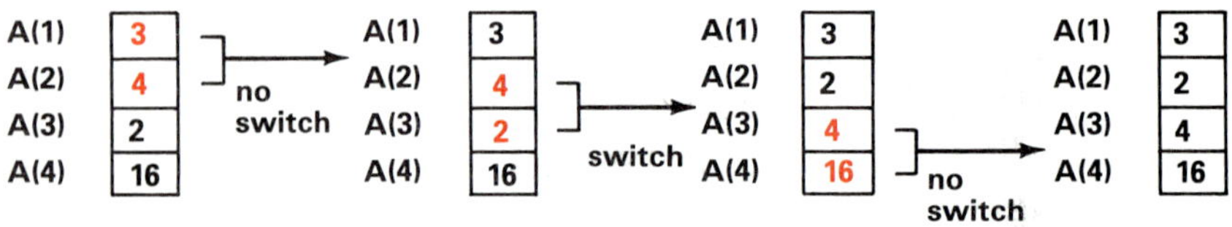

One more pass through the array will result in the correct numerical order:

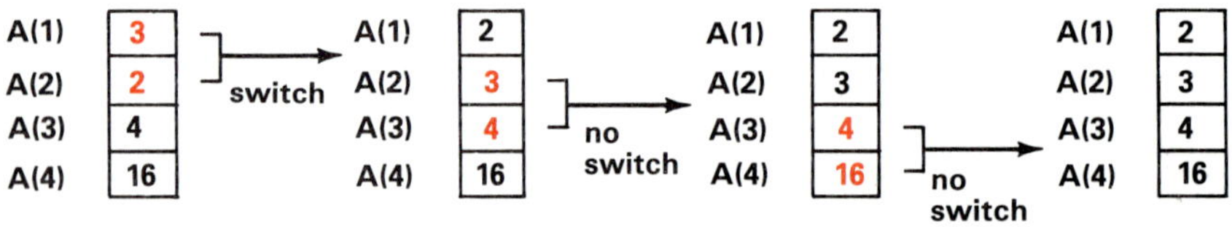

Exactly the same procedure can be followed to sort a string array into alphabetical order. How many times do we need to go through a four-element array to get it in order? Well, on the first pass through array A, the biggest number went to the bottom of the list. On the second pass, the second biggest number went to the position second from the bottom. On the third pass, the third biggest (second smallest) ended up in the second position, and necessarily the smallest was on top. Therefore, three passes will completely sort a four-element array (depending on the original order, even fewer may be needed). In general, if an array has N elements, then N − 1 passes will always put it completely in order.

An algorithm for a program to sort an N-element array into increasing order is on the next page.

Step 1 Fill array A with N elements.

Step 2 Make N − 1 passes through the array:

a. As I goes from 1 to N − 1, if A(I) > A(I + 1), then switch the contents of A(I) and A(I + 1).

b. Otherwise, leave A(I) and A(I + 1) alone.

Step 3 PRINT the sorted array.

In Step 2(a), the counter I goes only up to N − 1 because A(I) is being compared with A(I + 1); when I = N − 1, the element A(N − 1) is compared with A(N). The one part of the algorithm that needs further explanation is the switching of the contents of A(I) and A(I + 1). You might think that the instructions

```
110 LET A(I + 1) = A(I)
120 LET A(I) = A(I + 1)
```

would accomplish this. Suppose, however, that initially A(I) = 5 and A(I + 1) = 2:

A(I)	5
A(I + 1)	2

Then line 110 will assign A(I + 1) the value 5 and leave A(I) alone:

A(I)	5
A(I + 1)	5

The value 2 has been lost! How do you keep a value from being lost in a program? You assign it to a variable. Here are three lines that accomplish the switch, using a temporary third variable called TEMPO:

```
110 LET TEMPO = A(I + 1)
120 LET A(I + 1) = A(I)
130 LET A(I) = TEMPO
```

A fragment of a RUN chart should convince you that this temporary variable method works:

Line	A(I)	A(I + 1)	TEMPO	
	5	2	0	← *initial values*
110			2	
120		5		
130	2			

Here is the program. It uses the DATA . . . READ technique with a trailer value and counter to fill array A.

Program 1

Statement	Remark
10 PRINT "SIMPLE BUBBLE SORT"	
20 DIM A(10)	
30 GOSUB 100: REM * FILL THE ARRAY	
40 GOSUB 200: REM * SORT THE ARRAY	
50 GOSUB 300: REM * PRINT THE ARRAY	
60 END	
95 REM ** SUBROUTINE TO STORE N ELEMENTS **	
100 LET I = 1	*Count the elements.*
110 READ A(I)	
120 IF A(I) <> −999 THEN LET I = I + 1: GOTO 110	*−999 is the trailer value.*
130 LET N = I − 1	*Last number READ doesn't count.*
140 RETURN	
195 REM ** SUBROUTINE TO SORT ARRAY A **	
200 FOR PASS = 1 TO N − 1	*Go through array N − 1 times.*
210 FOR I = 1 TO N − 1	
220 IF A(I) <= A(I + 1) THEN GOTO 260	*If order correct, leave alone.*
230 LET TEMPO = A(I + 1)	
240 LET A(I + 1) = A(I)	*Switch the elements.*
250 LET A(I) = TEMPO	
260 NEXT I	
270 NEXT PASS	
280 RETURN	
295 REM ** SUBROUTINE TO PRINT ARRAY A **	
300 PRINT	
310 PRINT "HERE IS THE SORTED DATA:"	
315 PRINT	
320 FOR K = 1 TO N	
330 PRINT A(K)	
340 NEXT K	
350 RETURN	
360 DATA 5, 18, −3, 12, 17, 469, −12	
370 DATA 24, 0, 56, −999	

Output

```
SIMPLE BUBBLE SORT

HERE IS THE SORTED DATA:

-12
-3
0
5
12
17
18
24
56
469
```

Do you see how to change the program so that it will sort the data into *decreasing* (largest number to smallest) order? What changes need to be made so that the program will sort an array of strings?

The bubble sort is probably the easiest sorting algorithm to understand and to code into BASIC, but it is extremely slow when used with large arrays having hundreds or thousands of elements. The algorithm presented here can be made somewhat more efficient (some comparisons are unnecessary; see Exercises 9 and 10), but an entirely different approach is necessary for significantly greater speed. Nevertheless, some of the fastest sorting techniques make use of a bubble sort as part of a more complex algorithm.

Avoiding Pitfalls

The following portion of a program will *not* switch the contents of the variables A and B:

```
470  LET A = B
480  LET B = A
```

If these lines are executed, both A and B will end up with the original value of B. Instead, use a temporary variable, say T, as follows:

```
470  LET T = A
475  LET A = B
480  LET B = T
```

Summary

The *bubble sort* is a technique for arranging an array in numerical or alphabetical order. If the array contains N elements, then the array is sorted by making N − 1 passes through the array, each time comparing adjacent pairs of elements and switching them if they are out of order.

Exercises 10-3

A **1.** Sort the arrays shown below by hand into increasing numerical or alphabetical order. Use the bubble sort algorithm, writing down each step in the format shown in this example:

pass #1:	D	C	C	C
	C	D	D	D
	Q	Q	Q	A
	A	A	A	Q
pass #2:	C	C	C	C
	D	D	A	A
	A	A	D	D
	Q	Q	Q	Q
pass #3:	C	A	A	A
	A	C	C	C
	D	D	D	D
	Q	Q	Q	Q

a.	**b.**	**c.**
B	5	1
R	2	2
A	7	3
T	−3	

d.	**e.**	**f.**
Q	3	EAT
U	1	ANT
A	−6	AUNT
K	−12	BEND
E	1	ALPS

2. Tell whether each of the portions of a program in (a)–(h) can be used to switch the values of the variables A and B. If necessary, assign initial values to A and B and construct a RUN chart fragment.

a.
```
100 LET A=B
110 LET B=A
```

b.
```
100 LET A=T
110 LET B=A
120 LET T=A
```

c.
```
100 LET A=B
110 LET T=A
120 LET B=T
```

d.
```
100 LET T=A
110 LET B=A
120 LET A=T
```

e.
```
100 LET T=A
110 LET A=B
120 LET B=T
```

f.
```
100 LET T=B
110 LET B=A
120 LET A=T
```

g.
```
100 LET T=A
110 LET B=T
120 LET A=B
```

h.
```
100 LET T1=A
110 LET T2=B
120 LET A=T2
130 LET B=T1
```

3. What one-line change can be made to Program 1 so that it PRINTs the unsorted array before putting it in order and PRINTing the result?

4. Tell what changes are necessary in Program 1 so that it will sort an array of strings into alphabetical order.

5. Change Program 1 so that it will sort the data into *decreasing* numerical order (largest number to smallest).

6. Assume that the array A has N = 4 elements and has already been filled with these values:

Array A

A(1)	5
A(2)	18
A(3)	−3
A(4)	9

Construct a RUN chart for each of the following subroutines. Be sure there is a column for each of the subscripted variables A(1), A(2), A(3), and A(4), as well as for P, I, and T.

a.
```
2010 FOR P=1 TO N-1
2020 FOR I=1 TO N-1
2030 IF A(I)<=A(I+1) THEN
        GOTO 2070
2040 LET T=A(I+1)
2050 LET A(I+1)=A(I)
2060 LET A(I)=T
2070 NEXT I
2080 NEXT P
2090 RETURN
```

b.
```
2010 FOR P=1 TO N-1
2020 FOR I=1 TO N-P
2030 IF A(I)<=A(I+1) THEN GOTO 2070
2040 LET T=A(I+1)
2050 LET A(I+1)=A(I)
2060 LET A(I)=T
2070 NEXT I
2080 NEXT P
2090 RETURN
```

c.

```
2010 FOR P = 1 TO N - 1
2020 FOR I = N - 1 TO P STEP -1
2030 IF A(I) <= A(I + 1) THEN
       GOTO 2070
2040 LET T = A(I + 1)
2050 LET A(I + 1) = A(I)
2060 LET A(I) = T
2070 NEXT I
2080 NEXT P
2090 RETURN
```

d.

```
2010 FOR P = 1 TO N - 1
2020 FOR I = P TO 1 STEP -1
2030 IF A(I) <= A(I + 1) THEN GOTO 2080
2040 LET T = A(I + 1)
2050 LET A(I + 1) = A(I)
2060 LET A(I) = T
2070 NEXT I
2080 NEXT P
2090 RETURN
```

Example (d) is called the *shuttle sort*, which is similar to the bubble sort. Explain how it works differently from the bubble sort.

7. Using the format illustrated in the example in Exercise 1, sort the following array by hand using each of the subroutines in parts (a)–(d) of Exercise 6 above:

A(1)	6
A(2)	4
A(3)	−2
A(4)	3

8. a. Change subroutine 100 of Program 1 so that it fills array A with 10 random integers, each between 0 and 99.

b. Change subroutine 100 again so that it fills array A with 10 random strings of five letters each. Have the program sort the strings into increasing alphabetical order.

9. As observed in this section, one pass through an array in a bubble sort will always put the largest number in the last position of the array (when sorting in increasing order). Therefore, on the second pass, there is no need to compare the last two numbers of the array; they have to be in order already. Similarly, on the third pass, the program need not check whether the last three numbers are in order, and so forth. Change subroutine 200 in Program 1 so that such unnecessary comparisons are avoided. (*Hint:* You need only change line 210.)

10. If an array is almost in order to begin with, just a few passes may be needed to order it completely. Change subroutine 200 of Program 1 so that it uses a variable, say FLAG, to count how many switches are made on a given pass. If zero switches are made, then the array must be in order; have the subroutine RETURN in that case. (*Hint:* Eliminate the FOR PASS = 1 TO N − 1 . . . NEXT PASS loop; at line 270 have the program GOTO 210 if no switches have occurred.)

B **11.** Write a program that will sort three INPUT numbers A, B, and C into increasing order using this outline of a simplified (non-array) bubble sort:

Step 1 Get values of A, B, and C from the user.
Step 2 If A >= B, then switch A and B.
Step 3 If B >= C, then switch B and C.
Step 4 If A >= B, then switch A and B.
Step 5 PRINT the values of A, B, and C.

Construct a RUN chart to test your program for several values of A, B, and C. Do you see how this algorithm is a bubble sort? Why is it not necessary to complete the second pass? (That is, why is it not necessary to include this as step 4(b): If B >= C, then switch B and C?)

12. In Program 1, the data file used contained only one field (array A). More complex data files may be sorted according to any *key field.* For example, if a data file is stored in Program 1 in the arrays A, B$, and C, then the file may be sorted with array C as the key field by a simple modification of subroutine 200: if C(I) > C(I + 1), then not only must C(I) and C(I + 1) be switched but also B$(I) and B$(I + 1), and A(I) and A(I + 1).

a. Change Program 1 so that it creates a data file consisting of a list of ten persons' names, their ages, and their heights; have the program sort the file using the age field as the key.

b. Change the program to sort the file alphabetically using the name field as the key.

13. Write a program to fill a single array (using READ . . . DATA) with ten names, each consisting of a first name, a space, and a last name. The program should sort the names alphabetically according to last name. (*Hint:* Separate first and last names into two fields of a single data file, then sort according to the last-name field. Have the program PRINT the entire data file. See Exercise 12 above.)

14. Write a program to fill arrays with the data file containing the names of people and their favorite books (see page 520). Then have the program sort according to the book field.

15. Change subroutine 200 of Program 1 so that each pass through the array is from bottom to top (thus, the first comparison will be between A(N) and A(N − 1), the second will be between A(N − 1) and A(N − 2), and so forth).

16. You have probably noticed in following the bubble sort algorithm by hand that the larger numbers in the array move down quite rapidly, but smaller ones "bubble" to the top rather slowly. (Of course, this situation is reversed if the passes through the array are from bottom to top, as in Exercise 15.) Change subroutine 200 of Program 1 so that the first pass through the array is from top to bottom, the second pass is from bottom to top, the third from top to bottom, and so on.

17. Write a program that READs the data of the numerical array D shown below, sorts the elements into decreasing order, then PRINTs the third largest element of the array.

Array D

D(1)	12
D(2)	4
D(3)	50
D(4)	31

C 18. Write a program that READs the data of the two numerical arrays A and B shown below, then merges them into a single array C that is in increasing numerical order.

Array A

A(1)	4
A(2)	−2
A(3)	12
A(4)	0

Array B

B(1)	6
B(2)	2
B(3)	20
B(4)	−1

19. *Challenge:* An algorithm that is somewhat faster (in most cases) than the bubble sort — called the *selection sort* — involves finding the smallest number of the array and putting it in the first position, then finding the second smallest number (the smallest number of the rest of the array) and putting it in the second position, and so forth. Rewrite subroutine 200 of Program 1 to follow this algorithm:

As START goes from 1 to N − 1 (N = the number of elements of the array A):

a. Set SMALLEST = START. (SMALLEST will be the subscript of the smallest element among A(START), A(START + 1), . . . , A(N).)
b. As I goes from START + 1 to N, if A(I) > A(SMALLEST) then leave the elements alone.
c. Otherwise, set SMALLEST = I, then switch A(START) and A(SMALLEST). (Thus, the smallest element among A(START), A(START + 1), . . . , A(N) will end up in location A(START).)

Construct a RUN chart for array A shown below to verify that the subroutine works correctly.

Array A

A(1)	9
A(2)	4
A(3)	−1
A(4)	2

Lab Activity

An Illustrated Bubble Sort

In this Lab Activity, you will use a program that will sort (in increasing order) a graphically represented array using the bubble sort algorithm. The program chooses an array A of random X-coordinates and at the same time plots points on the screen corresponding to these random numbers. In particular, when the element A(1) is chosen, the point (A(1), 0) is plotted. When A(2) is chosen, the point (A(2), 3) is plotted. When A(3) is chosen, the point (A(3), 6) is plotted, and so forth. As you can see, only every third row on the screen is used. This is done so that the sorting process can be seen clearly.

Once all the points are plotted, the first two points (with X-coordinates A(1) and A(2)) are highlighted on the screen with short line segments on each side. If A(1) > A(2) is true, then according to the bubble sort algorithm the two elements (and their points) should be switched. This is exactly what happens when you press the space bar the first time. When you press the space bar again, the next two points, corresponding to A(2) and A(3), are highlighted and compared, and so forth. Graphically, then, the sorting process moves the left-most points (smallest A(I)) to the top of the screen and the right-most points (largest A(I)) to the bottom of the screen.

```
10  PRINT "GRAPHICAL BUBBLE SORT"
20  PRINT "PRESS THE SPACE BAR AT ANY TIME TO CONTINUE"
30  GOSUB 3000: REM * WAIT FOR SPACE BAR PRESS
40  LET XMAX =   : REM * FILL IN BIGGEST X-COORDINATE ON SCREEN
50  LET N =   : REM * FILL IN NUMBER OF ELEMENTS IN ARRAY TO BE SORTED; MAY
       NOT EXCEED 1 / 3 OF THE BIGGEST Y-VALUE ON THE SCREEN
60  GOSUB 1000: REM * SET UP GRAPHICS SCREEN
70  GOSUB 1500: REM * FILL ARRAY A, PLOT POINTS
80  GOSUB 2000: REM * SORT THE POINTS
90  END
990  REM ** SUBROUTINE TO SET UP GRAPHICS SCREEN **
1000  (Instructions to clear the screen
  .       and do graphics on your
  .       computer.)
  .
1050  RETURN
```

Program continued on next page.

```
1490 REM ** SUBROUTINE TO FILL ARRAY A WITH X-COORDINATES;
          PLOT THE POINTS **
1500 DIM A(N)
1510 FOR I = 1 TO N
1520 LET X = INT((XMAX — 5) * RND(1)) + 3: REM * RANDOM INTEGER
       FROM 3 TO XMAX — 3
1530 LET A(I) = X: REM * A(I) IS X-COORDINATE OF POINT IN ITH ROW
1540 LET Y = 3 * I — 1: REM * Y-COORDINATE EVERY THIRD ROW
1550 (Instruction to plot the point X, Y on your computer.)
1560 NEXT I
1570 RETURN

1990 REM ** SUBROUTINE TO BUBBLE SORT THE POINTS **
2000 FOR PASS = 1 TO N — 1
2010 FOR I = 1 TO N — 1
2020 LET Y = 3 * I — 1
2030 GOSUB 2500: REM * HIGHLIGHT THE ELEMENTS BEING COMPARED
2040 GOSUB 3000: REM * WAIT FOR SPACE BAR PRESS
2050 IF A(I) <= A(I + 1) THEN GOTO 2220: REM * IN ORDER; LEAVE ALONE
2060 (Instructions to erase the points A(I), Y and A(I + 1), Y + 3.)
  .
  .
  .
2100 GOSUB 2600: REM * ERASE HIGHLIGHTS
2110 LET T = A(I): REM * SWITCH A(I) AND A(I + 1)
2120 LET A(I) = A(I + 1)
2130 LET A(I + 1) = T
2140 (Instructions to plot the points A(I), Y and A(I + 1), Y + 3.)
2200 GOSUB 2500: REM * HIGHLIGHT NEW POINTS
2210 GOSUB 3000: REM * WAIT FOR SPACE BAR PRESS
2220 GOSUB 2600: REM * ERASE HIGHLIGHTS
2230 NEXT I
2240 NEXT PASS
2250 RETURN

2490 REM ** SUBROUTINE TO HIGHLIGHT ELEMENTS BEING COMPARED **
2500 (Instructions to plot the points
  .  (A(I) — 2, Y), (A(I) — 3, Y), (A(I) + 2, Y), (A(I) + 3, Y)
  .  (A(I + 1) — 2, Y + 3), (A(I + 1) — 3, Y + 3), (A(I + 1) + 2, Y + 3), and
  .  (A(I + 1) + 3, Y + 3).)
2580 RETURN
```

```
2590  REM ** SUBROUTINE TO ERASE HIGHLIGHTS **
2600  (Instructions to erase the points
 .        in subroutine 2500.)
 .
 .
2680  RETURN
2990  REM ** SUBROUTINE TO WAIT FOR SPACE BAR TO BE PRESSED **
3000  GET A$    Apple     or     3000  LET A$ = INKEY$         } TRS-80 and IBM
                                3010  IF A$ = "" THEN 3000   }
3020  RETURN
```

Problems

1. RUN the program with N = 6 (line 50), pressing the space bar repeatedly to see the progress of the sort. Describe what happens when the top point of the two currently being compared is located to the left of the bottom one. Describe what happens when the top point is located to the right of the bottom one. Describe the location of points on the screen when the sort ends.

2. RUN the program again with N as big a number as possible for your screen (N = 1/3 * *biggest Y-value allowed*). At each step, predict whether the two points should be switched.

3. You probably will have noticed that after the sort has been going on for a while, no switches occur toward the bottom of the screen. The reason is that during the first complete pass through the array, the largest element arrives at the last position (thus, the right-most point moves to the bottom of the screen). In the second and later passes, there is no reason to compare A(N − 1) with A(N), since A(N) is certain to be larger. Similarly, in pass number PASS, there is no reason to compare A(N − PASS + 1) with A(N − PASS + 2) since they will already be in order.

   Change line 2010 to:

   ```
   2010  FOR I = 1 TO N - PASS
   ```

   RUN the program to verify that this change in the final counter value avoids the extra comparisons and speeds up the sort.

4. Change the program so that it does not wait for you to press the space bar each time it compares or switches two elements of the array. RUN the program several times with line 2010 in the form given in Problem 3, and then several more times with the original version of 2010. Use a watch or clock with a second hand to time how long each version takes. Compare the average times for the two versions.

10-4 A Faster Sort: The Shell Algorithm

The bubble sort is rather slow for ordering any sizable array (see the Lab Activity for this section). The reason is that smaller numbers near the bottom of the list take a long time to "bubble" to the top. For example, consider this array:

Array A

A(1)	27
A(2)	14
A(3)	7
A(4)	17
A(5)	6
A(6)	12
A(7)	5
A(8)	2
A(9)	1

The number 1, initially stored in A(9), will take 8 passes to get to the position A(1). In an algorithm designed by D. L. Shell, smaller numbers are skipped to the top of the list much more quickly, thereby saving a lot of time. This is done by breaking or *partitioning* the entire array into sublists, each of which is bubble sorted. The number of sublists is given by INT(N / 2), where N is the number of elements in the array. For array A above N = 9, so the number of sublists is INT(9 / 2) = 4. Each sublist is obtained by taking every fourth element of the array.

Here are the four sublists:

First Partition

	First Sublist		Second Sublist		Third Sublist		Fourth Sublist
A(1)	27	A(2)	14	A(3)	7	A(4)	17
A(5)	6	A(6)	12	A(7)	5	A(8)	2
A(9)	1						

Now each sublist is bubble sorted. This sort is quick, involving at most two passes per sublist, since a first-partition sublist can contain no more than three elements. (As another example, if a list has 391 elements, then the first partition will create INT(391 / 2) = 195 sublists; the first 390 elements will be distributed evenly into the 195 sublists (2 each), and the 391st element will be the third member of the first sublist. How many sublists will there be if N = 500? How many elements will be in each sublist?)

Here are the four bubble-sorted sublists:

	First Sublist		Second Sublist		Third Sublist		Fourth Sublist
A(1)	1	A(2)	12	A(3)	5	A(4)	2
A(5)	6	A(6)	14	A(7)	7	A(8)	17
A(9)	27						

Thus, array A now looks like this:

	Array A
A(1)	1
A(2)	12
A(3)	5
A(4)	2
A(5)	6
A(6)	14
A(7)	7
A(8)	17
A(9)	27

A lot has been accomplished in this one set of short sorts; three of the smaller numbers got to the top half of the list, and three of the larger ones moved to the bottom half. (There is a faster algorithm, called the *quick sort,* which makes sure that *all* the smaller numbers get to the top half and *all* the bigger numbers get to the bottom half. See the Lab Activity.)

The next stage in the Shell sort is to partition the entire array again — this time into half as many sublists as before:

Second Partition

	First Sublist		Second Sublist
A(1)	1	A(2)	12
A(3)	5	A(4)	2
A(5)	6	A(6)	14
A(7)	7	A(8)	17
A(9)	27		

As in the first partition, each sublist is bubble sorted. The sublists are longer than before, but they are rather close to being in order already, so that relatively few time-consuming switches of consecutive elements need to be made. (In fact, in the example, the first sublist is already in order.) At the end of the two sorts, the entire array looks like this:

First Sublist

A(1)	1
A(3)	5
A(5)	6
A(7)	7
A(9)	27

Second Sublist

A(2)	2
A(4)	12
A(6)	14
A(8)	17

Array A

A(1)	1
A(2)	2
A(3)	5
A(4)	12
A(5)	6
A(6)	14
A(7)	7
A(8)	17
A(9)	27

Again, the array is partitioned into half as many sublists as before. In this example, that means there is only one sublist. Once that sublist is bubble sorted, which is quickly done, the Shell sort is finished. Here is the sorted array:

Array A

A(1)	1
A(2)	2
A(3)	5
A(4)	6
A(5)	7
A(6)	12
A(7)	14
A(8)	17
A(9)	27

A first outline of an algorithm for a program using the Shell sort could go like this:

Step 1 Fill array A with N elements.

Step 2 Do Shell sort on array A.

- **a.** Let NSUB (number of sublists) = INT(N / 2).
- **b.** Bubble sort each of the NSUB sublists.
- **c.** Divide the number of sublists in half; LET NSUB = INT(NSUB / 2).
- **d.** If NSUB is not yet zero, then go back to Step 2(b).

Step 3 PRINT the sorted array.

Notice that once the number of sublists (NSUB) equals 1 and the entire array has been bubble sorted for the last time, the instruction LET NSUB = INT(NSUB / 2) in Step 2(c) will give NSUB the value 0. Therefore, the condition in Step 2(d) will be false, and the results will be PRINTed in Step 3.

Step 2(b) of the outline needs elaboration. Certainly, a loop of the form FOR SUB = 1 TO NSUB . . . NEXT SUB can control the program's sorting of one sublist after another. What is the form of the algorithm for bubble sorting sublist number SUB? Of course, we follow the ideas discussed in Section 10–3, but the details are a little different. Suppose, for example, that array A has 9 elements and therefore is initially partitioned as shown below:

First Sublist	Second Sublist	Third Sublist	Fourth Sublist
A(1)	A(2)	A(3)	A(4)
A(5)	A(6)	A(7)	A(8)
A(9)			

Since NSUB = 4, the sublists can alternatively be described as follows:

First Sublist	Second Sublist	Third Sublist	Fourth Sublist
A(1)	A(2)	A(3)	A(4)
A(1 + NSUB)	A(2 + NSUB)	A(3 + NSUB)	A(4 + NSUB)
A(1 + NSUB + NSUB)			

As you can see, sublist number SUB can be described by

SUBth Sublist
A(SUB)
A(SUB + NSUB)
A(SUB + NSUB + NSUB)
.
.
.

(continuing until the next subscript would be bigger than N = 9).

In the bubble sort of sublist number SUB, therefore, A(SUB) is compared with A(SUB + NSUB) and the two are switched if out of order. Then A(SUB + NSUB) is compared with A(SUB + NSUB + NSUB), and so forth, until there are no elements left in the sublist. This sequence of comparisons can of course be handled by a loop. If I initially has the value SUB, then the program can compare A(I) with A(I + NSUB). After the appropriate action is taken, NSUB can be added to I and the new A(I), which is now the element A(SUB + NSUB), can be compared with A(I + NSUB), which is now the element A(SUB + NSUB + NSUB). This process is continued until I + NSUB becomes larger than N, the number of elements in the array.

Finally, as a time-saving device, we will have the program continue to pass through the sublist only until no more switches are made (then the sublist is completely sorted). The program can keep track of switches by using a *flag variable* (we'll call it SWFLAG, for *switch flag*) that equals 1 if a switch has been made in the current pass, and 0 otherwise.

Here is our elaboration of Step 2(b) in the algorithm outline:

Step 2(b) Bubble sort each of the NSUB sublists.
FOR SUB = 1 TO NSUB:

- **i.** Initialize SWFLAG = 0 (no switches have occurred in current pass).
- **ii.** Initialize I = SUB (the subscript of the first element of sublist number SUB).
- **iii.** If A(I) > A(I + NSUB), then switch A(I) and A(I + NSUB) and set SWFLAG = 1 (switch has now occurred).
- **iv.** Add NSUB to I (I is now the subscript of the next element in the sublist).
- **v.** If I + NSUB < = N, then go back to (iii).
- **vi.** Otherwise (current pass is finished), if SWFLAG = 1, go back to (i) (new pass).
- **vii.** Otherwise (no more switches to make — sublist is in order), exit from bubble sort subroutine.

NEXT SUB

Here is the program:

Program 1

Statement

```
10  PRINT "SHELL SORT"
20  GOSUB 1000: REM * FILL ARRAY WITH DATA
30  GOSUB 2000: REM * SORT THE ARRAY
40  GOSUB 3000: REM * PRINT THE ARRAY
50  END
1000  REM ** SUBROUTINE TO FILL ARRAY A **
1010  READ N: REM * NUMBER OF ELEMENTS
1020  DIM A(N)
1030  FOR C = 1 TO N
1040  READ A(C)
1050  NEXT C
1060  RETURN
```

```
2000 REM ** SUBROUTINE TO SHELL SORT ARRAY A **
2010 LET NSUB = INT(N / 2): REM * NUMBER OF SUBLISTS
2020 FOR SUB = 1 TO NSUB
2030 GOSUB 2500: REM * BUBBLE SORT SUBLIST NUMBER SUB
2040 NEXT SUB
2050 LET NSUB = INT(NSUB / 2): REM * HALF AS MANY SUBLISTS NEXT TIME
2060 IF NSUB > 0 THEN GOTO 2020: REM * SORT NEW SET OF SUBLISTS
2070 RETURN
2500 REM ** SUBROUTINE TO BUBBLE SORT SUBLIST NUMBER SUB **
2510 LET SWFLAG = 0: REM * NO SWITCHES YET ON THIS PASS
2520 LET I = SUB: REM * SUBSCRIPT OF FIRST ELEMENT OF SUBLIST SUB
2530 IF A(I) <= A(I + NSUB) THEN GOTO 2580: REM * IN ORDER — NO SWITCH
2540 LET TEMPO = A(I): REM * MAKE THE SWITCH
2550 LET A(I) = A(I + NSUB)
2560 LET A(I + NSUB) = TEMPO
2570 LET SWFLAG = 1: REM * SWITCH HAS NOW OCCURRED
2580 LET I = I + NSUB: REM * NEXT ELEMENT OF SUBLIST
2590 IF I + NSUB <= N THEN GOTO 2530: REM * NOT DONE YET
2600 IF SWFLAG = 1 THEN GOTO 2510: REM * DO ANOTHER PASS
2610 RETURN
3000 REM ** SUBROUTINE TO PRINT SORTED ARRAY **
3010 PRINT "SORTED ARRAY:"
3020 FOR C = 1 TO N
3030 PRINT A(C)
3040 NEXT C
3050 RETURN
4000 DATA 9, 27, 14, 7, 17, 6, 12, 5, 2, 1
```

Output

```
SHELL SORT
SORTED ARRAY:
1
2
5
6
7
12
14
17
27
```

Avoiding Pitfalls

When using a *flag* variable to keep track of switches in a sorting routine, be sure to reset the flag to its initial value before making another pass through the array (or sublist of the array).

Summary

The Shell algorithm is a relatively fast sorting technique that moves items of an array quickly into the general neighborhood of their final positions. This is done by partitioning the array into sublists, and then bubble sorting each sublist. At first, the sublists are extremely short, but their length doubles after each bubble sort is complete. Finally, there is only one sublist — the entire array — and one last, quick bubble sort finishes the ordering of the array.

Exercises 10-4

A **1.** Sort the lists at the top of the next page by hand into increasing numerical or alphabetical order, using the Shell algorithm. At those points where the algorithm calls for a bubble sort of a sublist, give full details. Here is an example to follow:

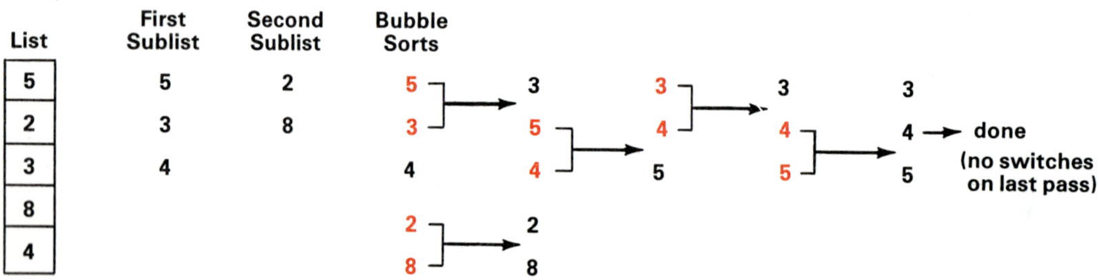

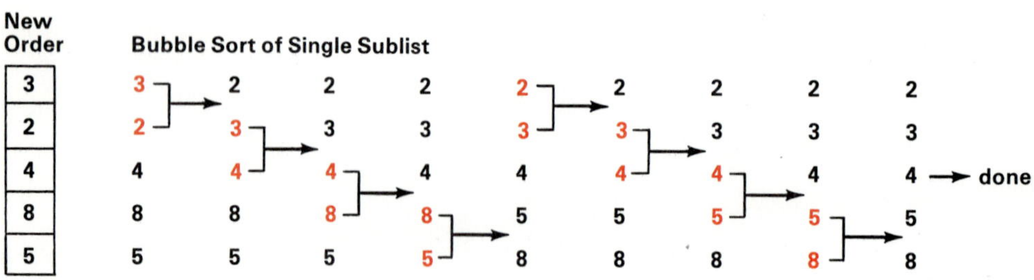

a.

1
5
9
2
3

b.

−3
1
2
−6
5
1

c.

C
Q
A
Z

2. Sort the following lists by hand into increasing numerical or alphabetical order. Use the Shell algorithm, but when each sublist is bubble sorted, leave out the details; just summarize the result of the sort. For example:

List	Four Sublists		Bubble Sorts		New Order
−5	−5 8 7 2	→	−5 3 6 2	→	−5
8	9 3 6 2		9 8 7 2		3
7					6
2					2
9					9
3					8
6					7
2					2

Two Sublists		Bubble Sorts		New Order	Bubble Sort of Single Sublist
−5 3		−5 2		−5	−5
6 2	→	6 2	→	2	2
9 8		7 3		6	2
7 2		9 8		2	3
				7	6
				3	7
				9	8
				8	9

a.

4
−7
3
2
8
−6

b.

−2
7
8
7
7
6
−4
3
−8

c.

MY
DOG
HAS
MANY
MANY
FLEAS
AND
NO
COLLAR

3. Change subroutine 2000 of Program 1 so that it sorts the array A into *decreasing* numerical order.

4. Change Program 1 so that it fills and sorts a string array A$ containing eleven names.

B 5. a. Write a program that INPUTs a list of people's heights in centimeters, Shell sorts the data in decreasing order, then PRINTs the third largest height.

b. Change the program in (a) to PRINT the *middle* height if there is an odd number of INPUT heights, or the *average of the two heights closest to the middle* if there is an even number of INPUT heights.

6. Write a program that generates a list of twenty random strings, each having between two and six letters, then PRINTs the list in alphabetical order. (Use a Shell sort.)

7. Write a program that puts a list of words into a string array A$ in random order (the same string may be used more than once). Have the program PRINT the list of words in this random order, then in alphabetical order. Use a Shell sort. (*Hint:* First READ the list into an array B$ in the order in which they appear in the DATA statements. Then for each subscripted variable in the array A$, choose randomly one of the elements of B$.)

8. Write a program that uses INPUT to set up a data file for a cassette tape collection. Each record of the file should consist of three fields: the title of the tape, the recording group, and the year the tape was bought. Have the program Shell sort the file alphabetically according to recording group, and then PRINT the entire data file. (See Exercise 12, on page 541, for hints on how to handle a file consisting of more than one array.)

9. Rewrite the program in each of the following exercises from Section 10–3 so that it uses a Shell sort.

a. Exercise 12, page 541 b. Exercise 13, page 541 c. Exercise 14, page 541

C 10. Write a program that uses READ . . . DATA to fill an array A as follows:

A(1)	4
A(2)	7
A(3)	12
A(4)	15
A(5)	17

(Notice that array A is already sorted.) Have the program INPUT a number B, then insert B into array A at the correct position so that the resulting extended array is still in order. (*Hint:* One way to do this is to start at the bottom of the array, moving numbers *down* until a number is found that is less than or equal to B (or the array is used up). Then B is inserted at the position right below that.) A step-by-step illustration is at the top of the next page.

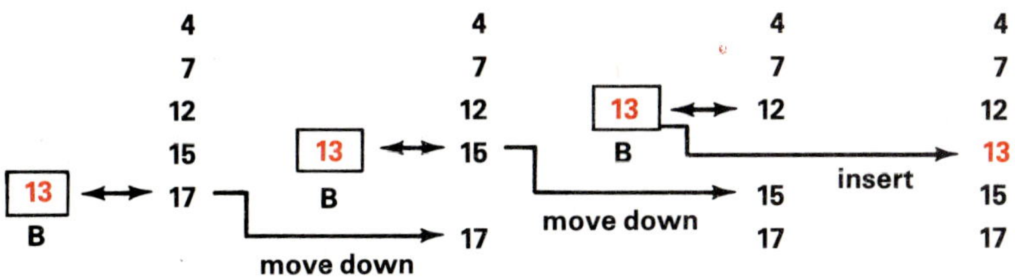

11. *Challenge:* Another sorting algorithm, called the *insertion sort,* involves inserting each number of the array into the proper position among all the numbers that come before it. Here is an example:

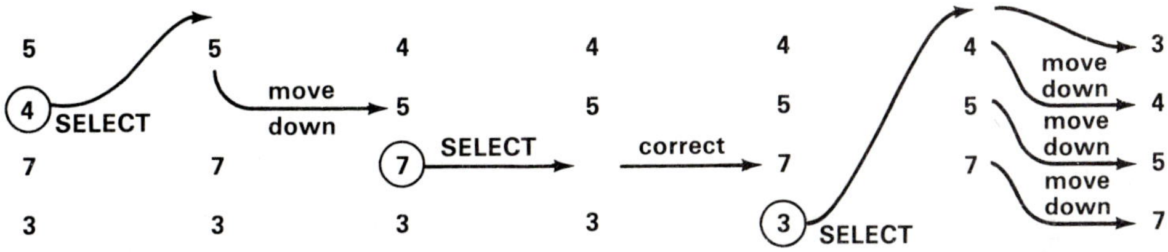

Here, the second number (4) is first selected. It is inserted above the 5 (that is, the 5 is moved down and the 4 is put in its place). At this point, the first two numbers are in order relative to each other. Then the third number (7) is selected. It comes after the 5, so no change is required. Finally, the fourth number (3) is selected. Since it goes before the 4, all the other numbers are moved down and the 3 is inserted at the beginning of the array. Write a program that uses INPUT to fill an array A with a list of numbers, then sorts the array using the insertion sort and PRINTs the results. (*Hint:* At the Ith stage, LET SELECT = A(I). Then compare SELECT with A(I − 1); if SELECT < A(I − 1) is true, then move A(I − 1) down one position in the array and compare SELECT with A(I − 2), and so on. The first time SELECT > = A(J) is true for some J, insert SELECT into the array at position J + 1. If SELECT < A(J) is true for all J < = I − 1, then SELECT goes into position A(1).)

12. *Challenge:* Rewrite the program in Exercise 7 so that no string is repeated on the list.

Lab Activity

Comparing Sorts

In Section 10–3, you studied the bubble sort, a relatively slow technique for sorting large amounts of data. An improvement, the Shell sort, moves items on the list being sorted more rapidly to the general area of their final positions.

Another algorithm, called the *quick sort,* does an even more efficient job of moving smaller items to the top of the list and larger items to the bottom. In the quick sort, the list is partitioned into two non-overlapping sublists, the top one containing all of the smaller items and the bottom one containing all of the larger items. Each sublist is partitioned in turn, the process continuing until there are no sublists left to partition; when this happens, the entire array is sorted. Since the computer can do only one thing at a time, the sublists left to be partitioned must be saved somehow; this is done in an array called a *stack* (see line 3010 of the program below). We will give no further explanation of the quick sort here. It is difficult; you will be in a better position to understand it after a more advanced computer course, although you might learn something valuable by studying subroutine 3000 in the program below.

The purpose of this Lab Activity is to compare the times required to sort an array by using the three algorithms that have been discussed: the bubble sort, the Shell sort, and the quick sort. The program given here does any of these sorts on any (reasonable) size array of random integers from 0 to 999.

```
10  PRINT "COMPARING SORTS"
20  (Fill in randomization instruction for your computer.)
30  PRINT "TYPE 1 FOR BUBBLE SORT"
40  PRINT "TYPE 2 FOR SHELL SORT"
50  PRINT "TYPE 3 FOR QUICK SORT"
60  INPUT "WHICH SORT:  "; SEL
70  IF NOT((SEL = 1) OR (SEL = 2) OR (SEL = 3)) THEN PRINT "INCORRECT
      RESPONSE": GOTO 60
100  PRINT
110  INPUT "TYPE NUMBER OF ARRAY ELEMENTS:  "; N
120  PRINT
130  PRINT "NOW ASSIGNING RANDOM DATA"
140  DIM A(N)
150  FOR I = 1 TO N
160  LET A(I) = INT(1000 * RND (1)) <—— On TRS-80 computers, use RND(0)
                                         instead of RND(1).
170  NEXT I
180  PRINT
190  INPUT "START TIMING WHEN YOU PRESS <RETURN> OR <ENTER>"; A$
200  ON SEL GOSUB 1000, 2000, 3000 <—— See page 574 for an explanation of
                                        ON . . . GOSUB.
210  PRINT
220  PRINT "DONE"
```

```
230  PRINT
240  PRINT "THE SORTED ARRAY IS:"
250  FOR I = 1 TO N
260  PRINT A(I); "  ";
270  NEXT I
280  PRINT
290  END

1000  REM ** SUBROUTINE TO BUBBLE SORT ARRAY A **
1010  FOR PASS = 1 TO N - 1
1020  FOR I = 1 TO N - PASS: REM * N - PASS IS MORE EFFICIENT THAN N - 1
1030  IF A(I) <= A(I + 1) THEN GOTO 1070: REM * ORDER OKAY; LEAVE ALONE
1040  LET TEMPO = A(I + 1): REM * SWITCH ELEMENTS
1050  LET A(I + 1) = A(I)
1060  LET A(I) = TEMPO
1070  NEXT I
1080  NEXT PASS
1090  RETURN

2000  REM ** SUBROUTINE TO SHELL SORT ARRAY A **
2010  LET NSUB = INT(N / 2): REM * NUMBER OF SUBLISTS
2020  FOR SUB = 1 TO NSUB
2030  GOSUB 2500: REM * BUBBLE SORT SUBLIST NUMBER SUB
2040  NEXT SUB
2050  LET NSUB = INT(NSUB / 2): REM * HALF AS MANY SUBLISTS NEXT TIME
2060  IF NSUB > 0 THEN 2020: REM * SORT NEW SET OF SUBLISTS
2070  RETURN

2500  REM ** SUBROUTINE TO BUBBLE SORT SUBLIST NUMBER SUB **
2510  LET SWFLAG = 0: REM * NO SWITCHES YET ON THIS PASS
2520  LET I = SUB: REM * SUBSCRIPT OF FIRST ELEMENT OF SUBLIST SUB
2530  IF A(I) <= A(I + NSUB) THEN GOTO 2580: REM * IN ORDER; NO SWITCH
2540  LET TEMPO = A(I): REM * SWITCH ELEMENTS
2550  LET A(I) = A(I + NSUB)
2560  LET A(I + NSUB) = TEMPO
2570  LET SWFLAG = 1: REM * SWITCH HAS NOW OCCURRED
2580  LET I = I + NSUB: REM * NEXT ELEMENT OF ARRAY
2590  IF I + NSUB <= N THEN GOTO 2530: REM * NOT DONE YET
2600  IF SWFLAG = 1 THEN GOTO 2510: REM * DO ANOTHER PASS
2610  RETURN
```

Program continued on next page.

```
3000 REM ** SUBROUTINE TO QUICK SORT ARRAY A **
3010 DIM STACK(20): REM * TO SAVE TOPS, BOTTOMS OF SUBLISTS
3020 LET PNTR = 0: REM * POINTER TO TOP OF STACK
3030 LET T = 1: REM * TOP OF SUBLIST
3040 LET B = N: REM * BOTTOM OF SUBLIST
3050 LET DIR = -1: REM * MOVE UP IF -1, DOWN IF +1
3060 LET DOWN = T: REM * SUBSCRIPT MOVING DOWN
3070 LET UP = B: REM * SUBSCRIPT MOVING UP
3080 IF A(DOWN) <= A(UP) THEN GOTO 3130: REM * IN CORRECT ORDER
3090 LET TEMPO = A(DOWN): REM * SWITCH ELEMENTS
3100 LET A(DOWN) = A(UP)
3110 LET A(UP) = TEMPO
3120 LET DIR = - DIR: REM * CHANGE DIRECTION OF MOTION
3130 IF DIR = - 1 THEN LET UP = UP - 1: GOTO 3150
3140 LET DOWN = DOWN + 1
3150 IF UP > DOWN THEN 3080: REM * SUBLIST NOT COMPLETELY PARTITIONED
3160 IF (UP - T) > (B - UP) THEN GOTO 3200
3170 LET STACK(PNTR + 1) = UP + 1: REM * PUSH TOP, BOTTOM OF
       BIGGER SUBLIST
3180 LET STACK(PNTR + 2) = B
3185 LET B = UP: REM * BOTTOM OF NEW SUBLIST
3190 GOTO 3220
3200 LET STACK(PNTR + 1) = T
3210 LET STACK(PNTR + 2) = UP - 1
3215 LET T = UP: REM * TOP OF NEW SUBLIST
3220 LET PNTR = PNTR + 2
3230 IF T < B THEN GOTO 3050: REM * DO SUBLIST
3240 IF PNTR = 0 THEN GOTO 3300: REM * STACK EMPTY;  ALL DONE
3250 LET B = STACK(PNTR): REM * POP BOTTOM, TOP OF NEW SUBLIST
3260 LET T = STACK(PNTR - 1)
3270 LET PNTR = PNTR - 2
3280 GOTO 3230
3300 RETURN
```

Problems

1. RUN the program and have it do a bubble sort on an array of 10 elements. Time as carefully as you can how long it takes for the sort to be accomplished. (A stop watch will work best. A very workable alternative is a

watch with a second display held near your computer screen. If you watch the seconds go by, you will be able to see out of the corner of your eye the moment when the sorted array starts being printed out. If you are working with a partner, one of you can watch the screen while the other watches the time.)

2. Time as carefully as possible how long it takes the program to sort an array of 10 elements first using the Shell sort and then the quick sort. Record the results.

3. Time how long it takes for each of the three algorithms — the bubble sort, the Shell sort, and the quick sort — to sort an array of 20 elements. Do each sort at least twice and record the results.

4. RUNning the program repeatedly, complete the following table:

Time in Seconds

Number of Elements	Bubble Sort	Shell Sort	Quick Sort
10			
20			
40			
80			
160			

5. The bubble sort is said to be an N-squared sort; as the number of elements in the array is doubled, the time it takes to do the sort is quadrupled (the square of 2 is 4). Verify that the time required to sort a 20-element array using the bubble sort is approximately one-fourth of the time required to sort a 40-element array. Does the same approximate relationship apply to the times required to sort arrays with 40, 80, and 160 elements using the bubble sort? (The quick sort is much faster than an N-squared sort; it is an N log(N) algorithm.)

10-5 Efficient Data Retrieval: The Binary Search

In Section 10–2, you learned how to write a program to find information in a data file using a linear search. As you recall, a linear search starts at the beginning of the file and looks at the key field of all the records in order until the desired item is found. For a large file, this is a very inefficient procedure; if the records of the file have been put in numerical or alphabetical order according to the key field, a much faster algorithm is possible.

The Binary Search

A method for searching an *ordered* file, which is much more efficient than the linear search, involves making a guess of the location of the item sought, then modifying the guess on the basis of what is found in that location. For example, suppose that we are seeking the string JABBER in an alphabetized array called A$, and that we guess that JABBER will be the contents of A$(18). If it turns out instead that A$(18) = "WOCKY", then we know that we should look among A$(1), A$(2), . . . , and A$(17) for JABBER, since "JABBER" < "WOCKY". On the other hand, if A$(18) = "ALICE", then JABBER must be among A$(19), A$(20), . . . , if it is in the array at all.

The question is: What should the first guess be, and exactly how should future guesses be modified on the basis of what is found in the array? The best answer, in the long run anyway, is always to guess the middle value among those that have not yet been ruled out (or as close to the middle as possible). For example, in trying to find JABBER in the 20-element array A$, we first should look at A$(10). If A$(10) turns out to have the value "HATTER",

A$(1)
.
.
.
A$(10) "HATTER"
.
.
.
A$(20)

then we know that we should look next among A$(11), A$(12), . . . , and A$(20), since "JABBER" > "HATTER". We choose to look at A$(15) next. (A$(15) and A$(16) are both in the middle. We will always take the first value in case of ties.) If A$(15) = "WALRUS",

A$(11)
.
.
.
A$(15) "WALRUS"
.
.
.
A$(20)

then we know that if JABBER is in the array at all, it must be among A$(11), A$(12), A$(13), and A$(14), since "JABBER" < "WALRUS".

We look next at A$(12). If A$(12) = "MAD",

A$(11)
A$(12) "MAD"
A$(13)
A$(14)

then the only remaining possibility for JABBER is A$(11).

The algorithm described above is called a *binary search;* "binary", of course, means "two." The algorithm repeatedly divides the remaining possibilities into *two* parts as evenly as possible. Unless there is some clue as to the location of the *target* (the string or number desired), a binary search is the best strategy for searching an ordered array. The most you can expect of any search strategy in the long run is to cut the number of possible locations of the target in half with each guess, and that is just what a binary search does.

Here is an outline of an algorithm for a program that uses a binary search to determine the location of an INPUT one-word string in an alphabetized array of strings.

Step 1 Fill array A$ with N elements.

Step 2 INPUT the string to be located; call it TARGT$.

Step 3 Search for TARGT$ in the array A$:

a. Set SMALL = 1 and BIG = N. (TARGT$ must lie between A$(SMALL) and A$(BIG).)

b. Set GUESS = the average of SMALL and BIG, rounded down to the nearest integer.

c. If TARGT$ = A$(GUESS), then set SUB = GUESS and RETURN. (SUB is the location of TARGT$.)

d. Otherwise, if TARGT$ < A$(GUESS), then set BIG = GUESS − 1. (TARGT$ must be between A$(SMALL) and A$(GUESS − 1), if it is in the array at all.)

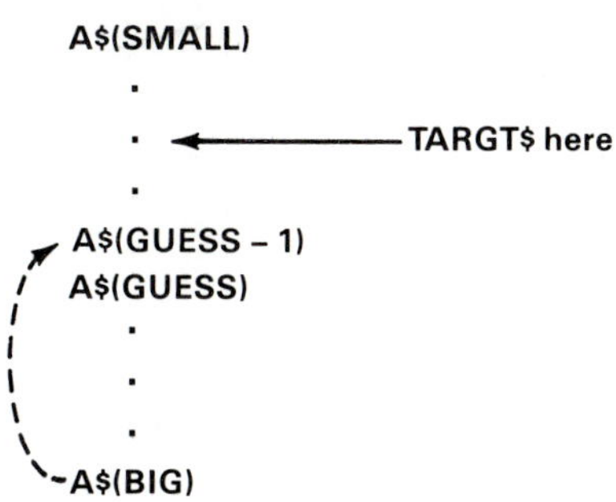

e. Otherwise, set SMALL = GUESS + 1. (TARGT$ must be between A$(GUESS + 1) and A$(BIG).)

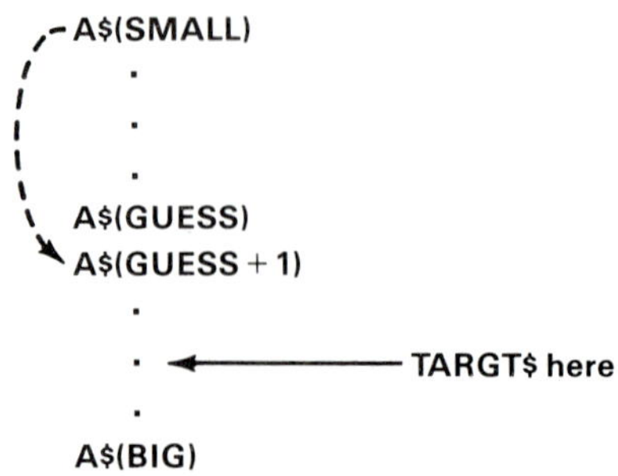

f. If SMALL < = BIG then go back to Step 3b (go to the next guess).

g. Otherwise, set SUB = 0 (to indicate that TARGT$ was not found) and RETURN.

Step 4 PRINT the location (SUB) of TARGT$ if found; PRINT the message NOT ON THE LIST if not found.

In this algorithm, the string sought, TARGT$, always lies between A$(SMALL) and A$(BIG) if it is in the array at all. Step 3(b) makes GUESS as close as possible to halfway between SMALL and BIG. Steps 3(d) and 3(e) assign new values to SMALL and BIG according to what is found at the guessed location. The process is repeated until either the target string is found (Step 3(c)) or BIG and SMALL have passed each other (Step 3(g)), in which case TARGT$ must not be in the array. The subroutine outlined in Steps 3(a) to 3(g) communicates the result of the search to the main routine by using the variable SUB. If SUB = 0, then the target string was not found in the array. Otherwise, TARGT$ = A$(SUB).

Here is the program:

Program 1

Statement

```
10  PRINT "BINARY SEARCH"
20  GOSUB 1000: REM * FILL ARRAY A$
30  PRINT
40  INPUT "TYPE STRING TO BE FOUND:  "; TARGT$
50  GOSUB 2000: REM * PERFORM SEARCH
60  PRINT
70  IF SUB = 0 THEN PRINT TARGT$; "  IS NOT ON THE LIST": GOTO 90
80  PRINT TARGT$; "  IS ITEM NUMBER  "; SUB; "  ON THE LIST"
90  END
```

```
1000 REM ** SUBROUTINE TO FILL ARRAY A **
1010 DIM A$(30)
1020 READ A$(1): REM * READ FIRST WORD
1030 LET N = 1: REM * COUNT THE NUMBER OF ELEMENTS
1040 READ A$(N + 1)
1050 IF A$(N + 1) >= A$(N) THEN LET N = N + 1: GOTO 1040: REM * STILL
       IN ORDER — KEEP READING
1060 RETURN: REM * STOP READING WHEN AN ELEMENT IS OUT OF ORDER
2000 REM ** SUBROUTINE TO SEARCH A$ FOR TARGT$ **
2010 LET SMALL = 1: REM * TOP OF SEARCH INTERVAL
2020 LET BIG = N: REM * BOTTOM OF SEARCH INTERVAL
2030 LET GUESS = INT((SMALL + BIG) / 2): REM * HALFWAY BETWEEN TOP
       AND BOTTOM
2040 IF TARGT$ = A$(GUESS) THEN LET SUB = GUESS: GOTO 2090
2050 IF TARGT$ < A$(GUESS) THEN LET BIG = GUESS — 1: GOTO 2070: REM *
       TARGT$ MUST BE BETWEEN A$(SMALL) AND A$(GUESS — 1)
2060 LET SMALL = GUESS + 1: REM * TARGT$ MUST BE BETWEEN
       A$(GUESS + 1) AND A$(BIG)
2070 IF SMALL <= BIG THEN GOTO 2030: REM * NEXT GUESS
2080 LET SUB = 0: REM * SIGNIFYING TARGT$ NOT FOUND
2090 RETURN
4000 DATA CAT, CATERPILLAR, CHESHIRE, CURIOUSER
4005 DATA DEE, DODO, DUCHESS, DUM
4010 DATA GRYPHON, HATTER, JABBER, MAD
4015 DATA TWEEDLEDEE, TWEEDLEDUM
4020 DATA WALRUS, WILLIAM
4025 DATA WOCKY, WONDERLAND
4030 DATA YOUTH, AAAA
```

Output

```
BINARY SEARCH

TYPE STRING TO BE FOUND:   ? JABBER

JABBER IS ITEM NUMBER 11 ON THE LIST

RUN
BINARY SEARCH

TYPE STRING TO BE FOUND:   ? LOOKING GLASS

LOOKING GLASS IS NOT ON THE LIST
```

Avoiding Pitfalls

Be sure that the numbers (or strings) in an array are in numeric (or alphabetical) order before performing a binary search.

Summary

The *binary search* algorithm is a method of searching an array that is in numerical or alphabetical order for a particular target number or string. If the location of the target has been narrowed down to a certain interval in the array, then the middle element in the interval is examined. Depending on its value, half of the interval is eliminated as possible locations of the target. This process of examining middle values of smaller and smaller possible intervals is repeated until the actual location is pinpointed, or it is shown that the target must not be in the array.

Exercises 10-5

A **1.** Construct a RUN chart for the following binary search subroutine, using array A$ shown below and the target string specified in (a)–(c).

```
5000  LET SMALL = 1
5010  LET BIG = N
5020  LET GUESS = INT((SMALL + BIG) / 2)
5030  IF TARGT$ = A$(GUESS) THEN PRINT GUESS: RETURN
5040  IF TARGT$ < A$(GUESS) THEN LET BIG = GUESS — 1: GOTO 5060
5050  LET SMALL = GUESS + 1
5060  IF SMALL <= BIG THEN GOTO 5020
5070  PRINT "NOT FOUND"
5080  RETURN
```

A$(1)	A
A$(2)	C
A$(3)	D
A$(4)	H
A$(5)	Q
A$(6)	R
A$(7)	T
A$(8)	Z

a. TARGT$ = "R" **b.** TARGT$ = "A" **c.** TARGT$ = "P"

2. Repeat Exercise 1, using array A$ and the target string given in (a)–(d).

a.

A$(1)	BRIDGE
A$(2)	DOWN
A$(3)	FALLING
A$(4)	IS
A$(5)	LONDON
A$(6)	MOTHER

TARGT$ | IS |

b. TARGT$ = "MOTHER" c. TARGT$ = "RHYME" d. TARGT$ = "GOOSE"

3. You can describe a binary search by writing, at each stage, the interval in the list that has not yet been eliminated, and identifying the middle number that should be compared next with the target. For example, consider a binary search of the following list for the target 16:

1		
3		
5		
12 ⟵ too small		
16	16	16 found!
19	19 ⟵ too big	
30	30	

Write a binary search in the manner illustrated above for each of the following lists and targets:

a. Same list as in the example; target = 1.
b. Same list as in the example; target = 6.
c. 2
17 target = 300
34
106
227
229
300
320
d. Same list as in (c), target = 34.
e. Same list as in (c), target = 500.

4. a. Using a binary search, find the maximum number of steps required to find any number in this list: 1, 2, 3, 4, 5, 6, 7, 8. Which numbers in the list require this maximum number of steps? (You can use the technique of Exercise 3 to write down each step of the search.)
b. Repeat part (a) with a 16-element ordered array and then with a 32-element ordered array.
c. Predict the maximum number of steps required to find any element in a binary search of a 64-element array and a 100-element array.

B **5.** Write a program that INPUTs 20 strings from the user, then sorts them into alphabetical order using a bubble sort. Have the program INPUT a target string from the user, then perform a binary search and PRINT the position of the target on the ordered list, or a message that the target is not on the list. The program should repeatedly INPUT targets until an appropriate trailer value is typed by the user.

6. Modify the program of Exercise 5 so that if the target is not on the list, it will be inserted at the appropriate alphabetical position. (You must move strings in the list *down* to make room for the new string. See Exercise 10, page 554.)

7. Modify the program of Exercise 6 so that if the target *is* on the list, it will be *deleted* from the list. Have the program PRINT the resulting array.

8. Modify the program of Exercise 5 so that if the target occurs on the list more than once, the position (subscript) of *each* occurrence is PRINTed. (*Hint:* When the target is found, have the program do a linear search of the *entire* array to find all other occurrences.)

9. Write a program that uses READ . . . DATA to set up a data file consisting of the names and telephone numbers of 10 people, alphabetized according to the name field. Have the program do a binary search for an INPUT target name, then PRINT the corresponding telephone number, or a message that the target is not on the list.

10. Modify the program of Exercise 6, page 554, so that after sorting the strings, it performs a binary search for a target that is INPUT from the user.

11. Write a program that uses INPUT to set up a data file of ten states and their annual wheat production in tons. Have the program sort the file alphabetically according to state. The program should INPUT the name of a target state, then perform a binary search and PRINT the wheat production of that state. (See Exercise 12, page 541, for hints on how to sort a data file consisting of more than one array.)

12. Write a program that uses READ . . . DATA to set up a data file of the names of 15 people and their places of birth. Have the program sort the file according to name. The program should INPUT a target name, then PRINT the place where the person was born.

13. Modify the program in Exercise 12 to sort the file according to place of birth. The program should then search for an INPUT city target and PRINT the names of *everybody* born in that city (see Exercise 8).

C **14.** Write a program that asks the user to type a positive integer N, then sets up and sorts an array of N random integers, each between 0 and 9999. The program should then ask the user for a target number between 0 and 9999, and ask whether the user wants a linear or a binary search. It should then perform the kind of search requested, and PRINT the result.

Lab Activity

Solving Equations by Binary Search

The binary search technique, modified slightly, can be used to find approximate solutions to equations. This is especially important when dealing with equations that are difficult or impossible to solve algebraically, such as $x^6 + 3x - 1 = 0$.

As with the array-searching algorithm discussed in this section, our equation-solving algorithm continually cuts an interval in half, narrowing down the search rapidly. In the array-searching algorithm, the interval at each stage consists of all the remaining possible subscripts of the target. In this equation-solving algorithm, the interval consists of possible (real number) solutions to the equation. For instance, to solve $x^6 + 3x - 1 = 0$ by hand, note that one solution must lie between $x = 0$ and $x = 1$, since the polynomial $x^6 + 3x - 1$ is negative (equals -1, in fact) at $x = 0$, but is positive (having the value 3) at $x = 1$. There must be a number between 0 and 1 where $x^6 + 3x - 1$ has the value 0, and that number is the solution we seek.

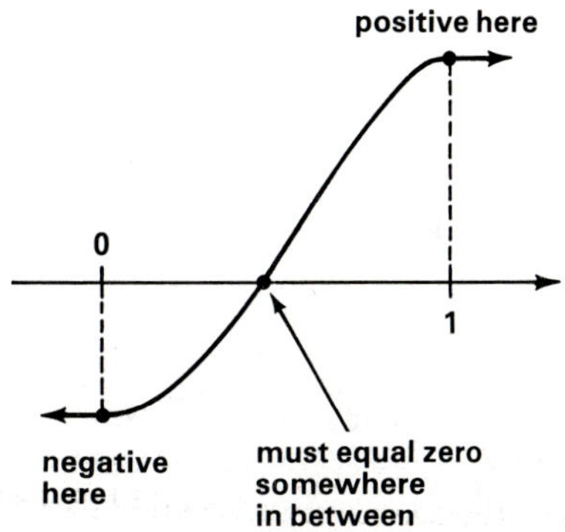

Next, we cut the interval in half: at $x = .5$, the polynomial has the value $(.5)^6 + 3(.5) - 1 \approx .515625$, which is positive. Since the polynomial is negative at 0, but positive at .5, it must be equal to 0 somewhere in between. We cut this interval in half: at $x = .25$, the polynomial has the approximate value $-.249756$, so the solution we are seeking is between .25 and .5. We can continue this process until the interval is extremely small. If three-decimal-place accuracy is desired, we can keep dividing the intervals in half until the length of the final interval is less than .0001. Here is the program:

```
10 PRINT "SOLUTION BY BINARY SEARCH"
20 PRINT "INTERVAL IN WHICH A SOLUTION MAY BE FOUND: "
30 INPUT "TYPE LEAST NUMBER:  "; LX
40 INPUT "TYPE GREATEST NUMBER:  "; GX
50 IF LX >= GX THEN PRINT "OOPS": GOTO 20
60 LET X = LX
```

Program continued on next page.

```
70  GOSUB 1000: REM * GET Y-VALUE OF FUNCTION AT X
80  LET LY = Y: REM * VALUE OF FUNCTION AT LEAST X
90  LET X = GX
100  GOSUB 1000: REM * GET Y-VALUE OF FUNCTION AT X
110  LET GY = Y: REM * VALUE OF FUNCTION AT GREATEST X
120  IF LY * GY > 0 THEN PRINT "SOLUTION NOT POSSIBLE": GOTO 20: REM *
        NEED INTERVAL IN WHICH FUNCTION CHANGES SIGN
130  LET X = (LX + GX) / 2: REM * MIDDLE OF THE INTERVAL
140  GOSUB 1000: REM * GET Y-VALUE OF FUNCTION AT MIDPOINT
145  IF Y = 0 THEN GOTO 180
150  IF LY * Y < 0 THEN LET GX = X: LET GY = Y: GOTO 170: REM * FUNCTION
        CHANGES SIGN BETWEEN LX AND X; CUT OUT RIGHT HALF OF INTERVAL
160  LET LX = X: LET LY = Y: REM * FUNCTION CHANGES SIGN BETWEEN X
        AND GX; CUT OUT LEFT HALF OF INTERVAL
170  IF GX - LX >= .0001 THEN GOTO 130: REM * CONTINUE UNLESS
        INTERVAL IS TOO SMALL
180  PRINT "SOLUTION =  "; INT(1000 * X + .5) / 1000: REM * ROUND
        TO 3 DECIMAL PLACES
190  END
1000  REM ** SUBROUTINE TO CALCULATE Y-VALUE OF FUNCTION AT X **
1010  LET Y = X ↑ 6 + 3 * X - 1
1020  RETURN
```

Problems

1. RUN the program and find the solution to $x^6 + 3x - 1 = 0$ that is between 0 ("LEAST NUMBER") and 1 ("GREATEST NUMBER"). You should get the answer .333.

2. RUN the program and find the solution to $x^6 + 3x - 1 = 0$ that is between -2 and -1.

3. Calculate the value of $y = x^6 + 3x - 1$ at $x = 1$ and at $x = 2$. Study the program and predict the output if you type 1 and 2 as the least and greatest numbers in the interval. RUN the program to verify your prediction.

4. Calculate algebraically the solution to the equation $3x + 5 = 0$. Use the program to find the solution (change line 1010 and use the interval -2 to -1). Does the program's output agree with your prediction?

5. Calculate algebraically the two solutions to the equation $6x^2 + x - 1 = 0$. (*Hint:* Factor.) Use the program to find the two solutions. Does the program's output agree with your solutions?

6. Use the program to find as many roots as you can of $x^4 + 3x^2 - x - 5 = 0$.

7. Show that the function $y = \frac{x+1}{x-0.4}$ is negative at $x = 0$, but positive at $x = 1$. RUN the program to find a solution of $\frac{x+1}{x-0.4} = 0$ between 0 and 1. Examine the function carefully. What is wrong with the solution you get? Why doesn't the program work correctly for this function?

10-6 Handling Data Files

In this section, we will write a program to create a data file with several fields. Depending on the user's wishes, the program will sort the data file or perform a binary search in any field. The purpose of the file is to keep track of items contributed to a local hospital to be auctioned off to raise money. Each record of the data file will consist of the name of the contributed item, the contributor's last name, and the suggested retail price to the nearest dollar.

In previous sections of this chapter, we handled such a data file by using three arrays (say ITEM$, CO$, and PRICE), one for each field in the data file. Note, however, that if the program is to be capable of sorting the data file keyed on each of these fields, three different sorting subroutines would be required (one for each of the arrays ITEM$, CO$, and PRICE). A better method is to use a two-dimensional array — we'll call it INFO$. In INFO$(I, J), the first subscript refers to the record number and the second subscript refers to the number of the field within that particular record:

Array INFO$

	Item	Contributor	Price
record #1	INFO$(1, 1)	INFO$(1, 2)	INFO$(1, 3)
record #2	INFO$(2, 1)	INFO$(2, 2)	INFO$(2, 3)
record #3	INFO$(3, 1)	INFO$(3, 2)	INFO$(3, 3)
	⋮	⋮	⋮

INFO$(3, 1) stores the *name* of the 3rd item, INFO$(3, 2) stores the name of the *contributor* of the 3rd item, and INFO$(3, 3) stores the suggested retail *price* of the 3rd item (represented as a string, so that it can be stored in a string array). If we want to sort the data file according to, say, contributor's last name, then the goal is to have the contributor's name that comes first in alphabetical order stored in INFO$(1, 2), the contributor's name that comes second in alphabetical order stored in INFO$(2, 2), and so on.

Indexed Sorting

In the standard sorting algorithms, individual elements in an array are repeatedly interchanged. In sorting a data file with several fields, each of the fields for two records must be switched. For example, if the second and third records in our example must be switched, then actually three interchanges are required:

INFO$(2, 1) ⟷ INFO$(3, 1)
INFO$(2, 2) ⟷ INFO$(3, 2)
INFO$(2, 3) ⟷ INFO$(3, 3)

This can be coded into a simple FOR . . . NEXT loop, but it will make for an unnecessarily long sort. A more efficient technique, called *indexed sorting,* saves a considerable amount of time, especially if each record contains a large number of fields. Indexed sorting makes use of an *index array,* we'll call it INDEX, that contains the record numbers (subscripts or indexes) of all the elements in the data file.

At any given time, the INDEX array gives the current order of the file: INDEX(1) is the record number of the first record in the file, INDEX(2) is the number of the second record, and so on. Since the values in the INDEX array determine the order of the file, the order can be changed (as in sorting) by simply interchanging the values in the INDEX array. The actual information stored in INFO$ need not be moved at all.

To make this clear, suppose that the second column of INFO$ looks like this:

INFO$(1, 2) = "T"
INFO$(2, 2) = "B"
INFO$(3, 2) = "W"
INFO$(4, 2) = "R"

Then the INDEX array initially reflects this order:

INDEX(1) = 1
INDEX(2) = 2
INDEX(3) = 3
INDEX(4) = 4

To interchange the first two strings (T and B), as required by the bubble sort algorithm, simply interchange the values of INDEX(1) and INDEX(2):

INDEX(1) = 2
INDEX(2) = 1
INDEX(3) = 3
INDEX(4) = 4

The preceding values for the INDEX array correspond to this order:

INFO$(INDEX(1), 2) = INFO$(2, 2) = "B"
INFO$(INDEX(2), 2) = INFO$(1, 2) = "T"
INFO$(INDEX(3), 2) = INFO$(3, 2) = "W"
INFO$(INDEX(4), 2) = INFO$(4, 2) = "R"

After the next interchange, between W and R, the array INDEX will have these values:

INDEX(1) = 2
INDEX(2) = 1
INDEX(3) = 4
INDEX(4) = 3

This corresponds to the following order:

INFO$(INDEX(1), 2) = INFO$(2, 2) = "B"
INFO$(INDEX(2), 2) = INFO$(1, 2) = "T"
INFO$(INDEX(3), 2) = INFO$(4, 2) = "R"
INFO$(INDEX(4), 2) = INFO$(3, 2) = "W"

The process is continued until the file is completely sorted (in this case, keyed on the second field).

Here is the program. We'll omit the steps in the algorithm this time, since the program uses many of the techniques developed thoroughly in previous sections of this chapter. Read the program carefully, starting with the main routine. Compare the subroutines with previous programs of this chapter. You will be asked questions about the program in the exercises.

Program 1

Statement

```
10 PRINT "HOSPITAL-AUCTION FILE"
20 GOSUB 1000: REM * SET UP DATA FILE
30 GOSUB 1500: REM * SET UP INDEX ARRAY
40 LET LFLD = 0: REM * LAST FIELD SORTED (NONE SO FAR)
50 GOSUB 2000: REM * PRESENT OPTIONS, GET COMMAND
60 IF COMM = 0 THEN GOTO 90: REM * QUIT
70 ON COMM GOSUB 2500, 3000: REM * IF COMMAND = 1 THEN GOSUB
      2500 (SORT); IF COMMAND = 2 THEN GOSUB 3000 (SEARCH)
80 GOTO 50
90 END
```

Program continued on next page.

```
1000  REM ** SUBROUTINE TO SET UP FILE INFO$ **
1010  READ N: REM * NUMBER OF RECORDS
1020  DIM INFO$(N, 3)
1030  FOR REC = 1 TO N
1040  FOR FLD = 1 TO 3
1050  READ INFO$(REC, FLD)
1060  NEXT FLD
1070  NEXT REC
1080  RETURN

1500  REM ** SUBROUTINE TO SET UP INDEX ARRAY **
1510  DIM INDEX(N)
1520  FOR REC = 1 TO N
1530  LET INDEX(REC) = REC: REM * PRESENT ORDER OF RECORDS
        OF THE DATA FILE
1540  NEXT REC
1550  RETURN

2000  REM ** SUBROUTINE TO GET COMMAND FROM USER **
2010  PRINT
2020  PRINT "TYPE 0 TO QUIT"
2030  PRINT "TYPE 1 TO SORT"
2040  PRINT "TYPE 2 TO SEARCH"
2050  PRINT
2060  INPUT "WHICH DO YOU WANT (0, 1, 2):  "; COMM
2070  IF NOT ((COMM = 0) OR (COMM = 1) OR (COMM = 2)) THEN PRINT
        "ERROR": GOTO 2050
2080  RETURN

2500  REM ** SUBROUTINE TO SORT INFO$ **
2510  IF COMM = 2 THEN GOTO 2550: REM * SEARCH COMMAND,
        PRELIMINARY SORT IS REQUIRED
2520  PRINT
2530  INPUT "SORT ON WHICH FIELD (1, 2, OR 3):  "; KY
2540  IF NOT ((KY = 1) OR (KY = 2) OR (KY = 3)) THEN PRINT
        "ERROR": GOTO 2520
2550  IF KY = LFLD THEN RETURN: REM * DATA FILE HAS ALREADY BEEN
        SORTED ON THIS FIELD
2560  LET LFLD = KY: REM * THIS IS THE FIELD ON WHICH THE DATA FILE
        WILL BE SORTED
```

```
2600 REM ** STANDARD SHELL SORT, USING INDEX ARRAY **
2610 LET NSUB = INT(N / 2): REM * NUMBER OF SUBLISTS
2620 FOR SUB = 1 TO NSUB
2630 GOSUB 2800: REM * BUBBLE SORT SUBLIST NUMBER SUB
2640 NEXT SUB
2650 LET NSUB = INT(NSUB / 2): REM * HALF AS MANY SUBLISTS NEXT TIME
2660 IF NSUB > 0 THEN GOTO 2620: REM * SORT NEW SET OF SUBLISTS
2670 RETURN

2800 REM ** SUBROUTINE TO BUBBLE SORT SUBLIST NUMBER SUB **
2810 LET SWFLAG = 0: REM * NO SWITCHES YET ON THIS PASS
2820 LET I = SUB: REM * SUBSCRIPT OF FIRST ELEMENT OF SUBLIST SUB
2830 IF INFO$(INDEX(I), KY) <= INFO$(INDEX(I + NSUB), KY) THEN
       GOTO 2880: REM * IN ORDER, NO SWITCH
2840 LET TEMPO = INDEX(I): REM * SWITCH INDEX(I) AND INDEX(I + NSUB)
2850 LET INDEX(I) = INDEX(I + NSUB)
2860 LET INDEX(I + NSUB) = TEMPO
2870 LET SWFLAG = 1: REM * SWITCH HAS NOW OCCURRED
2880 LET I = I + NSUB: REM * NEXT ELEMENT OF SUBLIST
2890 IF I + NSUB <= N THEN GOTO 2830: REM * NOT DONE YET
2900 IF SWFLAG = 1 THEN GOTO 2810: REM * ADD ANOTHER PASS
2910 RETURN

3000 REM ** SEARCH SUBROUTINE **
3010 PRINT
3020 INPUT "SEARCH WHICH FIELD (1, 2, OR 3):  "; KY
3030 IF NOT ((KY = 1) OR (KY = 2) OR (KY = 3)) THEN PRINT
       "ERROR": GOTO 3010
3040 GOSUB 2500: REM * SORT ON THE KEY FIELD, IF THAT HAS NOT
       ALREADY BEEN DONE
3050 PRINT
3060 INPUT "TYPE TARGET VALUE:  "; TARGT$

3100 REM ** BINARY SEARCH, USING INDEX ARRAY **
3110 LET SMALL = 1: REM * TOP OF SEARCH INTERVAL
3120 LET BIG = N: REM * BOTTOM OF SEARCH INTERVAL
3130 LET GUESS = INT((SMALL + BIG) / 2): REM * HALFWAY BETWEEN TOP
       AND BOTTOM
3140 IF TARGT$ = INFO$(INDEX(GUESS), KY) THEN GOTO 3210: REM * FOUND
       TARGET
```

Program continued on next page.

```
3150  IF TARGT$ < INFO$(INDEX(GUESS), KY) THEN LET BIG = GUESS - 1:
        GOTO 3170: REM * ELIMINATE BOTTOM HALF
3160  LET SMALL = GUESS + 1: REM * ELIMINATE TOP HALF
3170  IF SMALL <= BIG THEN GOTO 3130: REM * NEXT GUESS
3180  PRINT
3190  PRINT TARGT$; "  NOT IN THE FILE"
3200  RETURN
3210  REM * FOUND IT
3220  PRINT
3230  PRINT "ITEM:  "; INFO$(INDEX(GUESS), 1)
3240  PRINT "CONTRIBUTOR:  "; INFO$(INDEX(GUESS), 2)
3250  PRINT "SUGGESTED PRICE:  "; INFO$(INDEX(GUESS), 3)
3260  RETURN
4000  DATA 12
4010  DATA "TAPE, ADHESIVE", NIGHTINGALE, 42
4020  DATA "BIRDLIFE MAGAZINE, 500 ISSUES", FINCH, 30
4030  DATA "WINDOWPANE, CRACKED", KRAYZEE, 2
4040  DATA "ROPE, FRAYED", FOLLEN, 8
4050  DATA "CARPET TACKS, RUSTY", FOOTE, 5
4060  DATA "CABOOSE, RED", MCLAST, 23000
4070  DATA "BRIDGE, BROOKLYN", TRUSTME, 20000
4080  DATA "SOUP, ALPHABET", XZQWE, 1
4090  DATA "LIGHTBULBS, 40 SLIGHTLY DENTED", NOTLIKELY, 4
4100  DATA "SLICER-DICER, HANDY", POSTPAID, 12
4110  DATA "CRACKERS, DAMP", AFIRESALE, 3
4120  DATA "HUB CAP COLLECTION, SHINY", CARR, 1328
```

In line 70, a new instruction, ON . . . GOSUB, is used. The statement

```
45  ON I GOSUB 500, 700, 9000, 400
```

works as follows: If I = 1, then GOSUB 500 is executed (and RETURN from that subroutine is to the next statement after line 45). If I = 2, then GOSUB 700 is executed. If I = 3, then GOSUB 9000 is executed, and if I = 4, then GOSUB 400 is executed. There is also an ON . . . GOTO instruction that works similarly. The variable I can be replaced by any numerical expression. (See the Lab Activity to determine what happens if I has values other than 1, 2, 3, or 4.)

Program 1 is said to be *menu-driven.* The list of options PRINTed in subroutine 2000 is called a *menu.* This technique, along with the ON . . . GOSUB instruction, is useful for organizing complex programs that perform several different tasks.

Avoiding Pitfalls

In the statements

```
100  ON I GOSUB 500, 700, 9000, 400, 790
```

or

```
100  ON I GOTO 500, 700, 9000, 320, 6000
```

you should be sure that I will equal 1, 2, 3, 4, or 5. Also, be certain that each line number listed in line 100 corresponds to an actual statement in the program. An error message will be printed and the program will stop if I = 2, say, but there is no line 700 in the program.

Summary

Data files with several fields often can be most easily manipulated by storing them in a two-dimensional array. The first subscript can give the number of the record and the second subscript the number of the field.

Long time-consuming interchanges of records, required in sorting data files, can be minimized by using the technique of *indexed sorting,* in which an array of subscripts (indexes) keeps track of the order of the records.

The instruction ON K GOTO 100, 100, 300 causes the computer to GOTO line 100 if K = 1 or 2, or to GOTO line 300 if K = 3.

The instruction ON K GOSUB 100, 150, 10000 causes the computer to GOSUB 100 if K = 1, to GOSUB 150 if K = 2, or to GOSUB 10000 if K = 3.

A *menu* is a list of options presented to the user of a program. The action the program executes depends on the option the user chooses.

Exercises 10-6

A

1. If the user of Program 1 wants to search the data file, why does line 3040 of subroutine 3000 call subroutine 2500?

2. In line 2550 of Program 1, why is it unnecessary to sort the file if KY = LFLD?

3. In Program 1, what happens if the user types 0 as the command?

4. Why are quotation marks necessary around the names of contributed items in the DATA lines of Program 1? If the user wants to search for an item name, must quotation marks be used in responding to the INPUT statements of subroutine 3000? Explain your answers.

5. Predict the exact output of Program 1, assuming that the user wants to first sort the file according to the third field, then search for the target 1328, then quit.

6. Predict the output of each of the following programs:

a.
```
10  LET X=2
20  ON X GOTO 30, 50, 70
30  PRINT X
40  GOTO 80
50  PRINT X+2
60  GOTO 80
70  PRINT X-3
80  END
```

b.
```
10  READ X
20  ON X GOTO 10, 30, 40, 50
30  PRINT X
40  GOTO 10
50  PRINT X
60  DATA 1, 3, 2, 4, 5
70  END
```

c.
```
10  FOR A=1 TO 4
20  ON A GOTO 30, 50, 70, 90
30  PRINT "ONE"
40  GOTO 100
50  PRINT "TWO"
60  GOTO 100
70  PRINT "THREE"
80  GOTO 100
90  PRINT "DONE"
100  NEXT A
110  END
```

d.
```
10  LET B=1
20  ON B GOTO 40, 40, 70, 90
40  LET B=B+1
50  PRINT B
60  GOTO 20
70  PRINT B
80  GOTO 40
90  PRINT B
100  END
```

7. The ON . . . GOTO . . . instruction can be eliminated from any program by using IF . . . THEN statements. Rewrite the programs in Exercise 6 in this way.

8. Predict the output of each of the following programs:

a.
```
10  READ X
20  ON X GOSUB 40, 60, 70
30  IF X<3 THEN GOTO 10
35  END
40  PRINT "FIRST"
50  RETURN
60  PRINT "SECOND"
70  PRINT "THIRD"
80  RETURN
90  DATA 1, 2, 3, 4
```

b.
```
10  FOR I=1 TO 3
20  ON I GOSUB 50, 70, 90
30  NEXT I
40  PRINT "SELL"
45  END
50  PRINT "BUY"
60  RETURN
70  PRINT "LOW"
80  RETURN
90  PRINT "DON'T"
100  RETURN
```

9. Rewrite the programs in Exercise 8, replacing the ON . . . GOSUB instructions with one or more IF . . . THEN statements.

B 10. Set up a data file of information on seven employees of a small business in a two-dimensional array EMPL$. Each record should consist of the following fields: last name, first name, middle initial, hours worked, and pay rate per hour. Then give the value of each of the following:

a. EMPL$(2, 4) **b.** EMPL$(5, 1) **c.** EMPL$(3, 5) **d.** EMPL$(4, 3)

11. An indexed sort can be carried out by hand. Here is an example:

list	*index*
A	1
Q	2
P	3
D	4

If the list to be sorted is as above, then the index array initially corresponds to the original order of the list. Using the bubble sort algorithm, the first two elements of the index array are first singled out.

Of course, the indexes themselves aren't compared; instead, the corresponding elements "A" and "Q" of the list are examined. Since these are in the correct order, no switch occurs.

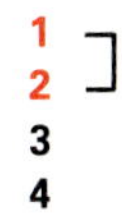

Next, the list elements corresponding to indexes 2 and 3 (namely "Q" and "P") are compared. These are out of order, and therefore the corresponding indexes are switched.

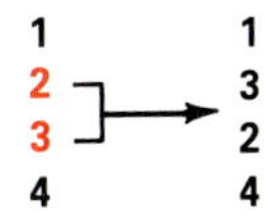

Next, "Q" and "D", corresponding to the indexes 2 and 4, are compared. Since they are out of order, their indexes are switched.

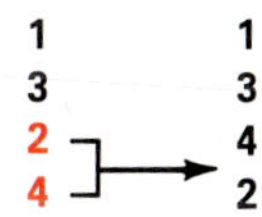

Here is the rest of the sort. Examine each step carefully.

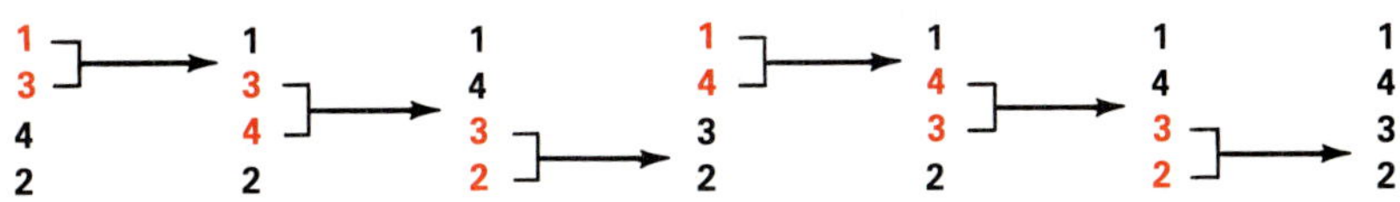

The final arrangement of indexes corresponds to the list order A, D, P, Q, which is in alphabetical order. Follow the procedure above to index sort by hand the following lists, using the bubble sort algorithm:

a. PIG
ANT
LAMB
FROG
GIGANTISAUROS

b. GAME
ALOOF
STAR
MOAN
MOOSE
ENERGY

12. Index sort the lists in Exercise 11 by hand using the Shell algorithm.

13. After subroutines 1000 and 1500 of Program 1 are executed, find the values of each of these variables:

a. INFO$(1, 1) b. INFO$(12, 3)
c. INFO$(1, 2) d. INDEX(2)
e. INFO$(1, 3) f. INDEX(7)
g. INFO$(2, 1) h. INFO$(INDEX(4), 2)
i. INFO$(6, 2) j. INFO$(INDEX(9), 1)

14. After subroutine 1000 of Program 1 is executed, assume that the index array looks like this:

INDEX(1)	3	INDEX(7)	2
INDEX(2)	12	INDEX(8)	7
INDEX(3)	1	INDEX(9)	8
INDEX(4)	6	INDEX(10)	11
INDEX(5)	5	INDEX(11)	4
INDEX(6)	9	INDEX(12)	10

Find the values of each of the following:

a. INFO$(INDEX(1), 2) b. INFO$(INDEX(4), 1)
c. INFO$(INDEX(6), 3) d. INFO$(INDEX(12), 2)

Is there any element of the INFO$ data file that is still in its original position (that is, INFO$(I, J) = INFO$(INDEX(I), J), for J = 1, 2, and 3)?

15. After Program 1 sorts the data file with field 1 (name of contributed item) as the key, give the values of each of the following:

a. LFLD b. KY
c. INDEX(1) d. INDEX(3)
e. INFO$(INDEX(1), 1) f. INFO$(INDEX(12), 1)

16. Show how to add a command option to Program 1 that would PRINT the entire data file in the current order (as indicated by the INDEX array).

17. What changes would be necessary in Program 1 to add a command option to find the total retail value of all the contributed items in the file? (Use VAL to change all the prices, stored as strings, into numbers.)

18. Change Program 1 so that when a search is made, *all* records matching the target are PRINTed. (See Exercise 8, page 566. Of course, there are no such duplications in the DATA assigned in subroutine 1000, but there could be duplications in a real file.)

C 19. Change Program 1 so that a fourth field, color of contributed item, is added to each record. Provide for sorting and searching with this new field as the key.

20. Show how to add another command option to Program 1 that would allow records to be added to the end of the file. The program should check to see that the record to be added is not already in the file (all three fields). This could be done with a linear search. Can you see how to do it with a binary search? Note that the DIM statements in lines 1110 and 1510 must be changed. Also, LFLD should be set equal to 0 when a record is added to the data file (why?), N should be changed, and INDEX(N) defined.

21. Change Program 1 so that in searches keyed on field 1 (name of contributed item), a record will be retrieved and PRINTed as long as the value typed for TARGT$ (line 3060) is an *initial substring* of the actual target string. (For example, AWA is an initial substring of AWAY WE GO, but BX is not a substring at all. WE is a substring of AWAY WE GO, but it is not an *initial* substring. Thus, if the value typed for TARGT$ were say, SLICER, then the program would PRINT the entire record shown in the DATA statement at line 4100.)

Lab Activity

ON . . . GOTO and ON . . . GOSUB Errors

Problems

1. Write and RUN a program that will help you find out what happens if I = 0 when ON I GOTO . . . is executed. Repeat for ON I GOSUB . . . . Summarize your results.

2. Determine experimentally what happens if I is too big for the number of options (for instance, if I = 4 when ON I GOTO 40, 30, 50 is executed).

3. Determine experimentally what happens if I is not an integer (for instance, try I = 1.2 and I = 1.8).

4. Determine what happens if one of the line numbers in an ON I . . . GOTO does not correspond to an actual line in the program.

5. Find out if it is possible for the I to be replaced by a constant such as: ON 6 GOTO . . . . (Can you think of any use for this?)

6. Find out if it is possible for the I to be replaced by an arithmetic expression such as: ON (I + 2) GOTO . . .

7. Find out if it is possible for the line numbers to be replaced by variables:

```
ON I GOSUB J, K, L
```

Chapter Summary

In computer data processing, information is usually organized into a data file consisting of a list of *records* (rows). All of the records have the same form: they are divided into one or more *fields* (columns), each of which is one small piece of information (number or string). In the computer's memory, each of the separate fields is stored in a separate array.

In a *linear search,* a string or number is INPUT from the user. Then a specific field, called the *key,* is examined in each record to see if it matches the INPUT value. The records are examined in order, starting with the first one in the file.

The *bubble sort* is a technique for arranging an array in numerical or alphabetical order. If the array contains N elements, then the array is sorted by making N − 1 passes through the array, each time comparing adjacent pairs of elements and switching them if they are out of order.

The *Shell* algorithm is a relatively fast sorting technique that moves items of an array quickly into the general neighborhood of their final positions. This is done by partitioning the array into sublists, and then bubble sorting each sublist. At first, the sublists are extremely short, but their length doubles after each bubble sort is complete. Finally, there is only one sublist — the entire array — and one last, quick bubble sort finishes the ordering of the array.

The *binary search* algorithm is a method of searching an array that is in numerical or alphabetical order for a particular target number or string. If the location of the target has been narrowed down to a certain interval in the array, then the middle element in the interval is examined. Depending on its value, half of the interval is eliminated as possible locations of the target. This process of examining middle values of smaller and smaller possible intervals is repeated until the actual location is pinpointed, or it is shown that the target must not be in the array.

Long time-consuming interchanges of records, required in sorting data files, can be minimized by using the technique of *indexed sorting,* in which an array of subscripts (indexes) keeps track of the order of the records in the data file.

The instruction ON K GOTO 100, 100, 300 causes the computer to GOTO line 100 if K = 1 or 2, or to GOTO line 300 if K = 3.

The instruction ON K GOSUB 100, 150, 10000 causes the computer to go to subroutine 100 if K = 1, to subroutine 150 if K = 2, or to subroutine 10000 if K = 3.

Chapter Test

1. Create a data file consisting of a list of the names of five of your friends and their favorite record albums. Write a program to fill two arrays with the fields of the data file. Have the program INPUT a friend's name, then do a linear search and PRINT the friend's favorite record album.

2. Sort the list below by hand into increasing numerical order. Use the bubble sort algorithm, writing down each step of each pass through the list.

   3
   −9
   6
   12
   −7
   0

3. Sort the list below by hand into alphabetical order. Use the Shell algorithm. At those points where the algorithm calls for a bubble sort of a sublist, give full details.

   A
   M
   S
   P
   T
   K
   Q

4. **a.** Create a data file consisting of a list of world-wide cities and the major language spoken in each of the cities. Write a program that READs the data below and fills two arrays with the fields of the data file.

```
500 DATA AMSTERDAM, DUTCH, QUEBEC, FRENCH, ROME, ITALIAN
510 DATA LONDON, ENGLISH, RIO DE JANIERO, PORTUGUESE
515 DATA PARIS, FRENCH
520 DATA VENICE, ITALIAN, VIENNA, GERMAN, SYDNEY, ENGLISH
530 DATA BARCELONA, SPANISH, WARSAW, POLISH
540 DATA MONTE CARLO, FRENCH
```

   b. Add a subroutine to the program that bubble sorts the file into alphabetical order with the city-field as the key.

   c. Add a subroutine to the program in (b) that binary searches the ordered file for an INPUT target city, then PRINTs the corresponding language.

   d. Add a subroutine to the program in (c) that does a linear search for *all* cities that speak an INPUT target language, and then PRINTs the results.

Computer Applications

Artificial Intelligence

Research in AI

Can you rearrange the letters of BROOTS to form a word that is used in connection with computers? Can you write a program to repeat what you have done? If you try to write the algorithm for the program, you may have difficulty putting it into words. When you solve this type of problem, you usually chance upon one or two syllables and then recognize the solution. How, then, could you write a program capable of "recognizing the solution"? These questions are at the heart of current research in a branch of computer science called *artificial intelligence* (AI, for short). AI researchers study the processes involved in human thinking, then design programs to simulate human intelligence. The main goal of AI researchers is to make computers more useful by having them "behave" more intelligently.

Applications of AI

Many interesting and useful AI programs have been developed. For example, many computers have been programmed to speak in natural languages such as English and to engage in "dialogue" on limited subjects. Programs have been created that enable computers to teach themselves new concepts by following sequences of instructions. Similarly, robots have been developed that can recall plans and adapt them to new situations. A computer program, used in conjunction with a camera, has been written to allow a computer to "see" a simple drawing. The program is capable of telling you whether an object in the drawing is behind or below another object in the drawing.

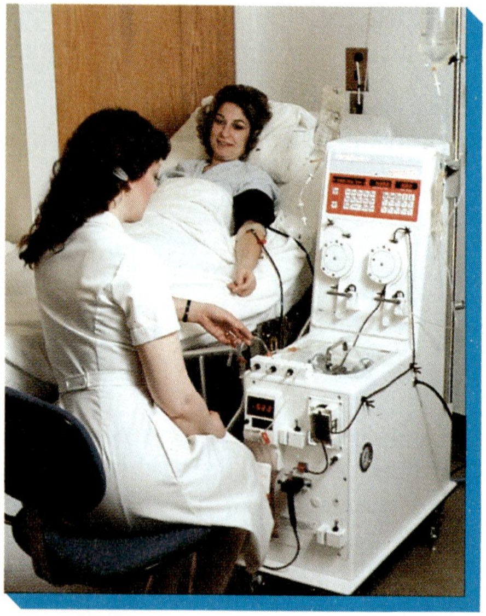

Nurse monitoring "expert system" used to help prescribe drug therapy through blood diagnosis

Although some of the more spectacular applications of artificial intelligence are still under development in research laboratories, many AI systems have found their way into everyday use. There are systems used as adaptive devices for people with physical handicaps. Other systems help doctors prescribe the correct drug therapy for cancer patients, or diagnose bacterial blood infections and recommend treatment. Researchers have created bionic noses that can distinguish differences in fragrance, and a system that reads printed material with an optical scanner, picking out key words previously selected by the management of a company as important. AI systems currently available can help with many personal, social, financial, and business problems. Certainly you would not want a computer to make your decisions for you, but you could use these AI systems to get advice to help make more intelligent choices.

AI systems, such as the one to prescribe drug therapy, are called *expert systems*. These systems combine textbook knowledge with rules of thumb based on experience to mimic human intelligence and make informed decisions. Researchers build these systems by consulting authorities in each field to determine how these experts reach their conclusions. Then, they build each system by assembling the data in thousands of conditional rules. The programs, written in a language such as LISP (see the Computer Language feature on page 584), are quite long and very complex.

Goals of AI Research

As we enter into the next generation of computers, some of the goals that AI researchers have set are developing an optical scanner that can read both type and pictures, an automatic translating machine that can convert one language to another, and a typewriter that can be operated by human speech rather than touch. Up to this point, no computer has been able to cope with the variety of pronunciations and accents of languages. If people are to get the full benefit of computers, the machines will have to be able to communicate in a natural language like English. The enormous convenience of being able to tell computers what you want them to do assures that AI researchers will continue to work toward solving this problem.

Another problem that AI experts face is teaching a computer common sense. A computer must be programmed with the most basic facts, facts that human beings perceive instinctively. You could tell a computer robot about the effects of gravity, but the robot still would not anticipate the resulting damage that would occur if it walked off a cliff. One other problem that AI researchers are investigating is how to teach a computer to "forget" nonimportant information. As you know, modern computers store large quantities of data. When the computer is searching for a solution to a problem, it must search through much of the data that has been stored. If AI researchers can develop a way for the computer to "forget" the useless information, the searching process will be much faster.

AI researchers are convinced that the problems facing them will be solved in the near future.

Farm surveillance-system image created by AI program that discerns shapes

LISP

The programming language LISP, which stands for LISt Processing, was developed about 1960 by John McCarthy as a result of his studies at the Massachusetts Institute of Technology. McCarthy had studied computer programming concepts and a branch of mathematics called lambda calculus that deals only with functions. (You are familiar with the built-in functions of BASIC.) He combined ideas from this mathematical system along with the programming concept of *list processing* to design his programming language. LISP has only one kind of statement — a function call. The biggest advantage is that the value returned by a function can be another function.

Let's examine a few of the beginning concepts of LISP. Both programs and data in LISP are structured as lists. A *list* is defined as a set of *items* (objects, symbols, or elements) in a specific order, enclosed by parentheses. Every item in a list is either an *atom* or another list. An *atom* is the name used for any string of characters. For example, the string OLD is an atom, and the string 39 is an atom.

Here are two examples of *lists:*

(THIS IS CALLED A LIST) ⟵ This list contains 5 items called atoms: THIS, IS, CALLED, A, and LIST.

(OLD IS 39) ⟵ This list contains 3 items, all of which are atoms.

It is also possible for a list to contain other lists. For instance,

((OLD IS NOT) 39) ⟵ This list has two items: The first (OLD IS NOT) is a list and the second (39) is an atom.

(THIS IS (A LIST WHICH HAS (THREE ITEMS IN IT))) ⟵ This list contains 3 items: 2 atoms (THIS and IS) and a list (the rest of the line) that itself contains 4 atoms and another list.

LISP was specifically designed for the manipulation of non-numeric data that changes in length and structure during the running of a program. It offers a convenient way of representing data that is in the form of English sentences, logic statements, and mathematical formulas.

Although LISP was not designed with mathematical calculations in mind, they can certainly be done. Compare the following notations for an expression written in both BASIC and LISP. Notice the list structure and the reverse notation of the LISP instruction.

BASIC: X + 4 * Y − 3 / Z LISP: (+ X(− (* 4 Y)(/ 3Z)))

As a programming language, LISP is favored by researchers in artificial intelligence (AI). AI is a branch of computer science that attempts to understand the nature of intelligent thinking by simulating it on a computer. AI research involves more symbol manipulation than number processing, therefore researchers usually prefer the symbol manipulations that are possible with LISP.

LISP, like Forth, can be extended by adding to the existing language. LISP lets the programmer add definitions that become an integral part of the original language. This ability of LISP to redefine itself, treating all contents of its memory (including the program) as lists, is a feature well-suited for artificial intelligence programming. The redefining ability allows the initial program to be designed so as to "learn" from experience, functioning in a manner similar to thought processes in the human brain.

LISP can be described, like Forth, as a high-level machine language. It requires attention to detail, but allows the programmer freedom to manipulate the program and data contained in it. Remember, most programming languages were developed with a particular application in mind. When looking for a language to study and explore, consider the application for which you want to use it.

Artificial intelligence programs are usually written in LISP.

Projects

(See page 258 for details on what should be included in a computer project.)

1. Write a program to simulate a dart-board game. Have the program set up a circular target board and allow for 2 to 4 players. Each player should have three turns tossing 3 darts (by pressing a specified key), and the program should PRINT the scores after each round. The position where the dart lands on the board should be determined randomly. Use graphics and animation to show the dart's movement to the target.

2. Write a program that randomly PRINTs three different geometric shapes on the screen each time a player presses a specified key. Have the program award 5 points if two of the geometric shapes match, and 10 points if all three match. Allow for 1 to 4 players, and PRINT the name of the player who first scores 100 points.

3. Write a "shake-the-bank" program. Have the player "shake" the bank (by pressing a specified key) to release randomly some of the coins in the bank. The program should PRINT the number of coins that fall out and their total value. Then the player should have several tries to guess the actual number of each kind of coin (pennies, nickels, dimes, and so on) that fell out of the bank.

4. Write a scrambled-word program that PRINTs words with the letters all mixed up. Have the user select one of five subjects from a menu; then have the program PRINT five scrambled words READ randomly from a DATA list of 30 words related to the chosen subject. Allow for two players, and PRINT the final results on the screen. (The words should appear in their normal form on the DATA list and not be scrambled until after they are READ from the DATA list.)

5. Develop a "huckle-buckle-beanstalk" game. Draw a closed figure on the screen and within its boundaries hide (randomly) a hidden treasure. The treasure should be chosen randomly from a group of at least ten treasures. Limit the number of tries that a player has to name the coordinates of the hidden treasure. Give clues based on the guesses — very cold, cold, lukewarm, warm, very warm, and so forth — until the correct answer is given, and then PRINT the phrase "huckle-buckle-beanstalk." If a player is not successful after the number of tries you have allowed, be sure to PRINT the type of treasure left undiscovered and its correct location.

6. Write a program in which a customer "shops" at a specialty clothing store that has 5 aisles and 6 different articles of clothing along each aisle. Have the customer "shop" by selecting an item from a menu of 30 items, and then being told the item's exact location (aisle no., position in aisle). If the next item chosen by the customer is *beside* the previously chosen one, then a 15% discount should be given on the least expensive of the two items. Once the shopping is finished, an itemized bill should be PRINTed showing the appropriate discount and cost of all items. Each time a player shops, the items in the store should be randomly located in different positions.

7. Ms. Adviser, a guidance counselor, needs a computer program to help keep track of weekly appointments with students. She has time only on Tuesdays through Fridays, since Mondays are reserved for other meetings. She works seven periods a day, with one period for lunch. Write a program that will let students choose a day and period to see Ms. Adviser. If a particular time slot is full, the student should be told to make another appointment. If the time slot is available, the student's name should be recorded. Once all the students have made their appointments for the week, Ms. Adviser should get a printout of the time schedule.

8. Write a program that converts numbers into decimal, binary, and hexadecimal form. Have the user choose which type of number to convert from a menu. Once that is determined, the user should type a number, and the program should PRINT its equivalent form in each of the other two number bases. The second part of this program should reverse the process: the program PRINTs a number (randomly) in any one of the three bases, and the user must type its equivalent form in each of the other two bases. Allow for 2 users and use a quiz format.

9. Write a program to survey people on their favorite recording group. Poll at least 20 people and ask them to rate six recording groups on a scale of 1 (best) to 5 (worst). Keep a separate tally of the responses of each male and female, and place the data in a DATA list. The user should have these three options of PRINTing the results of the poll: each group's rating based on the number of females voting for them, on the number of males voting for them, or a composite rating of both males and females. Graphics can be used to display the results in the form of a bar graph.

CHAPTER

11 Files

Computer simulation and computer-aided design (CAD) are currently being used in a wide range of fields. Here, a forest simulation is used to give forestry students experience in thinning groups of trees to maximize overall growth.

Introduction

In Chapter 10, you learned how to set up a data file using READ . . . DATA or INPUT statements. In many applications involving large quantities of data, it is convenient to store data permanently on a disk. (Disks are made of thin plastic covered with magnetic material. Information is recorded as extremely small magnetized regions on the surface of the disk.) In this chapter, you will learn the BASIC instructions needed for the *Apple, IBM,* or *TRS-80* computers to record data on a disk and to retrieve data from a disk. It will be assumed that you already know how to boot disks and how to save and load programs.

11-1 Disk Files: Sequential and Random-Access

When a data file is stored on a disk, it is called a *disk file.* Data from a disk file can be read into the computer's memory and then be processed by a program using the sorting and searching techniques explained in the preceding chapter.

The major advantage of a disk file is that the information (data) in the file may be used over and over again, even by different programs, without retyping DATA (or INPUT) statements each time.

Let's assume that you want to set up a disk file to store some friends' names and telephone numbers, as listed in the data file below. As you learned in the previous chapter, each record in a file is made up of fields; in this case, there are two fields, a name field and a telephone-number field, as illustrated in the diagram below.

Fields

	name	telephone number
record #1	RUDOLPH	262–8101
record #2	BLITZEN	873–4184
record #3	DASHER	615–8237
	.	.
	.	.
	.	.

Before the data in this file is stored on the disk, each name and telephone number (that is, data from the individual fields) is moved into a reserved area of the computer's memory called a *buffer.* The buffer is a holding location for data coming to and from the disk. Then the information in the buffer is written magnetically onto the disk. The disk is organized into tracks, which are similar to the grooves on a phonograph record. The diagram below illustrates the idea of storing data on a disk. (Of course, the data is actually stored as binary digits.)

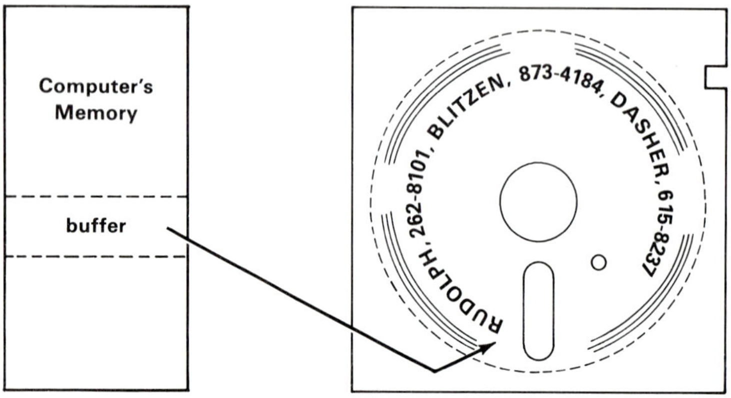

Notice that the data is recorded on the disk as one continuous stream of information with one field followed immediately by the next field. This type of disk file is called a *sequential file.* (Sequential means *one after another.*) Although the fields of each record in a data file can be stored on the disk in any sequence, they are ordinarily arranged in some order based upon a key field. In the example above, the records are recorded on the disk with the name field as the key. A sequential file should be used for data that will require few changes, because fields in this type of file are retrieved sequentially. In order to read the last record, the computer must read through the entire file from the beginning. With large amounts of data, this can be very time consuming.

Another type of disk file is the *random-access file,* in which records can be stored or retrieved in any order. If data must be retrieved from a random location inside the file (for example, a single card from a library's catalog), then a random-access file is a better choice than a sequential file. This type of file is also better suited to data that will need to be changed frequently or accessed quickly. Since random-access files are more difficult to use than sequential ones, they will be explained later in the chapter in Section 11–6.

Avoiding Pitfalls

Before writing a program to set up a disk file, you should decide whether a sequential or random-access file is better suited for the application you have in mind. It is difficult to change the file type at a later date.

Summary

A data file that is stored on a disk is called a *disk file.* The information in a disk file can be used in any number of different programs without retyping it.

A *sequential file* is a file in which the records are recorded and retrieved in order one after another. This type of file should be used for data that will require few changes, because retrieving data sequentially can be very time consuming.

A *random-access file* is a file in which the records may be recorded and retrieved in any order. This type of file is better suited to data that will need to be changed frequently or accessed quickly.

A *buffer* is a part of the computer's memory that is used as a holding area for data coming to and from the disk.

Exercises 11-1

A

1. What is a disk file?

2. What are the major differences between sequential and random-access files?

3. What is the location in the computer's memory called that temporarily holds data coming to and from a disk file?

4. List three applications in which disk files could be used by your local school system.

5. In each of the following, tell whether a sequential or random-access file seems more appropriate to store the data. Explain your answer.

a. a file to store strings to be used in a word-guessing game;

b. a file to store responses to a student survey regarding a dress code;

c. a file to store 100 employees' names, their rate of pay per hour, and the number of hours they work per week;

d. a file to store the names of the players on a basketball team, the number of minutes they each play per game, and the number of points they score per game;

e. a file to store the inventory list of a hardware store that includes an item's name, the number currently in stock, and its cost.

Lab Activity

PEEK and POKE

The memory of your computer consists of several thousand "locations," each of which stores a binary number. The number of locations and the maximum size of the numbers that can be stored in each one vary from computer to computer. BASIC variables use several memory locations each to store their values. BASIC programs are stored in coded form in memory locations. The machine language programs that control every action of the computer are also stored in memory locations.

The memory locations of your computer are numbered consecutively, starting with 0. The number of a location is called its *address.* BASIC has a way of examining the contents of any location and of changing the contents of many of them. For example, the command LET X = PEEK(10000) assigns to the variable X the contents of the memory location with address 10000. Similarly, PRINT PEEK(102) outputs the contents of location number 102.

The contents of a memory location can be changed by using the POKE instruction. POKE has this form: POKE *where, num.* This instruction puts the number *num* into location *where.*

Problems

(Load DOS into memory before proceeding.)

1. Type the following commands to verify the description of PEEK and POKE given above:

```
PRINT PEEK(10000)
POKE 10000, 46
PRINT PEEK(10000)
```

   (*Note:* On the *TRS-80,* use 30000 instead of 10000 in each command.)

2. Experiment to find out the largest number that can successfully be POKEd into location 10000. (Use location 30000 on *TRS-80* computers.)

3. (*Apple* and *TRS-80* users only) Some of the memory of your computer cannot be changed by POKE or by any other means. This area of memory, called ROM *(read only memory),* contains mostly machine language programs that remain in the machine even when the power is turned off. (The rest of memory, which *can* be changed, is called RAM — short for *random access memory.*)

By POKEing and PEEKing at some high addresses (low addresses on *TRS-80* computers), find out as much as you can about the location of ROM in your computer. (You are looking for locations where POKE has no effect.)

4. Clear the screen and then POKE several different values into location 1064. Describe what happens. (On *TRS-80* computers use location 15480. On *IBM* computers, first type DEF SEG = 45056, then use location 45100.)

5. (*Apple* users only) Type NEW, and then the following simple program:

```
10 PRINT "MOE"
20 END
```

Now type POKE 2051, 12. Now type LIST. What happened to line 10? Change the first line number to 30 by typing POKE 2051, 30. Does the program LIST correctly?

6. Turn off your machine and then turn it on again to remove any damage your POKEs may have done. Then RUN the following program that uses the memory directly to store an INPUT string one character at a time.

```
10 INPUT "TYPE STRING:  "; A$
20 FOR I = 1 TO LEN(A$)
30 POKE 9999 + I, ASC(MID$(A$, I, 1)) <---- (TRS-80: Use 30000 instead of 9999.)
40 NEXT I
50 POKE 10000 + LEN(A$), 0 <---- (TRS-80: Use 30000 instead of 10000.)
60 END
```

In line 30, the program takes the Ith character of A$ and POKEs its ASCII code into memory location 9999 + I (location 30000 + I on *TRS-80*). In line 50, a 0 is POKEd at the end of the string as a kind of trailer value.

7. Type NEW, then type and RUN this program, which retrieves and PRINTs the string typed in Problem 6:

```
10 LET L = 10000 <---- (TRS-80: Use 30000 instead of 10000.)
20 LET T = PEEK(L)
30 IF T = 0 THEN GOTO 70
40 PRINT CHR$(T);
50 LET L = L + 1
60 GOTO 20
70 END
```

In line 20, the program retrieves each of the ASCII codes and PRINTs the corresponding character until the trailer value 0 is reached. Notice an advantage to this POKE technique for storing values — a string or number stored in a *variable* would be lost when the second program was RUN.

11-2 Setting Up a Sequential File

In order to set up a sequential disk file, three steps are required:

Step 1 Open the file.
Step 2 Write data to the file.
Step 3 Close the file.

Opening a disk file provides essential information about the file and sets up a buffer. After the file is opened, special instructions are used to send data to the disk file rather than to the screen. After the data has been transferred, the file must be closed in order to write on the disk any information remaining in the buffer, and to release the buffer for other uses.

Opening the File

A file is opened by use of the OPEN statement. The exact form of this statement varies from computer to computer.

Apple

On Apple computers, all commands that refer to the operation of the disk drives are part of the DOS (*D*isk *O*perating *S*ystem). To include a DOS command such as OPEN in a program, you put the command inside quotation marks in a PRINT statement. Ordinarily, of course, PRINT statements cause output to go to the screen. Since this is not desired, there is a way to indicate to the computer that the string inside the quotation marks is a DOS command and not an ordinary message. A special character, CHR$(4), is placed at the beginning of the instruction. (CHR$(4) can also be produced by holding down the < CTRL > key and pressing the < D > key.) The OPEN command has the following form:

100 PRINT CHR$(4); "OPEN *file name*"

The file name following OPEN may be up to 30 characters in length and must start with a letter. Since both programs and disk files can be stored on the disk, different names should be given to each program and disk file.

TRS-80 and IBM

On these computers, the OPEN statement has this form:

10 OPEN "O", 1, "*file name*"

The letter "O" following the word OPEN indicates that the file is a sequential file and that data is to be sent (output) to the disk. The letter must be enclosed in quotation marks. Following the file type is a comma and then the *buffer number.* Each file in a program must have a buffer assigned to it. If there is one file, then one buffer is needed. If there are two files, then two buffers are needed, and so forth. The buffer numbers may range from 1 to 15, but if a buffer number bigger than 3 will be used, then that number must be specified at the time BASIC is loaded into memory. (See your computer's manual.) Following the buffer number is another comma and then the *file name* enclosed in quotation marks. The file name may be up to 8 characters in length and must start with a letter. (Punctuation marks should be avoided.) Since both programs and disk files can be stored on the disk, different names should be used for each program and disk file.

Sending Data to the Disk and Closing the File

The OPEN statement prepares a disk file for use. Special instructions must be given to put data into the file and to close the file.

Apple

On *Apple* computers, the DOS command WRITE is used to tell the computer to send data to the disk. For example, the statements

```
20 PRINT CHR$(4); "OPEN file name"
30 PRINT CHR$(4); "WRITE file name"
```

will cause all PRINT statements after line 30 to send information to the disk file specified rather than to the screen. Information will continue to go to the disk until another DOS command is given or the file is closed. Here is a program that OPENs a sequential file called SLEIGH and stores some friends' names and telephone numbers:

Program 1

Statement

```
10  REM * PROGRAM TO SET UP SEQUENTIAL FILE SLEIGH
20  PRINT CHR$(4); "OPEN SLEIGH": REM * OPEN FILE
30  FOR J = 1 TO 4
40  INPUT "TYPE NAME:  "; NAM$
50  INPUT "TYPE PHONE NO.:  "; NUM$
60  PRINT CHR$(4); "WRITE SLEIGH": REM * SEND DATA TO DISK
70  PRINT NAM$: REM * PUT NAME IN FILE
80  PRINT NUM$: REM * PUT PHONE NO. IN FILE
90  PRINT CHR$(4): REM * STOP WRITING TO DISK
100  NEXT J
```

Program continued on next page.

```
110 PRINT CHR$(4); "CLOSE SLEIGH": REM * CLOSE THE FILE
120 PRINT "THE DATA IS IN THE FILE."
130 END
```

Output

```
TYPE NAME:  ? RUDOLPH
TYPE PHONE NO.:  ? 262-8101
TYPE NAME:  ? BLITZEN
TYPE PHONE NO.:  ? 873-4184
TYPE NAME:  ? DASHER
TYPE PHONE NO.:  ? 615-8237
TYPE NAME:  ? DANCER
TYPE PHONE NO.:  ? 262-8103
THE DATA IS IN THE FILE.
```

Each time the user types a name and phone number, the WRITE command in line 60 causes the PRINT statements in lines 70 and 80 to send the name and phone number to the disk file. Then the statement PRINT CHR$(4) in line 90 causes the program to stop writing to the disk. This statement is necessary so that the messages in lines 40 and 50 will not be put in the disk file the next time through the loop.

When the FOR . . . NEXT loop in lines 30–100 is completed, the DOS command CLOSE in line 110 closes the file. Any file that has been opened must be closed. The effect of the CLOSE statement is to clear the buffer, so that all the data left in the buffer is transferred to the disk. Both the command CLOSE and the file name following it must be enclosed in quotation marks.

TRS-80 and IBM

On *TRS-80* computers, the command PRINT # is used to tell the computer to send data to the disk file. On *IBM* computers, the command WRITE # is used. For example, the statements

TRS-80

```
30 OPEN "O", 2, "file name"
40 PRINT #2, N$
50 PRINT #2, K
```

IBM

```
30 OPEN "O", 2, "file name"
40 WRITE #2, N$
50 WRITE #2, K
```

will cause the current values of N$ and K to be sent to the disk file specified instead of to the screen. The number 2 following PRINT # (or WRITE #) in lines 40 and 50 is a buffer number. This buffer number must match the buffer number named in the OPEN statement. The buffer number is followed by a comma, then a single string or numeric variable.

It is possible to write the value of more than one variable to the disk file using just a single PRINT # or WRITE # command. See your computer's manual for the precise punctuation that is needed.

Here is a program that OPENs a sequential file called SLEIGH and stores some friends' names and telephone numbers:

Program 1

Statement

```
5  REM * PROGRAM TO CREATE SEQUENTIAL FILE SLEIGH
10 OPEN "O", 1, "SLEIGH": REM * OPEN FILE, BUFFER NO. 1
20 FOR N = 1 TO 4
30 INPUT "TYPE NAME:  "; NAM$
40 INPUT "TYPE PHONE NO.:  "; NUM$
50 PRINT #1, NAM$ }                  50 WRITE #1, NAM$ }
60 PRINT #1, NUM$ } TRS-80    or     60 WRITE #1, NUM$ } IBM
70 NEXT N
80 CLOSE 1: REM * CLOSE THE FILE
90 PRINT "THE DATA IS IN THE FILE."
100 END
```

Output

```
TYPE NAME:  ? RUDOLPH
TYPE PHONE NO.:  ? 262-8101
TYPE NAME:  ? BLITZEN
TYPE PHONE NO.:  ? 873-4184
TYPE NAME:  ? DASHER
TYPE PHONE NO.:  ? 615-8237
TYPE NAME:  ? DANCER
TYPE PHONE NO.:  ? 262-8103
THE DATA IS IN THE FILE.
```

Each time the user types a name and telephone number, the PRINT # (or WRITE #) statements in lines 50 and 60 cause the name and phone number to be sent to the disk file. Once the FOR . . . NEXT loop in lines 20–70 is completed, the CLOSE statement in line 80 closes the file.

The effect of the CLOSE statement is to clear the buffer in the computer's memory, so that all the data left in the buffer is transferred to the disk. The CLOSE instruction must be followed by the buffer number named previously in the OPEN statement.

Deleting a File

If there already was a sequential file called SLEIGH on the disk when Program 1 for your machine was RUN, the new data would have been recorded over the old data (destroying some or all of the old data). Since some of the old data might still remain in the file after the new data has been recorded, it is always best to delete (erase) the old file before re-using the name for the new file. The statements needed to do this in a program are given below for each computer.

Apple

```
10  PRINT CHR$(4); "DELETE SLEIGH"
20  PRINT CHR$(4); "OPEN SLEIGH"
 .
 .
 .
```

TRS-80 and IBM

```
10  KILL "SLEIGH"
20  OPEN "O", 1, "SLEIGH"
 .
 .
 .
```

Avoiding Pitfalls

1. If a WRITE PROTECT error occurs when you are sending data to the disk, then you need to remove the tab that covers the notch on the corner of the disk.

2. If a DISK FULL error occurs when you are sending data to the disk, then to make room for more data, you need to delete some of the files on the disk. Or, you may prefer to start over again by putting another formatted disk in the drive to store the data.

3. When naming the file in the OPEN statement, you should choose a name different from the one you are going to use to save the BASIC program setting up the file.

4. *(Apple)* When an *Apple* WRITE command is in effect, the DOS command PRINT CHR$(4) must be used if a subsequent PRINT or INPUT statement is intended to go to the screen rather than to the disk file.

5. A file should not be OPENed a second time unless it has been CLOSEd in the meantime.

6. SYNTAX ERRORs are common when writing a program to set up a disk file. Be sure that you use the correct punctuation marks in all of the statements. If an error occurs when the program to set up the file is RUN, you should CLOSE the file (as an immediate mode command) before debugging the program. Otherwise, data stored previously may be destroyed and thus need to be retyped, or unwanted data may end up in the file.

Summary

Apple

The statements needed to open a sequential file, record data, and close the file are of this form:

```
20  PRINT CHR$(4); "OPEN file name"
 .
 .
 .
60  PRINT CHR$(4); "WRITE file name"
70  PRINT variable
80  PRINT variable
 .
 .
 .
110  PRINT CHR$(4); "CLOSE file name"
 .
 .
 .
```

The WRITE command in line 60 will cause subsequent PRINT statements to send data to the disk file until another DOS command is given, or the file is CLOSEd. The instruction PRINT CHR$(4) is a DOS command that causes a program to stop writing to the disk file.

TRS-80 and IBM

The statements needed to open a sequential file, send data to the disk, and close the file are of this form:

```
10  OPEN "O", 1, "file name"
20  PRINT #1, variable  }              20  WRITE #1, variable  }
30  PRINT #1, variable  }  TRS-80  or  30  WRITE #1, variable  }  IBM
 .
 .
 .
90  CLOSE 1
 .
 .
 .
```

The PRINT # (or WRITE #) instructions in lines 20 and 30 tell the computer to send the values of the specified variables to the disk file rather than to the screen.

Exercises 11-2

A 1. What is the purpose of the OPEN statement?

2. What is the purpose of the CLOSE statement?

3. Using the program listed for your computer, answer parts (a)–(f) below.

Apple

```
10  REM * SEQUENTIAL FILE
20  PRINT CHR$(4); "OPEN EXAMPLE"
30  FOR J = 1 TO 4
40  INPUT "TYPE NAME:  "; N$
50  INPUT "TYPE GRADE:  "; G
60  PRINT CHR$(4); "WRITE EXAMPLE"
70  PRINT N$
80  PRINT G
90  PRINT CHR$(4)
100  NEXT J
110  PRINT CHR$(4); "CLOSE EXAMPLE"
120  END
```

TRS-80 and IBM

```
5  REM * SEQUENTIAL FILE
10  OPEN "O", 2, "EXAMPLE"
20  FOR J = 1 TO 4
30  INPUT "TYPE NAME:  "; N$
40  INPUT "TYPE GRADE:  "; G
50  PRINT #2, N$ }                  50  WRITE #2, N$ }
60  PRINT #2, G  } TRS-80    or     60  WRITE #2, G  } IBM
70  NEXT J
80  CLOSE 2
90  END
```

a. What is the name of the sequential file?

b. What type of data is being stored in the file?

c. How many records are being stored in the file?

d. *(Apple)* What is the purpose of the statement in line 90?

e. *(TRS-80* and *IBM)* What does the letter "O" in line 10 indicate?

f. *(TRS-80* and *IBM)* What does the number 2 in line 80 indicate?

4. The programs below contain several errors. Change the program listed for your computer so that it will correctly store 10 names and ages in the sequential file NOGO.

Apple

```
10  REM * SEQUENTIAL FILE NOGO
20  PRINT CHR$(4); OPEN NOGO
30  FOR K=1 TO 10
40  INPUT "TYPE NAME, AGE:  "; NM$, A
50  PRINT CHR$(4); "WRITE NOGO"
60  PRINT NM$
70  PRINT A
80  NEXT K
90  PRINT CHR$(4); "CLOSE NOGO"
100  END
```

TRS-80 and IBM

```
5  REM * SEQUENTIAL FILE NOGO
10  OPEN "O", 2, NOGO
20  FOR K=1 TO 10
30  INPUT "TYPE NAME, AGE:  "; NM$, A
40  PRINT #1, NM$ }                 40  WRITE #1, NM$ }
50  PRINT #1, A   } TRS-80    or    50  WRITE #1, A   } IBM
60  NEXT K
70  CLOSE 1
80  END
```

B

5. Write a program that INPUTs the names of all the subjects you are currently studying and stores them in a sequential file called CLASS. (Use a FOR . . . NEXT loop to control the number of INPUTs.)

6. Write a program that READs the titles of five books from DATA statements and stores them in a sequential file called BOOK. Use the trailer value ZZZZ to indicate the end of the list.

7. Write a program that INPUTs the name of each class you are enrolled in, the teacher's name, and the number of the room where the class meets. Have the program continue to store each field in a sequential file called SCHOOL until the trailer value NO MORE is INPUT for the name.

8. Write a program that generates 12 random integers, each between 50 and 100, and puts them into an array R. (Use a FOR . . . NEXT loop.) Then have the program set up a sequential file called RAND to store the random numbers.

9. a. Write a program that INPUTs the names of a team's soccer players into an array PLAYER$ and the number of goals each scored during the last year into an array GOAL. Use the double trailer value XXXX and −1 to stop INPUTting values. Have the program store each field in a sequential file called SOCCER.
   b. Change the program in (a) so that the double trailer value XXXX, −1 is stored at the end of the file SOCCER.

10. (Graphics)
   a. Write a program to set up a sequential file called PICTURE that stores the coordinates of the points used to draw the picture shown at the right. Have the program READ the coordinates X, Y from DATA statements, stopping when the double trailer value −1, −1 is READ.
   b. Change the program in (a) so that the double trailer value −1, −1 is stored at the end of the file PICTURE.

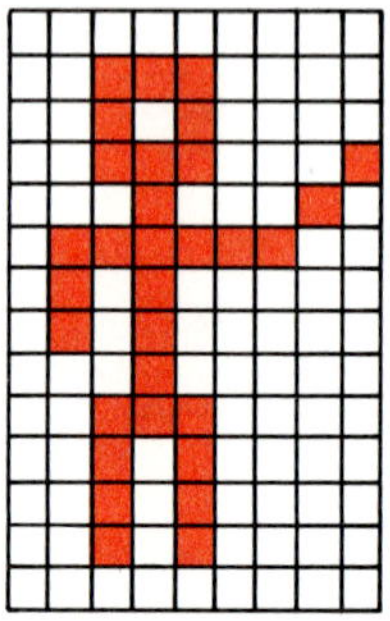

C 11. *Challenge:* Change the SNAIL program (see the Lab Activity for Section 9–6, page 506) to include the additional option of saving a SNAIL "program" as a sequential file with a name of the user's choosing.

Lab Activity

Writing Data with Commas to a File

(for use with *Apple* computers)

In the Lab Activity for Section 3–3, page 94, you learned that the INPUT statement will not accept a string containing a comma unless quotation marks are typed around the entire string. Similarly, such strings PRINTed to a sequential file must be enclosed in quotation marks using a special technique.

First, here is a review of how INPUT treats strings containing commas. Type the program below into the computer:

```
10 INPUT NAM$
20 PRINT NAM$
30 END
```

Problems

1. RUN the program and type the string WASHINGTON, GEORGE (be sure to include the comma). What does the computer PRINT in the output? If you typed the string correctly, then the result should have been an EXTRA IGNORED error message and then only WASHINGTON printed by the instruction in line 20.

2. RUN the program again, but this time type the name enclosed in quotation marks: "WASHINGTON, GEORGE". Now does the program PRINT the string correctly?

As you will learn, INPUT is also used to retrieve information from a disk file. Therefore, strings containing commas must be PRINTed to the file with quotes around them. Since quotation marks are used to enclose strings that are to be PRINTed on the screen (or on a printer), the only way they themselves can be PRINTed is by using CHR$(34). Specifically, after a file is OPENed and a WRITE statement is executed, the instruction

```
PRINT CHR$(34); N$; CHR$(34)
```

will write the string N$ to the file enclosed in quotation marks.

3. Write a program that writes strings containing commas to a file called SENTENCE. Then RUN the program and store the two following strings (enclosed in quotation marks):

```
"WHY, GEORGE, WHAT HAPPENED TO THE CHERRY TREE?"
"YOU CAN SEE, SURELY, THAT IT FELL DOWN!"
```

4. Type the following program that uses commands you will learn in the next section to read in the two strings from the file that you set up in Problem 3 above.

```
5  REM * READING A FILE
10  PRINT CHR$(4); "OPEN SENTENCE"
20  PRINT CHR$(4); "READ SENTENCE"
30  INPUT A$
40  INPUT B$
50  PRINT A$
60  PRINT B$
70  PRINT CHR$(4); "CLOSE SENTENCE"
80  END
```

RUN the program. Were the commas in the two strings stored correctly?

Lab Activity

Writing Data with Commas to a File

(for use with *TRS-80* and *IBM* computers)

In the Lab Activity for Section 3–3, page 94, you learned that the INPUT statement will not accept a string containing a comma unless quotation marks are typed around the entire string. The *TRS-80* and *IBM* computers have another way of handling this problem.

First, here is a review of how INPUT treats strings containing commas. Type the program below into the computer:

```
10  INPUT NAM$
20  PRINT NAM$
30  END
```

Problems

1. RUN the program and type the string WASHINGTON, GEORGE (be sure to include the comma). What does the computer PRINT? If you entered the string correctly, the result should have been an error message such as REDO FROM START.

2. Since the comma is used to separate data, the INPUT statement cannot be used to enter data that contains a comma. Instead, the LINE INPUT statement can be used. Change line 10 above to read:

   ```
   10  LINE INPUT NAM$
   ```

   Now RUN the program and type: WASHINGTON, GEORGE. Does the program PRINT the string correctly? (*Note:* With LINE INPUT you must have separate statements for each variable INPUT. A statement such as 10 LINE INPUT NAM$, TEL$ will result in a SYNTAX ERROR message.)

When you want to store data that contains commas in a file, you should use the LINE INPUT statement to get the data from the keyboard, and then use the PRINT # statement to put the string in the file. (*IBM* users should note that PRINT # is used instead of WRITE #.) The form of the PRINT # statement is:

PRINT # *buffer number, string variable*

Separate PRINT # statements should be used for each string that might contain a comma.

3. Write a program that writes strings containing commas to a file called SENTENCE. RUN the program and store the two following strings:

```
WHY, GEORGE, WHAT HAPPENED TO THE CHERRY TREE?
YOU CAN SEE, SURELY, THAT IT FELL DOWN!
```

4. You will learn in the next section how to read data from a sequential file using the command INPUT #. To accommodate commas in the strings in a file, you can use LINE INPUT # instead. Type the following program to read in the two strings from the file you set up in Problem 3.

```
10 OPEN "I", 2, "SENTENCE"
20 LINE INPUT #2, A$
30 LINE INPUT #2, B$
40 CLOSE 2
50 PRINT A$
60 PRINT B$
70 END
```

RUN the program. Were the commas in the two strings stored correctly?

11-3 Reading a Sequential File

Now that you know how to set up a sequential file, let's consider how to retrieve data from the disk. Three steps are required:

Step 1 Open the file in which the data is stored.
Step 2 Read data from the file back into the computer's memory.
Step 3 Close the file.

The instructions to accomplish these steps vary from computer to computer.

Apple

On *Apple* computers, the OPEN statement to read data from a sequential file is the same as that for creating the file. The difference here is that you are OPENing a file that already exists, so the computer uses the file as a source of data. The DOS command READ tells the computer that subsequent INPUT statements are to get their information from a disk file rather than from the keyboard. For example, if the file SLEIGH exists, the statements

```
20 PRINT CHR$(4); "OPEN SLEIGH"
30 PRINT CHR$(4); "READ SLEIGH"
```

will cause the computer to read data from the file SLEIGH when it encounters subsequent INPUT statements after line 30.

Here is an *Apple* program that OPENs the file SLEIGH created in Program 1, page 595, and PRINTs the names and telephone numbers stored there. The data being sent from the disk file will be placed in arrays so that the information can be manipulated easily.

Program 1

Statement

```
10 REM * PROGRAM TO READ AND PRINT DISK FILE SLEIGH
15 DIM NAM$(4), NUM$(4)
20 PRINT CHR$(4); "OPEN SLEIGH"
30 PRINT CHR$(4); "READ SLEIGH": REM * GET DATA FROM DISK
40 FOR K = 1 TO 4
50 INPUT NAM$(K): REM * GET NAME FROM DISK FILE, PUT IN NAME FIELD
60 INPUT NUM$(K): REM * GET PHONE NO., PUT IN NUMBER FIELD
70 NEXT K
80 PRINT CHR$(4); "CLOSE SLEIGH"
90 PRINT "NAME", "PHONE NO."
100 FOR I = 1 TO 4
110 PRINT NAM$(I), NUM$(I)
120 NEXT I
130 END
```

Output

```
NAME            PHONE NO.
RUDOLPH         262-8101
BLITZEN         873-4184
DASHER          615-8237
DANCER          262-8103
```

The DOS command READ is given in line 30. Therefore, the INPUT statements in lines 50 and 60 cause the computer to send the data in the file SLEIGH back to the computer's memory in the arrays NAM$ and NUM$. Once all the data is stored in the arrays, the file is CLOSEd (line 80). Although the program at this point simply PRINTs the data (lines 100–120), it would be possible also to manipulate the data using the sorting and searching techniques explained in Chapter 10.

TRS-80 and IBM

On these computers, the OPEN statement to read data from a sequential disk file is of this form:

```
10 OPEN "I", 1, "file name"
```

The letter "I" is used instead of "O" following the word OPEN to indicate that the data is to be sent (input) from the disk to the computer. The actual statement used to read information from the sequential file is INPUT #. Here is a program that OPENs the file SLEIGH created in Program 1, page 597, and PRINTs the names and telephone numbers stored there. The data being sent from the disk file will be placed in arrays so that the information can be manipulated easily.

Program 1

Statement

```
5  REM * PROGRAM TO READ AND PRINT DISK FILE SLEIGH
7  DIM NAM$(4), NUM$(4)
10  OPEN "I", 1, "SLEIGH": REM * OPEN DISK FILE TO SEND DATA
20  FOR K=1 TO 4
30  INPUT #1, NAM$(K): REM * GET NAME FROM DISK FILE, PUT IN NAME FIELD
40  INPUT #1, NUM$(K): REM * GET PHONE NO., PUT IN NUMBER FIELD
50  NEXT K
60  CLOSE 1
70  PRINT "NAME", "PHONE NO."
80  FOR J=1 TO 4
90  PRINT NAM$(J), NUM$(J)
100  NEXT J
110  END
```

The INPUT # statements in the FOR . . . NEXT loop in lines 20–50 cause the computer to send the data in the file SLEIGH back to the computer's memory, and to store the names in the array NAM$ and the telephone numbers in the array NUM$. Once all the information is stored in the arrays, the file is CLOSEd (line 60). Although the program at this point simply PRINTs the data (lines 80–100), it would be possible also to manipulate the data using the sorting and searching techniques explained in Chapter 10.

Disk Files and Trailer Values

In the programs used to set up and read the file SLEIGH, the exact number of data items in the file was known and a FOR . . . NEXT loop was used to control the number of times the computer sent data to or from the disk. When setting up a disk file containing many data items, you may not know the exact number. In this case, the use of a trailer value is more practical than a FOR . . . NEXT loop. We will illustrate how a trailer value can be used to signal the end of data by revising the programs that created and read the file SLEIGH.

Apple

Here is the revised version of Program 1, page 595, that created the file SLEIGH using a FOR . . . NEXT loop. This version uses the double trailer value ZZZZ, −1.

Program 2

Statement

```
10  REM * SET UP FILE SLEIGH USING TRAILER VALUES
20  PRINT CHR$(4); "OPEN SLEIGH": REM * OPEN FILE
30  INPUT "TYPE NAME (ZZZZ TO QUIT):   "; NAM$
35  IF NAM$ = "ZZZZ" THEN LET NUM$ = "—1": GOTO 50
40  INPUT "TYPE PHONE NO.:   "; NUM$
50  PRINT CHR$(4); "WRITE SLEIGH": REM * SEND DATA TO DISK
60  PRINT NAM$: REM * PUT NAME IN FILE
70  PRINT NUM$: REM * PUT PHONE NO. IN FILE
80  PRINT CHR$(4): REM * STOP WRITING TO DISK
90  IF NAM$ <> "ZZZZ" THEN GOTO 30: REM * ZZZZ AND
        —1 ARE TRAILERS
100  PRINT CHR$(4); "CLOSE SLEIGH"
110  PRINT "THE DATA IS IN THE FILE."
120  END
```

Notice that with the trailer-value method the user can send as many names and phone numbers as desired to the file, whereas in a FOR . . . NEXT loop the final counter value limits the amount of data that can be sent. Notice also that the trailer values ZZZZ and −1 are included at the end of the file. Can you think of a reason why this might be important?

Here is the revised version of Program 1, page 606, that read data from the file SLEIGH using a FOR . . . NEXT loop. In this version, the computer continues to read data from the file until the double trailer value ZZZZ, −1 signals the end of the data.

Program 3

Statement

```
5  REM * READ DATA FROM FILE WITH TRAILERS
10  DIM NAM$(50), NUM$(50)
20  PRINT CHR$(4); "OPEN SLEIGH"
30  PRINT CHR$(4); "READ SLEIGH": REM * GET DATA FROM DISK
35  LET K = 1: REM * K IS THE COUNTER
```

```
40  INPUT NAM$(K): REM * GET NAME, PUT IN NAME FIELD
50  INPUT NUM$(K): REM * GET PHONE NO., PUT IN NUMBER FIELD
60  IF NAM$(K) <> "ZZZZ" THEN LET K=K+1: GOTO 40
70  PRINT CHR$(4); "CLOSE SLEIGH"
80  PRINT "NAME", "PHONE NO."
90  FOR I=1 TO K-1
100  PRINT NAM$(I), NUM$(I)
110  NEXT I
120  END
```

This program uses a counter (K) to keep track of the number of records read by the loop in lines 40–60. The name field and telephone-number field are PRINTed by the FOR . . . NEXT loop in lines 90–110. Since the final counter value in the FOR statement is K − 1, the trailer values ZZZZ and −1 will not appear in the fields in the output.

TRS-80 and IBM

Here is the revised version of Program 1, page 597, that created the file SLEIGH using a FOR . . . NEXT loop. This version uses the double trailer value ZZZZ, −1.

Program 2

Statement

```
5  REM * SET UP FILE SLEIGH USING TRAILERS
10  OPEN "O", 1, "SLEIGH": REM * OPEN FILE, BUFFER NO. 1
20  INPUT "TYPE NAME (ZZZZ TO QUIT):  "; NAM$
25  IF NAM$ = "ZZZZ" THEN LET NUM$ = "-1": GOTO 40
30  INPUT "TYPE PHONE NO.:  "; NUM$
40  PRINT #1, NAM$ }               or   40  WRITE #1, NAM$ }
50  PRINT #1, NUM$ }  TRS-80            50  WRITE #1, NUM$ }  IBM
60  IF NAM$ <> "ZZZZ" THEN GOTO 20: REM * ZZZZ AND
       -1 ARE TRAILERS
70  CLOSE 1: REM * CLOSE THE FILE
80  PRINT "THE DATA IS IN THE FILE."
90  END
```

Notice that with the trailer-value method the user can send as many names and phone numbers as desired to the file, whereas in a FOR . . . NEXT loop the final counter value limits the amount of data that can be sent. Notice also that the trailer values ZZZZ and −1 are included at the end of the file. Can you think of a reason why this might be important?

Here is the revised version of Program 1, page 607, that read data from the file SLEIGH using a FOR . . . NEXT loop. In this version, the computer continues to read data from the file until the double trailer value ZZZZ, −1 signals the end of the data.

Program 3

Statement

```
5  REM * READ DATA FROM FILE WITH TRAILERS
7  DIM NAM$(50), NUM$(50)
10  OPEN "I", 1, "SLEIGH"
20  LET K=1: REM * K IS THE COUNTER
30  INPUT #1, NAM$(K): REM * GET NAME, PUT IN NAME FIELD
40  INPUT #1, NUM$(K): REM * GET PHONE NO., PUT IN NUMBER FIELD
50  IF NAM$(K) <> "ZZZZ" THEN LET K=K+1: GOTO 30
60  CLOSE 1
70  PRINT "NAME", "PHONE NO."
80  FOR J=1 TO K-1
90  PRINT NAM$(J), NUM$(J)
100  NEXT J
110  END
```

The program uses a counter (K) to keep track of the number of records read by the loop in lines 30–50. The name field and telephone-number field are PRINTed by the FOR . . . NEXT loop in lines 80–100. Since the final counter value in the FOR statement in line 80 is K − 1, the trailer values ZZZZ and −1 will not appear in the fields in the output.

Avoiding Pitfalls

1. If an error stops your program while it is reading data from a disk file, you should CLOSE the file (as an immediate mode command) before debugging the program. Otherwise, a bad file may result.

2. If you RUN a program to read data from a sequential disk file and a FILE NOT FOUND error occurs, then check that you have used the correct file name in the OPEN statement. If the file name is correct, then check that the file is actually stored on the disk currently in the disk drive.

3. To avoid bad files, you should not attempt to read data from a sequential file and then write data to it without first CLOSing the file and then reOPENing it.

Summary

Apple

The statements needed to read data from a sequential disk file are of this form:

```
20  PRINT CHR$(4); "OPEN file name"
30  PRINT CHR$(4); "READ file name"
40  INPUT variable
50  INPUT variable
 .
 .
 .
90  PRINT CHR$(4); "CLOSE file name"
```

The DOS command READ in line 30 will cause all subsequent INPUT statements to send data from the disk file to the computer's memory until another DOS command is given or the file is CLOSED.

TRS-80 and IBM

The statements needed to read data from a sequential disk file are of this form:

```
10  OPEN "I", 2, "file name"
20  INPUT #2, variable
30  INPUT #2, variable
 .
 .
 .
90  CLOSE 2
```

The INPUT # instructions in lines 20 and 30 tell the computer to send data values from the disk file to the computer's memory and store them in the specified variables.

Exercises 11-3

A **1.** **a.** Describe the steps needed to read data from a sequential file.

b. Tell why it might be useful to read data from a disk file into arrays.

c. When is the trailer-value technique of setting up a disk file more appropriate to use than a FOR . . . NEXT loop?

2. Using the program listed for your computer, answer (a)–(f) below.

Apple

```
10  REM * READING FROM A SEQUENTIAL FILE
20  PRINT CHR$(4); "OPEN EXAMPLE"
30  PRINT CHR$(4); "READ EXAMPLE"
40  FOR J = 1 TO 4
50  INPUT N$(J)
60  INPUT G(J)
70  NEXT J
80  PRINT CHR$(4); "CLOSE EXAMPLE"
90  PRINT "NAME", "GRADE"
100  FOR K = 1 TO 4
110  PRINT N$(K), G(K)
120  NEXT K
130  END
```

TRS-80 and IBM

```
5  REM * READING FROM A SEQUENTIAL FILE
10  OPEN "I", 1, "EXAMPLE"
20  FOR K = 1 TO 4
30  INPUT #1, N$(K)
40  INPUT #1, G(K)
50  NEXT K
60  CLOSE 1
65  PRINT "NAME", "GRADE"
70  FOR J = 1 TO 4
80  PRINT N$(J), G(J)
90  NEXT J
100  END
```

a. What is the name of the sequential file containing the data to be read?
b. What type of data is stored in the file?
c. *(Apple)* What does the statement in line 30 tell the computer?
d. *(Apple)* What is the purpose of the statements in lines 50 and 60?
e. *(TRS-80* and *IBM)* What does the letter "I" in line 10 tell the computer?
f. *(TRS-80* and *IBM)* What is the purpose of the statements in lines 30 and 40?

3. The programs below contain errors. Change the program listed for your computer so that it will correctly read the names of the 12 months of a year from the disk file MONTHS, then PRINT the names.

Apple

```
10  DIM MO$(12)
20  PRINT CHR$(4); "OPEN MONTHS"
30  FOR X = 1 TO 12
40  INPUT MO$(X)
50  NEXT X
55  PRINT CHR$(4); "CLOSE MONTHS"
60  PRINT "NAMES OF MONTHS"
70  FOR Y = 1 TO 12
80  PRINT MO$(Y)
90  NEXT Y
100  END
```

TRS-80 and IBM

```
10  DIM MO$(12)
20  OPEN "O", 1, "MONTHS"
30  FOR X = 1 TO 12
40  INPUT #2, MO$(X)
50  NEXT X
55  CLOSE 1
60  PRINT "NAMES OF MONTHS"
70  FOR Y = 1 TO 12
80  PRINT MO$(Y)
90  NEXT Y
100  END
```

4. The programs below contain errors. Change the program listed for your computer so that it will correctly read data from the sequential file CAL and store it in the string array DAY$. Assume that CAL contains the names of the seven days of the week and has the trailer value XXXX stored at the end.

Apple

```
10 REM * PROGRAM TO READ DATA FROM CAL
20 DIM DAY$(8)
30 PRINT CHR$(4); "OPEN DAY$"
40 PRINT CHR$(4); "READ CAL"
50 LET J = 1
60 INPUT DAY$(J)
70 IF DAY$(J) = "XXXX" THEN LET J = J + 1: GOTO 60
80 PRINT CHR$(4); "CLOSE DAY$"
90 END
```

TRS-80 and IBM

```
5 REM * PROGRAM TO READ DATA FROM CAL
10 DIM DAY$(8)
20 OPEN "I", 1, "DAY$"
30 LET J = 1
40 INPUT #1, DAY$(J)
50 IF DAY$(J) = "XXXX" THEN LET J = J + 1: GOTO 40
60 CLOSE CAL
70 END
```

B 5. Modify Program 3 so that, after reading the file into memory, it performs a linear search for an INPUT name. If the name is found, have the program PRINT the name and corresponding telephone number; otherwise, PRINT the message NAME NOT FOUND.

6. Write a program that reads data from a sequential file called CLASS, then PRINTs the data. Assume that CLASS contains the names of all the subjects you are currently studying, and that it was created using a FOR . . . NEXT loop. (See Exercise 5, page 601.)

7. Write a program that reads data from a sequential file called BOOK, then PRINTs the data. Assume that BOOK contains the titles of five books and has the trailer value ZZZZ stored at the end. (See Exercise 6, page 601.)

8. (Graphics) Write a program that reads data from a sequential file called PICT, then draws the picture (that is, the X, Y coordinates) stored there. (See Exercise 10, page 602.)

9. Write a program that reads data from a sequential file called RAND, then sorts the data into increasing order and PRINTs the result. Assume that the file RAND was created using a FOR . . . NEXT loop and has 12 numeric values, but no trailer value. (See Exercise 8, page 601.)

10. a. Write a program that reads data from a sequential file called SCHOOL, then PRINTs the data. Assume that SCHOOL contains fields in this order: first, the name of each class you are enrolled in; then the teacher's name; and then the room number where the class meets. (See Exercise 7, page 601.)
    b. Change the program in (a) so that after reading the data from the disk, it searches the class-name field for the string HISTORY. Have the program PRINT the message FOUND if the string is located and NOT FOUND otherwise.

11. a. Write a program that reads data from a sequential file called SOCCER, then PRINTs the data. Assume that SOCCER contains fields in this order: first, the name of each member of the soccer team; then the number of goals scored by each member in the last year. (See Exercise 9, page 602.)
    b. Change the program in (a) so that it sorts the data keyed on the goals-scored field, then PRINTs the corresponding name of the team member who scored the most goals.

12. You have seen that it is always essential to know either how many records are in a sequential file, or to have a known trailer value stored at the end of it. One technique, not mentioned thus far, is to reserve the first record of the file for the number of records in the file. For example, if a file VERBS is to be created by INPUTting words from the user, the words can be counted as they are stored in an array. Then the *number* of elements in the array can be written to the disk file as the first record, followed by all of the array elements. When the file is subsequently read back into the computer, the first record INPUT is the number of records (words) in the file. This number can then be used as the final counter value in a FOR . . . NEXT loop to read the rest of the records from the file.

    a. Write a program to set up a file called VERBS as outlined above.
    b. Write a program to read the file VERBS back into the computer.
    c. Add to the program in (b) so that it also sorts the array of words, then sends it back to the disk.

13. Modify Program 3 so that it asks the user for the name of a person, then finds the record for that person. The program should then INPUT from the user a new telephone number for that person and write the new version of the file to the disk.

C 14. *Challenge:* Change the SNAIL program (see Exercise 11, page 602) so that it will read SNAIL "programs" previously saved on the disk.

Lab Activity

Detecting the End of a File

When you read data from a sequential file using the techniques explained in this section, you must know the exact number of records in the file (so that a finite loop can be used) or the exact form of the trailer value. A third possibility exists; as usual, the technique varies from computer to computer.

When your computer writes data to a sequential file, it places a special number, called the *end of file marker,* at the end. When a new piece of information is written to the file, the file marker is moved to make room for it, and the marker is again placed at the end. When data is read from a file, if the end of file marker is detected by the Disk Operating System, an OUT OF DATA or INPUT PAST END error occurs, and the program ENDs prematurely. By detecting the end of file marker, you can stop INPUTting data and avoid the error. How this is done is explained below for *Apple, TRS-80,* and *IBM* computers.

Apple

Any error, including OUT OF DATA, can be detected in an *Apple* program by use of an instruction of this form:

5 ONERR GOTO *line number*

This statement is placed early in the program, before the file is read into the computer by the usual finite (but not FOR . . . NEXT) loop. When the end of file marker is reached, the ONERR GOTO instruction directs the computer to the number of the line that begins the rest of the program.

Problems

1. Type and RUN the following *Apple* program that creates a sequential file with no trailer value. (The program uses a trailer value to end the INPUT, but does not put it in the file.)

```
10 PRINT CHR$(4); "OPEN ANYTHING FILE"
20 INPUT "TYPE ANYTHING (999 TO END):  "; A$
30 IF A$ = "999" THEN GOTO 100
40 PRINT CHR$(4); "WRITE ANYTHING FILE"
50 PRINT A$
60 PRINT CHR$(4): REM * CANCEL WRITING
```

Program continued on next page.

```
70 GOTO 20
100 PRINT CHR$(4); "CLOSE ANYTHING FILE"
110 END
```

(*Note:* SAVE the programs in Problems 1 and 2 for later use with the Lab Activity following Section 11–4.)

2. Type and RUN the following *Apple* program that reads the file into the computer, and then PRINTs it on the screen using the ONERR GOTO technique:

```
10 ONERR GOTO 200
20 PRINT CHR$(4); "OPEN ANYTHING FILE"
30 PRINT CHR$(4); "READ ANYTHING FILE"
40 INPUT A$
50 PRINT A$
60 GOTO 40
200 PRINT CHR$(4); "CLOSE ANYTHING FILE"
210 END
```

A disadvantage of the ONERR technique is that any error, including a disk problem or a syntax error, will cause the program to GOTO the line specified. This can make debugging very difficult. There is a way to have your program determine what kind of error occurred, so that it can handle different errors in different ways. (A SYNTAX ERROR, for instance, might cause an appropriate message to be PRINTed and the program to END.) See your computer's manual for an explanation.

3. Change the program in Problem 2 so that it INPUTs the data into an array, counts how many elements are in the array, then PRINTs the entire array when the end of the file is detected.

TRS-80 and IBM

On these computers, there is a built-in function called EOF (which stands for *end of file*) that can be used to detect the end of file marker. EOF(*N*) is equal to −1 if the file with buffer number *N* has reached the end. (That is, if the next INPUT # instruction to read the file will find nothing left in the file.) EOF(*N*) is equal to 0 if there is more to be INPUT from the file.

Problems

1. Type and RUN the program at the top of the next page. The program creates a sequential file with no trailer value. (The program uses a trailer value to end the INPUT, but does not put it in the file.)

```
10  OPEN "O", 2, "ANYTHING"
20  INPUT "TYPE ANYTHING (999 TO END):  "; A$
30  IF A$ = "999" THEN GOTO 100
40  PRINT #2, A$  TRS-80  or  40  WRITE #2, A$  IBM
50  GOTO 20
100  CLOSE 2
110  END
```

(*Note:* SAVE the programs in Problems 1 and 2 for later use with the Lab Activity following Section 11–4.)

2. Type and RUN the following program that uses the EOF function to detect the end of the ANYTHING file.

```
10  OPEN "I", 2, "ANYTHING"
20  IF EOF(2) = —1 THEN GOTO 100
30  INPUT #2, A$
40  PRINT A$
50  GOTO 20
100  CLOSE 2
110  END
```

(Since −1 is the code for the Boolean value *true* — see the Lab Activity for Section 7–6, page 400 — line 20 can be written in this more simple way: 20 IF EOF(2) THEN GOTO 100.)

3. Change the program in Problem 2 so that it INPUTs the data into an array, counts how many elements are in the array, and then PRINTs the entire array when the end of the file is detected.

11-4 Changing a Sequential File

There are many serious applications of disk files. They almost always involve not only storing and retrieving information but also adding, deleting, and changing the stored data in the file. To do any of these modifications with a sequential file, the easiest procedure is to read the entire file into one or more arrays, alter the arrays, then write the arrays back to the disk. There are other techniques that can be used; some will be explored in the Lab Activity and the exercises for this section.

Here is a program that uses a menu to allow the user to add to the file SLEIGH, to delete from the file, or to change individual records in the file. It first reads the file into the arrays NAM$ and NUM$, and alters the file as requested. Then when the QUIT option is chosen, the program writes the file back to the disk.

We will present the main routine of the program first, then the subroutines one at a time. The disk-handling subroutines will, as usual, differ from computer to computer.

Program 1 (Main Routine)

Statement

```
5  REM * PROGRAM TO CHANGE THE FILE SLEIGH
10  GOSUB 1000: REM * READ FILE INTO ARRAYS
20  GOSUB 1500: REM * PRINT MENU AND GET
       COMMAND COMM
30  ON COMM GOSUB 2000, 3000, 4000, 5000: REM * ADD, DELETE,
       CHANGE, OR QUIT
40  GOTO 20
```

Reading the File

The subroutine to read the file is a straightforward application of what you have learned in this chapter. We will assume that the file SLEIGH was already created by another program, and that it ends with the double trailer value ZZZZ, −1.

Apple

```
999  REM ** SUBROUTINE TO READ FILE SLEIGH INTO
            ARRAYS NAM$ AND NUM$ **
1000  DIM NAM$(50), NUM$(50)
1010  PRINT CHR$(4); "OPEN SLEIGH"
1020  PRINT CHR$(4); "READ SLEIGH"
1030  LET NREC = 1: REM * NREC IS NO. OF RECORDS
1040  INPUT NAM$(NREC)
1050  INPUT NUM$(NREC)
1060  IF NAM$(NREC) <> "ZZZZ" THEN LET NREC = NREC + 1: GOTO 1040
1070  LET NREC = NREC - 1: REM * TRAILER VALUE IS NOT A REAL DATA VALUE
1080  PRINT CHR$(4): REM * CANCEL READ INSTRUCTION
1085  PRINT CHR$(4); "CLOSE SLEIGH"
1090  RETURN
```

Here is the subroutine to read the file SLEIGH into two arrays (for *TRS-80* and *IBM* computers).

TRS-80 and IBM

```
999  REM ** SUBROUTINE TO READ FILE SLEIGH INTO
               ARRAYS NAM$ AND NUM$ **
1000 DIM NAM$(50), NUM$(50)
1010 OPEN "I", 1, "SLEIGH"
1020 LET NREC = 1: REM * NREC IS THE NUMBER
       OF RECORDS
1030 INPUT #1, NAM$(NREC)
1040 INPUT #1, NUM$(NREC)
1050 IF NAM$(NREC) <> "ZZZZ" THEN LET NREC = NREC + 1:
       GOTO 1030
1060 LET NREC = NREC - 1: REM * TRAILER VALUE IS NOT A
       REAL DATA VALUE
1065 CLOSE 1
1070 RETURN
```

PRINTing the Menu

Here is the menu-printing subroutine; except for small modifications, it works on any computer.

```
1499 REM ** SUBROUTINE TO PRINT MENU AND
               GET COMMAND COMM **
1500 HOME (or CLS)
1520 PRINT "OPTIONS"
1530 PRINT
1535 PRINT
1540 PRINT "TYPE 1 TO ADD TO THE FILE"
1550 PRINT "TYPE 2 TO DELETE FROM THE FILE"
1560 PRINT "TYPE 3 TO CHANGE A RECORD"
1570 PRINT "TYPE 4 TO SAVE THE FILE AND QUIT"
1580 PRINT
1590 INPUT "TYPE YOUR CHOICE:  "; COMM
1600 IF (COMM <> 1) AND (COMM <> 2) AND (COMM <> 3) AND
       (COMM <> 4) THEN GOTO 1500
1620 HOME (or CLS)
1630 RETURN
```

Adding to the File

The subroutine that allows information to be added to the file looks somewhat like the subroutine that reads information from the disk (and works on any computer):

```
1999 REM ** SUBROUTINE TO ADD TO THE FILE **
2000 LET NREC = NREC + 1: REM * NEW DATA ADDED TO NEXT POSITION IN ARRAYS
2010 INPUT "TYPE NAME (ZZZZ TO END):  "; NAM$(NREC)
2020 IF NAM$(NREC) = "ZZZZ" THEN GOTO 2050
2030 INPUT "TYPE TELEPHONE NUMBER:  "; NUM$(NREC)
2040 GOTO 2000
2050 LET NREC = NREC — 1: REM * DON'T COUNT THE TRAILER VALUE
2060 RETURN
```

The subroutine above does not put the file on the disk; that will be taken care of when all the changes are done and the QUIT option is chosen.

Deleting from the File

The subroutine to handle deletions from the file first asks for the name to be deleted and finds the name in the NAM$ array. Then the subroutine replaces that name in the array with the string XXXX. This special *flag* will indicate to the QUIT subroutine that this record should not be saved on the disk. The subroutine itself uses another subroutine (3500) to perform a linear search of the file for the name to be deleted.

```
2999 REM ** SUBROUTINE TO INPUT NAME (TRGT$) TO BE DELETED, THEN
            REPLACE THAT NAME WITH THE STRING XXXX **
3000 INPUT "TYPE NAME TO BE DELETED:  "; TRGT$
3010 GOSUB 3500: REM * FIND NAM$(I) MATCHING TRGT$
3020 LET NAM$(I) = "XXXX"
3030 RETURN
3499 REM ** SUB. TO FIND SUBSCRIPT I SUCH THAT NAM$(I) = TRGT$ **
3500 LET I = 1
3510 IF NAM$(I) = TRGT$ THEN GOTO 3540: REM * FOUND MATCH, SO RETURN
3520 LET I = I + 1
3530 GOTO 3510: REM * LOOK AT NEXT NAME
3540 RETURN
```

What will happen if the user types in a name that is not in the NAM$ array (that is, the name is not in the file)? In the exercises, you will be asked to change the program to consider this possibility.

Changing the File

The subroutine (4000) to change a record in the file is very similar to the deleting subroutine. It must first do a search for the target name. Then, rather than changing NAM$(I) to XXXX, the subroutine must INPUT a new name and phone number to be assigned to the variables NAM$(I) and NUM$(I). You will be asked to write this subroutine in the exercises.

Writing the File to the Disk

The final subroutine (5000) to write the file back to the disk is similar to what was done in Section 11–3, except that we must exclude any record for which the name field was changed to XXXX by the deleting subroutine (3000).

Apple

```
4999 REM ** SUBROUTINE TO SAVE FILE ON DISK AND QUIT **
5000 PRINT CHR$(4); "DELETE SLEIGH": REM * TAKE OLD VERSION OFF DISK
5005 PRINT CHR$(4); "OPEN SLEIGH"
5010 PRINT CHR$(4); "WRITE SLEIGH"
5020 FOR I = 1 TO NREC
5030 IF NAM$(I) = "XXXX" THEN GOTO 5060
5040 PRINT NAM$(I)
5050 PRINT NUM$(I)
5060 NEXT I
5070 PRINT "ZZZZ"
5080 PRINT "—1"
5090 PRINT CHR$(4) "CLOSE SLEIGH"
5095 END
```

TRS-80 and IBM

```
5000 KILL "SLEIGH": REM * TAKE OLD VERSION OFF DISK
5010 OPEN "O", 1, "SLEIGH"
5020 FOR I = 1 TO NREC
5030 IF NAM$(I) = "XXXX" THEN GOTO 5060
5040 PRINT #1, NAM$(I) }            WRITE #1, NAM$(I) }
5050 PRINT #1, NUM$(I) } TRS-80  or WRITE #1, NUM$(I) } IBM
5060 NEXT I
5070 PRINT #1, "ZZZZ" }            WRITE #1, "ZZZZ" }
5080 PRINT #1, "—1"   } TRS-80  or WRITE #1, "—1"   } IBM
5090 CLOSE 1
5095 END
```

Avoiding Pitfalls

When you write subroutines to delete or add records to a file stored in arrays, you must be very careful that the counter that keeps track of the number of records in the file is accurate. In particular, the (double) trailer value must not be counted as meaningful data.

Summary

Altering a sequential file that ends with a trailer value is most easily accomplished by reading the file into one or more arrays (one for each field), then manipulating the data in the array(s), and finally writing the data back to the disk.

Exercises 11-4

A

1. Describe the steps necessary to add records to a sequential file that has one or more trailer values stored at the end.

2. Using the program listed for your computer, answer parts (a)–(f) on the next page.

Apple

```
10  PRINT CHR$(4); "OPEN TEST"
20  PRINT CHR$(4); "READ TEST"
30  FOR J = 1 TO 10
40  INPUT T$(J)
50  NEXT J
60  PRINT CHR$(4)
70  PRINT "WHICH NAME IS SPELLED WRONG?"
80  INPUT SP$
90  LET J = 1
100  IF SP$ = T$(J) THEN GOTO 140
110  LET J = J + 1
120  IF J <= 10 THEN GOTO 100
130  GOTO 200
140  INPUT "CORRECT SPELLING:  "; T$(J)
150  PRINT CHR$(4); "DELETE TEST"
155  PRINT CHR$(4); "OPEN TEST"
```

```
160  PRINT CHR$(4); "WRITE TEST"
170  FOR J = 1 TO 10
180  PRINT T$(J)
190  NEXT J
200  PRINT CHR$(4); "CLOSE TEST"
210  END
```

TRS-80 and IBM

```
10  OPEN "I", 2, "TEST"
20  FOR J = 1 TO 10
30  INPUT #2, T$(J)
40  NEXT J
50  CLOSE 2
60  PRINT "WHICH NAME IS SPELLED WRONG?"
70  INPUT SP$
80  LET J = 1
90  IF SP$ = T$(J) THEN GOTO 130
100  LET J = J + 1
110  IF J <= 10 THEN GOTO 90
120  GOTO 190
130  INPUT "CORRECT SPELLING:  "; T$(J)
140  KILL "TEST"
150  OPEN "O", 1, "TEST "
160  FOR J = 1 TO 10
170  PRINT #1, T$(J)   TRS-80     or     170  WRITE #1, T$(J)   IBM
180  NEXT J
190  CLOSE 1
200  END
```

a. What is the name of the file?

b. What type of data is stored in the file?

c. How many data items are stored in the file?

d. (*TRS-80* and *IBM*) What is the purpose of the statement in line 90?

e. How many data items are in the file TEST after the program is RUN?

f. Why is the file TEST deleted *before* the data items are sent back to the disk?

3. Change the program listed in Exercise 2 for your computer so that if no match is found for the INPUT string SP$, the computer PRINTs the message NO SUCH WORD IN THIS FILE.

4. Change subroutine 3500 of Program 1 so that it uses a flag variable (call it FLAG) to indicate if a search for an INPUT name is unsuccessful. Have the program PRINT the message NAME NOT FOUND if that is the case.
(*Hint:* Set the FLAG variable initially to 0. If the name to be deleted is found, then set FLAG = 1. Upon RETURN to subroutine 3000, check to see if the FLAG variable still equals 0. If it does, then the search must have been unsuccessful.)

B

5. Write subroutine 4000 for Program 1.

6. a. Add an option to Program 1 that will alphabetize the file keyed on the name field. Use one or more subroutines to do the sorting.

   b. Change the search strategy in subroutine 3500 of Program 1 to a binary search.

7. Write a program that adds 5 more random numbers to a sequential file called RAND, then PRINTs the extended file. Assume that RAND contains 12 random numbers and that it was created using a FOR . . . NEXT loop. (See Exercise 8, page 601.)

8. Write a program to delete an INPUT data item from a sequential file called CLASS. Assume that CLASS contains the names of all the subjects you are currently studying and that it was created using a FOR . . . NEXT loop. (See Exercise 5, page 601.)

9. a. Write a program that INPUTs the names of four soccer players and their number of goals scored, then adds them to a sequential file called SOCCER (use INPUT PLAYER$, GOALS). Assume that SOCCER contains the names of 5 players and their number of goals scored, and was created using a FOR . . . NEXT loop.

   b. Modify the program in (a) so that data in the file can be updated. Have the program INPUT the name of the player whose number of goals scored has changed. Then after the new number of goals is stored in the file, have the program PRINT the player's name whose number of goals has changed.

10. Write a program to update data in a file called INV (short for inventory). Assume that INV contains fields in this order: first, the part number of a particular hardware item; then the number of that item currently in stock. The double trailer value 9999, −1 is stored at the end of the file. The user should be able to type the part number of a hardware item and then correct the number of that item in stock.

11. Write a program that INPUTs the titles of books, then adds them to a sequential file called BOOK. Assume that BOOK contains the titles of books and has the trailer value ZZZZ stored at the end. Be sure to include the trailer value ZZZZ at the end of the new file.

12. a. Write a program that INPUTs the names of sandwiches and their prices, then adds them to a sequential file called MENU. Assume that MENU contains fields in this order: first, the name of a sandwich, and then its price. The double trailer value YYYY and 00, stored at the end of the original file, should be included at the end of the new file.
    b. Add to the program in (a) so that the data in the extended file MENU is read into two arrays, SNDWCH$ and PRICE$. Then have the program sort the data keyed on the array SNDWCH$ and PRINT the results.

C 13. Although it is convenient to read an entire sequential file into arrays before altering it, this is not always necessary. (For example, a simple way to add items to a file called ORIGINAL is described in the Lab Activity for this section.) To delete a record from a file, the following strategy could be used:

Step 1 OPEN ORIGINAL (Assume the file ends with a trailer value.)

Step 2 OPEN TEMPO, a temporary new version of the file.

Step 3 INPUT item to be deleted from the user.

Step 4 READ a record from ORIGINAL. If it is the trailer value, CLOSE the file and END.

Step 5 If the file item is *not* the one to be deleted, write it to the file TEMPO and GOTO Step 4.

Step 6 Finish reading the records from ORIGINAL and writing them to TEMPO until the trailer value is reached. (Leave out the deleted item, of course.)

Step 7 Finish up by erasing ORIGINAL from the disk and renaming TEMPO, giving it the name ORIGINAL.

Write a program, following the algorithm outlined here, to delete selected records from the file SLEIGH.

14. Rewrite the program in Exercise 2 so that it avoids the use of arrays. (See Exercise 13 for hints on how this could be done).

Lab Activity

Extending a File

If a sequential file has no trailer value (see the Lab Activity for Section 11–3 and Exercise 12, page 614, for two methods of handling such files), there is an easy way to add to the end of the file. The commands used are variations of the OPEN command, and are different for different computers.

Apple

On an *Apple* computer, you can add to the end of an existing sequential file by using the command APPEND in place of OPEN. Then WRITE and PRINT are used as usual to put new items in the file. Finally, the file is CLOSEd.

Problems

1. If you have available the file you created in the Lab Activity for Section 11–3, page 615, you may skip this step. Otherwise, go back and use the program in Problem 1 of that Lab Activity to create a file. Use the program in Problem 2 of that Activity to read the file.
2. Change the program in Problem 1 of the Lab Activity for Section 11–3 by changing the statement in line 10 to read as follows:

   ```
   10 PRINT CHR$(4); "APPEND ANYTHING FILE"
   ```

   RUN the program and add some strings to the end of the file.
3. RUN the program in Problem 2 of the Lab Activity for Section 11–3 to see that the strings you typed were added to the end of the file.

TRS-80 and IBM

On *TRS-80* computers, you can add to the end of an existing sequential file by using the letter "E" (which stands for *extend*) in place of "O" in the OPEN statement. On *IBM* computers, use the letter "A" (which stands for *append*) in place of "O" in the OPEN statement. Then the instructions PRINT # *(TRS-80)* and WRITE # *(IBM)* are used as usual to put new items in the file. Finally, the file is CLOSEd.

Problems

1. If you have available the file you created in the Lab Activity for Section 11–3, page 615, you may skip this step. Otherwise, go back and use the program in Problem 1 of that Lab Activity to create a file. Use the program in Problem 2 of that Activity to read the file.
2. Change the program in Problem 1 of the Lab Activity for Section 11–3 by changing the statement in line 10 to read as follows:

   `10 OPEN "E", 2, "ANYTHING"` *TRS-80* or `10 OPEN "A", 2, "ANYTHING"` *IBM*

   RUN the program and add some strings to the end of the file.
3. RUN the program in Problem 2 of the Lab Activity for Section 11–3 to see that the strings you typed were added to the end of the file.

11-5 Merging Sequential Files

Have you ever received any "junk mail"? You know, the kind of flyer that asks you to buy a handy-dandy kitchen gadget, or subscribe to a certain magazine for a "once-in-a-lifetime" price. Many companies keep a computerized list of names of potential customers to whom they send their advertising brochures. These mailing lists usually are stored in alphabetical order.

If a company wants to expand its mailing, then it can buy another company's (alphabetized) mailing list. This new list then must be "merged" with the old one. In this section you will learn how to merge the data in two sequential files, both already in order according to some key field, to create a third sequential file ordered on that same key field.

We will illustrate the merge technique by considering the sequential files REINDEER and HELPERS, listed in alphabetical order below. The ZZZZ in both files is a trailer value.

REINDEER	HELPERS
COMET	BASHFUL
DANCER	DOC
RUDOLPH	GRUMPY
VIXEN	SLEEPY
ZZZZ	SNEEZY
	ZZZZ

If we name the merged file COMBO, then the goal is to have the data of COMBO stored in the following order:

COMBO

BASHFUL
COMET
DANCER
DOC
GRUMPY
RUDOLPH
SLEEPY
SNEEZY
VIXEN
ZZZZ

One way to merge the two files would be to read one of the files into an array, add the other file to the end of the array, sort the entire array, and then write it to the disk. Since sorting takes a lot of time, at least for long files, it is more efficient if we take advantage of the fact that both of the input files are already in alphabetical order. It is possible to save even more time if we avoid arrays altogether.

The merging algorithm can be illustrated by referring to the two files just discussed. After REINDEER and HELPERS are OPENed, the first record in each file is read into the computer (into two different string variables).

input files *memory*

REINDEER

COMET
DANCER
RUDOLPH
VIXEN
ZZZZ

→ COMET → BASHFUL

HELPERS

BASHFUL
DOC
GRUMPY
SLEEPY
SNEEZY
ZZZZ

Since BASHFUL comes alphabetically before COMET, BASHFUL is put in the merged file COMBO, and the next record (DOC) is read from HELPERS.

input files *memory* *output file*

REINDEER

COMBO

COMET
DANCER
RUDOLPH
VIXEN
ZZZZ

BASHFUL

→ COMET → DOC

HELPERS

BASHFUL
DOC
GRUMPY
SLEEPY
SNEEZY
ZZZZ

Next, COMET and DOC are compared; COMET is sent to COMBO and the next record (DANCER) is read from REINDEER, as illustrated in the diagram below:

input files	*memory*	*output file*
REINDEER		COMBO
COMET		BASHFUL
DANCER		COMET
RUDOLPH		
VIXEN		
ZZZZ		
	→ DANCER → DOC	
HELPERS		
BASHFUL		
DOC		
GRUMPY		
SLEEPY		
SNEEZY		
ZZZZ		

At the next stage, DANCER is sent to COMBO and RUDOLPH is read from REINDEER. The significant thing to notice is that when a record from REINDEER is sent to the merged file, then a new record is read from REINDEER; if the record sent came from HELPERS, then the new record is read from HELPERS.

The process described above is continued until one of the files is used up (that is, the trailer value is reached). At that point, the remainder of the other file is put into the merged file.

Program 1 follows this algorithm. It starts by INPUTting the names of the input files (using the subscripted variables FILE$(1) and FILE$(2)) and the name of the resulting merged file (which is put into the string variable MRGD$). Thus, the program is able to merge *any* two ordered sequential files that have records consisting of a single field and that end with the trailer value ZZZZ.

The BASIC code is kept relatively short by using arrays not only for the names of the input files but also for the records read from the files. (X$(1) is used for file number 1 and X$(2) is used for file number 2.) Therefore, a single subroutine (1500) can read from either file (by giving the variable I the value 1 or 2), and another subroutine (2000) can write either of X$(1) or X$(2) to the merged file. The main routine of the program is at the top of the next page.

Program 1 (Main Routine)

Statement

```
10 REM ** PROGRAM TO MERGE TWO ALPHABETIZED SEQUENTIAL FILES **
20 GOSUB 500: REM * GET NAMES (FILE$(1), FILE$(2), MRGD$) OF FILES
30 GOSUB 1000: REM * OPEN FILES
40 LET I = 1: GOSUB 1500: REM * READ X$(1) FROM FILE #1
50 LET I = 2: GOSUB 1500: REM * READ X$(2) FROM FILE #2
60 IF X$(1) = "ZZZZ" THEN LET I = 2: GOTO 200: REM * FILE #1 IS
     FINISHED; NOW READ IN THE REST OF FILE #2
70 IF X$(2) = "ZZZZ" THEN LET I = 1: GOTO 200: REM * FILE #2 IS
     FINISHED; NOW READ IN THE REST OF FILE #1
80 IF X$(1) < X$(2) THEN LET I = 1: GOTO 100: REM * X$(1) GOES ON
     MERGED FILE
90 LET I = 2: REM * X$(2) GOES ON MERGED FILE
100 GOSUB 2000: REM * PUT X$(I) ON MERGED FILE
110 GOSUB 1500: REM * READ X$(I) FROM FILE #I
120 GOTO 60
199 REM * ONE FILE IS FINISHED; MOVE FILE #I TO MERGED FILE
200 IF X$(I) = "ZZZZ" THEN GOTO 300: REM * THIS FILE IS ALSO FINISHED
210 GOSUB 2000: REM * PUT X$(I) ON MERGED FILE
220 GOSUB 1500: REM * READ X$(I) FROM FILE #I
230 GOTO 200
299 REM * BOTH FILES ARE FINISHED
300 GOSUB 2000: REM * PUT ZZZZ TRAILER VALUE ON MERGED FILE
310 GOSUB 2500: REM * CLOSE THE FILES
320 END
```

The first subroutine (500) works with slight modification on any computer.

```
499 REM ** SUBROUTINE TO GET NAMES OF FILES **
500 HOME (or CLS)
510 DIM FILE$(2): REM * NAMES OF TWO INPUT FILES
520 FOR I = 1 TO 2
530 PRINT "NAME OF INPUT FILE #"; I
540 INPUT FILE$(I)
550 NEXT I
560 INPUT "NAME OF MERGED OUTPUT FILE   "; MRGD$
570 DIM X$(2): REM * ITEMS X$(I) WILL BE FROM INPUT FILE #I
580 RETURN
```

The disk-handling subroutines, as usual, are different for different computers. They illustrate how several files can be OPEN at the same time. Notice also how they use variables as file names (and thus the slightly different format in the OPEN, READ, WRITE, and CLOSE statements).

Apple

```
999  REM ** SUBROUTINE TO OPEN THE FILES **
1000 PRINT CHR$(4); "OPEN"; FILE$(1)
1010 PRINT CHR$(4); "OPEN"; FILE$(2)
1020 PRINT CHR$(4); "OPEN"; MRGD$
1030 RETURN
1499 REM ** SUBROUTINE TO READ X$(I) FROM INPUT FILE #I **
1500 PRINT CHR$(4); "READ"; FILE$(I)
1510 INPUT X$(I)
1520 PRINT CHR$(4): REM * CANCEL READ INSTRUCTION
1530 RETURN
1999 REM ** SUBROUTINE TO PUT X$(I) IN OUTPUT FILE **
2000 PRINT CHR$(4); "WRITE"; MRGD$
2010 PRINT X$(I)
2020 PRINT CHR$(4): REM * CANCEL WRITE INSTRUCTION
2030 RETURN
2499 REM ** SUBROUTINE TO CLOSE ALL FILES **
2500 PRINT CHR$(4); "CLOSE"; FILE$(1)
2510 PRINT CHR$(4); "CLOSE"; FILE$(2)
2520 PRINT CHR$(4); "CLOSE"; MRGD$
2530 RETURN
```

TRS-80 and IBM

```
999  REM ** SUBROUTINE TO OPEN THE FILES **
1000 OPEN "I", 1, FILE$(1)
1010 OPEN "I", 2, FILE$(2)
1020 OPEN "O", 3, MRGD$
1030 RETURN
1499 REM ** SUBROUTINE TO READ X$(I) FROM INPUT FILE #I **
1500 INPUT #I, X$(I)
1510 RETURN
1999 REM ** SUBROUTINE TO PUT X$(I) IN OUTPUT FILE **
2000 PRINT #3, X$(I) TRS-80      or      2000 WRITE #3, X$(I) IBM
2010 RETURN
```

Program continued on next page.

```
2499 REM ** SUBROUTINE TO CLOSE ALL FILES **
2500 CLOSE 1
2510 CLOSE 2
2520 CLOSE 3
2530 RETURN
```

Avoiding Pitfalls

1. When you use the techniques explained in this section to merge two files, be sure that both files are stored in alphabetical order and have trailer values. (You can also use the EOF technique explained in the Lab Activity on page 615.)
2. *(TRS-80* and *IBM)* When you have more than one file OPEN, be sure to assign each file a different buffer number. (To have more than three files OPEN at a time, you must tell the computer the number of buffers needed when BASIC is loaded into memory — see your computer's manual.)
3. *(Apple)* When more than one file is OPEN, be very careful to cancel WRITE and READ commands at appropriate times by using the instruction PRINT CHR$(4); otherwise, the data can easily be mixed up in the various files. (To have more than three files OPEN at a time, you must include in your program the instruction

   ```
   PRINT CHR$(4); "MAXFILES n"
   ```

   where *n* is the maximum number of files that will be OPEN at one time.)

Summary

To merge two input files (in alphabetical or numerical order) into a single output file (in alphabetical or numerical order):

Step 1 OPEN all three files.

Step 2 READ the first item from each input file.

Step 3 Compare the items to determine which one should be written first to the output file. Read the next item from the same input file.

Step 4 Continue to read and compare items from the files to be merged, writing the smaller item to the new file, until one of the trailer values is reached. Then transfer the rest of the data from the remaining file to the output file.

Step 5 CLOSE the files.

Exercises 11-5

A 1. Write the corresponding statement number(s) from Program 1 that accomplishes each of the following:

   a. OPENs the files to be merged;
   b. OPENs the file that will contain the merged data;
   c. Tests to determine which name is to be written to the merged file;
   d. Reads the next name from FILE #2 if the preceding name came from FILE #2;
   e. Writes the rest of FILE #1 to COMBO;
   f. CLOSEs each file.

2. Add another subroutine to Program 1 that PRINTs the merged file. Name the merged file COMBO.

3. Modify Program 1 to include two fields each in the two input files. Assume that the files are ordered with the first field as the key. Have the program store both fields in the merged file.

4. Change Program 1 so that it will merge three files that are each in alphabetical order.

5. Change Program 1 so that it reads the two input files into separate arrays, merges the two arrays into a single array, then writes the combined array to the disk.

6. Change Program 1 so that each record that is in FILE #1 only is put in the merged file, but all records that are in both input files are left out.

B 7. Another way to merge two files is to read all the data in the two files into an array (two arrays if there are two fields) and bubble (or Shell) sort on some key field. Write a program to merge the files REINDEER and HELPERS using this method. Do the original files have to be in alphabetical order to use this method?

8. Use the method of Exercise 7 to merge two files called RAND1 and RAND2. Assume that each of these files contains 20 random integers between 1 and 100. Have the program PRINT the merged file (in ascending order).

9. Write a program that will automatically update the file SLEIGH; both SLEIGH and another file, UPDATE, have name and telephone-number fields and are ordered according to the name field. Each name in UPDATE is to be found in SLEIGH and the telephone number in SLEIGH is to be changed to the one contained in UPDATE.

Lab Activity

Binary Files

(for use with *Apple* and *IBM* computers)

When you use the disk files described in this chapter, your computer's Disk Operating System (DOS) does a lot of work for you automatically. It sets up buffers, stores your data in them in the appropriate locations, and copies the buffers to the disk when they fill up. It is possible for you to have your program manage buffers directly by POKEing data directly into memory (see the Lab Activity for Section 11–1). The buffers can be transferred to and from your disk using special instructions. The resulting files are called *binary files* because as far as DOS is concerned, the data in them consists of nothing but binary numbers, with no special meaning as normal text characters or decimal numbers. Binary files use relatively little memory and the computer can handle them quickly. Of course, there are more details for the programmer to worry about, and therefore many more opportunities for bugs to creep into a program. The instructions for saving a binary file on disk vary.

Apple

The *Apple* DOS command to save a binary file on disk has the form

BSAVE *name*, A *location*, L *number*

where *name* is a legal file name (the same rules apply as for program and sequential file names), *location* is the base 10 address of the beginning of the file in memory, and *number* is the number of *bytes* (memory locations) in the file. (A is short for AT, and L stands for LENGTH.)

IBM

The IBM DOS command to save a binary file on disk has the form

BSAVE "*name*", *location*, *length*

where *name* is a legal file name (the same rules apply as for sequential file names), *location* is the base 10 address of the beginning of the file in memory, and *length* is the number of bytes (memory locations) in the file.

Problems

(Load DOS into memory before proceeding.)

1. Type and RUN the program at the top of the next page. The program POKEs the ASCII codes of the alphabet into memory starting at address 7000, then writes the file to disk.

```
   10 FOR I = 0 TO 25
   20 POKE 7000 + I, ASC("A") + I
   30 NEXT I
   40 PRINT CHR$(4); "BSAVE ALPHABET, A 7000, L 26" ←—— Apple
or 40 BSAVE "ALPHABET", 7000, 26 ←—— IBM
   50 END
```

Notice that when I = 0 in line 30, the ASCII code of the letter "A", which is 65, is put into location 7000 + 0 = 7000. When I = 1, the number ASC("A") + 1 = 66 is put into location 7000 + 1 = 7001, and so forth.

2. Type CATALOG *(Apple)* or FILES *(IBM)* to see that your file is on the disk. Now POKE some values other than 65 to 91 (such as 200) into a few locations between 7000 and 7025 to destroy the alphabet stored there by the program in Problem 1. (The purpose of this step is to make it clear that when the program below loads the alphabet from the disk, the letters that are in memory actually come from the binary file on the disk, and weren't just left over from the program in Problem 1.) Type and RUN the following program that reads the ALPHABET file back into memory and then PRINTs it on the screen.

```
   10 PRINT CHR$(4); "BLOAD ALPHABET" ←—— Apple
or 10 BLOAD "ALPHABET" ←—— IBM
   20 FOR I = 0 TO 25
   30 PRINT CHR$(PEEK(7000 + I)): REM * CHARACTER WITH
        ASCII CODE AT LOCATION 7000 + I
   40 NEXT I
   50 END
```

3. Write, type, and then RUN a program that INPUTs a string, POKEs it into memory starting at address 10000 (complete with trailer value 0), and then writes it to the disk. (See page 593, Problems 6 and 7.)

4. POKE some new values into locations 10000 and 10001 to destroy your message. Then write, type, and RUN a program to read the binary file created in Problem 3 into memory, and then PRINT it on the screen.

11-6 Random-Access Files

In the first section of this chapter another type of disk file was mentioned, the random-access file. Unlike sequential files, the records in random-access files can be written and read in any order. For example, if you want to retrieve the 15th record of a random-access file, you can do this directly, without first reading the prior 14 records. Random-access files tend to be longer than sequential files because all the records must be the same length (the same number of characters). For example, a file of names might be set up that allows 20 characters for each record. If a name consisting of 12 characters is put in the file, then the 8 remaining spaces are blank.

Apple Random-Access Files

On *Apple* computers, commands you are already familiar with — OPEN, WRITE, READ, and CLOSE — are used with random-access files in much the same way as they are used with sequential files. The only difference is that the commands now must include such information as the record number and the length of each record.

OPENING A RANDOM-ACCESS FILE

The OPEN statement for a random-access file is the same as for a sequential file except that the length of each record in the file must be specified. For example, the following statement OPENS a random-access file PRICING, which the owner of a grocery store might use to store the names and prices of some grocery items:

```
20  PRINT CHR$(4); "OPEN PRICING, L25"
```

The number 25 following the letter L (short for *Length*) tells the computer that the records of the file are 25 characters long. This means that each record of PRICING can contain a maximum of 25 characters, including spaces and a carriage return character (a < RETURN > key press) at the end of each field. (Each digit of a number counts as one character.) Here is an illustration showing how the records of PRICING might be stored on the disk (of course, the data is actually stored as binary digits):

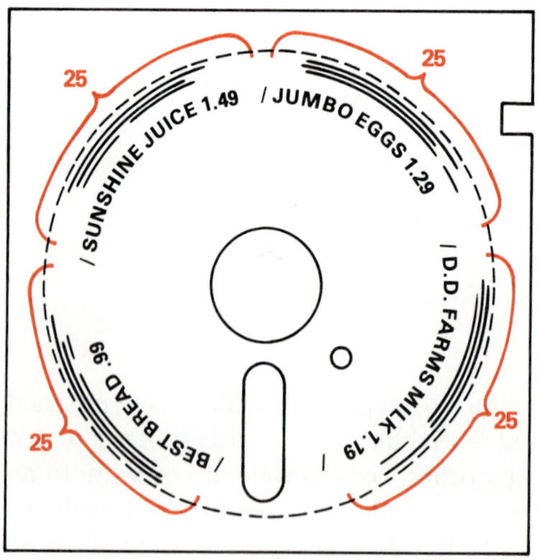

As you can see, each record has space for 25 characters even though none of the records shown uses all 25. When specifying the length of the records in the OPEN statement, keep in mind that each field ends with a < RETURN > character (ASCII code 13), which takes one space in the record.

WRITING DATA TO A RANDOM-ACCESS FILE

The WRITE statement for a random-access file is the same as for a sequential file except that a record number must be added to the end of the statement. For example, the statement

```
200  PRINT CHR$(4); "WRITE PRICING, R16"
```

directs the output of following PRINT statements to record number 16 of the file PRICING. If you want to use a variable, say NUM, to indicate the record numbers, then the statement has this form:

```
200  PRINT CHR$(4); "WRITE PRICING, R"; NUM
```

CLOSING A RANDOM-ACCESS FILE

The CLOSE statement for a random-access file is exactly the same as for a sequential file. Here is a program to set up the random-access file PRICING, in which each record after the first has two fields, a name field and a price field. Because individual records of a random-access file are easy to access, it is convenient to use the first record to store the number of records in the file.

Program 1

Statement

```
10  REM * PROGRAM TO SET UP RANDOM FILE PRICING
20  PRINT CHR$(4); "OPEN PRICING, L25": REM * RECORD LENGTH 25
30  INPUT "TYPE NO. OF RECORDS TO STORE:  "; REC
40  PRINT CHR$(4); "WRITE PRICING, R1": REM * FIRST RECORD IS NO. OF RECORDS
50  PRINT REC
60  PRINT CHR$(4): REM * STOP WRITING TO DISK
70  FOR K = 2 TO REC + 1: REM * REC RECORDS TO STORE (2 FIELDS EACH)
80  INPUT "TYPE ITEM:  "; ITEM$
90  INPUT "TYPE PRICE:  "; PRICE
100  PRINT CHR$(4); "WRITE PRICING, R"; K
110  PRINT ITEM$
120  PRINT PRICE
130  PRINT CHR$(4): REM * STOP WRITING TO DISK
140  NEXT K
```

Program continued on next page.

```
150 PRINT CHR$(4); "CLOSE PRICING"
160 PRINT "ALL RECORDS STORED"
170 END
```

Output

```
TYPE NO. OF RECORDS TO STORE:   ? 4
TYPE ITEM:   ? BEST BREAD
TYPE PRICE:   ? .99
TYPE ITEM:   ? SUNSHINE JUICE
TYPE PRICE:   ? 1.49
TYPE ITEM:   ? JUMBO EGGS
TYPE PRICE:   ? 1.29
TYPE ITEM:   ? D.D. FARMS MILK
TYPE PRICE:   ? 1.19
ALL RECORDS STORED
```

Since the number of records in the file was stored as the first record (lines 30–50), the counter K (line 70) had to go from 2 to REC + 1 instead of from 1 to REC in order to write REC records into the file. The technique of storing the number of records can be used instead of trailer values to control the number of records to be placed in the file. With this technique, the file can be changed easily.

In Program 1, notice that each record of a random-access file is like a short sequential file in that it may consist of several fields, each created by a separate PRINT statement, as in lines 110 and 120.

READING A RANDOM-ACCESS FILE

The READ statement for a random-access file is the same as for a sequential file except that the number of the record to be read must be added to the end of the statement. For example, the statement

```
50 PRINT CHR$(4); "READ PRICING, R1"
```

will read the data stored in record number 1 when the next INPUT statement is encountered. It is also possible to use a variable for the record number, as in

```
50 PRINT CHR$(4); "READ PRICING, R"; J
```

where J represents the number of the record from which data is to be read. This instruction directs the computer to take as the next INPUTs the fields of record J.

Program 2 at the top of the next page lets the user read any record from the file PRICING.

Program 2

Statement

```
10  REM * PROGRAM TO READ ANY RECORD OF PRICING
20  PRINT CHR$(4); "OPEN PRICING, L25"
30  PRINT CHR$(4); "READ PRICING, R1": REM * READ FIRST RECORD
40  INPUT REC: REM * NUMBER OF RECORDS IN THE FILE
50  PRINT CHR$(4): REM * CANCEL READING
60  INPUT "WHICH RECORD DO YOU WANT:   "; NUM
70  IF NUM < 1 OR NUM > REC THEN PRINT "NO SUCH RECORD": GOTO 60
80  PRINT CHR$(4); "READ PRICING, R"; NUM
90  INPUT ITEM$: REM * FIRST FIELD OF RECORD NUM
100  INPUT PRICE: REM * SECOND FIELD OF RECORD NUM
110  PRINT CHR$(4): REM * CANCEL READING
120  PRINT "RECORD #"; NUM: "  IS:   "; ITEM$; "    "; PRICE
130  PRINT CHR$(4); "CLOSE PRICING"
140  END
```

Output

```
WHICH RECORD DO YOU WANT:   ? 3
RECORD #3 IS:   SUNSHINE JUICE   1.49

RUN
WHICH RECORD DO YOU WANT:   ? 2
RECORD #2 IS:   BEST BREAD   .99
```

As you learned earlier in this chapter, when you are using a sequential file you cannot read a record, make changes in it, and write it back to the disk file immediately. Instead, the usual updating procedure is to read the entire file into an array, change individual elements of the array, and then write the array back to the disk. With random-access files, however, you can mix the reading and writing processes. For example, if you add the following lines to Program 2, the record read in will be changed on the disk:

```
122  PRINT CHR$(4); "WRITE PRICING, R"; NUM
124  PRINT "STORE BRAND"
126  PRINT PRICE —.25
135  PRINT "RUN THE PROGRAM AGAIN TO SEE NEW RECORD"
```

Do you see that these lines change the record so that it contains the reduced price (a 25 cents savings) of the store brand?

TRS-80 and IBM Random-Access Files

On *TRS-80* and *IBM* computers, the process of setting up a random-access file is somewhat more complicated than setting up a sequential file:

Step 1 OPEN the file: Use the OPEN statement to specify a random-access file, the buffer number, the file name, and the lengths of the records in the file.

Step 2 Write data to the disk:

a. Use the FIELD statement to indicate the names and lengths of the fields.
b. Use the LSET statement to transfer data from the program into the buffer.
c. Use the PUT statement to transfer data from the buffer to the disk file.

Step 3 CLOSE the file.

OPENING A RANDOM-ACCESS FILE

The OPEN statement for a random-access file is similar to that for a sequential file except that the letter "R" (for *R*andom) is used after OPEN, and the length of the records in the file is specified at the end. For example, here is the statement to OPEN a file called PRICING, which the owner of a grocery store might use to store the names and prices of some items:

```
20  OPEN "R", 1, "PRICING", 30
```

The number 30 at the end of this OPEN statement tells the computer that the records of the file are 30 characters long. This means that each record of PRICING can contain a maximum of 30 characters, including spaces and a carriage return character (an < ENTER > key press) at the end of each field. Unlike sequential files, random-access files store all information as strings. Therefore, all numeric data must be converted to strings (using STR$) before being stored. Here is an illustration showing how the records of PRICING might be stored on the disk (stored as binary digits, of course):

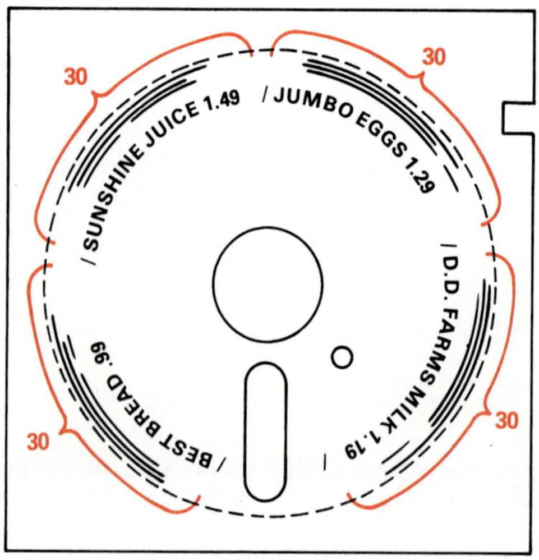

As you can see, each record has space for 30 characters, even though none of the records shown uses the full 30 characters.

WRITING DATA TO A RANDOM-ACCESS FILE

The first step in sending data to the disk is to give the name and specify the length of each field in the file. This is done with the FIELD statement. Here is a FIELD statement for our grocery store example:

```
30  FIELD 1, 20 AS NAM$, 10 AS PRICE$
```

This statement sets aside the first 20 character spaces of each record in buffer 1 for the string variable NAM$, and the next 10 spaces for the variable PRICE$. NAM$ now represents the name field and PRICE$ the price field of each record. Since random-access files can store only strings, all of the variables in the FIELD statement *must* be string variables.

After the buffer has been "fielded," the next step in sending data to the disk is to use the LSET statement to transfer data from the program into the buffer. For example, if we want to send the data B$ = "BEST BREAD" and C$ = ".99" into the current record of the buffer, we can use these LSET statements:

```
70  LSET NAM$ = B$
80  LSET PRICE$ = C$
```

In line 70, the string B$ is placed into the buffer in the field NAM$; in line 80, C$ is placed into the field PRICE$. The LSET statement places characters into the buffer starting at the left, adding blank spaces on the right to make sure that the string properly fits the space specified in the FIELD statement. For example, the string BEST BREAD in line 70 above uses 10 character spaces, so 10 blank spaces need to be added to bring the total to 20, the number specified in the FIELD statement. The LSET statement will drop off extra characters from the right end of a string that has too many characters to fit in the available space.

The final step in sending data to the disk is to use the PUT statement to transfer the contents of the buffer to the disk. For example, the statement

```
90  PUT 1, 3
```

will cause the strings (fields) assigned by the preceding LSET statements (BEST BREAD and .99, in our example) to be stored as record number 3. The number 1 after PUT is the buffer number.

CLOSING A RANDOM-ACCESS FILE

The CLOSE statement for a random-access file is exactly the same as for a sequential file.

Here is a program to set up the random-access file PRICING. Each record of the file has two fields, a name field and a price field. Because individual records of a random-access file are easy to access, it is convenient to use the first record to store the number of records in the file. The first record, therefore, will use only the name field to store the number of records (in string form). The price field of the first record will be filled with blank spaces.

Program 1

Statement

```
10  REM * PROGRAM TO SET UP RANDOM FILE PRICING
20  OPEN "R", 1, "PRICING", 30: REM * RANDOM-ACCESS FILE/RECORD LENGTH 30
30  FIELD 1, 20 AS NAM$, 10 AS PRICE$: REM * SPECIFY FIELD NAMES AND LENGTHS
40  INPUT "TYPE NO. OF RECORDS TO STORE:  "; REC
50  LET X$ = STR$(REC): REM * CONVERT REC TO A STRING
60  LSET NAM$ = X$: REM * MOVE NAM$ TO BUFFER
70  PUT 1, 1: REM * FIRST RECORD IS NO. OF RECORDS
80  FOR K = 2 TO REC + 1: REM * REC RECORDS TO STORE
90  INPUT "TYPE ITEM:  "; ITEM$
100  INPUT "TYPE PRICE:  "; CST$
110  LSET NAM$ = ITEM$: REM * MOVE NAME TO BUFFER
120  LSET PRICE$ = CST$: REM * MOVE PRICE TO BUFFER
130  PUT 1, K: REM * STORE FIELDS IN RECORD NO. K
140  NEXT K
150  CLOSE 1
160  PRINT "ALL RECORDS STORED"
170  END
```

Output

```
TYPE NO. OF RECORDS TO STORE:  ? 3
TYPE ITEM:  ? BEST BREAD
TYPE PRICE:  ? .99
TYPE ITEM:  ? SUNSHINE JUICE
TYPE PRICE:  ? 1.49
TYPE ITEM:  ? JUMBO EGGS
TYPE PRICE:  ? 1.29
ALL RECORDS STORED
```

The number of records typed by the user (line 40) is converted to a string in line 50, and then is stored as the first record by the LSET and PUT statements in lines 60 and 70. Therefore, the counter K in line 80 must go from the value

2 to REC + 1 instead of from 1 to REC in order to send REC records to the file. The technique of storing the number of records as the first record can be used instead of trailer values to control the number of records to be placed in the file. With this technique, the file can be changed easily.

READING A RANDOM-ACCESS FILE

To read data from a random-access file, the file must first be OPENed and its fields set up by a FIELD statement. Data is transferred from the disk to the buffer by the GET command. For example, the program fragment

```
700  OPEN "R", 3, "CRAZY", 25
710  FIELD 3, 10 AS FUN$, 15 AS HAHA$
720  GET 3, 16
```

reads the 16th record of the file CRAZY into buffer number 3. It assigns the first 10 characters of the record to FUN$ and the next 15 to HAHA$. Here is a program that lets the user read any record from the file PRICING:

Program 2

Statement

```
10  REM * PROGRAM TO READ ANY RECORD OF PRICING
20  OPEN "R", 2, "PRICING", 30
30  FIELD 2, 20 AS NAM$, 10 AS PRICE$
40  GET 2, 1: REM * GET FIRST RECORD
50  LET REC = VAL(NAM$): REM * CONVERT TO NUMBER
60  INPUT "WHICH RECORD DO YOU WANT:  "; NUM
70  IF NUM < 1 OR NUM > REC THEN PRINT "NO SUCH RECORD": GOTO 60
80  GET 2, NUM: REM * GET RECORD NO. NUM INTO NAM$, PRICE$
90  PRINT "RECORD #"; NUM; " IS: "; NAM$; "  "; PRICE$
100  CLOSE 2
110  END
```

Output

```
WHICH RECORD DO YOU WANT:  ? 3
RECORD # 3 IS: SUNSHINE JUICE 1.49
```

Notice that the variables NAM$ and PRICE$ specified in the FIELD statement may be used as ordinary string variables (see lines 50 and 90). The GET statement assigns them their values from the file. As you learned earlier in this chapter, when you are using a sequential file you cannot read a record, make changes in it, and write it back to the disk file immediately. Instead, the usual updating procedure is to read the entire file into an array, change individual elements of the array, and then write the array back to the disk.

With random-access files, however, you can mix the reading and writing processes. For example, if you add the following lines to Program 2, the record read in will be changed on the disk:

```
92  LSET NAM$ = "STORE BRAND"
94  LSET PRICE$ = STR$(VAL(PRICE$) — .25)
96  PUT 2, NUM
105  PRINT "RUN THE PROGRAM AGAIN TO SEE NEW RECORD"
```

Do you see that line 94 reduces the price by 25 cents?

Avoiding Pitfalls

1. When typing a program to set up or read a random-access file, be careful to type the correct punctuation. If an error does occur, CLOSE the file (as an immediate mode command) before debugging the program. Otherwise, a bad file may result.
2. When working with a random-access file, be sure that the total number of characters in a record does not exceed the length specified in the OPEN statement. Otherwise, part of your data may be destroyed.

Summary

Apple

The statements needed to open a random-access file, write data to the disk, and close the file are of this form:

```
  .
  .
  .
120  PRINT CHR$(4); "OPEN file name, L number" ←—— Number is the
  .                                                record length.
  .
  .
160  PRINT CHR$(4); "WRITE file name, R"; K ←——Causes subsequent
170  PRINT variable                              PRINT statements to
180  PRINT variable                              send data to record
  .                                              number K.
  .
  .
210  PRINT CHR$(4); "CLOSE file name"
```

To read data from a random-access file, change the WRITE command to READ in line 160, and change the PRINT commands in lines 170 and 180 to INPUT commands.

TRS-80 and IBM

The statements needed to open a random-access file, write records (with two fields, represented by A$ and B$) to the disk, and close the file are of this form:

```
.
.
.
110 OPEN "R", buffer number, "file name", number ←—— Number is the
                                                       record length.
120 FIELD buffer number, length AS A$, length AS B$ ←—— Specifies field
.                                                          names and
.                                                          sets length.
.
170 LSET A$ = string variable ⎫
180 LSET B$ = string variable ⎭ ←—— Sends data to the buffer.
190 PUT buffer number, K ←—— Stores fields in LSET statements in record
.                            number K.
.
.
230 CLOSE buffer number
```

To read data from a random-access file, change the PUT command in line 190 to GET. The LSET statements in lines 170 and 180 are no longer needed and may be deleted.

Exercises 11-6

A **1.** Write an OPEN statement to set up each of the following random-access files:

a. A file called CLASS, in which each record contains a single field: the name of a student in your computer class (maximum name length 18).

b. A file called PARTY, in which each record contains these two fields: a person's last name (maximum length 12), and his or her date of birth (in the string form month/day/year).

c. A file called INV (short for INVentory), in which each record contains these three fields: a part number (maximum length 5), a description of the part (maximum length 30), and the number currently in stock (maximum length 3).

d. (*TRS-80* and *IBM*) Write a FIELD statement for each of the files in (a) through (c).

2. Change Program 1 for your computer so that it continues to INPUT information from the user and to put it in the file until the double trailer value NOTHING, 00 is typed. Do not store the number of records as the first record, but include the double trailer value as the last record.

3. Change Program 2 for your computer so that it continues to INPUT record numbers and retrieve data until the user types −1.

4. a. Change Program 1 for your computer so that the records include a third field: a number to indicate in which aisle the item is located (maximum length 2).

   b. Change Program 2 for your computer so that it reads records from the file created in part (a).

5. Change Program 2 for your computer so that it reads all the records of the file and stores the fields in two arrays. Then have the program sort the file with the name field as the key.

B

6. a. Write a program to set up a random-access file called POEM. Have the program INPUT eight records, each of which contains a single string that is one line from your favorite poem (maximum length 40).

   b. Write a program to read and PRINT all eight records of the file POEM.

7. a. Write a program to set up a random-access file called ZIP. Have the program INPUT records containing these two fields: the names of streets in a large city (maximum length 20), and the Zip Codes for the streets (length 5). The first record should store the number of records.

   b. Write a program to search ZIP for an INPUT street name. If the street is found, then PRINT the corresponding Zip Code. Otherwise, PRINT the message NO SUCH STREET. (*Hint:* A random-access file is like a large array on disk, with record numbers in place of subscripts.)

8. Write a program to read records of a random-access file called CAR, which was created by an automobile dealer. Assume that the file contains 100 records and that the first record stores the number of records. Each record after the first contains these three fields: the car's make (maximum length 15), the year (length 4), and the color (maximum length 10). Have the program INPUT record numbers and PRINT the corresponding data, continuing until −1 is typed. Use error trapping to reject INPUT record numbers for which there are no records.

9. a. Write a program that reads all the records of a random-access file called TOURIST and stores the fields in arrays. Assume that the first record stores the number of records. Each record contains these four fields: a state's name, its annual income from tourism, the season when most tourists visit, and its major tourist attraction. (You decide on an appropriate record length.) Have the program sort the file with the state-name field as the key.

b. Modify the program in Exercise 9(a) so that when a user (say, a travel agent) INPUTs the name of a state, the program does a binary search, then PRINTs the information about tourism in that state.

10. Write a program to add an INPUT number of records to the end of the file PRICING of Program 1.

11. a. Write a program to delete an INPUT record from the file PRICING of Program 1.

b. Modify Program 2 so that if the user types the number of a deleted record, an appropriate message is PRINTed.

c. Change the program in (a) so that it replaces the deleted record by the last record in the file (and of course changes record number 1 appropriately).

C **12.** A random-access file can be sorted by first reading it into arrays. However, practical files are often too big to fit in the memory of any reasonable-sized computer. Treating the file as a kind of large array on disk, you can sort directly on the disk, using the computer's memory only for comparisons and interchanges. Write a program using this technique to perform a bubble sort on the name field of the file PRICING. (*Hint:* To compare record number I with record number I + 1, read the two records into two sets of variables, such as N1$, P1 for record number I and N2$, P2 for record number I + 1. If these two records need to be switched, this is easily accomplished by writing N2$, P2 to record number I + 1 and N1$, P1 to record number I.)

13. Change Program 2 for your computer so that if the user types in the name of an item, the program finds (if possible) the item in the file, then updates the price according to the user's wishes.

Lab Activity

Linked Files: an Alternative to Sorting

(for use with *Apple* computers)

For many data processing applications, files must be kept in alphabetical order. Sorting is very time-consuming, especially if the files are long. Disk access is relatively slow, so that files too big for the memory of the computer take a particularly long time to sort. Sorting can be avoided if the file can be kept in order as new data is being added. This is easily accomplished; when a new record is to be added, its alphabetical place in the file is found by a linear or binary search of the file for a matching record. If no match is found, at least the place where the new item should be inserted has been located. For example, suppose that a simple random-access file GROCERY contains the following items:

record number	*item*
1	APPLE
2	TURKEY
3	VEGETABLE SOUP

To add the item PARSLEY, a program can perform a search, ending up with "APPLE" < "PARSLEY" but "PARSLEY" < "TURKEY", so that the new item should be inserted between record #1 and record #2. (Record #1 is called the *predecessor* of PARSLEY, and record #2 is its *successor.*) What must be done, of course, is to move TURKEY and VEGETABLE SOUP down one position each (to record #3 and record #4, respectively), and put PARSLEY in the newly-vacated record #2. But moving all those records down is exactly what takes so much time in a sort!

One way to avoid time-consuming moving of records is to add another field to each record, called the *link* field. The link for a given record is simply the record number of the alphabetically next record (that is, of its successor). For example, in the GROCERY file (before PARSLEY is added), the link for record #1 is 2, since record #2 comes alphabetically right after record #1. (That is, record #2 is the *successor* of record #1.) The link for record #2 is 3, since record #3 is the *successor* of record #2, and so forth:

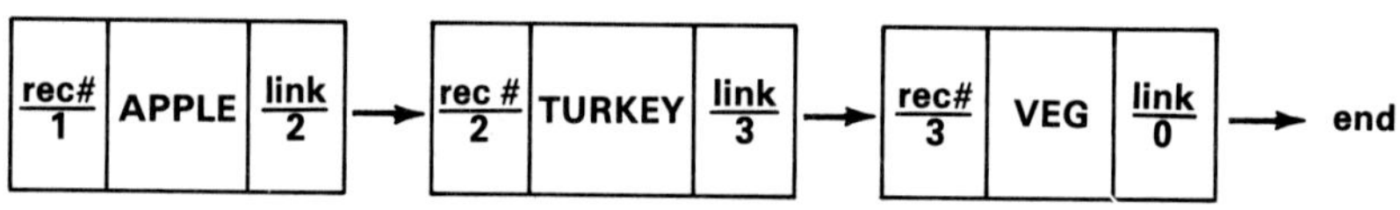

(The link for record #3 is set to 0 because VEGETABLE SOUP has no successor in the file.) To add PARSLEY to the file without moving any records, we simply put it in record #4 and change one link; APPLE's link will become 4, since PARSLEY is now the successor of APPLE. What is PARSLEY's link? The successor of PARSLEY is TURKEY, so PARSLEY's link will be 2:

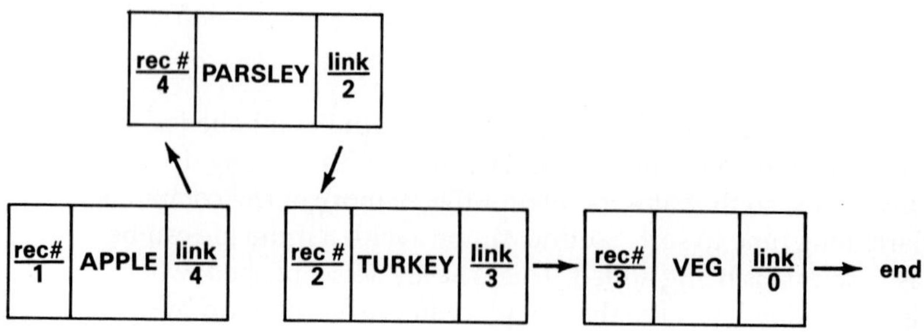

The insertion process for a linked file, then, involves first finding the predecessor and successor of the item to be inserted. The item is put in the next available record at the end of the file. Its link is the old link of its predecessor (PARSLEY took APPLE's old link). Its predecessor gets a new link, namely the record number where the new item is inserted.

It may have occurred to you that an item to be inserted may have no predecessor. (For example, the item ALMONDS belongs at the beginning of the file.) A related question is: in performing an alphabetical search, how does the program know where to start? After all, the first item in the file will not always be alphabetically first. To solve this difficulty, it is necessary to have a special record in the file that contains the link to the alphabetically first item in the file. We will use record #0.

We can also put in record #0 the number of records currently in the file, as is usually done with random-access files. Thus, *before* PARSLEY is added, record #0 will contain the following:

record #0: link = 1, number of records = 3

After PARSLEY is added, record #0 will contain these values:

record #0: link = 1, number of records = 4

What will happen if we add ALMONDS to the file? It will be put into record #5, as explained earlier. Its link will become the old link of record #0, since APPLE (the old first item) is its successor. The new link of record #0 will become 5 because ALMONDS is a new first item in the file:

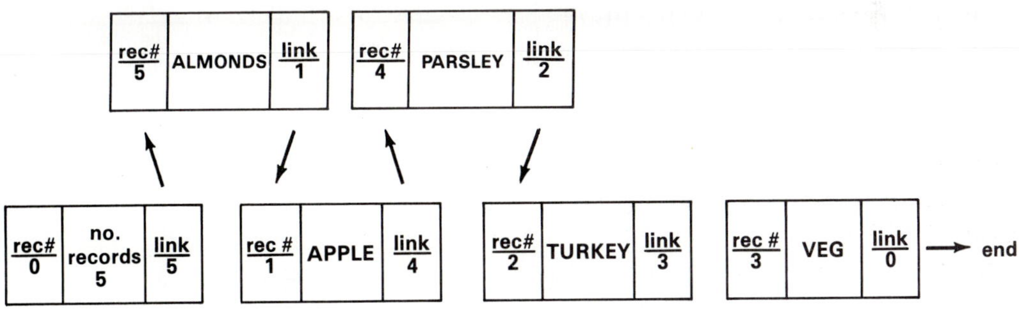

Problems

1. Work out in a diagram how the GROCERY file shown above will look after SQUASH is added.
2. How will the GROCERY file diagrammed in Problem 1 look after the string ZUCCHINI is added?

3. Type and then RUN the following program that simply puts an empty GROCERY file on your disk. (Record #0 will indicate a 0 link and 0 records in the file.)

```
10  PRINT CHR$(4); "OPEN GROCERY, L25"
20  PRINT CHR$(4); "WRITE GROCERY, R0": REM * RECORD #0
30  PRINT 0: REM * LINK TO NON-EXISTENT SUCCESSOR
40  PRINT 0: REM * NUMBER OF RECORDS IN FILE
50  PRINT CHR$(4); "CLOSE GROCERY"
60  END
```

4. Type and RUN the following program that allows you to add items to the GROCERY file. Notice in the program that a linear search is carried out in subroutine 1000; the variable START (line 1010) is the link to the alphabetically first item in the file. At all times in the search, the variable PRED is the candidate for the record number of the predecessor of the inserted item, and the variable SUCC is the candidate for the record number of the successor.

   When a possible successor item from the file (line 1060) is still beyond the inserted item (TARGT$), then the program moves forward in the file in this way: It makes the new predecessor be the old successor, and the new successor be the successor of the current file item (lines 1100 and 1110). The actual insertion of the new item is carried out in subroutine 1500. The links are adjusted as outlined in the previous discussion.

```
10  PRINT CHR$(4); "OPEN GROCERY, L25"
20  INPUT "ITEM (ZZZZ TO END):  "; TARGT$
30  IF TARGT$ = "ZZZZ" THEN GOTO 70
40  GOSUB 1000: REM * FIND RECORD NUMBER PRED OF PREDECESSOR,
       RECORD NUMBER SUCC OF SUCCESSOR
50  GOSUB 1500: REM * PUT NEW ITEM ON FILE
60  GOTO 20
70  PRINT CHR$(4); "CLOSE GROCERY"
80  END
990  REM ** SUBROUTINE TO FIND PREDECESSOR AND SUCCESSOR **
1000  PRINT CHR$(4); "READ GROCERY, R0": REM * GET SPECIAL RECORD
1010  INPUT START: REM * LINK TO ALPHABETICALLY FIRST RECORD
1020  LET PRED = 0: REM * NO PREDECESSOR YET
1030  LET SUCC = START: REM * LINK TO POSSIBLE SUCCESSOR
1040  INPUT REC: REM * NUMBER OF RECORDS
1050  IF SUCC = 0 THEN GOTO 1130: REM * AT END OF FILE
1060  PRINT CHR$(4); "READ GROCERY, R"; SUCC: REM * GET NEXT RECORD
```

```
1070 INPUT LINK
1080 INPUT ITEM$
1090 IF TARGT$ < ITEM$ THEN GOTO 1130: REM * PASSED TARGET, FOUND
        POSITION ON FILE
1100 LET PRED = SUCC: REM * MOVE FORWARD
1110 LET SUCC = LINK
1120 GOTO 1050
1130 RETURN

1490 REM ** SUBROUTINE TO ADD NEW RECORD AND LINKS **
1500 LET REC = REC + 1: REM * ONE MORE RECORD
1520 IF PRED = 0 THEN LET START = REC: GOTO 1590: REM * IF NO
        PREDECESSOR, THIS IS NEW FIRST RECORD
1530 PRINT CHR$(4); "READ GROCERY, R"; PRED: REM * GET PREDECESSOR
        RECORD
1540 INPUT X: REM * OLD LINK; DISCARD
1550 INPUT ITEM$
1560 PRINT CHR$(4); "WRITE GROCERY, R"; PRED: REM * PUT LINK TO NEW
        RECORD
1570 PRINT REC: REM * PRINTS TO NEW RECORD
1580 PRINT ITEM$: REM * PUT ITEM BACK IN
1590 PRINT CHR$(4); "WRITE GROCERY, R"; REC: REM * PUT NEW RECORD
        AT END OF FILE
1600 PRINT SUCC: REM * LINK TO SUCCESSOR
1610 PRINT TARGT$: REM * NEW ITEM
1620 PRINT CHR$(4); "WRITE GROCERY, R0": REM * PUT NEW INFO IN
        RECORD #0
1630 PRINT START: REM * LINK TO ALPHABETICALLY FIRST ITEM
1640 PRINT REC: REM * NUMBER OF RECORDS
1650 PRINT CHR$(4): REM * CANCEL WRITE
1660 RETURN
```

5. Write a program to read the file GROCERY and PRINT it in alphabetical order. (See subroutine 1000 for *hints* on how to accomplish this. Note that the file is done when the next LINK is 0.)

6. *Challenge:* Write a program to allow deletions from the file GROCERY. (*Hint:* INPUT from the user an item name. Find a match by doing a linear search, following the links as in subroutine 1000. Then move the physically — not alphabetically — last item in the file into the newly-vacated space and adjust all the necessary links.) Test your program thoroughly.

Chapter Summary

A data file that is stored on a disk is called a *disk file.* The information in a disk file can be used in any number of different programs without retyping it. A *sequential file* is a file in which the records are recorded and retrieved in order one after another. A *random-access file* is a file in which the records may be recorded and retrieved in any order.

APPLE SEQUENTIAL FILES

The statements needed to open an *Apple* sequential disk file, record (write) data, and close the file are summarized on page 599. The statements needed to read data from the disk file are summarized on page 611.

TRS-80 AND IBM SEQUENTIAL FILES

On these computers, the statements needed to open a sequential disk file, send data to the disk, and to close the file are summarized on page 599. The statements needed to read the data are summarized on page 611.

Altering a file that ends with a *trailer value* is most easily accomplished by reading the file into one or more arrays (one per field), then manipulating the data in the array(s), and finally writing the data back to the disk.

To *merge* two ordered input files into a single ordered output file:

Step 1 OPEN all three files.
Step 2 Read the first item from each input file.
Step 3 Compare the items to determine which one should be written first to the output file. Read the next item from the same input file.
Step 4 Continue to read and compare items from the files to be merged, writing the smaller item to the new file, until one of the trailer values is reached. Then transfer the rest of the data from the remaining file to the output file.
Step 5 CLOSE the files.

APPLE RANDOM-ACCESS FILES

The statements needed to open an *Apple* random-access file, write data to the disk, read data from the disk, and close the file are summarized on page 644.

TRS-80 AND IBM RANDOM-ACCESS FILES

On these computers, the statements needed to open a random-access file, write data to the disk, read data from the disk, and close the file are summarized on page 645.

Chapter Test

1. Answer questions (a)–(g) below for the program listed for your computer.

Apple

```
10 PRINT CHR$(4); "OPEN HEAR"
20 PRINT CHR$(4); "READ HEAR"
30 FOR M = 1 TO 4
40 INPUT K(M)
50 NEXT M
60 PRINT CHR$(4); "CLOSE HEAR"
70 END
```

IBM and TRS-80

```
10 OPEN "I", 1, "HEAR"
20 FOR T = 1 TO 4
30 INPUT #1, K(T)
40 NEXT T
50 CLOSE 1
60 END
```

a. What is the name of the sequential file?
b. What type of data is stored in the file?
c. How many records are stored in the file?
d. *(Apple)* Explain the purpose of the statement in line 20.
e. *(TRS-80* and *IBM)* Explain the purpose of the letter "I" in line 10.
f. *(Apple)* Explain the purpose of the statement in line 40.
g. *(TRS-80* and *IBM)* Explain the purpose of the statement in line 30.

2. Write the program that reads data from a sequential file called TV, then PRINTs the data. Assume that TV contains the names of 5 favorite television programs and that it was created using a FOR . . . NEXT loop.

3. Write a program that READs data from a sequential file called POETRY, loads the data into arrays, then PRINTs the data. Assume that POETRY contains fields in this order: first, the poet's name; then the name of the poem; and then the first line (verse) of the poem. The first record of POETRY contains the number of records stored in the file.

4. Write a program that will add records to a pre-existing sequential file called ELEVATE, then PRINT the extended file. Assume that ELEVATE contains the names of famous magicians and has the trailer value XXXX stored at the end of the file.

5. A bank officer wants to find out if there is any duplication of account numbers in recent accounts opened at two branch offices. Write a program to merge the account numbers stored in two sequential files, say BRANCH1 and BRANCH2. Assume that each account number is a 9-digit string and that both files are stored in ascending order.

6. Write a program to create a random-access file called KITE that keeps track of the inventory of a kite stop. Have the program INPUT records containing these 3 fields: type of kite (maximum length 12), manufacturer's name (maximum length 20), and current number in stock (maximum length 3). The first record should store the number of records.

"Chaining" Computers

Microcomputers are having a major impact on businesses throughout the world. Whether these types of computers are being used for word processing, financial analysis, data processing, or for presenting information graphically, their ease of use has made them the choice of office managers, particularly those who might be overwhelmed by the complexity of bigger mainframe computers. In most large companies, virtually all important business data is stored on "hard" disks used with mainframe computer systems. The transmitting of this data from the mainframe computer's data bank to the microcomputers in a company's local business centers, and then back to the mainframe computer, can be accomplished through a *computer network.* A computer network is set up by connecting or "chaining" computers to allow the transfer of information. The components of a network may consist of large mainframe computers, minicomputers, microcomputers, and video display terminals, all electronically linked together. Vast quantities of information can be input, stored, processed, output, and shared.

Telephone modem and output devices

School computers are often networked.

Forming a Network

One way that computers can be connected to form a network is directly through electrical wires. (This is called *hard-wiring.*) If all the computers are in the same room, or even in the same building, they are frequently connected in this manner. In many school computer labs, computers are connected by hard-wiring.

Another way that computers can be networked is to have them communicate through telephone lines or satellites. Computers networked in this way usually require an additional piece of equipment called a *modem.* A modem (*mo*dulator/*dem*odulator) is a coupling device that converts computer signals (data) into high-frequency signals, which allows computer-to-computer communication over a telephone line. The rate of speed at which the information is transmitted or received is called the *baud rate.* A baud rate of 1200, for example, indicates that 1200 *bits* (binary digits) per second are being transmitted or received. Common baud rates for today's computers range from 110 to 9600.

Besides a modem, some type of software (program) is needed to support the use of the modem. This program usually directs the computers to say "hello" to each other. Once this is done, users can then retrieve information to process or create new information to be stored or output to a printer.

Methods of Networking

A computer network can be set up in different ways. One method involves connecting the computers so that they operate from a central "control" computer (a mainframe, perhaps) that receives and transmits all data within the network. One advantage to this arrangement is that if any computer other than the control computer breaks down, the rest of the network can continue to operate. The disadvantage, of course, is that if the control computer "goes down," then the entire network fails.

A second method of arranging a network is to connect the computers in a circular fashion, resulting in a closed loop. This type of network does not use a control computer; however, if any computer in the loop malfunctions, the whole network breaks down.

In a third type of computer network, only a limited number of computers at one time are allowed to use the lines. With this arrangement, certain computers are often given priority to receive or send data before any others, or blocks of time are scheduled so that different computers in the network have priority at different times.

Networking Home Computers

Large businesses are not the only ones who form and use computer networks. Home computer owners can connect to a network using a telephone modem. There are many companies that sell information and services through computer networks. These commercial data bases provide news, weather, sports information, financial information (including stock price quotes), and reference sources. Computer networks also provide services such as catalog shopping and home banking. Thus, home computer owners can take advantage of the extremely large data banks of mainframe computers.

Networks can send stock-price quotes.

Computer Languages — APL

APL was developed by Kenneth E. Iverson in the late 1950's while he was teaching at Harvard. APL was first published in 1962 in a book entitled *A Programming Language.* IBM first used APL in 1966 in its time-sharing system for the IBM/360 computer. Since that time, APL has been used by many different computer companies with a variety of computer systems.

APL is a concise and compact language that uses symbols common to algebra, but the language also contains many useful functions that cannot be expressed with conventional mathematical symbols. Therefore, a special keyboard designed specifically for APL is needed:

Notice on the keyboard that the numbers and alphabetical characters are in the usual positions, but there are many additional symbols not ordinarily found on a regular typewriter. These symbols are specific to the APL language.

In APL, as in BASIC, there are two modes of operation: immediate mode and program mode. In immediate mode, APL works like a powerful hand-held calculator. As soon as an APL expression is typed and entered, the computer gives an immediate response. Here are some examples:

	APL Command	*Output*
1.	2 3 ρ 2 1 5 3 7 4	2 1 5 3 7 4
2.	4 ⌈ 7	7
3.	4 ⌊ 7	4
4.	5 0 –22 15 ⌈ 3 7 8 2	5 7 8 15
5.	+ / 2 4 3 7 5 6 8	35
6.	? 6	3

In the first example, the symbol ρ *(rho)* is used to set up a *matrix,* (a rectangular array of numbers). In this case, the numbers to the left of ρ indicate the number of rows (2) and columns (3) in the matrix, and the numbers to the right of ρ are the values to be placed in the matrix. If you study examples (2) and (3), you should be able to discover the meaning of the symbols used there. ⌈ is used to compare numbers and give the *maximum value* and ⌊ is used to give the *minimum value.* Note how ⌈ is used in the fourth example. In example (5), the symbol +/ stands for *plus reduction,* which means the numbers following it are to be added. The ? in example (6) is referred to as *roll.* It is used as a random number generator and in this example could be thought of as simulating the roll of a die.

In program mode, it is possible to write an APL program to perform several mathematical computations in a single program line. The APL program below compares two numeric values and then prints whether the value on the left is less than, greater than, or equal to the value on the right.

Program

```
        ∇ COMPR [⎕] ∇
  ∇ X CMPR Y
[1] ((X < Y) / 'LESS'), ((X > Y) / 'GREATER'), ((X = Y) / 'EQUAL')
  ∇
```

Output

```
   (comparing 7 and 22)
   7 CMPR 22
LESS
   (comparing 14 and 14)
   14 CMPR 14
EQUAL
```

APL is an *interpreted* high level language. This means that when an APL program is RUN, the APL interpreter translates the program, one line at a time, into machine language instructions. As the interpreter moves on to the next program statement, it "forgets" the line previously executed. This process is repeated each time the program is RUN. Even though an interpreted program will usually run slower than a *compiled* program, in which the entire program is first converted to machine language instructions before execution, an interpreted program is easier to debug.

Error Messages

commodore is same as apple

Apple	TRS-80	IBM
BAD SUBSCRIPT ERROR IN *line no.*	SUBSCRIPT OUT OF RANGE IN *line no.*	SUBSCRIPT OUT OF RANGE IN *line no.*
DIVISION BY ZERO ERROR IN *line no.*	DIVISION BY ZERO IN *line no.*	DIVISION BY ZERO IN *line no.*
EXTRA IGNORED	EXTRA IGNORED	REDO FROM START
FILE NOT FOUND	FILE NOT FOUND	FILE NOT FOUND
ILLEGAL QUANTITY ERROR IN *line no.*	ILLEGAL FUNCTION CALL IN *line no.*	ILLEGAL FUNCTION CALL IN *line no.*
NEXT WITHOUT FOR ERROR IN *line no.*	NEXT WITHOUT FOR IN *line no.*	NEXT WITHOUT FOR IN *line no.*
OUT OF DATA ERROR IN *line no.*	OUT OF DATA IN *line no.*	OUT OF DATA IN *line no.*
OUT OF DATA ERROR IN *line no.*	INPUT PAST END IN *line no.*	INPUT PAST END IN *line no.*
OUT OF MEMORY ERROR IN *line no.*	OUT OF MEMORY IN *line no.*	OUT OF MEMORY IN *line no.*
OVERFLOW ERROR IN *line no.*	OVERFLOW IN *line no.*	OVERFLOW IN *line no.*
REDIM'D ARRAY ERROR IN *line no.*	REDIMENSIONED ARRAY IN *line no.*	DUPLICATE DEFINITION IN *line no.*
REENTER	REDO	REDO FROM START
RETURN WITHOUT GOSUB ERROR IN *line no.*	RETURN WITHOUT GOSUB IN *line no.*	RETURN WITHOUT GOSUB IN *line no.*
SYNTAX ERROR IN *line no.*	SYNTAX ERROR IN *line no.*	SYNTAX ERROR IN *line no.*
TYPE MISMATCH ERROR IN *line no.*	TYPE MISMATCH IN *line no.*	TYPE MISMATCH IN *line no.*
UNDEF'D STATEMENT ERROR IN *line no.*	UNDEFINED LINE NUMBER IN *line no.*	UNDEFINED LINE NUMBER IN *line no.*

Appendix: Mathematical Applications

Chapter 2

In each of the following exercises, write a program using only the PRINT statement, with commas and semicolons when necessary.

Algebra One

1. Write a program that illustrates the addition properties of the real numbers. Have the output appear as follows:

```
CLOSURE:
23 + 51 = 74, A REAL NUMBER
COMMUTATIVE:
3 + 4 = 7            4 + 3 = 7            3 + 4 = 4 + 3
ASSOCIATIVE:
(5 + 4) + 2 = 11     5 + (4 + 2) = 11     (5 + 4) + 2 = 5 + (4 + 2)
IDENTITY:
12 + 0 = 12          0 + 12 = 12          0 IS IDENTITY FOR +
INVERSE:
17 + (-17) = 0       (-17) + 17 = 0       17 AND -17 ARE + INVERSES
```

2. Write a program that illustrates the multiplication properties of the real numbers. Have the output appear as follows:

```
CLOSURE:
23 * 51 = 1173, A REAL NUMBER
COMMUTATIVE:
3 * 4 = 12           4 * 3 = 12           3 * 4 = 4 * 3
ASSOCIATIVE:
(5 * 4) * 2 = 40     5 * (4 * 2) = 40     (5 * 4) * 2 = 5 * (4 * 2)
IDENTITY:
12 * 1 = 12          1 * 12 = 12          1 IS IDENTITY FOR *
INVERSE:
17 * (1 / 17) = 1    (1 / 17) * 17 = 1    17 AND 1 / 17 ARE * INVERSES
```

3. Write a program that illustrates the distributive property. Have the output appear as follows:

```
DISTRIBUTIVE:
4 * (5 + 7) = (4 * 5) + (4 * 7)
            = 20 + 28
            = 48
```

4. Write a program that has the following output:

   713.8 * 23.62 = 16859.956
   12 * 38 − 6 * (15 + 4) = 342
   12 * 38 − 6 * 15 + 4 = 370
   12 * (38 − 6) * 15 + 4 = 5764

5. Write a program that has the following output:

   −(12 + 5) = −17
   −(12 − 5) = −7
   −(5 − 12) = 7
   (−12) * 5 = −60
   (−12) * (−5) = 60

Geometry

In each of the following exercises, include appropriate messages in the output, such as "PERIMETER: ", "SIDE: ", and so forth.

6. PRINT the perimeter and area of a right triangle of sides 9, 12, and 15.
7. PRINT the perimeter and area of a square of side 13.
8. PRINT the perimeter and area of a rectangle of sides 23 and 37.
9. PRINT the perimeter and area of a parallelogram of sides 12 and 15, and height 9.
10. PRINT the perimeter and area of an isosceles trapezoid of bases 15 and 25, and altitude 12.

Chapter 3

In each of the following exercises, write a program using LET, INPUT, or READ . . . DATA to assign values to the variables. Use the GOTO statement when needed, and include appropriate PRINT messages in the output. Document the program. (In this chapter, an OUT OF DATA message is acceptable for programs using GOTO with READ . . . DATA.)

Algebra One

1. PRINT the average of four numbers assigned to the variables A, B, C, and D in LET statements.
2. PRINT the average of six numbers READ (all at one time) from a DATA list.
3. PRINT the amount of money you will have if you INPUT P pennies, N nickels, D dimes, and Q quarters.

4. Evaluate $5x^2 - 3xy + 7y^2$ for three sets of values of X and Y READ from a DATA list.

5. Show that the distributive property is true for three sets of values of A, B, and C READ from a DATA list.

6. INPUT a positive integer M, and then PRINT the value of P + 1, where P = M(M + 1)(M + 2)(M + 3). What kind of a number is P + 1?

7. PRINT the batting average of a player making H hits in B times at bat for three sets of values of H and B READ from a DATA list.

8. If Y varies directly as X and Y = 12 when X = 4, then PRINT the value of Y for an INPUT value of X.

9. If Y varies inversely as X and Y = 2 when X = 3, then PRINT the value of Y for an INPUT value of X.

Geometry

10. PRINT the area of a right triangle for INPUT values of the legs X and Y.

11. PRINT the perimeter and area of a square for an INPUT value of a side S.

12. PRINT the perimeter and area of a parallelogram for INPUT values of the sides L1 and L2, and the height H.

13. PRINT the area of a rhombus for INPUT values of the lengths of the diagonals D1 and D2.

14. PRINT the perimeter and area of an isosceles trapezoid for INPUT values of the bases B1 and B2, the sides S1 and S2, and the height H.

15. PRINT the circumference and area of a circle of radius R for values of R READ from a DATA list.

16. PRINT the sum of the measures of the interior and exterior angles of a polygon of N sides for an INPUT value of N.

17. PRINT the measure of each interior angle of a regular polygon of N sides for values of N READ from a DATA list.

18. PRINT the total surface area and volume of a cube of side S for an INPUT value of S.

19. PRINT the total surface area and volume of a right prism for INPUT values of the sides L1, L2, and L3.

20. **a.** PRINT the total surface area of a pyramid if the base is a square of side S and the slant height is H. READ three sets of values of S and H from a DATA list.
    b. PRINT the volume of the pyramid in (a) for an INPUT value of the height (say, HEI) of the pyramid.

21. PRINT the total surface area and volume of a right circular cylinder for INPUT values of the radius R and height H.

22. PRINT the volume of a sphere for an INPUT value of the radius R.

23. PRINT the number of degrees in the complement and the supplement of an INPUT angle A.

24. PRINT the measures of the base angles of an isosceles triangle ABC for an INPUT measure of the vertex angle A.

25. Given $\triangle ABC \sim \triangle DEF$, with sides as shown in the diagram.

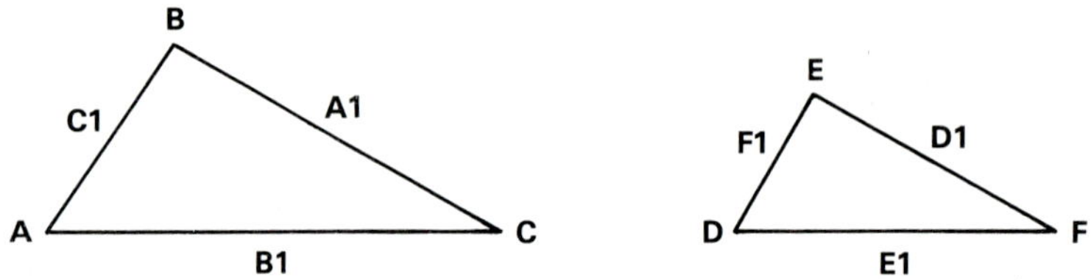

a. PRINT the value of D1 for INPUT values of C1, F1, and A1.
b. PRINT the perimeter of $\triangle DEF$ for INPUT values of C1, A1, B1, and F1.
c. In part (b), PRINT the ratio of the areas of $\triangle ABC$ and $\triangle DEF$.

26. Use the diagram for parts (a) and (b) below.

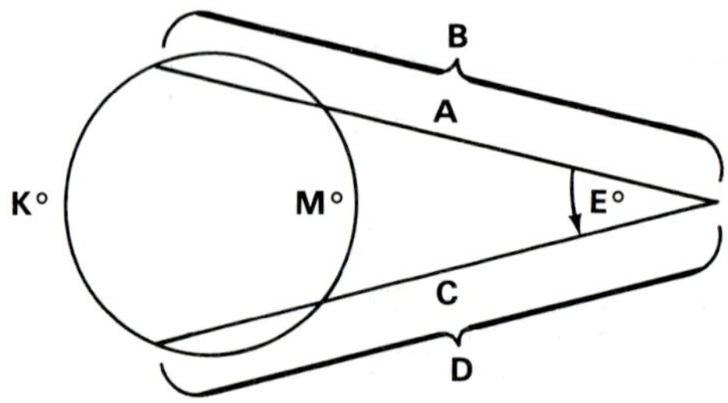

a. PRINT the measure of angle E for INPUT values of K and M.
b. PRINT the length of D for INPUT values of A, B, and C.

Algebra Two

27. For an INPUT point P with coordinates (X, Y), PRINT the coordinates of the point P1 that is symmetric to P with respect to the:

a. y-axis **b.** origin **c.** x-axis **d.** line $y = x$

28. If P dollars are invested at R% annual rate of interest, compounded D times a year, then the amount A earned at the end of N years is given by: $A = P(1 + R / 100D)^{ND}$. PRINT the value of A for INPUT values of P, R, D, and N.

29. Recall that $i = \sqrt{-1}$, $i^2 = -1$, $i^3 = -i$, and so on, and PRINT the value of i^N for INPUT values of N.

30. For two complex numbers Z1 = A + Bi and Z2 = C + Di, INPUT values for A, B, C, and D, and then PRINT the value of the following:

   a. Z1 + Z2   b. Z1 − Z2   c. Z1 * Z2   d. Z1 / Z2

31. For two INPUT roots X1 and X2 of a quadratic equation, PRINT the equation in the form $Ax^2 + Bx + C = 0$.

Chapter 4

In each of the following exercises, write a program using IF . . . THEN in addition to all of the statements that you have been using in Chapters 2 and 3. Include appropriate PRINT messages in the OUTPUT, and document the program. Use trailer values to signal the end of INPUT or READ . . . DATA, and use error trapping for unwanted INPUTs.

Algebra One

1. PRINT the solution to the linear equation $Ax + B = C$ for INPUT values of A, B, and C (where $A \neq 0$).

2. PRINT the solution to the linear inequality $Ax + B < C$ for three sets of values of A, B, and C ($A \neq 0$), READ from a DATA list.

3. PRINT the coordinates (X, Y) of the points that lie on the line $2x + 3y = 6$ for the x-values −3, −2, −1, 0, 1, 2, and 3, READ from a DATA list.

4. PRINT a message telling whether an INPUT integer X is positive, negative, or zero.

5. PRINT a message telling whether A / B is greater than, less than, or equal to C / D for INPUT values of A, B, C, and D ($B \neq 0$, $D \neq 0$).

6. READ three numbers from a DATA list, then PRINT the numbers in order from smallest to largest.

7. INPUT values of X1, Y1, A, B, and C, then PRINT a message telling whether the point with coordinates (X1, Y1) lies on the line $Ax + By = C$. (Remember, A and B cannot both be equal to 0.)

Geometry

8. PRINT a message telling whether an INPUT angle A between 0° and 180° is acute, right, or obtuse.

9. PRINT a message telling whether three INPUT numbers A, B, and C could represent the lengths of the sides of a triangle.

10. INPUT the lengths A, B, and C of the sides of a triangle, then PRINT a message telling whether the triangle with those sides is scalene, isosceles, or equilateral.

11. INPUT the measures X, Y, and Z of the angles of a triangle, then PRINT a message telling whether the triangle is acute, right, or obtuse.

12. READ the coordinates (X1, Y1), (X2, Y2), (X3, Y3) of three points from a DATA list, then PRINT a message telling whether the three points are collinear.

13. READ values for the lengths L and widths W of two rectangles from a DATA list, then PRINT a message telling whether the rectangles are similar.

Algebra Two

14. **a.** PRINT the slope M1 of the line passing through the points with coordinates (X1, Y1) and (X2, Y2), for INPUT values of X1, Y1, X2, and Y2. (Be sure to consider the case when X1 = X2.)
    b. PRINT the slope M2 of the line perpendicular to the line in part (a). (Be sure to consider the case when Y1 = Y2.)
    c. PRINT the coordinates of the midpoint of the line segment joining (X1, Y1) and (X2, Y2).

15. PRINT the equation of the line (in the form $y = \mathrm{M}x + \mathrm{B}$) passing through the points with coordinates (X1, Y1) and (X2, Y2), for INPUT values of X1, Y1, X2, and Y2.

16. PRINT the x- and y-intercepts of the line $\mathrm{A}x + \mathrm{B}y = \mathrm{C}$ for three sets of values of A, B, and C READ from a DATA list.

17. Use *Cramer's Rule* to solve and PRINT the solution to the linear system

$$\mathrm{A}x + \mathrm{B}y = \mathrm{C}$$
$$\mathrm{D}x + \mathrm{E}y = \mathrm{F}$$

for INPUT values of A, B, C, D, E, and F. PRINT a message for the case in which the system has no solution or more than one solution.

18. PRINT a message telling whether the point with coordinates (X1, Y1) lies above, on, or below the graph of the parabola $y = \mathrm{A}x^2 + \mathrm{B}x + \mathrm{C}$, for INPUT values of X1, Y1, A, B, and C.

19. PRINT a message telling whether the quadratic equation $\mathrm{A}x^2 + \mathrm{B}x + \mathrm{C} = 0$ has two, one, or no real roots, for three sets of values of A, B, and C READ from a DATA list.

Chapter 5

In each of the following exercises, write a program using FOR . . . NEXT and subroutines in addition to all the statements that you have been using in previous chapters. Include appropriate PRINT messages in the OUTPUT, and document the program.

Algebra One

1. PRINT a table of the even numbers from 2 to 100, inclusive. Use a FOR . . . NEXT loop.

2. PRINT a table of powers of 2 from 2 to 20, inclusive. Use a FOR . . . NEXT loop.

3. a. PRINT a table of even numbers and the sums of those even numbers from 2 to 100. Use a FOR . . . NEXT loop. Have the OUTPUT appear as follows:

NUMBER	SUM
2	2
4	6
6	12
.	.
.	.
.	.

   b. PRINT the average of the even numbers in part (a).

4. PRINT a table verifying the commutative property of addition for the first four positive integers. Use a double nested loop.

5. PRINT the sum X + Y for all integer pairs (X, Y) such that $-4 \le X \le 4$ and $0 \le Y \le 5$.

Geometry

6. Use a FOR . . . NEXT loop to PRINT the length X of a side of a cube, the area of one face of the cube, and the volume of the cube. Use the statement FOR X = A TO B, where the values of A and B are INPUT. Then PRINT the output in 3 columns.

7. Use a double nested loop to approximate the length L and width W of the maximum rectangular area that can be enclosed using 52 m of fencing.

8. Use a triple nested loop to find the total number of triangles that can be constructed using sides of integer lengths less than 10. (Try to eliminate unnecessary tests by choosing appropriate initial and final counter values in the FOR statements.)

9. Approximate π by finding the perimeters of regular N-gons inscribed in a circle of radius 1 / 2. Use N = 4, 8, 16, . . . , 512.

10. A formula for generating $\frac{\pi}{4}$ is given by:

$$\frac{\pi}{4} = 1 - \frac{1}{3} + \frac{1}{5} - \frac{1}{7} + \frac{1}{9} - \cdots + \frac{(-1)^{N-1}}{2N - 1} \cdots$$

Use a loop to add successive terms. Include an IF-THEN statement in the loop to test when the difference between two successive approximations is less than a very small number, such as .00001. Then multiply by 4 and PRINT the approximation of π.

Algebra Two

11. a. PRINT the Nth term of an arithmetic sequence for INPUT values of the first term A1, the common difference D, and N.

    b. In part (a), PRINT the sum of the first N terms of the corresponding arithmetic series.

12. PRINT N arithmetic means between A1 and AN. Use an INPUT statement for N and READ four sets of values for A1 and AN from a DATA list.

13. Use a FOR . . . NEXT loop to find the sum $S = 1^2 + 2^2 + 3^2 + \ldots + N^2$, for any INPUT positive integer N. Compare the result with that found by using this formula:

$$S = \frac{N(N + 1)(2N + 1)}{6}$$

14. N factorial (written N!) is defined by

$$N! = N(N - 1)(N - 2) \ldots \cdot 3 \cdot 2 \cdot 1.$$

(0! = 1.) Use a FOR . . . NEXT loop to calculate N! for INPUT nonnegative values of N.

15. The number of permutations P of N different objects taken R at a time is given by this formula:

$$P = N! / (N - R)!$$

PRINT the value of P for INPUT values of N and R ($R < N$). Use a subroutine to calculate N!.

16. Use a FOR . . . NEXT loop with successive STEP refinements (start with STEP 1, then STEP .1, . . . , STEP .0001) to approximate the zeros of the polynomial function $y = 2x^3 - 6x^2 - 18x + 1$. Use −5 and 5 for the initial and final counter values in the FOR statement to determine the two values of x between which the function first changes sign.

Chapter 6

In each of the following exercises, write a program using the formatting and graphics techniques explained in Chapter 6, in addition to all of the statements that you have been using in previous chapters.

Algebra One

1. Using the graphics capability of your computer, draw a line segment connecting any two pairs of coordinates having these slopes:

a. 2 **b.** $\frac{3}{5}$ **c.** -2 **d.** $\frac{1}{2}$

(Since the screen coordinates (0, 0) are in the top left-hand corner, the segments will look upside-down from their plotted position in the coordinate plane.)

2. Suppose you want to use your home computer to keep track of your family's monthly budget. Write a program using PRINT TAB and PRINT USING that has output formatted as below. READ the information in the first three columns from a DATA list.

CATEGORY	INCOME	OUTGO	% INCOME	BALANCE
Salary	+2000.00			2000.00
Interest	+ 158.17			2158.17
Dividends	+ 235.50			2393.67
Mortgage		−341.87	14.3%	2051.80
Taxes		−502.67	21.0%	1549.13
Utilities		− 92.81	3.9%	1456.32
Food		−158.34	6.6%	1297.98
Clothing		− 83.50	3.5%	1214.48
Personal		− 21.55	0.9%	1192.93
Education		−100.00	4.2%	1092.93
Savings		−100.00	4.2%	992.93

Geometry

3. Use PRINT TAB and asterisks to draw each of the following:

a. octagon **b.** decagon

4. *(Apple* and *IBM)* In graphics mode, use HPLOT *(Apple)* or LINE *(IBM)* to draw each of the following:

a. octagon **b.** decagon

Algebra Two

5. Using the graphics capability of your computer, draw a line segment perpendicular to the midpoint of each of the segments drawn in Exercise 1 above.

Chapter 7

In each of the following exercises, write a program using the BASIC built-in functions along with statements you have learned in previous chapters. Include appropriate PRINT messages in the output, and document the program.

Algebra One

1. INPUT a positive real number X, then PRINT the value of the square root of X in three columns using SQR(X), X ↑ (1 / 2), and X ↑ .5.
2. Use the ABS function and a FOR . . . NEXT loop with initial counter value 5 to help decide whether each of the following is always true:

   a. $|A + B| \leqslant |A| + |B|$
   b. $|A - B| = |A| - |B|$
   c. $|A - B| \geq |A| - |B|$
   d. $|A - B| = |B - A|$
   e. $|A * B| = |A| * |B|$

3. INPUT two integers A and B, then use the SGN function to decide whether A + B, A − B, A * B, and A / B is positive, negative, or zero.

Geometry

4. INPUT two positive integers A and B, then PRINT the geometric means of A and B.
5. Use the diagram of right triangle ACB in parts (a)–(d).

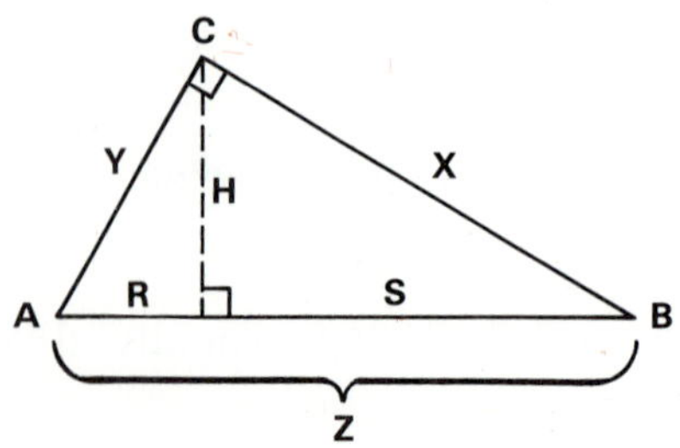

a. INPUT X and Y, then PRINT the value of Z.
b. INPUT Y and Z, then PRINT the value of X.
c. INPUT R and S, then PRINT the value of H.
d. INPUT H and R, then PRINT the value of S, Z, Y, and X.

6. INPUT the length of a side S of an equilateral triangle, then PRINT:

a. the length H of the altitude b. the area A of the triangle

7. INPUT the length D of a diagonal of a square, then PRINT:

a. the length S of a side b. the area A of the square

8. Use the diagram of a cube in parts (a) and (b) below.

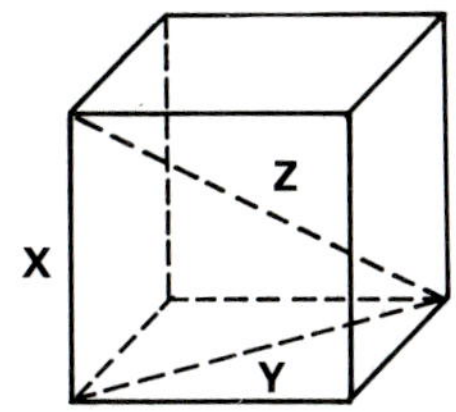

a. INPUT X, then PRINT the value of Y and Z.
b. INPUT X, then PRINT the volume of the cube and the total surface area.

9. Given a line L with equation $Ax + By = C$ and a point P1 with coordinates (X1, Y1), you can find the perpendicular distance D from the point P1 to the line L by using the formula $D = \frac{|A * X1 + B * Y1 + C|}{\sqrt{A^2 + B^2}}$. READ A, B, and C from a DATA list, INPUT X1 and Y1, and then PRINT the distance from P1 to L.

Algebra Two

10. INPUT values of coefficients A, B, and C for the quadratic equation $Ax^2 + Bx + C = 0$ ($A \neq 0$), then PRINT the real roots of the equation. If the roots are complex, then PRINT an appropriate message.

11. Use the diagram of triangle ABC below to do parts (a) and (b) at the top of the next page.

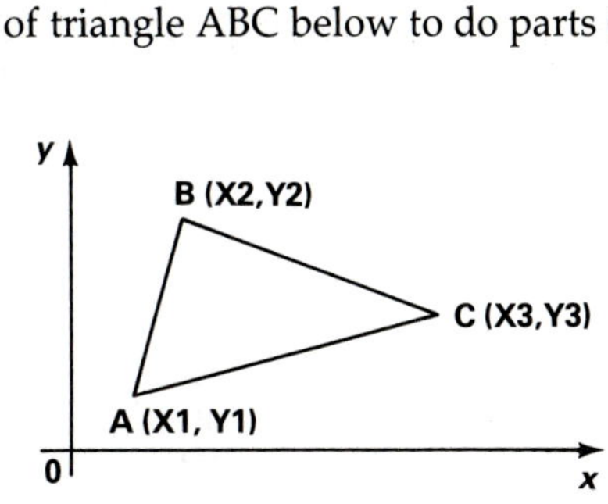

a. READ the coordinates of A, B, and C from a DATA list, then PRINT the equations of the three altitudes in general form.
b. Use *Cramer's rule* to solve the system of any two equations in part (a), and then check the solution in the third equation. PRINT the solution as the ordered pair (X4, Y4). This point is called the *orthocenter* of the triangle.

12. An ellipse has foci at (C, 0), y-intercepts (0, B) and (0, −B), and x-intercepts (A, 0) and (−A, 0). INPUT values of B and C, then PRINT the equation of the ellipse in the form $x^2 / A^2 + y^2 / B^2 = 1$.

13. A hyperbola has foci at (C, 0) and (−C, 0), and x-intercepts (A, 0) and (−A, 0). INPUT values of A and C, then PRINT the equation of the hyperbola in the form $x^2 / A^2 - y^2 / B^2 = 1$. Also, PRINT the equation of the asymptotes of the hyperbola.

Advanced Math

14. Given a line

$$A1x + B1y = C$$

and a parabola

$$y = A2x^2 + B2x + C2,$$

PRINT the solution set of the system for INPUT values of the coefficients. If there is no solution, PRINT an appropriate message.

15. Given an ellipse $\frac{x^2}{A1^2} + \frac{y^2}{B1^2} = 1$ and a parabola $y = A2x^2 + B2x + C2$, PRINT the solution set of the system for INPUT values of A1, B1, A2, B2, and C2. If there is no solution, PRINT an appropriate message.

16. The half-life of a radioactive substance is the time required for a given amount of the substance to decompose to one half the original amount. The half-life of radioactive Carbon-14 is approximately 5730 years. In dating famous paintings, for example, one can compare the ratio (say R) of the level of radioactivity of the pigments in the paint, which were originally derived from plants, to the level of radioactivity of living plants. Then an estimate can be given for when a particular painting was drawn. The formula used for the ratio is R = (.5) * T / 5730, where T is the number of elapsed years. Solving for T gives this result:

$$T = 5730 * (LOG(R) / LOG(.5))$$

Use this formula to write a program that estimates the year a painting was drawn. INPUT R-values of .965, .955, .945, .935, .925, and .915. How many years difference are there in a 1% change of the ratio, say, from 95.5% to 94.5%?

17. The computer calculates values of the built-in exponential function EXP using an infinite series, such as:

$$e^x = 1 + x + \frac{x^2}{2!} + \frac{x^3}{3!} + \cdots + \frac{x^n}{n!} \cdots$$

PRINT the value of e^1, $e^{1.5}$, e^2, $e^{2.5}$, . . . , $e^{4.5}$, and e^5 using the series, and compare each value to that obtained using the built-in function EXP.

18. a. Two numbers are *relatively prime* if they have no common factor other than one. For example, 8 and 15 are relatively prime numbers. INPUT two positive integers greater than one, then PRINT whether they are relatively prime.
    b. INPUT three positive integers A, B, and C, and then PRINT whether they are relatively prime.

19. a. INPUT integer X-values from −3 to 3, and then PRINT the slope of the tangent line T for the user-defined function FNF(X) = X * X. Round the values of T to 3 decimal places. What do you notice about the values of T at −3 and 3, at −2 and 2, and at −1 and 1? What is the value of T at X = 0?
    b. Use the program in (a) to PRINT the slope of the tangent line T for the user-defined function FNF(X) = X ↑ 3 − 6 * X ↑ 2 − 15 * X + 2 at the INPUT X-values −2, −1, 0, . . . , and 6. Are there any values of X where T is (approximately) equal to 0? Is FNF(X) a relative maximum or a relative minimum at these X-values?

Chapter 9

In each of the following exercises, write a program using subscripted variables and arrays. Include appropriate PRINT messages in the output and document the program.

Algebra One

1. READ 10 numbers from a DATA list into an array A, then PRINT the average of the numbers.

2. Use a two-dimensional array A and a double nested loop to PRINT a 9×9 multiplication table. Use TAB to align the columns.

3. INPUT 10 numbers into an array Y, then PRINT the elements with an odd subscript.

4. INPUT 20 numbers and store the positive numbers in an array POS and the negatives in an array NEG, then PRINT both arrays (ignore zeros).

Geometry

5. INPUT the X- and Y-coordinates of the vertices of a rectangle and store the X-values in array X and the Y-values in array Y. Then PRINT the perimeter of the rectangle.

Algebra Two

6. READ 20 numbers from a DATA list into an array P. INPUT a number X, then PRINT the number of times X occurs in the array.

7. READ 2 numbers A and B from a DATA list, then insert three arithmetic means and store the sequence of five numbers in an array M.

8. PRINT a two-dimensional array P such that the elements of P are the elements of the two-dimensional array Q in reverse order. READ the values for the elements of array Q from a DATA list.

9. PRINT the factors of the quadratic polynomial $P(x) = x^2 + Bx + C$, where B and C are integers. (*Hint:* $(x - a)$ is a factor of $P(x)$ if and only if a is a root of the equation $P(x) = 0$.)

Advanced Math

10. a. In the *Fibonacci sequence,* each term from the third on is the sum of the two preceding terms (the first two terms are both 1):

$$1, 1, 2, 3, 5, 8, 13, 21, \ldots$$

INPUT an integer N, then store the first N terms of the sequence in an array FIBB. PRINT the array.

b. PRINT the sum of the first N terms of the sequence in (a).

11. INPUT a base-10 integer N, then PRINT the number N in its binary, or base-2, form.

12. INPUT the digits of a base-2 number X, then PRINT the base-10 equivalent of the number X.

13. a. If the 2×2 matrices A and B are as follows,

$$A = \begin{bmatrix} a_{11} & a_{12} \\ a_{21} & a_{22} \end{bmatrix} \qquad B = \begin{bmatrix} b_{11} & b_{12} \\ b_{21} & b_{22} \end{bmatrix}$$

then the *sum* A + B is defined by:

$$A + B = \begin{bmatrix} a_{11} + b_{11} & a_{12} + b_{12} \\ a_{21} + b_{21} & a_{22} + b_{22} \end{bmatrix}$$

READ values for the two matrices A and B from a DATA list and store them in 2 two-dimensional arrays A and B. PRINT the sum A + B.

b. Modify the program in 13(a) so that it also PRINTs the sum B + A. Is 2 × 2 matrix addition commutative?

c. Modify the program in (a) so that it PRINTs the difference A − B. (A − B is equivalent to A + (−B), where the values in (−B) are the opposite of the ones in B.) Does A − B = B − A?

14. a. The product of the two 2 × 2 matrices A and B in Exercise 13 is defined by:

$$A * B = \begin{bmatrix} a_{11} & a_{12} \\ a_{21} & a_{22} \end{bmatrix} \begin{bmatrix} b_{11} & b_{12} \\ b_{21} & b_{22} \end{bmatrix} = \begin{bmatrix} a_{11}b_{11} + a_{12}b_{21} & a_{11}b_{12} + a_{12}b_{22} \\ a_{21}b_{11} + a_{22}b_{21} & a_{21}b_{12} + a_{22}b_{22} \end{bmatrix}$$

READ values for the two matrices A and B from a DATA list and store them in 2 two-dimensional arrays A and B. Then have the program PRINT the product A * B.

b. Modify the program in (a) so that it also PRINTs the product B * A. Is 2 × 2 matrix multiplication commutative?

Chapter 10

In each of the following exercises, write a program using the sorting and searching techniques explained in this chapter. Include appropriate PRINT messages in the output and document the program.

Algebra One

1. INPUT a list of integers in which an element can occur more than once (use −999 as the trailer value). Store the numbers in an array NUM, and then PRINT the array with any repetitions eliminated.

Algebra Two

2. INPUT 10 numbers and store them in an array P. Then PRINT the array with the following elements switched: P(1) and P(10), P(2) and P(9), P(3) and P(8), and so on.

3. READ 15 numbers from a DATA list into an array D. For any three numbers in a row, the middle one is to be compared with the other two. PRINT the number only if it is greater than both of them.

4. READ the digits 9, 5, and 3 from a DATA list and store them in an array M. Then PRINT all 3-digit numbers that can be constructed using those digits. PRINT an asterisk in front of any number in which there is no repetition of digits.

Advanced Math

5. If a list of numbers contains an odd number of values, and they are arranged in numerical order, then the *median* M is that number such that one half the values are above M and one half below M. If the list contains an even number of values, then the median is the average of the two middle values. INPUT values into an array M, then PRINT the median whether an even or odd number of values were entered.

6. The *mode* of a list of numbers is the number(s) that occurs most often. READ numbers from a DATA list, then PRINT the mode.

7. The *standard deviation* SD is a number that measures the amount of dispersion, or "spread," from the arithmetic mean M of a set of data. It can be calculated using the formula

$$SD = \sqrt{\frac{\sum_{I=1}^{N}(A(I) - M)^2}{N}},$$

where A(I) − M represents the difference between the mean M and each value A(I), FOR I = 1 TO N. PRINT the standard deviation of a set of N numbers READ from a DATA list.

8. The mean and standard deviation can be used to convert a set of data to *standard scores,* or *T-scores.* Changing the original data to T-scores makes the mean equal to 0 and the standard deviation equal to 1. In this way, different sets of data can easily be compared to each other. T-scores can be calculated using this formula:

$$T(I) = \frac{A(I) - M}{SD}$$

Use a FOR . . . NEXT loop with FOR I = 1 TO N to convert a DATA list of N numbers into T-scores.

Glossary

ABS(X) (p. 345) ABS(X) gives the absolute value of X.

action (p. 136) The action is the instruction that immediately follows THEN in an IF . . . THEN statement. It is executed only if the condition is true.

algorithm (p. 129) An algorithm is a list of steps a program will follow.

animation (p. 313) Animation is a process of plotting and erasing points so that graphics shapes appear to move.

APPEND *(Apple)* (p. 626) APPEND is the instruction that replaces OPEN when new items are to be added to the end of an existing sequential file.

array (p. 456) An array is a collection of subscripted variables with the same variable name.

ASC(A$) (p. 429) ASC(A$) gives the ASCII code of the first letter of A$.

ASCII (p. 153) ASCII stands for *A*merican *S*tandard *C*ode for *I*nformation *I*nterchange and includes special code numbers for keyboard characters.

ATN(X) (p. 385) ATN(X) gives the principal value of the arctangent of X.

BASIC (p.1) The abbreviation for *B*eginner's *A*ll-Purpose *S*ymbolic *I*nstruction *C*ode; BASIC is a simple problem-solving language for use with computers.

binary (p. 427) The binary or base-2 number system uses only 0's and 1's. All information is stored in the computer as sequences of binary numbers.

binary search (p. 560) The binary search is a method of searching an array that is in alphabetical or numerical order for a particular target number or string.

bit (p. 64) A bit is a binary digit; that is, a 0 or 1.

bubble sort (p. 532) The bubble sort is a method for arranging an array in numerical or alphabetical order.

buffer (p. 589) A buffer is a holding location for data coming to and from the disk.

bug (p. 184) A bug is an error in a computer program.

byte (p. 64) A byte usually consists of eight bits.

CATALOG *(Apple)* (p. 73) CATALOG is the command to list the names of the programs stored on a disk.

CHR$(N) (p. 429) CHR$(N) gives the character with ASCII code value N.

CIRCLE *(IBM)* (p. 312) The CIRCLE command, used in medium resolution graphics with BASICA loaded, will draw a circle with a specified center and radius.

CLOSE (p. 596) The CLOSE statement closes the file and clears the buffer so that all the remaining data is transferred to the disk.

CLS *(IBM, TRS-80)* (p. 30) CLS, short for "Clear Screen", is the BASIC instruction to erase all characters from the screen.

CMD "D:d" *(TRS-80)* (p. 73) CMD "D:1" is the DOS command to list the names of the programs stored on the disk in drive 1.

COLOR *(Apple)* (p. 45) COLOR is a low resolution graphics command that sets the color of the dots to be plotted.

concatenation (p. 422) Concatenation is the process of linking strings together. The strings are joined using the + symbol.

condition (p. 136) A condition is a comparison of two numerical values or strings and immediately follows the IF in an IF . . . THEN statement.

CONT (p. 184) CONT is the command that tells a program to resume or CONTinue running from where it was STOPped.

COS(X) (p. 380) COS(X) gives the value of the cosine of X, where X is in radian measure.

cursor (p. 18) The cursor indicates where the next character will appear on the screen.

cursor keys (p. 19) These are special keys on a computer used to aid in editing.

DATA (p. 101) The DATA statement contains a list of values to be used with a READ statement.

data file (p. 519) A data file contains records a program is to use.

data processing (p. 519) Data processing is the name for the applications of computers that involve changing and manipulating large amounts of information.

debugging (p. 131) Debugging is the process of correcting errors in a program.

DEF FNS(X) (p. 394) DEF FNS(X) is a user-defined function in which S is the name of the function and X is the "dummy" variable.

DELETE *(Apple)* (p. 73) DELETE is the command used to remove a program from a disk.

DIM (p. 469) DIM, short for *dimension,* is the statement that tells the computer how many memory spaces to reserve for an array. DIM must be used when subscripts of an array will exceed 10.

disk file (p. 589) A disk file is a data file stored on disk. The information in the file can be reused without retyping it.

documentation (p. 91) Documentation provides the purpose of the program, the role of important lines, and instructions on how to use the program. This information is usually given in REM or PRINT statements.

DOS (p. 70) DOS, short for *Disk Operating System,* is a control program that interprets the diskette commands and relays information between the computer's memory and the diskette.

doubly-subscripted variable (p. 488) This variable describes the location of each element in a two-dimensional array. The first subscript refers to the row and the second subscript refers to the column in which an element is located.

EDIT *(IBM, TRS-80)* (p. 120) This command allows the programmer to change a part of a line.

editing (p. 19) Editing is the process of making changes and corrections in a program.

END (p. 28) END is the statement in a program that tells the computer to stop executing the program.

ELSE *(IBM, TRS-80)* (p. 293) ELSE is an extension of the IF . . . THEN instruction.

<ENTER> *(IBM, TRS-80)* (p. 17) This key is used to enter typed information into the computer.

EOF *(IBM, TRS-80)* (p. 616) EOF is a built-in function that can be used to detect the end of file marker.

error trapping (p. 136) Error trapping involves using IF . . . THEN statements to reject unwanted INPUT values.

exponential form (p. 21) Exponential form, or E-form, is a variation of scientific notation and is used to express very large or very small numbers.

EXP(X) (p. 383) EXP(X), the built-in exponential function, calculates the value of e^x, where e is a special constant having the approximate value 2.71828.

FIELD *(IBM, TRS-80)* (p. 641) The FIELD statement specifies the length of each field in a random-access file.

fields (p. 519) Fields are the columns of a data file.

FILES *(IBM)* (p. 73) FILES is the command used to list the names of the programs stored on the disk.

FLASH *(Apple)* (p. 292) The FLASH command displays flashing text characters on the screen.

flowchart (p. 162) A flowchart is a diagram that shows the logical flow of a program.

FOR (p. 211) FOR is the beginning statement in a FOR . . . NEXT loop. The statement names the counter and assigns its initial and final values.

FORMAT *(IBM, TRS-80)* (p. 70) This command records indexing information on a new disk and completely erases old information on a used disk.

formatting string *(IBM, TRS-80)* (p. 286) The formatting string is used with the PRINT USING statement to reserve spaces and to specify the exact form of output.

function (p. 335) A function is a routine that takes a value, string, or number as an input and produces a single (usually different) value as an output.

GET *(Apple)* (p. 442) GET is the command that puts a blinking cursor on the screen and causes the computer to wait until a single key is pressed.

GET *(TRS-80, IBM)* (p. 643) GET is the command that transfers data from the disk to the buffer for a random-access file.

GOSUB *line number* (p. 243) GOSUB is the instruction that tells the computer to go to the subroutine beginning at the specified line number and continue executing statements until RETURN is reached.

GOTO (p. 110) The GOTO statement changes the order in which the computer executes the statements in a program.

GR *(Apple)* (p. 45) The abbreviation for GRaphics is a command to prepare the computer to do low resolution graphics.

hardware (p. 5) The physical equipment of the computer system is its hardware.

HCOLOR *(Apple)* (p. 298) The HCOLOR statement, used in high resolution graphics, designates the color of points to be plotted.

HGR *(Apple)* (p. 298) The HGR command prepares the computer to do high resolution graphics.

HLIN *(Apple)* (p. 295) The HLIN statement, used in low resolution graphics, instructs the computer to draw a horizontal line.

HOME *(Apple)* (p. 30) HOME is the command to clear the screen and move the cursor to the top left-hand corner.

HPLOT *(Apple)* (p. 298) The HPLOT statement is used in high resolution graphics to plot both points and lines.

HTAB *(Apple)* (p. 271) The HTAB statement specifies the column number to which the cursor will be moved.

IF . . . THEN (p. 136) The IF . . . THEN statement contains a *condition* that compares numerical values or strings to determine whether an *action* will be executed.

immediate mode command (p. 19) This is any instruction that the computer executes immediately after the RETURN or ENTER key is pressed.

increment (p. 194) The increment is the amount the counter will be increased or decreased each pass through the loop.

INIT *(Apple)* (p. 70) INIT is the command that formats or initializes a disk with indexing information. The command completely erases old information on a used disk.

initialize (p. 70) Initializing a counter assigns it a starting value.

INKEY$ *(IBM, TRS-80)* (p. 442) INKEY$ is the command that puts a blinking cursor on the screen and causes the computer to wait until a single key is pressed.

INPUT (p. 86) The INPUT statement puts a ? on the screen and allows the user to enter data for assignment to variables while the program is running.

input device (p. 5) A device used to enter information and instructions into the computer.

INPUT$ *(IBM, TRS-80)* (p. 607) This statement is used to read information from a sequential file.

INSTR *(IBM, TRS-80)* (p. 426) The INSTR function searches a string for substrings.

INT(X) (p. 335) The INTeger function, INT, rounds a number X *down* to the nearest integer.

INVERSE *(Apple)* (p. 292) The INVERSE command displays dark text characters on a light screen.

key field (p. 526) The key field is the specific field being examined in each record during a search to find a target value or string.

KILL *(IBM, TRS-80)* (p. 73) KILL is the command used to remove a program from a disk.

**LEFT$** (p. 410) LEFT$ is the function that extracts the left portion of a string up to a specified number of characters.

LEN (p. 409) LEN is the function that gives the *length* of a string, the number of characters in the string including spaces.

LET (p. 74) LET is a statement that assigns values to a variable.

linear search (p. 526) A linear search is a process that starts at the beginning of a data file and looks at the key field in each record until the desired information is found or the data is used up.

LINE *(IBM)* (p. 302) The LINE statement, used in medium and high resolution graphics, draws lines connecting any two points.

LINE INPUT *(IBM, TRS-80)* (p. 604) This statement is used to input a string containing commas.

LIST (p. 28) LIST is an immediate mode command that tells the computer to display the entire program that is currently in its memory.

LLIST *(IBM,TRS-80)* (p. 74) This command replaces LIST and tells the computer to print a paper copy of a program listing.

LOAD (p. 72) LOAD is the command used to put a new program into memory; it erases the old program from memory.

LOCATE *(IBM)* (p. 271) LOCATE is the command used to position the cursor anywhere on the screen.

loop (p. 110) A loop is a set of statements executed repeatedly by the computer.

LOG(X) (p. 383) LOG(X) calculates the value of $\log_e x$ (the natural logarithm of x), for x a positive number.

LPRINT *(IBM, TRS-80)* (p. 74) This command replaces PRINT and tells the computer to print a paper copy of the output.

LSET *(IBM, TRS-80)* (p. 641) The LSET statement transfers data from the program to the buffer for the OPENed random-access file.

menu (p. 507) A menu is a list of options presented to the user of a program.

microchip (p. 5) This is a small piece of silicon crystal containing integrated circuits with as much processing power as a computer of the 1950's.

**MID$** (p. 415) MID$ extracts a specified number of characters from any part of a string.

nested loops (p. 231) In nested loops, one FOR . . . NEXT loop is completely enclosed within another FOR . . . NEXT loop.

NEW (p. 30) NEW is an immediate mode command that erases the program currently in the computer's memory.

NEXT (p. 211) NEXT is the final statement in a FOR . . . NEXT loop. It increments and tests the counter (on most computers).

NORMAL *(Apple)* (p. 292) The NORMAL command displays light text characters on a dark screen.

NOTRACE *(Apple)* (p. 185) NOTRACE is a command to turn off TRACing.

null string (p. 77) The string containing no characters.

numeric variable (p. 67) A numeric variable is a variable that has a number value.

OPEN (p. 594) OPEN is a statement used to open and prepare sequential and random-access files.

output (p. 17) Output is information a computer sends to a screen, printer, or storage device.

output device (p. 5) A device used to communicate information from the computer to the user.

palette *(IBM)* (p. 51) The two palettes contain ranges of color for the points to be plotted in medium resolution graphics.

PEEK(N) (p. 592) This command gives the contents of memory location N.

PLOT *(Apple)* (p. 46) PLOT is a low resolution graphics command used to plot points.

POKE (p. 592) POKE is a command that changes the contents of a memory location.

PRINT (p. 17) The PRINT command tells the computer to print the strings or the values of the BASIC numerical expressions that follow PRINT.

PRINT@ *(TRS-80)* (p. 271) The PRINT@ statement specifies the starting location where output will be printed on the screen.

PRINT# *(TRS-80)* (p. 596) PRINT# is the command used to send data to a disk file.

PRINT TAB (p. 263) The PRINT TAB statement specifies the starting column where output will be printed on the screen.

PRINT USING *(IBM, TRS-80)* (p. 286) The PRINT USING statement specifies how digits of a number will appear in the output of a program.

PR#0 *(Apple)* (p. 74) This command tells the computer to send output to the screen.

PR#1 *(Apple)* (p. 74) This command tells the computer to send output to the printer.

program (p. 1) A program is a sequence of instructions a computer can follow.

PSET *(IBM)* (p. 52) PSET is a graphics command used to plot points.

PUT *(IBM, TRS-80)* (p. 641) The PUT statement transfers the contents of the buffer to the disk for a random-access file.

RAM (p. 6) *R*andom-*a*ccess *m*emory is working memory that contains information that can be changed.

RANDOM *(TRS-80)* (p. 359) RANDOM is the statement given at the beginning of a program that causes a different sequence of random numbers to be generated each time the program is run.

RANDOMIZE *(IBM)* (p. 359) See RANDOM.

random-access file (p. 590) This file is a disk file in which information can be recorded and retrieved in any order.

READ (p. 101) The READ statement is used to assign values to variables; the values are read from a DATA list.

records (p. 519) Records are the rows of a data file.

recursion (p. 250) Recursion in BASIC is a subroutine that contains a GOSUB to itself.

REM (p. 89) The REM statement is used to place explanatory remarks or other documentation in a program.

RESTORE (p. 104) The RESTORE statement tells the computer to go back to the beginning of the DATA list.

RETURN (p. 242) The RETURN statement ends a subroutine and instructs the computer to go back to the program line immediately following the GOSUB statement.

<RETURN> (p. 17) This key is used to enter typed information into the computer.

**RIGHT$** (p. 410) RIGHT$ is the function that extracts the right (last) portion of a string up to a specified number of characters.

RND(0) *(TRS-80)* (p. 358) RND(0) is used to generate random numbers from 0 to .999999.

RND(1) *(Apple, IBM)* (p. 358) RND(1) is a function that generates random numbers from 0 to .999999999.

ROM (p. 6) *R*ead-*o*nly *m*emory contains the control program for the computer and other information that cannot be changed.

RUN (p. 27) RUN is an immediate mode command that tells the computer to execute the statements in a program.

SAVE (p. 71) SAVE is the command used to store a program on a disk.

SCREEN 1 *(IBM)* (p. 53) This instruction prepares the computer for medium resolution graphics.

SCREEN 2 *(IBM)* (p. 304) This instruction prepares the computer for high resolution graphics.

sequential file (p. 590) A sequential file is a disk file in which the records are stored and retrieved in order, one after another.

SET *(TRS-80)* (p. 48) The SET statement is used to plot points on the *TRS-80* graphics screen.

SGN (p. 348) SGN is a function that can determine if a number is positive, negative, or zero.

Shell sort (p. 546) The Shell sort is a relatively fast method for arranging an array in numerical or alphabetical order by partioning the array into sublists.

SIN(X) (p. 380) SIN(X) gives the value of the sine of X, where X is in radian measure.

software (p. 5) Software is the term used to describe computer programs.

SQR(X) (p. 346) SQR(X) gives the principle square root of a non-negative number X.

STEP (p. 222) STEP is an instruction that tells the computer how much to increment the counter in a FOR . . . NEXT loop.

STOP (p. 184) The STOP command halts program execution.

**STR$** (p. 436) STR$ is a function that converts numbers to strings.

string (p. 17) A string is a sequence of characters enclosed in quotation marks.

String variable (p. 67) A string variable is a variable that has a string as its value.

subroutine (p. 242) A subroutine, part of a main program, is a set of statements that performs a specific task.

subscripted variable (p. 455) This type of variable describes the location of an element in an array.

TAN(X) (p. 380) TAN(X) gives the value of the tangent of X, where X is in radian measure.

TEXT *(Apple)* (p. 47) The TEXT instruction ends graphics and returns the computer to text mode.

Time-delay loop (p. 221) A time-delay loop is a FOR . . . NEXT loop with nothing in the body of the loop.

top-down design (p. 129) This synonym for structured programming is a systematic approach to developing an algorithm for a computer program.

TRACE *(Apple)* (p. 185) The TRACE command, a debugging device, lists line numbers on the screen in the order in which they were executed.

trailer value (p. 155) A trailer value is a special number or string that signals the end of input or a data list.

TROFF *(IBM, TRS-80)* (p. 185) TROFF is a command to turn off TRON and return to the program.

TRON *(IBM, TRS-80)* (p. 185) The TRON command, a debugging device, lists line numbers on the screen in the order in which they were executed.

two-dimensional arrays (p. 488) Two-dimensional arrays can be used to store and process data that can be arranged in rows and columns.

VAL (p. 437) VAL is a function that converts a string to a number.

variable (p. 67) A variable is a storage location in the memory of a computer. A variable name consists of either a single letter, or a letter followed by other letters or the digits 0 to 9.

VLIN *(Apple)* (p. 296) The VLIN statement, a low resolution graphics command, is used to draw vertical lines.

VTAB *(Apple)* (p. 271) The VTAB statement specifies the row number to which the cursor will be moved.

wrap-around (p. 21) Wrap-around results when more letters are typed than can fit on one line on the screen.

WRITE *(Apple)* (p. 595) WRITE is a DOS command that tells the computer to send data to a disk file.

WRITE # *(IBM)* (p. 596) WRITE # is a command that tells the computer to send data to the disk file.

Index

A

B

C

D

E

F

G

H

I

J

K

L

M

N

O

P

Q

R

S

T

U

V

W

Z

Selected Answers

Chapter 2 Computer Output

Exercises 2-1, pages 19–20 **3. a.** 5 + EIGHT **b.** 13 **c.** syntax error; PRINT "FIVE AND 8" **5. a.** SIX MINUS FOUR **b.** 2 **c.** 6 − 4 **9.** PRINT "HERE WE GO"

Exercises 2-2, pages 24–25 **1. c.** −1230 **f.** .000003001 **i.** 426305000 **2. c.** −13 **f.** 4 **i.** 46 **3. c.** PRINT 2 ↑ 2 − 5; −1 **f.** PRINT 12 / 3 − 4 / 2; 2 **i.** PRINT 2 * (3 + 4); 14

Exercises 2-3, pages 32–33 **7.** 10 PRINT "I'M FINE THANKS"
11. 15 PRINT 4 * 5 / 10
15.
```
99
IS A SECRET AGENT
```

20.
```
10  PRINT "1"
20  PRINT "■2"
30  PRINT "■■3"
40  PRINT "■2"
50  PRINT "1"
60  END
```

Exercises 2-4, pages 42–44 **3.** 5   3   1END **5.** EYE TO EYE **7.** SUM IS: 5 **15. a.** PRINT "MUR", "MUR", "MUR" **c.** PRINT "MUR"; "MUR", "MUR"; "MUR", "MUR"; "MUR"

Exercises 2-5, pages 55–56 **2. a.** *(Apple)* no error; *(TRS-80)* negative numbers not allowed 100 SET(5, 7); *(IBM)* parentheses not allowed 100 SCREEN 1, 1 **c.** *(Apple)* illegal quantity 80 PLOT 6, 39; *(TRS-80)* illegal quantity 28 SET(90, 40); *(IBM)* palette number can only be 1 or 0 50 COLOR 9, 1

3. b.

(Apple)	*(TRS-80)*	*(IBM)*
10 GR	10 CLS	10 CLS
20 HOME	20 SET(4, 2)	20 SCREEN 1, 0
30 COLOR = 7	30 SET(3, 3)	30 COLOR 7, 1
40 PLOT 4, 2	40 SET(4, 3)	40 PSET(4, 2), 1
50 PLOT 3, 3	50 SET(5, 3)	50 PSET(3, 3), 1
60 PLOT 4, 3	60 SET(2, 4)	60 PSET(4, 3), 1
70 PLOT 5, 3	70 SET(4, 4)	70 PSET(5, 3), 1
80 PLOT 2, 4	80 SET(6, 4)	80 PSET(2, 4), 1
90 PLOT 4, 4	90 SET(4, 5)	90 PSET(4, 4), 1
100 PLOT 6, 4	100 SET(4, 6)	100 PSET(6, 4), 1
110 PLOT 4, 5	110 SET(4, 7)	110 PSET(4, 5), 1
120 PLOT 4, 6	120 END	120 PSET(4, 6), 1
130 PLOT 4, 7		130 PSET(4, 7), 1
140 END		140 END

Chapter 3 Computer Input

Exercises 3-1, pages 68–69 **1. a.** valid **e.** valid **i.** invalid; + is not a valid character **r.** invalid *(Apple)* — reserved word **2. c.** string variable; value = "JUNIOR" **d.** numeric variable; value = 8

Exercises 3-2, pages 81–84 **1. b.** type mismatch; 5 LET H$ = "ORANGES" **g.** variable needs to be on left-side of equation; 40 LET AB = 18 **2. c.** 9 **g.** 5 7 **4. b.**

LINE	K	OUTPUT
10	5	
20	4	
30		4
40	1	
50		1
60		0

Exercises 3-3, pages 91–94 **1. a.** valid **d.** invalid

4. a.
```
TYPE A NOUN:  ? DOG
TYPE ANOTHER NOUN:  ? FLEAS
MY DOG HAS FLEAS
```

7.
```
? 4
? 6
? 7
13
```

Exercises 3-4, pages 99–101 **1. c.** valid **f.** invalid; 10 INPUT A$, B3 **i.** valid **3. a.** 10 PRINT "TYPE NAMES OF THREE FRIENDS: "; F1$, F2$, F3$ **5.**
```
10 INPUT "TYPE FIRST NAME: "; N1$
20 INPUT "TYPE LAST NAME: "; N2$
30 PRINT N2$; " , "; N1$
```

Exercises 3-5, pages 106–108 **1. b.** change: 10 READ Y$, X

3. b. PLUTO IS A DOG
AND A PLANET

d. MARS SATURN **5.** same output

Exercises 3-6, pages 115–118 **1. a.** *i.* 10, 20, 30, 40, 20, 30, 40, 20 . . .

ii.
```
ABC
CDE
CDE
.
.
.
```

d. *i.* 10, 20, 50

ii. FORWARD

3.
```
TELEPHONE DIRECTORY
NAME        NUMBER
JACOBS      876-3020
NAME        NUMBER
JENSEN      413-6972
NAME        NUMBER
JONES       612-0084
NAME        NUMBER
OUT OF DATA IN 30
```

5. a.
```
LIMERICK
NOUN:  ? HOUND
PLACE:  ? ORLEANS
THERE ONCE WAS A HOUND
FROM ORLEANS
THERE ONCE WAS A HOUND
FROM ORLEANS
.
.
.
```

Chapter 4 Branching

Exercises 4–1, pages 132–133 **1.** Step 1: a. Sit up in bed b. Wish you didn't have to get up c. Reach for alarm d. Push button to turn off alarm Step 2: a. Turn towards side of bed b. Wish you didn't have to get up c. Swing feet over edge of bed d. Place feet on floor e. Stand Step 3: a. Decide what clothes to wear b. Go to closet and dresser to get clothes c. Go to washroom to bathe and brush teeth d. Change from night clothes **5.** Step 1: Gather necessary equipment a. Make sure dog isn't looking b. Gather soap and bucket c. Clear path to warm water spigot d. Fill bucket with warm water e. Get goodies to coax dog back to bucket Step 2: Wash a. Put leash on dog b. Pet dog with lathered soap in hand c. Vigorously scrub d. Let lather set a few minutes Step 3: Rinse a. Get clear water b. If dog is in a good mood and it is warm outside, then hose down; otherwise gently sprinkle water on dog c. Inspect for soap. If soap remains, then continue with Step 3. Step 4: Dry dog; towel dog down Step 5: Clean up a. Put soap, bucket, towels away b. Empty soapy water c. Get dog inside so dog stays clean

10. Inputs: 3 letters (L1$, L2$, L3$)

Outputs:
```
L1$ L2$ L3$
L1$ L3$ L2$
L2$ L1$ L3$
L2$ L3$ L1$
L3$ L1$ L2$
L3$ L2$ L1$
```

Step 1. INPUT the 3 letters
Step 2. PRINT all possible outputs as outlined already.

Coding:
```
10  PRINT "LETTER COMBINATIONS"
20  INPUT "TYPE IN THREE LETTERS  "; L1$, L2$, L3$
30  PRINT "POSSIBLE COMBINATIONS:"
40  PRINT L1$; L2$; L3$
50  PRINT L1$; L3$; L2$
60  PRINT L2$; L1$; L3$
70  PRINT L2$; L3$; L1$
80  PRINT L3$; L1$; L2$
90  PRINT L3$; L2$; L1$
100  END
```

Exercises 4–2, pages 139–142 **3. c.**
```
2
3
4
5
6
```
f.
```
4
OK
4
```

5. change: 50 IF W1 = W2 THEN PRINT "YOU WEIGH THE SAME"

9. change:
```
40 IF X < 0 THEN GOTO 130
50 IF X > 20 THEN GOTO 130
60 IF Y < 0 THEN GOTO 130
70 IF Y > 20 THEN GOTO 130
```
add:
```
130 PRINT "OUT OF BOUNDS"
140 GOTO 30
```

11. a.
```
10 INPUT "HOURS WORKED:  "; HRS
20 IF HRS <= 8 THEN WAGES = HRS * 10
30 IF HRS > 8 THEN WAGES = 8 * 10 + (HRS - 8) * 15
40 PRINT "WAGES FOR  "; HRS; "  HOURS:  "; WAGES
50 END
```

Exercises 4–3, pages 148–153 **3. a.**
```
ORANGE      JUICE
THAT'S ALL
```

6. b.

LINE	CONDITION	A$	B$	OUTPUT
10		ALPHA		
20			BETA	
30	false			
40	true			
60				DONE
65				BYE

7. add:
```
45 IF N1$ = N2$ THEN GOTO 70
70 PRINT "NAMES ARE THE SAME"
80 GOTO 60
```

Exercises 4–4, pages 159–161 **5. a.**
```
? BRAVE
? COURAGEOUS
? BOLD
? XXX
ADJECTIVES:  3
```

9.
```
30 READ NUM
75 DATA 56, 48, -999
```

Exercises 4–5, pages 169–173 **5. a.** different output if A < 5 and B < 4. In first program, output is YES. Second program would print NO. **d.** same output **7.** change: 30 INPUT "TYPE X, Y COORDINATES (BETWEEN 0 AND 20; –999, –999 TO END)"; X, Y add: 35 IF X = –999 THEN GOTO 90

9.
```
10 REM * ALIKE OR NOT?
20 INPUT A$, B$, C$
30 IF (A$ = B$) AND (B$ = C$) AND (A$ = C$) THEN PRINT
     "MATCH"
40 IF (A$ <> B$) OR (B$ <> C$) OR (A$ <> C$) THEN PRINT
     "NOT ALIKE"
50 END
```

Exercises 4–6, pages 179–183 **2. a.** 2 **d.** GONE WITH
3

4. b. different output for S$ >= "MMM"

8. a. change:
```
20 IF NDOGS = 0 THEN PRINT "TOO BAD, ANY CATS?":
     GOTO 300
30 IF NDOGS = 1 THEN PRINT 'THAT'S  NICE": GOTO 300
40 IF NDOGS = 2 THEN PRINT "WELL, WELL": GOTO 300
```
delete: lines 70–200

Chapter 5 Looping

Exercises 5-1, pages 197–200 **5. a.** counter is PE **b.** line 10 **c.** line 20 **d.** line 30 **e.** line 40 **f.**

```
2    4
4   16
6   36
```

7. a. change: 50 IF N < = 12 THEN GOTO 30

d. add: 10 READ NME$, NUM change: 50 IF N < = NUM THEN GOTO 30
55 DATA SANDY, 21

13. a.

```
COUNTDOWN
10

BLASTOFF!!
```

16. b.

```
10  INPUT P
20  LET J = 27 <initialization>
30  PRINT J - 1; "  PINATAS" <body>
40  LET J = J - 1 <increment>
50  IF J > = P THEN GOTO 30 <test>
60  PRINT "DIFFERENT"
70  END
```

Exercises 5-2, pages 205–209 **1. c.**

```
1   1
3   4
```

f. C = 2 S = 13

5.

```
COUNTING THE'S
TYPE A WORD:  ? THE
TYPE A WORD:  ? AN
TYPE A WORD:  ? THE
TYPE A WORD:  ? .
YOU USED 'THE' 0 TIMES.
```

11. add: 25 LET COUNT = 0
75 PRINT "AVERAGE OF THESE NUMBERS = "; SUM / COUNT
change: 50 IF NUM > = 30 THEN LET SUM = SUM + NUM:
LET COUNT = COUNT + 1
70 PRINT "SUM OF NUMBERS THAT ARE 30 OR GREATER = "; SUM

15. change: 40 IF A$ < > "999" THEN LET COUNT COUNT + 1: GOTO 30
delete: lines 50 and 60

Exercises 5-3, pages 216–220 **3. a.**

```
10  FOR I = 1 TO 11
20  PRINT "HI, KID"
30  NEXT I
40  END
```

6. a.

```
10  FOR J = 2 TO 9
20  PRINT "I HAVE  "; J;
      "  MARBLES."
30  NEXT J
40  PRINT "I HAVE LOST MY MARBLES."
50  END
```

b. add: 5 PRINT "I HAVE 1 MARBLE."

8. b.

```
10  FOR AB = 1 TO 10
20  PRINT AB, AB ↑ 2
30  NEXT AB
40  PRINT "SQUARES ARE DONE"
50  END
```

11. change: 10 PRINT "AVERAGING DATA" 80 PRINT "AVERAGE IS "; SUM / N
14. a. change: 10 FOR K = –4 TO 20

Exercises 5-4, pages 226–227
1. c. valid **h.** valid **j.** invalid
4. add: 25 NEXT N change: 10 FOR N = 10 TO 20 STEP 2
8.

```
10  LET SUM = 0
20  FOR X = 2 TO 100 STEP 2
30  LET SUM = SUM + X
40  NEXT X
50  PRINT "SUM =  "; SUM
60  END
```

Exercises 5-5, pages 234–240 **3. c.** no error **g.** NEXT without FOR; exchange lines 70 and 90
4. b. change: 30 FOR J = 4 TO 5
40 PRINT J, K
d. change: 20 FOR K = 1 TO 2
30 FOR J = 1 TO 3

6. a. *(Apple)*

```
5   GR
10  HOME
15  COLOR = 7
20  LET Y = 20
30  FOR X = 0 TO 39
40  PLOT X, Y
50  NEXT X
60  END
```

(IBM)

```
5   SCREEN 1, 1
10  CLS
20  LET Y = 20
25  FOR X = 0 TO 319
30  PSET(X, Y)
40  NEXT X
50  END
```

(TRS-80)

```
10  CLS
20  LET Y = 20
30  FOR X = 0 TO 127
40  SET (X, Y)
50  NEXT X
60  END
```

Exercises 5-6, pages 246–249 **2. a.**

```
9
25
5
```

c.

```
3
CORRECT
6
CORRECT
9
CORRECT
```

5. a.

```
10  PRINT "THIS
    CALCULATES AVERAGES."
20  INPUT "NO.'S:  "; X, Y
30  GOSUB 100: REM * GET AVERAGE
40  PRINT "AVERAGE IS  "; AVG
50  END
100  LET AVG = (X + Y) / 2
110  RETURN
```

6. a.

```
1000  PRINT " * * * * * "
1010  RETURN
```

b.

```
2000  FOR X = 1 TO 3
2010  PRINT " * "
2020  NEXT X
2030  RETURN
```

Chapter 6 Formatting; Graphics

Exercises 6-1, pages 267–269

3. (answer may vary depending on whether or not your computer places a blank space before no.'s.)

```
. . . 14 15 16 17 18 19 20 21 22 . . .
         A =           1  0

         T H A T ' S    I T
```

7.

```
. . . 16 17 18 19 20 21 22 23 24 25
       T  T  T  T  T  T  T  T  T
       T  T  T  T  T  T  T  T  T
       T  T  T  T  T  T  T  T  T
                T  T  T
                T  T  T
                T  T  T
                T  T  T
                T  T  T
                T  T  T
```

11. *(Apple)*

```
10  LET X = 20
20  HOME
30  FOR I = 7 TO 1 STEP -1
40  READ L$
50  PRINT TAB(X + I); L$
60  NEXT I
70  DATA  A, B, C, D, E, F, G
80  END
```

(IBM)

```
10  LET X = 40
20  CLS
```

(TRS-80)

```
10  LET X = 32
20  CLS
```

Exercises 6-2, pages 280–283

2. b. *(Apple)*

```
10  HOME
20  FOR X = 2 TO 8 STEP 2
30  HTAB 11: VTAB X: PRINT "ARE YOU TRYING?"
40  NEXT X
50  END
```

(IBM)

```
10  CLS
20  FOR X = 2 TO 8 STEP 2
30  LOCATE X, 11: PRINT "ARE YOU TRYING?"
40  NEXT X
50  END
```

(TRS-80)

```
10  CLS
15  LET S = 64
20  FOR X = 1 TO 4
30  PRINT @ 11 + S, "ARE YOU TRYING?"
35  LET S = S + 64
40  NEXT X
50  END
```

Exercises 6-3, pages 289–291 **1. c.** 25 **f.** 74.37

3. SPECIAL FORMAT

```
  5        23.60
100         4.00
 12         8.33
```

Exercises 6-4, pages 307–310

2. b. *(Apple)* *(IBM)*

```
(Apple)                    (IBM)
10 HOME                    10 CLS
20 GR                      20 SCREEN 1, 0
30 COLOR = 7               30 COLOR 7, 1
40 FOR X = 10 TO 12        40 FOR X = 10 TO 12
50 VLIN 6, 11 AT X         50 LINE (X, 6)-(X, 11), 1
60 NEXT X                  60 NEXT X
70 END                     70 END
```

Exercises 6-5, pages 323–325

3. change:

```
(Apple)                        (IBM)
50  FOR X = 37 TO 3 STEP -1    50  FOR X = 317 TO 3 STEP -1
510 PLOT 37, Y                 500 PSET(317, Y), 1
520 HLIN 36, 38 AT Y + 1       510 LINE (316, Y + 1)-(318, Y + 1), 1
530 HLIN 35, 39 AT Y + 2       520 LINE (315, Y + 2)-(319, Y + 2), 1
620 PLOT X + 1, Y + 1          610 PSET(X + 1, Y + 1), 0
630 PLOT X + 2, Y + 2          620 PSET(X + 2, Y + 2), 0
710 PLOT X - 1, Y              700 PSET(X - 1, Y), 1
720 PLOT X - 2, Y + 1          710 PSET(X - 2, Y + 1), 1
730 PLOT X - 3, Y + 2          720 PSET(X - 3, Y + 2), 1
```

```
(TRS-80)
50  FOR X = 125 TO 3 STEP -1
500 SET(125, Y)
520 SET(124 + A, Y + 1)
550 SET(123 + B, Y + 2)
610 RESET(X + 1, Y + 1)
620 RESET(X + 2, Y + 2)
700 SET(X - 1, Y)
710 SET(X - 2, Y + 1)
720 SET(X - 3, Y + 2)
```

Chapter 7 Numeric Functions

Exercises 7-1, pages 338–341 **1. c.** 5 **h.** −1 **3. b.** true **e.** false

5. d. −1.2 **h.** 2.667

6. d.

```
TYPE THE NUMERATOR: ? 22
TYPE THE DENOMINATOR: ? 4
QUOTIENT = 5
REMAINDER = 2
```

Exercises 7-2, pages 350–353 **1. d.** 9 **h.** 3.2 **k.** 1

3. b.
```
? -23
? -6.5
PRODUCT IS POSITIVE
```

5. a.
```
500 REM * SUBROUTINE FOR SGN
510 IF X > 0 THEN LET Y = +1
520 IF X = 0 THEN LET Y = 0
530 IF X < 0 THEN LET Y = -1
540 RETURN
```

Exercises 7-3, pages 362–364 **1. c.** integers 5 to 9, inclusive

3. a. *(Apple)*

change:
```
20 HGR
30 HOME
40 HCOLOR = 3
100 LET X = 140
110 LET Y = 80
130 IF DIR = 1 AND Y > 0 THEN LET Y = Y - 1
140 IF DIR = 2 AND X > 0 THEN LET X = X - 1
150 IF DIR = 3 AND Y < 159 THEN LET Y = Y + 1
160 IF DIR = 4 AND X < 279 THEN LET X = X + 1
170 HPLOT X, Y
```

(IBM)

change:
```
20 SCREEN 1, 1
30 CLS
100 LET X = 160
110 LET Y = 100
130 IF DIR = 1 AND Y > 0 THEN LET Y = Y - 1
140 IF DIR = 2 AND X > 0 THEN LET X = X - 1
150 IF DIR = 3 AND Y < 199 THEN LET Y = Y + 1
160 IF DIR = 4 AND X < 319 THEN LET X = X + 1
170 PSET(X, Y)
```

(TRS-80)

change:
```
20 CLS
100 LET X = 64
110 LET Y = 24
120 LET DIR = INT(4 * RND(0)) + 1
130 IF DIR = 1 AND Y > 0 THEN LET Y = Y - 1
140 IF DIR = 2 AND X > 0 THEN LET X = X - 1
150 IF DIR = 3 AND Y < 47 THEN LET Y = Y + 1
160 IF DIR = 4 AND Y < 127 THEN LET X = X + 1
170 SET(X, Y)
```

Exercises 7-4, pages 373–377 **1. c.** false **e.** true

3. c.
```
? 144
? 36
GCF IS:  36
```

5. a. SUMMING
SUM IS: 45

8. a.
```
10  REM * DIVISIBILITY TEST
20  INPUT "NUMBER:  "; NUM
30  IF NUM / 5 = INT(NUM / 5) THEN PRINT
    "DIV. BY 5": GOTO 50
40  PRINT "NOT DIVISIBLE BY 5"
50  END
```

Exercises 7–5, pages 386–390 **1. d.** LET Y = EXP(–.5 * (LOG(X))

4.
```
10  REM * IDENTITY 2
20  PRINT "SIN(X)  COS(X)"
30  PRINT "------------ = TAN(X)"
40  PRINT "1 – (SIN(X)) ↑ 2"
45  PRINT: PRINT
50  FOR X = 0 TO 3.1 STEP .1
60  PRINT (SIN(X) * COS(X)) / (1 – (SIN(X)) ↑ 2), TAN(X)
70  NEXT X
80  END
```

Exercises 7–6, pages 398–400 **3. a.** POINTS ON A LINE

K	FNS(K)
1	–1
2	1
3	3
4	5
5	7

5. b. DEF FNB(X) = SQR(ABS(X))

9. DEF FNRTEN(BOTT) =
INT(RND(1) * 11) + BOTT

Chapter 8 String Functions

Exercises 8–1, pages 412–414 **3. b.** no error **f.** Assignment statement needs variable on left and function on right: LET P = LEN(A$).
5. c. ELION **f.** ANDELION **j.** N **7. a.** change: 40 PRINT RIGHT$(A$, I)

Exercises 8–2, pages 418–420 **1. d.** T HAND **h.** 5
3. a. works correctly **5. a.**
```
MYSTERY
STRING:  ?LAUGH
LAUGH
```

6.
```
10  PRINT "EVERY OTHER LETTER"
20  INPUT "STRING:  "; S$
30  FOR I = 1 TO LEN(S$) STEP 2
40  LET L$ = MID$(S$, I, 1)
50  PRINT L$;
60  NEXT I
70  END
```

Exercises 8–3, pages 424–426
1. b. APRIL SHOWERS
e. EMAYPOL

5.
```
10  INPUT "FIRST NAME:  "; F$
20  INPUT "MIDDLE NAME:  "; M$
30  INPUT "LAST NAME:  "; L$
```

```
40 LET IN$ = LEFT$(F$, 1) + "." +
   LEFT$(M$, 1) + "." + LEFT$(L$,
   1) + "."
50 PRINT "ARE THE INITIALS OF"
60 PRINT F$; "  "; M$; "  "; L$
70 END
```

Exercises 8-4, pages 432–433 **3. b.** BUNNY
5. a. 73 **7.** change: 70 LET N = N + 2
84 add: 85 IF N = 92 THEN LET N = 66
83

Exercises 8-5, pages 439–440 **1. b.** −6.03 (as a string) **g.** 68 **k.** 36
3. change: 10 PRINT "CASTING OUT NINES"
90 IF SUM = 9 THEN PRINT "DIVISIBLE BY 9": GOTO 95
add: 85 IF SUM > 9 THEN N$ = STR$(SUM): GOTO 50
92 PRINT "NOT DIVISIBLE BY 9"

Exercises 8-6, pages 444–445

3. *(Apple)*

```
10 REM * FILL THE LINE
20 HOME
30 GET A$
40 IF ASC(A$) = 13 THEN GOTO 90
50 FOR J = 1 TO 40
60 PRINT A$;
70 NEXT J
80 GOTO 30
90 END
```

(IBM and *TRS-80)*

```
10 REM * FILL THE LINE
20 CLS
30 LET A$ = INKEY$
40 IF A$ = "" THEN GOTO 30
50 IF ASC(A$) = 13 THEN
   GOTO 90
60 FOR J = 1 TO 80
   (TRS-80: FOR J = 1 TO 64)
65 PRINT A$;
70 NEXT J
80 GOTO 30
90 END
```

Chapter 9 Arrays

Exercises 9-1, pages 458–459 **1. d.** illegal **i.** illegal **l.** legal
3. b. AB(10) **e.** MICE$(7) **4. a.** COMPASS

Exercises 9-2, pages 464–466
2. b. I HAVE HAD IT WITH YOU
OKAY
4. add: 42 FOR J = 1 TO 5 STEP 2
44 PRINT KIT$(J)
46 NEXT J

Exercises 9-3, pages 471–473 **2.** 10 DIM AN$(11)
5. a. change: 20 FOR X = 0 TO 14
6. b. 10 DIM REC$(100), PRC$(100)

Exercises 9-4, pages 480–484 **1. f.** SUPERDOOPER
MEGAMAGNIFICENT
EXTRAORDINARY

3. a.
```
10 PRINT "PRODUCT OF THE ELEMENTS"
20 DIM P(20)
25 LET PROD = 1
30 GOSUB 100: REM * FILL ARRAY
40 GOSUB 200: REM * FIND PRODUCT
50 PRINT "PRODUCT IS:  "; PROD
55 END
100 REM ** SUBROUTINE TO FILL ARRAY P **
110 FOR L = 1 TO 20
120 READ P(L)
130 NEXT L
140 RETURN
200 REM ** SUBROUTINE TO FIND PRODUCT **
210 FOR L = 1 TO 20
220 LET PROD = PROD * P(L)
230 NEXT L
240 RETURN
```

Exercises 9–5, pages 493–496 **1. b.** 150 **e.** 140 **3. a.** E * OR

5. add:
```
80 FOR X = 1 TO 4
90 READ NM$(X)
100 NEXT X
110 FOR ROW = 1 TO 4
120 PRINT NM$(ROW);
130 FOR COL = 1 TO 3
140 PRINT TAB(12 * COL); D(ROW, COL)
150 NEXT COL
160 PRINT
170 NEXT ROW
235 DATA "FRESHMEN", "SOPHOMORES", "JUNIORS", "SENIORS"
```

Exercises 9–6, pages 503–506 **1. b.** −14

2. b.
```
100 REM * * SUM THIRD ROW * *
110 FOR COL = 1 TO 3
120 LET SUM = SUM + K(3, COL)
130 NEXT COL
140 RETURN
```

Chapter 10 Sorting and Searching

Exercises 10–1, pages 521–523

2. b.

	Fields		
	Student	Class	Lunch Period
record #1	Alphie B. Soup	Sophomore	5C
record #2	B. K. Bean	Senior	5A
record #3	B. R. Sprout	Junior	5B

f.

	Name	Number
record #1	Abbott's of Oshkosh	980-7118
record #2	Abel, Caren	624-3915
record #3	Abel, George	432-6121
record #4	Arny's Rental	865-4700
⋮	⋮	

(Fields)

5.

	Card No.	Borrower	Title of Book	Author's Name	Due Date
record #1	10036524	Luis Campos	European History	Norton	June 25
record #2	10037246	Heather Dun	⋮	⋮	⋮
record #3	10039815	Jian Lin			
⋮					

(Fields)

The file could be used to list all overdue books so that overdue notices can be sent or to list all books checked out on a particular card. The data file could search for the name of a borrower if a card no. is INPUT. The file could also conceivably search for a book that has not yet been returned, so that the borrower could be notified that another person had requested the book.

Exercises 10-2, pages 528–530 **1. b.** TYPE A MARKET: ? PRODUCE CITY

3. 60 IF LEFT$(ANS$, 1) = "Y" THEN GOTO 30
65 IF LEFT$(ANS$, 1) <> "N" THEN GOTO 50

Exercises 10-3, pages 538–542 **1. b.**

pass #1:

```
 5 ┐      2       2       2
 2 ┘→     5 ┐     5       5
 7        7 ┘→    7 ┐    -3
-3       -3      -3 ┘→    7
```

pass #2:

```
 2 ┐      2       2       2
 5 ┘→     5 ┐    -3      -3
-3       -3 ┘→    5 ┐     5
 7        7       7 ┘→    7
```

pass #3:

```
 2 ┐     -3      -3      -3
-3 ┘→     2 ┐     2       2
 5        5 ┘→    5 ┐     5
 7        7       7 ┘→    7
```

7. c. pass #1:

```
 6        6       6 ┐    -2
 4        4 ┐    -2 ┘→    6
-2 ┐     -2 ┘→    4       4
 3 ┘→     3       3       3
```

pass #2:

```
-2       -2      -2
 6        6 ┐     3
 4 ┐      3 ┘→    6
 3 ┘→     4       4
```

pass #3:

```
-2       -2
 3        3
 6 ┐      4
 4 ┘→     6
```

Exercises 10–4, pages 552–555 **1. c.**

List	First Sublist	Second Sublist	Bubble Sorts	
C	C	Q	C →	A
Q	A	Z	A	C
A			Q →	Q
Z			Z	Z

New Order	Bubble Sort of Single Sublist						
A	A	A	A	A	A	A	A
Q	Q	Q	C	C	C	C	C
C	C	C	Q	Q	Q	Q	Q
Z	Z	Z	Z	Z	Z	Z	Z

Exercises 10–5, pages 564–566

3. c.

	target = 300	
2		
17		
34		
106 ← too small		
227	227	
229	229 ← too small	
300	300	300 ← found!
320	320	320

Exercises 10–6, pages 575–579 **5.** HOSPITAL AUCTION FILE

TYPE 0 TO QUIT
TYPE 1 TO SORT
TYPE 2 TO SEARCH

WHICH DO YOU WANT (0, 1, 2): ? 1

SORT ON WHICH FIELD (1, 2, OR 3): ? 3

TYPE 0 TO QUIT
TYPE 1 TO SORT
TYPE 2 TO SEARCH

WHICH DO YOU WANT (0, 1, 2): ? 2

SEARCH WHICH FIELD (1, 2, OR 3): ? 3

TYPE TARGET VALUE: ? 1328

ITEM: HUB CAP COLLECTION, SHINY
CONTRIBUTOR: CARR
SUGGESTED PRICE: 1328

6. c. ONE
TWO
THREE
DONE

9. b.

```
10 FOR I = 1 TO 3
20 IF I = 1 THEN PRINT
     "BUY"
30 IF I = 2 THEN PRINT
     "LOW"
40 IF I = 3 THEN PRINT
     "DON'T"
50 NEXT I
60 PRINT "SELL"
70 END
```

Chapter 11 Files

Exercises 11–1, page 591 **3.** buffer **5. c.** random-access

Exercises 11–2, pages 600–602 **5.**

(TRS-80 and *IBM)*

```
10  REM * CREATE CLASS FILE
20  OPEN "0," 1, "CLASS"
30  FOR K = 1 TO 5
40  INPUT "TYPE CLASS:  "; C$
50  PRINT #1, C$ (TRS-80)
or 50  WRITE #1, C$ (IBM)
60  NEXT K
70  CLOSE 1
80  END
```

(Apple)

```
10  REM * CREATE CLASS FILE
20  PRINT CHR$(4); "OPEN CLASS"
30  FOR K = 1 TO 5
40  INPUT "TYPE CLASS:  "; C$
50  PRINT CHR$(4); "WRITE CLASS"
60  PRINT C$
70  PRINT CHR$(4)
80  NEXT K
90  PRINT CHR$(4); "CLOSE CLASS"
100  END
```

Exercises 11–3, pages 611–614 **3.** *(Apple)* add: 25 PRINT CHR$(4); "READ MONTHS"

(TRS-80 and *IBM)* change: 20 OPEN "I", 1, "MONTHS"

Exercises 11–4, pages 622–625 **3.** *(Apple)* add: 125 PRINT "NO SUCH WORD IN THIS FILE."

(TRS-80 and *IBM)* add: 115 PRINT "NO SUCH WORD IN THIS FILE."

Exercises 11–5, page 633 **1. a.** 1000, 1010 **b.** 1020 **c.** 80 **d.** 1500
e. 200, 210, 220, 230 **f.** 2500, 2510, 2520

2. add: 315 GOSUB 3000
change: 510 DIM FILE$(2), N$(20)

(Apple)

```
2999  REM * * PRINTING MRGD$ * *
3000  PRINT CHR$(4); "OPEN"; MRGD$
3010  PRINT CHR$(4); "READ"; MRGD$
3020  LET C = 1
3030  INPUT N$(C)
3040  IF N$(C) < > "ZZZZ" THEN LET
      C = C + 1: GOTO 3030
3050  PRINT CHR$(4); "CLOSE"; MRGD$
3060  FOR I = 1 TO C - 1
3070  PRINT N$(I)
3080  NEXT I
3090  RETURN
```

(TRS-80 and *IBM)*

```
2999  REM * * PRINTING MRGD$ * *
3000  OPEN "I", 1, MRGD$
3010  LET C = 1
3020  INPUT #1, N$(C)
3030  IF N$(C) < > "ZZZZ" THEN
      LET C = C + 1: GOTO 3020
3040  CLOSE 1
3050  FOR I = 1 TO C - 1
3060  PRINT N$(I)
3070  NEXT I
3080  RETURN
```

Exercises 11–6, pages 645–647 **1. c.** *(Apple)* PRINT CHR$(4); "OPEN INV, L38"
(TRS-80 and *IBM)* OPEN "R", 1, "INV", 38

2. *(Apple)* delete: lines 30, 40, 50, 60, 70
change: 140 IF ITEM$ < > "NOTHING" THEN GOTO 80
(TRS-80 and *IBM)*
delete: lines 40, 50, 60, 70, 80
change: 140 IF ITEM$ < > "NOTHING" THEN GOTO 90

Acknowledgments

Cover concept by Ligature Publishing Services, Inc.
Cover photograph, © Walter Wright, Science Source/Photo Researchers, Inc.

Technical Art by Graphics Etcetera; Omnigraphics, pp. 8, 656

Photos: Page iv, © Walter Wright/Photo Researchers, Inc.; x, "Escher" (detail) © David Em, 1979; 1 left, © Van Bucher, Science Source; 1 right, File Photo; 2 top, The Bettmann Archive; 2 bot., © Bill Pierce/Rainbow; 3 top, The Computer Museum, Boston, MA; 3 bot., Courtesy of IBM; 4 top, Paul Donaldson/Harvard Univ.; 4 bot., Univ. of Penn. Archives; 5 left, Don Carroll/The Image Bank; 5 right, Bill Gallery/Stock Boston; 7 top, Frank Wing/Stock Boston; 7 bot., Edith G. Haun/Stock Boston; 10 left, Brad Hess/Black Star; 10 top, Peter J. Kaplan/The Stock Shop; 10 bot., © Joseph Nettis/Photo Researchers, Inc.; 12 bot., Dick Luria/The Stock Shop; 12 top, Eric Preau/SYGMA; 13, © Hank Morgan/Rainbow; 15, © Michal Heron 1983; 16, Courtesy of Computervision Corp., Bedford, MA; 62 left, Roger Ressmeyer/Wheeler Pictures; 62 right, © Dan McCoy/Rainbow; 63 top, Bill Gallery/Stock Boston; 63 bot., Robert Goldstein/Medichrome; 65 top, Erich Hartmann/Magnum; 65 bot., Courtesy of Sperry Corp.; 66, Howard Sochurek; 124 bot., © Michal Heron 1983; 124 top, FPG/Bob Evans; 125, Howard Sochurek; 126, © Dan McCoy/Rainbow; 127, © Dan McCoy/Rainbow; 128, Daimler Benz, Evans & Sutherland; 189 top, Nike; 189 bot., © Dan McCoy/Rainbow; 190, Roger Ressmeyer/Wheeler Pictures; 191, Merrell Wood/The Image Bank; 192, Roger Ressmeyer/Wheeler Pictures; 254 bot., Ken Lax/The Stock Shop; 254 top, James H. Simon/The Picture Cube; 255 bot., John McGrail/Wheeler Pictures; 255 top, Lee Foster/Bruce Coleman Inc.; 256, Chuck O'Rear/Woodfin Camp & Assocs.; 257, Graph courtesy of ISSCO; 258, Melvin L. Prueitt, Los Alamos Nat'l Laboratory, author of *Art and the Computer,* McGraw-Hill, 1984; 330, Edith G. Haun/Stock Boston; 331 top, Liane Enkelis/Stock Boston; 331 bot., Carol Lee/The Picture Cube; 333, © 1982 Walt Disney Productions; 334, © SPL/Photo Researchers, Inc.; 404 bot., Mechanical Dynamic Inc., Evans & Sutherland; 404 top, Courtesy of Computervision Corp., Bedford, MA; 405 bot., Tom Tracy/The Stock Shop; 405 top, Lockheed-Georgia, Evans & Sutherland; 406, © Michal Heron 1983; 407, Graph courtesy of ISSCO; 408, Nelson Max, Univ. of Calif., Lawrence Livermore Nat'l Laboratory, Dept. of Energy; 450 bot., Aerospace Corp., Evans & Sutherland; 450 top, © Hank Morgan/Rainbow; 451 top, Daimler Benz, Evans & Sutherland; 451 bot., Wash. State Historical Society, Tacoma, WA; 452 top, Brown Brothers; 452 bot., Michael Collier/Stock Boston; 453, FPG/B. Barnes; 454, Graph courtesy of ISSCO; 514 bot., Jonathan L. Barkan/The Picture Cube; 514 top, Liane Enkelis/Stock Boston; 515, © 1985 Bill Gallery; 516 top, The Granger Collection, New York; 516 bot., The Bettmann Archive; 517, Science Museum in London; 518, © SPL/Photo Researchers, Inc.; 582, Richard Wood/The Picture Cube; 583, Erich Hartmann/Magnum; 585, Photo by Steve Grohe, LISP Machine, Inc.; 586, Purdue Univ., Evans & Sutherland; 654 bot., Gregory Heisler/The Image Bank; 654 top, David W. Hamilton/The Image Bank; 655, William Rivelli/The Image Bank;